THE EARLY MODE

The Early Modern Subject explores the understanding of self-consciousness and personal identity—two fundamental features of human subjectivity—as it developed in early modern philosophy. Udo Thiel presents a critical evaluation of these features as they were conceived in the seventeenth and eighteenth centuries. He explains the arguments of thinkers such as Descartes, Locke, Leibniz, Wolff, and Hume, as well as their early critics, followers, and other philosophical contemporaries, and situates them within their historical contexts. Interest in the issues of self-consciousness and personal identity is in many ways characteristic and even central to early modern thought, but Thiel argues here that this is also an interest that continues to this day, in a form still strongly influenced by the conceptual frameworks of early modern thought. In this book he attempts to broaden the scope of the treatment of these issues considerably, covering more than a hundred years of philosophical debate in France, Britain, and Germany while remaining attentive to the details of the arguments under scrutiny and discussing alternative interpretations in many cases.

Udo Thiel is Professor of the History of Philosophy at the University of Graz.

The Early Modern Subject

Self-consciousness and personal identity from Descartes to Hume

UDO THIEL

OXFORD
UNIVERSITY PRESS

Great Clarendon Street, Oxford, OX2 6DP,

Oxford University Press is a department of the University of Oxford.
It furthers the University's objective of excellence in research, scholarship,
and education by publishing worldwide. Oxford is a registered trade mark of
Oxford University Press in the UK and in certain other countries

© Udo Thiel 2011

The moral rights of the author have been asserted

First published 2011
First published in paperback 2014

All rights reserved. No part of this publication may be reproduced,
stored in a retrieval system, or transmitted, in any form or by any means,
without the prior permission in writing of Oxford University Press,
or as expressly permitted by law, by licence or under terms agreed with the appropriate
reprographics rights organization. Enquiries concerning reproduction
outside the scope of the above should be sent to the Rights Department,
Oxford University Press, at the address above

You must not circulate this work in any other form
and you must impose this same condition on any acquirer

Published in the United States of America by Oxford University Press
198 Madison Avenue, New York, NY 10016, United States of America

British Library Cataloguing in Publication Data
Data available

Library of Congress Cataloging in Publication Data
Data available

ISBN 978-0-19-954249-9 (Hbk)
ISBN 978-0-19-870440-9 (Pbk)

Contents

Detailed list of contents	vii
Preface to the Paperback Edition	xii
Acknowledgements	xiv
Introduction: aims and issues	1

PART I. THE SEVENTEENTH-CENTURY BACKGROUND

1. The ontological view of the self: Scholastic and Cartesian conceptions — 35
2. Metaphysical alternatives: conceptions of identity, morality, and the afterlife — 61

PART II. LOCKE'S SUBJECTIVIST REVOLUTION

3. Locke on identity, consciousness, and self-consciousness — 97
4. Locke on personal identity: consciousness, memory, and self-concern — 121

PART III. PROBLEMS WITH LOCKE: CRITIQUE AND DEFENCE

5. The notion of a person and the role of consciousness and memory — 153
6. The charge of circularity and the argument from the transitivity of identity — 190

PART IV. SUBJECTIVITY AND IMMATERIALIST METAPHYSICS OF THE MIND

7. The soul: human and universal — 224
8. Relating to the soul, pure thought, original sin, and the afterlife — 248

PART V. SUBSTANCE, APPERCEPTION, AND IDENTITY: LEIBNIZ, WOLFF, AND BEYOND

9. Individuation and identity, apperception and consciousness in Leibniz and Wolff — 279

10. Beyond Leibniz and Wolff: from immortality to the necessary 'unity of the subject' — 315
11. From the critique of Wolffian apperception to the idea of the 'pre-existence' of self-consciousness — 343

PART VI. BUNDLES AND SELVES: HUME IN CONTEXT

12. Hume and the belief in personal identity — 383
13. Hume and the bundle view of the self — 407

Conclusion: beyond Hume and Wolff — 431

Bibliography — 438
Index — 471

Detailed list of contents

Introduction: aims and issues   1
   I.1. The aims   1
   I.2. The literature   3
   I.3. The issues   5
      I.3.1. Consciousness and self-consciousness   5
      I.3.2. Individuation and identity   18
      I.3.3. The person and personal identity   26
   I.4. The general development   30

PART I. THE SEVENTEENTH-CENTURY BACKGROUND

1. The ontological view of the self: Scholastic and Cartesian conceptions   35
   1.1. Descartes and the Cartesians on the person and the soul   36
   1.2. Descartes and the Cartesians on consciousness   43
   1.3. The trinity, human personality, and self-consciousness: the debate between Sherlock and South   54
   1.4. Essayistic alternatives: Pascal and La Rochefoucauld   60

2. Metaphysical alternatives: conceptions of identity, morality, and the afterlife   61
   2.1. Spinoza on individuation, identity, and consciousness   61
   2.2. Cambridge Platonism: Cudworth's account of consciousness   67
   2.3. The subjectivist treatment of identity: Clauberg, Hobbes, and Boyle   72
   2.4. Personality and moral responsibility: Hobbes and Pufendorf   76
   2.5. The afterlife: the immortality of the soul and the resurrection of the body   81
      2.5.1. Immortality   82
      2.5.2. The resurrection of the body   85

PART II. LOCKE'S SUBJECTIVIST REVOLUTION

3. Locke on identity, consciousness, and self-consciousness   97
   3.1. Locke and his 'sources'   97
   3.2. Locke and the subjectivist treatment of identity   102

3.3.	Locke on man, soul, and person	106
3.4.	Locke on consciousness	109
3.5.	Locke on consciousness, self-consciousness, and intuition	118

4. Locke on personal identity: consciousness, memory, and self-concern   121

4.1.	Personal identity: consciousness and memory	121
4.2.	Personal identity: self-concern and moral and legal responsibility	127
4.3.	Original sin	131
4.4.	Self-concern and the afterlife	132
4.5.	The resurrection of the body: Locke's controversy with Stillingfleet	134
4.6.	Repentance and moral miracles	139
4.7.	Thinking matter and personal identity. Locke and his followers: Collins, Voltaire, and Cuenz	144

PART III. PROBLEMS WITH LOCKE: CRITIQUE AND DEFENCE

5. The notion of a person and the role of consciousness and memory   153

5.1.	Person, man, soul, and the resurrection of the body	156
	5.1.1. 'Identity of person as apply'd to man': Felton 157	
	5.1.2. Watts on staminal particles, the resurrection, and the man–person distinction 160	
	5.1.3. The person as soul and the resurrection of the body: Lee 163	
	5.1.4. Defending Locke on the resurrection 165	
	5.1.5. Conclusion: the resurrection of the body and the immortality of the soul 166	
5.2.	The debate about the role of consciousness and memory	168
	5.2.1. Consciousness, reflection, memory, and the 'ill consequences' of Locke's theory: Lee 170	
	5.2.2. Consciousness, drunkenness, and moral responsibility: Becconsall 172	
	5.2.3. Consciousness, 'real forgetfulness', and 'fancied memory': Watts 175	
	5.2.4. Actual and potential consciousness: Berkeley 176	
	5.2.5. Consciousness and self-concern: Shaftesbury 177	
	5.2.6. Consciousness and the personality of infants: Roche 181	
	5.2.7. Ploucquet's commentary on Locke 184	
	5.2.8. The anonymous *Essay on Personal Identity* 186	
	5.2.9. Conclusion 189	

6. **The charge of circularity and the argument from the transitivity of identity** — 190
   6.1. The charge of circularity against Locke — 190
       6.1.1. Sergeant on Locke on individuation and personal identity 191
       6.1.2. Lee's version of the charge 195
       6.1.3. Other versions of the charge 196
       6.1.4. Butler's critique of Locke 198
       6.1.5. Defending Locke against Butler 201
           6.1.5.1. Perronet's failed attempt at defending Locke 203
           6.1.5.2. Law: the notion of a person as 'solely a creature of society' 205
       6.1.6. Conclusion 209
   6.2. Locke and the transitivity of identity — 210
       6.2.1. Three versions of the argument: Berkeley, the anonymous *Essay*, and Reid 211
       6.2.2. Responses to the argument from transitivity 213
   6.3. Conclusion — 220

PART IV. SUBJECTIVITY AND IMMATERIALIST METAPHYSICS OF THE MIND

7. **The soul: human and universal** — 224
   7.1. Cartesian themes — 227
       7.1.1. An English Cartesian's account of personal identity: Emes 227
       7.1.2. Consciousness as an 'external imaginary denomination', and identity: Clarke 229
       7.1.3. The unity of consciousness and the 'moral man': Grove 234
       7.1.4. The importance of personal pronouns for the issue of personal identity: Watts 237
   7.2. The universal soul and human personal identity: Shaftesbury — 240

8. **Relating to the soul, pure thought, original sin, and the afterlife** — 248
   8.1. On relating to one's own soul — 248
       8.1.1. Consciousness versus reflection: Norris, Browne, and Berkeley 248
       8.1.2. Consciousness as the 'basis and foundation of all knowledge whatsoever': the *Essay on Consciousness* 253
   8.2. Berkeleian themes — 258
       8.2.1. The person as 'the concrete of the will and understanding': Berkeley 258
       8.2.2. Personal identity and original sin: Edwards 262

8.3. The senses of identity: Butler's epistemology and metaphysics
of personal identity and the future life   266
8.4. 'Pure thought' and identity: the anonymous *Essay on Personal
Identity*, and Tucker's critique   269
8.5. Conclusion   275

PART V. SUBSTANCE, APPERCEPTION, AND IDENTITY: LEIBNIZ, WOLFF, AND BEYOND

9. Individuation and identity, apperception and consciousness in Leibniz and Wolff   279

9.1. Leibniz on individuation and identity   280
9.2. Leibniz on personal identity   289
9.3. Problems with Leibniz: apperception and consciousness   295
9.4. Leibniz and Wolff   301
9.5. Wolff on consciousness, self-consciousness, and apperception   304
9.6. Wolff on consciousness, personal identity, and immortality   311

10. Beyond Leibniz and Wolff: from immortality to the necessary 'unity of the subject'   315

10.1. Wolffian accounts of immortality and identity   316
    10.1.1. Leibnizian 'footprints' and identity: Canz, Poley, and von Creuz   316
    10.1.2. Lockean leanings: Müller and Meier   322
    10.1.3. Wolffian accounts of immortality and the four main theses of rational psychology   327
10.2. Wolffian accounts of consciousness, the unity of the soul, and personal identity   328
    10.2.1. The necessary 'unity of the subject': Winckler, Knutzen, and Mendelssohn   329
    10.2.2. From unity to identity: Eberhard and Reimarus   332
    10.2.3. Consciousness and 'complete' identity: Tiedemann   339

11. From the critique of Wolffian apperception to the idea of the 'pre-existence' of self-consciousness   343

11.1. The primacy of consciousness: Rüdiger and Crusius *contra* Wolff and Klosse   343
11.2. On Wolffian self-consciousness: Hollmann and von Creuz   349
11.3. Self-consciousness and the body: Sulzer   354
    11.3.1. Sulzer on consciousness and self-consciousness   356
    11.3.2. Sulzer on self-consciousness and the body   358
    11.3.3. Sulzer on the consciousness of the unity and identity of the self   361

11.3.4. Sulzer and Herder: self-consciousness and the distinction between representation (*Vorstellung*) and feeling (*Empfindung*) 363
11.4. Towards Kant? Mérian on apperception and identity   365
    11.4.1. Mérian on personal identity 368
    11.4.2. Mérian on 'original apperception' as a necessary condition of thought 372
    11.4.3. Beyond Mérian 376

PART VI. BUNDLES AND SELVES: HUME IN CONTEXT

12. Hume and the belief in personal identity   383
12.1. The 'natural propension' to believe in personal identity   385
12.2. Time, change, and identity   388
12.3. Confounding identity with diversity: Hume, Shaftesbury, and Buffier   390
12.4. 'The identity which we ascribe to the mind of man'   393
12.5. Hume and Lockean theory   396
12.6. Hume's Appendix   398
12.7. The *Abstract*   402
12.8. Hume on consciousness and reflection   403

13. Hume and the bundle view of the self   407
13.1. Critique of the bundle view of the self: Beattie's and Reid's objections to Hume's account   407
13.2. Varieties of the bundle view. 'Anticipations' of the Humean position: Hutcheson, Bayle, Berkeley, Régis, Boulainviller, and Deschamps   410
13.3. What is Hume's bundle view of the self?   418
13.4. Personal identity 'as it regards our passions or the concern we take in ourselves': Hume and Kames   423
13.5. A note on Hume and Kant   428

Conclusion: beyond Hume and Wolff   431
C.1. *Sentiment intime* and *Selbstgefühl*   432
C.2. Materialism   433
C.3. Common Sense   434
C.4. Kantian thought   435

Bibliography   438
Index   471

Preface to the Paperback Edition

The warm welcome which greeted the hardback edition of this book, not only from philosophers of various kinds including analytical philosophers as well as historians of ideas, but also from academics in the literary disciplines, has been very encouraging. I believe that this indicates an interest in the theme that not only goes beyond specialists in seventeenth- and eighteenth-century philosophy, but even outside philosophy as such.

In any case, it is indeed very pleasing to have the book republished as a paperback!

Although it is tempting to use this occasion to consider new literature or to engage in detailed debate on scholarly disagreements, these activities must be postponed for another time as there is simply not enough space in a short Preface such as this. Rather, I am taking this opportunity to highlight just a few points of a very general nature mainly from the general Introduction below.

First of all, although the book focuses on only two of the most fundamental issues relevant to subjectivity or 'the subject', this in no way expresses an intention to devalue the many other issues or questions that one could ask about this theme. In particular, it is surely undisputed that disciplines other than philosophy have examined issues to do with self-consciousness and diachronic personal identity, and that these accounts are valuable in their own right. Not only that, even as a historian of philosophy, with my focus naturally on the philosophical debates, I do consider some of these other areas (dealing, for example, with theological issues) in so far as they help explain the philosophical debates and their impact. Nevertheless, this book is a work in the history of philosophy, and it is not, then, mainly concerned with disciplines such as theology, nor even with pre- and early modern fiction. Nor is it concerned with the more general question of when 'the subject' emerged. Some valuable publications relating to these questions are cited in the Introduction, but this is not the focus of the present volume.

Further, I would like to emphasise that although this study concentrates on early modern debates, it does not claim that its theme is special to early modern thought in the sense either that it was not discussed prior to that, or that pre-modern philosophers simply ignored or neglected it. Far from it; the Introduction outlines ancient, medieval and other pre-modern thought not only on the specific topic of this volume, but also on related issues. In addition, some Chapters review earlier debates in order to consider more precisely the relationship between specific pre-modern and early modern accounts (see, for example, pp. 97–102, 280–285).

As argued in the Introduction, however, the relationship between pre-modern and early modern discussions is not as straightforward as one might think. For example, are Stoic discussions of identity essentially the same as those of the seventeenth and eighteenth centuries, or at least sufficiently similar so that they can reasonably count as 'anticipations' or even as having 'influenced' the later debates? Care needs to be taken with such claims. It is not enough to rely on outward and seeming similarities.

Preface to the Paperback Edition

In addition, the scope of what is called 'early modern' varies in different disciplines, and even within philosophy. For the purposes of this book, 'early modern' has been used to refer to the period roughly from Descartes to Hume, with the term 'roughly' here accounting for the fact that there is some discussion of both pre-Descartes and post-Hume material. Still, with respect to the issues of self-consciousness and diachronic personal identity, it makes sense to begin the detailed study with Descartes, as his account is most relevant to the debates that follow.

Finally, the Introduction also outlines the general development of thought on these issues within early modern philosophy, but both here and in the individual Chapters, the notion of *development* must not be confused with that of *progress*. As indicated in the Conclusion, I do not accept the not uncommon view, held especially in the German speaking world, that early modern philosophy developed towards Kant and Kantianism as a goal. While I reject the idea that some kind of progressive or hierarchical structure underlies the early modern discussions, I do claim, however, that it is possible to identify a number of (major and minor) turning points in the early modern debates about self-consciousness and personal identity. Some of these are explained in the Introduction, others are highlighted in individual Chapters. This means that there was not just random change, but a development of thought in the sense that, for example, a thinker or group of thinkers may have adopted a new perspective on the topic; or that a philosopher may have introduced some new conceptual distinctions; or that a thinker, such as Leibniz, may even have coined some new terminology in his attempt to deal with the issue of self-consciousness. In short, I believe that one can identify important turning points in early modern thought, but identifying such turning points is not the same as claiming that there was a development towards a particular goal.

The text has not been altered for this paperback edition, except for the correction of typographical errors, the updating of references to works that were listed as forthcoming and that have since been published, and the like.

I would like to take this opportunity to express my sincere thanks to Hannes Fraissler and Rudolf Mösenbacher, both of the University of Graz, for their invaluable help with these matters: Danke vielmals!

November 2013   Udo Thiel

Acknowledgements

Having worked on this book intermittently over many years, I have, unsurprisingly, used some (often heavily revised) material from my previously published papers. I am grateful to those who gave the appropriate permissions to make use of the following articles: 'Cudworth and Seventeenth-Century Theories of Consciousness', in S. Gaukroger (ed.), *The Uses of Antiquity. The Scientific Revolution and the Classical Tradition* (Dordrecht: Kluwer, 1991), pp. 79–99, by permission of the publisher (Springer Science+Business Media B.V.); 'Leibniz and the Concept of Apperception', *Archiv für Geschichte der Philosophie*, 76 (1994), 195–209, by permission of the publisher (de Gruyter); 'Hume's Notions of Consciousness and Reflection in Context', *British Journal for the History of Philosophy*, 2 (1994), 75–115, by permission of the publisher (Taylor & Francis Group); 'Between Wolff and Kant: Merian's Theory of Apperception', *Journal of the History of Philosophy*, 34 (1996), 213–32, by permission of the publisher (Johns Hopkins University Press); '"Epistemologism" and Early Modern Debates about Individuation and Identity', *British Journal for the History of Philosophy*, 5 (1997), 353–72, by permission of the publisher (Taylor & Francis Group); 'Individuation', in D. Garber and M. Ayers (eds.), *The Cambridge History of Seventeenth-Century Philosophy* (Cambridge: University Press, 1998), pp. 212–62, by permission of the publisher; 'Personal Identity', in D. Garber and M. Ayers (eds.), *The Cambridge History of Seventeenth-Century Philosophy* (Cambridge: University Press, 1998), pp. 868–912, by permission of the publisher; 'Locke and Eighteenth-Century Materialist Conceptions of Personal Identity, *The Locke Newsletter*, 29 (1998), 59–83, by permission of the editor (Roland Hall); 'Self-Consciousness and Personal Identity', in K. Haakonssen (ed.), *The Cambridge History of Eighteenth-Century Philosophy* (Cambridge: Cambridge University Press, 2006), pp. 286–318, by permission of the publisher; 'Der Begriff der Intuition bei Locke', in *Aufklärung*, 18 (2006), 95–112, by permission of the publisher (Meiner); 'Sulzer über Bewußtsein im Kontext', in F. Grunert and G. Stiening (eds.), *Johann Georg Sulzer. Aufklärung zwischen Christian Wolff und David Hume* (Berlin: Akademie Verlag, 2011), pp. 21–36, by permission of the publisher. I have also used material from the following publications of Oxford University Press: 'The Trinity and Human Personal Identity', in M. A. Stewart (ed.), *English Philosophy in the Age of Locke* (2000), pp. 217–43; 'Religion and Materialist Metaphysics: Some Aspects of the Debate about the Resurrection of the Body in Eighteenth-Century Britain', in Ruth Savage (ed.), *Philosophy and Religion in Enlightenment Britain: New Case Studies* (2012), pp. 90–111.

It is a pleasure to acknowledge the institutions that have supported me. The Australian National University in Canberra granted me leave several times while I was working on this project. The Duke August Library in Wolfenbüttel welcomed me as a *Stipendiat* and as a Visiting Scholar many times over the years, and I would like to thank especially Sabine Solf and Gillian Bepler from the research branch of the library for their support. The Institute for Advanced Studies in the Humanities at

Acknowledgements

the University of Edinburgh and its then Head, Peter Jones, also welcomed me several times as a Visiting Scholar, as did the Max Planck Institute for the History of Science in Berlin. I was also fortunate to spend some time at the History of Science Department at Harvard University as a Visitor when the project was in its infancy, and at the Department of Philosophy at Humboldt University in Berlin toward the end of the project. In October 2009 I took up my current position as the new Professor of the History of Philosophy at the University of Graz in Austria.

I have presented seminar papers relating to the theme of this book at all the institutions mentioned above. In addition I thank Manfred Baum, Reinhard Brandt, John Cottingham, Lothar Kreimendahl, Manfred Kuehn, and Dominik Perler for inviting me to present papers dealing with material from this project at their respective institutions. I have also presented talks relating to this project at several conferences, large and small, and I thank the organizers and the participants—too many to mention by name—for their comments, criticisms, and questions.

I am extremely grateful to the anonymous readers for Oxford University Press who read drafts of the manuscript and made many very helpful suggestions—most of which I have taken on board. I thank the editor, Peter Momtchiloff, for his interest in, and encouragement for, this project, and I thank the production team for their excellent work and patience.

At the University of Graz I thank Thomas Valentin Harb, Ingeborg Röllig, Sarah Tropper, and Nora Kreft for their help with various aspects of the editing process.

There are a number of people with whom I corresponded and/or conversed about matters relating to the theme of this book. These include Michael Ayers, Christian Barth, Manfred Baum, Reinhard Brandt, Stephen Buckle, Manfred Frank, Heiner F. Klemme, Lothar Kreimendahl, Manfred Kuehn, Martin Lenz, Stephan Schmid, Gideon Stiening, Pedro Stoichita, Kenneth P. Winkler, John Wright, and Falk Wunderlich. I am very grateful for their advice and many helpful comments.

I am particularly indebted to Knud Haakonssen and M. A. Stewart, who read and commented on large sections of the original manuscript, and to Galen Strawson, who read and commented, in considerable detail, on the entire manuscript, and engaged with me in a lively correspondence about this project. Their comments, insightful suggestions, and advice on various aspects of the book have been invaluable.

Last, but certainly not least, Hans-Joachim Wehmeier, who taught me philosophy and its history in my early years, has been a continuous source of support and friendship. Sheena Smith—the most important person in my life—has accompanied this work continuously with love as well as with a sharply critical eye ever since 2002. To her this book is dedicated with love.

Udo Thiel

Introduction: aims and issues

I.1. THE AIMS

This volume discusses two fundamental features of human subjectivity: self-consciousness and personal identity. This does not, however, exhaust the topic of human subjectivity, which can indeed touch on a dazzlingly wide variety of inter-related issues such as the mind–body problem, questions concerning agency, self-determination, moral and legal responsibility, and also the possibility of knowledge of an external world of physical objects, to name just a few. However, an essential feature of the human subject, presupposed by notions such as agency, concerns its ability to relate to itself in various ways, the most fundamental form of which is the awareness or consciousness of one's own self. Thus, the ability to determine our own self with respect to actions, and even the ability to reflect on our own past, presupposes that we are conscious of our own self in some way. Another related and equally fundamental feature of the human subject is that it thinks of itself as identical through time. For example, we assume such identity when we talk of a person's responsibility for past actions. So, for these reasons, this volume discusses these two fundamental features of human subjectivity: self-consciousness and personal identity. Further, it discusses them in what is commonly known as the early modern period in French, German, and British philosophy. That is to say, it deals with the treatment of these issues by seventeenth- and eighteenth-century thinkers such as Descartes, Locke, Leibniz, Wolff, and Hume, as well as their early critics, followers, and other philosophical contemporaries.[1] There are two reasons for this particular historical focus. First of all, interest in the issues of self-consciousness and personal identity is certainly characteristic and even central to early modern thought. And, secondly, this is an interest that continues to this day, in a form still strongly influenced by the conceptual frameworks of early modern thought on these issues.[2] It may

---

[1] The debates about these issues in the second half of the eighteenth century, from philosophers such as Condillac up to Priestley, Reid, Kant, and Reinhold, will be dealt with in a separate volume entitled *The Enlightened Subject* (in preparation). There does not seem to be much original discussion of these issues in Italy. Thomas Burford has attempted to reconstruct an account of personal identity in Vico (to whom he ascribes a narrative account), but provides no evidence of any explicit discussion of self-consciousness and personal identity in the texts. See Burford, 'A Theater of Memory: Vico's View of Personal Identity', *South Atlantic Philosophy of Education Society Yearbook*, 32 (1987), 69–76.

[2] Compare, for example, the discussion in Brinkmann, 'Consciousness, Self-Consciousness, and the Modern Self', *History of the Human Sciences*, 18 (4) (2005), 27–48, at 27.

be too strong to claim, with Michael Ayers, that 'for all the transformation of our motives, indeed of our general philosophical theory... the debate on personal identity has hardly moved on since the innovations of the seventeenth and eighteenth centuries'.[3] There can be no doubt, however, that self-consciousness and personal identity in the form in which they are so widely discussed today originate in the rich debates of the seventeenth and eighteenth centuries and are significantly informed by the latter.

Of course, various aspects that are relevant to early modern discussions of self-consciousness and personal identity were present prior to seventeenth-century thought. Some of these were consciously taken up and developed, while others may have affected early modern thought without being explicitly appealed to by particular thinkers. As is true of most philosophical issues, thought about this topic goes back as far as ancient Greek philosophy. Clearly, although early modern philosophers thought of themselves as making a fresh start, there are many points of contact with pre-modern thought.[4] Indeed, today no serious historian of philosophy would maintain that early modern philosophy was somehow created out of nothing or distinguishes itself from earlier periods by some huge divide. The attempt at making a fresh start was characterised by significant continuities with the past, and this includes the issues of self-consciousness and personal identity.[5]

As we shall see at various points, however, care needs to be taken when ideas in ancient thought appear to be essentially the same as ideas in early modern thought. For just as we tend to read present-day concerns into early modern philosophical thought, we tend to read the latter into the traditions of Platonist, Aristotelian, and Hellenistic and medieval philosophy.[6] Indeed, identifying the nature of the presence of these traditions in the early modern period is not always as straightforward as we might wish, since the impact of ancient traditions is often varied and diffused. Moreover, while the early modern period is essentially and obviously related to what went on before, the concerns of philosophers of this period, their ideas, and even their terminology, have also to be seen in their own immediate and specific contexts, for these are relevant to the way in which the ancient ideas were used and possibly modified. And there are, of course, genuine early modern contexts that are important to an understanding of the philosophical thought of that time.

---

[3] Ayers, *Locke* (1991), vol. 2, p. 281.

[4] For the impact of ancient thought on early modern philosophy, see the literature from Gaukroger (ed.), *The Uses of Antiquity* (1991), to Hedley and Hutton (eds.), *Platonism at the Origins of Modernity* (2008).

[5] This is even more obvious if our treatment of human subjectivity does not focus especially on issues concerning self-consciousness and the sense of identity. For example, Kobusch has emphasised the important and influential role of the Church Fathers in this context, as they assign the 'inner man' a central place in their philosophical thought: Kobusch, *Christliche Philosophie. Die Entdeckung der Subjektivität* (2006), pp. 18–19. Libera has argued that the idea of human subjectivity, understood simply in terms of ownership of mental states or agency, is not new in the early modern period but is present, for example, in Aquinas: Libera, 'When did the Modern Subject Emerge?', *American Catholic Philosophical Quarterly*, 82 (2008), 181–220.

[6] Witness, for example, Annas's statement in her otherwise excellent study *Hellenistic Philosophy of Mind* (1992), that the Stoic view about self-consciousness is 'the same' as Kant's, who merely uses different arguments to arrive at the 'same' conclusion.

While subjectivity as understood here is certainly a main issue in early modern thought, it is of course not the only one. Rather, to a large extent early modern philosophy is concerned with foundations for the new experiential sciences and with how the latter can be reconciled with the demands of theology.[7] Within this broad context, however, a debate emerged about self-consciousness and identity—if only slowly at first. Detailed discussions of personal identity did not begin until the late seventeenth century, and advanced in earnest in the eighteenth century. Similarly, in the early modern context, the very notions of consciousness and self-consciousness did not become an object of enquiry in their own right until the early eighteenth century. But the seventeenth century is absolutely essential to these developments, so a discussion of these issues in the early modern period must begin with Cartesian philosophy and how it relates to Scholastic and other seventeenth-century strands of thought. Certainly, and contrary to what some scholars have claimed, philosophical theory about human subjectivity was alive and well long before the beginnings of German Idealism around 1800.[8]

In short, then, this book's aim is twofold: (1) to provide an account of the development of its topic in the early modern period up to Wolff and Hume and their critics and followers, and critically to evaluate their contributions; and (2) to explain the philosophical arguments in their historical context. As will become apparent, there is a wealth of important material in this period, but some major developments and turning points as well as many connections relating to points of detail can be identified.

I.2. THE LITERATURE

To date there appear to be three groups of publications that deal with aspects of seventeenth- and eighteenth-century accounts of self-consciousness and personal identity. First, there are general overviews of the history of the notion of the self or mind covering several centuries, some of which range from antiquity to the present day.[9] These may include surveys and summaries of some eighteenth-century views relating to personal identity, self-consciousness, and connected issues, though they do not focus on

---

[7] Compare Harré, 'Knowledge', in Rousseau and Porter (eds.), *The Ferment of Knowledge: Studies in the Historiography of Eighteenth-Century Science* (1980), pp. 11–54, at p. 15.

[8] According to Henrich, genuine theory of the subject did not begin until the rise of German Idealism with the philosophy of Fichte. This, he claims, is the 'foundation period of the philosophy of the subject': Henrich, 'Die Anfänge der Theorie des Subjekts', in Honneth, McCarthy, Offe, and Wellmer (eds.), *Zwischenbetrachtungen im Prozeß der Aufklärung. Jürgen Habermas zum 60. Geburtstag* (1989), pp. 106–70, at p. 115.

[9] See, for example, Teichert, *Personen und Identitäten* (2000); MacDonald, *History of the Concept of Mind. Speculations about Soul, Mind and Spirit from Homer to Hume* (2003); MacDonald, *History of the Concept of Mind, Volume 2. The Heterodox and Occult Tradition* (2006); Martin and Barresi, *The Rise and Fall of Soul and Self. An Intellectual History of Personal Identity* (2006); Vidal, *Les sciences de l'âme xvi^e–xviii^e siecle* (2006). For earlier general overviews, see Carus, *Geschichte der Psychologie* (1808; reprinted, with an introduction by Rolf Jeschonnek, 1990); Blakey, *History of the Philosophy of Mind: embracing the Opinions of all Writers on Mental Science from the Earliest Period to the Present Time*, 4 vols. (1850).

the eighteenth century. They are very selective, providing only very brief summaries of a small amount of the material that is covered here. Second, at the other extreme, there is specialist literature on the accounts of identity and self-consciousness of only one or two individual 'major' thinkers of the period, such as Locke and Hume.[10] Clearly, there are some highly valuable and insightful contributions among these many treatments focusing on individual thinkers. But their concern is not with the development as a whole. In the present study, both more and less well known thinkers are dealt with in some detail, and they are read in their historical context and given a place in the early modern development of thought on these issues. Third, there are publications that focus more closely on the eighteenth century and deal with aspects of our topic. There are, for example, a number of investigations from a literary, linguistic, or broader cultural-studies perspective, some of which touch on philosophical issues relating to self-consciousness and personal identity. For the most part, however, these studies are restricted to only some of the relevant aspects, and focus on either France or Britain.[11] And among the more narrowly philosophical investigations, there are those that deal with the notion of consciousness but say nothing or very little on the issue of personal identity.[12] Some publications on eighteenth-century thought, however, do comment on the issue of personal identity, and also refer to the notions of consciousness and self-consciousness. Perhaps the most important earlier studies dealing with aspects relevant to our concern are B. L. Mijuskovic's *The Achilles of Rationalist Arguments* (1974) and R. Martin and J. Barresi's *Naturalization of the Soul: Self and Personal Identity in the Eighteenth Century* (2000). Both accounts are very selective, however. Mijuskovic

---

[10] For references to some of the most important contributions of this kind, see the relevant chapters below.

[11] See, for example, Fox, *Locke and the Scriblerians: Identity and Consciousness in Early Eighteenth-Century Britain* (1988). Fox's very interesting study focuses on the problem of personal identity and the significance which the debates on identity had for early eighteenth-century literature. See also Perkins, *The Concept of the Self in the French Enlightenment* (1969); and Davies, *Conscience as Consciousness. The Idea of Self-Awareness in French Philosophical Writing from Descartes to Diderot* (1990). Perkins comments occasionally on personal identity; but as the title of her book suggests, the focus is entirely on French material, and it mostly describes but does not analyse and discuss in any detail the relevant arguments. Davies's book provides a very useful and often insightful but largely linguistic and literary study of the notion of consciousness in France. For seventeenth-century French notions of consciousness, see also the earlier works by Lindemann, *Der Begriff der Conscience im französischen Denken* (1938), and (Rodis-)Lewis, *Le problème de l'inconscient et le Cartésianisme* (1950). For a treatment that focuses on identity and culture, see Wahrman, *The Making of the Modern Self. Identity and Culture in Eighteenth-Century England* (2004).

[12] The earliest study of importance here is Grau's contribution from the early twentieth century: *Die Entwicklung des Bewusstseinsbegriffs im XVII. und XVIII. Jahrhundert* (1916). Grau discusses Descartes, Hobbes, Locke, Berkeley, Hume, Leibniz, and Wolff and his followers and opponents. But he offers a history of philosophy of mind in general, rather than a detailed examination of the concept of self-consciousness, though obviously he does comment on questions relevant to this study. More recently, Frank's many and highly important publications dealing with self-consciousness focus, for the most part, on post-Kantian German thought. This post-Kantian perspective also informs his treatment of earlier material in Frank, *Selbstgefühl* (2002). Wunderlich's recent study, however, focuses very much on Kant and the pre-Kantian German notions of consciousness (and on Wolff in particular): see Wunderlich, *Kant und die Bewußtseinstheorien des 18. Jahrhunderts* (2005).

Introduction: aims and issues 5

discusses most of the selected authors very briefly indeed, and Martin and Barresi are concerned only with the development in Britain, focusing, as the title suggests, on the issue of the 'naturalization of the soul'.[13]

Certainly I owe a debt of knowledge to many of these publications. Insofar as they do cover similar material, however, my interpretations often differ significantly from theirs. Moreover, the present study also attempts to broaden the scope of the treatment of these issues considerably, and in more than one sense, by dealing, for example, with more than a hundred years of philosophical debate in France, Britain, and Germany, while at the same time not neglecting the details of the arguments as well as, in many cases, discussing alternative interpretations.

I.3. THE ISSUES

As indicated, the notions of self-consciousness and personal identity are closely connected. It would be difficult to account for the discussion of personal identity without invoking the notion of consciousness, understood as a relating to one's own self. The reverse does not apply, however. The notion of self-consciousness has a broader significance than its link to the issue of personal identity. Before analysing those connections and the details of the arguments and developments, it is important to provide some preliminary conceptual and historical background for the three central notions that are examined in this book: self-consciousness, identity, and person.

I.3.1. Consciousness and self-consciousness

There are very few explicit discussions of consciousness dating from the seventeenth century and the early part of the eighteenth century. In Britain, the term 'consciousness' was used extensively by a large number of philosophical and theological writers in the

---

[13] Martin and Barresi are to be congratulated in particular for having rediscovered Hazlitt's contribution to the issue of personal identity from the early nineteenth century (1805), which is outside the scope of the present volume. The earliest survey of British eighteenth-century accounts of personal identity seems to be an 86-page tract from 1827 by a certain Thomas Wallace, which covers Locke, Butler, Reid, Brown, and Stewart, but omits Hume: Wallace, *A Review of the Doctrine of Personal Identity* (1827). Other, more recent, book-length publications include Hauser's thesis *Selbstbewußtsein und Personale Identität* (1994), which deals with only Locke, Leibniz, Hume, and Tetens. Moreover, it has to be said that the standard of his analyses and arguments is not very high. For details, see my review in *Das Achtzehnte Jahrhundert*, 19 (1995), 243–5. There are a few relevant edited collections, such as Barber's and Gracia's *Individuation and Identity in Early Modern Philosophy. Descartes to Kant* (1994). This book does not deal with the issue of self-consciousness, however, and is very selective as far as the eighteenth century is concerned. It discusses the issue of *personal* identity only in relation to Locke and Hume. For a critical discussion of *Individuation and Identity*, see Thiel, ' "Epistemologism" and Early Modern Debates about Individuation and Identity', *British Journal for the History of Philosophy*, 5 (1997), 353–72. Cazzaniga's and Zarka's edited collection *L'individu dans la pensée moderne xvie–xviiie siècle*, 2 vols. (1995), has some relevant contributions on individual thinkers (such as Diderot and Condillac). Many of the contributions, however, are concerned with larger political and anthropological issues and with material from the sixteenth century.

1690s and in the early eighteenth century, but none of these authors examined the notion of consciousness itself in any detail. It was not until the 1720s that consciousness became an object of enquiry in its own right. In some contexts, consciousness was thought of as being concerned with external objects, but this was not how the notion was generally understood. In 1727, John Maxwell distinguished between three meanings of the term 'consciousness':[14] (a) 'the reflex Act, by which a Man knows his Thoughts to be his own Thoughts', (b) 'the Direct Act of Thinking; or (which is of the same Import;) simple Sensation', or (c) 'the Power of Self-motion, or of beginning of Motion by the Will'.[15] Maxwell insists that (a)—consciousness understood as a 'reflex act' on our own thoughts—is 'the strict and properest Sense of the Word'.[16] Consciousness, then, is understood here as a way of relating to one's own mental states. This inner-directed sense of consciousness dominated the eighteenth-century discussions, not only in Britain, but also in France and Germany.[17]

Although consciousness understood in this way is obviously a form of relating to one's own self, it has to be distinguished from *self*-consciousness—the consciousness of a self or subject or *I*.[18] This very distinction raises further questions, however, about the relation between these different forms of relating to one's own self. For example, can there be self-consciousness without consciousness? Or does self-consciousness require consciousness? Can there be consciousness without self-consciousness, or is the former always and necessarily accompanied by the latter?

---

[14] Discussed in more detail in Thiel, 'Cudworth and Seventeenth-Century Theories of Consciousness', in Gaukroger (1991), pp. 79–99, at pp. 80–1.

[15] *A Treatise of the Laws of Nature. By . . . Richard Cumberland . . . Made English from the Latin by John Maxwell, ... At the End is subjoin'd, An Appendix, containing two Discourses, 1. Concerning the Immateriality of Thinking Substance. 2. Concerning the Obligation, Promulgation, and Observance of the Law of Nature, by the Translator* (1727). (Cumberland's Latin original was first published in 1672.) The quoted passages are from the first discourse in the appendix (p. 5; separate pagination). The discourse's full title is *A Summary of the Controversy between Dr. Samuel Clarke and an anonymous Author* [Anthony Collins], *concerning the Immateriality of Thinking Substance*. The controversy between Clarke and Collins took place from 1706 to 1708, and was initiated by Henry Dodwell's *An Epistolary Discourse, proving from the Scripture and the first Fathers, that the Soul is a Principle naturally Mortal* (1706). In this controversy, extensive use was made of the term 'consciousness'. For Clarke and Collins, see Chapters 4 and 7 below.

[16] This is how Clarke defines 'consciousness' in *A Second Defense of an Argument made use of in a Letter to Mr. Dodwell* (1707), p. 42.

[17] Compare also the comment by the eighteenth-century American philosopher Jonathan Edwards, who says: 'Consciousness is the mind's perceiving what is in itself—ideas, actions, passions, and every thing that is there perceptible. It is a sort of feeling within itself': *'The Mind' of Jonathan Edwards: A Reconstructed Text*, ed. Howard (1963), p. 101. For a discussion of Edwards, see Chapter 8 below.

[18] Compare, for example, Frank's distinction between 'egological self-consciousness' and 'non-egological self-consciousness'. The former is the 'consciousness of the owner of consciousness (the *subject* or *I*)'; the latter is the consciousness of mental states. Non-egological self-consciousness can, in turn, relate either to the mental states, acts, or experiences themselves, or to the contents of these mental states—a distinction that is not always made explicit in early modern discussions. See Frank, 'Non-objectal Subjectivity', in *Journal of Consciousness Studies*, 14 (2007), 152–73. Here, what Frank calls 'non-egological self-consciousness' is simply called 'consciousness'; and his 'egological self-consciousness' is our 'self-consciousness'. Frank is of course, perfectly justified in referring to both as forms of self-consciousness, as both involve a relating to one's own self.

Early modern philosophers do not always formulate these kinds of question explicitly, but views and arguments about them can be identified in many of them, even if they hint only implicitly at the importance of various conceptual distinctions concerning the issue of relating to oneself.

In 1728 an essay solely devoted to the notion of consciousness understood essentially in the inner-directed sense, and dealing also with self-consciousness, was published anonymously in London.[19] The author, who has now been identified as a certain Charles Mein,[20] says that consciousness is 'that inward Sense and Knowledge which the Mind hath of its own Being and Existence, and of whatever passes within itself, in the Use and Exercise of any of its Faculties or Powers' (pp. 144–5). This essay seems to have been the first extensive and detailed treatment of the topic in the early modern context. The author himself appears to be aware of this, and finds it 'not a little surprising that They, who have search'd and ransack'd every nook and corner of the Mind, for *Ideas*... should never once happen to *Stumble* upon *Consciousness*' (ibid., p. 195). In Germany, Christian Wolff's empirical and rational psychologies of the 1720s and 1730s contain reflections on consciousness and self-consciousness, and by the 1730s these notions had come to be regarded as fundamental philosophical concepts. For Wolff, the issue of self-consciousness is central to his account of our knowledge of the external world: the problem of external objects cannot even be formulated without raising questions about our own self. Thus, Mein's *Essay* and the writings of Wolff constitute a turning point in the philosophical discussion of consciousness and self-consciousness. These notions now become central to the philosophical enterprise. And in the second half of the century—especially from the mid-1760s onwards, with the development of empirical psychology—consciousness was discussed not only in the context of other philosophical debates, but also in an increasing number of independent tracts devoted to consciousness itself. In 1778 Joseph Priestley could safely say that 'in all metaphysical subjects, there is a perpetual appeal made to *consciousness*'.[21]

The question is, however, what form of self-relation the 'reflex act' or 'inward Sense and Knowledge' called consciousness was held to be, and how it was thought to connect to other forms of relating to one's own self. This question is not as easy to answer as it may seem, and there appears to be no general agreement among early modern philosophers as to precisely what kind of self-relation terms such as 'consciousness' or 'self-consciousness' denote. It is important in this context to look at the etymological and conceptual connection between the notions of consciousness and conscience. Like English 'conscience', French 'conscience', and German 'Bewußtsein' and 'Gewissen', the term 'consciousness' derives from the Latin 'conscientia'—the

---

[19] Anon. [Charles Mein]. *Two Dissertations concerning Sense, and the Imagination. With an Essay on Consciousness* (1728). A modern edition of the *Essay, Pseudo-Mayne. Über das Bewusstsein 1728*, trans. and ed. Brandt (1983), contains an introduction and notes by the editor.

[20] Buickerood has made this identification in '*Two Dissertations concerning Sense, and the Imagination. With an Essay on Consciousness* (1728): A Study in Attribution', *1650–1850: Ideas, Aesthetics, and Inquiries in the Early Modern Era*, 7 (2002), 51–86.

[21] Price and Priestley, *A Free Discussion of the Doctrines of Materialism and Philosophical Necessity* (1778), p. 280.

noun for 'con-sc/i/re'. The details of the etymology of 'conscientia' are complex and controversial, but it seems that it is a translation of Greek terms—the main candidates being 'syneidesis,' 'synesis', and 'synaisthesis.'[22] Indeed, the first English writing philosopher to make extensive use of the noun 'consciousness' and to attach to it a particular philosophical meaning, the Cambridge Platonist Ralph Cudworth, uses the term as a translation of 'synaisthesis'.[23] Initially, Latin 'conscientia', Greek 'syneidesis', and even English 'consciousness' or being 'conscious', meant a perception or knowledge of something that one shares with someone else: being conscious meant being privy to something. In fact, this was how 'being conscious' was still defined occasionally in the seventeenth century, but it was clearly no longer the standard meaning. Rather, like Greek 'syneidesis' and Latin 'conscientia' (much earlier), 'consciousness' changed its meaning from 'knowing together with someone else' to 'knowing something with oneself': the person with whom I am privy to something else is not someone else but my own person. It came to be understood in a self-relating sense.

The English 'conscience' is much older than 'consciousness', and derives from a further development of 'conscientia' denoting a moral judgement of one's own actions and thoughts. In Scholastic thought, 'conscientia' formed a very special topic within moral theology.[24] This tradition was still relevant in the early modern period. In England in the first half of the seventeenth century there were countless sermons and tracts on the problem of 'conscientia'—especially in the context of Puritan teaching and its emphasis on the individual's conscience. The notion of *conscientia* applied here seems to be very similar to that in Scholastic thought. *Conscientia* as a whole was thought to consist of three parts or elements. The first is a set of objective moral principles which set the standard according to which we ought to direct our actions—sometimes referred to as the rational or pure part of conscience. The second

---

[22] For the etymology of 'conscientia', 'conscience', 'consciousness', and 'Bewußtsein', see Zucker, *Syneidesis-Conscientia* (1928); Jung, 'Syneidesis, Conscientia, Bewußtsein', in *Archiv für die Gesamte Psychologie*, 89 (1933), 525–40; Seel, 'Zur Vorgeschichte des Gewissens-Begriffes im altgriechischen Denken', in Kusch (ed.), *Festschrift Franz Dornseiff zum 65. Geburtstag* (1953), pp. 291–319; Hennig, *'Conscientia' bei Descartes* (2006), pp. 80–94. Hennig assumes that 'conscientia' is not a translation of 'syneidesis', and that the Greek background can be neglected (pp. 87–8). Even if this were acceptable for the interpretation of Descartes, such neglect would be highly problematic for an understanding of seventeenth-century notions of consciousness, given the importance of neo-Platonic sources in the early modern period. For the etymology of 'consciousness', see also Lewis, *Studies in Words* (1960), pp. 181–213.
[23] Cudworth, *True Intellectual System of the Universe* (1678; *imprimatur* 1671), p. 159. Thus, the following statement is obviously false: 'Outside of several minor uses of the word itself, the earliest written use of the term *consciousness* in the language is by John Locke' (Fox, 1988 p. 12). Cudworth's statements about consciousness are not so much part of an analysis of human subjectivity, but of a metaphysical account of nature in general—an account that relies heavily on Plotinus. See Plotinus, *Enneads*, III.8.4, V.8.11. On Plotinus, see Schwyzer, '"Bewusst" und "unbewusst" bei Plotin', in E. R. Dodds (ed.), *Les sources de Plotin* (1960), pp. 343–90; Warren, 'Consciousness in Plotinus', *Phronesis*, 9 (1964), 83–97; O'Daly, *Plotinus' Philosophy of the Self* (1973). For further comment on Cudworth on consciousness, see Chapter 2 below and Thiel (1991), pp. 79–99.
[24] For the history of the notion of conscience, see Stelzenberger, *Conscientia bei Augustinus: Studien zur Geschichte der Moraltheologie* (1959); Potts, *Conscience in Medieval Philosophy* (1980); Kittsteiner, *Die Entstehung des modernen Gewissens* (1995); Hennig (2006), pp. 96–183.

is a knowledge or remembrance of thoughts and actions performed by us. In 1621 Anthony Cade described it as 'a Chronicle, or register, roll or record' where all our 'thoughts, words, and actions be they good or evil' are set down. The third part is the moral judgement of our remembered actions on the basis of the moral principles.[25] Clearly, in this account a non-evaluative sense of relating to one's own self is present as the second part or element—as the remembering of our own thoughts and actions. This is a prerequisite for our moral judgement of our actions. But in this context *conscientia* as 'chronicle' is just an element of the moral '*conscientia*' theorem as whole.[26]

While in French there is only 'conscience' for the Latin '*conscientia*', in German and English two different terms for evaluative and non-evaluative *conscientia* respectively evolved: 'consciousness' and 'conscience'; 'Bewußtsein' and 'Gewissen'. While Cudworth introduced the term 'consciousness' into English philosophical terminology, Christian Wolff introduced the German 'Bewußtsein' for the non-evaluative relating to one's own self.[27] The fact that French and Latin texts of the time had only one term for both consciousness and conscience can create some confusion, and not just for present-day readers. It would be a mistake, however, simply to assume that all uses of '*conscientia*' and French 'conscience' should be understood in terms of conscience. Some philosophers writing in French and/or Latin only (Leibniz and Pierre Coste, for example) clearly struggled to distinguish between the two meanings of the one French or Latin term. It would seem that Descartes, too, makes use of '*conscientia*' or '*conscium esse*' in the non-evaluative sense—at least in some contexts.[28] Other seventeenth- and early eighteenth-century thinkers clearly made use of the non-evaluative sense of the French and Latin terms. Leibniz, for example, suggests in *Principes de la nature et de la grâce* (1714) that conscience is 'the reflective knowledge [connaissance réflexive]' of our inner states (§ 4). In *Nouveaux essais* he sometimes translates Locke's 'consciousness' as 'conscience', and at other times attempts to coin new terms (such as 'consciosité') to maintain the distinction

---

[25] Cade, *A Sermon on the Nature of Conscience* (1621), pp. 19–22. For Scholastic definitions, see Goclenius, *Lexicon philosophicum* (1613), p. 447; and Micraelius, *Lexicon philosophicum*, second edn. (1662; first edition, 1653), col. 321.
[26] Sometimes the term '*conscientia*' was used to denote the old notion of *sensus communis*. This is true, for example, of Herbert of Cherbury, who defines '*conscientia*' as the '*sensus communis* of the inner senses'. Here, too, however, the function ascribed to *conscientia* is mainly a moral one. See Herbert of Cherbury, *De veritate*, third edn. (1645; first edition, 1624), p. 104. *Conscientia* is said to be that by which we examine what is good and evil, and by means of which we apply the 'common notions' to particular cases.
[27] Wolff, *Vernünfftige Gedancken von Gott, der Welt und der Seele des Menschen, auch allen Dingen überhaupt* (1719), reprint of 1751, ed. Corr (1983); at Section 719. There are earlier versions of 'Bewußtsein'—for example, in Thomasius's German writings (see Chapter 11 below), but it was Wolff's usage that became influential in subsequent philosophical discussion.
[28] *Oeuvres de Descartes*, ed. Adam and Tannery (1964–76), vol. 10, p. 524; *Philosophical Writings*, ed. Cottingham, Stoothoff, Murdoch, and Kenny (1984–91), vol. 2, p. 418. See also *Oeuvres* (1964–76), vol. 7, p. 559; *Philosophical Writings*, vol. 2, p. 382. In *Philosophical Writings*, '*conscientia*' is translated as 'awareness'. It has been claimed, however, that in Descartes, *conscientia* is to be understood in an evaluative sense. Henning, for example, argues that all occurrences of '*conscientia*' and '*conscium esse*' in Descartes are to be understood in an evaluative sense of *conscientia*. See Hennig (2006), and the detailed discussion of Descartes on consciousness in Chapter 1 below.

between consciousness and conscience in French.[29] Samuel Christian Hollmann and Daniel Strähler make a point of distinguishing between what they call 'logical' 'conscientia' (consciousness) and 'moral' 'conscientia' (conscience).[30] La Forge and Malebranche also use the French term 'conscience' in a non-evaluative sense—as synonymous with 'sentiment intérieur'.[31] Malebranche says that we know our own thoughts and souls only through a 'sentiment intérieur' or 'conscience'.[32] Pierre Coste, whose French translation of Locke's *Essay Concerning Human Understanding* (1st edn. 1690) first appeared in 1700, translates Locke's 'consciousness' as 'conscience'. In later editions Coste remarks that Malebranche's 'conscience' corresponds to Locke's 'consciousness'.[33] Elsewhere, Gerard de Vries, for example, who in the late 1680s and 1690s published widely on ontology and pneumatology in general and on Descartes's philosophy in particular,[34] and who was influential in early eighteenth-century Britain,[35] makes use of the notion of non-evaluative *conscientia*. He defines thought in terms of *conscientia*, and holds that thought is always conscious of itself.[36] In spite of the

---

[29] For references and a detailed discussion of Leibniz, see Chapter 9 below.

[30] Hollmann, *Philosophia rationalis, quae Logica vulgo dicitur, multum aucta et emendate* (1746), p. 92. For a discussion of Hollmann, see Chapter 11 below. Strähler, *Prüfung der Vernünftigen Gedancken des Herrn Hof-Rath Wolffes von Gott, der Welt und der Seele des Menschen, auch allen Dingen überhaupt* (1723; reprinted, 1999), p. 557.

[31] La Forge speaks of 'cette conscience, ce tesmoignage, & ce sentiment interieur par lequel l'Esprit est aduertry de tout ce qu'il fait ou qu'il souffre': Clair (ed.), *Louis de La Forge (1632–1666). Oeuvres philosophiques* (1974), p. 134. The passage is from chapter 6 of La Forge's *Traité de l'esprit de l'homme* (1666). His use of 'conscience' is noted by Lewis (1960), p. 113; by Balz, *Cartesian Studies* (1951), p. 95; and by Davies (1990), pp. 13–14.

[32] Malebranche, *De la recherche de la vérité*, III.1.1: 'on ne connoît la pensée que par sentiment intérieur ou par conscience'. In III.2.7, Malebranche says about the soul: 'nous ne la connoissons que par *conscience*'. References to Malebranche's *Recherche* are to (Rodis-)Lewis (ed.), *Oeuvres de Malebranche* (1962), vol. 1.

[33] Coste, *Essai philosophique concernant L'entendement humain... Traduit de l'anglois de Mr. Locke* (1700), p. 404. For the remark on Malebranche, see, for example, the fifth edition (1755), p. 265. For a detailed discussion of Coste's translation of Locke's 'consciousness', see Davies (1990), pp. 26–38.

[34] de Vries, *De catholicis rerum attributis determinatones ontologica* (1687); *De natura dei et humanae mentis determinationes pneumatologicae* (1687); *Exercitationes rationales de deo divinisque perfectionibus: nec non philosophemata miscellanea, editio nova* (1695) (an expanded version with a treatise on innate ideas; the first edition appeared in 1685). *De R. Cartesii Mediationibus a Petro Gassendo impugnatis dissertatiuncula historico-philosophica* (1691). I refer to the 'sixth edition' of *De Naturae Dei et Humanae Mentis Determinationes Pneumatologicae* (1718) (abbr. *Pneumatology*). This edition was issued together with the 1718 edition of the work on ontology. The two works have continuous pagination.

[35] Watts, for example, cites 'that just censure, and that forbidding character, which the learned professor de Vries gives to the Metaphysics of the schools of former ages', in *Philosophical Essays on Various Subjects... To which is subjointed A Brief Scheme of Ontology* (1733). The quote is from the preface to the 'Brief Scheme'. There are also references to de Vries in Berkeley: *The Works of George Berkeley*, ed. Luce and Jessop (1948–57), vol. 1, p. 104 (entry nos. 887 and 888). For many years de Vries's books on ontology and pneumatology were used as textbooks at the University of Edinburgh. Thus it is very likely that Hume became familiar with some of de Vries's writings whilst studying there. M. A. Stewart drew my attention to this.

[36] See de Vries, *Pneumatology*, p. 72: 'Tale esse cogitandi facultatem, evincit, quae in hac omni semper involvitur, conscientia sui'; p. 76: 'Cogitatio actio cum conscientia est'. See also p. 83, where de Vries states that the intellect perceives 'cum conscientia'.

distinction that evolved between consciousness and conscience, there are some contexts in which the connection between the two notions must be taken into account. We shall see that this is the case, for example, with Locke. The moral significance he ascribes to personal identity relates to the connection between consciousness and conscience. Some authors explicitly distinguish between consciousness and conscience and explain how the two notions are related to one another.[37]

Apart from the distinctions between (inner-directed) consciousness and self-consciousness, and between consciousness and conscience, however, there remains the question about the nature of inner-directed consciousness itself. And here again, early modern thought relates to pre-modern philosophy. There are relevant sections in Plato's *Charmides*, for example, and especially in Aristotle's *De anima*.[38] As Victor Caston's seminal study has shown, although there seems to be no single term in their writings for what is called 'consciousness' in the early modern period or today, issues concerning the nature of consciousness as discussed in the early modern period and in current debates can be identified in Plato and in particular in Aristotle's discussion of perceiving that we perceive (*De anima*, 425b12–25).[39] This concerns, for example, a fundamental distinction between first-order and higher-order accounts of consciousness. According to the former, consciousness is an awareness of mental states that is an intrinsic and essential feature of those mental states—a feature which is not further analysable. According to the latter, consciousness consists in a higher-order thought or perception—that is to say, on this view, mental states become conscious in virtue of another, distinct mental state that is directed at the first mental state. This distinction is addressed by Aristotle who, as Caston argues, opts for a first-order account. Aristotle's argument against the higher-order accounts includes the issue of an infinite regress. For combined with the thesis that all mental states are conscious, higher-order accounts cannot, it seems, avoid an infinite regress of higher-order states. To avoid the infinite regress one must assume a higher-order state by which another state becomes conscious without being conscious itself (Caston, 2002, 754).

---

[37] Thus Grove, for example, argues that consciousness is the 'knowledge of the existence' of actions, while conscience is the knowledge of 'the moral Nature of Actions'. Therefore, he says, '*Consciousness* is a province of *Metaphysicks*, *Conscience* of *Morality*': Grove, *A System of Moral Philosophy*, ed. Amory, 2 vols. second edn. (1749; reprinted, 2000). Grove, *Ethical and Theological Writings*, ed. Sell, 6 vols. (2000). Vols. 5 and 6 contain Grove's *A System of Moral Philosophy* (1749). The quote is from *System* I, pp. 5–6. Grove's account of consciousness is discussed in detail in Chapter 7 below.

[38] For relevant discussions of Plato's *Charmides*, see, for example, Wellman, 'The Question posed at *Charmides* 165a–166c', *Phronesis* (1964), 107–13; Martens, *Das Selbstbezügliche Wissen in Platons 'Charmides'* (1973); Gloy, 'Platons Theorie der "episteme heautes" im *Charmides* als Vorläufer der modernen Selbstbewußtseinstheorien', *Kant-Studien*, 77 (1986), 137–64. For Aristotle see, for example, Kahn, 'Sensation and Consciousness in Aristotle's Psychology', *Archiv für Geschichte der Philosophie*, 48 (1966), 43–81; Oehler, *Subjektivität und Selbstbewußtsein in der Antike* (1997); Sihvola, 'The Problem of Consciousness in Aristotle's Psychology', in Heinämaa, Lähteenmäki, and Remes (eds.), *Consciousness: From Perception to Reflection in the History of Philosophy* (2007), pp. 49–65.

[39] Caston, 'Aristotle on Consciousness', *Mind*, 111 (2002), 751–815.

While it is difficult to determine with any certainty whether or not early modern philosophers were influenced by Aristotle's discussion, either directly or indirectly, these issues are present in early modern thought. Although the distinction between the two conceptions of consciousness is not made explicit, some thinkers clearly adopt a higher-order account of consciousness, while others opt for a first-order notion of consciousness. The issue of an infinite regress, too, is discussed in several early modern treatments of consciousness (for example, in Hobbes and Leibniz). Another issue, related to a first-order understanding of consciousness, concerns the notion of what is called today 'creature consciousness'. The idea that consciousness is an intrinsic feature of mental states might suggest that what is claimed here is that mental states such as perceptions are aware. The opposing view is that only the subjects or 'creatures' themselves who have the mental states can be conscious of something, no matter if we account for this consciousness in terms of a first-order or higher-order theory.[40] Again, in the early modern period, philosophers do not explicitly address this distinction between 'creature consciousness' and the notion that perceptions are aware, but the issue itself is present. While some formulate their views in such a way as to suggest that mental states are aware, it becomes clear in most cases that consciousness is understood as 'creature consciousness'. When Antoine Arnauld, for example, argues in *Des vrayes et des fausses idées* (1683) that 'our thought or perception is essentially reflective on itself',[41] he could be read as saying that the perception is aware. Elsewhere, however, he suggests that only 'creatures' such as human beings '*sunt conscia sui, et suae operationis*'.[42]

Apart from thematic points of contact between ancient and early modern accounts of consciousness, there are also direct borrowings of ancient theory and even terminology. Ralph Cudworth's seventeenth-century account (noted above) is deeply informed by neo-Platonic thought, and especially by Plotinus. Prior to Cudworth the English term 'consciousness' appeared only occasionally in philosophical contexts. One that is potentially significant concerns a translation of Stoic sources. Thomas Stanley, in his famous *History of Philosophy* (1656), translates 'syneidesis' in Diogenes Laertius's account of Chrysippus (*Lives*, VII, 85) as consciousness:

The first appetite of a living creature is to preserve it self, this being from the beginning proper to it by nature, as *Chrysippus* in his first Book of Ends, who affirms that the care of our selves, and consciousnesse thereof, is the first property of all living Creatures.[43]

---

[40] As Caston (2002) points out, Aristotle talks of *our* perceiving that we perceive, and thus assumes that consciousness is 'creature consciousness' (769).

[41] Arnauld, *Des vrayes et des fausses idées* (1683), chap. 6, p. 46: 'nostre *pensée ou perception* est essentiellement reflechissante sur elle même: ou, ce qui se dit plus heureusement en Latin, *est sui conscia*'. In a letter to Descartes he speaks of an 'intrinsic reflection of all thoughts': *Oeuvres* (1964–76), vol. 5, p. 213. For further discussion of Arnauld on consciousness, see Chapter 1 below.

[42] Arnauld, *Des vrayes et des fausses idées*, chap. 2, p. 11.

[43] Stanley, *The History of Philosophy, the Eighth Part, Containing the Stoick Philosophers* (1656), p. 60. Forschner has pointed out that the reading 'syneidesis' here is controversial. On the basis of other sources, he argues, 'synaisthesis' seems more plausible: Forschner, *Die Stoische Ethik* (1981), p. 146.

Introduction: aims and issues

Stanley then proceeds to account for this idea in terms of the notion of a sense of one's own self ('sensus sui') by presenting essentially a translation of a passage from Cicero's *De finibus* (III, 16):

> As soon therefore as a living Creature cometh into the World, it is conciliated to it self; commended to the conservation of it self and its own state, and to the election of such things as may preserve its state, but alienated from destruction, and from all such things as may destroy it... Neither could they desire any thing without having some sense of themselves, whereby they love themselves, and what belongs to them. Hence it is manifest, that the principle of this love is derived from themselves. (Stanley, *History*, Part 8, p. 60)

Other occurrences of 'consciousness' or 'conscientia' in early modern thought also point towards Stoic sources. When Spinoza, for example, speaks of the consciousness of one's drive of self-preservation ('mens sui conatus conscia', *Ethica*, III, prop. 9, dem.) he clearly appeals to Stoic ideas.[44] For example, he defines desire ('cupiditas') in man as a drive that is accompanied by the consciousness of this drive.[45] Moreover, even Cudworth's account of consciousness in terms of Plotinus's *synaisthesis* may well be linked to the Stoics, as it has been argued that Plotinus's notion of *synaisthesis* was inspired by Stoic doctrine.[46]

As these early modern references to the issue of relating to one's own self appeal to Stoic contexts, it is tempting to think that early modern thought about consciousness in general was inspired above all by Stoic doctrine.[47] As was indicated above, however, care needs to be taken here, as it can be seriously misleading to assimilate ancient sources to early modern concerns which are in general somewhat less alien to philosophical minds of the twenty-first century. In Stoic thought the notions of consciousness and 'sense of self' belong to the doctrine of *oikeiosis*—a doctrine that has been said to be the very 'foundation of Stoic ethics'.[48] Classical scholars note the difficulty of translating 'oikeiosis' into modern languages and therefore tend to transcribe rather than translate the term, but common English translations include 'familiarization' and 'appropriation'.[49] In any case, the doctrine is part of the Stoic account of moral development. The view is that this development begins with a basis that is natural to all human beings (indeed to all animals). The 'appropriation' to oneself or, rather, to one's own physical 'constitution' (*systasis/constitutio*) is part of

---

[44] This was noted by Pohlenz, *Die Stoa. Geschichte einer geistigen Bewegung*, vol. 2 (1949), p. 229.

[45] 'Cupiditas est appetitus cum eiusdem conscientia': Spinoza, *Ethica*, III, prop. 9, schol. In *Spinoza Opera*, ed. Gebhardt (1925), vol. 2.

[46] Pohlenz (1949), p. 190.

[47] Thus, Brandt has claimed that 'the whole of the modern philosophy of consciousness' was inspired by Stoic doctrine: 'Selbstbewusstsein und Selbstsorge. Zur Tradition der οἰκείωσις in der Neuzeit', *Archiv für Geschichte der Philosophie*, 85 (2003), 179–97, at 181. He does not, however, cite any of the sources in Stanley, Spinoza, and Cudworth given here and elsewhere to support this claim. Rather, he speculates that there are three Stoic 'succession-fragments' in Locke and Kant. Even if these speculations were convincing, they would hardly prove the rather sweeping claim about 'modern philosophy' in general.

[48] Pohlenz (1949), p. 113.

[49] Compare Gill, *The Structured Self in Hellenistic and Roman Thought* (2006), p. 37. The Latin notion used, for example, in Cicero, *De finibus*, III, 16, and Seneca, *Epistulae Morales*, ltr. 121, para. 16, is 'conciliatio'. The Loeb translation of Seneca uses 'adaptation'.

this process. Its natural basis concerns the desire to preserve our own physical constitution. Animals, including humans, are naturally adapted to develop in a way that preserves their being or constitution (Gill, 2006, p. 36). Such a desire is said to require a feeling of affection, concern for, or attachment ('appropriation') to our constitution.[50] The affection or concern for our constitution in turn requires an elementary sense or 'consciousness' that we all have of our own self or our own constitution.[51] At first, this 'appropriation' to one's own constitution is expressed by our acceptance of what is 'appropriate' to us and what preserves our life (ibid., p. 37). But the striving for self-preservation is only the *prote horme*—the first impulse (Diogenes Laertius on Chrysippus, *Lives*, VII, 85). A later development concerns the striving of reason and relates to the whole cosmos. In adult humans, preservation is not restricted to oneself but includes others and is informed by reason (see Gill, 2006, p. 36). And reason is understood here as the bearer of insight and moral striving (Forschner, 1981, p. 150). Thus the doctrine of *oikeiosis* is sometimes described in terms of 'two faces'—'an inward looking one and an outward looking one'.[52]

In spite of the occasional explicit and implicit references to this Stoic doctrine, however, the differences between early modern thought on consciousness and related ideas in Stoic philosophy are more significant than the (seeming) similarities.[53] Early modern philosophers' discussions of consciousness are concerned with the consciousness of mental states such as thoughts, memories, and emotions, and not primarily with Stoic self-preservation. As we shall see, this applies even to an admirer of ancient thought such as Ralph Cudworth. Although Cudworth develops his account of consciousness in terms of the notion of plastic nature rather than that of an individual subject, when applied to human subjects, consciousness, for Cudworth, relates to thoughts and actions rather than to the physical nature or constitution of its being. In Descartes, Locke, and other early modern thinkers too, consciousness is understood as an individual human subject's relating to its thoughts, feelings, and actions. It is not—or at least is not primarily—a consciousness of the essence of one's physical nature or constitution for which one then can feel affection, which is in turn the basis for the desire to preserve that constitution.

The Stoic material and, indeed, the notion of conscience, relates more to the issue of self-consciousness than to merely the consciousness of mental states. And it is with

---

[50] Compare Diogenes Laertius's account of this: 'The dearest thing 'proton oikeion' to every animal is its own constitution and the consciousness thereof': *Lives*, VII, 85 (transl. Hicks (1925)).

[51] This is the 'sensus sui' in Cicero, *De finibus*, III, 16. Seneca speaks of the sense of our own constitution: *Epistulae Morales*, ltr. 121, para. 9.

[52] G. B. Kerferd, 'The Search for Personal Identity in Stoic Thought', Bulletin of the John Rylands University Library of Manchester, 55 (1972), 177–96, at 179.

[53] This has been pointed out by several classical scholars who seem to be more sensitive to these differences than are writers on early modern thought such as Brandt (2003). See, for example, Long, 'Hierocles on Oikeiosis and Self-Perception', in Long, *Stoic Studies* (1996), pp. 250–63, at pp. 156–7. See, especially, the detailed study by Gill (2006), pp. 363–4. As Gill notes, the Stoic doctrine 'runs counter to the assumption typical of post-Cartesian thought that certain types of reflexive or self-related experiences notably self-consciousness have a special status as an expression of personhood'.

respect to self-consciousness in particular that early modern thought has been said to distinguish itself from pre-modern thought. Thus, Klaus Brinkmann argues that what distinguishes modern from pre-modern conceptions of subjectivity is precisely that only with the former does self-consciousness become a necessary condition of object-awareness.[54] But the relation between what modern thought calls consciousness and self-consciousness was debated well before the early modern period. Again, this debate can be said to go back to Aristotle. For Aristotle the consciousness we have of our own self and its thoughts and actions is dependent on and derived from the consciousness of objects. We arrive at a consciousness of our own self only on the basis of a consciousness of objects.[55] Self-consciousness, by this account, requires an activity of distinguishing oneself from the objects to which consciousness primarily relates—an idea that became relevant with Christian Wolff in the eighteenth century, as we shall see.[56] Aristotle also speaks of a self-relation that is not mediated through a consciousness of outer things, but this is possible only for the divine being.[57] In Stoic sources one can identify the view that all external experience or consciousness of outer things requires self-consciousness. It seems, however, that self-consciousness as included in external experience could not exist without or independently of such external experience, and is in this sense dependent on the latter.[58] Aquinas takes up the Aristotelian idea when dealing with the question of how 'the intellect knows itself', and says, referring approvingly to Aristotle's *De anima*: 'What is first known by the human intellect is this object; then, in the second place, the act by which the object is known is itself known; and finally, by way of the act, the intellect itself, of which the act of understanding is the perfection, is known'. Thus the primary objects of knowledge are external objects, and the intellect 'comes to a knowledge of all else from these'.[59] This view—that the consciousness of external things has priority over the consciousness of one's own self—was widely held by early modern thinkers who tended towards empiricist lines of thought.

Thus, when Aquinas says that the 'mind knows itself by means of itself', this is not to be understood as an immediate or direct form of self-awareness, as 'by means of itself' is to be understood as 'by means of its acts', and these relate to objects which are 'what is first known by the human intellect'.[60] The notion of an immediate and

---

[54] Brinkmann (2005), 27–48, at 32–5. Brinkmann maintains that this view is present in Descartes. As we shall see, however, Descartes does not even investigate the notion of consciousness in any detail. The view is present in Wolff, whom Brinkmann does not discuss.

[55] Compare *De anima*, 415a16. Aristotle suggests here that we first know the objects, then the acts that relate to the objects, and then the capacities for those acts. Compare, for example, the discussion in Oehler (1997), pp. 20, 22ff., 38, 39; and Owens, 'The Self in Aristotle', *Review of Metaphysics*, 41 (1988), 707–22.

[56] For the importance of the activity of distinguishing in Aristotle's discussion of self-consciousness, see Schmitt, 'Synästhesie im Urteil aristotelischer Philosophie', in Adler and Zeuch (eds.), *Synästhesie. Interferenz-Transfer-Synthese der Sinne* (2002), pp. 109–47, at pp. 122–30.

[57] Its 'thinking is a thinking of thinking': *Metaphysica*, 1074b34. Compare Oehler (1997), pp. 40ff.

[58] See the discussion of Chrysippus, Cicero, and Seneca, in Annas (1992), pp. 56–61.

[59] Aquinas, *Summa theologiae*, 1a.87.3; transl. Gilby et al. (1964–80), pp. 115–17.

[60] Aquinas, *Summa theologiae*, 1a.87.1; p. 109; and 1a.87.3, p. 115.

direct relating to one's own thought and soul, also present in early modern thought, is typically associated with Augustine, but, as Deborah Black has shown, can also be found, for example, in Avicenna.[61] Augustine suggests (in the context of an account of the trinity) that the knowledge of one's own existence is immediate and direct. The mind knows itself simply by being 'present to itself'.[62] It does not require the bodily senses or prior knowledge of external things. Moreover, mental faculties, such as memory, intelligence, and the will, are mutually related to one another but also essentially self-reflexive. Importantly, this internal reflexivity that is present in all mental acts is distinguished from thinking about or reflecting on those mental acts.[63] It seems that Augustine even ascribes to the mind what is called a pre-reflective knowledge of itself—for example, when he states in *De trinitate*: 'When the mind seeks to know itself, it already knows that it is a mind'.[64] These apparently very modern thoughts have tempted scholars to read Augustine through a variety of much later developments, including Kantian transcendental philosophy and twentieth-century phenomenology.[65] Avicenna's discussion of consciousness is less well known than Augustine's (and is independent of the latter), but his so-called 'Flying Man' argument is often seen as a precursor of the Cartesian *cogito*. The argument attempts to show that the human soul is always aware of itself, quite independently of its awareness of other objects. Moreover, Avicenna appears to hold that such self-awareness is primitive and involved in, and presupposed by a more explicit knowledge of myself as well as of my awareness of other things.[66]

In Descartes and in Cartesian thought more generally too, consciousness or knowledge of self does not seem to depend on the consciousness or knowledge of objects. In the framework of his 'methodical' doubt Descartes famously argues that the knowledge of one's own existence is fundamental, and that this knowledge is based on the immediate knowledge we have of our own thinking activity. The knowledge we have of the external world is secured only after the existence of the

---

[61] See Black, 'Consciousness and Self-Knowledge in Aquinas's Critique of Averroes's Psychology', *Journal of the History of Philosophy*, 31 (1993), 349–85, at 351–2; and especially Black, 'Avicenna on Self-Awareness and Knowing that One Knows', in Rahman, Hassan, and Street (eds.), *The Unity of Science in the Arabic Tradition* (2008), pp. 63–87.

[62] Augustine, *De trinitate*, X.9.12. *The trinity*, transl. Mckenna (1963). See the discussion, for example, in Matthews, 'Si fallor, sum', in Markus (ed.), *Augustine. A Collection of Critical Essays* (1972), pp. 151–67, at pp. 159–60.

[63] Augustine, *De trinitate*, X.11.17–18. Christoph Horn has drawn attention to the historical importance of this distinction in Augustine: Horn, 'Seele, Geist und Bewusstsein bei Augustinus', in Crone, Schnepf, and Stolzenberg (eds.), *Über die Seele* (2010), pp. 77–93, at pp. 87–8. See also Horn, 'Selbstbezüglichkeit des Geistes bei Plotin und Augustinus', in Brachtendorf (ed.), *Gott und sein Bild. Augustins 'De Trinitate' im Spiegel gegenwärtiger Forschung* (2000), pp. 81–103.

[64] Augustine, *De trinitate*, X.4.6.

[65] See, for example, Delahaye, who links Augustine to Kant on self-consciousness: Delahaye, *Die 'memoria interior'-Lehre des heiligen Augustinus und der Begriff der 'transzendentalen Apperzeption' Kants. Versuch eines historisch-systematischen Vergleichs* (1936). Hölscher reads Augustine through twentieth-century phenomenology: Hölscher, *The Reality of the Mind. Augustine's Philosophical Arguments for the Human Soul as a Spiritual Substance* (1986).

[66] See the discussion in Black (2008), 65–70. See also Sorabji, *Self. Ancient and Modern Insights about Individuality, Life and Death* (2006), pp. 222–6. Sorabji argues that the views of Augustine and Avicenna on these matters may have a common source in Porphyry (pp. 226–9).

self and that of God have been proved. But Descartes's position on this issue is not as clear as it may seem, as he does not seem to deal with the question of whether those thoughts, through the knowledge of which I come to know my own existence, are primarily inner-directed or outer-directed. Moreover (as we shall see), Descartes does not present any detailed account of precisely what kind of self-relation the 'knowledge' of one's own thinking (and of one's own self as subject of these thoughts) is supposed to be, nor how it may be related to other forms of relating to the self.

Early modern accounts of self-consciousness in general have been criticized by philosophers such as Dieter Henrich and other members of the so-called Heidelberg School.[67] Henrich argues that early modern philosophy is guilty of accounting for self-consciousness in terms of what he calls a 'reflection theory', according to which the self 'knows itself by entering into a relation to itself; that is, by turning itself back into itself' (Henrich, 1982, 20).

This theory begins by assuming a subject of thinking and emphasizes that this subject stands in a constant relationship to itself. It then goes on to assert that this relationship is a result of the subject's making itself into its own object; in other words, the activity of representing, which is originally related to objects, is turned back upon itself and in this way produces the unique case of an identity between the activity and the result of the activity. (ibid., p. 19)

Henrich argues that this 'theory of the Self as reflection... continually turns in a circle' (ibid., pp. 19–20). For if we assume, as we must, that the subject that reflects on itself is really a self, then that subject would already be conscious of itself, prior to any act of reflection. As Henrich argues, 'anyone who sets reflection into motion must himself already be both knower and the known' (ibid., p. 20). In this way the reflection theory is viciously circular, in that it presupposes what it sets out to explain. Reflection, Henrich argues, presupposes a prior, pre-reflective 'familiarity' of the self with itself: 'The self knows itself in an original way, not through exhortations or clever inferences' (ibid., p. 21).[68] This original self-consciousness cannot first be brought about by reflection. Reflection is merely a 'secondary phenomenon' (ibid., p. 22).

Now Henrich maintains that all early modern treatments of self-consciousness are in terms of reflection, so that 'an entire epoch' has fallen into the trap of the reflection theory.[69] Fichte, Henrich argues, was the first philosopher who not only recognized the circularity of the reflection theory but also developed a philosophy of the self that

---

[67] Henrich, 'Fichte's Original Insight', *Contemporary German Philosophy*, 1 (1982), 15–53; first published as 'Fichte's ursprüngliche Einsicht', in Henrich and Wagner (eds.), *Subjektivität und Metaphysik, Festschrift für Wolfgang Cramer* (1966), pp. 188–232. Quotations are from the English translation.

[68] See also Frank, *What is Neo-Structuralism?* (1989): 'Reflection can recognize as identical to itself only that whose identity it already previously has known. This prior familiarity with itself cannot, however, be the work of autonomous reflection itself, for all reflection is relative; i.e. it is the relation of *two* to each other, and these two are thus to this extent not simply *one*' (p. 280).

[69] Henrich (1982), 19–20. Henrich writes about the philosophy from Descartes to Kant that 'all of these theories... are guided by the very same idea of the structure of the Self' in terms of the reflection-theory (p. 19). See also Frank, *Selbstbewußtseinstheorien von Fichte bis Sartre* (1991), pp. 427, 435, 446–7.

'successfully avoids' this circularity (ibid., pp. 21, 27).[70] Even assuming that Henrich's analysis and critique of the reflection theory of self-consciousness are valid, however, we shall see that his rather sweeping statements about early modern philosophy are highly problematic. Although, possibly, some early modern thinkers (Descartes, Leibniz, Mein) can be reconstructed in terms of the reflection theory, this does not apply to several other thinkers of the period. These include Locke, with his account of self-consciousness in terms of intuition, for example, and philosophers such as Mérian, who speaks of a pre-reflective, 'original' apperception that is presupposed by any reflective turning to one's own self.[71]

It is plain, then, that early modern discussions of consciousness and self-consciousness are more complex than we may like to think. Recasting them in terms of later philosophical thought without qualification will fail to do them justice.

I.3.2. Individuation and identity

The problem of identity in general—that is, the problem of what constitutes the identity of any object—is the historical as well as the systematic basis of the special issue of the identity of persons. The issue of identity was not always clearly distinguished by philosophers of the seventeenth and eighteenth centuries from a closely related issue: the problem of individuation. Indeed, identity often came to be discussed under the heading of 'individuation'. But the latter issue is about what it is that makes an individual the individual that it is, and distinguishes it from all other individuals of the same kind. The search for a principle of individuation is the search for a cause or principle of the individuality of individuals. The question about identity, by contrast, concerns the requirements for an individual's remaining the same through time and partial change. The search for a principle of individuation was of course a standard topic in medieval philosophy. And the medieval disputes about the principle of individuation formed a large part of the background to seventeenth-century discussions of the issue. It is important to note, however, that the main concern of Locke and other seventeenth- and eighteenth-century philosophers is the question of identity through time, and not the problem of individuation.

The disputes about individuation and identity were not purely philosophically motivated. Both in medieval and in early modern philosophy problems of individuation and identity were rarely discussed in isolation from theological issues and related moral issues. Quite often, in both periods, the issue of individuation was explored in the course of an explanation of the doctrine of the trinity. Indeed, early medieval discussions of individuation arose out of the trinitarian debates: If there is one God, how can there be three divine persons—Father, Son, and Holy Spirit? This

---

[70] In a later article, Henrich assigns Karl Leonhard Reinhold a role in this discovery. See Henrich, 'Die Anfänge der Theorie des Subjekts (1789)', 1989, pp. 106–70, at pp. 139ff.
[71] There are problems with the Heidelbergers' own positive account of self-consciousness in terms of an original 'familiarity' of oneself with oneself. For a discussion of these, see Zahavi, 'The Heidelberg School and the Limits of Reflection', in Heinämaa, Lähteenmäki, and Remes (eds.), *Consciousness: From Perception to Reflection in the History of Philosophy* (2007), pp. 267–85.

question led to an examination of the distinction between the common (divine) nature and the individual (divine) person. In the seventeenth century too, many theologians and philosophers enquired into concepts such as individuality, substance, person, and so on as a preliminary to their explanation of the unity of three persons in God.[72] Theological issues which gave rise to disputes over identity through time were the doctrines of the transubstantiation of bread and wine in the Eucharist, the resurrection of the body, and the immortality of the soul. Clearly, the issues of life after death, moral responsibility, and reward and punishment continued to be relevant to discussions of the problem of personal identity in early modern thought, as Christian ideas such as that of individual immortality continued to be central to philosophical accounts of personal identity.

The medieval disputes over the principle of individuation too, can be traced to ancient Greek philosophy, and especially to Aristotle. It was Boethius, however, who introduced the problem into metaphysical discussions in the context of the debates over the trinity. Although Boethius himself does not deal with the problem in a systematic way, his various remarks on issues that belong to the topic proved to be immensely influential in subsequent discussions.[73] Individuation presented itself as a problem to those philosophers who adopted a realist position on the ontological status of universals. For 'Platonic' or extreme realists, universals (essences, forms) have reality independently of individual beings. In fact, it is claimed that, strictly speaking, only universals have reality. On this view, individuals belong to the realm of mere appearance; and their individuality is constituted by collections of accidents. Among the early medieval philosophers who adopted this position was John Eriugena.[74] Of more importance in the present context are the moderate or 'Aristotelian' realists. According to their version of realism, universals have no independent reality; they are real only in so far as they are in individual beings. For these realists (such as Aquinas), each particular natural being partakes in a general (substantial or accidental) 'form' or essence, by which it is the kind of thing it is. Since this essence is something that each particular being shares with all other members of the same kind, the question arises of what constitutes or accounts for the individuality of each individual of a given kind.

Among the medieval treatments of individuation within the realist framework, the best known and perhaps the most influential are those of Aquinas on the one hand, and of Duns Scotus and his followers on the other. Aquinas took up remarks that

---

[72] Thus, Brandt is completely wrong in asserting (and without engaging with any of the relevant literature) that the trinitarian debates are of no importance to discussions of human personal identity: 'John Lockes Konzept der persönlichen Identität. Ein Resümee', *Aufklärung*, 18 (2006), 37–54.

[73] For an overview of the medieval disputes, see Assenmacher, *Die Geschichte des Individuationsprinzips in der Scholastik* (1926); and Gracia, 'The Centrality of the Individual in the Philosophy of the Fourteenth Century', *History of Philosophy Quarterly*, 8 (1991), 235–51, and *Individuation in Scholasticism* (1994). For a detailed account of the debate in the early Middle Ages, see Gracia, *Introduction to the Problem of Individuation in the Early Middle Ages* (1984). Gracia gives a detailed interpretation of Boethius's contribution to the debate, and in particular emphasises the importance of Boethius's *De trinitate* in this respect (pp. 65–121, 255–62).

[74] For discussions of Eriugena, see Assenmacher (1926), pp. 15–16, and especially Gracia (1984), pp. 129–35.

Aristotle had made on the issue of individuality. For Aristotle there are two intrinsic causes of being—form and matter—and he indicates that whereas the form makes a thing a member of a certain kind, it is matter that brings about individuality and makes a being distinct from others of the same kind: 'All things which are many in number have matter; for many individuals have one and the same intelligible structure, for example, man, whereas Socrates is one'.[75] Aquinas agrees that in composite beings, such as human beings, matter individuates; but he modifies Aristotle's theory in arguing that it is not matter as such, but designated matter ('materia signata') which individuates. And by 'designated matter' he means 'that which is considered under determined dimensions. This kind of matter is not part of the definition of man as man, but it would enter into the definition of Socrates if Socrates could be defined'.[76] Matter as *materia communis* is common to all material things of a kind; it is 'undesignated matter'. The essence of man, for example, which is common to all human beings, includes undesignated matter: 'The definition of man, on the contrary, does include undesignated matter. In this definition we do not put this particular bone and this particular flesh, but bone and flesh absolutely, which are the undesignated matter of man'.[77] Part of this theory of individuation is that with respect to pure spirits (angels), whose 'definition' does not include matter, there is no plurality of beings within a species: each spirit constitutes a separate kind. Angels differ from one another specifically as well as numerically, and there are as many kinds as there are individuals.

According to the Averroists too, matter is the principle of individuation; and like Aquinas they hold that spirits, since they are pure forms, are not multiplied within a kind. Unlike Aquinas, however, they apply this account to the human soul as well, and they can therefore argue that after death—after the separation from the body—there is no individuality of souls and, consequently, no individual immortality. Aquinas tries to defend the individuality of human souls after death without giving up the 'material' principle of individuation by arguing that the soul retains its 'aptitude' to inform a particular body and thereby retains its individuality among other spiritual beings of the same kind. The complete human individual is restored at the resurrection of the body.

In contrast to both Aquinas and the Averroists, Duns Scotus and his followers look for a principle of individuation that will allow a plurality of spirits within a kind. Scotus vehemently rejects Aquinas's theory of individuation. He argues that the human soul must be a complete individual being prior to, and independently of its union with a body: 'In the order of nature the soul is an individual in virtue of its own singularity before its union with something material'.[78] For Scotus, the issue of

---

[75] *Metaphysica*, 1074a, as translated in Aristotle, *Metaphysics*, ed. Tredennick (1936); see also *Metaphysics*, 1016b3.
[76] Aquinas, *De ente et essentia* (ed. Boyer, 1946, ed. Mavrer, 1968), chap. 2.
[77] Aquinas, *De ente et essentia*, chap. 2. See also Aquinas's commentary on Aristotle, in *In duodecim libros metaphysicorum Aristotelis expositio*, ed. Cathala and Spiazzi (1950); *Commentary on the Metaphysics of Aristotle*, ed. and transl. Rowan (1961), bk. 4, lesson 8, commentary 876.
[78] Duns Scotus, *Quaestiones quodlibetales*, ed. and transl. Wolter (1968); *God and Creatures. The Quodlibetal Questions*, ed. and transl. Alluntis and Wolter (Princeton, NJ: Princeton University Press, 1975), q. 2, para. 16: quoted from (1975), p. 35.

Introduction: aims and issues 21

individuality has to be explained by analogy to that of the species: the species (such as man) is constituted by the addition of the specific difference to the genus (such as animal); and the individual (such as Socrates) in turn is constituted by the addition of the individual difference to the species. This individual difference ('thisness', 'haecceitas') is the principle of individuation: man becomes Socrates by the addition of the individual nature or character, the 'Socratity'. The individual nature constitutes the final difference of beings. By ascribing individuation to 'individual natures' the Scotists identify a positive reality or formal ground as the cause of individuality: in addition to the generic and specific forms there is a form of thisness which constitutes the ultimate reality of a being. And since, by this doctrine, matter is not required for individuation, there is no problem in allowing for a plurality of individual spirits within a kind.

Individuality was not considered problematic by proponents of the various versions of nominalism (or conceptualism). According to the nominalist/conceptualist doctrine (most famously in Ockham), there are no real universals, which means there are no (accidental or substantial) forms or essences in reality, but only individuals; therefore there arises no question as to what brings about individuality within a kind: everything that exists is individual by itself and essentially. Universals are merely names or concepts to which nothing corresponds in reality. Consequently, nominalists regard the search for a principle of individuation as superfluous. In the context of the trinitarian debates, nominalists were often accused of tritheism. It was argued that since they denied real common natures, talk of three divine persons must have meant to them that there are three distinct gods.

The main Scholastic theories concerning individuation were drawn together and discussed in detail towards the end of the sixteenth century in the fifth of Francisco Suárez's fifty-four *Disputationes metaphysicae* (1597). Suárez's two volumes proved to be immensely influential in seventeenth-century metaphysics—especially, but not only, in the metaphysical textbooks of the Scholastic university philosophy of the time.[79] This is also true of Suárez's fifth metaphysical Disputatio, *De unitate individuali eiusque principio*. One aspect of its considerable influence on seventeenth-century debates over individuation and identity is that it provided a rich source for the various Scholastic views and arguments concerning the issue.[80] The impact of Suárez's *Disputationes* was wider than that on Scholastic university philosophy. More independent thinkers such as Leibniz and, to some extent, Descartes, were impressed by the Suárezian solution of the problems of individuation and identity.

---

[79] Suárez's influence is evidenced by the then widely used metaphysical textbooks by Timpler, Combach, Scheibler, and others. Freedman has counted 97 citations of Suárez in Timpler's *Metaphysicae systema methodicum*, which first appeared in Steinfurt in 1604: Freedman, *European Academic Philosophy in the Late Sixteenth and Early Seventeenth Centuries: the Life, Significance, and Philosophy of Clemens Timpler*, 2 vols. (1988), vol. 1, p. 142. For the impact of Suárez on seventeenth-century metaphysics in general, see Grabmann, *Mittelalterliches Geistesleben* (1926–56), vol. 1, pp. 525–60; Lewalter, *Spanisch-jesuitische und deutsch-lutherische Metaphysik des 17. Jahrhunderts*, second edn. (1967); Wundt, *Die deutsche Schulmetaphysik des 17. Jahrhunderts* (1939), pp. 41–7.
[80] I have used the editions, translations, and commentaries by Specht (Suárez, 1976) and Gracia (Suárez, 1982). Translations are from the latter.

According to Suárez, the question about individuation 'concerns what basis or principle the individual difference has in reality' (*Disputationes*, V.3.2), and he looks for a principle of individuation which is the same 'in all created substances' (ibid., V.6.1). That is to say, he searches for one principle that applies to spiritual as well as to material, to simple as well as to composite substances, and, indeed, to non-substances ('accidents'). For Suárez, all 'actual beings' are individual; and actual beings are things 'that exist or can exist immediately'. Suárez adds 'immediately' in order to exclude the common nature of beings, which, as such, cannot immediately exist or have actual entity, except in singular and individual entities. If these are removed, it is impossible for anything real to remain (ibid., V.1.4).

By arguing that things which *can* exist immediately have individuality, Suárez precludes the view about existence as the principle of individuation—a view which he ascribes to Henry of Ghent.[81] For Suárez, individuality does not depend on actual existence. Possible beings (beings which are conceived by God as alternatives to existent beings) must have individuality too. He argues, however, that 'existence' can be interpreted to mean the 'actual entity of a thing', and in this sense the view about existence as the principle of individuation coincides with his own position (ibid., V.5.2). This is that in all created substances it is the very entity of a thing—those intrinsic principles which compose it—that make it the individual it is. That which individuates 'cannot be distinguished from the entity itself'. Whatever it is that composes a being is also that which brings about its individuality: 'There is no other principle of individuation in addition to its entity, or in addition to the intrinsic principles which constitute its entity'. A simple substance is individual 'from itself ['ex se'] and from its simple entity' (ibid., V.6.1, last three quotations). Composite beings, such as men, horses, dogs, and so on, which consist of 'matter and form united' (ibid., V.6.1), are individuated neither by their form alone, nor by their matter alone, but by 'this matter and this form united to each other' (ibid., V.6.15).

Thus, Suárez rejects any view according to which the principle of individuation is to be identified with only one of the two Aristotelian intrinsic causes of being (matter and form): he accepts neither the Thomists's position about 'designated matter', nor the theory that the substantial form alone constitutes individuality—a theory which he ascribes to Averroes and Avicenna. Nevertheless, Suárez makes some concession to the latter view in holding that in composite substances the form is the primary principle of individuation. A particular composite being is what it is through its form. The form is primary 'because this form is most proper to this individual, and because it is what completes numerically this whole substance' (ibid., V.6.16). Suárez points out that the distinction between individual human beings, for example, is due to their distinct souls (form), rather than their distinct bodies (matter). While this emphasis on the form as the primary principle of individuation is obviously and decidedly anti-Thomistic, Suárez attempts to accommodate even the Thomists's view with his own theory by arguing that if we ask how we know the individuality and distinctness of

---

[81] For Henry of Ghent, see Assenmacher (1926), pp. 30–2.

things (rather than what constitutes individuality in reality), then the Thomists's answer makes sense: 'For, with respect to us, who derive our knowledge from material things, the distinction among individuals is often taken from matter or from the accidents which follow matter, such as quantity and other properties' (ibid., V.6.17).

As Aristotelian versions of realism about universals were widespread among seventeenth-century metaphysicians, especially in Germany,[82] the principle of individuation continued to be discussed at the universities and in the Scholastic textbooks, and there are lengthy entries on the topic in the philosophical dictionaries of the time.[83] There were representatives of most of the traditional answers to the problem of individuation. In his *Scientiae metaphysicae compendiosum systema*, Bartholomaeus Keckermann, for instance, defends the view that existence individuates, arguing that this means that space and time are the individuating principles.[84] Other metaphysicians, such as Christoph Scheibler, Johannes Scharf, and Franco Burgersdijk, adopt Suárez's position. In his *Institutiones metaphysicae*, Burgersdijk, for example, argues against the accounts of individuation of both Scotus and Aquinas; his own position is that the individual essence (Suárez's 'entity') is the principle of individuation.[85] Also, Leibniz's teachers Daniel Stahl and Jakob Thomasius identify the unity of 'this form and this matter' as the principle of individuation, and thus adopt a Suárezian position on the issue.[86]

Nominalism (or the view that everything that exists is individual) reigned supreme in the English-speaking world. At least, all of the seventeenth-century English philosophers who are still well known today—Bacon, Hobbes, Locke—adopted some form of nominalism.[87] In France too, major thinkers such as Pierre Gassendi and Antoine Arnauld were committed to the nominalist position.[88] And so these thinkers too, do not consider individuation within a kind as a problem. As they deny real universals, a genuine issue of how the individuality of individuals is constituted within a natural kind does not arise.

Even if we accept that individuation within a kind does not require a special principle, it does not follow, however, that identity through time requires no principle either. Indeed, from about the middle of the seventeenth century, many philosophers tended to neglect the original issue of individuation and instead focus on the issue of identity through time. Thus it is true that in the early modern period the debate about individuation in general declined.[89] In the course of the eighteenth

---

[82] See Wundt (1939), pp. 210–13. According to Wundt, Werner Capella was the only nominalist among the many university metaphysicians in seventeenth-century Germany.
[83] Goclenius, *Lexicon philosophicum*, pp. 231–2; Micraelius, *Lexicon philosophicum*, cols. 613–14.
[84] Keckermann, *Scientiae metaphysicae compendiosum systema* (1614), vol. 1, cols. 2016–17.
[85] Burgersdijk, *Institutiones metaphysicae* (1675), bk. 1, chap. 12, esp. pp. 68–71. See Scheibler, *Metaphysica* (1636), p. 97; Scharf, *Metaphysica exemplaris, seu Prima philosophia*, fourth edn. (1643), p. 199.
[86] For Stahl and Thomasius, see Wundt (1939), pp. 143–4, 213.
[87] Bacon, *Novum organum*, ed. Fowler (1878) II, 2; Hobbes, *Leviathan*, ed. Macpherson (1968) iv; Locke, *Essay*, ed. Nidditch (1975) III, iii and vi. Compare Milton, 'John Locke and the Nominalist Tradition', in Brandt (ed.) *John Locke: Symposium 1979* (1981), pp. 128–45.
[88] Gassendi, *Opera omnia* (1658), vol. 3, p. 159; Arnauld and Nicole, *La logique* ed. Clair and Girbal (1965), pt. 1, chap. 6.
[89] Here I agree with Barber and Gracia. See Barber and Gracia (1994), pp. 4–7. But they neglect the status of personal identity in the philosophical debates of the second half of the eighteenth century. See also my critical discussion of their book, in Thiel (1997b), 353–72.

century, however, the related issue of identity, and especially that of personal identity, achieved a status that equals that of individuation in the Middle Ages. Of course, issues to do with identity through time also extend back to antiquity. Several 'puzzles' about identity were discussed in antiquity, and some of these were taken up explicitly in the early modern period. The best known of these is perhaps that of the 'Ship of Theseus'. Plutarch reports in his *Life of Theseus* that the Athenians preserved the ship on which Theseus sailed, and comments: 'They took away the old timbers from time to time, and put new and sound ones in their places, so that the vessel became a standing illustration for the philosophers in the mooted question of growth, some declaring that it remained the same, others that it was not the same vessel'.[90] Indeed, the Ship of Theseus case continues to be a 'standing illustration' in discussions of identity to this day, and in early modern philosophy thinkers as diverse as Hobbes, Clauberg, and Leibniz explicitly refer to it in their discussions of identity. The 'question of growth' that Plutarch mentions in this passage sparked off discussions of identity in Hellenistic thought (see Gill, 2006, pp. 64–73). Thus, Academic sceptics, in criticizing Stoic ideas, argue that living entities when they grow cannot retain their determinate identity, as growing includes a change of their physical nature.[91] The Stoic Chrysippus responds by maintaining that living beings are not characterized solely by their material nature but also as individuals, by being 'peculiarly qualified' (ibid., pp. 67–8). Thus, the growing argument apparently fails to undermine the Stoic account because it only addresses the question of material change. A puzzle that is especially relevant to the discussions of early modern thought, as it relates to the question of death and life after death, is from Epicureanism, and is offered by Lucretius in his *De rerum natura* (Bk. 3, pp. 845–61; compare Gill, 2006, pp. 69–71). Lucretius states that if after death our matter will be brought back together exactly as it is now and life restored to us, that afterlife would be of no concern to us if we would have lost all memory or recollection of our previous life. The interpretation of this passage is of course controversial among classicists; but on the face of it, it seems to anticipate ideas that are developed in early modern thought—not least those of Locke—and the text was certainly present in seventeenth- and eighteenth-century discussions of identity.[92] Again, however, care

---

[90] Plutarch, *Theseus*, chap. xxiii, in Plutarch, transl. and ed. Perrin (1959), p. 49.

[91] See the discussion by Gill (2006), pp. 64–8. Compare also Sedley, 'The Stoic Criterion of Identity', *Phronesis*, 27 (1982), 255–75; Bowin, 'Chrysippus' Puzzle about Identity', *Oxford Studies in Ancient Philosophy*, 24 (2003), 239–51. See also Lewis, 'The Stoics on Identity and Individuation', *Phronesis*, 40 (1995), 89–108; and Irwin, 'Stoic Individuals', *Philosophical Perspectives*, 10 (1996), 459–80.

[92] Lucretius, *On the Nature of Things*, ed. and trans. Rouse and Smith (1992) An influential English translation of Lucretius was published with commentaries by Thomas Creech in 1682; a second edition appeared in 1714. T. Lucretius Carus, *Of the Nature of Things, In Six Books, Translated into English Verse; by Tho. Creech... In two Volumes, explain'd and illustrated with Notes and Animadversions, being a compleat System of the Epicurean Philosophy*, 2 vols. For direct references to the relevant passages in eighteenth-century texts, see, for example, Grove and Tucker. Grove, *Ethical and Theological Writings*, ed. Sell (2000), vol. 3, pp. 369–70. Tucker, *The Light of Nature Pursued*, vol. 7 second edn. (1805), pp. 11–14. Creech's commentary is discussed in Chapter 2 below, and Grove and Tucker are discussed in Chapters 7 and 8 respectively. Bayle, of course,

needs to be taken when making claims about anticipations. As we shall see, the overlap between the ancient and early modern concerns turns out to be rather limited in this case (see also Gill, 2006, pp. 67, 73). As indicated above, the uses made of such sources in early modern thought must be seen in their immediate context.

In the Middle Ages too, the issue of identity over time was discussed in connection with the afterlife, but here of course in the context of Christian thought that is also relevant to early modern accounts. The idea of individuality and especially that of individual immortality is central in Christian thinking. And here, Aristotelian realism, with its insistence that forms exist only in individuals, is clearly more compatible with Christian thinking than the extreme, Platonic form of realism. If matter individuates, as the Thomists held, then the sameness of the body is required at the resurrection; individual immortality is completed at the resurrection. Some versions of Aristotelian realism, however, clashed with the Christian idea of individual immortality. The doctrine of Averroes and his followers in the thirteenth century (such as Siger of Brabant) is a version of Aristotelianism which most sharply contrasts with Christianity in this respect. According to them, there is only one single universal spirit in which all human souls inhere, and there is no individual immortality: after death, human souls become part of the one universal and eternal spirit. This doctrine was still an object of debate in the seventeenth-century. Leibniz, for example, attacked Averroes (as well as those seventeenth century theories which he thought led in the same direction, such as that of Spinoza), and he made it quite clear that he did so in the interest of the Christian idea of individual immortality.

Another position that has echoes in early modern ideas, is present in Suárez's account of identity. We saw above that for Suárez, the form is the primary principle of individuation in composite substances such as human beings. In his account of the problem of identity over time and through partial change, he notes the importance of this view to the theological issue of the resurrection. A man, he argues, is rightly judged to be the same man when his body has changed, as long as his soul is still the same (since it is the primary principle of individuation in men):

For if to Peter's soul, for example, there should be united a body composed of matter distinct from the body which it first had, although the composite would not be in all its parts the same it was before, nevertheless... the individual is said to be the same by reason of the same soul. (*Disputationes*, V.4.4; see also ibid., V.6.16)

As the debate in the early modern period moved away from individuation to identity through time, there was another shift in discussions of these issues: a marked shift, around the middle of the seventeenth century, away from a primarily ontological to a more subjective treatment of the topic: our concepts of those things whose identity is in question came to be regarded as crucial for dealing with problems of individuation and identity. Locke was the most important thinker to make this shift towards the

---

has a long entry on Lucretius in his *Dictionnaire historique et critique* (1697), and discusses the cited passage relating to the afterlife. See the selection by Gawlick and Kreimendahl (eds.), Pierre Bayle, *Historisches und Kritisches Wörterbuch. Eine Auswahl* vol. 2 (2006), pp. 404–8. The entry is not in Popkin's selection: Bayle, *Historical and Critical Dictionary* (1965).

end of the seventeenth century, but there were others before him (see the discussion below in Chapter 2). While this marks an important strain in the development of the issue in early modern philosophy, the ontological treatment of identity continued to exist side by side with this subjective or 'epistemologist' treatment.[93]

The issue of the resurrection of the body (to which Suárez appeals in the cited passage) relates to the special issue of the identity of persons. And the various responses to the question of personal identity through time depend not only on views about identity in general, but also on which concept of person is being applied. Indeed, from the notion of person adopted by some philosophers a genuine problem about the identity of persons might not even arise. Hence, seventeenth-century notions of personal identity cannot be fully understood without some idea of which concept of person is being employed.

I.3.3. The person and personal identity

The term 'person' has a complex etymology, the early aspects of which can be bypassed for the purposes of our discussion. What is important to note, however, is that throughout the seventeenth century, 'person' most commonly referred to an individual human being: it was simply a term for the individual human subject. But in some philosophical discussions 'person' referred to a particular aspect, quality, or function of the individual human being. Indeed, the Latin term 'persona'—a translation of the Greek 'prosopon' (face)—originally signified the mask through which an actor communicated his 'role' to the audience. 'Persona' was then used to denote this role or character itself, and its denotation was transferred from the role on the stage to the role or function that an individual human being fulfils in real life.[94] Cicero, for example, formulated a theory of four *personae*, or roles, which apply to every individual human being.[95] And the distinction between individual human being and person implicit in this understanding of 'persona' as role or quality was not

---

[93] See my critical discussion of Barber and Gracia, in Thiel, 'Epistemologism' (1997), 353–72, esp. 372.

[94] On the history of the term 'persona', see Trendelenburg, 'Zur Geschichte des Wortes Person', *Kant-Studien*, 13 (1908), 1–17; Rheinfelder, *Das Wort 'Persona'. Geschichte seiner Bedeutungen mit besonderer Berücksichtigung des französischen und italienischen Mittelalters* (1928); Vogel, 'The Concept of Personality in Greek and Christian Thought', *Studies in Philosophy and the History of Philosophy*, 2 (1963), 20–60; Fuhrmann 'Persona, ein römischer Rollenbegriff', in Marquard and Stierle (eds.), *Identität* (1979); Greshake, 'Die theologische Herkunft des Personbegriffs', in Pöltner (ed.), *Personale Freiheit und Pluralistische Gesellschaft* (1981), pp. 75–86; Mauss, 'A Category of the Human Mind: The Notion of Person; the Notion of Self', transl. Halls, in Carrithers, Collins, and Lukes (eds.), *The Category of Person: Anthropology, Philosophy, History* (1985), pp. 1–25; Teichmann, 'The Definition of Person', *Philosophy*, 60 (1985), 175–85; Forschner, 'Der Begriff der Person in der Stoa', in Sturma (ed.), *Person. Philosophiegeschichte—Theoretische Philosophie—Praktische Philosophie* (2001), pp. 37–57; and Kreuzer, 'Der Begriff der Person in der Philosophie des Mittelalters', in Sturma (2001), pp. 59–77.

[95] Compare Fuhrmann (1979), pp. 97–102; and Gill, 'Personhood and Personality: The Four Personae Theory in Cicero, *De Officiis* I', *Oxford Studies in Ancient Philosophy*, 6 (1988), 169–99. See also Forschner (2001), pp. 37–57.

lost on the philosophers of the seventeenth century.[96] The meaning of 'persona' as role connects with the use of the term in moral and legal contexts: in Roman law *personae* were distinguished from *res* (things) as two distinct objects of law. 'Persona' simply referred to the individual human being insofar as he stands in a relationship to legal matters. In a later development, 'persona' was used to refer to all bearers of rights and duties, and as such the term applied to corporate bodies as well as to human individuals. The idea of the individual human being or person as a bearer of rights and duties is also central to the Christian tradition of natural law. It is therefore not surprising that many discussions of the problem of personal identity in the seventeenth century focused on moral and legal issues—a person being regarded as someone with rights and obligations, to whom actions are attributed, and who is held responsible for those actions.

The notion of person as responsible human agent is not necessarily tied to the old meaning of person as role, however. In fact, orthodox Christian and Scholastic doctrine was to reject the Roman understanding of 'persona' altogether and to replace it by a definition of person as an individual rational substance. This notion of person came onto the scene as a result of Christological and trinitarian debates in the early church. Thus, early medieval discussions of the notion of person arose out of problems relating to the doctrine of the trinity.[97] Tertullian is said to have coined the phrase 'una substantia tres personae' to explicate the trinity. Yet it seems unclear exactly what 'substantia' and 'persona' were supposed to mean. And although the use of 'persona' for Father, Son, and Holy Spirit had been accepted in the Christian church since the Council of Alexandria in 362, Augustine was reluctant to use the term in the trinitarian context.[98] His book on the trinity is relevant to later discussions of personality—not so much because it employs the term 'persona', but mainly because of the psychological arguments for the possibility of the trinity. Augustine argues that there are triads in the soul (for example, intelligence, memory, and will) which are consistent with the oneness of the soul, appealing to these triads as analogous to the divine trinity.[99] He conceives of the divine persons in relational terms, but does not seem to think of the human person in this way. Rather, he identifies the human person with a mind—being concerned with the mind that 'desires to know itself', as Augustine says in this context.[100] Important to subsequent discussion of subjectivity is also, of course, Augustine's famous discussion of memory and its various functions in the different context of his *Confessiones*, in which the mind is in some passages even identified with memory.[101]

---

[96] See Hobbes, *Leviathan*, xvi, pp. 217–18.
[97] See Gracia (1984).
[98] Augustine, *De trinitate*, V.9–10; VII.4.7–9.
[99] Ibid., X.11.17–18. Michael Schmaus reads Augustine's account of the trinity as a 'psychological doctrine': *Die Psychologische Trinitätslehre des heiligen Augustinus* (1927).
[100] Augustine, *De trinitate*, X.2.4. Compare the discussion in Lloyd, 'On Augustine's Concept of a Person', in Markus (1972), pp. 191–205, at pp. 203–4. See also O'Daly, *Augustine's Philosophy of Mind* (1987), especially pp. 42, 57–8, 135ff., 148–51.
[101] Augustine, *Confessiones*, X.14, X.17. It has been argued that Augustine's *Confessiones* introduces a notion of personality that is different from the one discussed in the trinitarian context. *Confessiones* tells a story of a person, thereby bringing into play 'the exemplary narration of (the development of) the identity of an individual consciousness': Kreuzer (2001), pp. 71–2, also

The term 'persona' received its classical definition around 500, when Boethius began using it to refer to an Aristotelian first substance whose essence consists in rationality. He defines 'person' as 'the individual substance of a rational nature'. Applying this definition to the trinity, Boethius speaks of 'one essence, three substances, and three persons of the Godhead'.[102] He also applies 'persona' to individual human beings as consisting of 'soul and body, not [of] soul or body separately'.[103] What makes human beings persons, however, is, Boethius insisted, not their corporeity, but their rationality. Obviously, the old Roman notion of person as role is not present in Boethius. It is equally obvious that Boethius's concept of a person is not identical with the modern notion of a self-conscious subject. His 'ontological' view of person as a thing or individual substance, with its emphasis on rationality, proved to be immensely influential, however. It dominated not only medieval Scholastic thought, but also metaphysical disputes about the person throughout the seventeenth century—even when no explicit reference to the problem of the trinity was made.[104]

This notion of a person as a rational substance, however, was linked by some to the old moral and legal contexts. This issue appears to have become prominent in Christological discussions of the first half of the thirteenth century.[105] Thus, Alexander of Hales distinguishes three modes of being in Christ: *subiectum*, relating to his 'natural being', consisting of soul and body; *individuum*, relating to his rational nature; and *persona*, which concerns his 'moral being'. The moral being in turn is connected to notions such as freedom and dignity.[106] Theo Kobusch has argued that these medieval discussions about *persona* as a moral being constitute not only the beginnings of a tradition of a *metaphysica moralis*, but also 'the origin of the modern notion of a person'—a notion that functions today as the 'foundation of the law, of constitutions and of world-wide declarations of human rights'.[107] Kobusch concedes, however, that the thirteenth-century contributions to which he refers belong to the framework of a traditional 'Aristotelian ontology of natural things' or 'ontology of substance'.[108]

---

p. 62. This needs to be distinguished, however, from a theoretical account of the nature of personhood.

[102] *Liber contra Eutychen et Nestorium*, in Boethius, *The Theological Tractates*, transl. and ed. Stewart, Rand, and Tester (1973), pp. 84–5, 90–1. On Boethius, see Rheinfelder (1928), pp. 159–71, esp. pp. 169–71. See also Chadwick, *Boethius: The Consolations of Music, Logic, Theology, and Philosophy* (1981), pp. 190–202.

[103] *De trinitate*, in Boethius, *The Theological Tractates* (1973), pp. 10–11.

[104] Discussions of the notion of person in mainly trinitarian contexts continued well into the eighteenth century. See, for example, Clendon, *Tractatus philosophico-theologicus de persona, or, A Treatise of the Word Person* (1710); Robertson, *An Attempt to explain the Words Reason, Substance, Person, Creeds, Orthodoxy, Catholic-Church, Subscription, and Index expurgatorius* (1766).

[105] For a discussion of this material, see Kobusch, *Die Entdeckung der Person. Metaphysik der Freiheit und modernes Menschenbild*, 2nd. edn. (1997), pp. 23–54.

[106] Ibid., pp. 23–6. See also Principe, *Alexander of Hales' Theology of the Hypostatic Union* (1967); and Hufnagel, 'Die Wesensbestimmung der Person bei Alexander von Hales', *Freiburger Zeitschrift für Philosophie und Theologie*, 4 (1957), 148–74.

[107] Kobusch (1997), pp. 11, 23, 28–9.

[108] Ibid., p. 54.

Aquinas cites these discussions, but mainly appeals to Boethius when discussing the notion of person in the context of his own account of the trinity. Like Boethius, Aquinas applies the term 'persona' to substances other than the divine ones, emphasising rationality as the main characteristic of persons: 'Among all other substances individual beings with a rational nature have a special name, and this is "person".' And because of their rationality, persons are substances which 'have control over their actions' and 'act of their own initiative'.[109] Thus rationality is linked to moral issues such as action-ascription and responsibility. In applying 'persona' to human beings, Aquinas emphasises corporeity more strongly than does Boethius. According to Aquinas, 'persona' in relation to human nature refers to '*this* flesh, *these* bones, and *this* soul which are the sources ['principia'] of man's individuality; these are indeed part of what is meant by "a human person"'.[110] For Aquinas, 'a human person' is synonymous with 'individual human being', where 'man' or 'human being' is understood as being composed of soul (form) *and* body (matter). The soul as the form of man is said to be the principle of life and intellectual operations, but not, on its own, to constitute the human person. Although Aquinas argues that unlike other forms, human souls 'can exist apart' from matter, he insists that the soul alone does not make up the man or human person: 'We can neither define it [the soul] nor speak of it as a "person".'[111]

Suárez, too, adopts the Boethian notion of person in his influential *Disputationes metaphysicae* (1597). He cites the relevant passages from both Boethius and Aquinas, and defines 'person' as a *suppositum* or first substance of an 'intellectual or rational nature'.[112] Elsewhere, however, Suárez emphasises the moral aspect of personality. Persons are beings who are subject to the laws of a community. Here he introduces an important distinction between a true and a fictional person ('persona vera' and 'persona ficta'), thus anticipating similar distinctions in Hobbes and Pufendorf between natural and artificial persons.[113] The individual human being is a *persona vera*; a body politic with moral unity is a *persona ficta*. Both types of person are subject to the law.

Scholastic views about what individuates persons vary, of course, with the general theory of individuation that was adopted. If all composite beings are individuated by 'designated matter' (Aquinas), then this applies to human beings as well. If it is the whole 'entity' or 'this matter and this form united to each other' which brings about individuation (Suárez), then this of course includes the individuation of human beings.[114] And if the soul is the 'primary' principle of individuation in composite

---

[109] Aquinas, *Summa theologiae*, 1a.29.1. See *Summa theologiae*, 1a.29.3, for references to the discussion of *persona* as moral being. Compare Kobusch (1997), pp. 25–6; Ruello, 'Remarques sur la notion thomiste de personne', *Revue des faculté catholique de l'ouest*, 2 (1963), 3–32.
[110] Aquinas, *Summa theologiae*, 1a.29.4.
[111] Ibid., 1a.29.1.
[112] Suárez, *Disputationes*, XXXIV.1.13.
[113] Kobusch has drawn attention to this distinction in Suárez and its importance to subsequent thought: Kobusch (1997), pp. 63–6. Suárez, *De legibus* (1612), I.6.7, in *Opera omnia* (1856–78), vols. 5 and 6. The distinction between *persona vera* and *persona ficta* appears in vol. 5 (1856), p. 25.
[114] Suárez, *Disputationes*, V.6.15.

substances (Suárez), then despite bodily changes, 'the individual is said to be the same by reason of the same soul'.[115] Although the various Scholastic philosophers disagree on the principle of individuation, most of them seem to adopt what is essentially a Boethian concept of a (natural) person, even when distinctions are made between a person's moral and natural mode of being.

As was indicated above, the question of human personal identity is closely related to another theological issue that was much discussed in the seventeenth century: the doctrine of life after death. Philosophers and theologians realized that for the idea of a future life to make sense one needs to assume (if not to argue) that after death we shall be the *same* persons that we are now: in other words, what is now sometimes referred to as the 'identity condition' needs to be satisfied.[116] This condition is also important for the reason that, according to Christian doctrine, we shall be judged and punished or rewarded by God for actions we performed in this life: the divine rewards or punishments can be said to be *just* only if the same person who acted in this life will be punished or rewarded for these acts in the next life. Thus, the problem of personal identity is closely linked to the two related questions of the immortality of the soul and the resurrection of the body. The issue of the identity condition raises the further question about what is required for the same person to exist in the future life. And on this question some philosophers argued that it is sufficient that the same human soul continues to exist, whereas others believed that in addition the very same body a person had on earth must be resurrected.

The problem of identity through time is central to the above-mentioned moral and legal issues concerning the notion of person. Obviously, the identity condition needs to be satisfied not only in relation to divine judgement, but also in relation to the judgements of human courts of law. Thus, moral and legal problems led to more fundamental, metaphysical questions about what constitutes a person and its identity through time. Prior to Locke, however, the 'right answers' to these metaphysical questions were often simply assumed, rather than argued for, when the context of the discussion was primarily moral and legal.

I.4. THE GENERAL DEVELOPMENT

Unsurprisingly perhaps, most philosophers in the early modern period did not discuss the whole range of issues related to the problem of personal identity and self-consciousness. Some focused on the issue of consciousness and self-consciousness, without treating in any detail the issue of personal identity, while others, dealing with personal identity, concentrated on theological topics. And still others focused on moral and legal points, or gave priority to the metaphysical questions. Quite often the

---

[115] Ibid., V.4.4.
[116] For an overview of seventeenth- and eighteenth-century views on immortality, see Mijuskovic (1974), pp. 19–57. For systematic discussions of the 'identity condition', see Williams, *Problems of the Self* (1973), pp. 91ff., and Perrett, *Death and Immortality* (1987), pp. 93–6. The expression 'identity condition' is from Perrett.

issue of personal identity was addressed along the way, as part of a larger theological or metaphysical argument. Locke was the first to attempt to formulate a comprehensive theory of personal identity that could deal with all those various issues to which the problem of personal identity is related (with the exception of the trinity).

Clearly, the relevant seventeenth- and eighteenth-century material is rich as well as diffuse, but some major developments and turning points can be identified even on the basis of the very general sketch so far. Although prior to Locke there are few detailed seventeenth-century treatments of self-consciousness and personal identity, there is a vast amount of material that addresses these and related issues in some form that is important in its own right and also as essential background to what follows. (This material will be discussed in Chapters 1 and 2). As indicated, a major turning point in the debate is the publication of Locke's chapter on identity which he added to the second edition of his *An Essay Concerning Human Understanding* (1694). This chapter contains the most detailed and original contemporary treatment of the problem, challenging traditional views about both personality and identity. It was, indeed, 'revolutionary', in part at least, for the reason that Locke accounts for personal identity in terms of inner-directed consciousness. And it was Locke's account that sparked off the discussions of this and related issues in the eighteenth century. Therefore, Locke's theory deserves a detailed treatment in the early modern context (Part 2, Chapters 3 and 4).

Locke's theory aroused controversy very soon after its first publication. Indeed, as indicated, it dominated the disputes over personal identity in the late seventeenth century and throughout the eighteenth century. Chapters 5 and 6 examine eighteenth-century responses to Locke's account insofar as they are concerned with either defending or criticizing and rejecting Locke's theory. Most of the responses to Locke examined here are argued from a metaphysical standpoint about the nature of the soul; that is, from the perspective either of a materialist or an immaterialist philosophy of mind. The metaphysical positions are not always explicitly invoked in the responses to Locke; but it is plain that the various answers to the question of what constitutes personal identity through time depend to a considerable extent on the views adopted about the nature of the human mind. And here, the battle between materialist and immaterialist philosophers of the mind is of central importance.[117]

A large number of thinkers in the first half of the eighteenth century dealt with the issues of personal identity and self-consciousness from an immaterialist perspective. Within this group, however, there is considerable variety in the treatment of these issues. Moreover, in the context of the development in Britain (Chapters 7 and 8) there is the important turning point in the debate about consciousness with the first detailed early modern treatment of the topic in the anonymously published *Essay on Consciousness*—even if its immediate impact seems to have been limited.

---

[117] Here I use the terms 'immaterialism' and 'immaterialist' to refer not to the position, according to which there is no material world independently of spiritual or immaterial substance (Berkeley's position), but to refer to the view that the human soul or mind is an immaterial substance—which is a view that Berkeley and many others share.

Leibniz is the best known and the most important contemporary critic of Locke, but he had developed his own ideas about consciousness and identity well before dealing with Locke's *Essay*. Although Leibniz adopts the notion of an immaterial mental substance, unlike most other immaterialists of the time, he distinguishes between the identity of a mental substance or soul and personal identity. His views and arguments concerning personal identity and self-consciousness were taken up by Christian Wolff—at least to a considerable extent (both are discussed in chapter 9). Certainly, the debate about the Wolffian philosophy which dominated Germany in the middle of the century meant that a basically Leibnizian position was of central importance prior to the influence of Lockean views and the development of materialist accounts in Germany in the second half of the eighteenth century (chapter 10). While the Leibnizian account is important in its own right, the critics of Leibniz and Wolff in particular moved the debate forward significantly (chapter 11), and in a way that became crucial to the discussions in the second half of the eighteenth century.

The last turning point in the debates covered in this volume comes with the most important British contribution of the eighteenth century: that of David Hume. Hume seems to argue, at least on the standard reading, that there is no such thing as personal identity at all. Like Locke's discussion, Hume's treatment of the topic continues to engage philosophers and scholars—partly because of its philosophical importance, but also partly because of difficult questions concerning the interpretation of his text. Hume's account and the arguments of his early critics are discussed in chapters 12 and 13.

Of course, this is a very general outline of the developments, and the details must be spelt out in the chapters that follow. And, obviously, early modern discussions of self-consciousness and personal identity do not end with the debates about Wolff and Hume. The conclusion of this book points towards the further developments to be dealt with in detail in the sequel to this volume: *The Enlightened Subject*. These new developments began to emerge especially from the 1760s onwards, when the heyday of empirical psychology led to fresh investigations of empirical personal identity not only in Britain but also in France and Germany. The strengthening of materialist lines of thought, often associated with empiricist approaches in psychology, sparked off discussions from a then unusual and for the most part unpopular perspective. Towards the end of the century there were the Scottish Common Sense school's accounts of these issues, and in Germany the debates centred on Kant's philosophy of the subject.

PART I

THE SEVENTEENTH-CENTURY BACKGROUND

1

The ontological view of the self: Scholastic and Cartesian conceptions

This Chapter introduces seventeenth-century treatments of the self relating to consciousness and personal identity, and the main themes in the context of which these issues were discussed. The next chapter will focus on alternative seventeenth-century accounts of the soul, consciousness, identity, and related issues such as moral responsibility and the afterlife. Apart from contributions that are important in their own right, this material constitutes essential background to Locke and the eighteenth-century debates.

As indicated in the Introduction, Boethius's definition of person as 'the individual substance of a rational nature', although sometimes modified, became standard in Scholastic thought. And it was through influential Scholastics such as Suárez that the Boethian definition of person made its way into the metaphysical textbooks and dictionaries of the seventeenth century. In these textbooks, *persona* was mainly treated as a theological concept and discussed in connection with the immaterial kinds of being, God, angels, and souls (as substantial forms). The Boethian definition was adopted by Catholic and reformation philosophers alike. For example, the influential Christoph Scheibler, who became known as the 'protestant Suárez', adopted the Boethian notion of person in his *Metaphysica* (first published in 1617), in which he points out the importance of this notion to the problem of the trinity.[1] And in the middle of the century Johann Micraelius still defined 'persona' as 'an individual, incommunicable substance of an intellectual nature, which subsists independently'.[2] There were dissenting voices, however, especially in the context of the anti-Scholastic humanist movement in the fifteenth and sixteenth centuries. Lorenzo Valla and, later, Michael Servetus, rejected the orthodox notion of person as substance and attempted to rehabilitate the old Roman concept of person as role or quality which they also wanted to apply to the doctrine of the trinity.[3] However,

---

[1] See Scheibler, *Metaphysica* (1636), 'Prooemium', and bk. 2, chap. 2, pp. 444–52.
[2] Micraelius, *Lexicon philosophicum* (1662), col. 991. See also Scharf, *Metaphysica exemplaris, seu prima philosophia* (1643), p. 251. On German seventeenth-century university metaphysics and the notion of person, see Wundt, *Die deutsche Schulmetaphysik des 17. Jahrhunderts* (1939), pp. 171, 220ff.; and Lewalter, *Spanisch-jesuitische und deutsch-lutherische Metaphysik des 17. Jahrhunderts* (1967), pp. 69ff., 73.
[3] Valla, *De linguae latinae elegantia*, bk. VI, chap. 34 (1688), pp. 519–21; Servetus *De trinitatis erroribus libri septem* (1531), pp. 29a and 36b; Servetus *Two Treatises of Servetus on the Trinity*, transl. Wilbur (1932), pp. 45, 57.

Melanchthon, another humanist, defended the Scholastic concept of person and publicly criticized Servetus.[4] Clearly, Scholastic doctrine about *persona* won the day, and it continued to dominate metaphysical thought until about the middle of the seventeenth century, by which time the Cartesians had developed a powerful rival theory. Even in the late seventeenth and early eighteenth century the Boethian notion of person was alive and well, and it can be found in philosophers who cannot be classed as simply neo-Scholastics. Gerard de Vries, for instance, whose textbooks were still used in the first half of the eighteenth century, defines 'persona' as a rational *suppositum*; and Stephanus Chauvin gives an account of the Boethian definition of 'persona' in his *Lexicon philosophicum* which first appeared in 1692.[5] Valla's critique of Boethius's definition of person continued to be discussed until late in the seventeenth century. By and large, Valla's position was rejected, and for theological reasons. Christoph Scheibler, for example, criticized Valla's notion of person in considerable detail,[6] and Richard Burthogge saw a need to defend explicitly Boethius's notion of person against Valla's critique in 1694.[7] And as late as 1710 John Clendon discussed Boethius's and Valla's accounts of the person, opting for a middle way between the two.[8]

1.1. DESCARTES AND THE CARTESIANS ON THE PERSON AND THE SOUL

Although the Cartesians had developed a powerful rival theory of person, they did not disagree with the notion of person as individual rational substance, and it was certainly not their concern to reintroduce the old notion of person as role or quality. Nevertheless, their theory differs markedly from Scholastic doctrine. Descartes does not use 'persona' or 'personne' as technical terms. In fact, like most of his followers, he rarely applies the terminology of person when discussing the notion of the self which is so central to his metaphysics.[9] And on the few occasions when he does use

---

[4] For Servetus, see Rheinfelder, *Das Wort 'Persona'* (1928), pp. 167–9. For Melanchthon's critique of the notion of person as quality, see Trendelenburg, 'Zur Geschichte des Wortes Person', *Kant-Studien*, 13 (1908), 13–14.

[5] de Vries, *De naturae dei et humanae mentis determinationes pneumatologicae*, sixth edn. (1718), p. 58. Chauvin, *Lexicon philosophicum*, second edn. (1713), p. 485.

[6] Scheibler, *Metaphysica*, pp. 444–6.

[7] Burthogge, *An Essay upon Reason, and the Nature of Spirits* (1694), pp. 277–80. See also Stillingfleet, *The Doctrine of the Trinity and Transubstantiation Compared: The Second Part* (1687), p. 25.

[8] Clendon, *Tractatus philosophico-theologicus de persona, or, A Treatise of the Word Person* (1710), pp. 95–7. 'The truth of the Matter...must lye betwixt them both, and *Persona* signifies the Accident or Quality, but in Conjunction with Substance' (p. 95). Clendon emphasises the distinction between 'person' and 'personality' in this context: '*Persona* is the Concrete; and does not only signifie the Quality whereby one Man differs from another, but it denotes likewise the Man that is so qualified and distinguish'd from another; whereas the Abstract *Personalitas* signifies the naked Qualification only' (p. 96).

[9] References to Descartes's writings are to *Oeuvres de Descartes*, ed. Adam and Tannery (1964–76), and to *René Descartes: Philosophical Writings*, ed. and transl. Cottingham, Stoothoff, Murdoch, and Kenny, 3 vols. (1984–91).

'persona' or 'personne', it is to refer to the individual human being as consisting of soul and body.[10] According to Descartes, body and soul are rightly thought of as a single individual being, 'because to conceive the union between two things is to conceive them as one single thing'.[11] Neither body alone, nor soul alone, constitutes the human being or person: 'The union which joins a human body and soul to each other is not accidental to a human being, but essential, since a human being without it is not a human being.'[12] This account of 'man' appears to be very similar to the Scholastic doctrine, and sometimes Descartes even makes use of the Scholastic terminology when discussing the mind–body relationship.[13] His theory differs from the Scholastic one in several respects, however. For Descartes, soul and body are not related to one another as form and matter, but as two independent substances. Although Aquinas too argues that the human soul is incorporeal, subsistent, and indestructible, he still thinks of it as form, and not, as does Descartes, as a complete substance in itself. Also, Descartes places much less importance on the bodily part of man than do the Scholastics. According to Descartes, the soul constitutes the essence of the self, whereas the body is something which the self merely 'has', to which it is 'very closely joined'.[14] Thus, Descartes implicitly distinguishes between the notion of human being or person which includes corporeity and the notion of the (essential) self, 'I', or soul, as something which is not necessarily linked to a body. While Aquinas insists that the soul alone cannot be regarded as that which makes up the self, Descartes argues that the self is the same, with or without the body: 'This I ['ce moi']—that is, the soul by which I am what I am—is entirely distinct from the body . . . and [the soul] would not fail to be whatever it is, even if the body did not exist'.[15] And the soul, that is, that 'by which I am what I am', is for Descartes a complete, simple, and immaterial substance.[16] Further, Descartes argues that thought is the 'principal property' of the soul: it is that which 'constitutes its nature and essence, and to which all its other properties are referred'.[17] The soul or mind (or self) is essentially a thinking thing—a *res cogitans*. Now, for Descartes, to say that thought is the essence of the soul is to say that the soul always thinks—not just that it has the faculty of thought: if the soul stopped thinking, it would cease to exist.[18] Descartes then defines thought in terms of consciousness, and sees consciousness as relating to one's own thoughts.

---

[10] See, for example, Descartes's letters to Princess Elizabeth, 28 June 1643: *Oeuvres*, vol. 3, p. 694; *Philosophical Writings*, vol. 3, p. 228; and 15 September 1645: *Oeuvres*, vol. 4, p. 293; *Philosophical Writings*, vol. 3, p. 266. Compare also (Rodis-)Lewis *Le problème de l'inconscient et le Cartésianisme* (1950), p. 237.
[11] *Oeuvres*, vol. 3, p. 692; *Philosophical Writings*, vol. 3, p. 227 (letter to Princess Elizabeth).
[12] *Oeuvres*, vol. 3, p. 508; *Philosophical Writings*, vol. 3, p. 209 (letter to Regius).
[13] For example, Descartes writes in a letter to Mesland that human bodies 'are numerically the same only because they are *informed* by the same soul' (my italics): *Oeuvres*, vol. 4, p. 167; *Philosophical Writings*, vol. 3, p. 243.
[14] *Meditationes*, VI: *Oeuvres*, vol. 7, p. 78; *Philosophical Writings*, vol. 2, p. 54.
[15] *Discours*, pt. IV: *Oeuvres*, vol. 6, p. 33; *Philosophical Writings*, vol. 1, p. 127.
[16] For a more detailed account of Descartes's notion of the soul, see, for example, Garber, 'Soul and Mind: Life and Thought in the Seventeenth Century', in Garber and Ayers (eds.), *The Cambridge History of Seventeenth-Century Philosophy* (1998), pp. 759–95.
[17] *Principia philosophiae*, I, 53: *Oeuvres*, vol. 8A, p. 25; *Philosophical Writings*, vol. 1, p. 210.
[18] See Descartes's letter to Gibieuf, 19 January 1642: *Oeuvres*, vol. 3, pp. 478ff.; *Philosophical Writings*, vol. 3, p. 203.

I use this term ['thought', 'cogitatio'] to include everything that is within us in such a way that we are immediately conscious of it. Thus all the operations of the will, the intellect, the imagination and the senses are thoughts. I say 'immediately' so as to exclude the consequences of thoughts: a voluntary movement for example, originates in a thought but is not itself a thought.[19]

Since the mind or soul always thinks, and since thought is always accompanied by consciousness, it follows that the soul is always conscious: for the duration of its existence, the soul is continuously engaged in conscious activity. Our understanding of ourselves as thinking things is based on this consciousness which always accompanies thought. And this self-understanding is in turn the basis of our knowledge of ourselves as individual selves:

From the mere fact that each of us understands himself to be a thinking thing and is capable, in thought, of excluding from himself every other substance, whether thinking or extended, it is certain that each of us, regarded in this way, is really distinct from every other thinking substance and from every corporeal substance.[20]

In the last analysis, then, consciousness understood as a relating to one's own thoughts is the basis of our knowledge not only of the distinctness from the body of the soul, or self, as a thinking thing, but also of the distinctness of the self from all other thinking things.[21] It is important to note, however, that Descartes does not say that consciousness is what individuates the soul: all he claims is that we derive our *knowledge* of the individuality of our souls from the consciousness we have of our own thoughts. Descartes's argument implies that the individuality of the soul is given prior to the consciousness of thoughts: he assumes the soul's individuality as given, and fails to give an account of what brings about this individuality. Descartes does not argue that souls are individuated through their union with their bodies. Indeed, he could not have argued this, because according to his theory, souls are complete individual substances by themselves, independently of matter. Rather, the identity of the human body depends on the identity of the human soul. It is because the self is equated with the unextended, immaterial part of man that a problem of personal identity through time does not arise. The real self is a simple, immaterial, 'pure' substance: its body and its 'accidents'—that is, its thoughts—may change, but it does not thereby lose its identity: 'For even if all the accidents of the mind change, so that it has different objects of the understanding and different desires and sensations, it does not on that account become a different mind.'[22]

---

[19] Descartes's Second Set of Replies to his *Meditationes*: *Oeuvres*, vol. 7, p. 160; *Philosophical Writings*, 2, p. 113. See also *Principia philosophiae*, I, 9: 'By the term "thought" I understand everything which we are conscious of as happening within us': *Oeuvres*, vol. 8A, p. 7; *Philosophical Writings*, vol. 1, p. 195. *Philosophical Writings* translates 'conscium esse' as 'to be aware'.

[20] *Principia philosophiae*, I, 60, in *Oeuvres*, vol. 8A, pp. 28–9; *Philosophical Writings*, vol. 1, p. 213.

[21] For Descartes's notion of consciousness, see the discussion in the next section. For discussions of the *cogito* argument see, for example, Schmaltz, 'The Cartesian Refutation of Idealism', *British Journal for the History of Philosophy*, 10 (2002), 513–40.

[22] 'Synopsis' of the *Meditationes*: *Oeuvres*, vol. 7, p. 14; *Philosophical Writings*, vol. 2, p. 10.

Descartes discusses in some detail the issue of the diachronic identity of the human body, but that discussion leads back to the unresolved question of the individuation and identity of the human soul.[23] When he comes to discuss the identity of complex bodies over time, he gives two different accounts, depending on a distinction between two kinds of complex body. If by 'body' we mean merely an individual quantity of matter, just a 'determinate part of matter, a part of the quantity of which the universe is composed',[24] then the identity of a body over time depends on the sameness of that quantity of matter: an individual body is no longer numerically the same individual as soon as even 'the smallest amount of that quantity' which constitutes the individual is removed.[25] Unlike both individual souls and matter in general, particular bodies, understood as individual quantities of matter, are perishable as the individual entities that they are. In one passage Descartes applies this notion of the individual to the human body; here, he even suggests that 'a human body loses its identity merely as a result of a change in the shape of some of its parts'. And he concludes that a human body 'can very easily perish'.[26]

Descartes argues elsewhere, however, that there is a sense in which human bodies differ from other kinds of bodies in that they are something more unitary and remain identical through change of size and shape. The context of this argument is a discussion of the Catholic doctrine of transubstantiation in the Eucharist.[27] As contemporary critics (Arnauld and Mesland) had pointed out to Descartes, his philosophy of matter appears to be inconsistent with that doctrine. One question that was raised had to do with Descartes's account of the individual body in terms of its local extension: if the individual body is the same as its local extension, how, then, can it be that in the Eucharist Christ's body is present within the dimension of the bread, rather than with its own extension which, by Descartes's theory, makes it the particular body it is? In response to this question, Descartes introduces a distinction between human and non-human bodies: the individuality of non-human bodies is simply their being determinate portions of universal extension; 'and if any particle of the matter were changed, we would at once think that the body was no longer quite the same, no longer *numerically the same*'.[28] Descartes points out, however, that a

---

[23] For a fuller account of Descartes's accounts of the individuation of bodies, see Thiel, 'Individuation', in Garber and Ayers (eds.), *The Cambridge History of Seventeenth-Century Philosophy* (1998), pp. 224–7.
[24] Letter to Mesland: *Oeuvres*, vol. 4, p. 166; *Philosophical Writings*, vol. 3, p. 243. See ibid.: 'a determinate part of matter, or one that has a determinate size'. See also *Principia philosophiae*, I, 65: *Oeuvres*, vol. 8A, p. 32; *Philosophical Writings*, vol. 1, p. 216.
[25] Letter to Mesland: *Oeuvres*, vol. 4, p. 166; *Philosophical Writings*, 3, p. 243.
[26] 'Synopsis' of the *Meditationes*: *Oeuvres*, vol. 7, p. 14; *Philosophical Writings*, vol. 2, p. 10.
[27] Letter to Mesland: *Oeuvres*, vol. 4, pp. 162–70; *Philosophical Writings*, vol. 3, pp. 241–4. For a fuller account of the Cartesian debate about transubstantiation, see (Rodis-)Lewis (1950), pp. 5–7, 68–74; Watson 'Transubstantiation among Cartesians', in Lennon, Nicholas, and Davis (eds.), *Problems of Cartesianism* (1982), pp. 127–48; Armogathe, *Theologia Cartesiana. L'explication physique de l'eucharistie chez Descartes et Dom Desgabets* (1977); Watson, *The Breakdown of Cartesian Metaphysics* (1987), pp. 155–70; and especially Nadler, 'Arnauld, Descartes, and Transubstantiation: Reconciling Cartesian Metaphysics and Real Presence', *Journal of the History of Ideas*, 49 (1988), 229–46. For a discussion of the intellectual context, see Ariew, *Descartes and the Last Scholastics* (1999), pp. 140–54. Ariew argues against the common view that Descartes wrote about transubstantiation against his will.
[28] Letter to Mesland: *Oeuvres*, vol. 4, p. 166; *Philosophical Writings*, vol. 3, pp. 242–3.

human body is not just an isolated portion of general matter, but a body joined to a particular soul. And the soul is said to function as the body's principle of unity: Descartes argues that it is through its union with a soul that a human body remains the same through change. The soul is individual by itself and continues to be numerically the same 'pure substance'; therefore, although there is not 'any particle of our bodies which remains *numerically* the same for a single moment... our body, *qua* human body, remains always *numerically* the same so long as it is united with the same soul'. Descartes thinks this explains why we are justified in saying that 'we have the same bodies as we had in our infancy, although their quantity has much increased, and... there is no longer in them any part of the matter which then belonged to them, and even though they no longer have the same shape'.[29] No matter how much its shape and size have changed over time, it is still the same human body as long as it is united to the same individual soul.[30] Both the individuation and the identity over time of the body '*qua* human body' are secured through its union to an individual soul. Considered independently of a soul, the body does not remain the same from one moment to the next. Descartes applies this theory to the Eucharist. The bread becomes Christ's body, even though it does not have the extension of Christ's body, by being unified with his soul: 'The miracle of transubstantiation which takes place in the Blessed Sacrament consists in nothing but the fact that the particles of bread and wine... are informed by his soul simply by the power of the words of consecration'.[31]

Although this account seemed to Descartes to be 'quite elegant',[32] he anticipated that to orthodox theologians 'this explanation will be shocking at first'.[33] Descartes obviously realized that it practically denies the real presence of Christ's body in the sacrament. He tries to accommodate his own explanation to the traditional accounts by making use of the traditional Scholastic terminology of form and matter, when he says, for example, that human bodies 'are numerically the same only because they are *informed* by the same soul'.[34] Indeed, Descartes's account of the individuation of a human body is reminiscent of Suárez's account. As we saw above, for Suárez too, the identity of a human body is preserved by the identity of the soul—the soul being the form and primary principle of individuation in humans.[35] It is important to note, however, that despite the similar terminology in this context, Descartes's notion of

---

[29] Letter to Mesland: *Oeuvres*, vol. 4, pp. 166–7; *Philosophical Writings*, vol. 3, p. 243, last two quotations.

[30] Thus I disagree with Kemmerling, who ascribes to Descartes the view that the identity of the human body is constituted independently of the soul and that the identity of the person, therefore, is not constituted by the soul alone. See Kemmerling, 'Was macht den Begriff der Person so besonders schwierig?' in Thomas and Schüle (eds.), *Gegenwart des Lebendigen Christus* (2007), pp. 541–65, at pp. 556–7.

[31] Letter to Mesland, *Oeuvres*, vol. 4, p. 168; *Philosophical Writings*, vol. 3, p. 244.
[32] Letter to Mesland, *Oeuvres*, vol. 4, p. 165; *Philosophical Writings*, vol. 3, p. 242.
[33] Letter to Mesland, *Oeuvres*, vol. 4, p. 169; *Philosophical Writings*, vol. 3, p. 244.
[34] Letter to Mesland, *Oeuvres*, vol. 4, p. 167; *Philosophical Writings*, vol. 3, p. 243 (my italics).
[35] Suárez, *Disputationes metaphysicae* (1597), V.4.4. See the discussion of Suárez in the Introduction.

the soul is quite different from that of the Scholastics. For Descartes the soul is not the form of man but a complete, individual, and independent substance. Also, unlike Suárez, Descartes does not search for a principle of individuation that applies to all beings. None of Descartes's accounts of individuation appeals to the Suárezian notion of 'entity' or the intrinsic principles which compose a being that is, 'this matter and this form united to each other'.[36] To summarize, there is no unitary account of individuation in Descartes. There are several strains in his thought concerning individuality in the material world. And although the individuality and identity of the human body are explained as dependent on the identity of the human soul, Descartes fails to account for the individuality of the soul itself.

The view that the identity of the human body depends on its being united to the same soul was a common one throughout the seventeenth century; and the vocabulary in which it was usually presented indicates that in most cases it derived from the Scholastic tradition itself rather than from Descartes. Sir Kenelm Digby, for example, makes the same point as Descartes, but with a much more pronounced Scholastic flavour. The context of Digby's discussion is the problem of the resurrection, which is why he concentrates on identity over time. According to Digby, it is true in general that 'that which giveth the numerical individuation to a *Body*, is the substantial forme. As long as that remaineth the same, though the matter bee in a continuall flux and motion, yet the thing is still the same.'[37] Consequently, in the case of human beings where the soul is the form, the body remains identical no matter how much it has changed, as long as it has 'the same distinguisher and individuator; to wit, the same forme, or *Soule*'.[38] This view was restated frequently and in various forms, depending on the concept of soul that was employed. As late as 1697, John Sergeant, who saw himself as defending the 'Peripatetick School', argued, against John Locke's theory of identity, that the soul preserves the identity of the human body.[39] This view is present in its Cartesian version in Robert Boyle. Boyle criticized Scholastic talk of 'substantial forms' vehemently, and he adopted the Cartesian distinction between soul and body. As to the identity of an individual man, he argued, like Descartes, that 'the same soul being united to a portion of duly organised matter is said to constitute the same man, notwithstanding the vast differences of bigness that there may be at several times between the portions of matter whereto the human soul is united'.[40]

Many of Descartes's followers were dissatisfied with his account of the mind–body relationship, and so developed alternative theories.[41] Nevertheless, they accepted

---

[36] Ibid., V.6.15.
[37] Digby, *Observations upon Religio Medici* (1643), p. 82. Page numbers refer to the second edition (1644).
[38] Digby, *Observations*, p. 84.
[39] Sergeant, *Solid Philosophy Asserted* (1697), p. 258.
[40] *Some Physico-Theological Considerations about the Possibility of the Resurrection* (1675), in Boyle *Selected Philosophical Papers*, ed. Stewart (1979), p. 205. For Boyle's notion of the soul, see Anstey, *The Philosophy of Robert Boyle* (2000), pp. 187–204.
[41] See Garber and Wilson, 'Mind–Body Problems', in Garber and Ayers (eds.), *The Cambridge History of Seventeenth-Century Philosophy* (1998), pp. 833–67.

Descartes's general dualistic picture of man, locating the real self in the soul understood as a *res cogitans* and an immaterial substance. Arnold Geulincx, for example, distinguishes between ethical and metaphysical considerations of the self: the self as human being, that is, as an embodied mind, is the object of ethics, while the true self, the self as mind or simple, immaterial, thinking substance, is the object of metaphysics.[42] Nicolas Malebranche argues that the knowledge we have of the self is imperfect, precisely because it is based on consciousness only ('sentiment intérieur ou conscience'), and not on ideas mediated through God.[43] Yet, although knowledge based on consciousness is imperfect, it is certain and sufficient to yield the most important characteristics of the human soul, such as its liberty, spirituality, and immortality. Like other Cartesians, Malebranche does not address, in any detail, the question of personal identity through time.

Pierre-Sylvain Régis, in his *Système de philosophie* (1690),[44] also adopts a version of mind–body dualism, but unlike Descartes and other Cartesians he argues that minds are individuated by their bodies. Here it is important to recall that according to one strain in Descartes's thought concerning the individuation of bodies (but not human bodies), the material world, in contrast to the mental world, is not understood to be a plurality of individual substances at all: body or matter, 'considered in general', is just one substance whose essence consists in extension.[45] On this account, the term 'corporeal substance' does not refer to a particular body, but to extension in general, to a universally extended substance or the totality of matter. Régis extends the notion of just one substance to the mental world. For Régis, individual minds are modal, rather than substantial beings. He distinguishes between *l'esprit* (spirit or mind) and *l'âme* (soul): 'esprit' or 'spirit' denotes thinking substance in general, whereas 'soul' denotes an individual or particular spirit. For Régis, a soul (the individual being) is essentially related to an organic body:

> By *Soul* I do not mean spirit considered in itself and according to its absolute being, according to which it is a substance which thinks, but I mean only the relation which the spirit has to the organic body with which it is united; from which it follows that the soul taken abstractly is nothing *but the union of the spirit with an organic body.*[46]

A soul is constituted, says Régis, through the spirit's relation to an organic body. He recognizes that it is also a feature of the soul that its thoughts have a particular form and are not just 'thinking in general'. But again, the particularity of a soul's thoughts is said to depend on the body:

---

[42] See Geulincx *Opera philosophica*, 3 vols., ed. Land (1891–93), vol. 3, p. 219.

[43] Malebranche, *De la recherche de la vérité* (1674–75), III. 2. 7. References to Malebranche's *Recherche* are to (Rodis-)Lewis (ed.), *Oeuvres complètes de Malebranche* (1962), vol. 1.

[44] All references are to vol. 1 (of 3 vols.). Translations are mine unless indicated otherwise.

[45] *Principia philolophiae*, II,4; *Oeuvres*, vol. 8A, p. 42; *Philosophical Writings*, vol. 1, p. 224. See also 'Synopsis' of the *Meditationse*, 'body, taken in the general sense, is a substance': *Oeuvres*, vol. 7, p. 14; *Philosophical Writings*, vol. 2, 10; and *Principia philolophiae*, II.23; *Oeuvres*, vol. 8A, pp. 52–3; *Philosophical Writings*, vol. 1, p. 232. See also Thiel, 'Individuation' (1998), 224.

[46] The original reads 'par *Ame* je n'entendray pas l'esprit considéré en luy-même & selon son estre absolu, selon lequel il est une substance qui pense, mais j'entendray seuelement le rapport que l'esprit a au corps organique avec lequel il est uni; d'où il s'ensuit que l'ame prise abstractivement ne sera autre chose *Que l'union de l'esprit avec un corps organique*': Régis, *Système*, p. 113.

The ontological view of the self: Scholastic and Cartesian conceptions 43

My soul which is a particular spirit does not only have thought which is the essential attribute of spirit considered in itself, but it must also have some particular form 'façon' of thinking which determines that thought to be of a certain kind 'manière', to be for example in the form of desire, fear, or hope, in accordance with what the body occasions.[47]

This means that a soul's particular thoughts must be seen in relation to the body with which it is united. This account is confirmed by Régis's discussion of self-knowledge. He says: 'As the soul only acts in dependence on the body with which it is united, so it cannot know itself but in dependence of this body.' For the soul to know itself as a soul (as an individual), it is not sufficient that it knows itself as a substance which thinks; that is, as spirit. It must also know that 'its sentiments and imaginings depend on the body with which it is united'.[48] Thus, Régis's notion of the individual self or soul differs markedly from that of other Cartesians. Like other Cartesians, however, he does not discuss, in any detail, the issue of personal identity through time.[49]

According to Régis, then, the body functions as the individuating principle of the soul. Unlike Régis, Descartes does not have the notion of just one spiritual substance, which needs to be individuated (particularized) by being united with organic bodies. For Descartes, a soul is a complete individual substance by itself, prior to, and independently of, any relation to a body. It is the identity of the human body, rather, which depends on that of the soul. The problem is, of course, that Descartes's failure to account for the individuality of souls undermines his account of the identity of the body.

1.2. DESCARTES AND THE CARTESIANS ON CONSCIOUSNESS

In the previous section it was assumed that in Descartes the terms 'conscius' and at least some occurrences of 'conscientia' can be read in terms of the English notions of 'conscious' and 'consciousness', rather than in the evaluative sense of 'conscience'. Of course, it is possible that when Descartes says that we know our own thoughts through *conscientia* 'or internal testimony which everyone experiences within himself'[50] that he has in mind a moral evaluation; but this seems highly implausible. Descartes himself does not explain the notions of *conscius* and *conscientia* in any

---

[47] 'mon ame qui est un esprit particulier, n'a pas seulement la pensée qui est l'attribut essentiel de l'esprit considéré en soy, mais elle doit avoir encore quelque façon particuliere de penser qui détermine cette pensée à estre d'une certain maniere, à estre par exemple sous la forme du desir, de la crainte, ou de l'espérance selon que le corps luy en donne l'occasion': Régis, *Système*, p. 132.
[48] 'Comme l'ame n'agit que dépendamment du corps auquel elle est unie, elle ne peut aussi se connoître elle-même que dépendamment de ce corps ... ses sentiments et ses imaginations dépendent du corps auquel elle est unie': Régis, *Système*, p. 161.
[49] For a critical discussion of Lennon's reading of Descartes and Régis on the individuation of minds, see Thiel, '"Epistemologism" and Early Modern Debates about Individuation and Identity', *British Journal for the History of Philosophy*, 5 (1997), 353–72, esp. 357–60.
[50] *Recherche de la vérité*, *Oeuvres*, vol. 10, p. 524; *Philosophical Writings*, vol. 2, p. 418. See also *Oeuvres*, vol. 7, p. 559; *Philosophical Writings*, vol. 2, p. 382. In *Philosophical Writings*, 'conscientia' is translated as 'awareness'.

detail, but his writings seem to suggest that in several contexts at least he uses these terms in the non-evaluative sense of consciousness.[51] This is also how Descartes's seventeenth-century critics and followers seem to have understood his statements about 'conscium esse' and 'conscientia' and related terms.[52] Of course, this reading is consistent with the claim that there is a conceptual connection between Descartes's *conscientia* and the moral life. For Descartes, I have *conscientia* not only of perceptions but also of my acts of free will.[53]

Assuming, then, that Descartes works with a non-evaluative notion of consciousness, understood as a relating to one's own thoughts, it is not clear what kind of

---

[51] Hennig has criticized the consciousness-reading of Cartesian 'conscientia' in a book-length study of the topic: *'Conscientia' bei Descartes* (2006). See also Hennig's article which summarizes the argument of the book in English: 'Cartesian *Conscientia*', *British Journal for the History of Philosophy*, 15 (2007), 455–84. Hennig concedes that on the basis of Descartes's texts 'we are not able to establish the meaning of "*conscientia*"' ('Cartesian *Conscientia*', 466). His strategy is to look at earlier accounts of the notion—in particular in Augustine, Aquinas, and a certain Martin Bresser, who published a book *De conscientia libri IV* (1638)—and then to 'simply insert the traditional explanation of "*conscientia*"' into Descartes's doctrine ('Cartesian *Conscientia*', 481). It is not surprising, then, that Hennig ends up reading Descartes's 'conscientia' in terms of an evaluative notion. Descartes's notion is not identical with moral conscience, Hennig argues, but should be construed in analogy with the latter. Although Descartes is 'not interested in the moral value of thought', he is interested in 'values that apply to thoughts as such: truth, validity, coherence and so on' (ibid., 481–2). *Conscientia* is an evaluation of something in us as a thought (ibid., 483). But since human evaluation can only be imperfect, *conscientia* is not a particular human thought. It is not simply the individual human subject that has *conscientia*. Rather '*conscientia* is *shared knowledge*. The mind always and necessarily knows *that* its thoughts are subject to an evaluation by objective criteria'; that is, by an 'ideal observer' (ibid., 484). And this 'ideal observer and evaluator of our thoughts' is God (ibid.). On this interpretation, then, my consciousness of the thought that I am walking (*Oeuvres*, vol. 7, p. 352; *Philosophical Writings*, vol. 2, p. 244) *is* a knowledge and an evaluation that this walking-thought is subject to an evaluation by an ideal observer. Hennig's interpretation is learned, subtle, and complex, but it is also highly speculative. There is simply no textual evidence on the basis of which one could ascribe such a loaded notion of consciousness to Descartes's terms 'conscius' and 'conscientia'. Also, Hennig provides no evidence that Martin Bresser, to whose book he attaches considerable importance, was relevant to Descartes's thought at all. The fact that Bresser 'lived, spatially and temporally, rather close to Descartes' ('Cartesian *Conscientia*', 478) is hardly sufficient as evidence for establishing such a connection. Moreover, there seem to be several passages that speak against Hennig's reading. In the passage quoted above, where Descartes speaks of 'conscientia, vel interno testimonio' (*Oeuvres*, vol. 10, p. 524: *Philosophical Writings*, vol. 2, p. 418), he appeals to everybody's experience and makes no reference, implicitly or explicitly, to an 'ideal observer' or a knowledge about evaluation. *Conscientia* here is only the human subject's own 'internal testimony' of its thoughts. If Descartes had adopted the notion that Hennig ascribes to him, there would have been many opportunities for him to explain it to his contemporary critics (such as Hobbes) who read him differently. But Descartes did no such thing. Moreover, even if we were to accept Hennig's interpretation it remains unclear what kind of relating to our own thoughts is involved when we 'know' that 'our thoughts are subject to evaluation by objective criteria'.

[52] Baker and Morris, in *Descartes' Dualism* (1996), pp. 100–38, assert that 'Descartes' conception of *conscientia* is in most respects very close to the Scholastic one' (p. 101), but fail to discuss the Scholastic material on the issue in any detail, and thus are unable to justify their claim. Most of their references are to sources post Descartes.

[53] Anstey has emphasised this connection in Descartes between 'being *conscius* of something and moral character'. See Anstey, '*De Anima* and Descartes: Making up Aristotle's Mind', *History of Philosophy Quarterly*, 17 (2000), 237–60, at 250–1.

The ontological view of the self: Scholastic and Cartesian conceptions   45

relation to our thoughts consciousness is. As indicated, Descartes defines thought in terms of consciousness.[54] But what is consciousness? Is it a relating to our thoughts *via* a distinct, second-order act of perception or thought, or is it an inherent reflexivity that belongs to the thoughts themselves? As noted in the general Introduction above, this question relates to present-day debates about higher-order theories of consciousness, but is present also in early modern thought. There is no explicit discussion of this question in Descartes, however. On the basis of his writings it may not be possible to give a definite answer to it, although many commentators have of course given such an answer on Descartes's behalf. There are some passages which would suggest a higher-order account of consciousness.[55] Thus, in the *Conversation with Burman* Descartes states that 'to be conscious is both to think and to reflect upon one's thought'.[56] The terminology of reflection here suggests a second-order activity, but 'to reflect' in this passage should not be read in terms of a particular type of second-order thought called 'reflection'. That is, it should not be read in terms of what Descartes elsewhere calls 'reflection' when he speaks of it 'as a kind of pondering' (*Oeuvres*, vol. 7, p. 559; *Philosophical Writings*, vol. 2, p. 382) or when he gives an account of 'reflective knowledge, or the kind of knowledge that is acquired by means of demonstrations' (*Oeuvres*, vol. 7, p. 422; *Philosophical Writings*, vol. 2, p. 285). Rather, the comment to Burman indicates that the consciousness or 'inner knowledge' ('cognitio interna') of our thinking involves a second-order activity that precedes such 'pondering' or 'reflective knowledge'.[57] Also, we should not link 'to reflect' in the *Conversation with Burman* to Descartes's notion of 'reflective thoughts' which he distinguishes from 'direct thoughts'. This distinction is commonly made in seventeenth-century Scholastic university textbooks in which *reflexio* is said to be an explicit return of the mind or intellect to itself.[58] And Descartes, writing to Arnauld, states:

---

[54] See, for instance, *Principia philosophiae*, 1, 9: *Oeuvres*, vol. 8A, p. 7; *Philosophical Writings*, vol. 1, p. 195.
[55] Proponents of this reading include, for example, Cottingham, 'Descartes on "Thought"', *Philosophical Quarterly*, 28 (1978), 208–14, at 211–14. Schmaltz notes, rightly, that Descartes 'was not entirely clear...on the nature of our consciousness of thoughts', but in the end opts for an interpretation in terms of a second-order understanding of consciousness; see Schmaltz, *Malebranche's Theory of the Soul: A Cartesian Interpretation* (1996), pp. 18, 21.
[56] 'Conscium esse est quidem cogitare et reflectere supra suam cogitationem' (*Oeuvres*, vol. 5, p. 149; *Philosophical Writings*, vol. 3, p. 335). In *Philosophical Writings* 'conscium esse' is translated as 'to be aware'. See also Cottingham (ed.), *Descartes' Conversation with Burman* (1976), p. 7. Doubts have been raised occasionally about the authenticity of the *Conversation with Burman*, but as no one has shown, or attempted to show, that the text is not authentic, it is assumed here, in line with the standard view, that it is genuine.
[57] *Oeuvres*, vol. 7, p. 422; *Philosophical Writings*, vol. 2, p. 285. *Philosophical Writings* translates 'cognitio interna' as 'inner awareness', thus identifying it with 'conscientia', which is also translated as awareness.
[58] See, for example, Goclenius, *Lexicon philosophicum* (1613), p. 971. Early in the eighteenth century John Norris spends a whole chapter on the topic: *An Essay towards the Theory of the Ideal or Intelligible World*, vol. 2 (1704), pp. 117–23. Norris says that in the 'reflex way of thinking...the Mind retiring as it were from all Ideas turns its view as I may say inwards, and in a very wonderful manner considers what passes there' (pp. 120–1). At p. 120 he states that in reflection 'there seems to be a kind of return of the Mind upon it self', and that in reflection the mind 'terminates upon it self, or is its own Object'.

> We make a distinction between direct and reflective thoughts... I call the first and simple thoughts of infants *direct* and not reflective... But when an adult feels something, and simultaneously perceives that he has not felt it before, I call this second perception *reflection*, and attribute it to the intellect alone.[59]

The passage in the *Conversation with Burman* implies that the consciousness of *all* thoughts, be they direct or reflective, involves a second-order activity of 'reflecting'. Thus, 'to reflect' in that passage should not be identified with a particular kind of thought called 'reflective thought'. Clearly, Descartes does not use the terminology of 'reflexio' consistently, and we should not simply appeal to other comments on 'reflection' to explain 'conscium esse' in the *Conversation with Burman*. Still, the passage suggests that consciousness is an act distinct from the act to which it relates— a second-order act of perception or thought. It is pointless to reject this interpretation on the grounds that *we* may think that such a claim about consciousness is 'fantastical and unnecessary'.[60] Even if there are good reasons for rejecting that claim, that would not (obviously) be a sufficient reason for not ascribing it to Descartes. Moreover, it is not as obvious as some may think that the idea of consciousness as a higher-order activity is 'fantastical and unnecessary'. Many philosophers of mind today argue for a higher-order theory of consciousness.

There are, however, passages in which Descartes seems to hold that consciousness is not a second-order act, but an integral part or attribute of every thought as such— an 'immanent reflexivity' of thought itself.[61] Passages that are often cited in support of such an interpretation are contained in Descartes's replies to the seventh set of objections against his *Meditationes* (by Bourdin). Here, Descartes rejects Bourdin's claim that 'to enable a substance to be superior to matter... it is not sufficient for it to think: it is further required that it should think that it is thinking, by means of a reflective act, or that it should have a consciousness ('conscientia') of its own thought'. This idea, Descartes comments, is 'deluded' (*Oeuvres*, vol. 7, p. 559; *Philosophical Writings*, vol. 2, p. 382). It needs to be noted, however, that Bourdin interprets Descartes's notion of consciousness in terms of a particular type of reflection: he believes that for Descartes, to be conscious of thinking means 'to contemplate and consider your thought' (*Oeuvres*, vol. 7, p. 533; *Philosophical Writings*, vol. 2, p. 364). As we saw above, however, Descartes does not adopt this notion of reflection when he explains 'conscium esse' in terms of 'reflectere' to Burman. Descartes rejects Bourdin's claim because the latter thinks of consciousness

---

[59] *Oeuvres*, vol. 5, pp. 220–1; *Philosophical Writings*, vol. 3, p. 357.
[60] Hennig (2007), 462; see also Kemmerling, *Ideen des Ichs* (1996), p. 179.
[61] Alanen adopts the expression 'immanent reflexivity' from Frankfurt, and ascribes it to Descartes's notion of consciousness, without, however, analysing relevant passages: *Descartes's Concept of Mind* (2003), pp. 100–1. Scholars who adopt a first-order reading of Descartes's notion of consciousness include (Rodis-)Lewis (1950), pp. 40–2; Radner, 'Thought and Consciousness in Descartes', *Journal of the History of Philosophy*, 26 (1988), 439–52, at 446; Aquila, 'The Cartesian and a certain "Poetic" Notion of Consciousness', *Journal of the History of Ideas*, 49 (1988), 543–62; Balibar, *Identité et différence* (1998), p. 41; and Simmons, 'Changing the Cartesian Mind: Leibniz on Sensation, Representation and Consciousness', *The Philosophical Review*, 110 (2001), 31–75, at 35–6.

The ontological view of the self: Scholastic and Cartesian conceptions 47

in terms of deliberate reflection, contemplation, or consideration. Obviously, Descartes suggests, 'this kind of pondering or reflecting' (ibid.; *Philosophical Writings*, vol. 2, p. 382) is not essential to thought and consciousness and is 'not required in order for a thinking substance to be superior to matter' (*Oeuvres*, vol. 7, p. 559; *Philosophical Writings*, vol. 2, p. 382). He leaves open the question of whether consciousness involves a second-order activity that is different from reflection understood as contemplation. He comments further:

> The initial thought by means of which we become aware ['advertimus'] of something does not differ from the second thought by means of which we become aware ['advertimus'] that we were aware of it, any more than this second thought differs from the third thought by means of which we become aware ['advertimus'] that we were aware that we were aware. (ibid.)

Again, Descartes seems to suggest here that awareness and the act to which it relates are one and the same act. According to Richard Aquila, for example, Descartes here 'proposes an identification' of the two acts.[62] It is not as obvious as many seem to think, however, that the passage supports this kind of interpretation. Although Descartes says that the various acts of awareness do not differ and that they *appear* to be indistinguishable from each other, he does not suggest that they are not distinct acts. What he is saying, rather, is that they are of the same kind. He explicitly distinguishes between the original thought or perception, the perception of the perception, and the perception of the perception of the perception as mental acts (1), (2), and (3). He does not identify them.

Moreover, Descartes does not even use the terminology of 'conscientia' or 'conscium esse' here. When Descartes explains 'conscium esse' to Burman he is referring to an activity that is simultaneous with the act to which it relates. The quoted passage in the response to Bourdin seems to concern a different kind of relating to one's own thoughts. The second and third thoughts to which Descartes refers here relate to past thoughts: 'the second thought by means of which we become aware that we *were* aware of it' (my italics). It is doubtful, therefore, that this passage can be read as a comment on *conscientia* as understood by Descartes at all, let alone as one that endorses a first-order account of consciousness. Rather, his point is to argue that thinking, not the capacity to contemplate and consider one's thought, is what 'differentiates corporeal things from incorporeal things'.[63]

In any case, the response to Bourdin is consistent with the passage in the *Conversation with Burman*, where Descartes accounts for consciousness in terms of an activity of 'reflecting' (not contemplating) that relates to one's own thought as its object:

> It is correct that to be conscious is both to think and to reflect on one's thought. But it is false that this reflection cannot occur while the previous thought is still there. This is so because . . . the soul is capable of thinking of more than one thing at the same time, and of continuing with a particular

---

[62] Aquila (1988), 547. Hennig rejects this interpretation, but appeals to this passage as evidence against the second-order act interpretation: Hennig (2007), 465.
[63] *Oeuvres*, vol. 7, p. 559; *Philosophical Writings*, vol. 2, p. 382. In the latter, the Latin 'considerent' is translated as 'reflect'.

thought which it has. It has the power to reflect on its thoughts as often as it likes, and to be conscious of its thought in this way.[64]

This passage strongly suggests a second-order understanding of consciousness, emphasising that the act of consciousness can be simultaneous with the act 'reflected' upon. Descartes could also have used this point against Hobbes, who argues that Descartes's position leads to an infinite regress. As noted in the general Introduction above, this (old) problem arises for theories, according to which (1) relating to oneself through consciousness is a mental act distinct from the act to which it relates, and (2) each mental act is simultaneously accompanied by an act of consciousness. If (1) and (2) are accepted, it follows that each act of consciousness is in turn accompanied by another act of consciousness, and so on *ad infinitum*. Hobbes argues in his second objection to Descartes:

Although someone may think that he *was* thinking... it is quite impossible for him to think that he *is* thinking, or to know that he is knowing. For then an infinite chain of questions would arise: 'How do you know that you know that you know...?'[65]

Hobbes points out that the problem arises only if consciousness is said to be simultaneous with the act which is its object; and he concludes that knowledge of our own thoughts and actions can relate only to the past. It seems that Descartes, however, does not regard the infinite regress as a problem, as he does not address it in any detail in his response to Hobbes. From the passage in the *Conversation with Burman*, however, it is clear why the infinite regress is not a problem for him. The soul 'has the power to reflect on its thoughts as often as it likes, and to be conscious of its thoughts in this way' because 'the soul is capable of thinking of more than one thing at the same time, and of continuing with a particular thought which it has'.[66]

It seems, then, that a second-order interpretation of Descartes's understanding of consciousness is the most plausible one.[67] Like most seventeenth-century thinkers, however, Descartes does not elaborate on the notion of consciousness, and in his case it seems difficult to determine precisely, on the basis of his writings, what kind of self-relation consciousness is.[68] After Descartes, consciousness continued to be understood

---

[64] *Oeuvres*, vol. 5, p. 149; *Philosophical Writings*, vol. 3, p. 335.
[65] *Oeuvres*, vol. 7, p. 173; *Philosophical Writings*, vol. 2, pp. 122ff.
[66] *Oeuvres*, vol. 5, p. 149; *Philosophical Writings*, vol. 3, p. 335.
[67] There are other isolated passages in Descartes which may seem to suggest a first-order account of consciousness. For example, Descartes says in *Les passions de l'âme* that 'it is certain that we cannot will anything without thereby perceiving that we are willing it', and that 'this perception is really one and the same thing as the volition': *Oeuvres*, vol. 11, p. 343; *Philosophical Writings*, vol. 1, pp. 335–6. As Christian Barth has pointed out, however, volition and the perception thereof cannot, strictly speaking, be identical for Descartes, as perceptions belong to the passive intellect, while volitions originate in the activity of the will. Volitions, then, are represented by a distinct perception with which they are connected: Barth, 'Bewusstsein bei Descartes', *Archiv für Geschichte der Philosophie*, 93 (2011), 162–94.
[68] Lähteenmäki argues in a very thoughtful article that first-order and second-order interpretations of Descartes on consciousness can be reconciled: Lähteenmäki, 'Orders of Consciousness and Forms of Reflexivity in Descartes', in Heinämaa, Lähteenmäki, and Remes (eds.), *Consciousness: From Perception to Reflection in the History of Philosophy* (2007), pp. 177–201. In order to achieve such reconciliation

The ontological view of the self: Scholastic and Cartesian conceptions 49

as a form of relating to one's own thoughts, but for the most part the concept itself was left unexplained.

This applies, for example, to comments on consciousness that were made in discussions between Cartesians and Scholastics over the question of animal souls.[69] Here the capacity to reflect, considered as unique to human souls, features strongly. Again, however, 'reflection' is used in more than one sense. Sometimes it is equated with reasoning, contemplating, or deliberately reflecting on our thoughts, while at other times it is understood as an activity by which thoughts become conscious in the first place. Indeed, some of the misunderstandings in this debate are due to this ambiguity in the terminology of 'reflection'.

Among the main players in the seventeenth-century debate are Ignace-Gaston Pardies on the Scholastic side, and Antoine Dilly on the Cartesian side. Pardies believes in animal souls, but emphasises that they differ in nature from human souls. Animal souls are capable of a basic sensory knowledge, but do not have any spiritual or intellectual knowledge which involves the capacity to reflect on one's own thoughts.[70] This means, moreover, that unlike human souls, animal souls do not have a consciousness of their own self and are not able to say 'I'.[71] For Pardies, then, thought is not necessarily accompanied by reflection. Antoine Dilly, by contrast, argues that the distinction between animal and human souls in terms of the capacity

---

Lähteenmäki attempts to show that Descartes distinguishes between three types of consciousness: 'rudimentary consciousness', 'reflexive consciousness', and 'consciousness achieved by deliberate, attentive reflection'. The relation of consciousness to its object can vary, according to this reading, depending on the type of consciousness. For example, there is a structural difference between the consciousness of perceptions and the consciousness of volitions. The former can be rudimentary consciousness or a combination of the latter and reflexive consciousness; consciousness of volitions, however, is always reflexive consciousness. Moreover, reflexive consciousness accompanies most perceptions in adults. In children, consciousness of perception is exclusively rudimentary consciousness. Barth (2011) differs from Lähteenmäki in points of detail, but accepts the general point that the 'deep structure' of consciousness varies in Descartes's account. There are several problems with this interpretation, however. One is that Descartes's comments on various ways of 'reflecting' are used to explain what he means by 'conscientia' and 'conscium esse'. It is true, of course, that Descartes makes use of notions of relating to one's own self that are different from *conscientia*. We noted above the notions of 'pondering', 'reflective thought', 'reflective knowledge', 'contemplation', and 'consideration', but, as also noted above, these must not be mixed up with the kind of second-order activity that is involved in *conscientia*. Moreover, there is no reason to believe that 'to think' in the Burman passage is not to be understood in the broad sense of *cogitatio* that includes 'all the operations of the will, the intellect, the imagination and the senses': *Oeuvres*, vol. 7, p. 160; *Philosophical Writings*, vol. 2, p. 113.

[69] For a general account of this debate, see, for example, Rosenfield, *From Beast-Machine to Man-Machine. Animal Soul in French Letters from Descartes to La Mettrie* (1968). See especially pp. 80–6, 252–6, 270–3.

[70] Pardies, *Discours de la connaissance des bestes* (1672), pp. 149ff.

[71] Pardies says about the human soul: 'Elle se sentira donc elle-même, puisque rien ne lui est si intimement appliqué; & en se sentant ainsi, elle se pourra nommer, pour ainsi dire, elle-même, & se dire *Moi*; Moi qui me sens & qui m'apperçois; Moi qui sens la douleur, ou qui remarque cét objet': *Discours de la connaissance des bestes*, pp. 81–2. A note in the margin of p. 82 refers to Augustine, *De trinitate*, 14, chap. 4.

50   *The Early Modern Subject*

to reflect does not work, because any thought—even thought that is involved in mere sensory knowledge—involves an element of reflexivity, conceived of as an immediate consciousness of such thoughts.[72] In short, if we ascribe any thought at all to animals, then we are forced to ascribe to them the capacity to reflect, which was meant to be the distinguishing mark of human souls, on Pardies's own account. Therefore one should not ascribe any thought of whatever kind to animals. If we do, we cannot distinguish between human and animal souls, as Pardies himself wishes to do.

It is plain that the terminology of 'reflection' is used differently, as described above, by the two sides. What may not be so obvious is whether the kind of reflexivity that Dilly ascribes to all thought is to be understood as a first-order inherent reflexivity or as a second-order activity that is essentially connected with all thought. Some passages, however, suggest a reading in the former sense. Thus, Dilly notes that thinking consists in mental operations 'of whose existence one is immediately certain' by those operations themselves and at the time when these are performed.[73] Pierre Bayle, who commented on the issue of animal souls towards the end of the century in his *Dictionnaire historique et critique*, clearly implies a distinction between consciousness as a first-order reflexivity and other, second-order activities relating to our own thoughts. Like Dilly, Bayle argues that the Scholastic position would allow animals the power of reflection. He holds that 'every substance that has any sensations knows that it has them', and proceeds to refer to this reflexive knowledge in terms of a first-order relation to one's own thoughts when he says that 'all the acts of the sensitive faculty are reflexive upon themselves'.[74] He does not, however, confound this kind of reflexivity with the capacity to reflect deliberately on one's thought. Rather, he argues that beings to which we ascribe the first-order type of reflexivity that belongs to thinking as such must also be able to engage in higher-order reflections on their own thoughts: 'As soon as a soul is capable of *one* thought, it is capable of *any* thought.'[75]

Nicolas Malebranche, too, does not comment on the notion of consciousness in any detail. As noted in the Introduction, Malebranche says that we know our own thoughts and souls through a 'sentiment intérieur' or 'conscience'.[76] Although he does not elaborate on the notion of *conscience* understood as inner sentiment or feeling, he appears to believe that it is an immediate relating to our own self and

---

[72] Dilly, *De l'ame des bêtes* (1676). See especially chaps. 2, 3, 11, and 13.
[73] 'Penser, c'est avoir des opérations de l'existence desquelles on est certain immédiatement par elles mêmes dans le moment qu'on les a': Dilly, *Traité*, p. 8. Compare the discussions in (Rodis-)Lewis (1950), pp. 112–13; Balz, *Cartesian Studies* (1951), p. 131; and Rosenfield, *From Beast-Machine to Man Machine* (1968), pp. 271–3.
[74] Bayle, *Dictionnaire historique et critique* (1697; fifth edn., 1740). *Historical and Critical Dictionary. Selections*, ed. Popkin (1965), entry 'Rorarius', note E.
[75] Ibid.
[76] *De la recherche de la vérité*, III.1.1: 'on ne connoît la pensée que par sentiment intérieur ou par conscience'. In III.2.7, Malebranche says about the soul: 'nous ne la connoissons que par *conscience*'.

The ontological view of the self: Scholastic and Cartesian conceptions 51

thoughts and does not involve ideas. He holds that we can know external objects through *ideas* that represent them and that are mediated through God, but that this does not apply to our relating to our own souls and thoughts. *Sentiment intérieur* as an immediate and direct relating to our own self is the only way in which we know our souls and thoughts. And as we are not able to acquire knowledge of the soul and its thoughts through divinely mediated ideas but only through *conscience*, Malebranche argues—against Descartes—that we cannot arrive at 'a complete knowledge of our soul'.[77] Although knowledge based on *conscience* is imperfect, however, Malebranche asserts that it is certain and provides sufficient evidence for the most important characteristics of the human soul, such as its liberty, spirituality, and immortality.

Moreover, there are passages in which he suggests that other forms of relating to one's own soul, apart from *conscience*, are possible. For example, in the *Traité de morale* (1684) he emphasises the importance of knowledge (indeed of a *science*) of human nature, adding that this can only be an experimental science—a science which is the result 'of a reflection which one makes on what passes in one's own self'.[78] And in the *Recherche* too, he maintains that it is necessary 'to study and observe one's own self'.[79] He appeals to readers of his work that they take the trouble to 'make some reflections on what they feel in themselves'. He also states in this context that many often forget to think about themselves—'that they make no reflection on what they feel and that they do not search at all for the reasons of that which passes in their mind'.[80] He does not say much, however, about the nature of relating to one's own self through reflection. He could not (and does not) say that reflection produces ideas of the soul and its modifications, for he rejects the possibility of such a self-relation. Reflection seems to relate to a scientific study and the nature of thought in general. Yet the passage in which he says that one should study and observe one's own self clearly concerns a relating to one's own self as an individual being. What he seems to be saying is that those mental contents to which we have access through *conscience* can become objects of reflection.

In any case, it remains unclear what the relationship between the various forms of relating to one's own self is in Malebranche. It may be that the self-relation *via réflexion* is even the same as *conscience* or *sentiment intérieur*. He certainly makes no attempt at explicitly distinguishing between *conscience* and *réflexion*. Also, it is not clear whether he regards *sentiment intérieur* (or *conscience*) as a second-order act of perception or as an element of thought itself. The fact that he ascribes immediacy to *conscience* does not help in this respect. All that the notion of immediacy explains

---

[77] 'une entière connaissance de nôtre âme': *De la recherche de la vérité*, III.2.7.
[78] 'de la réflexion qu'on fait sur ce qui se passe en soi même': *Traité de morale*, pt. I, c. 5, § 17; *Oeuvres completes*, vol. 11, ed. Adam (1966), p. 67.
[79] 'de s'étudier et de s'observer soi-même': *De la recherche de la vérité*, V.2.
[80] 'de faire quelques réflexions sur ce qu'ils sentent dans eux-mêmes'; 'les hommes s'oublient souvent si fort eux-mêmes, qu'ils ne font pas de réflexion sur ce qu'ils sentent et qu'ils ne rechercherent point les raisons de ce qui se passe dans leur esprit'. Both quotations are from *De la recherche de la vérité*, V.2.

is that, unlike the perception of external things, the relating to one's own self is not mediated through ideas.[81]

It seems that the earliest explicit, if brief, discussion of consciousness and its distinction from other forms of relating to one's own thoughts in the broad Cartesian context can be found in Louis de La Forge, and especially, somewhat later, in Antoine Arnauld. In his *Traité de l'esprit de l'homme* (1666) La Forge holds that the nature of thought consists in non-evaluative *conscience* or *sentiment intérieur*, emphasising that the relationship of *conscience* to thought is characterized by immediacy: *conscience* always and immediately accompanies mental events.[82] We saw that Descartes defines thought as that of which we are immediately conscious only in order to exclude 'voluntary movement' from the notion of thought, without explaining the nature of this immediacy.[83] We have seen that Malebranche too leaves the immediacy of *conscience* unexplained; it seems to refer only to the fact that *conscience* is not a form of relating to one's own self through divinely mediated ideas. La Forge, by contrast, explains that *conscience* is not a separate act but an element of thought itself: *conscience* is a reflexivity inherent in thought as such.[84] Thus, here the notion of an 'immanent reflexivity' of thought that has been ascribed to Descartes by some commentators is appropriate. Moreover, La Forge explicitly distinguishes between *conscience* and the 'reflection we sometimes make on our thoughts'. Unlike *conscience*, reflection is not an element of thought as such; reflection, rather, is just a particular type of thought. *Conscience* is an element inherent in all acts of reflection; but acts of reflection are not necessarily accompanied by another act of reflection.[85] Thus, although the expression *sentiment intérieur* might suggest the notion of a separate act of *sentiment* or feeling distinct from those acts that are felt, this is not how La Forge understands that notion.

Later in the century, Antoine Arnauld accounts for consciousness in essentially the same way as does La Forge. Although Arnauld makes use of the terminology of 'conscientia' in its non-evaluative sense, he explains consciousness mainly in terms of two types of *réflexion*. In his *Des vrayes et des fausses idées* (1683) he draws a distinction between *réflexion virtuelle* and *réflexion expresse*. The notion of *réflexion virtuelle* is the

---

[81] Schmaltz notes that there are some passages in Malebranche which can be used to support second-order interpretations, and others that suggest a first-order understanding of *conscience*. In the end, however, he believes that Malebranche was influenced by La Forge in this regard, and 'simply assumed' that *conscience* is an aspect of thought itself: Schmaltz (1996) pp. 18–19. On this basis he ascribes to Malebranche a distinction between *direct consciousness* and *reflexive consciousness* (p. 21).
[82] La Forge, *Traité de l'esprit de l'homme* (1666), p. 54.
[83] *Oeuvres*, vol. 7, p. 160; *Philosophical Writings*, vol. 2, p. 113.
[84] See La Forge, *Traité*, p. 54.
[85] It is worth quoting the relevant passage in full: 'Ie dis immediatement, afin de vous faire connoistre que ce témoignage & ce sentiment interieur n'est pas different de l'action ou de la passion, & que ce sont elles mesmes qui l'auertissent de ce qui se fait en luy; et qu'ainsi vous ne confondiez pas ce sentiment interieur auec la Reflexion que nous faisons quelquefois sur nos actions, laquelle ne se trouue pas dans toutes nos pensées, dont elle est seulement vne espece': La Forge, *Traité*, p. 54. See p. 318, where La Forge says that in order to compare ideas with one another the mind needs to make a 'reflexion mentale'.

The ontological view of the self: Scholastic and Cartesian conceptions 53

notion that 'our thought or perception is essentially reflective on itself, or, as it is said more aptly in Latin, *est sui conscia*'.[86] Elsewhere he states that human beings are intelligent beings who '*sunt conscia sui, et suae operationis*'.[87] The latter formulation and other passages suggest that *réflexion virtuelle* involves an immediate relating also to one's own self as the subject of one's thoughts or perceptions.[88] Arnauld does not, however, elaborate on this aspect of *réflexion virtuelle*. He distinguishes consciousness (or *réflexion virtuelle*) understood as the essential reflexivity of thought from reflection proper (understood as a second-order act of perception) by pointing out 'that there is a more explicit reflection, by which we examine our perception by another perception'.[89] This more explicit reflection is Arnauld's *réflexion expresse*. Further, Arnauld links *réflexion expresse* to that reflection which is, to him, characteristic of scientific enquiry.[90] Arnauld, too, does not examine the notion of consciousness in much detail, but at least he explicitly accounts for it as an immanent reflexivity of thought rather than as a second-order act of perception or reflection.[91]

This notion of an immediate form of relating to oneself is hinted at and appealed to if not explained or discussed in any detail by other Cartesian philosophers at the end of the seventeenth century—by Pierre Sylvain Régis and François Lamy, for example.[92] It is used by later Cartesians such as Régis in discussions concerning the issue of infinite regress. Critics of the Cartesian philosophy, such as the Jesuit Pierre Daniel Huet, clearly assuming a second-order notion of consciousness, argued that Cartesians cannot avoid an infinite regress of thought, as on the Cartesian view all thought is accompanied by consciousness, and consciousness itself is a form of thinking. Régis notes, however, that there is no such commitment to an infinite regress in the Cartesian position, because relating to one's own thinking does not require a distinct mental act. Rather, the soul knows its thoughts through those thoughts themselves.[93]

---

[86] Arnauld, *Des vrayes et des fausses idées* (1683), chap. 6, p. 46: 'nostre *pensée ou perception* est essentiellement reflechissante sur elle même: ou, ce qui se dit plus heureusement en Latin, *est sui conscia*. Car je ne pense point, que je ne sçache que je pense'. Arnauld appeals to Augustine, *De trinitate*, X, 10, in this context. In a letter to Descartes he speaks of an 'intrinsic reflection of all thoughts': *Oeuvres*, vol. 5, p. 213.
[87] Arnauld, *Des vrayes et des fausses idées*, chap. 2, p. 11.
[88] Ibid.: 'Et la pensée que nostre ame a de soy-même, par ce que, quoy que ce soit que je connoisse, je connois que je le connois, par une certaine reflexion virtuelle qui accompagne toutes mes pensées. Je me connois donc moy même, en connoissant toutes les autres choses.'
[89] Ibid., chap. 6, p. 46: 'La 2. est qu'outre cette reflexion qu'on peut appeler *virtuelle*, qui se rencontre dans toutes nos perceptions, il y en a une autre plus *expresse*, par laquelle nous examinons nostre perception par une autre perception.' On the distinction between *réflexion virtuelle* and *réflexion expresse*, see also chap. 13, p. 123.
[90] Ibid., chap. 6, p. 46.
[91] In contrast to our above reading of Descartes, Nadler holds that Arnauld's distinction between *réflexion virtuelle* as a first-order reflexivity of thought and *réflexion expresse* 'is one which is found in Descartes': *Arnauld and the Cartesian Philosophy of Ideas* (1989), p. 120.
[92] Régis, *Système de philosophie* I, p. 68; Lamy, *Traité de la connaissance de soi-même* (1694). On Régis's and Lamy's terminology, see also (Rodis-)Lewis (1950) pp. 113, 119; and Davies, *Conscience as Consciousness* (1990), pp. 11, 18–19.
[93] Huet, *Censura philosophiae cartesianae* (1689; fourth edn., 1691), pp. 35–7. Régis, *Système*, I, p. 150; Régis, *Réponse au livre qui a pour titre, P. Danielis Huetii... Censura philosophiae*

54   The Early Modern Subject

We noted above that the distinction between consciousness and reflection is appealed to by Pierre Bayle in his *Dictionnaire historique et critique*. He draws this distinction explicitly elsewhere, without, however, making use of the terms 'conscience' or 'conscientia' in this context. For the immediate relating to one's own thoughts through consciousness, Bayle, like Arnauld, employs the notion of an essential reflexivity of all thought. In his early *Système abrégé de philosophie*, published posthumously in the fourth volume of his *Oeuvres diverses* (1731), he distinguishes this inherent or immanent reflexivity of thought from acts of reflection 'by which the soul examines its acts'. In these acts of reflection one thought is said to be the *object* of another thought.[94] We shall see in Chapter 3 that La Forge's understanding of *conscience* and Arnauld's *réflexion virtuelle* are also relevant to Locke's account of consciousness.

1.3. THE TRINITY, HUMAN PERSONALITY, AND SELF-CONSCIOUSNESS: THE DEBATE BETWEEN SHERLOCK AND SOUTH

Scholastic doctrine of the person was not defunct in the second half of the century. This is well illustrated by a debate that took place in England in the early 1690s between two theologians: William Sherlock and Robert South. Significantly, both Sherlock and South deal with the issue of individuation and the notion of person in general, making use of the notions of consciousness and self-consciousness in this context. There are some references to personal identity through time, but as they are concerned with the issue of the trinity, their discussions focus on individuation. Their dispute created widespread interest and controversy at the time, and many other theologians and philosophers contributed to it: for example, Richard Burthogge, Edward Stillingfleet, and Francis Gastrell, to name only the philosophically most important ones. The importance of this debate consists not only in the fact that it helps to illuminate further the difference between the Scholastic and the Cartesian accounts of the person, but also in the fact that it foreshadows arguments very similar to those that were very soon to be discussed in relation to Locke's new theory—this despite the fact that unlike Sherlock and South, Locke's concern is mainly with diachronic personal identity, and not with individuation. It is against

---

cartesianae (1691), pp. 35, 41. Régis assures his critics that for Cartesians 'il n'y a point de connaissance plus directe que celle que l'esprit a de sa propre pensée, puisqu'il la connoist par elle-même' (*Réponse*, p. 46). For a discussion of Régis and other Cartesians responding to Huet, such as Schotan and Schweling, invoking a first-order understanding of consciousness, see (Rodis-)Lewis (1950), pp. 117–23.

[94] Bayle states that 'il faut observer que toute pensée est essentiellement un acte réfléchi, c'est-à-dire qu'elle est connue par elle même, en sorte que par cela même qu'elle connoît un objet, elle sait qu'elle le connoît, & connoît par conséquent l'acte de connoître qu'elle produit. Mais il y a encore des connoissances qu'on appelle réfléchies dans un autre sens, savoir celles par lesquelles l'ame examine ses actes, tellement qu'une pensée soit l'objet d'une autre pensée': *Oeuvres diverses*, vol. IV, ed. Labrousse (1968), p. 457.

the background of this debate that Locke's theory can be seen to distinguish itself from both Cartesian and Scholastic theories.

In discussing the doctrine of the trinity, South makes it clear that he wishes to defend the 'schoolmen's' account; whereas Sherlock's position, by contrast, is labelled 'Cartesian' by his contemporaries—and rightly so.[95] As indicated, Sherlock and South preface their arguments concerning the trinity with philosophical enquiries into the concept of the person in general, and into what constitutes the individuality of a human person. In doing so, both Sherlock and South appeal to the standard Boethian definition of a person as an 'individual substance of a rational nature'. Both hold the view that when applied to human beings, the term 'person' denotes the individual human being as a whole, consisting of soul and body. However, whereas South regards the body as an essential element of the person and argues that souls, when separated from their bodies, are not persons,[96] Sherlock maintains that the soul constitutes the person when united to a body, and *is* the (same) person when separated from the body.[97] And the soul or person is, for Sherlock, 'a simple uncompounded thing...which cannot consist of parts':[98] a person, human or divine, is essentially an individual spiritual substance. Thus, like Descartes, Sherlock distinguishes the notion of an individual human being or person as including corporeity from the notion of the essential self or soul as an incorporeal entity. Unlike Descartes, however, Sherlock also applies the term 'person' to this incorporeal spiritual entity—which may be confusing. When Sherlock comes to account for the individuality of persons, he does so in terms of consciousness: and here he seems to go further than Descartes, who argued that our knowledge of the soul's individuality is derived from consciousness. Sherlock seems to be saying that consciousness actually brings about the individuality of the person: 'Now this Self unity of the Spirit... can be nothing else but *Self-consciousness*: That it is conscious to its own Thoughts, Reasonings, Passions, which no other finite Spirit is conscious to but itself: This makes a finite Spirit numerically one, and separates it from all other Spirits.'[99] Sherlock, it seems, thinks that consciousness, understood as a unifier of thoughts and actions, individuates persons or finite spirits.[100]

---

[95] For a more detailed discussion of the Sherlock–South debate over the notion of person, see Thiel, *Lockes Theorie der Personalen Identität* (1983), pp. 63–4, 107–16; and, especially, Thiel, 'The Trinity and Human Personal Identity', in M. A. Stewart (ed.), *English Philosophy in the Age of Locke* (2000), pp. 217–43. This article also discusses the historical context of the debate and its role in Locke's writing of the chapter on identity. For a different account of the debate, see Wedeking, 'Locke on Personal Identity and the Trinity Controversy of the 1690s', *Dialogue*, 29 (1990), 163–88. Critical comments on Wedeking's reading are in Thiel (2000).

[96] South, *Animadversions upon Dr. Sherlock's Book, Entituled A Vindication of the Holy and Ever Blessed Trinity* (1693), p. 75; South, *Tritheism Charged upon Dr. Sherlock's New Notion of the Trinity* (1695), pp. 115–16.

[97] Sherlock, *A Defence of Dr. Sherlock's Notion of a Trinity in Unity* (1694), p. 47.

[98] Ibid., p. 45.

[99] Sherlock, *A Vindication of the Doctrine of the Holy and Ever Blessed Trinity* (1690), pp. 48–9.

[100] In order to account for the unity of the three divine persons, Sherlock introduces the notion of 'mutual consciousness'. The divine persons have a mutual consciousness of one another, in addition to self-consciousness, 'and therefore are as essentially One, as a Mind or Spirit is One with itself': Sherlock, *A Vindication*, p. 68. For a similar account of the roles of self-consciousness and

South rejects this theory of the individuation of persons, arguing instead that a person must have individuality prior to being conscious of thoughts and actions, and that, therefore, consciousness cannot constitute this individuality.[101] In other words, South accuses Sherlock's theory of circularity; for according to South, Sherlock introduces as a principle of individuation that which in fact presupposes individuality. For South, consciousness presupposes an individual person because consciousness is an 'action' that 'issues from' the person: there must be a person before there can be acts (like those of consciousness) which originate in the person. Further, South holds that consciousness presupposes other personal acts which are its objects. Since consciousness is a 'Reflex Act' on thoughts and feelings of the person, it 'must needs in Order of Nature be Posterior to the Act reflected upon by it. And therefore *Self-Consciousness*, which is by two degrees Posterior to Personality, cannot possibly be the *formal Reason* of it.'[102] This argument indicates that for South the 'Reflex Act' of consciousness is to be understood in terms of a second-order act of perception. It is on the basis of this understanding of consciousness that South argues that consciousness presupposes other mental acts (those on which the mind reflects or of which it is conscious), as well as a unitary mind in which both first-order and second-order acts of perception originate.

Sherlock responds to this second argument by drawing an important distinction between self-consciousness and self-knowledge—that is, by rejecting South's identification of self-consciousness with reflection or an 'act of knowledge'. Sherlock's distinction corresponds to the old Platonic distinction between sense and knowledge in general—a distinction which the Cambridge Platonist Ralph Cudworth draws explicitly in *A Treatise concerning Eternal and Immutable Morality* (as we shall see in the next chapter).[103] Indeed, Sherlock himself relates his point about self-consciousness to the generic distinction between what he calls 'speculation' and 'sensation'. Self-knowledge and self-consciousness, he says, stand in the same relation to one another as do 'Speculation and Sensation' in general (*A Defence* p. 77). He emphasises that he does not mean to say that acts of reflection or self-knowledge constitute the individuality of a person, arguing that self-knowledge is an objectifying consideration of the self. In order

---

mutual consciousness before Sherlock, see John Turner *A Discourse Concerning the Messiah. To Which is Prefixed a Large Preface, Asserting and Explaining the Doctrine of the Blessed Trinity, against the Late Writer of the Intellectual System* (1685), pp. clii–cliii; also pp. cxxv–cxxvii. For a detailed discussion of the originality of Sherlock's account in terms of self-consciousness, see Thiel (2000), pp. 224–31. I argue that Sherlock's account of individual personality in terms of self-consciousness has its sources not only in Descartes, but also and especially in the revival of neo-Platonic thought in Cambridge in the second half of the seventeenth century, and that his theory has an immediate predecessor in the work of John Turner.

[101] South, *Animadversions*, pp. 71, 94.

[102] Ibid., p. 71. Similar arguments were brought forward against Sherlock by Richard Burthogge and Edward Stillingfleet. See Burthogge, *Essay*, p. 273, and Stillingfleet, *A Discourse in Vindication of the Doctrine of the Trinity: With an Answer to the Late Socinian Objections against it from Scripture, Antiquity and Reason* (1697), pp. 71–2.

[103] This work was published posthumously in 1731 (see esp. p. 170). It is unlikely, then, that Cudworth was Sherlock's source here. The relevant distinction is also present in Augustine, of course, but Sherlock does not appeal to Augustine in this context. For comments on Augustine, see the comments in the Introduction above.

to acquire self-knowledge we produce a 'copy' or an 'image' of our own self which becomes an object of contemplation. Self-consciousness, by contrast, is an immediate relating to one's own self—a 'feeling' of our own thoughts and passions. It is this immediate relation of oneself to oneself which is relevant to the individuation of persons:

Self-Knowledge properly signifies to contemplate our own Natures in their Idea, to draw our own Image and Picture as like the Original as we can, and to view our selves in it: But *Self-consciousness* is an *intellectual Self Sensation*, when we feel our selves, and all the Thoughts, Knowledge, Volitions, Passions of our Minds, and know what is Self, and what belongs to Self by feeling it.[104]

Sherlock believes that this distinction between two different ways of relating to oneself is crucial to an understanding of the issue at hand: 'He, who knows not the difference between intellectual Sence [*sic*] and Knowledge, is as unfit to meddle in this Controversie, as a Blind-Man is to dispute of Colours' (ibid., p. 77). The fact that he draws this distinction is, indeed, of considerable historical importance; for while the general distinction between 'sense' and 'speculation' or knowledge was not new, we have seen that most seventeenth-century philosophers did not explicitly distinguish between different ways of relating to oneself.[105] It is doubtful, however, that Sherlock's emphasis on self-consciousness as a feeling or internal sensation can help him in his defence against South. For he still seems to think of self-consciousness as a second-order act of perception; and that means that South's critique remains valid.

Sherlock's appeal to the distinction between self-knowledge and self-consciousness does not constitute the main line of his defence, however. About the first (and main) point of South's critique Sherlock says that he is not, as South assumes, concerned with the constitution or 'formal reason' of personality, but with what individuates a person. But neither is this Sherlock's main argument,[106] and South has no problems in dealing with this (weak) defence. From the Scholastic point of view (which is South's point of view) Sherlock's distinction between the 'formal reason' and the 'principle of individuation' is spurious. South points out that what he

---

[104] Sherlock, *A Defence*, p. 77. See also p. 7, where he identifies self-consciousness with 'Internal Sensation'.

[105] In *A Defence* (p. 39) Sherlock introduces the term 'self-feeling' to explain his understanding of self-consciousness. Unlike 'self-consciousness', this term was not taken up in subsequent debates about the self and personal identity. The German translation of Sherlock's 'self-consciousness' seems to be one of the earliest occurrences of the term in German—a term that became very important in post-Kantian philosophy. Rambach's preface to his edition of Sherlock's sermons translates Sherlock's term as 'Selbstbewustheit' (slightly different from the later and now standard 'Selbstbewußtsein' Sherlock, *Auserlesene Zeugnisse von den wichtigsten Grundwahrheiten der Christlichen Religion*, transl. Rambach (1744)). 'Self-feeling' is occasionally used again towards the end of the eighteenth century—for example, in Crichton *An Inquiry into the Nature and Origin of Mental Derangement* (1798), vol. 1 p. 113. Crichton makes no reference to Sherlock, however. Rather, his 'self-feeling' is an attempt to translate literally the German *Selbstgefühl*, which was a much-used term in the German psychology of the 1770s. On the notion of *Selbstgefühl* and its origin, see Thiel, 'Varieties of Inner Sense. Two Pre-Kantian Theories', *Archiv für Geschichte der Philosophie*, 79 (1997), 58–79.

[106] Thus I am in disagreement with Wedeking, who believes that Sherlock's distinction between the 'formal reason' and the 'principle of individuation' is his 'main . . . line of defence': Wedeking (1990), 167–8.

'affirms to be the *formal Reason* of a Thing' is precisely that 'which gives it Being, Unity in it self, and distinction from all others'.[107] The 'formal reason' of a thing is also that which individuates it. Even Sherlock himself concedes that if South means by 'the formal Reason of Personality... that which makes a Mind, Spirit, or Person one, and either distinguishes or separates it from all other Minds, Spirits or persons, I do affirm, that Self-consciousness is this formal Reason' (Sherlock, *A Defence*, p. 38).

What, then, is Sherlock's main argument? It appears that in setting out to defend his theory against South's charge, Sherlock in fact modifies it, but without acknowledging that his argument amounts to a modification of his original theory. He retreats to a position according to which consciousness is not, as he seemed to be saying, the *ratio essendi* of individual personality, but merely its *ratio cognoscendi*. He bases his position on a sceptical view about human knowledge of essence: all we know about spiritual substance is 'what we feel in our Selves' (ibid., p. 6). This feeling or consciousness is the only means available to us for discovering the unity of our own self; and this is what it means to say that the individuality of persons has its foundation in consciousness. Sherlock makes it clear that he does not wish to say that consciousness is the real ground of personal identity: he agrees with South's criticism, saying that:

> there must be a Person, before there can be any *actual Self-consciousness*; that is to say, there must be a Self (which in this Dispute is all that can be meant by Person) before this Self can feel it Self, and by this Self-feeling distinguish Himself from all other Selfs. (ibid., p. 39)

Despite this concession, Sherlock thinks we can determine *a priori* what the real ground of personal identity is, and he continues to employ the terminology of consciousness in his discussion of the topic. Nevertheless, it becomes clear that he modifies his original position. For he argues that 'the principle of Self-consciousness' (or '*Self-consciousness* in the *Abstract*', ibid., p. 40), rather than actual consciousness, individuates a person (ibid., p. 66). And this 'principle' of consciousness is, of course, the soul itself, as 'the Soul is the seat of Personality, the only Principle of Reason, Sensation, and a Conscious life'. (ibid., p. 60) Through actual consciousness we discover our individuality as persons, and 'by this actual *Self-consciousness* every Person feels himself to be himself, and not to be another' (ibid., p. 62). But Sherlock agrees with South that actual self-consciousness 'cannot make the Person' (ibid.). It is 'the principle of Self-consciousness' that does 'distinguish between Self-conscious Persons' (ibid., p. 66).

South notices that by moving from the 'acts' to the 'principle' of self-consciousness in dealing with the charge of circularity, Sherlock thereby had altered the state of the debate (South, *Tritheism*, p. 99). More importantly, in attempting to explain the individuality of the person (= soul) in terms of the 'principle of self-consciousness' (= soul), Sherlock quite obviously fails to account for the individuality of the person understood as an immaterial substance—just as Descartes himself fails to account for the individuation of the soul as an immaterial substance. And so, despite his un-Cartesian appeal to scepticism about essence, Sherlock's position on the self is very close to the standard Cartesian position. The self is conceived of as an

---

[107] South, *Tritheism*, p. 98. There is no reference to this book in Wedeking (1990).

immaterial thinking substance, and its individuality is said to be known on the basis of consciousness; but what constitutes this individuality is left unexplained.

As indicated above, given the trinitarian context of the debate, both Sherlock and South focus on the problem of individuation and do not address at any length the issue of identity through time. For Sherlock, just as for Descartes, no genuine problem of personal identity through time arises. The human body may change constantly, but since the essence of the self is located in the soul or immaterial thinking substance, these changes do not affect personal identity through time:

> Whatever change there be in the Body, the Person is the same still, which could not be, were the Body part of the Person, for then the change of the Body would be a partial Change of the Person too; and yet our Bodies are in a perpetual Flux, and change every day.[108]

South occasionally addresses the issue of personal identity through time. Indeed, in examining Sherlock's notion of 'the personality of the soul', South refers to the issue of human personal identity through time, and related issues such as the afterlife, the resurrection of the body, and responsibility (*Animadversions*, pp. 76–8). Further, South's argument, that the soul alone does not constitute the person (ibid., pp. 73–5), and the question he puts to Sherlock, 'whether the *Soul*, or *Mind* of Man be *one Person*, and the Man himself *Another*' (ibid., 83), are reflected in Locke's treatment of personal identity (for example, *Essay*, II.xxvii.21), as we shall see. But for South, consciousness obviously can play no constitutive role for personal identity through time.

Thus, Sherlock's account of personhood turns out to be Cartesian in two important respects: (1) he places a characteristically non-Scholastic emphasis on consciousness understood as a relating to one's own thoughts and actions;[109] but (2) he does not ascribe to consciousness a constitutive function for the self as a person. The latter point

---

[108] Sherlock, *A Defence*, p. 51.
[109] Baker, in his critical discussion of *The Cambridge History of Seventeenth-Century Philosophy*, states that the Scholastic notion of *conscientia* is the notion of a 'vital cognitive power of the rational soul'. On this basis he criticizes my statement in the chapter 'Personal Identity', which I repeat here, that 'the Cartesians place a characteristically *non-scholastic* emphasis on consciousness and self-consciousness' (Baker's emphasis): *British Journal of the History of Philosophy*, 8 (2000), 364–5. In response to this criticism, the following points need to be emphasised. First, the comment quoted by Baker relates to the concept of a *person* as discussed in that chapter, including the debate between Sherlock and South. And it is clear that the Scholastic definition of person does not include the notion of consciousness. The difference between Sherlock and South, as documented there as well as here, however, relates to a large extent to the notion of consciousness. Second, and more importantly, Baker's identification of *conscientia* with a *cognitive* power is highly problematic. As noted in the Introduction above, the Scholastic notion of *conscientia* formed a special topic in moral theology. The *conscientia* theorem involves the knowledge or memory of one's own past actions, but is not identical with it. Third, this knowledge is not the same as consciousness in Sherlock, Cudworth, and Locke. Again, as noted in the Introduction, the history of the term 'conscientia' and its cognates is very complex, as is its function in the philosophical debates (for example, the term may refer to conscience or to consciousness or to both, depending on the context). Baker's comments display no awareness of the relevant primary and secondary material (some of which is cited above in the Introduction). Lastly, he fails to distinguish between memory and consciousness, self-knowledge and self-consciousness and *conscientia*, as well as other forms of relating to one's own self. For these reasons, his remark that the *Cambridge History* in the passages he cites 'shows little understanding of conscientia' is somewhat misplaced, to put it mildly.

means that despite the differences between Scholastic and Cartesian theories of the person, as illustrated by the Sherlock–South debate, the two share the 'ontological' view of the self as thing or substance.

1.4. ESSAYISTIC ALTERNATIVES: PASCAL AND LA ROCHEFOUCAULD

The human self was approached from an entirely different perspective by Michel Montaigne in the sixteenth century, and, for example, by Pascal and La Rochefoucauld in the seventeenth century.[110] They see the person as an object not of abstract metaphysical thought, but of psychological observation. They are somewhat sceptical about reason as a means of grasping the nature of the self, and instead emphasise the constant changes that human beings undergo and the elusiveness of the self as an object of enquiry. For these authors, the emotional side of persons, rather than questions about their metaphysical make-up, is central. Pascal points out that metaphysically speaking, whatever the essence of a person is, what matters is that we love a person because of his or her observable qualities:

What is the self? . . . if someone loves me for my judgement or my memory, do they love me? *me*, myself? No, for I could lose these qualities without losing my self. Where then is this self, if it is neither in the body nor the soul? And how can one love the body or the soul except for the sake of such qualities, which are not what makes up the self, since they are perishable? Would we love the substance of a person's soul, in the abstract, whatever qualities might be in it? That is not possible, and it would be wrong. Therefore we never love anyone, but only qualities.[111]

This focus on 'qualities' is reminiscent, of course, of the old Roman notion of person. Pascal, however, does not elaborate on this point. And although his and La Rochefoucauld's psychological observations, presented in aphoristic style, amount to a description of what they take to be the nature of human persons—for example, that they have characteristics such as vanity and weakness, that they are formed by outward influences and custom, and so on—neither of them enquires systematically into the concept of a person, nor develops a theory about what it is to be a person and what would be required for a person to remain the same through time. But this is precisely the question that other philosophers of the time investigated—as we shall see in the following Chapters.

---

[110] For a detailed discussion of Pascal and La Rochefoucauld, see Krailsheimer, *Studies in Self-Interest. From Descartes to La Bruyère* (1962). See also Thweatt, *La Rochefoucauld and the Seventeenth-Century Concept of the Self* (1980); and Bürger, *Das Verschwinden des Subjekts* (1998), pp. 32–7 (Montaigne), pp. 44–8 (Pascal), and pp. 48–51 (La Rochefoucauld).

[111] Pascal, *Pensées*, transl. Krailsheimer (1966), no. 688.

2

Metaphysical alternatives: conceptions of identity, morality, and the afterlife

We have seen that although the Cartesians assign an important role to the notion of consciousness and self-consciousness, they do not ascribe to consciousness a constitutive function for the self as person. This is true also of those seventeenth-century philosophers prior to Locke who cannot be classed as either Scholastics or Cartesians, such as the Cambridge Platonists and Spinoza. Both, however, contribute to the debate in various ways.

2.1. SPINOZA ON INDIVIDUATION, IDENTITY, AND CONSCIOUSNESS

Spinoza does not discuss the issue of human personal identity in any detail. His account of 'man', although influenced by Descartes, differs from both Scholastic and Cartesian doctrine. He holds that human beings consist of mind and body,[1] but this is neither a union of form and matter, nor a union of two distinct and independent substances. For Spinoza, human beings (like other individuals) are not, strictly speaking, substances at all. They are individual things (*res singulares*) existing in the one divine substance: the human self consists of body understood as a mode of the divine attribute of extension, and of mind understood as a mode of the divine attribute of thought.[2] The individuality of human beings is constituted, like that of other *res singulares*, by a limitation or negation of divine attributes. And so Spinoza explains the union of mind and body in terms of modes of the divine attributes of thought and extension, not as a substantial union: 'The Mind and the Body, are one and the same Individual, which is conceived now under the attribute of Thought, now under the attribute of Extension' (*Ethica*, II, prop. 21, schol.).

Spinoza seems to assume that under normal circumstances an individual person remains the same through time and partial change. He makes only few occasional

---

[1] Spinoza, *Ethica*, II, prop. 13, dem., cor.: *Spinoza Opera*, ed. Gebhardt (1925), vol. 1; *The Collected Works of Spinoza*, ed. Curley (1985), vol. 1.
[2] Spinoza, *Ethica*, II, prop. 21, schol.; II, prop. 7, schol.

remarks on the topic. He does, however, discuss the individuation of bodies.[3] Clearly, for Spinoza bodies do not differ with respect to their substance: rather, they have this in common that they 'involve the concept of one and the same attribute'—the divine attribute of extension.[4] Like Descartes, Spinoza assumes that extension essentially entails mobility: all bodies are either in motion or rest. And he argues that the individuation of bodies can be explained in these terms—another idea he takes up from Descartes: 'Bodies are distinguished from one another by reason of motion and rest, speed and slowness, and not by reason of substance.'[5] Of course, Spinoza does not say that motion and rest as such individuate bodies, for all bodies have this in common that they are essentially in a state of motion or rest. Rather, it is the particular proportion of motion and rest that individuates a body: 'there is no other mode in extension than motion and rest, and ... each particular corporeal thing is nothing but a certain proportion of motion and rest, so much so that if there were nothing in extension except motion alone, or nothing except rest alone, there could not be, or be indicated, in the whole of extension, any particular thing'.[6] Further, each particular body is determined to its proportion of motion or rest by another body, and this body in turn 'has also been determined to motion or rest by another, and that again by another, and so on, to infinity'.[7] In other words, the individuality of each body is determined by its causal relations to other bodies. Spinoza, then, does not account for individuation in terms of intrinsic constituents of a being, considered in isolation from other beings. On his theory, rather, the individuality of all 'things' is constituted by their interrelatedness in the one divine substance.

With respect to composite bodies (such as the human body) there is an additional cause for their individuation. While the relation to other bodies remains relevant, the relationship between those bodies which make up the composite body itself is of special importance here: a composite body 'is distinguished from the others by this

---

[3] For Spinoza's account of the individuation of bodies and his argument for the oneness of substance, see Thiel, 'Individuation', in Garber and Ayers (eds.), *The Cambridge History of Seventeenth-Century Philosophy* (1998), pp. 229–31. For a more detailed account, see Woolhouse, *Descartes, Spinoza, Leibniz. The Concept of Substance in Seventeenth-Century Metaphysics* (1993), pp. 28–53. Compare also Garrett, 'Spinoza's Theory of Metaphysical Individuation', in Barber and Gracia (eds.), *Individuation and Identity in Early Modern Philosophy* (1994), pp. 73–101.

[4] *Ethica*, II, prop. 13, lem. 2 dem.

[5] *Ethica*, II, prop. 13, lem. 1; for extension and mobility see *Ethica*, II, prop. 13, ax. 1 and 2. See also *Ethica*, II, prop. 13, lem. 3, dem.: Bodies 'are singular things which ... are distinguished from one another by reason of motion and rest.'

[6] Spinoza, *Korte Verhandeling* [*Short Treatise on God, Man, and His Well Being*] *Spinoza Opera* (1925), vol. 1, p. 120; *The Collected Works of Spinoza* (1985), vol. 1, p. 155. See also *Spinoza Opera*, vol. 1, p. 52; *The Collected Works of Spinoza*, vol 1, p. 95: 'Each and every particular thing that comes to exist becomes such through motion and rest ... The differences between [one body and another] arise only from the different proportions of motion and rest, by which one is so, and not so, is this and not that.'

[7] *Ethica*, II, prop. 13, lem. 3. Compare the demonstration to lem. 3. See also *Ethica*, II, prop. 31, dem: 'For each singular thing, like the human Body, must be determined by another singular thing to exist and produce effects in a certain and determinate way, and this again by another, and so to infinity.'

union of bodies'; that is, by the particular relationship that holds between its component parts.[8] This notion enables Spinoza to explain what constitutes the identity of composite bodies over time and through the change of its parts. Since it is the relationship among its parts, rather than the parts themselves, which individuates a composite body, the numerical identity of the components is not required for the diachronic identity of the composite body. The nature of the composite can be retained by different parts, as long as they (fulfil the same function and) stand in the same relation to one another as did the previous ones: 'If the parts composing an Individual become greater or less, but in such a proportion that they all keep the same ratio of motion and rest to each other as before, then the Individual will likewise retain its nature, as before, without any change of form.'[9]

Spinoza's account of the individuality of minds and human beings or persons has the same general features as does his theory of the individuation of bodies: it is an account of individuals as non-substantial entities, and one in terms of their relationships to other individuals and to the component parts that make up the individual.[10] The mind is understood as the 'idea of the body'; it consists in awareness of bodily events: 'The object of the idea constituting the human Mind is the Body.'[11] And since the mind is an idea (in God) of the body, the individuation and identity of the mind must run parallel to the individuation and identity of the body. Since the mind is nothing but the idea or knowledge of the body, the connections between ideas correspond to connections on the side of the body.[12] Thus, Spinoza argues that imagination and memory are dependent on the body: 'The Mind can neither imagine anything, nor recollect past things, except while the Body endures.'[13] He suggests, further, that a human being loses his or her identity through loss of memory. He relates a story about a Spanish poet who, after having recovered from a disease, does not remember anything of his past life and who for that reason cannot be regarded as the same man as before the amnesia.[14] So, human personal (or

---

[8] Spinoza, *Ethica*, II, prop. 13, lem. 3, dfn.
[9] Ibid., II, prop. 13, lem. 5. Spinoza realizes that his views on the individuation of body would require further clarification and argument. He points out that the topic is merely a digression, or rather a preliminary to what follows in the argument of *Ethica*, and that it is not central to his main interest in that work. 'If it had been my intention to deal expressly with body, I ought to have explained and demonstrated these things more fully. But I have already said that I intended something else, and brought these things forward only because I can easily deduce from them the things I have decided to demonstrate': *Ethica*, II, prop. 13, lem. 7, schol.
[10] For further comment on this, see Saw, 'Personal Identity in Spinoza', *Inquiry*, 12 (1969), 1–14; and especially Rice, 'Spinoza on Individuation', in Mandelbaum and Freeman (eds.), *Spinoza: Essays in Interpretation* (1975), pp. 195–214; Gilead, 'Spinoza's *Principium Individuationis* and Personal Identity', *International Studies in Philosophy*, 15 (1983), 41–57; and Den Uyl and Rice, 'Spinoza and Hume on Individuals', *Reason Papers*, 15 (1990), 91–117.
[11] Spinoza, *Ethica*, II, prop. 13.
[12] Ibid., II, prop., 19 dem. In the early *Korte Verhandeling* [*Short Treatise on God, Man, and His Well-Being*] Spinoza states that change in our body 'which arises in us from the fact that other bodies act on ours, cannot occur without the soul's becoming aware of it, since it, too, changes constantly' *Spinoza Opera* (1925), vol. 1, p. 52n; *The Collected Works of Spinoza* (1985), vol. 1, p. 95.
[13] Ibid., V, prop. 21.
[14] Ibid., IV, prop. 39, schol.

mental) identity requires continuity of memory; and continuity of memory depends on continuity of the body. And since the mind or soul is 'only an Idea, knowledge etc. of a body', it follows that if the body is destroyed the individual mind or person is destroyed too.[15] Nevertheless, Spinoza indicates that there is a sense in which the mind is eternal: the mind is eternal insofar as it is a mode or idea in the one divine substance.[16] As an individual being, however, the human mind is not eternal; there is no personal immortality. This is, obviously, a position which differs significantly from both Cartesian and Scholastic conceptions of the self. Cartesians and Scholastics alike argue for personal immortality, and they regard the substantiality of the self as necessary to secure personal immortality (see the last section of this Chapter). Spinoza's theory of the oneness of substance implies that the human self is not a substantial being; and this denial of the substantiality of the self undermines the basis of traditional theories of personal immortality. This is why Leibniz accuses Spinoza of Averroism, for Spinoza 'who recognizes only one single substance, is not far from the doctrine of a single universal spirit'.[17] Spinoza's denial of personal immortality may well be the reason that he does not discuss the issue of personal identity in any detail: since there is no personal immortality, personal identity through time does not constitute a pressing problem.

It has been suggested that in remarking that personal identity cannot be retained through amnesia, Spinoza 'anticipates' Locke's theory according to which personal identity depends on consciousness.[18] It is doubtful, however, that Spinoza's story about the Spanish poet really amounts to such an anticipation. It is true that both Spinoza and Locke link personal identity to consciousness in some way, although Spinoza speaks of memory here, rather than consciousness. Yet, Spinoza's story can be read as indicating merely that the poet has changed so much through his disease as to have lost his identity, and that as a *result* of this loss of identity he does not remember anything of his past life.[19] Locke, as we shall see, argues that the loss of consciousness *brings about* the loss of personal identity, because consciousness is what constitutes personal identity. There is a different, and perhaps more important, similarity between the two philosopher's accounts of the self: if Spinoza can be said to 'anticipate' Locke's revolutionary theory, this may be not because of Spinoza's occasional remark about amnesia, but because he does not conceive of human personality in terms of substantiality. The question of substantiality or non-substantiality of personality reappears, although in a very different systematic context, in Locke's theory of personal identity.

Although Spinoza makes use of the notion of consciousness in his account of the human mind, he provides no detailed discussion of that notion. Most scholars seem

---

[15] *Korte Verhandeling, Spinoza Opera* (1925), vol. 1, p. 52n.
[16] For Spinoza's views on the eternity of mind, see the concise account in Curley, *Behind the Geometrical Method: A Reading of Spinoza's Ethics* (1988), pp. 83–6.
[17] Leibniz, *Die Philosophischen Schriften*, ed. Gerhardt (1978), vol. 6, pp. 529–30; Leibniz, *Philosophical Papers and Letters*, ed. Loemker (1969), pp. 554–5.
[18] Curley (1988), p. 86.
[19] This is how Rice (1975), pp. 209–10, interprets the story.

to agree that Spinoza does not have a 'theory' of consciousness, and many think that the notion is only marginal to this philosophy.[20] Even scholars who believe Spinoza has something to contribute to the debates about consciousness concede that he does not have 'an explicit and perfectly consistent account of consciousness'.[21] For example, he defines desire ('cupiditas') as appetite together with the consciousness of the appetite ('appetitus cum eiusdem conscientia'), but does not examine *conscientia* in its own right.[22] He uses 'conscientia' in its non-evaluative sense, but it mostly occurs in the context of discussions of the emotions, and so seems to refer to a recording of one's own mental states that indicates the emotional quality of the latter.[23] In any case, although 'conscientia' is clearly a relating to one's own mental states,[24] it remains unclear what kind of relation to one's own mental states, emotional or otherwise, *conscientia* is meant to be in Spinoza.

Spinoza does, however, comment on relating to one's own thought in his doctrine of reflexive ideas or *ideae idearum*.[25] Some argue that this doctrine amounts to an account of consciousness, even if the terminology of *conscientia* is not used here.[26] In the early *Short Treatise on God, Man, and His Well-Being*, Spinoza indicates that feeling ('gevoel') gives rise to a 'reflexive Idea, or knowledge of oneself, experience, and reasoning',[27] without, however, distinguishing clearly between 'reflexive idea' and 'self-knowledge'.[28] In *Ethica* Spinoza argues that there is not only an idea for

---

[20] Compare, for example, Miller, who argues that that the concept of consciousness is 'not very central at all' to Spinoza's thought: 'The Status of Consciousness in Spinoza's Concept of Mind', in Heinämaa, Lähteenmäki, and Remes (eds.), *Consciousness: From Perception to Reflection in the History of Philosophy* (2007), pp. 203–20, at p. 208.

[21] Nadler, 'Spinoza and Consciousness', *Mind*, 117 (2008), 575–601, at 575.

[22] Spinoza, *Ethica*, III, prop. 9, schol.

[23] Renz points this out in *Die Erklärbarkeit von Erfahrung. Realismus und Subjektivität in Spinozas Theorie des menschlichen Geistes* (2010), p. 251. Contrary to what she suggests, however, it is not the case that Spinoza uses the terminology of 'conscientia' *only* when the consciousness of emotions is at issue. Compare, for example, *Ethica*, V, prop. 39, schol.

[24] According to Nadler there is an ambiguity in Spinoza's understanding of consciousness. In some contexts the term 'conscientia' seems to refer to a 'raw qualitative awareness'—for example, in the passage quoted above, where Spinzoa defines desire as appetite together with the *conscientia* of the appetite (*Ethica*, III, prop. 9, schol.). Elsewhere (V, prop. 39, schol.) he seems to use the terminology of 'conscientia' to refer to the awareness that one is in a certain mental state, 'thus importing an element of *self*-consciousness': Nadler (2008), 580. It is not clear, however, that the *conscientia* of my own appetite does not similarly involve a relating to my own self, and thus an 'element of self-consciousness.'

[25] *Ethica*, II, prop. 20–3.

[26] See, for example, Wilson, 'Objects, Ideas and "Minds": Comments on Spinoza's Theory of Mind', in Wilson, *Ideas and Mechanism: Essays on Early Modern Philosophy* (1999), pp. 126–40.

[27] 'een weerkeerige Idea, of de kennisse syns zelfs, de ervaring, en reedenering': *Spinoza Opera* (1925), vol. 1, p. 121; *The Collected Works of Spinoza* (1985), vol. 1, p. 156. Hampshire discusses the *cognitio reflexiva* or reflexive knowledge of the *Tractatus de intellectus emendatione* (*Spinoza Opera*, vol. 2, p. 16; *The Collected Works of Spinoza*, vol. 1, p. 19), indicating that there *may be* an implicit distinction in Spinoza between different types of reflection: Hampshire, *Spinoza* (1951), pp. 97–8. For further discussion, see also (Rodis-)Lewis, *Le problème de l'inconscient et le Cartésianisme* (1950), pp. 123–35.

[28] Rice reads too much into this passage when he says that Spinoza says here that reflexive ideas 'make self-knowledge and clear understanding possible': 'Reflexive Ideas in Spinoza', *Journal of the History of Philosophy*, 28 (1990), 201–11, at 205–6.

every mode of extension but also for every mode of thought. There is in God an idea of the mind, just as there is an idea of the human body. As thought is an attribute of God, there must be in God an idea of thought and of all its affections (*Ethica*, II, prop. 20, dem.). But what is the relation between the idea of an idea and the idea that is its object? The expression 'idea of an idea' seems to indicate that it is a separate, second-order idea. And Spinoza seems to refer to the issue of an infinite regress in this context without, however, considering the regress as a problem: 'As soon as someone knows something, he knows that he knows this; and at the same time he knows that he knows what he knows, and so on, in infinitum.'[29] But, when Spinoza says that 'the idea of the mind and the mind itself are one and the same thing' (ibid.), he seems to suggest that there is some sort of identity between the idea of an idea and the idea that is its object,[30] or at least a kind of unity between the two ideas. Again, however, it remains unclear wherein exactly this unity is meant to consist.

Moreover, it has been argued that as an account of consciousness, the 'ideas of ideas' doctrine is problematic, as it does not allow for differences in degrees of consciousness throughout nature. According to the 'ideas of ideas' doctrine, every mind is accompanied by an idea of an idea to the same degree; and yet Spinoza seems to appeal to different degrees of consciousness in nature.[31] For this reason, some scholars have argued that one should look elsewhere for Spinoza's account of consciousness—at passages, that is, that take the parallelism between the human body and the human mind as their starting point and comment on bodily capacities.[32] One such passage is the following:

He who like an infant or a boy, has a body capable of very few things and very heavily dependent on external causes, has a mind which considered solely in itself is conscious of almost nothing of itself, or of God, or of things. On the other hand he who has a body capable of a great many things, has a mind which considered only in itself is very much conscious of itself, and of God, and of things. (*Ethica*, V, prop. 39)

This passage seems to suggest that as the body develops more capacities, the mind becomes more excellent and that this excellence is a higher degree of consciousness. It seems, then, that 'human or higher consciousness for Spinoza is nothing but the mental correlate of the superlative complexity of the human body.'[33] And so we may have here 'the seeds or outline' of a 'naturalistic account of consciousness' (Nadler, 2008, 586–7). While such a reading of Spinoza may well make his thought relevant

---

[29] *Ethica*, II, prop. 21, schol. Compare also *Tractatus de intellectus emendatione*. *Spinoza Opera* (1925) vol. 2, p. 14; *The Collected Works of Spinoza*, vol. 1, pp. 17–18.

[30] This is what Nadler (2008) argues, 582–3, linking Spinoza's 'ideas of ideas' to Arnauld's 'virtual reflection.' Nadler concedes, however, that 'this is certainly an obscure element of Spinoza's thought', and that for Spinoza 'there presumably still is a second idea involved—albeit one that occurs at the same level or order as the original idea and is inseparable from it.'

[31] Nadler (2008), 585.

[32] Such scholars include Nadler (2008), and Garrett, 'Representation and Consciousness in Spinoza's Naturalistic Theory of the Imagination', in Charles Huenemann (ed.), *Interpreting Spinoza: Critical Essays* (2008), pp. 4–25.

[33] Nadler (2008), 587. For Garrett, by contrast, the passage suggests that 'degrees of power of thinking are to be identified with degrees of consciousness': Garrett (2008), p. 23.

to 'the kind of empirical, scientific inquiry into consciousness that characterizes contemporary neuroscience and (some) recent philosophy of mind' (Nadler, 2008, 586), it also raises several questions. One question concerns the relation of this account of consciousness to the 'ideas of ideas' doctrine. It has been suggested that the latter may not concern consciousness but 'a cognition of oneself and of one's mental states',[34] but if Spinoza wanted to distinguish between the two accounts and relate them to one another in this way, he certainly failed to do so explicitly. Moreover, the quoted passage again raises the question of what 'consciousness' even means in Spinoza. It is assumed that, as in other thinkers of the time, the term refers to a relating to one's own self or mental states, even if the nature of this relating is left unexplained. This is what the 'ideas of ideas' doctrine, understood as an account of consciousness, indicates. But the objects of consciousness in the quoted passage include not only one's own self but also God and 'things.' In short, the passage does not help at all in answering the question of what consciousness is for Spinoza. What is the nature of relating to one's own self and ideas? What are the different forms of such relating to one's own self? To these questions Spinoza does not seem to provide an answer.

It is Spinoza's contemporary, the Cambridge Platonist Ralph Cudworth, for one, who assigns the notion of consciousness an important place in his, quite different, metaphysical system.

2.2. CAMBRIDGE PLATONISM: CUDWORTH'S ACCOUNT OF CONSCIOUSNESS

The Cambridge Platonists also reject both Scholastic doctrine and a Cartesian-type dualism. Like Descartes, one of the leading thinkers of that school, Ralph Cudworth, distinguishes sharply between the corporeal and the incorporeal.[35] Unlike Descartes, however, he holds that all life is incorporeal and that incorporeal life is not to be equated with thought and consciousness. Cudworth postulates a general plastic nature that is immaterial and acts according to divine wisdom and fulfils divine purposes, but that lacks knowledge of the reasons for its actions as well as the consciousness of the fact that it performs the actions it does perform. Indeed, as mentioned above in the Introduction, Cudworth was the first English-writing philosopher to make extensive use of the noun 'consciousness' and to attach to it a particular philosophical meaning. In applying this notion Cudworth makes explicit recourse not so much to Cartesian but to Neo-Platonic sources—especially to Plotinus. Cudworth uses 'consciousness' as a translation of the Greek 'synaisthesis', indicating a feeling or awareness of one's own thoughts and actions.[36]

---

[34] Nadler (2008), 595.
[35] Cudworth, *The True Intellectual System of the Universe* (1678). The reading of Cudworth's notion of consciousness presented here elaborates on my interpretation in Thiel, *Lockes Theorie der Personalen Identität* (1983), and in Thiel, 'Cudworth and Seventeenth-Century Theories of Consciousness', in Gaukroger (ed.), *The Uses of Antiquity* (1991), pp. 79–99.
[36] Cudworth, *True Intellectual System*, p. 159. Compare Plotinus, *Enneads*, III.8.4 and V.8.11.

Cudworth's notion of consciousness is introduced not as part of an analysis of human subjectivity, but of a metaphysical account of reality in general—an account which affirms the traditional idea of a scale of nature, drawing heavily on Plotinus (*True Intellectual System*, p. 648).[37] As indicated, in his discussion of the plastic nature Cudworth points out two deficiencies that are relevant here: (1) the plastic nature lacks knowledge of the reasons and purposes for its actions; (2) it does not know that it performs the actions it does perform (ibid., pp. 155–65, §§ 11 and 12). It is to describe this second kind of 'knowledge' that Cudworth uses the terminology of consciousness. He says that the plastic nature is not '*Clearly and Expresly Conscious of what it doth*' (ibid., p. 158). It has 'no Express *synaisthesis*, Con-sense or Consciousness of what it doth' (ibid., p. 159).[38]

Cudworth also speaks of unconscious plastic natures, analogous to the plastic nature of the universe, that are at work in each individual living being (ibid., pp. 167, 171).[39] For Cudworth, as for Descartes, human souls are immaterial beings. Yet by employing the notion of consciousness he distinguishes two kinds of incorporeal life: a pure rational part of the soul which is conscious, and an unconscious 'plastic' power of the soul which is responsible for organic functions, reflex actions, habits, and dreams.[40] Thus, although he agrees with Descartes that 'Consciousness... [is] essential to Cogitation' (ibid., p. 871), he disagrees with Descartes's view that conscious activity is essential to the soul. On the Cartesian position, Cudworth argues, one could not explain how the soul during sound sleep and fainting fits is without consciousness and still exists—and it is obvious that the soul exists in such states. He concludes: 'Now if the Souls of Men and Animals be at any time without

---

[37] Cudworth does not, of course, claim originality for the notion of a plastic nature. Other Cambridge thinkers such as Henry More adopt it (he calls it the 'Spirit of Nature'), and Cudworth goes to great length and detail in attempting to show that the notion can be found in ancient Greek thought: *True Intellectual System*, pp. 151–4. For the notion of plastic nature and its history, see for example, Hunter, 'The Seventeenth Century Doctrine of Plastic Nature', *Harvard Theological Review*, 43 (1950), 197–213; Aspelin, *Ralph Cudworth's Interpretation of Greek Philosophy* (1943), pp. 13–15, 26–31; Jacob, 'The Neoplatonic Conception of Nature in More, Cudworth, and Berkeley', in Gaukroger (ed.), *The Uses of Antiquity* (1991), pp. 101–21.

[38] Compare Plotinus, *Enneads*, III.8.4. For the notion of consciousness in Plotinus, see Schwyzer, '"Bewusst" und "unbewusst" bei Plotin', in *Les sources de Plotin. Entretiens sur l'antiquité classique*, V (1960), pp. 343–90, esp. at pp. 355ff. Compare also, Warren, 'Consciousness in Plotinus', *Phronesis*, 9 (1964), 83–97; O'Daly, *Plotinus' Philosophy of the Self* (1973). Davies notes that Cudworth's term 'con-sense' here goes back to 'consensus' or 'consensia'—terms by which Ficino translates Plotinus's *synaisthesis*. Davies, *Conscience as Consciousness* (1990), pp. 42–3.

[39] Carter emphasises the theological context of Cudworth's discussion of consciousness—in particular, the 'theological disputes over the place and extent of human freewill within an overarching system of providence': Carter, 'Ralph Cudworth and the Theological Origins of Consciousness', *History of the Human Sciences*, 23(3) (2010), 29–47, at 30. Carter argues that 'Cudworth's thought developed in strong reaction to the voluntarism of the Calvinism that [William] Perkins represents', relating Cudworth's understanding of consciousness to his 'account of providence', and thereby linking it to the notions of conscience and moral responsibility. Our account below, focusing on the conceptual distinctions, confirms the thesis about a link between consciousness and conscience in Cudworth.

[40] Cudworth, *True Intellectual System*, pp. 160–1.

Consciousness and *Self-perception*, then it must needs be granted, that Clear and Express *Consciousness* is not Essential to *Life*' (ibid., p. 160).

Cudworth's 'cogitations' include sense-perceptions ('sensitive cogitations') and what he calls 'pure cogitations': concepts which have their origin in the understanding itself, such as concepts of relations.[41] He points out the importance of this self-relation via consciousness: it is most fundamental because it is that 'which makes a Being to be Present with it self' (*True Intellectual System*, p. 159). These passages suggest that the self-relation *via* consciousness is characterized by immediacy, but it remains unclear wherein precisely this immediacy consists. For Cudworth almost always qualifies consciousness by adjectives such as 'clear' and 'express' (ibid., pp. 159–60), suggesting thereby that it is an explicit relating to oneself where the act of being conscious is distinct from the thought to which it relates—rather than a reflexivity that belongs to this thought itself. He states that 'a Duplication...is included in the Nature of *synaisthesis*, Con-sense, and Consciousness' (ibid., p. 159), thus indicating that the self is the subject (that which is conscious) as well as the object of consciousness.[42] It is this presence to oneself through consciousness that makes states of happiness and misery possible: it makes a being 'to perceive it self to Do or Suffer, and to have a Fruition or Enjoyment of itself' (ibid.).

Some of the passages quoted above would seem to suggest that for Cudworth consciousness is at the same time self-consciousness, i.e. consciousness of the subject of thought, and occasionally he even uses expressions such as 'Self-perception' (ibid., p. 160, cited above) and 'self-conscious.' For example, he says that 'all cogitative beings as such are self-conscious.'[43] It is plain, however, that 'self-perception' in the cited passage is used synonymously with the 'consciousness' that relates to cogitations, and there is no reason to read 'self-conscious' differently. It refers to the consciousness of one's own cogitations rather than to the existence of the self as the subject of thought. Indeed, Cudworth makes it clear that consciousness as *synaisthesis* is not itself self-consciousness. Rather, consciousness is the more fundamental relation to one's own self, and it is that which makes self-consciousness and other forms of relating to the self possible. As far as knowledge of our own existence as thinking subjects is

---

[41] *Treatise concerning Eternal and Immutable Morality* (1731; posthumously published), pp. 81, 154–5.

[42] Cudworth himself does not explain what he means by 'duplication.' Lähteenmäki discusses this notion extensively, but his account is somewhat speculative: 'Cudworth on Types of Consciousness', *British Journal for the History of Philosophy*, 18 (2010), 9–34. Lähteenmäki holds that 'duplication' is to be understood 'as a purely structural characterisation of an internal reflexivity that is within a single consciousness'—conceding, however, that the textual basis for this reading is thin and that the relevant passage 'is not entirely clear.' Further, he believes that the immediacy that Cudworth ascribes to consciousness precludes a reading in terms of a second-order act relating to other mental acts. But immediacy does not have to be understood in terms of an inherent reflexivity, and as indicated, Cudworth does not explain wherein this immediacy consists. Certainly, neither the notion of immediacy, nor Cudworth's use of the term 'duplication', helps in determining whether his 'consciousness' is to be understood as a second-order act or an 'inherent reflexivity.' The fact that he consistently qualifies 'consciousness' as an 'express' or an explicit act of relating to one's own cogitations does not suggest the idea of an inherent reflexivity.

[43] Cudworth, *A Treatise of Freewill* (1838; posthumously published), p. 71.

concerned, Cudworth says: 'we are certain of the Existence of our own Souls, partly from an inward Consciousness of our own Cogitations, and partly from that Principle of Reason, That Nothing can not Act' (*True Intellectual System*, p. 637). One's own existence, then, is inferred from a general principle and the consciousness of thinking. This means, moreover, that only rational beings—beings with the ability to infer and understand general principles—have self-consciousness in this sense, whereas all sentient beings have consciousness or *synaisthesis*.

With respect to rational beings Cudworth distinguishes further forms of self-relation in addition to consciousness and self-consciousness—one of which concerns the distinction mentioned above between knowing the reasons and purposes of one's actions and simply being aware of them. This relates to Cudworth's implied distinction between consciousness and reflection. The fact that Cudworth seems to conceive of consciousness as a second-order act or perception does not, of course, mean that he identifies it with reflection.[44] Reflection, too, involves a 'duplication' of the self, but on a higher, rational level. In reflection we contemplate and objectify our own self. 'We are certain by inward sense that we can reflect upon ourselves and consider ourselves, which is a reduplication of life in a higher degree; for all cogitative beings as such are self-conscious' (*Treatise of Freewill*, p. 71). Further, reflection is the basis of, and can result in a judgement of our own self. For the latter Cudworth uses 'conscience' (ibid.). Thus it can be seen how the etymologically related terms 'consciousness' and 'conscience' are related in Cudworth. The two notions belong to two different levels of life. Beings that have conscience, however, must also have consciousness, as it is presupposed by conscience. As Cudworth says, it is through consciousness that we become 'Attentive to . . . (our) own actions, or Animadversive of them' (*True Intellectual System*, p. 159). For conscience to be possible, the capacity to reflect and the knowledge of the distinction between right and wrong must be presupposed in addition to mere consciousness. Conscience, Cudworth argues, is 'attributed to rational beings only, and such as are sensible of the *discrimen honestorum* or *turpium* when they judge of their own actions according to that rule, and either condemn or acquit themselves' (*Treatise of Freewill*, p. 71). Lastly, relating to one's own self *via* consciousness and reflection points at least to the possibility of another self-relation: namely, to the possibility of self-determination with respect to actions. Against the determinists' argument that self-determination is conceptually impossible because one and the same being cannot be the subject (that which is determining) as well as the object of the determination (ibid., p. 69), Cudworth argues that we have no reason to believe that such a relation of oneself to oneself is impossible; for there is an analogous 'duplication' or relation to oneself involved in consciousness and reflection. A being that obviously can relate to itself in those ways should also be capable of being active on itself by determining its own actions: 'Wherefore that which is thus conscious to itself, and reflexive upon itself, may also well act upon itself, either as fortuitously determining its own activity, or else as

---

[44] Lähteenmäki, by contrast, believes that if consciousness were a second-order activity for Cudworth, then it would be the same as reflection: 'Lähteenmäki (2010).

intending and exerting itself more or less in order to the promoting of its own good' (ibid., p. 71).

We saw that for Cudworth, consciousness or *synaisthesis* is a relating to one's own self that is more fundamental than self-consciousness, reflection, conscience, and self-determination. But in places Cudworth seems to assume another, even more fundamental self-relation than consciousness. Although he says that the plastic nature has no 'clear and express' consciousness of what it does, he seems to concede that nature has some basic sense of its own actions. He appeals to Plotinus for this, quoting *Enneads*, III, 8, 4, and translating:

If any will needs attribute some kind of Apprehension ['synesis'] or Sense ['aesthesis'] to Nature, then it must not be such a Sense or Apprehension, as is in Animals, but something that differs as much from it, as the Sense or Cogitation of one in a profound sleep, differs from that of one who is awake. (*True Intellectual System*, p. 160)

He adds that 'it cannot be denied but that the *Plastick Nature* hath a certain *Dull* and *Obscure Idea* of that which it Stamps and Prints upon Matter' (ibid.). Nature, then, according to Plotinus and Cudworth, has 'a kind of self-perception' ('hoion synaisthesis', ibid.); a basic awareness of itself; a dim or dull feeling of itself which does not involve a duplication or a division of a being into subject and object, as 'clear' and 'express' consciousness seems to do. This basic awareness, we are told by Plotinus—Cudworth can be compared to that of a sleeping man who is in peace with himself. Cudworth does not elaborate on this notion of a basic self-awareness, however, and is content to quote Plotinus as an authority on this. The notion itself remains somewhat dull and obscure.[45]

Thus, in contrast to Descartes and other philosophers of the time, such as Spinoza, there are in Cudworth clear distinctions between consciousness, self-knowledge, reflection, and other forms of relating to the self, and these distinctions may well have had an impact on thinkers such as Locke and Leibniz and many others who were familiar with his work, even if they did reject his general metaphysical outlook. Yet although there are these distinctions in Cudworth, like Descartes, he does not ascribe to consciousness a constitutive or individuating function for the human subject. Consciousness is taken to be merely the basis of knowledge of the self which presupposes the latter's individuality. It 'makes a being present to itself', but the being's individuality itself is presupposed by this self-relation. Also unlike Descartes, Cudworth makes frequent use of terms such as 'person' and 'personality' for the human subject; but he then equates 'person' and 'personality' with the soul, and argues that 'Personalities' are 'unquestionably *Substantial Things* and *Really Distinct* from Matter.'[46] And like Descartes, Cudworth holds that the identity of persons understood as immaterial substances is secured by their immateriality.[47]

---

[45] Possibly, this basic sense that nature has of its own actions, according to Cudworth, could be interpreted along the lines of the notion of an 'inherent reflexivity' that Lähteenmäki ascribes to Cudworth's notion of consciousness: Lähteenmäki (2010). Cudworth does not say enough, however, about this 'kind of self-perception' to justify such an interpretation.
[46] Cudworth, *True Intellectual System*, p. 750.
[47] See the section below on immortality.

2.3. THE SUBJECTIVIST TREATMENT OF IDENTITY: CLAUBERG, HOBBES, AND BOYLE

As noted in the Introduction, the problem of identity in general is the historical as well as the systematic basis for the special issue of the identity of persons. Also hinted at above was a certain development of the treatment of identity in early modern thought. Around the middle of the seventeenth century there was a shift away from a primarily ontological to a more subjective treatment of the topic: our concepts of those things whose identity is in question came to be regarded as crucial for dealing with problems of individuation and identity. This idea is not present in Spinoza and other philosophers whom we have discussed above. Moreover, while this marks an important strain in the development of the issue in early modern philosophy, the ontological treatment of identity continued to exist side by side with this subjectivist or 'epistemologist' treatment.[48] We shall see that the shift towards a subjectivist treatment of identity occurred in connection with another shift, also mentioned in the Introduction, from the issue of individuation to the question of identity through time.

The subjectivist treatment of identity is present in some philosophers who work within the Cartesian framework. Thus, the Dutch philosopher Johannes Clauberg, who attempts to reconcile Cartesian ideas with a Scholastic metaphysics of being in general, indicates that attributes such as identity and distinctness cannot be ascribed to objects independently of the mind which apprehends those objects.[49] He argues that, like all relations, those of identity and diversity are not real, but are *entia rationis*. This means for him that identity is based on the intellectual operations of comparing and judging. Numerical identity consists in this: that a perceived object is judged to be the same as a previously perceived object, and that we attach the same name to it (*Ontosophia*, chap. xviii, § 291). Whether or not we judge a thing to be the same at different points of time—that is, whether or not we attach the same 'name' to it—depends on our definition of the thing: on our 'naming' it. If the object is perceived to have changed only in respects which, on our definition of it, are not essential, then we rightly judge it to be identical. On the basis of our definitions we are able to judge men, plants, trees, and rivers to be identical at different points of time, even though they have changed in various respects. Clauberg concludes that the whole issue of identity and diversity pertains more to modes of thought and speech than to things as they are in themselves (*Ontosophia*, chap. xviii, §§ 292–4). A position similar to that of Clauberg can be found in another Dutch Cartesian, Arnold Geulincx. In his posthumously published *Metaphysica vera et ad mentem*

---

[48] See my critical discussion of Barber and Gracia, in Thiel, '"Epistemologism" and Early Modern Debates about Individuation and Identity', *British Journal for the History of Philosophy*, 5 (1997), 353–72.

[49] Clauberg's *Elementa philosophia sive Ontosophia* first appeared in 1647. In 1660 a new version was published, of which a third edition appeared in 1664 under the title *Metaphysica de ente, quae rectius ontosophia*. References are to chapters and paragraphs in this edition, which was included in Clauberg's *Opera omnia philosophica* (1691). The relevant passages are chap. xii, §§ 206–7, 216, and chap. xviii, §§ 291–4.

peripateticam (1691) he argues that, like all attributes of being, those of oneness ('unum') and identity are not attributes which belong to things as they are in themselves ('res in se'); rather, the human intellect ascribes them to things as a result of a unifying or identifying act.[50]

This idea was developed in England by Richard Burthogge, who was probably influenced by Geulincx when studying at the University of Leiden. For Burthogge, entity, substance, accident, whole, part, cause, effect, and so on, 'do not really exist without the mind'; rather, they are 'notions' under which we consider things as they appear to us (Burthogge, *An Essay upon Reason*, 1694, p. 69). And so, individuality and distinctness of things are to be understood in relation to the qualities of the latter as they appear to us, 'these being the Characters by, and under which alone, we do perceive and know, and by consequence, can only distinguish them' (ibid., p. 107). Burthogge does not deny, however, that there are 'things themselves' independent of our notions; for our notions 'have in things without us certain grounds or Foundations' (ibid., p. 70; also p. 92). Indeed, he even argues for the existence of a world-soul and of individual spirits. The latter are essentially united to matter; for all spirits, including angels (to which he refers as 'invisible animals') and human minds, are 'individuated by matter' (ibid., pp. 162, 168). He states explicitly the problem which arises from the Cartesian view that souls are individual immaterial substances independently of their union with a body: 'Were Spirits absolutely pure and simple, without any Concretion of Matter, there could be no distinction among them as to *Individuals*' (ibid., p. 167).[51] When addressing the Scholastic disputes over the principle of individuation directly, however, Burthogge does not refer to matter at all, and simply states that 'they seem to me to come nearest to the Truth, who do affirm, that a singular or individual becomes so, not by any distinct Principle of individuation, but immediately and *per se*, and in that, that it is in being' (ibid., p. 270). This is consistent with his earlier insistence on matter as individuating spirits, however, since his view is that spirits are only 'in being' once they are united to matter. To say that individuality belongs to beings 'immediately and *per se*' is obviously to adopt a nominalist position on the issue. Burthogge does not believe in the real existence of universals: 'Particular singular beings...are the only beings that compose the Universe, as members or parts of it...Universals...are not of Mundane existence' (ibid., p. 61). Thus, Burthogge's theory oscillates between an objectivist account of individuation of 'things themselves' and a subjectivist explication of individuality in terms of our distinguishing between them on the basis of perceived qualities.

The subjectivist treatment of identity was developed more elaborately by decidedly anti-Cartesian thinkers who worked within the framework of the atomist or corpuscular picture of the world, as it was revived in the context of the developing experimental sciences. The proponents of the 'corpuscular philosophy' aim to explain all phenomena of nature wholly in terms of 'matter and the accidents of

---

[50] Geulincx, *Opera philosophica*, ed. Land, 3 vols. (1891–93), vol. 2, pp. 272–3.
[51] Compare also Burthogge, *Essay*, p. 154: 'The Great work and Business of the Body is to *Singularize* and *Individuate* the *General Vital Principle* of the Universe, that it may become a *Soul*, or a Particular Vital Principle of a certain Particular Body.'

matter',[52] without reference to any such metaphysical entities as substantial forms. As indicated previously, their denial of real universal forms means that at least the issues of individuation *within a kind* does not present itself as a genuine problem to them. They share the basic nominalist (or conceptualist) assumption that everything that exists is individual by itself, and that a search for a principle that individuates within a kind is superfluous. Robert Boyle, for example, clearly implies that no 'principle' over and above the particular corpuscular constitution is required to account for the individuality of bodies. To Boyle, an individual body is simply a 'distinct portion of matter which a number of (corpuscles)... make up' (Boyle, *Selected Philosophical Papers*, p. 30). Hobbes at least addresses the issue of individuality, if only briefly. In doing so he makes use of the old theory according to which existence individuates. For Hobbes, to say an individual is individual by itself is to say that it is individual through its existence at a particular place and time: all things (namely individuals) exist in space and time, and they are the individuals they are, distinct from all other individuals by their very position in absolute space and time. As Hobbes says: 'it is manifest that no two bodies are the same; for seeing they are two, they are in two places at the same time; as that, which is the same, is at the same time in one and the same place' (Hobbes, *De corpore*, II.xi.2, in *Works*, 1962, vol. 1).

Since individuality is regarded as unproblematic by these philosophers, the attention shifts totally to the problem of identity over time. Both Boyle and Hobbes interpret what they refer to as the problem of 'individuation' as being concerned only with what constitutes identity over time. And this—the issue of how to determine what preserves the identity of bodies over time and through change—does present itself as a problem to proponents of the corpuscular philosophy. Hobbes states the problem thus:

But the same body may at different times be compared with itself. And from hence springs a great controversy among philosophers about the principle of individuation, namely, in what sense it may be conceived that a body is at one time the same, at another time not the same it was formerly. For example, whether a man grown old be the same man he was whilst he was young, or another man; or whether a city be in different ages the same, or another city. (Hobbes, *De corpore*, II.xi.7, in *Works*, 1962, vol. 1; 'principium' is translated as 'beginning')

As substantial forms are denied, it does not seem possible to pick out any constituent in the things themselves that can in all cases be regarded as that which is essential for securing identity over time, for 'matter and the accidents of matter' continuously change. There seems to be no simple straightforward answer as to what could replace the role of substantial forms. Robert Boyle, for one, sees clearly that 'it is no such easy way as at first it seems, to determine what is absolutely necessary and but sufficient to make a portion of matter, considered at different times or places, to be fit to be reputed the same body'.[53]

---

[52] Boyle, *The Origin of Forms and Qualities According to the Corpuscular Philosophy* (1666), in *Selected Philosophical Papers of Robert Boyle*, ed. Stewart (1979), p. 54.

[53] Boyle, *Some Physico-Theological Considerations about the Possibility of the Resurrection* (1675), in *Selected Philosophical Papers*, p. 193.

And this is how the shift of attention from individuation to diachronic identity is linked to the development of a subjectivist treatment of the issue: as substantial forms are denied and no 'principle' of identity could be discovered in the things themselves, it is recognized that their identity must depend on what we regard as their essential constituents; in other words, what becomes crucial now are our criteria for judging whether or not a body has remained the same through change. Scholastics such as Suarez, too, occasionally considered what the basis is for our identifying and distinguishing things. Importantly, the point is not merely that philosophers such as Hobbes put more emphasis on this issue; rather, on their view, the very problem of the identity of things over time can be answered only by reference to our concepts or 'naming' of those things whose identity is in question; for we have no knowledge of their internal real essence—that is, of an ontological basis of their identity. Therefore, it is regarded as crucial for any treatment of identity questions to be clear about our concepts of those things whose identity is under discussion—otherwise there would be hopeless confusion. According to Boyle, problems concerning identity over time arise, because:

> almost every man that thinks conceives in his mind this or that quality, or relation, or aggregate of qualities, to be that which is essential to such a body and proper to give it such a denomination; whereby it comes to pass that, as one man chiefly respects this thing, and another that, in a body that bears such a name, so one man may easily look upon a body as the same, because it retains what he chiefly considered in it, whilst another thinks it to be changed into a new body, because it has lost that which he thought was the denominating quality or attribute. (Boyle, *Selected Philosophical Papers*, p. 194)

Boyle does not develop any further the point that our concepts determine what is required for the identity of objects over time. But Hobbes had already explained it at some length. Although his discussion is couched in the traditional Scholastic terminology of 'form', 'matter', and 'accidents', he states the new view clearly. Hobbes begins by reviewing three rival theories of individuation: the theory according to which form individuates, the theory which takes matter to be the principle of individuation, and the view that the unity of the 'aggregate of all the accidents together' is what individuates bodies (Hobbes, *De corpore*, II.xi.7, in *Works*, 1962, vol. 1). He indicates that each of these three answers to the problem has absurd consequences. If we take matter to be the principle of individuation, it follows that 'he that sins, and he that is punished, should not be the same man, by reason of the perpetual flux and change of man's body.' If we assume that the form individuates, then 'two bodies existing both at once, would be one and the same numerical body' (ibid.).

Hobbes illustrates his point by way of discussing the ancient case of the Ship of Theseus, mentioned in the Introduction—an example that was discussed by several seventeenth-century philosophers, including Clauberg and Leibniz.[54] If a ship had been continuously repaired, 'in taking out the old planks and putting in new' until no single plank of the original remained, we would still speak of the same numerical ship, since it has retained its 'form' or structure. Now, if someone put together the

---

[54] Plutarch, 'Life of Theseus', in *Plutarch's Lives*, transl. and ed. Perrin (1959), p. 49.

old, discarded planks in the same order, then we would have a second ship which is also the same numerical ship as the previous one. Thus, we would have two bodies existing at the same time which are numerically identical. If we say that the aggregate of accidents individuates, then 'nothing would be the same as it was; so that a man standing would not be the same as he was sitting' (ibid.).

Having pointed out the problems with three rival theories of individuation, Hobbes goes on to argue that what is really essential for deciding questions about identity over time is whether we have named the object whose identity is in question with respect to its form or with respect to its matter. If it is clear under which aspect we consider the object, then the question of identity or diversity can be easily decided. For 'material' and 'formal' respects of naming provide different criteria of identity respectively. If we name an individual, Socrates, with respect to his form, then the question of identity relates to whether he is the same man at different times; if we name Socrates with respect to his matter, then the question relates to whether he is the same body. Our judgement about his identity differs according to the respect under which we consider him. Therefore we must always first be clear about the way we conceive of an individual before addressing the question of identity:

> But we must consider by what name anything is called, when we inquire concerning the *identity* of it. For it is one thing to ask concerning Socrates, whether he be the same man, and another to ask whether he be the same body; for his body, when he is old, cannot be the same it was when he was an infant, by reason of the difference of magnitude; for one body has always one and the same magnitude; yet, nevertheless, he may be the same man. (ibid.)

This idea—also crucial to Locke's treatment of the issue of identity, as we shall see—can be called 'subjectivist' in the sense that on this view the principle of identity is contained in our concepts of the things, and is not an aspect or feature of the things themselves.

2.4. PERSONALITY AND MORAL RESPONSIBILITY: HOBBES AND PUFENDORF

Hobbes is significant in this context also, of course, because he is among those philosophers who reject both Scholastic and Cartesian metaphysics of man discussed above. Since Hobbes argues that 'every part of the Universe, is Body',[55] the Cartesian notion of an immaterial substance is, to Hobbes, a contradiction in terms (*Leviathan*, xxxiv, pp. 428–9). According to Hobbes, man is simply a '*living Body*' who has the capacity to reason (ibid., xlvi, p. 691). He also employs the term 'person' to the human self, but he distinguishes the notion of person from that of man. In fact, his concept of person leads to the issue of moral responsibility and its connection with the problem of self-identity. Although Hobbes devotes a whole chapter of his *Leviathan* to the topic 'Of Persons, Authors, and things Personated' (ibid., xvi, pp. 217–22), he does not, however, set out to develop a theory of human personal identity. The main

---

[55] Hobbes, *Leviathan* ed. MacPherson (1968), xlvi, p. 689.

purpose of that chapter is, rather, to introduce the notion of 'artificial person' which Hobbes requires for his political theory. Nevertheless, what he has to say about 'person' in this context is, to some extent, also relevant to the notion of an individual human person. His definition of person in general reads: 'A PERSON, is he *whose words or actions are considered, either as his own, or as representing the words or actions of an other man, or of any other thing to whom they are attributed, whether Truly or by Fiction.*' (ibid., p. 217).

In the first case, that is, when the 'words or actions' are ascribed to the individual who utters or performs them, the individual is a '*Naturall Person*'; and in the second case, when the words and actions 'are considered as representing the words and actions of an other, then is he a *Feigned* or *Artificiall person.*' (ibid.) Thus, whereas Hobbes defines 'man' in metaphysical terms as a 'reasonable' living body, he defines 'person' in terms of action ascription or ownership of actions. He explicitly introduces the notion of authorship in this context: he regards *natural* persons as persons who are considered to be the *authors* of those actions they perform. He does not discuss the conditions of action attribution in any detail here; but he does point out that the 'use of reason' is one of them. For he argues that human beings who do not have the 'use of reason' are not to be considered the authors of their actions, and this means that they are not (natural) persons: 'Likewise Children, Fooles, and Mad-men that have no use of Reason, may be Personated by Guardians, or Curators; but can be no Authors (during that time) of any action done by them, longer then (when they shall recover the use of Reason) they shall judge the same reasonable.' (ibid., p. 219).

Although Hobbes does not explicitly draw a distinction between 'man' and 'natural person', his statements clearly imply this distinction. For what he says is basically this: in most cases 'natural person' and 'man' may be applied to the same individual being; yet even then, the two terms denote different aspects of the same being. Further, there are cases in which we may apply the term 'man' but not 'natural person' (such as 'mad-man'). When we consider an individual human being under the notion of person, we do not consider it with respect to its metaphysical make-up, but with regard to the actions attributed to that being; that is, under moral and legal aspects. Hobbes seems to take up the old legal usage of 'persona.' He reminds the reader of the history of the term 'persona', and appeals to Cicero's use of 'persona' as role. Yet he does not, in this context, address other issues that are relevant to the problem of moral responsibility such as that of the freedom of the will. Nor does he introduce the notion of person to his metaphysical discussion of identity in *De corpore* where, as we saw, he distinguishes between the identity of man and the identity of body.

Samuel Pufendorf, the German natural law theorist and critic of Hobbes, takes over, as we shall see, the distinction between man and person, but does not share the latter's materialism, and he discusses neither human personal identity through time, nor issues directly related to self-consciousness. Pufendorf has important things to say, however, that relate to the question of the ontological status of persons and indeed to Locke's later account of the notion of person. As his main concern is natural law, Pufendorf gives no detailed account of the metaphysics of man. He simply assumes that 'man consists of two parts'—the real self or soul which is 'the great principle and spring of human actions', and the body which is merely 'a subordinate instrument.'[56] He is interested, rather, in the human subject as a 'moral entity' or 'moral person': the individual human being insofar as he owns actions and is held to be responsible for them.[57] Thus Pufendorf, too, links the notion of person to that of action attribution and, thereby, to moral responsibility. Like other natural law theorists before him, Pufendorf cites freedom and reason as the general conditions of action attribution.

Pufendorf's fundamental distinction of '*ens*, or being in general' is between 'substance and mode' (*The Law and Nature of Nations*, I.i.3, p. 3). Unlike substances, modes 'have no self-subsistence' or do not subsist *per se*, 'but are founded in substances and their motions, and do only affect them after a certain manner.' Moreover, there are two fundamental kinds of mode. First, there are those that 'flow, as it were, naturally from the things themselves' and are produced 'by creation.' Second, there are modes that are 'superadded to natural things and motions by intelligent beings.' Intelligent beings 'can from the reflex knowledge of things, and from comparing them with one another, form such notions as may prove very serviceable in the direction of an agreeable and consistent faculty.' Such superadded modes are produced not by creation, but by acts of 'imposition' of intelligent beings, exercising their free will. Pufendorf's 'moral entities' are a kind of such modes that 'are added at the pleasure of intelligent creatures, to beings already perfect in nature... and obtain their whole existence from the determination of their authors' (ibid., I.i.iii and iv, p. 3). In short, like other superadded, notional entities, moral entities seem to be creatures of the mind. Pufendorf emphasises their importance at the outset:

Our business is to declare, how, chiefly for the direction of the will, a certain kind of attributes have been imposed on things and their natural motions; whence there springs up a peculiar agreement and convenience in the actions of mankind, a grateful order and comeliness for the ornament of human life. And these attributes are called moral entities, because the manners and the actions of men are judged and tempered with relations to them. (ibid., I.i.2, p. 2)

Moreover, while moral entities in general are, like all modes, to be distinguished from substances, there are some that are conceived by analogy to substances while others are 'formally' modes (ibid., I.i.17): we talk of them *as if* they were substances, and such moral entities 'are called moral persons' (ibid., I.i.12, p. 7).

Now though moral entities do not subsist of themselves, and for that reason ought not, in general, to be ranked under the class of *substances*, but of *modes*; yet we find many of them to be conceived in the manner of substances, because other moral things seem to be immediately

---

[56] Pufendorf, *De jure naturae et gentium* (1672), in Pufendorf, *Gesammelte Werke*, ed. Schmidt-Biggemann, pt. 4, vols. 1 and 2, ed. Böhling (1998), at vol. 1, II.4.1. Pufendorf *The Law of Nature and Nations*, trans. Kennett, with notes by Barbeyrac (1717), p. 154. All page numbers for Pufendorf refer to this translation.

[57] Ibid., I.1.12–13, pp. 7–8. For an account of Pufendorf's notion of personhood in the natural law context, see Haakonssen, *Natural Law and Personhood: Pufendorf and Social Explanation* (2010).

founded in them, just as quantities and qualities inhere in the real substance of bodies. (ibid., I.i.6, p. 4)

And with respect to moral persons we can distinguish again between two fundamental kinds: simple or natural persons which 'are particular men', and compound persons which consist of several individual human beings 'joined in one body by some moral tie.' Here, several human individual beings 'are supposed to have but a single will, and every action which they perform is construed as one only although a number of natural individuals concur in its production' (ibid., I.i.13, p. 8).[58] Among the important modes that are superimposed on persons there are various states in which the latter can be. Again Pufendorf points out the analogy to physical substances: 'As natural substances suppose some kind of space, in which they fix their existence; so in allusion to these, *moral persons* are especially said to be in some *state*, which in like manner contains them, and in which they perform their operations' (ibid., I.i.6, p. 4).

Thus, we seem to have the following structure:

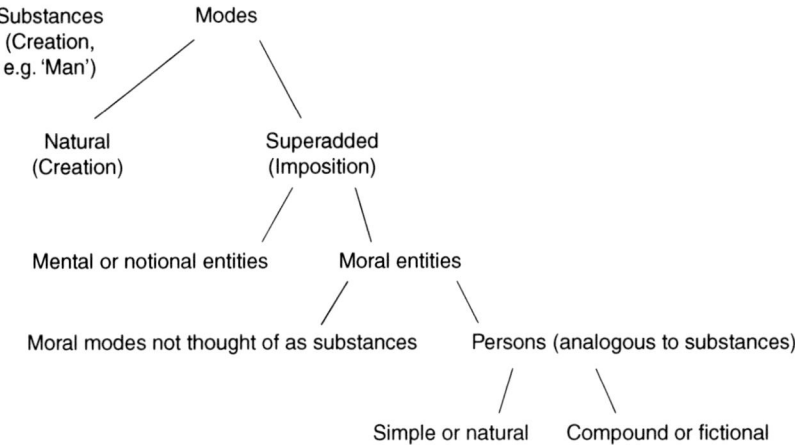

It is plain that Pufendorf's account implies a distinction between both substance and person, and man and person. It is important to note, however, that this distinction applies not only to compound and fictional persons, but also to simple or natural persons. Although Pufendorf says that simple persons 'are particular men' (quotation above), this does not mean than man and person are identical here. It remains true that 'particular men' are created beings, and simple persons are modes, produced by acts of imposition. A simple or natural person is an individual human being,

---

[58] Kobusch has drawn attention to a distinction in Suárez between the notions of a true and a fictional person—*persona vera* and *persona ficta*—and its importance to subsequent thought, including Pufendorf. See the remarks and references in the Introduction, section I.3.3.

considered under a particular aspect or quality: namely, 'with the state or office which they maintain in common life' (ibid., I.i.13, p. 8). As Pufendorf points out, a single man can sustain several persons:

> Concerning the nature of simple moral persons, we have farther to observe, that as one and the same man may be in several states together, provided they do not clash with each other, so he may sustain several persons together, upon supposition that the duties attending those persons may be performed together by him.

Not surprisingly, Pufendorf appeals to Cicero and his notion of *persona* as role here (ibid., I.i.14, p. 9).[59] In this context Pufendorf makes occasional remarks on a person's identity through time, without, however, treating the issue as problematic. Thus he notes that

> just as individual persons remain the same, although in the passage of time the body undergoes marked changes through various additions and losses of particles, so through the particular succession of individuals a society does not change but remains the same, unless at a single time such a change befall that it utterly destroys the true character of the former body or society.[60]

A question is raised by Pufendorf's account, however, relating to the relationship between moral entities (including persons) and other modal beings that are the result of acts of 'imposition', such as notional beings or *entia notionala*, or mental beings. Of course, moral entities differ from other *entia notionala* in terms of the different function they fulfil, but can they be distinguished from the latter in terms of their ontological status?[61] Pufendorf took over the notion of imposition from his teacher Erhard Weigel. But for Weigel, both *entia moralia* and *entia notionala* are grounded in acts of imposition and thus cannot be distinguished from one another in terms of their production and ontological status. And the same would seem to apply to Pufendorf.[62] If *entia moralia*, including persons, are constituted by acts of 'imposition', then *entia moralia* are difficult to distinguish from *entia notionala*, which also result from an act of imposition. Of course, even if moral persons are to be understood as *entia notionala*, it would still be possible to talk of them as if they were substances, by analogy.

This issue seems to be relevant to a debate concerning the nature of Pufendorfs's system. Some see his stance as decidedly 'anti-metaphysical',[63] while others regard his doctrine of *entia moralia* as a development of Scholastic ideas, and as a new kind of 'ontology' which serves as a 'metaphysical grounding of morality.'[64] In part at

---

[59] See also the passage in I.i.16, p. 10: 'men are conceived as different persons, upon account of their different state or office.' In his notes to I.i.14, Barbeyrac refers the reader to a later work on this issue, by Hirtius, *De uno homine plures sustinate personas* (1700), p. 9.

[60] Pufendorf, *Elementorum iurisprudentiae universalis libri duo* (1672/1931) I.iv.3.

[61] The issue is briefly discussed, but not resolved, by Kobusch, *Die Entdeckung der Person. Metaphysik der Freiheit und Modernes Menschenbild* (1997), pp. 73–4.

[62] See Röd, 'Erhard Weigels Lehre von den entia moralia', in *Archiv für Geschichte der Philosophie*, 51 (1969), 58–84; Kobusch (1997), p. 73.

[63] Hunter, *Rival Enlightenments. Civil and Metaphysical Philosophy in Early Modern Germany* (2001), p. 164.

[64] Kobusch (1997), pp. 71–2. For Hunter's rejection of this reading, see Hunter (2001), p. 165.

least, the difference seems to be a verbal one, relating in particular to the word 'metaphysics.' Both sides seem to accept that 'the ontology of substances and attributes' is not relevant to Pufendorf's understanding of 'the moral domain and the understanding of personhood.'[65] If *entia moralia* have the same status as *entia notionala*, however, then it would seem to be difficult to account for them in terms of an ontology. But it is possible, of course, to assume such a broad notion of metaphysics as to label Pufendorf's discussion of moral entities a 'metaphysics of the *ens morale*.'[66]

Regarding the notion of personhood, the following aspects of Pufendorf's account are especially relevant to subsequent discussions: the modal nature of personhood, the related revival of the Ciceronian notion of *persona* as role, the implied distinctions between man and person, and substance and person. Especially important to subsequent accounts, for example in Locke, is the idea that persons are modes that can be and are conceived of by analogy to substances, and talked of as if they were substances.

2.5. THE AFTERLIFE: THE IMMORTALITY OF THE SOUL AND THE RESURRECTION OF THE BODY

The notion of moral responsibility is, of course, part of the Christian doctrine of life after death which continued to be much discussed in the seventeenth century. According to this doctrine, we shall receive in the future life God's judgement and reward or punishment for our actions in this life. And philosophers have to make their views about the human self at least compatible with this doctrine. Thus, Ralph Cudworth holds that 'Rational Souls' have 'both *Morality* and *Liberty* of *Will*, and [are] thereby ... capable of *Rewards* and *Punishments*, and Consequently *Fit Objects* for the *Divine Justice* to display it self upon.'[67] Cudworth's appeal to rationality and freedom as grounds of action attribution obviously does not originate with him, since it can be found in traditional natural law thought. Cudworth takes for granted that the 'identity condition' is satisfied. Since God's rewards or punishments are, by definition, just, it is assumed that the person who will be rewarded or punished for actions in this life is the *same* person who committed those actions in this life. As the Christian doctrine of the afterlife holds that the whole man will live, it includes a belief in the immortality of the soul, as well as in the resurrection of the body.

---

[65] Hunter (2001), p. 164. This is consistent with the reading of Kobusch (1997), p. 71. Kobusch also emphasises that Pufendorf rejects Aristotelian Scholastic metaphysics, understood as a discipline that is restricted to natural things or substances.

[66] Kobusch (1997), p. 82.

[67] Cudworth, *True Intellectual System*, p. 869. Passmore argues that Cudworth is led to deny the Christian doctrine of *eternal* rewards and *eternal* punishments: 'For it is inconsistent with the nature of the human soul [according to Cudworth], which always contains within it the potentiality for good and evil, a potentiality which immortality could do nothing to remove': Passmore, *Ralph Cudworth: An Interpretation* (1951), pp. 77–8.

2.5.1. Immortality

Philosophers who adopt a Cartesian conception of man could regard the immortality of the soul and its identity into the next life as unproblematic: for them, both can be deduced from what was taken to be the nature of the soul; that is, from its immateriality and simplicity. The argument for the immortality of the soul from its immaterial nature was a common one in the seventeenth century. Seth Ward, for example, presents it in the form of a syllogism: 'Whatsoever substance is incorporeall it is immortall. But the souls of men are incorporeall substances, *Ergo*...'[68] And just as the Cartesian conception of the self as immaterial soul helps to avoid the problem of self-identity with respect to this life, so it does with regard to the future life. What is meant by 'immortality' was just the continued existence of the soul as an immaterial substance. For Descartes's own theory, however, the unresolved problem of the individuation of immaterial substances reappears in this context: since the disembodied soul lacks sensation as well as the memory of any sensory experience, the question arises as to how genuine personal immortality is possible. What distinguishes one disembodied soul from another? Descartes's introduction of the problematic notion of a purely intellectual memory which survives the death of the body does not resolve the issue.[69]

With the revival of Epicurean materialism in early modern thought, critical ideas relating to the very notion of immortality were expressed that relate to the notion of identity. Thus, in 1682 Thomas Creech published an influential translation and commentary of Lucretius's *De rerum natura*.[70] In a passage that may sound like an anticipation of Locke, Lucretius states that even if after death our matter will be brought back together exactly as it is now and life restored to us, that afterlife would be of no concern to us if we have lost all memory or recollection of our previous life (*De rerum natura*, III, 847–51). Creech's translation and comments bring together the notions of identity, memory, and self-concern. Thus, one of the relevant passages in his translation reads: 'Nay grant, the scatter'd Ashes of our Urn/ Be join'd again, and Life and sense return;/ Yet how can that concern us, when 'tis done;/ Since all the Mem'ry of past Life is gone?' (*Of the Nature of Things*, vol. I, p. 259). Note, however, that Creech does not identify memory, but the conjunction of particles as a criterion of identity. The interpretation of this and other related passages in Lucretius is a matter of debate among classicists.[71] But Creech's point is that without

---

[68] Ward, *A Philosophical Essay towards an Eviction of the Being and Attributes of God* (1652) p. 35.

[69] Daniel Garber drew my attention to the importance of the notion of intellectual memory in this context. Descartes speaks of intellectual memory in several places. See, for example, the letter to Huygens in which Descartes says that 'we have, on my view, an intellectual memory which is certainly independent of the body': *Oeuvres de Descartes*, ed. Adam and Tannery (1964–76), vol. 3, p. 598. For a detailed discussion of Descartes's notion of intellectual memory and the problem of immortality, see (Rodis-)Lewis, *Le problème de l'inconscient et le Cartésianisme* (1950), pp. 208–18.

[70] T. Lucretius Carus, *Of the Nature of Things, In Six Books, Translated into English Verse; by Tho. Creech... In two Volumes, explain'd and illustrated with Notes and Animadversions, being a compleat Ssystem of the Epicurean Philosophy*, 2 vols. (1682) (quoted from the 1714 edition).

[71] Compare Gill, *The Structured Self in Hellenistic and Roman Thought* (2006), pp. 69–71. Gill would endorse Creech's reading (p. 70). But Sorabji, for example, argues that there are passages in

memory such identity is of no concern to us. If the present life is to have any significance to my afterlife, the two lives must be connected by memory and not merely by the sameness of material particles. Memory, in addition to identity, would be required. As Creech elaborates in his notes on Lucretius:

> We are not solicitous concerning those, who formerly were the very and individual Beings we now are; nor are we solicitous neither for them, nor do we bear any part in their Affliction, who hereafter shall be moulded out of the same matter, which now composes this Frame of ours. Let us suppose, for instance, that another, yet the same Poet Lucretius had liv'd before this of ours, certainly this Lucretius was nothing troubled concerning him: And suppose further, that there has been since, or will be hereafter, a third Lucretius; certainly our Lucretius was not the least concern'd for him neither: So that neither they who have been, nor they who will be, even tho' they have been, or shall be ourselves, neither have contributed or will contribute, to our Grief and Joy. (ibid., p. 260)

Again, the identity of the individual subject can be accounted for in materialistic terms; but that alone is not sufficient for a meaningful notion of an afterlife. There must be a connection through memory or recollection, otherwise the future self (although identical with the present self) will be of no concern to us. I must be able to be concerned for my former or future self—and that requires memory; the identity of material particles alone cannot establish such a concern.

Other materialist philosophers such as Richard Overton, Henry Layton, and especially Hobbes, who prefers to speak of the 'Immortality of the Man', argue against the Cartesian doctrine of 'natural immortality' and hold that immortality depends on the grace of God.[72] Even anti-materialist critics of Hobbes such as Ralph Cudworth, however, reject the view that the immortality of the human soul can simply be deduced from its immaterial nature. To Cudworth, *all* life is essentially of an incorporeal nature, but is not thereby immortal. Whether the human soul lives after death depends on God's will; and our assurance of its immortality cannot be derived from syllogistic reasoning but requires faith.[73] Further, since the existence of an immaterial substance does not necessarily include conscious experience, the notion of immortality must, for Cudworth, contain more than that of the continued existence of substance. To say we will receive God's rewards or punishments and to speak of a future state of *life*, we must believe that God will make the future state a

---

Lucretius suggesting that 'the retention of memory is necessary for personal identity': *Self: Ancient and Modern Insights about Individuality, Life and Death* (2006), p. 98. For a seventeenth-century translation of Lucretius that may suggest this reading, see, for example John Dryden: 'Nay, tho our Atoms shou'd revolve by chance,/ And matter leape into the former dance;/ Tho' time our Life and motion cou'd restore,/ And make our Bodies what they were before,/ What gain to us wou'd all this bustle bring?/ The new made man wou'd be another thing;/ When once an interrupting pause is made,/ That individual Being is decay'd,/ We, who are dead and gone, shall bear no part/ In all the pleasures, nor shall feel the smart,/ Which to that other Mortal shall accrew,/ Whom of our Matter Time shall mould anew': *Sylvae* (1685), in *The Works of John Dryden* (1969), vol. 3, p. 48.

[72] Hobbes, *Leviathan*, xxxviii and xliv. Overton, *Mans Mortalitie* (of 1643–44), ed. Fisch (1968). For discussions of this 'mortalist' position, see Burns, *Christian Mortalism from Tyndale to Milton* (1972); Ball, *The Soul Sleepers: Christian Mortalism from Wycliffe to Priestley* (2008).

[73] Cudworth, *True Intellectual System*, pp. 45, 868–9.

state of consciousness. Recall that for Cudworth it is consciousness 'which makes a Being to be Present with it self... to perceive it self to Do or Suffer, and to have a *Fruition* or *Enjoyment* of it self.'[74] As with Lucretius/Creech, the identity of substance, be it material or immaterial, is not sufficient for a meaningful notion of the afterlife. The quoted passage in Cudworth is in line with Lucretius's comment, as translated by Creech: 'He that is Miserable, must Perceive, Whilst he is so: he then must Be and Live' (*Of the Nature of Things*, vol. I, p. 260).

Although Cudworth does not regard immateriality as sufficient for immortality, he insists, against the materialists, that it is necessary: it is necessary precisely because it is immateriality which secures the soul's unity and identity through time. Cudworth explicitly addresses the 'identity condition' when discussing the materialist challenge. If the soul were not immaterial, Cudworth argues, it could not even remain identical within this life. In fact, it could not be a simple substance at all; rather, it would consist of a '*Heap of Substances.*'[75] Since bodies consist of a large number of particles which change constantly, souls, if they were material, 'could not be Numerically the same throughout the whole space of their Lives... Which Reason may be also extended further to prove the Soul to be no Body at all.'[76] Thus, if the soul's immateriality is denied, its identity through time is made impossible also, and so are just divine rewards or punishment and a meaningful notion of life after death.

These latter consequences of the materialist position were emphasised by another anti-materialist thinker, Timothy Manlove, towards the end of the century. After having pointed out that the materialist position creates a problem of personal identity, Manlove says:

If the [materialist] Hypothesis which I am writing against, be true, no man can rationally believe a Future State of Retribution. You have heard already how Individuation and Personality are overthrown by it, and by consequence there can be no just room for Rewards and Punishments hereafter, because the Person when he died had not the same Soul that he

---

[74] Cudworth, *True Intellectual System*, p. 159. See also p. 847: 'It is certain, that without *Consciousness* or *Understanding* nothing can be *Happy* (since it could not have any *Fruition* of itself).'

[75] Ibid., p. 830. The argument that the materialist theory cannot account for the soul's unity and simplicity is not, of course, unique to Cudworth. See, for example, More, *An Antidote against Atheism*, in More, *A Collection of Several Philosophical Writings*, 2 vols. (1662; reprinted, 1978), vol. 1, p. 34: 'This is to make the *several particles* of the Brain so many *individual persons;* a fitter object for Laughter then the least measure of Belief.' Similarly, Bentley argues that on the materialist hypothesis the human self cannot be a unitary entity: 'For every single Atom of our Bodies would be a distinct Animal, endued with self-consciousness and personal Sensation of its own. And a great number of such living and thinking Particles could not possibly by their mutual contact and pressing and striking compose one greater individual Animal, with one Mind and Understanding, and a vital Consension of the whole Body': *The Folly and Unreasonableness of Atheism* (1699), p. 47. The Cambridge Platonist John Smith appeals to the 'knowledge which the soul retains in itself of things past, and in some sort prevision of things to come'; and he argues that only an immaterial soul 'can thus bind up past, present, and future time together': *Select Discourses*, third edn. (1821), pp. 88–9.

[76] Cudworth, *True Intellectual System*, p. 46. See also p. 799: 'It is certain, that we have not all the same Numerical Matter, and neither more nor less, both in *Infancy* and in Old Age, though we be for all that the self Same Persons.'

had a month before; and why should one Soul be *punished* for another's Crimes, and that other *go free*?[77]

These arguments show that the metaphysical position adopted concerning the composition of the human self was thought to be, at least by the anti-materialists, of paramount importance for securing the identity required for the self as a moral and immortal being: only if the soul is an immaterial entity, so it was argued (or assumed), can there be moral accountability and life after death.

Platonist thinkers such as Henry More, who revived the doctrine of the pre-existence of our souls, also assume that the identity of the self as immaterial substance transcends this present life. Critics of the doctrine of pre-existence—for example, Samuel Parker and Edward Warren—argue (among other things) that if there had been a previous life, there would be some trace of it in our memory now; since we have no memory whatsoever of a pre-existent state, it is unlikely that there was such a state.[78] More, however, rejects the implicit assumption that memory of the past is relevant to the continuous existence and identity of the soul, and says that our memory is often deficient even with respect to this life; yet no one wants to say that because of this the soul does not remain the same throughout this life.[79]

2.5.2. The resurrection of the body

To return to the Christian doctrine of life after death; this doctrine, as mentioned above, holds that the human being as a whole will live. That is, it includes a belief not only in the immortality of the soul but also in the resurrection of the body. The eighteenth-century debates about the resurrection have a long prehistory, going back to early Christianity when the notion of bodily resurrection was introduced into theological debates by the Pauline epistles, especially at I. Cor. xv.[80] The more immediate background of the eighteenth-century discussions, however, concerns the debates of the late seventeenth century.

Due to the obvious fact that the body is subject to constant change, the identity of the resurrection-body could not be maintained as straightforwardly as that of the immaterial soul. Thus metaphysical disputes arose about the conditions that must be fulfilled for there to be the same body at the resurrection, and these in turn led to more general discussions about the identity of the human body in this life and indeed personal identity in general. The doctrine of the resurrection, then, is a prime example of the close connection that existed between religion and metaphysics. This connection was seen clearly by eighteenth-century discussants of the topic. It

---

[77] Manlove, *The Immortality of the Soul Asserted, and Practically Improved* (1697), p. 55.
[78] Parker, *An Account of the Nature and Extent of the Divine Dominion* (1666), p. 49. Warren, *No Praeexistence: Or a Brief Dissertation against the Hypothesis of Humane Souls* (1667), p. 100.
[79] More, *Immortality of the Soule* (1659), pp. 252–6.
[80] Bynum, *The Resurrection of the Body in Western Christianity, 200—1336* (1995), pp. 3–4, 22. For the history of the topic, see also Alger, *A Critical History of the Doctrine of a Future Life* (1864). For a general historical overview, see Vidal, 'Un "desir de corps mort". Résurrection et identité des evangiles au *cyberspace*', *Equinoxe*, 15 (1996), 139–52.

was claimed not only that the metaphysical debates about personal identity 'have been gradually introduced by the doubts entertained concerning the resurrection of the *same* body',[81] but also that an examination of the metaphysics of identity is required for an understanding of the resurrection doctrine. It 'is a point which is inseparably connected with the resurrection of the body' and needs to be examined for a meaningful discussion of the latter.[82]

So, the question is whether the identity condition for the afterlife needs to be satisfied in relation to the body as well, or only with regard to the soul. Does the body possessed on resurrection have to be the very same body one had in this life for there to be the same person in the future life? There are countless tracts, sermons, and pamphlets on this topic from the seventeenth century. Most authors answer the question in the affirmative, as Aquinas had done much earlier. For, so it is argued, if there is to be life after death, there will have to be the same human being as in this life, and this requires that there be the same body as well as the same soul. In a book which was much read and often reprinted in the seventeenth century, John Pearson points out that it is part of the concept of the resurrection that the same body will be restored to life which a person had here; for, 'if either the same body should be joyned to another soul, or the same soul united to another body, it would not be the resurrection of the same man.'[83] Further, Pearson argues, since divine rewards or punishments relate to the body as well as to the soul, they could not be just rewards or punishments, if the resurrection-body were not the same as the pre-mortem body:

That which shall receive the reward, and be lyable to the punishment, is not onely the soul but the body; it stands not therefore with the nature of a just retribution, that he which sinned in one body should be punished in another, he which pleased God in his own flesh should see God with other eyes.[84]

The disputes about the identity of the resurrection-body concern the conditions that need to be satisfied for there to be the same body at the resurrection as in this life. And here there seem to be three main positions.[85] The first is that the resurrection-body has to consist of numerically the same particles as the pre-mortem body. This position was held by Sir Thomas Browne in *Religio medici*, for example, and by his critic Alexander Ross. Browne and Ross argue that we must

---

[81] Cooper, *Tracts, Ethical, Theological and Political* (1787), p. 307; reprinted in Thiel (ed.), *Philosophical Writings of Thomas Cooper*, vol. 1 (2001).

[82] Drew, *An Essay on the Identity and General Resurrection of the Human Body; in which the Evidences in Favour of these important Subjects are considered in Relation both to Philosophy and Scripture* (1809), p. 132.

[83] Pearson, *An Exposition of the Creed* (1659), p. 758.

[84] Ibid., p. 762.

[85] For the problem of the identity of bodies, see also Thiel, 'Individuation' (1998). For a detailed discussion of the early history of doctrine of the resurrection, see Bynum (1995). See also her 'Material Continuity, Personal Survival, and the Resurrection of the Body: A Scholastic Discussion in its Medieval and Modern Contexts', in *Fragmentation and Redemption. Essays on Gender and the Human Body in Medieval Religion* (1991), pp. 239–97. For a general historical overview, see Vidal (1996), 139–52.

ascribe to God the ability to reunite the same atoms that made up a human body in this life. As Ross says, God 'can with as great facility reunite these dispersed *atomes*, as he could at first create them.'[86] If the resurrection-body were not in this strict sense identical to the body in this life, Ross argues, there would be no resurrection at all, but rather a transmigration of the soul into a different body.[87] This position, which accounts for the sameness of the resurrection-body in terms of a reassembling of particles, seems to ignore the seed-metaphor in I. Cor. xv that inspired the theological debates in the first place.[88] The second position was that identity of the particles is *not* required for the body to be the same. Here there are several positions as to which aspects or parts of the body are essential to its identity. For example, there are Rabbinic theological speculations about the *luz* or 'resurrection-bone': the *luz* is a part of the human body which subsists and is not destroyed in death; it is a material substratum which guarantees the identity of the resurrection-body as a whole.[89] The third main view was that all that is required for the resurrection-body to be the same is that it will be united to the same soul (understood either as 'form' or as a complete substance).

A version of the second view, according to which the identity only of certain essential particles of the body is required for the identity of the resurrection-body with the pre-mortem body, is defended in a different way (in a different way from the *luz* theory, that is) by Humphrey Hody.[90] According to Hody, the identity of the body at the resurrection requires the restoration of at least some of the very particles that belonged to the pre-mortem body. It requires the restoration of those particles of the pre-mortem body that are necessary to restore the same *organic body*. He argues against Boyle who, according to Hody, maintains 'that the Body which rises, may be said to be the same with that which was buried, though it contain in it but a very small part of the same substance' (Hody, *Resurrection* p. 190). For Hody, Boyle's position is 'not to defend the Doctrine of the *Resurrection*, but to give it up to it's [*sic*] Adversaries, and to advance another Doctrine instead of it. For it is not true that a Body so made up, may be call'd the *same* with that which died' (ibid., p. 191). He argues that the sameness of the man is required for the resurrection, and that the sameness of the man cannot be reduced to the sameness of the soul. "Tis a great Mistake to imagine that the *Identity* or *Sameness* of a *Man* consists wholly in the *sameness* of the *Soul*. If *Euphorbus*, and *Homer*, and *Ennius*, had had *one and the same*

---

[86] Ross, *Medicus medicatus: Or the Physicians Religion Cured, by a Lenitive or Gentle Potion* (1645), pp. 98–9. See also *Sir Thomas Browne. The Major Works*, ed. Patrides (1977), pp. 120–1.
[87] Ross, *Medicus medicatus*, pp. 108–9.
[88] Bynum notes that this also applies to the medieval debates which 'to a large extent ignore or explicitly reject the seed metaphor of I Corinthians 15': Bynum (1995), p. 8.
[89] Menasseh ben Israel, *De resurrectione mortuorum* (1636), pp. 198ff. See McMurrich 'The Legend of the "Resurrection Bone"', *Transactions of the Royal Canadian Institute*, 9 (1913), 45–51; Stewart, *Rabbinic Theology* (1961). There is a reference to the notion of *luz* in Leibniz, *Nouveaux essais*, II.xxvii.6.
[90] Hody, *The Resurrection of the (Same) Body Asserted* (1694). The view that only certain essential particles of the body need to remain the same to guarantee the identity of the body at the resurrection was also considered and argued for in the eighteenth century.

Soul, yet they would not have been *one and the same,* but *Three distinct Men*' (ibid., p. 218). The sameness of the self as man is required for reward and punishment: 'If it be reasonable that we should be *Men* when we are punish'd or rewarded for what we did when *Men*; it seems much more reasonable that we should be then the *same Men*: But we cannot be the same Men unless we have the *same Bodies*' (ibid.).

Hody holds, moreover, that there are different criteria for the diachronic identity of the human body in this life on the one hand, and for the identity of the resurrection-body with the pre-mortem body on the other. The latter identity requires sameness of some essential particles; the former does not require identity of particles but only the same organism:

I have own'd already that the *Identity* of our Bodies in this Life, does not consist in the *Identity* of *Particles*: I have granted that our Bodies in *old age* are the *same* with those which we had when *Infants*, or in our Mothers Womb, tho' they have not in 'em any one Particle the same. But... it does not therefore follow that the rising Body may be the *same* with that which was buried, tho' it have not any, or but few, of the same Particles. The *Identity* of the Body here in this Life consists in a fit Construction and Organization of successively fleeting Particles of matter. The *Identity* of the *Rising* Body, or it's [*sic*] sameness with that which died, can consist in nothing else but in the Restauration of the same Particles of Matter, which made up the *necessary* Parts of the *dying* Body, to their former Construction.[91]

As indicated, Hody emphasises that not all particles need to be identical at the resurrection: 'it is not necessary that all the Particles of it [the body] should be *rais'd up*. "Tis enough that such Particles are *rais'd* as made up the *integrant* and *necessary* Parts of the Body. By *necessary* Parts, I mean those which remain after the utmost degree of *Maceration*, without which the Body would not be *Integral*, but *Imperfect*' (ibid., pp. 187–8). Those particles need to be restored that 'are necessary to Life' (ibid., p. 188). But Hody's position seems problematic to adopt. He does not seem to give any plausible argument for saying that identity means one thing in this life, and another at the resurrection.[92]

Some argue, however, that the resurrection-body need only be the same organism as in this life—another version of the second view. Robert Boyle, whom Hody criticizes, seems to adopt this view in *Some Physico-Theological Considerations about the Possibility of the Resurrection* (1675). Boyle points out 'that there is no determinate bulk or size that is necessary to make a human body pass for the *same.*'[93] And although he argues for the possibility of the identity of the resurrection-body with the pre-mortem body, he holds that sameness of the body in a 'strict and literal sense'

---

[91] Hody, *Resurrection*, pp. 191–2.

[92] He points out, however, the difference between gradual and total change in this context. See Hody, *Resurrection*, pp. 132–3: 'There is a great deal of difference betwixt a Body whose Particles are *gradually* chang'd in a continu'd union with the Soul, and a Body whose Particles are chang'd, not *gradually*, but all together' (p. 132). Thus, 'when the Soul is separated from the Body, if that Body be dissolv'd, and *new* Particles be form'd into a Body and united to a Soul, it cannot be said to be the *same*, or to *rise again*. I appeal to the common Sense of Mankind' (p. 133).

[93] Boyle, *Selected Philosophical Papers*, p. 199.

is not necessary for the resurrection to be possible: it is sufficient that the individual soul remains the same. In other words, he accepts the third main view on this issue, according to which all that is required for the resurrection-body to be the same is that it will be united to the same *soul*. Whether the body's material composition or structure will be the same is irrelevant. This position conforms to Descartes's account of human bodily identity.[94] Although Boyle rejects the Scholastic notions of 'form' and 'matter', he presents his view on the identity of the resurrection-man by making use of the old language:[95]

In regard that the *human soul* is the form of man—so that, whatever duly organised portion of matter it is united to, it therewith constitutes the same man—the import of the *resurrection* is fulfilled in this, that after death there shall be another state, wherein the soul shall no longer persevere in its separate condition.[96]

Before Boyle, similar views were held by Kenelm Digby, and after Boyle, by the Archbishop of Canterbury, John Tillotson.[97] Digby argues that the body, taken in separation from the soul, is never identical from one moment to the next; nevertheless, as Christians, 'wee must beleeve that we shall rise againe with the same body that walked about, did eate, drinke, and live here on earth.'[98] Digby argues that whatever matter is joined to the same soul constitutes the same human body; therefore, the identity of the body at the resurrection is secured if *any* matter is united to the same soul:

If *God* should joyne the *Soule* of a lately dead man ... unto a *Body* made of earth taken from some mountaine in *America*; it were most true and certaine that the body he should then live by, were the same Identicall body he lived with before his *Death* & late *Resurrection*. It is evident that *samenesse*, *thisnesse*, and *thatnesse*, belongeth not to matter by it selfe ... but onely as it is distinguished and individuated by the Forme. Which, in our case, whensoever the same *Soule* doth, it must be understood alwaies to be the same matter and body.[99]

Although authors such as Digby subscribe to the doctrine of the sameness of the resurrection-body, their position is really a thinly veiled version of the view that the identity of the body is not required for the restoration of the same self at the resurrection. Cudworth, for example, rejects the notion of a strict identity of the pre-mortem body with the resurrection-body by emphasising that at the resurrection the body is purified and 'transformed into a spiritual and heavenly body' (Cudworth, *True Intellectual System*, p. 799). He goes on to say:

---

[94] See Descartes's letter to Mesland, 9 February 1645: *Oeuvres*, vol. 4, pp. 162–70, esp. p. 166; *Philosophical Writings*, vol. 3, pp. 242–3. The context of Descartes's discussion is not the problem of the resurrection, but the doctrine of transubstantiation. See the section on Descartes in Chapter 1.
[95] Compare, for example, Suárez's position as discussed in the Introduction above. For Suárez 'the individual is said to be the same by reason of the same soul': *Disputationes metaphysicae* (1597), V.6.15; *Suarez on Individuation*, ed. and transl. Gracia (1982).
[96] Boyle, *Selected Philosophical Papers*, p. 206.
[97] See Tillotson, *The Possibility of the Resurrection asserted and proved* (1682), in Tillotson (1728), vol. 3, pp. 248–55.
[98] Digby, *Observations upon Religio Medici* (1644), pp. 78–9.
[99] Digby, *Observations upon Religio Medici* (1644), pp. 85–7.

We conclude therefore, that the *Christian Mystery, of the Resurrection of Life*, consisteth not in the Souls being reunited to these Vile Rags of Mortality, these *Groß Bodies* of ours (such as now they are) but in having them *changed into the Likeneß of Christ's Glorious Body*, and in *this Mortal's putting on Immortality*. (ibid.)

The view that the identity of the body is not required for the resurrection of the same self appealed to those philosophers and theologians who followed Descartes at least in this: that they regarded the body not as an essential element of the human subject, and thought that the soul alone, whether embodied or disembodied, constitutes the same self or person. This was not to deny that the resurrection concerns the body; but it was argued that since both human and divine courts judge only with respect to the same soul, the identity of the body is not required at the resurrection. As Arthur Bury, a defender of this view, wrote: 'if Human justice punish an old crime, though between the act and the discovery every particle of the body be chang'd, because the same soul makes him the same person; how can we doubt but Divine justice may at the resurrection do the same?'[100]

This issue of the resurrection is especially pressing for materialists who wish to remain Christians. Indeed, it has been claimed that the 'exigencies of a materialistic philosophy' created a 'motive for believing the resurrection of the body' (Alger, 1864, p. 502). Since to the materialist, death is 'the total destruction of man for the time', 'there was therefore plainly no alternative for him but either to abandon one of his fundamental convictions as a Christian and a philosopher, or else to accept the doctrine of a future resurrection of the body into an immortal life' (ibid., p. 503). And indeed, materialists such as Richard Overton argue that immortality is a gift of God received at the resurrection.[101] Clearly, if man is totally material, then the hope for an afterlife rests entirely on the resurrection. But as Joseph Priestley noted late in the eighteenth century, it was said 'that if all our hopes of a future life rest upon the doctrine of a *resurrection*, we place it on a foundation that is very precarious.' For after death:

the body putrefies, and the parts that composed it are dispersed, and form other bodies, which have an equal claim to the same resurrection...And where, they say can be the propriety of rewards and punishments, if the man that rises again be not identically *the same* with the man that acted and died?[102]

In attempting to respond to this question, materialists appeal to a variety of previous accounts as well as developing their own ideas. In the end, however, the development of materialist thought appears to result in a denial of numerical bodily or personal identity at the resurrection, combined with the claim that such identity is not even required for a plausible account of the resurrection.

William Coward was an early proponent of this view, arguing against the natural immortality of soul, and that the numerical identity of the body (meaning the

---

[100] Bury, *The Naked Gospel* (1690), p. 71.
[101] As Overton expresses it, 'all *hope* of future life and Being is in the Resurrection': *Mans Mortalitie*, p. 17.
[102] Priestley, *Disquisitions relating to Matter and Spirit* (1777), p. 156.

identity of its particles) is not required for the resurrection.[103] Of course, as a materialist he holds that an immaterial soul could not constitute the identity of the man. Although Coward published after Locke's main works had appeared, he does not take into account Locke's position on personal identity.[104] For example, unlike Locke he does not distinguish between the identity of the man and the identity of the person. Persons are 'living creatures' or men (*Second Thoughts*, p. 430). What he has in common with thinkers such as Boyle and Locke is just the thesis that the same numerical body is not required for the resurrection (third view listed above). What distinguishes his account from Locke's and from that of some other materialist thinkers is also the view that numerical identity of the *person* is not required at the resurrection. Rather, similarity or a 'specific identity' (*Farther Thoughts*, p. 85) is sufficient. With this view he anticipated the positions of later eighteenth-century materialists on the topic, such as Thomas Cooper.

Coward's argument can be analysed as follows. *First*, even if there were an immaterial soul, it could not in any way constitute the same man at the resurrection or even in this life. In this context Coward provides the standard anti-Cartesian argument that immaterial souls, if they did exist, could not be individuated.[105] And since an immaterial soul could not be individuated, it could not constitute the identity of the man through time:

If we had a transmigration of the *Souls*, he speculates, 'would that Man be the same Man in 50 different Bodies by reason of his *Identity of Soul*?' Certainly, no, my Friend, no. No more than if it should Transmigrate into a Beast, and claim to be denominated the *same Man*, because he possesses the *same Soul*. (ibid., pp. 82–3)

Second, as an immaterial soul cannot fulfil the function of constituting identity in the afterlife, Coward argues, that '*Identity of Body* must be the only requisite to make up *Identity of Man*' (ibid., p. 85).

Third, to count as the same as the pre-mortem body, Coward holds, the resurrection-body need only have a sufficient similarity with the pre-mortem body. Similarity appears to be relevant in two senses. (1) It is understood in terms of the 'exterior Likeness ... we are to enjoy at the Resurrection' (*Second Thoughts*, p. 439). (2) It relates to the particles that make up the body. Coward argues that although God would of course be able to reunite the same numerical particles of the pre-mortem body at the resurrection, this is not required for there to be the same body.[106] Rather,

---

[103] For an account of Coward's 'mortalism', see Ball (2008), pp.135–8. Ball does not discuss Coward's account of identity.

[104] Coward, *Second Thoughts concerning the Human Soul* (1702); Coward, *Farther Thoughts concerning the Human Soul* (1703).

[105] 'What Criterion have you to distinguish the dissimilitude of two *Immaterial Beings*, so as to denote them Identically different? That which usually distinguishes Man from Man are his Shape, or Figure, Qualities and Qualifications, according to the old Philosophical Maxim, *a Qualitate oritur Similitudo et Dissimilitudo*': Coward, *Farther Thoughts*, p. 84.

[106] 'Indeed God may, if he pleases, gather together the very *individual scattered Atoms* of every Man that has been buried and corrupted in the Grave, and *reunite* the same into the Form of that Living Creature they in this World composed, and raise the very *Numerical Man* as to every Particle he was made of, because this doth not exceed an Omnipotent Power; but yet I do not see that either

'a *Specifical Identity* is sufficient, not a *Numerical*, as to all the particles Man's Body was compounded of, when he died... nor do I take *Body* as a *part of Man* contradistinct to his Soul, but for a *Living Man*, when I apply it to Man' (*Farther Thoughts*, pp. 85–6).

Fourth, like some of his immaterialist opponents, Coward appeals to the notion of the spiritualization of our natural body (I. Cor. xv. 44) in order to support the idea that numerical identity is not required at the resurrection.[107] Here again he emphasises similarity. At the resurrection 'the *Similitude* of the same Man, compos'd of Spiritualiz'd Flesh, seems to be sufficient' (*Second Thoughts*, p. 434; my italics).[108] Whatever this 'spiritualization' may mean from a materialist standpoint, Coward insists that it is still a material being, not an immaterial entity.[109] Nor is this the sort of change that undermines the kind of identity that is required for just rewards or punishments:

So that the Change here meant, seems no ways to infer a Change of Man into some other different Being or Creature, but only from a State of Imperfection to one of great Perfection, *i.e. From a Natural Body to a Spiritual Body*, Man still retaining Body as when living upon Earth. (ibid., p. 439)

Fifth, Coward does not wish to exclude numerical difference. As far as numerical difference from other persons at the resurrection is concerned, 'Man will be distinguish'd by his Qualities and Qualifications from another, as he shall be rais'd a corporeal *Living Creature* again' (*Farther Thoughts*, p. 83).

Coward's account leaves many questions unanswered. What precisely are we to understand by a non-spiritual spiritualization of the body? And what degree of similarity or what kind of 'specifical identity' is sufficient for divine, just rewards and punishments? Nevertheless, aspects of his understanding of the resurrection were taken up later in the century. In the meantime, other materialists insisted on numerical bodily identity and attempted to make this compatible with their metaphysics.

---

by plain Scripture or Consequences drawn from any Texts therein contain'd, God says that he will do so, or has declared any such Ways of his in the reproduction of Man by a Resurrection, when he shall please to give him Life again': Coward, *Second Thoughts*, pp. 430–1.

[107] See also Coward, *Second Thoughts*, p. 430: 'when I say, *The Body will be raised*, I mean, *Man as he was once a living Creature will be so raised from the Grave again, and with the Eyes of* Flesh spiritualiz'd *will see God;* And *that God doth not, or is oblig'd to, or will require the* particular Particles of Bones or Flesh *that made Man, and was buried in the Grave and turn'd to Atomes, or Dust out of which he was first formed.*'

[108] See also Coward, *Second Thoughts*, p. 437: 'at the general Resurrection we shall All be raised in our former Human Likeness, but our Flesh and Blood must put on Incorruption, and be spiritualiz'd into such a Body, as will be capable of receiving those immense joys God has promised to the Righteous, or enduring those eternal Torments he has denounced against the impenitent hardened Sinners. And all this will be done to the very *same living Creature*, tho' the very flux Constitution of his mortal Nature be such, that as to *Identity of Particles* he is scarce ever the same from the Day of his Birth to the Day of his Death, or Corruption in the Grave.'

[109] 'But I tell you still, that it will be your *Body*, and not a *Spirit*, or *Spiritual Substance*, that will be so raised and spiritualiz'd': Coward, *Second Thoughts*, pp. 428–9.

The position John Locke adopts on this issue is very similar to that of those theologians who deny the identity of the resurrection-body. Yet he differs from them in that he does not regard the identity of the soul, as substance, as essential either; nor does he commit himself to a materialist position. Locke interprets the doctrine of life after death against the background of his new theory of personal identity.

PART II

LOCKE'S SUBJECTIVIST REVOLUTION

3

Locke on identity, consciousness, and self-consciousness

Locke's chapter on identity was published in May 1694 as Chapter 27 of the second Book of his *An Essay Concerning Human Understanding* (second edition). Locke composed the chapter in mid-1693 at the suggestion of his Irish friend William Molyneux, but he had sketched views on the topic much earlier. The first journal note dealing explicitly with it dates from as early as 1683, and there are some thoughts relevant to his later theory that appear in a note on immortality of 1682.[1] In the first edition of the *Essay* (1690) Locke makes several remarks on the topic when discussing the doctrine of the resurrection and the Cartesian doctrine that the soul always thinks.[2] Molyneux referred to these remarks when suggesting to Locke that he deal more extensively with the issue in the second edition. A passage in the first edition indicates that on Locke's view personal identity has to do with the 'Consciousness of our Actions and Sensations, especially of Pleasure and Pain, and the concernment that accompanies it'.[3] In the second edition Locke elaborates on this and presents a detailed theory of personal identity. The two central notions in the quoted first-edition comment, *consciousness* and *self-concern*, are also crucial to his theory as developed in the second-edition chapter. But Locke's theory is complex and intricate, and its interpretation is still a matter of debate.[4]

3.1. LOCKE AND HIS 'SOURCES'

Locke's account in terms of a self-relating consciousness challenges traditional views about personality and identity. He was certainly well aware of the traditional

---

[1] *Identy* [sic] *of persons* (5 June 1683), Bodleian Library, MS Locke f. 7, p. 107; facsimile in Thiel, *John Locke* (2000), p. 89. See Locke, *An Early Draft of Locke's Essay, together with Excerpts from His Journals*, ed. Aaron and Gibb (1936), pp. 121–3, for the 1682 note on immortality.
[2] Locke, *An Essay Concerning Human Understanding*, ed. Nidditch (1975), I.iv.4–5; II.i.11–12. See also Locke, 'Draft C' (1685), II.i.15–16.
[3] Locke, *Essay*, II.i.11.
[4] For a detailed discussion of Locke's theory in its historical context (and of the relevant secondary literature up to 1982), see Thiel, *Lockes Theorie der personalen Identität* (1983). See also Thiel, 'The Trinity and Human Personal Identity', in Stewart (ed.), *English Philosophy in the Age of Locke* (2000), esp. pp. 237–8.

conceptions of personal identity discussed above. Indeed, he obviously refers to earlier accounts of the issue when he notes the 'great deal of that Confusion, which often occurs about this Matter, with no small seeming Difficulties; especially concerning *Personal Identity*'.[5] Locke does not indicate which texts he has in mind, but it is plain that one of the debates to which he is referring is the heated controversy between William Sherlock and Robert South about the trinity, discussed above—a debate which took place just prior to the writing and publication of Locke's chapter and created widespread interest, and which concerned the identity of human persons and self-consciousness as well as the theological issue. I have argued elsewhere (Thiel, 1983, pp. 61–4, 105–18; Thiel, 2000) that while Locke separates the issue of human personal identity from that of the trinity and is concerned with diachronic personal identity rather than with individuation, there are good reasons to believe that when Locke composed the chapter he had both Sherlock's theory and South's critique thereof very much present to mind, and that his knowledge of South and Sherlock affected the way in which he presented his account of personal identity.[6] It is very probable that Locke knew of Sherlock's theory through South's *Animadversions* (1693). Thus he would have been able to take into account South's arguments against a theory that bases personality on the notion of consciousness. It remains true that Locke's treatment of personal identity was not in the first place inspired by the trinitarian debate between Sherlock and South, as he had sketched his theory much earlier. It is also true, however, that he did not work out a detailed theory until mid-1693. Most probably, his reading of Sherlock through South would have been of considerable importance to his thinking about the issue of personal identity. South's critique of Sherlock would have made him very much aware of the charge of circularity. In working out his account of personal identity in terms of the notion of consciousness, Locke would have wanted to ensure that his own theory be safe from this charge. I return to this issue and to the relation between Locke's theory and the Sherlock–South debate when, in Chapter 6, I come to discuss the charge of circularity against Locke.

Of course, the Sherlock–South debate is not the sole source of Locke's treatment of the topic. As indicated above, Locke was familiar with the traditional positions relevant to the issue. Indeed, the Sherlock–South controversy itself hints at the complexity of the historical context from which Locke's new theory emerged.[7] Some of the relevant background can be gleaned from references in Locke's text and has been discussed above: it includes debates about the Scholastic search for a principle of individuation and related debates about diachronic identity in general; discussions about the immortality of the soul and the resurrection of the body;

---

[5] Locke, *Essay*, II.xxvii.7. See also sect. 28, where Locke refers to 'the difficulty or obscurity, that has been about this Matter'.

[6] Thiel, 'The Trinity and Human Personal Identity' (2000), pp. 238–40.

[7] It is plain that the relevant context cannot be reduced to Descartes, Hobbes, More, and Boyle, as Forstrom claims. Indeed, her recent book-length study has little to add to the debate about Locke on personal identity. An indication of this is that the latest secondary source cited on this topic is from 1991. Forstrom, *John Locke and Personal Identity: Immortality and Bodily Resurrection in Seventeenth-Century Philosophy* (2010).

related views about the nature of the human soul and the human body, especially in Cartesian and anti-Cartesian early modern thought; and traditional notions of responsibility, the law, and just rewards and punishments in this life and the afterlife.

Other relevant background is not obvious from Locke's published text, which includes traditional ideas of consciousness and related notions such as conscience, memory, and debates about the very concept of a person from Boethius onwards. Regarding the notion of consciousness, we shall see that it relates to accounts in thinkers such as Antoine Arnauld and Louis de la Forge discussed in chapter 1 above. Moreover, Locke's journal note on immortality from 1682 reflects his reading of the Cambridge Platonist Ralph Cudworth who, as indicated above, introduced the very term 'consciousness' into the English philosophical terminology, using it as a translation of Plotinus's 'synaisthesis,' but understood as a relating to an entity's own thoughts and actions.[8]

Locke's note of 1683 echoes passages in Lucretius (cited in the previous Chapter in the section on immortality) that relate memory to the issue of identity.[9] Locke states in this note that:

Identy [sic] of persons lies not in haveing the same numericall body made up of the same particles, nor if the minde consists of corporeal spirits in their being the same. but in the memory & knowledg of ones past self & actions continued on under the consciousnesse of being the same person whereby every man ownes himself.[10]

This passage is not a summary of Locke's developed theory of ten years later. In terms of his later theory the expression 'consciousness of being the same person' would be open to the charge of circularity to which his mature theory is immune, as we shall see. The important point in the present context is that in this note Locke rejects the view that personal identity could be accounted for in terms of the identity of material particles or 'corporeal spirits'. Thus, although the passage is reminiscent of Lucretius, there is an important difference to the Lucretian view. For Locke, but not for Lucretius, memory, and consciousness (here 'knowledge') of the past are *constitutive* of identity. We saw that for Lucretius and his English commentator Creech the identity of a human subject can be accounted for in terms of material particles even through death, if we assume that the same matter can be gathered again after death. But memory of the past is required for the subject to be concerned in his past self and therefore for a meaningful notion of an afterlife. Unlike Lucretius, Locke, even in this early note, links the very notion of the identity of a person to consciousness and memory. For Locke, but not for Lucretius, the identity of persons cannot be established by the sameness of material particles at all, but requires consciousness

---

[8] See sections in the next Chapter on the theological aspects of Locke's theory.
[9] This has first been noted by Behan, 'Locke on Persons and Personal Identity', *Canadian Journal of Philosophy*, 9 (1979), 53–74. A possible connection between Locke and Lucretius on this issue (without reference to the Journal note) is also discussed in Warren, 'Lucretian *Palingenesis* Recycled', *Classical Quarterly*, 51 (2001), 499–508; Gill, *The Structured Self in Hellenistic and Roman Thought* (2006); and Sorabji, *Self: Ancient and Modern Insights about Individuality, Life and Death* (2006), pp. 95–9.
[10] Bodleian Library, MS Locke f. 7, p. 107; facsimile in Thiel, *John Locke* (2000), p. 89.

and memory of past thoughts and actions. For Locke, such a notion of identity is required for self-concern. The notion of self-concern does not appear in this early note. But Locke's mature account shows that self-concern is possible because consciousness fulfils a constitutive role for personal identity. Identity and self-concern are no longer potentially separate, as they would seem to be in the Lucretian account.[11]

Some have maintained that Locke's account must have been inspired by Stoic ideas, and in particular by the Stoic doctrine of *oikeiosis* discussed in the Introduction.[12] On the face of it this would seem to be a plausible suggestion, as there can be no doubt about the presence of other Stoic ideas in Locke's thought.[13] The textual evidence for the claim about the doctrine of *oikeiosis* is very slim, however. It is easy to see that although some of the terminology used may seem similar, Locke's concern with personal identity differs significantly from that of Stoic doctrine. In support of the Stoic reading of Locke it has been said that the Stoic doctrine contains the two central elements of Locke's theory: self-consciousness and self-concern (Brandt, 2003, 180). And as Locke makes use of terms such as 'appropriate' in his chapter on identity, the connection to Stoic doctrine seems obvious to some. Moreover, it has been claimed that the process that the Stoics describe in terms of the notion of *oikeiosis* 'is a process of self-recognition, and it is by self-recognition that a sense of personal identity is achieved'.[14] This again seems to suggest a close connection to early modern and in particular Lockean doctrine of personal identity.

It is plain, however, that even assuming that the gloss on the Stoic doctrine just quoted is correct, 'personal identity' thus understood is completely different from Locke's concern with a person's identity over time. The texts to which such readings appeal (see Introduction) also make it clear that the Stoic doctrine has little if anything in common with Locke's account, and is thus an unlikely source for the latter. It should be noted that the term 'appropriate' occurs only three times in Locke's long chapter on identity. More importantly, the 'appropriation' or

---

[11] Compare Gill (2006), p. 70, and Warren (2001). As noted in the previous Chapter, however, the interpretation of the relevant passages in Lucretius is a matter of debate. Sorabji (2006), for example, argues that some passages suggest that for Lucretius 'the retention of memory is necessary for personal identity'. As he notes, on this reading, Lucretius's view would be 'closer to that of John Locke' (p. 98). Locke owned three editions of Lucretius's *De rerum natura*: Harrison and Laslett, *The Library of John Locke* (1971).

[12] Brandt, 'Selbstbewusstsein und Selbstsorge. Zur Tradition der οἰκείωσις in der Neuzeit', *Archiv für Geschichte der Philosophie*, 85 (2003), 179–97. Brandt, 'John Lockes Konzept der persönlichen Identität. Ein Resümee', *Aufklärung*, 18 (2006), 43–5; Sorabji (2006), pp. 104–9. Sorabji's claim is more careful than Brandt's in that he speaks merely of 'reminiscences of Stoicism' in Locke (p. 107). For Brandt it is impossible to understand Locke's account of personal identity without taking into account its 'Stoic sources'.

[13] Compare, for example, Nuovo's careful study, 'Aspects of Stoicism in Locke's Philosophy', in Hutton and Schuurman (eds.), *Studies on Locke: Sources, Contemporaries, and Legacy* (2008), pp. 1–25. Nuovo does not discuss the doctrine of *oikeiosis*, however, and does not claim that Stoic ideas had any impact on Locke's account of personal identity.

[14] Kerferd, 'The Search for Personal Identity in Stoic Thought', *Bulletin of the John Rylands University Library of Manchester*, 55 (1972), 177–96, at 186.

'familiarization' of the Stoics relates to something that already exists: one's own physical constitution.[15] According to Cicero, desiring things that are conducive to oneself requires that a being feel an affection towards its constitution, and this in turn would not be possible without self-consciousness ('sensus sui').[16] In Seneca, too, the *sensus sui* or 'self-consciousness' relates to the physical constitution of animals.[17] Clearly, this *sensus sui* is not the consciousness of thoughts and actions that Locke is talking about in his account of personal identity, nor does it relate to anything like Locke's technical notion of a person. Against this it could be argued that Seneca appears to address the very issue of personal identity through time in the context of a discussion of *oikeiosis*. Seneca states:

But each age has its own constitution, different in the case of the child, the boy, and the old man; they are all adapted to the constitution wherein they find themselves... no matter what may be the constitution into which the plant comes, it keeps it, and conforms thereto'... The periods of infancy, boyhood, youth, and old age, are different; but I, who have been infant, boy, and youth, am still the same ['Alia est aetas infantis, pueri, adulescentis, senis; ego tamen idem sum, qui et infans fui et puer et adulescens']. Thus, although each has at different times a different constitution, the adaptation [or appropriation] of each to its constitution is the same ['Sic, quamvis alia atque alis cuique constitutio sit, conciliatio consitutionis suae eadem est'].[18]

As has been noted in the literature on this issue, however, Seneca's concern here is not with personal identity as understood by Locke and other early modern philosophers.[19] First, 'ego' does not refer to a Lockean person. Second, what Seneca is talking about is not an individual's identity through time in a Lockean sense. Rather, he is talking about the adaptation (or appropriation) at each period to one's own constitution. The notion of sameness relates to this adaptation, not to an 'I' and its diachronic identity. Seneca emphasises the continuity of the appropriation to one's own constitution at various times of a being's development. But this is not what Locke and other early modern thinkers have in mind when they discuss personal identity and self-consciousness. The passage in Seneca, then, is not concerned with the numerical identity of a Lockean person over time and related issues concerning accountability. It is, of course, still possible that Locke was positively inspired by a doctrine that is completely different from his own concern with the identity of

---

[15] This is confirmed even by Kerferd's own account of the Stoic idea. The self becomes 'conscious of the nature of the self that is already there waiting to be perceived': Kerferd (1972), 188.
[16] Cicero, *De finibus*, III, 16. See also Diogenes Laertius's account of Chrysippus (VII, 85). These are passages that are typically cited in accounts of Stoic *oikeiosis*.
[17] Seneca, *Ad Lucilium epistulae morales*, ed. and transl. Gummere (1953), vol. 3, pp. 397–411 (Latin, pp. 396–410), Letter 121, 5ff., on the instinct of animals. 'But that which art gives to the craftsman, is given to the animal by nature. No animal handles its limbs with difficulty, no animal is at a loss how to use its body. This function they exercise immediately at birth' (6). 'So all these animals have a consciousness of their constitution ['Ergo omnibus constitutionis suae sensus est'], and for that reason can manage their limbs as readily as they do; nor have we any better proof that they come into being equipped with this knowledge than the fact that no animal is unskilled in the use of its body' (9).
[18] Seneca, *Ad Lucilium*, Letter 121, 15 and 16; transl. as above.
[19] See Gill (2006), pp. 43–5.

human persons, but if we were to accept this, our search for possible 'inspirations' and 'influences' would become rather arbitrary and speculative. Certainly the claim that Locke's account could 'not be understood' without taking into account its 'Stoic sources' (Brandt, 2006, pp. 43, 48) is completely unwarranted, given that there is no evidence at all in Locke's text for an appeal to such sources.

3.2. LOCKE AND THE SUBJECTIVIST TREATMENT OF IDENTITY

For Locke, identity in general is an issue that pertains to our concepts of those things whose identity is in question. He rejects both the Scholastic and the Cartesian accounts of the problem, and breaks with the traditional ontological view of the person and of personal identity. He treats the special problem of personal identity in accordance with his general theory of identity. This is essentially a subjectivist treatment of the issue where our own concepts are crucial rather than the things themselves—a view discussed in the previous Chapter in relation to thinkers as diverse as Johannes Clauberg, Thomas Hobbes, and Robert Boyle.

As far as the issue of individuation within a kind is concerned, Locke, like other proponents of the corpuscular philosophy, regards this issue as unproblematic, as he too denies real universal forms. He adopts the basic nominalist assumption that everything that exists is individual by itself and that a search for a principle of individuation is superfluous. Like Hobbes, Locke argues that to say an individual is individual by itself is to say that it is individual through its existence at a particular place and time: all things (individuals) exist in space and time, and they are the individuals they are, and distinct from all other individuals, by their very position in space and time. Thus Locke thinks it is 'easy to discover' that the principle of individuation which 'is so much enquired after' is simply 'Existence it self'; for, existence 'determines a Being of any sort to a particular time and place incommunicable to two Beings of the same kind' (*Essay*, II.xxvii.3). This means that in contrast to Suárez's view, for example, individuality cannot be prior to existence; further, it means that individuality is not something that existent things may or may not have. For to exist is to be at a certain place and time, and by that itself any being is 'that very thing, and not another, which at the same time exists in another place, how like and undistinguishable soever it may be in all other respects' (II.xxvii.1). Of course, not everybody who holds that existence is the principle of individuation would have to be a proponent of the corpuscular hypothesis, but it is easy to see why proponents of the theory, such as Locke, would adopt that position. The postulated atoms or corpuscles themselves are, of course, to be thought of as distinct individual beings. Now, it is possible that two atoms are the same with respect to all their properties, except for their position in space and time. Only their different existence in space and time can guarantee their distinctness and individuality. As Locke points out against John Sergeant, the Aristotelian critic of his *Essay*: 'What complexion of accidents besides those of place & perhaps time can distinguish two attoms perfectly solid & round & of the same diameter?'[20] According to Locke, to hold that 'Existence it self' is the principle of individuation also has the advantage that one avoids having to postulate different individuating principles for different kinds of beings; for whatever the principle of individuation is, it must be 'the same in all the several species of creatures'.[21] And existence not only individuates atoms as well as composite bodies, but 'a Being of any sort' (II.xxvii.3).

While Hobbes restricts his brief discussion of individuation to bodies, Locke explicitly appeals to a distinction between three general kinds of substance in this context. He distinguishes, just like Descartes, between God, finite spirits, and bodies (II.xxvii.2), stressing that one thing excludes all other things of the same kind from its position in space and time. A body is individual and distinct from all other bodies through its spatio-temporal existence; it excludes all other bodies from its place and time.[22] Yet a body does not exclude a spiritual substance from its place. God is everywhere and eternal, but does not exclude finite substances, be they spiritual or material. In short, 'these three sorts of Substances, as we term them, do not exclude one another out of the same place' (II.xxvii.2).

Locke thinks that if we attend to the distinction between the three general kinds of things, there arises no real problem concerning individuation. It is 'Existence it self' that individuates in each case. And this principle is said to apply to non-substances as well. Locke does not adopt the traditional view that the individuation of accidents depends on that of substances: 'All other things being but Modes or Relations ultimately terminated in Substances, the Identity and Diversity of each particular Existence of them too will be by the same way determined'; that is to say, their individuation is determined, like that of substances, by their existence.[23] Locke does not elaborate any further, however, on the issue of the individuality of modes and relations in general.

Like Hobbes and Boyle, Locke thinks that what presents itself as a serious problem is not individuation but identity through time. He too argues that the answer to the question of identity has to do with our concepts of those things whose identity is in question. But Locke is more explicit about this than are thinkers such as Hobbes and Boyle. Rejecting substantial forms and denying that we have knowledge of the real essences of substances, he holds that the answer to the question of how much a thing may change without losing its identity must be in terms of 'nominal essences'; that is, in terms of our abstract ideas of those beings whose identity is under consideration.

---

[20] Locke's marginal notes in his copy of Sergeant, *Solid Philosophy Asserted, against the Fancies of the Ideists* (1697), p. 258. The notes are reproduced in the 1984 reprint of this book.
[21] Locke's response to Stillingfleet in Locke Works (1823), vol. 4, p. 439.
[22] This is, to Locke, a self-evident principle. See *Essay*, IV.vii.5; I.ii.18.
[23] Locke, *Essay*, II.xxvii.2. The corresponding passage in Wynne's *An Abridgement of Mr. Locke's Essay Concerning Human Understanding* (1731), which was authorized by Locke, makes this point more clearly: 'The Identity and Diversity of *Modes* and *Relations* are determined after the same Manner that Substances are' (p. 112). See also Coste's translation of the *Essay*: 'Toutes les autres choses, n'etant, après les Substances, que des *Modes* ou des *Relations* qui se terminent aux Substances, on peut determiner encore par la meme voie l'*identité* et la *diversité* de chaque existence particuliere qui leur convient': *Essai philosophique concernant l'entendement humain* (1755), p. 259.

Unlike Hobbes, Locke does not make use of the terminology of form and matter when discussing identity. According to Locke, identity over time is just as unproblematic as individuation, as long as we consider only simple substances such as finite spirits and atoms: just as the individuality of any being is provided by 'Existence it self', so is the identity of a simple substance over time secured by its continued existence; that is, by its spatio-temporal continuity:

> Let us suppose an Atom, *i.e.* a continued body under one immutable Superficies, existing in a determined time and place: 'tis evident, that, considered in any instant of its Existence, it is, in that instant, the same with it self. For being, at that instant, what it is, and nothing else, it is the same, and so must continue, as long as its Existence is continued: for so long it will be the same, and no other. (II.xvii.3)

At the beginning of its existence (as at all other points of time) any being excludes all other individuals of the same kind from its particular position in absolute space and time, and no two things of the same kind can begin to exist at the same spatio-temporal position. Neither can one thing have two beginnings of existence in space and time. Any simple substance's identity through time is secured all along because of its special relation to its own beginning of existence.[24]

Locke also mentions the identity of non-substances: namely, that of actions, in this context. He points out that their identity and distinctness too can be explained in terms of beginning of existence: it is the very nature of actions and motions that they exist only at one time and at one place:

> Only as to things whose Existence is in succession, such as are the Actions of finite Beings, *v.g. Motion* and *Thought*, both which consist in a continued train of Succession, concerning their Diversity there can be no question: Because each perishing the moment it begins, they cannot exist in different times, or in different places, as permanent Beings can at different times exist in distant places; and therefore no motion or thought considered as at different times can be the same, each part thereof having a different beginning of Existence'. (II.xxvii.2)

Thus, in respect of actions there can be no numerical identity at different points of time; for example, if a body moves continuously during the period t_1 to t_4, its movement at t_2 is not numerically identical with its movement at t_3.

Continued existence—that is, spatio-temporal continuity—is relevant not only to the identity of simple substances, but also to that of composite beings. Locke recognizes, though, that the fact that 'permanent Beings' (substances) are liable to change must be taken into account. And here again the question arises of how much a thing may change without losing its identity—the question about its essential constituents. Since Locke rejects substantial forms and denies that we have knowledge of the real essences of substances, he argues that the answer to this question must be determined by 'nominal essences' or abstract ideas. Abstract ideas, according

---

[24] For Locke (but not according to the Cartesian tradition), immaterial substances (if they exist) exist in space. This is implied by Locke's remark on the identity of spirits: 'Finite Spirits having had each its determinate time and place of beginning to exist, the relation to that time and place will always determine to each of them its Identity as long as it exists': *Essay*, II.xvii.2.

to Locke, are formed on the basis of observed similarities among objects. They signify kinds of things—what we take to be the essence of any being. Only our abstract ideas can tell us about the essential features of substances; that is, only our abstract ideas can determine the requirements for the identity of these beings. And this is why Locke believes it is crucial to adhere to that abstract (sortal) idea of any being whose identity we consider: 'Whatever makes the specifick *Idea*, to which the name is applied, if that *Idea* be steadily kept to, the distinction of any thing into the same, and divers will easily be conceived, and there can arise no doubt about it' (II.xxvii.28). The abstract, sortal, or 'specifick' idea tells us what is required for any individual falling under that idea to preserve its identity over time. In order to find out what constitutes identity through time, we have to determine exactly the abstract idea or nominal essence of that thing of which identity is to be predicated: 'To conceive, and judge of it [identity] aright, we must consider what *Idea* the Word it is applied to stands for: . . . for such as is the *Idea* belonging to that Name, such must be the *Identity*' (II.xxvii.7). According to Locke, then, when asking about the identity of a body we have first to be clear about what idea of 'body' we are applying. It makes a crucial difference whether by 'body' we mean an aggregate or collection of atoms or a living being (as a plant, an animal, or a human being): if we refer to a body as an aggregate of atoms, the preservation of the identity of that body requires that numerically the same atoms be retained. If, on the other hand, we refer to a living being, the sameness of all the particles is not required for identity. Locke says that in order to understand what makes an oak tree the same at different times, we have to 'consider wherein an Oak differs from a Mass of Matter' (II.xxvii.4). Since our idea of an oak tree is not that of an aggregate of atoms, different requirements of identity apply. An oak tree may lose some of its parts, and change its shape and size, without losing its identity. What is required for identity here is that the changing particles partake in the same organized life:

That being then one Plant, which has such an Organization of Parts in one coherent Body, partaking of one Common Life, it continues to be the same Plant, as long as it partakes of the same Life, though that Life be communicated to new Particles of Matter vitally united to the living Plant, in a like continued Organization, conformable to that sort of Plants. (II.xxvii.4)

Similarly, if we take the idea of a human being to be that of an 'organiz'd living Body' (II.xxvii.8), rather than that of a union of an immaterial and a material substance, then it is clear that the identity of a human being consists 'in nothing but a participation of the same continued Life, by constantly fleeting Particles of Matter, in succession vitally united to the same organized Body' (II.xxvii.6).

Despite Locke's explicit pronouncement concerning the role of the 'specifick idea' for questions of identity, however, his discussion of particular cases (oak, horse, man) could be read as suggesting that the specific idea does not, after all, play a role in determining identity. On this reading, Locke's account of identity is merely nominalistic in tone, but not in content. For (1) Locke seems to assume that there is just one very general principle of identity for plants, animals, and human beings alike;

that is, life. And (2), although it follows from the emphasis on the specific idea that people with different ideas of man will have different answers to questions about the identity of a man, Locke does not seem to suppose such a thing. Again, he seems to take it that everybody would accept the same general principle: namely, 'life'. Close attention to Locke's text, however, reveals that he consistently adheres to the view that the specific idea has a crucial function to fulfil in questions about identity. Regarding (1), although the identity of a man is secured by the same very general principle as is the identity of plants and animals—life—it is not the same sort of life in each case. Locke distinguishes between different sorts of life: horse-life is (obviously) not the same as oak-life; and that is, horse-identity is not the same as oak-identity. An oak is 'such a disposition of [particles of matter] as constitutes the parts of an Oak; and such an Organization of those parts, as is fit to receive, and distribute nourishment, so as to continue, and frame the Wood, Bark, and Leaves, etc. of an Oak, in which consists the vegetable Life'. The organization of particles which secures the identity of an oak is one that is 'conformable to that sort of Plants' (II.xxvii.4, last two quotations). Similarly, if our idea of man is that of a 'vital union of Parts in a certain shape' (in a human shape), then 'as long as that vital union and shape remains... it will be the same *Man*' (II.xxvii.29). Regarding (2): it is evident from sections 21 and 29 of the chapter on identity that Locke supposes that people with different ideas of man would have different answers to questions about the identity of a man. He says, 'supposing a rational Spirit be the *Idea* of a *Man*', then 'the *same Spirit*, whether separate or in a Body will be the *same Man*' (II.xxvii.29; see also sections 15 and 6). It is just that Locke believes that his notion of man is the most appropriate, and that it conforms to the idea of man 'in most Peoples Sense' (II.xxvii.8). So, there is no reason to believe that Locke disagreed with Boyle's statement, cited in the previous Chapter, that our concepts determine what is required for the identity of objects over time. Locke expresses this point again in the final sentence of the chapter: 'For whatever be the composition whereof the complex *Idea* is made, whenever Existence makes it one particular thing under any denomination, the same Existence continued, preserves it the same individual *under the same denomination*' (last emphasis mine) (II.xxvii.29). According to Locke, then, what constitutes the identity of a being through time is the continued fulfilment of those requirements which are specified by that abstract idea under which we consider the being: there can be no satisfactory treatment of identity through time independently of our abstract ideas of those things whose identity is in question.

3.3. LOCKE ON MAN, SOUL, AND PERSON

In accordance with this general theory Locke argues that we need to be clear about the concept of person in order to be able to determine what constitutes the identity of persons: 'To find wherein *personal Identity* consists, we must consider what *Person* stands for.'²⁵ And to be clear about the concept of person we have to distinguish it carefully from those of thinking substance or spirit, and of man or human being. Locke attaches considerable importance to these distinctions, both when he introduces the topic (II.xxvvii.7) and in his discussion of specific issues (for example, II. xxvii.15, 20, 21). Many of his critics—both in his own time and today—reject these distinctions; indeed, many commentators to this day do not accept that Locke meant to distinguish between person, spiritual substance, and man. But for Locke himself, as he makes clear enough, although these concepts are closely related and may be applied to the same individual being, they denote different aspects, respectively, under which we may consider the human subject; and they need to be distinguished from one another for an account of identity, for each of these concepts carries with it different identity criteria:

> But yet when we will enquire, what makes the same *Spirit*, *Man*, or *Person*, we must fix the *Ideas* of *Spirit*, *Man*, or *Person*, in our Minds; and having resolved with our selves what we mean by them, it will not be hard to determine, in either of them, or the like, when it is the *same*, and when not. (II.xxvii.15)

Earlier in the chapter, before going into the details of the personal identity issue, Locke emphasises:

> But to conceive, and judge of it [identity] aright, we must consider what *Idea* the Word it is applied to stands for: It being one thing to be the same *Substance*, another the same *Man*, and a third the same *Person*, if *Person*, *Man*, and *Substance*, are three Names standing for three different *Ideas*; for such as is the *Idea* belonging to that Name, such must be the *Identity*. (II.xxvii.7)²⁶

Locke's position is that 'man' and 'person' denote different abstract ideas which may be applied to the human subject—which has the consequence that there are different possible answers to the question about the identity of the human subject, depending on which abstract idea we apply. Locke says: 'If it be possible for the same Man to have distinct incommunicable consciousness at different times, *it is past doubt the*

---

[25] Locke, *Essay*, II.xxvii.9.
[26] Although Locke distinguishes explicitly between spiritual substances or 'finite spirits' and persons, several commentators persist in ascribing to Locke the view that identifies the two. Flew, for example, invents a 'Platonic–Cartesian' notion of substance and interprets Locke's concept of a person in terms of it: 'Locke and the Problem of Personal Identity', in Martin and Armstrong (eds.), *Locke and Berkeley: A Collection of Critical Essays* (1968), pp. 155–78. Compare, Loptson, 'Locke, Reid, and Personal Identity', *The Philosophical Forum*, 35 (2004), 51–63, at 60–1. According to Loptson, Locke's view is 'rather close' to that of his critics such as 'Butler and Reid' (61). For Locke, Loptson maintains, 'human persons are the same as...human finite spirits, and these are substances' (ibid.). See also Loptson, 'Man, Person, Spirits in Locke's *Essay*', *Eighteenth-Century Thought*, 3 (2007), 359–72, where he rejects the view of those who 'want to deny that *person*, for Locke, designates a substance' (369). For similar interpretations, see Mattern 'Moral Science and the Concept of Person in Locke', *Philosophical Review*, 89 (1980), 24–45; Atherton, 'Locke's Theory of Personal Identity', *Midwest Studies in Philosophy*, 8 (1983), 273–93; Gallie, 'The Same Self', *The Locke Newsletter*, 18 (1987), 45–62; Alston and Bennett, 'Locke on People and Substances', *Philosophical Review*, 97 (1988), 25–46; and Winkler, 'Locke on Personal Identity', *Journal of the History of Philosophy*, 29 (1991), 201–26.

same Man would at different times make different Persons.'[27] In other words, it is possible for *a* (at time *t*) to be identical with *b* (at time *t+n*) with respect to the notion of man, but not in regard to the notion of person, even though both notions may be applied to both *a* and *b*.[28] Some commentators, however, have argued that in Locke 'man' and 'person' do not denote two different ideas under which we may consider the human subject, but two distinct *things* occupying the same place; for on this reading of Locke there is never a case where an individual *a* is both the same man and not the same person as an individual *b*. And so, Locke is said to be committed to a 'doctrine of double existence'. At time *t* we do not have one subject to which different ideas may be applied, but two entities: one man and one person.[29] The following passage, for example, seems to suggest that Locke adopts the 'doctrine of double existence'. When distinguishing his account from the common sense view according to which 'man' and 'person' are synonymous terms, he says: 'I know that in the ordinary way of speaking, the same Person, and the same Man, stand for one and the same thing.'[30] This may be taken to imply that Locke's own view is that man and person are two distinct things. The passage need not be read that way, however. Rather, it may be interpreted as a statement about the use of the terms 'man' and 'person', which are said by Locke to denote distinct *ideas*—abstract ideas—which may be applied to the human subject.[31] The latter interpretation is confirmed by the moral and legal dimensions of Locke's theory (discussed below), which show that his concept of person (for which he also uses the term 'personality') comes close to the traditional notion of person as moral quality. There is thus a striking similarity between Locke's notion of person and Pufendorf's notion of the person as a moral and modal entity. As noted in the previous Chapter, the Pufendorfian notion of personality as a mode allows for thinking of persons *in analogy* to substances, *as if* they were substances. This would also apply to Locke's notion. In short, Locke

---

[27] Locke, *Essay*, II.xxvii.20 (my italics). Locke's man–person distinction is still a focus in twentieth-century debates over personal identity. See Wiggins, *Sameness and Substance* (1980), pp. 29, 37, 161; Chappell, 'Locke and Relative Identity', *History of Philosophy Quarterly*, 6 (1989), 69–83; Snowdon, 'Persons, Animals, and Ourselves', in Gill (ed.), *The Person and the Human Mind* (1990), pp. 83–107; Thornton, 'Same Human Being, Same Person?', *Philosophy*, 66 (1991),115–18; Ayers, *Locke* (1991), vol. 2, pp. 283ff.; and Baillie, 'Recent Work on Personal Identity', *Philosophical Books*, 34 (1993), 197.

[28] For a discussion of this reading, see also Thiel, 'Individuation', in Garber and Ayers (eds.), *The Cambridge History of Seventeenth-Century Philosophy* (1998), pp. 212–62.

[29] This is how Chappell interprets Locke's distinction between man and person. See especially Chappell (1989), 76–80. He bases his interpretation on an analysis of two of Locke's examples: the 'prince–cobbler case' (*Essay*, II.xxvii.15), and the 'day-and-night-man case' (*Essay*, II.xxvii.23). Similarly, Bolton holds that there is in Locke a 'duplication of individuals'—namely, of thinking substances and persons—claiming that this ontological distinction, rather than a conceptual distinction, is crucial to Locke's theory of personal identity. Bolton, 'Locke on Identity: The Scheme of Simple and Compounded Things', in Barber and Gracia (eds.), *Individuation and Identity in Early Modern Philosophy* (1994), pp. 103–31. For a discussion of Bolton's reading, see Thiel, '"Epistemologism" and Early Modern Debates about Individuation and Identity', *British Journal for the History of Philosophy*, 5 (1997), 353–72, esp. 363–6.

[30] Locke, *Essay*, II.xxvii.15.

[31] Chappell (1989), 72, concedes that Locke 'is of course notorious for his use of thing-language to refer to ideas'.

regards soul or spirit, man, and person(ality) as different abstract ideas under which we may consider the human subject.

With respect to the thinking substance or soul, Locke not only rejects the Cartesian view that the soul always thinks; he also argues more generally, as Gassendi and others before him, that we have no certain knowledge at all about the real essence of the soul: we know that we have the faculty of thought, but our knowledge does not go beyond the evidence of inner experience. We do not know whether the substance which thinks is an immaterial or a material being. Although Locke believes it is 'more probable' that the thinking substance is immaterial,[32] he regards it as possible that matter has the power to think. Accordingly, he does not definitely make up his mind between a Cartesian dualist account of man and the view of man as an 'organiz'd living Body'.[33] He favours the non-dualist position only insofar as our (ordinary) *idea* of man is concerned.[34] However, which account of man and of soul we choose is, to Locke, irrelevant to the problem of *personal* identity, for we have to distinguish the concept of person from both that of the soul and that of man in any case. We shall return to this important distinction between person, man, and spiritual substance in the next Chapter. As Locke accounts for persons and personal identity in terms of the notion of consciousness, the latter must be examined first.

3.4 LOCKE ON CONSCIOUSNESS

Locke argues that 'it is the consciousness...which makes the same *Person* and constitutes this inseparable *self*' (II.xxvii.17). For Locke, to consider the human subject as a person is to consider it with regard to all those thoughts and actions of which it is conscious. But what is consciousness according to Locke? This question cannot be as easily answered as it might seem. Some, like Thomas Reid, read Locke's notion of consciousness as memory. This view has had a considerable influence on the interpretation of Locke and his account of personal identity in particular. Others seem to think that consciousness is basically the same as reflection. On the reading presented here Locke equates consciousness neither with memory nor with reflection. But it has to be determined what consciousness is and how it is related to notions such as memory and reflection in order to understand the role that he assigns to that notion in his account of personal identity.

---

[32] Locke, *Essay*, II.xxvii.25.
[33] Ibid., II.xxvii.8. See also ibid., II.i.11, and II.xxvii.21.
[34] Wright has argued that Locke's thinking about the soul and the 'man' was influenced by a seventeenth-century Epicurean account of the material soul as the principle of life—that of Thomas Willis, in *Two Discourses Concerning the Souls of Brutes, which is also that of the Vital and Sensitive Part of Man*, trans. Pordage (1683; Latin original, 1672). See Wright, 'Locke, Willis, and the seventeenth-century Epicurean soul', in Osler (ed.) *Atoms, Pneuma, and Tranquillity: Epicurean and Stoic Themes in European Thought* (1991), pp. 239–58.

One reason for the problems of interpreting Locke's account of consciousness is that he does not say very much about it.[35] There is no chapter, no section in Locke's *Essay* entitled 'On consciousness'. In fact, even the term 'consciousness' does not occur very often at all in Locke's writings. In the *First Draft* of the *Essay* Locke uses 'consciousness' only once, and even in the *Essay* itself the term does not occur very often, except for the chapter on identity.[36] There are passages which may suggest that Locke simply equates consciousness with reflection, and many of his readers have interpreted his text in this way.[37] He may simply follow other writers of the time who identify consciousness with inner sense or reflection. Thus, John Wilkins states that the 'inward sense' is that 'by which we can discern *internal* objects, and are conscious to our selves, or sensible both of the impressions that are made upon our outward *senses*, and of the inward motions of our *minds*.'[38] Locke, in the first chapter of Book II, states that reflection is 'the Perception of the Operations of our own Minds within us' (sect. 4), and a few sections later that consciousness is 'the perception of what passes in a Man's own mind' (sect. 19). The two statements are not identical, but they would seem to be sufficiently similar to suggest that consciousness and reflection are the same thing for Locke. One could speculate about whether there is any real difference between 'operations of our own minds' and 'what passes within us'.[39] If there is no essential difference between the two, then perhaps we could equate consciousness and reflection in Locke. It should be noted that the term 'operations' here is to be understood in a very broad sense. It refers not only to 'Actions of the Mind about its *Ideas*', but also to 'some sort of Passions arising sometimes from them, such as is the satisfaction or uneasiness arising from any thought' (II.i.4). Thus some mental states are included under the title of 'operations'. Maybe for Locke all mental operations are something that 'passes in a Man's own mind', but not everything that 'passes in a Man's own mind' is a mental operation (it may be a state), so that the notion of consciousness is broader than that of reflection. Even if this were the case, however, it could still be argued that reflection and consciousness are the same kind of relating to operations and to other things that pass 'in a Man's own mind'. For Locke characterizes both reflection and consciousness in terms of the notion of perception. If there is a difference between consciousness and reflection at all, it would seem to be a difference that relates to the object, not to the nature of the activity involved.

---

[35] Thus, it is somewhat surprising that Kemmerling claims that Locke is a philosopher who 'schwelgt' in the terminology of consciousness: *Ideen des Ichs. Studien zu Descartes* (1996), p. 193.

[36] Strangely, Kulstad does not consider II.27 at all in his thirty-five page chapter on 'Locke on Consciousness and Reflection', in *Leibniz on Apperception, Consciousness and Reflection* (1991). His interpretation of Locke's understanding of consciousness is based on passages in the first chapter of the second book of the *Essay*.

[37] Kulstad (1991), p. 115, claims that Locke is confused: 'No consistent and definitive stand is taken one way or the other on the sameness or difference of reflection and consciousness of mental operations.'

[38] Wilkins, *Of the Principles and Duties of Natural Religion* (1677), p. 3.

[39] Kulstad (1991), for example, reflects on this (p. 88).

If we accept what the cited passages from *Essay* II.i.4 and 19 suggest, it would seem to be easy to determine what Locke's understanding of 'consciousness' is. Although Locke does not say much about consciousness, he does say a fair amount about reflection. And if consciousness is the same as reflection, then his account of reflection may also be applied to consciousness. He says about reflection that it is the only other experiential source of simple ideas, apart from sensation. It is 'the other fountain from which Experience furnisheth the Understanding with Ideas'. Our own mental operations, 'when the soul comes to reflect on and consider, do furnish the understanding with another set of *ideas*, which could not be had from things without: and such are *Perception, Thinking, Doubting, Believing, Reasoning, Knowing, Willing*, and all the different actings of our own Minds'. And: 'This source of *Ideas* every *Man* has wholly in himself: And though it be not Sense, as having nothing to do with external Objects, yet it is very like it, and might properly enough be call'd internal Sense.' He calls this source of ideas 'reflection' because 'the *Ideas* it affords being such only as the mind gets by reflecting on its own Operations within it self' (II.i.4).

According to Locke, then, in reflection we turn our own mental operations into objects of inner observation; and for this to be possible it is required that we turn our attention to these operations. 'The Understanding turns inwards upon it self, *reflects* on its own *Operations*, and makes them the Object of its own Contemplation' (II.i.8). 'Unless he turn his Thoughts that way, and considers them [Operations of his Mind] *attentively*', he will have no clear and distinct ideas of his operations. He has to apply '*himself with attention*' (II.i.7).[40] For Locke, therefore, reflection is a

---

[40] Lähteenmäki, 'The Sphere of Experience in Locke. The Relations between Reflection, Consciousness and Ideas', *Locke Studies*, 8 (2008), 59–100, claims that there are two distinct and clearly defined conceptions of reflection in Locke. (1) Reflection as a source of ideas which is completely passive: here, attention and what Locke calls 'contemplation' are not involved. And there are no mental operations on which we do not reflect in this sense, that is to say we acquire ideas of all of our mental operations (92ff.). (2) Reflection as an operation about ideas which is voluntary and attentive. It is only this type of reflection that Locke characterizes by the notion of 'contemplation' (59, 68–9). Only this type of reflection presupposes consciousness: namely, consciousness of the *ideas* which we have acquired through the first type of reflection (60). It is highly problematic, however, to ascribe this distinction to Locke. Although there are passages in which Locke uses the terminology of 'reflection' in a general and indeterminate sense that is not identical with the definition of reflection (in *Essay*, II.i.4) as a source of ideas (see, for example, II.xxviii.12; III. v.16), this does not justify the ascription of two clearly defined and distinct notions of reflection to Locke, as envisaged by Lähteenmäki. (Mishori, 'Locke on the Inner Sense and Inner Observation', *Locke Studies*, 4 (2004), 145–81, even distinguishes 'four meanings of Lockian reflection'.) Locke's text simply does not support Lähteenmäki's interpretation. For example, *pace* Lähteenmäki, the notion of contemplation is used by Locke to characterize reflection as a source of ideas. In *Essay*, II. i.7, Locke notes that if we contemplate the operations of the mind (the operations themselves), we will acquire ideas of them. In order to acquire ideas of mental operations, the mind 'turns its view inward upon it self, and observes its own Actions' (II.vi.1; see also II.I.24). Of course, 'contemplation' is broader than reflection understood as a source of ideas, so that not every contemplation can be explained in terms of reflection; but every act of reflection by which we acquire ideas of mental operations involves an activity that Locke characterizes through notions such as contemplation and attention. Finally, Locke nowhere states that we acquire ideas of all of our mental operations and that there are no unreflected-on operations. Rather, he says that it is 'pretty late, before most Children get *Ideas* of the Operations of their own Minds' (II.i.8), and that 'in time

mental act that is directed towards other mental acts—a higher-order perception (HOP) of other perceptions.[41] And if consciousness is to be equated with reflection, consciousness too must be a HOP. According to this reading, then, Locke is a proponent of a HOP account of consciousness. And many—both proponents and critics of the HOP account of consciousness—have read Locke in this way. According to William Lycan, for example, 'Locke put forward the theory of consciousness as 'internal sense' or 'reflection'—on which theory, consciousness is perception-like second order representing of our own psychological states'.[42] This reading of Locke's notion of consciousness in terms of a higher-order act of perception was, however, proposed much earlier. For example, it is present in Leibniz,[43] who simply assumes that 'consciousness' is the same as 'reflection' in Locke. This is obvious from Leibniz's critique of Locke in *Nouveaux essais* (II.i.19). In the corresponding passage in the *Essay*, Locke states that for him thought is always (and necessarily) conscious thought. Now, Leibniz takes Locke to be saying that thought is always accompanied by an act of reflection—a higher-order act of perception. It is clear from Leibniz's critique of Locke that he reads Lockean 'consciousness' in terms of reflection. He first translates Locke's 'being conscious' (of thoughts) as 's'apercevoir de'. But then he makes use of the terminology of reflection and says:

It is impossible that we should always reflect explicitly on all our thoughts; for if we did, the mind would reflect on each reflection, *ad infinitum*, without ever being able to move on to a new thought. For example, in being aware of ['en m'appercevant de'] some present feeling, I should have always to think that I think about that feeling, and further to think that I think of thinking about it, and so on *ad infinitum*. It must be that I stop reflecting on all these reflections, and that eventually some thought is allowed to occur without being thought about; otherwise I would dwell for ever on the same thing.[44]

---

the Mind comes to reflect on its operations about the *Ideas* got by *Sensation*, and thereby stores it self with a new set of *Ideas*' (II.i.24). We do not necessarily reflect on our mental operations, for Locke says: 'Whoever reflects on what passes in his own Mind, cannot miss it. And *if he does not reflect* [my italics], all the Words in the World cannot make him have any notion of it' (II.ix.2). On this point, then, I am in agreement with Scharp, who argues that for Locke, 'the mind does not reflect on all its mental operations'. See Scharp, 'Locke's Theory of Reflection', *British Journal for the History of Philosophy*, 16 (2008), 25–63, at 27, 34–6.

[41] For discussions of present-day HOP accounts of consciousness, see, for example, Gennaro (ed.), *Higher Order Theories of Consciousness: An Anthology* (2004).

[42] Lycan, 'Consciousness as Internal Monitoring', in Block, Flanagan, and Guzeldere (eds.), *The Nature of Consciousness: Philosophical Debates* (1997), pp. 755–71, at 755. For other ascriptions of a HOP account of consciousness to Locke, see, for example, Guzeldere, 'Is Consciousness the Perception of What Passes in a Man's own Mind?', in Metzinger (ed.), *Conscious Experience* (1995), pp. 335–58, at p. 335; Carruthers, 'HOP over FOR, HOT Theory', in Gennaro (2004), pp. 115–58, at p. 118.

[43] Thomas Reid claims that 'Mr. LOCKE has ... confounded reflection with consciousness, and seems not to have been aware that they are different powers': *Essays on the Intellectual Powers of Man*, ed. Brookes (2002), p. 421.

[44] The English translation is from *New Essays on Human Understanding*, trans. Remnant and Bennett (1981), p. 118. The French original reads: 'il n'est pas possible que nous reflechissions tousjours expressement sur toutes nos pensées; autrement l'Esprit feroit reflexion sur chaque reflexion à l'infini sans pouvoir jamais passer à une nouvelle pensée. Par exemple, en m'appercevant de quelque sentiment present, je devrois toujours penser que j'y pense, et penser

As a critique of Locke, this (old) argument from infinite regress makes sense only if it is assumed that consciousness is an act of reflection—a higher-order mental act. Leibniz's critique would be correct if Locke's conception of consciousness were indeed identical with reflection. For, as was indicated in the Introduction, the combination of a HOP account of consciousness with the thesis that all thought is accompanied by consciousness yields the infinite regress that Leibniz discusses. Locke would be saying, then, that thought is always accompanied by a higher-order act of perception.[45]

Indeed, even if we assumed a distinction between consciousness and reflection in Locke, this would by itself not be sufficient to defend Locke against Leibniz's critique. For it would still be possible that Locke conceives of consciousness in terms of a HOP, but of a kind that is different from reflection. This is an interpretation suggested by, for example, Mark Kulstad, who thinks that Locke is confused about the relation between consciousness and reflection,[46] but claims that if there is a distinction between the two in Locke it would be a distinction between two kinds of HOP.[47] On this reading, consciousness in Locke is a higher-order operation, but can give us merely 'obscure ideas' of our mental operations.[48] This is so because consciousness does not focus attention on the latter. Reflection, by contrast, is said to be 'equivalent to focusing attention on one's mental operations'; thus reflection, but not consciousness, provides us with 'clear and distinct ideas of operations of the mind'.[49] Therefore, if there is a distinction in Locke between consciousness and reflection, it is between two types of higher-order activity: in the one case (reflection) we focus attention on mental operations, and in the other case (consciousness) we do not focus our attention that way. This reading is not without its problems, for more than one reason, as it suggests that consciousness is a source of ideas, and thus

encor que je pense d'y penser, et ainsi à l'infini. Mais il faut bien que je cesse de reflechir sur toutes ces réflexions et qu'il y ait enfin quelque pensée qu'on laisse passer sans y penser; autrement on demeureroit tousjours sur la même chose' *Nouveaux essais*, II.i.19, Leibniz, *Die Philosophischen Schriften*, ed. Gerhardt, vol. 5).

[45] For a detailed discussion of this, see also Thiel, 'Leibniz and the Concept of Apperception', *Archiv für Geschichte der Philosophie*, 76 (1994), 195–209.

[46] Kulstad (1991), p. 115.

[47] Ibid., 86–7.

[48] Recently, Locke's statement that 'the Operations of our minds, will not let us be without, at least some obscure Notions of them. No Man, can be wholly ignorant of what he does, when he thinks' (*Essay*, II.i.25) has led to some debate. Does Locke say here that *consciousness* is a source of ideas, or is he talking about reflection? Does he perhaps identify reflection and consciousness here? As noted, Kulstad (1991), pp. 86–7, 108, thinks Locke has in mind consciousness understood as a higher-order activity, but as distinct from reflection. Lähteenmäki (2008), 70, assumes that Locke is referring to reflection, although the term is not even used in the relevant section. I tend to agree with Weinberg's reading that the 'obscure Notions' are due to consciousness understood as distinct from reflection and, more generally, as distinct from any second-order perception: 'The Coherence of Consciousness in Locke's *Essay*', *History of Philosophy Quarterly*, 25 (2008), 24, 28–9. Indeed, Locke's statement when explaining the 'obscure notions' we have of our mental operations is very similar to his account of consciousness as something that 'is inseparable from thinking, and as it seems to me essential to it: ... When we hear, see, smell, taste, feel, meditate, or will any thing, we know that we do so. Thus it is always as to our present Sensations and Perceptions' (*Essay*, II. xxvii.9).

[49] Kulstad (1991), p. 108.

introduces a third experiential source of simple ideas, apart from sensation and reflection which would contradict Locke's thesis that sensation and reflection are the only sources of such ideas. More problematic than this in the present context is that the introduction of this kind of distinction between consciousness and reflection cannot save Locke from Leibniz's critique. For the thesis that consciousness is a HOP (but different from reflection), combined with Locke's thesis that all thought is accompanied by consciousness, would still yield the infinite regress pointed out by Leibniz.

Recent defenders of the HOP account of consciousness may, perhaps with good reason, reject the thesis that all mental states are conscious and avoid the infinite regress issue this way, although this move would then raise the question of how the conscious can be grounded in the unconscious.[50] In any case, it would obviously not be an option for Locke, as that thesis is an essential feature of his account of consciousness. More recent discussions of Locke have instead rejected the standard reading of Locke discussed above, according to which Locke is a proponent of a HOP account of consciousness.[51] This is the reading defended here (and previously). If it is correct, Leibniz's critique in terms of the infinite regress issue misses the mark. But what is consciousness, according to Locke, if it is not a HOP, and how is it to be distinguished from reflection?

Although the two passages from *Essays*, II.i.4 and 19 seem to suggest that Locke equates consciousness with reflection, it is evident from a number of other passages in the *Essay* (i) that he implies a distinction between consciousness and reflection, and (ii) that this is not a distinction between two types of HOP. Locke says that 'consciousness... is *inseparable* from thinking, and as it seems to me essential to it... When we see, hear, smell, taste, feel, meditate, or will any thing, we know that we do so. Thus it is always as to our present Sensations and Perceptions'.[52] For Locke, 'being conscious' denotes an immediate awareness that is an integral part of all acts of thinking as such. Locke says that 'thinking *consists* in being conscious that one thinks' (my italics) (II.i.19). Consciousness is an essential element of thought and is 'inseparable' from it. And Locke makes it quite clear that what he means by 'reflection' is, unlike consciousness, not an essential element of thought as such. He does not say that thinking consists in reflection; he says it consists in consciousness. As we have seen, 'reflection' is Locke's technical term for inner sense; and reflection, he says, requires a special attention (II.i.24). His definition of reflection in terms of

---

[50] See Coventry and Kriegel, 'Locke on Consciousness', *History of Philosophy Quarterly*, 25 (2008), 225; Kriegel, 'Consciousness as Intransitive Self-Consciousness: Two Views and an Argument', *Canadian Journal of Philosophy*, 33 (2003), 103–32.

[51] See for example, Thiel, 'Leibniz and the Concept of Apperception' (1994), 195–209; Thiel, 'Hume's Notions of Consciousness and Reflection in Context', *British Journal for the History of Philosophy*, 2 (1994), 75–115; and Thiel, 'Der Begriff der Intuition bei Locke', *Aufklärung*, 18 (2006), 95–112. See also Mishori (2004), 145–81, at 160; Weinberg (2008), 21–39; and Coventry and Kriegel (2008), 221–42.

[52] Locke, *Essay*, II.xxvii.9; my italics. See also II.i.10: 'Our being sensible of it is not necessary to any thing, but to our thoughts; and to them it is; and to them it will always be necessary, till we can think without being conscious of it.'

inner sense means that reflection is not an immediate relation of oneself to oneself, and is not to be associated with consciousness. According to Locke, through reflection the mind relates to itself in the sense that it observes its own operations and produces ideas of them;[53] and he links reflection, but not consciousness, to contemplation.[54] In other words, consciousness is a presence of the mind to itself that is more fundamental than the objectifying reflection: the essential difference is that, unlike reflection, consciousness is not a HOP. Without consciousness, reflection would not have any objects upon which to reflect. Both sensation and reflection are conscious acts; but for Locke they are not necessarily accompanied by an act of reflection.[55]

Further evidence for ascribing to Locke a distinction between consciousness and reflection can be derived from changes that Locke made to later editions of the *Essay*. Consider for example the following passage from IV.iii.23. In editions 1–4 the passage reads: 'All the simple *Ideas* we have are confined... to those we receive from corporeal Objects by *Sensation*, and from the Operations of our own Minds, *that we are conscious of* in our selves' (last italics mine). This formulation could be read as saying that *consciousness* is the source of ideas of mental operations, and that consequently, consciousness is the same as reflection. Obviously, in order to avoid such a misinterpretation Locke changed the passage for the fifth edition by replacing the terminology of consciousness with that of reflection. Now he speaks of 'the Operations of our own Minds as the Objects of *Reflection*'.

Against this reading it can (and has been) objected that if, as this reading suggests, Locke would allow that consciousness relates directly to mental states and operations, then he would allow for objects of experience that are not ideas, and this would contradict his explicit thesis that only ideas can be objects of thought and experience.[56] As noted above, he nowhere suggests that consciousness is or could be an additional source of ideas. If consciousness can relate directly to mental states and operations without producing ideas of them, however, then, as the objection states, he would allow for objects of thoughts and experience that are not ideas. Instead, it is argued, when Locke speaks of the consciousness of mental states and operations he must mean the consciousness of *ideas* of mental operations and states, and not a direct relation of consciousness to mental states and operations.[57] Thus when Locke says that we cannot perceive without being conscious that we perceive, according to

---

[53] 'By REFLECTION then... I would be understood to mean, that notice which the Mind takes of its own Operations, and the manner of them, by reason whereof there come to be *Ideas* of these Operations in the Understanding': *Essay*, II.i.4. 'In time, the Mind comes to reflect on its own *Operations*... and thereby stores it self with a new set of *Ideas*, which I call *Ideas* of *Reflection*': *Essay*, II.i.24.
[54] See *Essay*, II.vi.1, II.i.4, II.i.7, and II.i.8.
[55] This does not mean, of course, that we must be conscious of all aspects and elements or details of these complex processes. Compare II.viii.10 on implicit judgements. I thank Martin Lenz for drawing my attention to this.
[56] Lähteenmäki (2008), 60–1, 73.
[57] Both Lähteenmäki and Scharp hold that for Locke, consciousness does not relate directly to mental operations but only to ideas of them which have been acquired by reflection. See Lähteenmäki (2008), 85–6; and Scharp (2008), 30, 42.

this reading, Locke is saying that we are conscious of the *idea* of perceiving, not of the act of perceiving itself. And this idea of perceiving must of course be an idea of reflection—an idea that we have acquired through the mental operation of reflection. According to this interpretation, then, consciousness of mental operations presupposes reflection on the latter. But this reading is very implausible. Of course, for Locke to have ideas means that we are conscious of these ideas or at least can become conscious of them. But does he say anywhere that mental operations and states become conscious only *via* ideas of reflection? On the contrary, we saw that for him consciousness is inseparable from thinking and is essential to *it* (not just to the idea of thinking acquired through reflection). Thinking—not just the idea of thinking—consists in being conscious that one thinks (II.i.19). The relation of consciousness to thought is not mediated through ideas, but is immediate in the sense that consciousness belongs to thought itself.

But what about the objection that such a direct relation of consciousness to mental states and operations means that there are for Locke objects of thought and experience that are not ideas—which would contradict Locke's thesis that ideas are the only objects of thought and experience? The problem with this objection is that it conceives of mental states and operations as *objects* of consciousness in the same way as such operations and states are objects of reflection. As suggested by the passages quoted above, Locke thinks of the relationship between consciousness and thought in a different way. Thinking and other mental operations are not 'objects' that are somehow separate from consciousness; rather, they are characterized by an inherent reflexivity which Locke calls consciousness (rather than reflection). This reflexivity is part of their nature as mental states and operations. Consciousness or inherent reflexivity is not a relation which may hold sometimes but not other times. One can distinguish conceptually between the content and the consciousness of thought, but this does not mean that the two aspects could be separated from each other in reality. Reflection but not consciousness is an extrinsic relation to thought. Rather, as indicated above, in order for reflection to be able to relate to operations and states, the latter must always already be characterized as *mental* operations; that is to say, by that inherent reflexivity that Locke calls 'consciousness'. Locke's statement in II.i.4 about reflection can be interpreted along these lines. We can produce ideas of mental operations because we are conscious of them ('which we being conscious of'), and can therefore consider them through an act of reflection. He illustrates his thesis that thinking consists in being consciousness that one thinks by an analogy with hunger and the feeling of hunger. To say we could think without being conscious of thinking is, Locke states, as absurd as to say we are hungry without feeling hungry. Rather, being hungry consists in this feeling of hunger—this feeling is not something that needs to be added to hunger 'itself'. In the same way, consciousness is not something that needs to be added to thinking externally; rather, it is an aspect of thinking itself.

It is plain, then, that Locke is not a proponent of a HOP account of consciousness, as the traditional reading has it. Recently, philosophers who accept the reading presented here have labelled Locke's account a Same-Order Perception (SOP) account of consciousness.⁵⁸ I have no objection to the label as such, but the SOP account that is ascribed to Locke is typically explained in terms of later phenomenological theory—in particular, that of Franz Brentano.⁵⁹ And indeed, Brentano too constructs consciousness as something intrinsic that belongs to the mental phenomena themselves. Experience has two objects: a primary and a secondary object. 'In the same mental phenomenon in which the sound is present to our minds we simultaneously apprehend the mental phenomenon itself... We can say that the sound is the *primary object* of the *act* of hearing, and that the act of hearing itself is the *secondary object*.'⁶⁰ It is not clear, however, that Locke's position can be usefully illuminated by appeals to Brentano and other phenomenologists. In fact it seems unlikely that Locke would have endorsed Brentano's formulation of the SOP account of consciousness, since for Brentano the mental phenomenon is still an *object* of consciousness, even if merely a secondary one. And to liken Locke's account too much to that of Brentano would mean that, unnecessarily, objections that have been raised against Brentano become relevant to a discussion of Locke.⁶¹ Rather, in terms of its historical relations, Locke's account would seem to be closer to earlier seventeenth-century views with which he was familiar.

We have seen above that Cudworth introduced the term 'consciousness' into English philosophical terminology, arguing that consciousness is an immediate relating to one's own self. As Locke was very familiar with Cudworth's work and other relevant writings of the time, there can be no doubt that Cudworth's understanding of consciousness, and the notion as employed by thinkers such as William Sherlock and Robert South, are relevant background to an understanding of Locke's notion. But the account of consciousness that is closest to Locke's understanding of consciousness can be found in thinkers who attempted, within the framework of Cartesianism, to further develop the notion of consciousness: thinkers such as Louis de La Forge and in particular Antoine Arnauld, discussed in Chapter 1. We saw there that La Forge accounts for *conscience* explicitly in terms of an inherent reflexivity of thought itself, rather than as a second-order act of perception.⁶² Arnauld makes the same point by explaining consciousness in terms of a *réflexion virtuelle*, as distinct from a *réflexion expresse*; that is to say, in terms of the notion that

---

⁵⁸ See Coventry and Kriegel (2008), 221–42. Weinberg does not make use of the SOP terminology, but speaks of 'one-level' theories, and her interpretation of Locke is similar to that of Coventry and Kriegel: Weinberg (2008), 21–39. She says that for Locke, consciousness is 'a reflexive and proprietary constituent of ordinary perception' (26), but like Coventry and Kriegel she links Locke's account to that of Brentano (27–8; compare Coventry and Kriegel (2008), 226).

⁵⁹ Caston has argued convincingly that Brentano's account was strongly influenced by Aristotle. See Caston, 'Aristotle on Consciousness', *Mind*, 111 (2002), 751–815. Coventry and Kriegel's (2008) suggestion, however, that Locke too may have been influenced by Aristotle on consciousness, is highly speculative (228ff.). It is more likely that Locke's immediate context is relevant.

⁶⁰ Brentano, *Psychology from an Empirical Standpoint*, trans. Rancurello, Terrell, and McAlister (1973), pp. 127–8.

⁶¹ Weinberg seems to acknowledge this, and mentions the problems in Brentano that have been discussed in the literature, saying that Locke's account is only 'a bit like Brentano': Weinberg (2008), 27–8.

⁶² La Forge, *Traité de l'esprit de l'homme* (1666) p. 134. See also pp. 82, 112, 156–7.

'our thought or perception is essentially reflective on itself'.[63] Locke was very much familiar with Arnauld's work, and, indeed, his notion of consciousness is best understood in terms of an Arnauldian *réflexion virtuelle*.[64] Also, consciousness for Locke is to be understood as 'creature consciousness'. It is not the perception that is conscious, but the subject of thought. As he states, 'when we see hear, smell, taste, feel, meditate, or will any thing, *we* know that we do so' (II.xxvii.9, my italics).

3.5. LOCKE ON CONSCIOUSNESS, SELF-CONSCIOUSNESS, AND INTUITION

So far we have discussed consciousness as relating to mental states and operations, but Locke also speaks of consciousness as relating to our own self as the *subject* that has such states and performs such operations. Just as we are always immediately aware of our own thought, we are also aware in every act of thought that our own self exists as the subject of thought. 'In every Act of Sensation, Reasoning, or Thinking, we are conscious to our selves of our own Being' (IV.ix.3). Sometimes Locke describes this immediate awareness of our own existence as 'self-consciousness'.[65] Clearly, the consciousness of states and operations on the one hand and the consciousness of one's own existence or self-consciousness on the other are very closely connected in Locke. Moreover, both consciousness and self-consciousness are linked by him to the notion of intuition. Intuition or intuitive knowledge, too, relates to thoughts and ideas as well as to the existence of the self or subject. Like consciousness, intuition is an immediate self-relation which is characterized by absolute certainty. As soon as we perceive an idea we immediately perceive not only its existence, but also the identity and distinctness of its content. Locke says: 'there can be no *Idea* in the Mind, which it does not presently, by an intuitive Knowledge, perceive to be what it is, and to be different from any other'.[66] Yet although consciousness and intuition share the properties of immediacy and certainty, they are not simply identical. There is one type of intuitive knowledge which has self-evident truths as its object; it is this kind of intuitive knowledge which is the basis and essential element of what Locke calls 'demonstrative knowledge'. And he does not relate 'consciousness' to the knowledge of self-evident truths. If intuition

---

[63] Arnauld, *Des vrayes et des fausses idées* (1683) chap. 6, p. 46.
[64] Arnauld's *réflexion expresse* is not, however, identical with Locke's technical concept of reflection. Locke's reflection serves as an experiential source of a certain set of simple ideas. This may be included in Arnauld's notion, but even if it is, the latter is broader than Lockean reflection.
[65] In a journal note of 1696, Locke states that 'our own existence is known to us by a certainty yet higher than our senses can give us of the existence of other things, and that is internal perception, a self-consciousness or intuition' (MS Locke, c.28, fols. 119r–120v); printed in King, *The Life of John Locke* (1830), vol. 2, pp. 138–9. In the *Essay* chapter on identity (II.xxvii.16), Locke uses 'self-consciousness' only once, and as a term that refers not to the intuition of our own existence but to the consciousness of states, experiences, and operations.
[66] *Essay*, IV.iii.8. See also IV.i.4, IV.ii.1, IV.ii.14, IV.iii.3, and IV.vii.19.

is not the same as consciousness, how are these notions related to one another in Locke? The *Essay* does not deal with this question.

The relationship between consciousness and intuition is directly addressed (and clarified), however, in John Wynne's correspondence with Locke.[67] Wynne published a very successful 'abridgement' of Locke's *Essay* which first appeared in 1696. Writing to Locke in March 1695 about his 'almost finished' *Abridgement* of the *Essay*, he adds the following 'querie':

> Whether the knowledge we have of our own Existence, and the perception of our Sensations, be not A sort of knowledge *Sui generis* as we say, and different from Intuitive; and might not more properly be accounted A distinct sort, under the name of consciousness. (*The Correspondence of John Locke*, ed. de Beer, vol. 4 (1979), no. 1869)

In other words, Wynne wishes to distinguish more sharply than does Locke between consciousness and intuition. Wynne proposes a fourth kind of knowledge, in addition to Locke's sensitive, demonstrative, and intuitive knowledge: namely, consciousness. 'Consciousness' should refer to the immediate knowledge of our own existence and of our perceptions, whereas 'intuition' should be restricted to knowledge of self-evident truths. Although Locke's reply to this letter has not survived, Wynne's next letter to Locke allows us to infer what Locke's answer is: here Wynne refers to 'What you have said in answer to the quare propos'd in my last' (ibid., no. 1884). According to Wynne, Locke comprehends 'under the general Name of Intuition, the Knowledge we have of our own existence and thoughts as well as of self-evident Truths'. They all belong to one kind of knowledge because of their immediacy and their 'equal degree of certainty'. A distinction between different kinds of intuitive knowledge can be drawn, however, in relation to the objects of intuitive knowledge; that is, between (1) 'the Internal perception or Sensation of our own Existence', (2) 'the Consciousness of our thoughts', and (3) 'the perception of Self-evident Truths'. Now everything falls into place: to Locke, although one may distinguish between these three kinds of knowledge (in relation to the object of knowledge), one should regard all three of them as forms of intuitive knowledge, because they are all characterized by immediacy and absolute certainty.[68]

Consciousness, then, is not identical with intuition as such, but only with that type of intuition that relates to ideas and perceptions. And self-consciousness relates to intuition only in the first sense, as an 'internal perception' of one's own existence. Clearly, self-consciousness in this sense is closely linked to the consciousness of mental states and operations. By way of the consciousness we have of mental states and operations, we perceive immediately—that is, intuitively—our own existence.

---

[67] The relevance of this correspondence to an understanding of Locke's concept of intuition was first discussed in Thiel, 'Leibniz and the Concept of Apperception' (1994), 203, and in Thiel, 'Hume's Notions of Consciousness and Reflection in Context' (1994), 75–115.

[68] Clearly, Locke's argument that consciousness is a type of intuition constitutes additional support for the view that he distinguishes between consciousness and reflection: for Locke does not link reflection to intuition, and he does not describe reflection in terms of the notions of immediacy and absolute certainty. Consciousness, but not reflection, is understood as an immediate form of relating to one's own self and said to be a quality of all thoughts as such.

Therefore, the knowledge of our own existence 'neither needs, nor is capable of any proof' (*Essay* IV.ix.3). Very much like Descartes, Locke states that 'if I doubt of all other Things, that very doubt makes me perceive my own *Existence*, and will not suffer me to doubt of that' (ibid.).[69] Performing a mental operation involves the consciousness of the latter, and this in turn involves the consciousness of the existence of the subject that performs the operation. 'If I know I *doubt*, I have as certain a Perception of the Existence of the thing doubting, as of that Thought, which I call *doubt*. Experience then convinces us, that *we have an intuitive Knowledge of our own Existence*, and an internal infallible Perception that we are' (ibid.).[70]

Unlike Descartes, however, Locke holds that we cannot know the nature or real essence of 'the thing doubting' or soul. This brings us back to his distinction, discussed above, between the notions of soul as substance, man, and person. As with all substances, Locke holds with respect to the thinking thing or substance that we can acquire ideas of their operations through experience (in this case, inner sense or reflection), and we know intuitively that there must be something—a 'thing' or substance—that performs these operations, though our knowledge does not extend to the nature of this substance called soul: ''Tis past controversy, that we have in us something that thinks, our very Doubts about what it is, confirm the certainty of its being, though we must content our selves in the Ignorance of what kind of *Being* it is' (IV.iii.6). In short, metaphysical questions about the material or immaterial nature of the soul are beyond human knowledge. Therefore, the question of the identity of the human subject should relate not to the soul as substance, but to what Locke calls the person or personality.

---

[69] In the early 'Drafts' (1671) for the *Essay* Locke explicitly refers to Descartes in this context, without, however, making use of the notion of intuition. See Nidditch and Rogers (eds.), *John Locke. Drafts for the Essay concerning Human Understanding and other Philosophical Writings. Drafts A and B* (1990), Draft A, §§10, 27; Draft B, §35.

[70] In some places, however, Locke seems to suggest that we know the existence of our own self inferentially rather than intuitively. See, for example, *Essay*, II.i.10. For a discussion of this, see Thiel (2006), 95–112, at 102–6.

4

Locke on personal identity: consciousness, memory, and self-concern

As indicated above, for Locke a person is the human subject considered with regard to all those thoughts and actions of which it is or can become conscious. The inner nature or real essence of this subject as soul or substance is irrelevant to its personality. And the identity of a person is constituted by this consciousness of thoughts and actions. Consciousness is that 'which makes the same *Person*, and constitutes this inseparable *self*'.[1]

4.1. PERSONAL IDENTITY: CONSCIOUSNESS AND MEMORY

Consciousness constitutes the person and its identity by unifying thoughts and actions (II.xxvii.16). We saw that for Locke, consciousness 'is inseparable from thinking, and... essential to it' (II.xxvii.9). By virtue of its presence in all acts of thinking, consciousness functions as a unifier of thoughts and actions. The latter are 'appropriated to me' by consciousness (II.xxvii.16). 'That with which the *consciousness* of this present thinking thing can join it self, makes the same *Person*' (II.xxvii.17). This is why speculations about the soul's materiality or immateriality are irrelevant to an understanding of the human subject as a person. Even if we knew for certain which account of thinking substance is correct, personal identity would still have to be determined in terms of consciousness. We saw that in the early manuscript note of 1683 Locke argues that even if the mind consisted of 'corporeal spirits', the identity of the person would not be constituted by 'their being the same', but by consciousness. And in the *Essay* Locke points out that "tis evident the *personal Identity* would equally be determined by the consciousness, whether that consciousness were annexed to some individual immaterial Substance or no' (II.xxvii.23). Whereas Cartesians and Platonists alike hold that the identity of the person is secured by the soul's unchanging immaterial nature, Locke argues that 'whether we are the same thinking thing; *i.e.* the same substance or no' is a question which 'concerns not *personal Identity* at all' (II.xxvii.10).[2]

---

[1] Locke, *An Essay Concerning Human Understanding*, ed. Nidditch (1975), II.xxvii.17.
[2] It is clear from the above and from Locke's account of consciousness that the latter relates to thoughts and actions and *via* these to the subject or substance that thinks and acts. That is how

Locke's position, then, can be described as follows: consciousness presupposes a thinking substance (or man) as the agent who performs acts of consciousness and those thoughts and actions to which consciousness relates; consciousness does not bring about the identity of the human subject as soul or man. While Cartesians and Scholastics identify either the soul or the man with the person as a *res* whose individuality is constituted independently of and prior to consciousness, Locke argues that there are good reasons for carefully distinguishing the unity of the person from both that of the soul, as substance, and from that of life (man). Neither of the latter unities is co-extensive with that of consciousness; and 'person' or 'personality' is the term for this unity of conscious thoughts and actions. For the Cartesians at least, consciousness is a basis for the discovery of the individuality of the self (soul); but Locke ascribes to consciousness a constitutive function: the unity and identity of the human subject as a person is not one that is constituted prior to acts of consciousness, but rather exists only by virtue of its being constituted by consciousness.[3] How does consciousness achieve this, however, and what, if any, is the role that memory fulfils in the constitution of personal identity?

It is obvious from what has been said in the previous Chapter that, contrary to what many writers on the topic have for a long time assumed,[4] consciousness in Locke's account of personal identity is not to be identified with memory. Consciousness is always involved in memory—so much so that one could even say the latter is a form of consciousness. Locke states that 'to remember is to perceive any thing with memory, or with a consciousness, that it was known or perceived before' (I.iv.20). This is what he seems to have in mind when he speaks in some places of consciousness as 'a present representation of a past Action' (II.xxvii.13). But this does not of course mean that consciousness is identical with memory. Consciousness is much broader than memory, as it is not restricted to relating to perceptions or experiences we have 'perceived before'.

Still, consciousness is meant to relate to the past in some way and thereby constitute personal identity through time. Locke several times speaks of 'the same

---

Locke's occasional remarks about consciousness uniting 'different Substances... into one Person' (*Essay*, II.xxvii.10) should be read. For personal identity the relating of consciousness to thoughts and actions is relevant: 'whatever has the consciousness of present and past Actions, is the same Person to whom they both belong' (II.xxvii.16). It is thus misleading to focus on the notion of substance and speak of a Lockean person and its 'constituent thinking substances'—as does, for example, Conn, in 'Locke's Organismic Theory of Personal Identity', *Locke Studies*, 2 (2002), 105–35, at 129.

[3] For a more detailed account of the constitutive function that Locke ascribes to consciousness, see Thiel, *Lockes Theorie der personalen Identität* (1983), chap. V. See also Thiel, 'Locke's Concept of a Person', in Brandt (ed.), *John Locke. Symposium Wolfenbüttel 1979* (1981), p. 184. Winkler, too, emphasises the Lockean concern with what he calls the 'subjective constitution of the self'. At the same time he holds that according to Locke, the person is a substance. Winkler, 'Locke on Personal Identity', *Journal of the History of Philosophy*, 29 (1991), 201–26.

[4] Reid, *Essays on the Intellectual Powers of Man* (1785) ed. Brookes (2002), III.6; Flew, 'Locke and the Problem of Personal Identity', in Martin and Armstrong (eds.), *Locke and Berkeley: A Collection of Critical Essays* (1968), pp. 155–78. More recently, Lännström has interpreted Locke's account in terms of the notion of memory: 'Locke's Account of Personal Identity: Memory as Fallible Evidence', *History of Philosophy Quarterly*, 24 (2007), 39–56.

consciousness' (II.xxvii.10, 15, 16, 21) and of 'the identity of consciousness' (II.xxvii.19, 23) as that which is responsible for personal identity. Yet it does not follow from this that he would argue (implausibly) that (acts of) consciousness at two different points of time are the same and that this is how consciousness constitutes personal identity. For he explicitly rejects the idea that 'the same Consciousness... [is] the same individual Action' (II.xxvii.13).[5] Thus, when he speaks of 'the same continued consciousness' (II.xxvii.25), this expression should be read not as referring to some unchanging property of the self, nor as suggesting that (acts of) consciousness at different points of time can be numerically identical, but rather in terms of the idea of a connectedness of distinct (acts of) consciousness, 'continued on for the future' (II.xxvii.25). Commentators who tend to read Lockean consciousness in terms of memory have suggested this reading as a revision of Locke's view.[6] It is believed that Locke's position can be usefully 'revised' by emphasising a distinction between the notion of the continuity of consciousness and direct memory connections. It is argued that Locke could hold that 'a person at time t_2 is the same as a person at time t_1 just in case the person at time t_2 is linked by continuity' of consciousness to the person at time t_1. This continuity can be accounted for in terms of the notion of 'overlapping chains' of direct consciousnesses.[7] This would not require that the person at time t_2 can *remember* what the person at time t_1 thought or did in order to be the same person. As John Mackie has expressed it, there would still be a unified mental history, for the various experiences at different times all belong to the same unity of consciousness.[8] As indicated, this view would seem to be present in Locke, and does not constitute a revision of his view. The notion of a continuity of consciousness is indeed emphasised by Locke himself. He notes that consciousness relates to the present (II.xxvii.10, II.xxvii.10, 24) as well as to the immediately preceding moment (II.xxvii.16)—and it is clear from this alone that he would not simply equate consciousness with memory. Moreover, he suggests that consciousness thus understood as relating to the present and the immediate past is 'continued on for the future' (II.xxvii.25). Given that he states that it is only consciousness that unites actions 'into the same Person' (II.xxvii.16), he would seem to suggest an account of personal identity in terms of the continuity of consciousness, rather than in terms of the ability to remember past experiences, as the traditional interpretation would have it. And indeed, some recent writers claim

---

[5] As noted in the previous Chapter Locke says: 'as to things whose Existence is in succession, such as are the Actions of finite Beings, *v.g. Motion* and *Thought*, both which consist in a continued train of Succession, concerning their Diversity there can be no question; Because each perishing the moment it begins, they cannot exist in different times, or in different places, as permanent Beings can at different times exist in distant places; and therefore no motion or thought considered as at different times can be the same, each part thereof having a different beginning of Existence' (*Essay*, II.xxvii.2). Clearly, this would apply also to the 'reflex acts' of consciousness.

[6] See also the material discussed below in Chapter 6, Section 2, on 'Locke and the transitivity of identity'.

[7] Noonan, *Personal Identity* (1989), pp. 10–12.

[8] Mackie, *Problems from Locke* (1976), p. 180.

that for Locke memory really plays no part at all in the constitution of personal identity.[9]

The problem with this reading, however, is that while it is true that Locke implies a distinction between consciousness and memory, he clearly holds that *both* are involved in constituting personal identity. Thus, the account of personal identity in terms of a continuity of consciousness would indeed be a 'revision' of Locke, if it is claimed that continuity of consciousness is all that is relevant to Lockean personal identity and that memory plays no role whatsoever. Locke notes the importance of memory when he speaks of a 'memory of a past consciousness' (II.xxvii.23; see also sections 16 and 25) and of consciousness as 'a present representation of a past Action' (II.xxvii.13) as relevant to personal identity. It is through this connection to present and past conscious experiences that personal identity is constituted (II.xxvii.16, 17, 24). For Locke to establish personal identity across time, it is not sufficient to point to a chain of direct, overlapping consciousness-links; it must also be possible that the past thoughts and actions be recalled, so they can be attributed to one's own self. As Locke notes, the human mind does not always think and is thus not always conscious (II.i.9ff.). Consciousness is often interrupted by periods of unconsciousness, such as dreamless sleep, for example.[10] Locke suggests that such gaps can be bridged through a 'memory of a past consciousness'. Moreover, consciousness is 'interrupted always by forgetfulness' (II.xxvii.10). The mind 'may sometimes part with its past consciousness, and be restored to it again' (II.xxvii.23). The restoration of past consciousness as well as the bridging of gaps created by states such as dreamless sleep can be achieved through memory. This means that to Locke, the memory of actions of the past, even 'very remote in time' (II.xxvii.16), is just as important to personal identity as is the chain of consciousness relating to the present and the 'immediately preceding moment(s)' (ibid.).[11]

The importance of memory becomes especially apparent when we consider the practical or 'forensic' aspect of Locke's account, discussed below. For Locke, to establish a guilty mind it would not be sufficient to point to an underlying chain of direct, overlapping consciousness-links. I must also be able to bring the past misdeed to mind. Perhaps I would not be able to do this if there was no underlying chain of direct consciousness-links. But this would be only a necessary, not a sufficient condition of moral personal identity. It is also required that there be an ability to recall the past action and thus to attribute it to one's own self, so that one can be held responsible for it. It must be possible that the past misdeed 'be brought home to the mind, and made present'—to use a formulation from Locke's chapter

---

[9] Schechtman, for example, is of the view that for Locke, memory plays no constitutive role in personal identity. She claims that although Locke seems to see some connection between memory and personal identity, he never talks about memory when he tells us what personal identity consists in: *The Constitution of Selves* (1996), p. 107.

[10] Compare Mackie (1976), pp. 180–1.

[11] Through its connection with 'concernment', consciousness can also relate to the future (*Essay*, II.xxvii.10, 26). See the relevant section below.

'Of Power' (II.xxi.37).¹² Indeed, it is because of this forensic aspect of personal identity that the ability to recall past experiences and actions—what is sometimes called 'experience-memory',¹³—rather than just other types of psychological continuity (such as continuity of consciousness), is important to Locke. Both the connectedness through memory and the continuity of consciousness are essential to personal identity.¹⁴

Locke seems to draw a strong analogy between consciousness and life. As just stated, it is through its relating to the past that consciousness and memory constitute the identity of the person over time: "'Tis plain consciousness... unites Existences, and Actions, very remote in time, into the same Person, as well as it does the Existence and Actions of the immediately preceding moment: So that whatever has the consciousness of present and past Actions, is the same Person to whom they both belong.' (II.xxvii.16) In other words, I am at present the same person as I was in the past—not because I am the same living body, nor because the same substance thinks in me, but only because my present conscious experience is connected with that of past conscious experience: they belong to one conscious life, and this means that they are part of one identical person. Locke seems to be saying that the same consciousness constitutes the same person in the same way as 'the same Life' unites 'different Bodies... into one Animal', and thus preserves the latter's identity (II.xxvii.10). Therefore it has been claimed that for Locke 'consciousness plays the same role in the case of persons as life plays in the case of organisms',¹⁵ or that 'consciousness is the life of persons'.¹⁶ The analogy is not as strong as it might first appear, however. Thus Locke's example of dreamless sleep, cited above, points to a crucial difference between life and consciousness.¹⁷ Moreover, the few passages in which Locke links consciousness and life should not lead us to neglect the important role that memory fulfils for personal identity.¹⁸

---

¹² Compare also *Essay*, II.xxvii.24. Here Locke says that for me to be the same person at different points of time, it must be possible for me 'upon recollection' to 'join' the past existence 'with that present consciousness, whereby I am now my *self*'. Locke says here that only those thoughts and actions which I can 'recollect' and 'by my consciousness make my own Thought and Action' are truly mine.
¹³ Noonan (1989), p. 11.
¹⁴ As mentioned above, Lännström (2007) accounts for Locke's theory in terms of memory only. Moreover, she argues that for Locke, the latter is not constitutive of personal identity, but functions merely as evidence. Further, she claims that memory is not the only type of evidence; the identity of the self as man or human being is another type of evidence for Lockean personal identity (45–6, 51–3). As we have argued, however, the constitutive function of consciousness (and memory) is a distinctive feature of Locke's theory. The view that Lännström ascribes to Locke is closer to that of his critics such as Leibniz and Butler, as we shall see in the Chapters below.
¹⁵ Conn (2002), 120. To make the analogy appear stronger, Conn ascribes to Locke talk of a 'stream of consciousness' (123)—an expression not, however, used by Locke himself.
¹⁶ McCann, 'Locke on Identity: Matter, Life, and Consciousness', *Archiv für Geschichte der Philosophie*, 69 (1987), 54–77, at 68. For McCann, in Locke, 'consciousness makes for personal identity in just the way life makes for animal or vegetable identity' (68–9).
¹⁷ This has been pointed out by Ayers in *Locke* (1991), vol. 2, p. 265.
¹⁸ Conn believes that the analogy between consciousness and life allows us to ascribe a four-dimensionalist account of personal identity to Locke. Conn (2002), 105–35, esp. 119–34. See also Conn's book on the topic, *Locke on Essence and Identity* (2003). On the four-dimensionalist view,

But the importance that Locke attaches to memory raises the issue of amnesia. Indeed, as indicated, Locke recognizes the fact that there is 'no moment of our Lives wherein we have the whole train of all our past Actions before our Eyes in one view'. Our 'forgetfulness', Locke concedes, 'seems to make the difficulty' (II.xxvii.10): for would one really be justified in saying, as one would have to on Locke's theory, that I am not the same person now as I was ten years ago, only because I do not remember what I did then? Does amnesia turn me into a different person? Locke argues that the difficulty arises only if we confuse the terms 'man' and 'person': if we stick firmly to the relevant conceptual distinctions, 'forgetfulness' does not pose a problem to his theory:

We must here take notice what the Word *I* is applied to, which in this case is the Man only. And the same Man being presumed to be the same Person, *I* is easily here supposed to stand also for the same Person. But if it be possible for the same Man to have distinct incommunicable consciousness at different times, it is past doubt the same Man would at different times make different Persons. (II.xxvii.20)

I am still the same human being as before the loss of memory, for my identity as 'man' does not require that I am conscious of my past, but I am not the same person: the subject or referent of 'I' can be identical at different points of time with respect to the notion of man, while being non-identical with regard to the notion of person. It should be noted, however, that Locke speaks here of 'distinct *incommunicable* consciousness' (my italics), not of mere forgetfulness. As discussed above, moral personal identity requires the ability to recall past experiences and actions. Only if past experiences are irretrievably lost so that they can no longer 'be brought home to the mind, and made present' (II.xxi.37) would this affect personal identity.

---

persons (as well as physical objects) are extended not only in space but also in time, and thus can be said to have temporal parts. That is to say, at one point of time only part of me exists, in the same way in which the parts of my body exist only in their respective spatial regions. This means that an object or person 'perdures' in time (exists at different times by having distinct temporal parts at these times), rather than 'endures' (exists wholly at every moment of its existence). There are several problems, however, with ascribing four-dimensionalism to Locke. (1) Locke distinguishes explicitly between, on the one hand, events and actions that are obviously extended in time, and 'permanent Beings', on the other hand, whose identity conditions he investigates (*Essay*, II.xxvii.2). (2) In support of his interpretation, Conn (2002), 133, appeals to II.xxvii.21, where Locke distinguishes between three notions of *man*; but Conn mistakes this to be an account of 'human persons', concluding that 'Lockian persons are... composed of (diachronically compounded) organisms' and have 'both spatial and temporal extent' (ibid., 134). (3) Conn's account neglects the importance of memory to Lockean personal identity. (4) Conn concedes that four-dimensionalism or perdurantism 'represents a radical departure from how we normally speak and think' (ibid., 109), but this means that Locke could not adopt four-dimensionalism. For the importance he attaches to issues such as agency, self-concern, and moral and legal responsibility requires an approach that is consistent with 'how we normally speak and think'. (5) There is the more general problem of ascribing to Locke a complex position that was developed in the second half of the twentieth century and that is itself a matter of much controversy. Indeed, it is so controversial that even the very distinction between four-dimensionalism and three-dimensionalism has been called into question. It has been argued that the two approaches are 'intertranslatable' and thus 'effectively equivalent' (Lowe, 'Review of Christopher Hughes Conn', *Locke Studies*, 4 (2004), 243–53, at 246–7, 253). Obviously, if this is correct then the attempt at determining whether or not Locke was a four-dimensionalist about persons is a rather futile enterprise.

4.2. PERSONAL IDENTITY: SELF-CONCERN AND MORAL AND LEGAL RESPONSIBILITY

As already mentioned, the difference between the identity of the human subject as man and as person is crucial also to the moral and legal aspects of Locke's theory. Like others before him, Locke explicitly links the notion of person to that of moral and legal responsibility. For Locke, 'person' or 'personality' is not just a cognitive unity of thoughts and actions. Rather, the term refers also to that aspect or quality of a human subject with respect to which it is morally and legally responsible; it is a 'Forensick Term' (II.xxvii.26). In this context the notion of self-concern plays an important role.[19] Its main function is to relate the present human subject, as person, to its own future; for the consciousness of thoughts and sensations includes the consciousness of pleasure and pain; and 'that which is conscious of Pleasure and Pain' desires 'that that *self*, that is conscious, should be happy' (II.xxvii.26). Therefore Locke says that a 'concern for Happiness' is 'the unavoidable concomitant of consciousness' (ibid.). And it is through its link with self-concern that consciousness relates to the future person: we are now motivated to act in such a way as to avoid future pain and to attain happiness. This includes the desire that I will not have to ascribe actions to myself which will result in punishment—that is, misery.[20]

This raises a central interpretative question about the relationship between the cognitive side of Locke's account in terms of consciousness and the practical or moral and legal aspects in terms of the notion of self-concern. For a long time (up to the 1970s), most commentators focused almost exclusively on the cognitive side of Locke's account and the notion of consciousness or memory that is relevant here, and made Locke a predecessor of twentieth-century discussions of interesting 'puzzle cases' about identity.[21] At the other end, some more recent writers have emphasised the practical aspect of Locke's theory to such an extent that they ascribe to self-concern and related moral and legal notions even a certain priority over consciousness in the constitution of personal identity.[22] Both extremes are problematic—and

---

[19] Thiel (1983), pp. 128–51; Thiel, 'Personal Identity', in Garber and Ayers (eds), *The Cambridge History of Seventeenth-Century Philosophy* (1998), pp. 868–912, at pp. 894–7.

[20] Brandt asserts without argument that Locke's notion of self-concern is the same as the Stoic *cura*: 'John Lockes Konzept der persönlichen Identität. Ein Resümee', *Aufklärung*, 18 (2006), 37–54.

[21] Flew's famous article is representative of this line of interpretation. Flew (1968).

[22] See, for example, Brandt (2006), 41. Yaffe holds that Locke endorses a 'susceptibility-to-punishment theory' of personal identity: 'Locke on Ideas of Identity and Diversity', in Newman (ed.), *The Cambridge Companion to Locke's Essay Concerning Human Understanding* (2007), pp. 192–230. According to Yaffe, personal identity in Locke is determined by the appropriateness of rewards and punishments, and he sees Locke as 'reversing the assumed order of priority of the metaphysical and the moral' (p. 228). It is plain, however, that this reading is not consistent with Locke's text. For Locke, punishment is 'annexed to personality, and personality to consciousness' (*Essay*, II.xxvii.22). Schechtman (1996) also tends to neglect the cognitive aspect of Locke's account, stressing what she calls the '*affective* side of consciousness' (p. 108). For critical comments on Brandt, see Thiel, 'Das "Gefühl *Ich*". Ernst Platner zwischen Empirischer Psychologie und Transzendentalphilosophie', in *Aufklärung*, 19 (2007), 139–61, at 148–9. For a critical

neither is compatible with Locke's text. For Locke, both consciousness (including memory) and self-concern are central, but consciousness has priority. Locke notes that 'it is impossible to make personal Identity to consist in any thing but consciousness' (II.xxvii.21). Moreover, it is clearly not only morally and legally relevant experiences that make up the '*personal self*' (II.xxvii.11); purely cognitive experiences such as that of having seen 'an overflowing of the *Thames* last Winter' (II.xxvii.16) also belong to it. The cognitive aspect of the 'personal self' is linked to the practical feature through self-concern, but in the end self-concern is, as noted, merely an 'unavoidable concomitant of consciousness' (II.xxvii.26), and it reaches only 'as far as . . . consciousness extends' (II.xxvii.17).

Locke argues elsewhere in his *Essay* that human beings are free—that is, capable of rational self-determination with respect to their actions (II.xxi). In the chapter on identity he indicates that 'person' can be applied only to such free, rational beings that we hold responsible for their actions: the term 'belongs only to intelligent Agents capable of a Law, and Happiness and Misery' (II.xxvii.26). Locke also points out that the identity of the person is the foundation of 'all the Right and Justice of Reward and Punishment' (II.xxviii.30). This claim that the 'identity condition' needs to be satisfied for just rewards and punishment is of course not original to Locke. Within the framework of Cartesian doctrine, for example, the identity required for moral and legal responsibility is seen as guaranteed by the metaphysical composition of the self as an immaterial substance. As Locke rejects Cartesian metaphysics, however, he cannot, as Descartes and his followers could, simply assume that the 'identity condition' is secured by the metaphysical make-up of the self. In Locke, the notion of self-identity required for moral and legal purposes takes on an entirely new meaning: morally and legally relevant action attribution requires *consciousness* in addition to freedom and reason. Thus, he links his practical considerations concerning the person to his theoretical or 'speculative' ones in terms of consciousness. For Locke to say that responsibility and just rewards or punishments are founded in self-identity is to say that it is required both that I was conscious of what I was doing when I performed the action, and that I am now conscious of what I did then: we are liable to punishment for past crimes on account of our identity as persons (in Locke's sense), and not on account of our identity as thinking substances or human beings; for it is 'consciousness, whereby [one] becomes concerned and accountable, owns and imputes to [oneself] past Actions' (II.xxvii.26).

As indicated in the previous Chapter, if one wishes to place Locke's notion of person in relation to traditional ones, it is clear that it comes closest to that of person as (moral) quality or a Pufendorfian moral entity: 'person' or 'personality' denotes that aspect or quality of a human subject with respect to which it may be morally and legally judged. A person is a human subject, but considered with respect to the consciousness of its thoughts and actions and self-concern, rather than with respect

---

discussion of Yaffe's interpretation, see Anderson, 'Susceptibility to Punishment: A Response to Yaffe', in *Locke Studies,* 8 (2008), 101–6.

to its being a man or a thinking substance. To use the formulation of one of Locke's eighteenth-century defenders: when we apply the term 'person' to an individual human subject, we do not treat this subject 'absolutely, and in gross; but under a particular relation or precision'.[23] This is consistent with the fact that 'in the ordinary way of speaking' (II.xxvii.15) we may not always clearly distinguish between the human subject as moral entity or person and as man or rational substance. Following Pufendorf, it seems, Locke allows for the fact that we think and talk of persons in analogy to substances, *as if* they were substances.

Several commentators argue, however, that 'person' in Locke denotes the idea of a rational substance.[24] In support of this interpretation, reference is sometimes made to a passage which does not appear in the chapter on identity, but in Book III of the *Essay* in which Locke introduces the notion of 'moral man', understood as the idea of a '*corporeal rational Being*' (II.xi.16). This notion of 'moral man' is then linked to Locke's concept of moral person(ality) in the chapter on identity, and it is argued that the latter is to be understood in essentially the same way as that of 'moral man'—namely, as a rational substance.[25] It is not clear, however, why the 'moral man' passage should lead to such an understanding of Locke's notion of person. The point of the passage in Book III is to argue that the bodily shape of a being should not be a relevant consideration when deciding whether that being can be classed with 'man' in a moral sense (although bodily shape *is* relevant to the notion of man 'in a physical Sense'). We may class the being as a 'moral man', if it has rationality (and, that is, freedom).[26] Yet rationality and freedom are only neccessary but not sufficient conditions of personhood: the personality or that aspect of the human subject, in relation to which it may be morally and legally judged, is constituted through the consciousness of a rational substance. Thus it is misleading to liken Locke's notion of person(ality) to that of 'moral man'. The consciousness of a rational substance constitutes personality, and the latter is not itself a substance.

---

[23] Law, *A Defence of Mr. Locke's Opinion Concerning Personal Identity* (1769), p. 2. For a fuller account of Law's reading of Locke, see Chapter 6 below.

[24] See also the comments in the previous Chapter, in the section 'Locke on Man, Soul, and Person'. Loptson, for example, holds that '*person*, for Locke, designates a substance'. To think otherwise, he maintains, would mean to ascribe to Locke an 'innovative contribution', but it would be 'completely wrong' to do so. Locke should not be seen as 'particularly or impressively *original*' here: 'Man, Person, Spirits in Locke's *Essay*', *Eighteenth-Century Thought*, 3 (2007), 359–72, at 369–70. Even if it were true, however, that Locke's account is not very original, this would not speak against the interpretation presented here. Loptson ignores the fact that the notion of person as a spiritual substance was only one relevant tradition. As was noted above in the Introduction, the Ciceronian notion of person was a powerful rival tradition that was very much present in the seventeenth century—for example, in Pufendorf. Locke appears to take this up, modifying it in terms of his notion of consciousness.

[25] Mattern, 'Moral Science and the Concept of Persons in Locke', *Philosophical Review*, 89 (1980), 24–45, at 38–40; Winkler (1991), 215–16.

[26] As Locke says: 'For were there a Monkey, or any other Creature to be found, that had the use of Reason, to such a degree, as to be able to understand general Signs, and to deduce Consequences about general *Ideas*, he would no doubt be subject to Law, and, in that Sense, be a *Man*, how much soever he differ'd in Shape from others of that Name' (*Essay*, III.xi.16).

Locke's idea that 'punishment [is] annexed to personality, and personality to consciousness' (II.xxvii.20) means, of course, that actions of which I have no consciousness are not part of my personality, and that consequently I cannot justly be held responsible for them: I do not have to accept authorship of actions which are not united to my personality through consciousness, and I cannot justly be punished for criminal acts which I do not ascribe to myself through consciousness. Appealing to the insanity defence Locke holds that his theory, with its distinction between man and person, can explain and justify the practice of the law where the sane man is not punished for what he did when temporarily insane.[27] According to Locke, the sane man is not punished because he is not the same *person* as he was when insane; he is the same human being, but since he was 'besides himself', as Locke expresses it, when he committed the crime, there is no link of consciousness—that is, no *personal identity*—and consequently no justification for punishment (II.xxvii.20). As some of Locke's early critics noticed, however, other cases Locke discusses seem to suggest that his theory is actually inconsistent with the practice of the law in his time. Locke raises the case of the drunkard. Since it is the practice of the law to punish the sober man for what he did when drunk, the man drunk and the man sober would have to be the same person on Locke's view; but since the man drunk committed the crime while being 'besides himself' and the sober man in any case may not remember what he did when drunk, Locke's theory does not *allow* that the man sober and the man drunk be regarded as the same person and that the former be punished for what the latter did. Locke attempts to reconcile his theory with legal practice by arguing that in the case of the drunkard human courts of law do not have to accept lack of consciousness as a plea, because they cannot know for certain whether the plea is genuine: 'They cannot distinguish certainly what is real, what counterfeit' (II.xxvii.22). And since I cannot prove my lack of consciousness, human courts will justly punish me if the fact that I committed the crime is proved against me, for example by an eye-witness. The courts are justified in simply assuming that my plea is not genuine and punishing me 'with a Justice suitable to their way of Knowledge' (ibid.).

Locke's friend William Molyneux challenges Locke on this point.[28] He argues that crimes committed by someone when drunk are punishable not for the reason Locke gives, but because drunkenness is itself a crime which is committed voluntarily, and because one crime that brings about another crime cannot be used as an excuse for the latter. Now, it is certainly true that Molyneux's arguments are more in line with English seventeenth-century legal thought than are Locke's: drunkenness is a punishable offence, and it is not accepted as an excuse for a crime that results from it. The drunkard is thought of as *voluntarius daemon*; and, according to Coke, 'he hath... no priviledge thereby [by his drunkenness]; but what hurt or ill soever he

---

[27] For the history of the insanity defence, see Walker, *Crime and Insanity in England* (1968).
[28] See Molyneux's letters in *The Correspondence of John Locke*, ed. de Beer, 8 vols. (1976–89), vol. 4, pp. 767–8 (letter no. 1685), and vol. 5, pp. 20–2 (letter no. 1712).

doth his drunkenness doth aggravate it'.[29] Locke, however, in responding to the criticism, says that Molyneux's argument, 'how good soever', cannot be used by him: 'For what has this to do with consciousness? nay, it is an argument against me, for if a man may be punish'd for any crime which he committed when drunk, whereof *he is allow'd not to be conscious*, it overturns my hypothesis.'[30] Locke concedes to Molyneux 'that drunkenness being a voluntary defect, want of consciousness ought not to be presum'd in favour of the drunkard';[31] but he still wants to accommodate the drunkard case to his theory: the person, in this case, is *not* 'allow'd not to be conscious'. Rather, courts are justified in basing their judgement on the assumption that the person was conscious of what he did, because lack of consciousness cannot be proved in favour of the accused. This defence concedes that just punishment or reward does not have to be based on the *actual* self-ascription of actions through consciousness. It seems, however, that for Locke, courts do not have to accept that we have a case of 'distinct incommunicable consciousness' (II.xxvii.20) here, where the past action is irretrievably lost. Rather, on the basis of other evidence courts may assume that the action can still 'be brought home to the mind and made present' (II.xxi.37).

Still, consideration of the drunkard case gives rise to a more general problem for Locke's theory. Since personal identity is the basis of judgements of human courts, and since personal identity is constituted only through inner consciousness, the question arises of how human courts can *in principle* distinguish between genuine and pretended lack of consciousness: since a person's ability to self-ascribe actions through consciousness is beyond the courts' knowledge, how can they ever 'distinguish certainly what is real, what counterfeit?' The only means available to them for identifying the individual are those that relate to the individual as human (bodily) being. In other words, they can judge only with regard to the identity of the self as human being, not as person. But if this is so, does Locke's claim that *personal* identity is the foundation of 'all the Right and Justice of Reward and Punishment' still make sense? To answer this, we have to take into account the theological aspects of Locke's theory.

4.3. ORIGINAL SIN

It is plain from Locke's account of moral responsibility that he cannot accept the doctrine of original sin. Moral responsibility is founded in personal identity and personal identity in consciousness. Thus for Locke, on Judgement Day 'no one shall be made to answer for what he knows nothing of' (II.xxvii.22). We can be held responsible only for actions which we ascribe to ourselves through consciousness. All this implies the rejection of the doctrine of original sin. The latter is rejected

---

[29] Coke, *The First Part of the Institutes of the Laws of England*, ninth edn. (1684), p. 247 (a); Bk. 3, chap. 6, sec. 405.
[30] *The Correspondence of John Locke*, vol. 4, p. 785 (letter no. 1693); my italics.
[31] Ibid., vol. 5, p. 58 (letter no. 1744).

explicitly in Locke's *Reasonableness of Christianity*. The doctrine of original sin is inconsistent, Locke argues, with divine goodness and justice. 'Some men', he says, 'would have all Adam's posterity doomed to eternal, infinite punishment, for the transgression of Adam, whom millions had never heard of, and no one had authorised to transact for him, or be his representative' which is 'little consistent with the justice or goodness of the great and infinite God'.[32] Rather, what was lost through Adam's fall is immortality (ibid., pp. 5–6). 'Death came on all men by Adam's sin' (ibid., p. 6); but death is not necessarily a state of eternal torment. The defenders of original sin take it to be 'a state of guilt, wherein not only he [Adam], but all his posterity was so involved, that every one descended of him deserved endless torment, in hell-fire' (ibid., p. 6). But death does not equal 'eternal life in misery' (ibid., p. 6). God cannot be supposed, 'as a punishment of one sin, wherewith he is displeased, to put man under the necessity of sinning continually, and so multiplying the provocation' (ibid., p. 6); 'and therefore, though all die in Adam, yet none are truly punished, but for their own deeds' (ibid., p. 8). Jesus restores the dead to life, and then they are put on trial on the basis only of their own actions (ibid., pp. 9–10).[33]

4.4. SELF-CONCERN AND THE AFTERLIFE

Locke attempts to explain the way in which we at present relate to the future life and the divine judgement. For Locke, when pursued rationally, the 'concern for happiness' discussed above relates to happiness in the afterlife. For according to Locke (and Christian doctrine), only the happiness of the future life is true happiness (*Essay*, II.xxi.38, 60, 70). And since our happiness or misery in the future life depends on God's judgement of our actions in this life, we are concerned to be able to ascribe actions to ourselves which please God; that is, actions which conform to the divine moral law—a law available to us through reason and revelation.

Thus, Locke's talk of personal identity being the ground of just reward or punishment relates, in the last result, to the Last Judgement. And here the problem of the genuineness of self-ascription of actions through consciousness (raised above) does not arise. Locke appeals to the belief that we shall have a purified consciousness free from all error: 'The Secrets of all Hearts shall be laid open', and 'no one shall be made to answer for what he knows nothing of'.[34] According to Locke, God will not only ensure that we shall not lack consciousness of actions we in fact committed consciously, but also that we shall not wrongly ascribe actions to ourselves which we did not commit: divine justice and goodness 'will not by a fatal Error of theirs [God's

---

[32] *The Reasonableness of Christianity, as delivered in the Scriptures*, in *The Works of John Locke*, 10 vols., new edn., corrected (1823; reprinted, 1963), vol. 7, p. 4.

[33] Later, Jonathan Edwards attempts to link the doctrine of original sin in a positive way to an account of diachronic personal identity. For Edwards, see Chapter 8, Section 2.2.

[34] *Essay*, II.xxvii.22. See 1 *Corinthians*, 14, 25.

creatures] transfer from one to another, that consciousness, which draws Reward or Punishment with it' (II.xxvii.13). Therefore, in relation to the Last Judgement, Locke can safely say: 'The Sentence shall be justified by the consciousness all Persons shall have, that they *themselves* in what Bodies soever they appear, or what Substances soever that consciousness adheres to, are the *same*, that committed those Actions, and deserve that Punishment for them' (II.xxvii.26). It is important to note that Locke's reference to the Last Judgement is an essential element of his theory: only by relating the question of moral responsibility and reward or punishment to the Last Judgement can he avoid all those problems which would arise from his position that consciousness-based personal identity alone is the foundation of just reward and punishment. Thus, although it is correct to say that Locke's theory is 'revolutionary' in some respects—for example, in that he distinguishes personal identity from identity of substance—it is clear that in other respects it must be understood in the context of the traditional Christian doctrine of life after death.

Having said that Locke's theory must be understood in the context of the traditional Christian doctrine of life after death, it must be pointed out that at the same time his conception of the afterlife is based on his new theory of the person, and thereby differs considerably from some traditional views about the future life. Debates about the immortality of the soul centred to a large extent around the question of the soul's nature; that is, around the question whether the soul is a material or an immaterial substance. Some theologians and philosophers argued that the 'identity condition' required by a meaningful conception of the afterlife can be satisfied only if the soul is immaterial. Since Locke argues that questions about the essence of the soul are irrelevant to personal identity in this life, he also regards them as irrelevant to personal immortality.[35] We are assured of our immortality, he says, through revelation.[36] And like Cudworth, he argues that by immortality 'is not meant a state of bare substantial existence and duration', but 'a state of sensibility'.[37] This means that immortality is a state in which we shall live as *persons*—as beings who are conscious of pleasure and pain. Locke argues that even if the soul or mental substance is indestructible and continues to exist forever, this on its own does not mean that the *person* enjoys immortal life.[38] For Locke, the belief in immortality is

---

[35] Thus Locke states, for example, that 'all the Great Ends of Morality and Religion, are well enough secured, without philosophical Proofs of the Soul's Immateriality' (*Essay*, IV.iii.6).

[36] Locke, *The Works* (1823), vol. 4, p. 476.

[37] Locke, *An Early Draft of Locke's Essay, together with Excerpts from His Journals*, ed. Aaron and Gibb (1936), p. 121.

[38] As Locke seems to reject the idea of a 'natural' immortality of the soul here, some have linked his views to the 'mortalist' position of Richard Overton and Thomas Hobbes, according to which immortality is a gift by God at the resurrection. See, for example, Snobelen, 'Socinianism, Heresy and John Locke's *Reasonableness of Christianity*', *Enlightenment and Dissent*, 20 (2001), 88–125. It is plain, however, that Locke does not endorse Overton's and Hobbes's materialism. Still, the point is that for Locke, immateriality is in any case no guarantee for immortality, so that immateriality is compatible with the mortality of the soul. On this, see also Marshall, 'Locke, Socinianism, "Socinianism", and Unitarianism', in Stewart (ed.) *English Philosophy in the Age of Locke* (2000), pp. 111–82, at pp. 158–60. For further discussion of Locke and mortalism, see Ball, *The Soul Sleepers. Christian Mortalism from Wycliffe to Priestley* (2008).

the belief that God 'can and will restore us to the like state of Sensibility in another World, and make us capable there to receive the Retribution he has designed to Men, according to their doings in this Life' (*Essay*, IV.iii.6). If the future state were not a state of consciousness or 'sensibility', there would be no distinction for us between reward and punishment; no distinction between heaven and hell.[39] Also, if the future life were merely 'a state of bare substantial existence and duration' we would not now be concerned for our future life and, consequently, not determine our actions accordingly. The identity condition which needs to be satisfied for a meaningful conception of a future life relates to the *person*, not to mental substance: it is required that present and future life form a unity of consciousness—that the consciousness of divine reward or punishment will be part of the same person who was constituted in this life by the consciousness of those actions which are the objects of divine judgement.

Locke's distinction between substance and person enables him even to handle the doctrine of the pre-existence of souls. Unlike other critics of the doctrine, Locke does not appeal to the fact that we do not remember anything of our pre-existent life in order to refute the belief in pre-existence. To Locke, however, lack of consciousness of the past life means that the pre-existent state—assuming there was one—is completely irrelevant to the self as person in this life. If there had been a pre-existent state of our soul, our soul now and then would constitute different persons, because the two states do not form a unity of consciousness: 'So that personal Identity reaching no farther than consciousness reaches, a pre-existent Spirit not having continued so many Ages in a state of Silence, must needs make different Persons' (*Essay*, II.xxvii.4). A pre-existent state would only matter, Locke holds, if it were accessible to consciousness now; but this is not the case, as the proponents of the doctrine themselves seem to concede.

4.5. THE RESURRECTION OF THE BODY: LOCKE'S CONTROVERSY WITH STILLINGFLEET

As with the idea of the immortality of the soul, Locke reinterprets the doctrine of the resurrection of the body against the background of his theory of personal identity. Since life after death means that the same *person* will be restored, he does not think it necessary that the resurrection-body be the very same as the pre-mortem body. Locke does not deny that we shall have a body, yet he argues that its identity is not essential; the crucial point for life after death is that our personal identity is retained. In his *Essay* he says: 'And thus we may be able without any difficulty to conceive, the same Person at the Resurrection, though in a Body not exactly in make or parts the same which he had here, the same consciousness going along with the Soul that inhabits

---

[39] Locke *Early Draft*, p. 122.

it.'[40] Clearly, he is in agreement with thinkers such as Arthur Bury, who hold that bodily identity is not required by the doctrine of the resurrection. Yet he disagrees with Bury in arguing that the identity of the mental substance is not necessary either. All that is required, according to Locke, is that present and future life will form a unity of consciousness.

The most prominent contemporary theological critic of Locke—Edward Stillingfleet, Bishop of Worcester, with whom Locke entered into a long controversy over the *Essay* as a whole in the late 1690s—argues not only that Locke's account of personal identity is inconsistent with the Christian doctrine of the resurrection, but also that Locke's 'Way of *Certainty by Ideas*' that he considers to be '*wholly New*'[41] cannot explain the traditional distinction between nature and person that is crucial to the doctrine of the trinity.[42] As indicated above, Locke attempts to separate the issue of human personal identity from the problem of the trinity. He does not want to become embroiled in a debate about this theological issue, and it is not surprising, therefore, that he does not mention explicitly the trinitarian controversy that was so much on everyone's mind at the time when he composed his chapter on identity. Nor is it surprising that despite his efforts he was drawn into a debate about the trinity by Stillingfleet after the publication of that chapter in the second edition of the *Essay*.

In the context of discussing the doctrine of the trinity, Stillingfleet briefly examines the issue of individuation in general.[43] He argues against Locke's view that existence in space and time is the principle of individuation. Like Leibniz and other later critics, Stillingfleet concedes that spatio-temporal location is a means by which we can distinguish between individuals, but insists that this is merely an external difference between them and cannot constitute individuality itself. Individuality must have an intrinsic ground independently of spatio-temporal location—'antecedent to such accidental Differences as are liable to our Observation by our Senses'.[44] According to Stillingfleet, if we suppose that there be no external difference, such as the difference of place, between two individuals, there would still be two distinct individuals. It follows that there must be an intrinsic principle which makes them the individuals that they are—two distinct beings of the same kind. In his reply Locke maintains that he cannot accept the supposition on which Stillingfleet bases this argument: he holds that the notion of numerical distinctness between

---

[40] Locke, *Essay*, II.xxvii.15. See also Locke's letter to Daniel Whitby, 17 January 1698/99: 'I being fully perswaded of the resurrection and that we shall have bodys fitted to that state it is indifferent to me whether any one concludes that they shall be the same or not.' *The Correspondence of John Locke*, vol. 6, p. 548 (letter no. 2536). For a different account of Locke's view about the resurrection, see Pitassi, 'Une résurrection pour quel corps et pour quel humanité? La réponse lockienne entre philosophie, exégèse et théologie', *Rivista di storia della filosofia* (1998), pp. 45–61.

[41] Stillingfleet, *An Answer to Mr. Locke's Second Letter; Wherein his Notion of Ideas is Prov'd to be Inconsistent with It Self, and with the Articles of the Christian Faith* (1698), p. 120.

[42] Stillingfleet, *A Discourse in Vindication of the Doctrine of the Trinity* (1697), p. 260. See also Locke, *The Works* (1823), vol. 4, pp. 92–3, 148–9.

[43] See also Stillingfleet, *The Doctrine of the Trinity and Transubstantiation Compared... The Second Part* (1687), p. 27.

[44] Stillingfleet, *An Answer to Mr. Locke's Second Letter*, p. 171.

individuals of a kind entails that of external differences between the individuals: 'I cannot, I find, suppose, that there is no such external difference between Peter and James, as difference of place; for I cannot suppose a contradiction; and it seems to me to imply a contradiction to say, Peter and James are not in different places.'[45]

Stillingfleet's own account of individuation is in terms of the Scholastic notions of common natures or essences and particular subsistence.[46] He indicates that 'in gross and material Beings' this individuality and distinctness is brought about by a complex of 'peculiar Modes and Properties, which distinguish them from each other'.[47] In the case of human beings individuality is constituted, according to Stillingfleet, by the particular union of soul and body.[48] Locke replies, however, that Stillingfleet's position violates the principle that whatever it is that brings about individuation must be 'the same in all the several species of creatures, men as well as others'. Further, Locke argues that on Stillingfleet's account it is not clear how body and soul can be individuals before they are united into one human being.[49] This issue is connected to the topic of the resurrection and the diachronic identity of the person. On the traditional view which Stillingfleet endorses, the resurrection consists of a union of a material substance—the body—with an immaterial substance—the soul.

Stillingfleet holds that the identity of the body at the resurrection is an article of the Christian faith with which Locke's interpretation of the doctrine and his theory of personal identity on which that interpretation is based are not consistent.[50] He notes, correctly, that in Locke, 'the article of the *Resurrection* is Resolved into your *Idea* of *Personal Identity*',[51] but argues that 'if the Scripture be the sole foundation of our Faith, this is an Article of it, and so your *Idea* of *Personal Identity* is inconsistent with it; for it makes the same Body which was here united to the Soul not to be necessary to the Doctrine of the *Resurrection*'.[52] In short, his complaint is that Locke denies the identity of the resurrection-body with the pre-mortem body.

Stillingfleet's argument assumes the Scholastic notion of a human person as a 'compleat intelligent Substance, with a peculiar manner of Subsistence', meaning that both soul and body are required to make up the person and that the soul alone does not constitute the person—a view for which Robert South argued against William Sherlock.[53] Like South, Stillingfleet appeals here to the Scholastic view that body and soul are incomplete entities. He argues that 'we take *Person* with Relation to *Soul* and *Body* united together. And so the *Identity* of *Person* must take in

---

[45] Locke, *The Works* (1823), vol. 4, p. 173.
[46] See, for example, Stillingfleet, *An Answer to Mr. Locke's Second Letter*, pp. 157–65; Stillingfleet, *The Doctrine of the Trinity*, p. 27.
[47] Stillingfleet, *The Doctrine of the Trinity*, p. 27.
[48] Stillingfleet, *An Answer to Mr. Locke's Second Letter*, p. 171.
[49] 'And upon this ground it will be very hard to tell what made the soul and the body individuals (as certainly they were) before their union.' Locke, *The Works* (1823), vol. 4, p. 439.
[50] Stillingfleet, *An Answer to Mr. Locke's Second Letter*, pp. 33–44.
[51] Ibid., p. 33.
[52] Ibid., p. 44.
[53] Stillingfleet, *A Discourse*, p. 261.

both, not only here, but at the Resurrection'.[54] Thus, Stillingfleet rejects Locke's distinction between man and person. To him, 'person' is a term that refers to what Locke lists as one of the three senses of 'man' in *Essay*, II.xxvii.21; namely, a unity of soul and body. Self-consciousness plays no definitional role in Stillingfleet's account of the person. To him, then, it is the unity, peculiar to each individual person, of soul and body, that grounds individuation and identity in persons: 'the true Reason of Identity in Man is the vital Union of Soul and Body: And since every Man hath a different Soul united to different Particles of Matter, there must be a real Distinction between them, without any respect to what is accidental to them'.[55]

Stillingfleet maintains that at the resurrection we shall have the same body—the same material substance which was united to the soul in this life.[56] Of the three main views about the identity of the body at the resurrection outlined in Chapter 2, Stillingfleet subscribes to the view that sameness of the bodily organization, but not sameness of material particles, is required for the identity of the resurrection-body with the pre-mortem body:

> In things capable of any sort of Life, the *Identity* is consistent with a continued succession of Parts... And thus the Alteration of the Parts of Body at the *Resurrection* is consistent with its *Identity*, if its *Organization* and *Life* be the same; and this is a *Real Identity* of the Body which depends not on *Consciousness*. From whence it follows, that to make the same Body, no more is required but restoring Life to the *Organized Parts* of it. (*An Answer to Mr. Locke's Second Letter*, p. 42)

Thus Stillingfleet makes use of an account of the identity of living bodies that Locke himself endorses. He is very much aware of this, pointing out that the latter accounts similarly for the identity of living beings, and, moreover that the identity of the body *at the resurrection* must be understood in terms of the identity of the human body as a living being. Sameness of body is, for Stillingfleet, the sameness of an organism.

In his extensive response to the arguments about the resurrection, Locke tries to defend his position partly by restating some of his philosophical arguments—partly by producing textual evidence from the Bible in support of his view. He rejects Stillingfleet's theory as well as the latter's appeal to his own account of the identity of living beings in the *Essay*, and emphasises that he distinguishes between 'man' and 'body': the identity of man consists in the sameness of the organization of parts, the identity of the body in the identity of material particles (Locke, *The Works* (1823) vol. 4, pp. 320, 323). And the question raised by Stillingfleet concerns the same *body* at the

---

[54] Stillingfleet, *An Answer to Mr. Locke's Second Letter*, p. 175.
[55] Ibid., p. 171. This point is also related to Stillingfleet's complaint about Locke's treatment of the notion of substance in general. For an account of the afterlife, Stillingfleet insists, we have to assume the immortality of the soul, and for that to be possible we need to be able to determine the nature or real essence of the soul as (immaterial) substance: 'It is no easie matter to give an account, how the Soul should be capable of *Immortality*, unless it be an *Immaterial Substance*' (p. 57). For a discussion of the general issue of substance in the Locke–Stillingfleet controversy, see Kort, 'Stillingfleet and Locke on Substance, Essence, and Articles of Faith', *Locke Studies*, 5 (2005), 149–78.
[56] 'It must be the same material Substance which was vitally united to the Soul here.' Stillingfleet, *An Answer to Mr. Locke's Second Letter*, p. 35.

resurrection—the question whether the same particles will be reunited (ibid., pp. 305, 309). Thus, in contrast to Stillingfleet, Locke (in this context) conceives of 'body' and 'material substance' not in terms of the notion of organism or living bodies, but in terms of 'mass of matter'.[57] For Locke, the issue of the resurrection of the same body must relate to 'body' in this sense, not to the question of the same man. For 'man' (which Stillingfleet equates with 'person') is accounted for by Stillingfleet in terms of the *union* of soul and body, but the resurrection as understood by himself and others is meant to relate to the body only.

Locke's main argument against Stillingfleet, however, is that neither the identity of the body nor that of the man is required for the identity of the self at the resurrection. Although 'God may, if he pleases, give to every one a body consisting only of such particles as were before vitally united to his soul' (*The Works*, 1823, vol. 4, p. 332), what matters is only the identity of the self as a person. It is the person that will be rewarded or punished. And to identify us as persons God need not apply external bodily criteria. 'It suffices, that all the dead shall be raised, and every one appear and answer for the things done in this life' (ibid., p. 312). Thus Locke emphasises that the resurrection concerns the person, not the body: 'The Scripture being express, that the same persons should be raised and appear before the judgment-seat of Christ, that every one may receive according to what he had done in his body' (ibid., p. 324; see also p. 304).

Thus, although Locke does not doubt 'that the dead shall be raised with bodies',[58] he points out to Stillingfleet that when St Paul 'speaks of the resurrection, he says, you, and not your bodies. l. Cor.vi.14'.[59] In fact he states that 'I do not remember in any place of the New Testament (where the general resurrection at the last day is spoken of) any such expression as the resurrection of the body, much less of the same body' (ibid., p. 304). He tells Stillingfleet that he will change the passages in the *Essay* in which he has spoken of the resurrection of the body, and use the expression 'resurrection of the dead' instead (ibid.).[60] To count a body as 'my' body—that is, as a body of the same person at different points of time—Locke argues, it is not required that it remains the same through time. This applies to this life as much as to the afterlife. Locke writes to Stillingfleet:

The body he had, and did things in, at five or fifteen, was no doubt his body, as much as that which he did things in at fifty was his body though his body were not the very same body at those different ages: and so will the body, which he shall have after the resurrection be his body, though it be not the very same with that which he had at five, or fifteen, or fifty. (ibid., p. 308)

---

[57] Kaufman points out that Locke's thinking on the ontological status of organisms is rather muddled. In the *Essay*, Locke suggests in many places that organisms are substances, but in the correspondence with Stillingfleet he seems to equate material substance with mass of matter and thus distinguishes it from organisms. See Kaufman, 'The Resurrection of the Same Body and the Ontological Status of Organisms: What Locke Should Have (and Could Have) Told Stillingfleet', in Hoffman, Owen, and Yaffe (eds.), *Contemporary Perspectives on Early Modern Philosophy: Essays in Honor of Vere Chappell* (2008), pp. 191–214.

[58] Locke, *The Works* (1823), vol. 4, p. 334.

[59] Ibid., p. 304.

[60] Compare Locke, *Essay*, IV.xviii./ and IV.xvii.23.

And because 'whatever matter is vitally united to his soul, is his body' (ibid., p. 314) it makes sense to call that body the 'same' body, although it does not consist of the same particles and is, strictly speaking, not the same: 'For being his body both before and after the resurrection, every one ordinarily speaks of his body as the same, though in a strict and philosophical sense, as your lordship speaks, it be not the very same' (ibid., p. 324).

We have seen that Locke's account of the resurrection is part of his new theory of personal identity in terms of consciousness. But Stillingfleet rejects Locke's idea that consciousness can account for the sameness required at the resurrection. He points out that according to Locke, 'a Material Substance may .... have *Self-consciousness* in it' (Stillingfleet, *An Answer to Mr, Locke's second Letter*, pp. 35–6), arguing that this view affects the resurrection issue:

For, if it may be only a Material Substance in us that thinks, then this Substance, which consists in the Life of an Organiz'd Body, must cease by Death; for how can that, which consisted in Life, be preserved afterwards? And if the *Personal Identity* consists in a *Self-consciousness* depending on such a Substance as cannot be preserved without an Organiz'd Body, then there is no Subsistence of it separate from the Body, and the Resurrection must be giving a new Life. To whom? To a Material Substance which wholly lost its Personal Identity by Death. So that there can be no *Personal Identity* at all; unless you say the very same Life which was long since at an end can be Reproduced. Which I suppose you will not assert. (ibid., p. 36)

The problem with this critique is of course that Stillingfleet assumes what Locke challenges: namely, that the identity of substance underlying self-consciousness is required for the identity of the person. Stillingfleet acknowledges that Locke holds that it is at least 'the more probable Opinion' that consciousness depends on an immaterial substance (which Stillingfleet simply assumes as true). According to Stillingfleet, however, this does not help to make Locke's account of the resurrection more satisfactory, for, as we saw, in his view there must be the same material substance at the resurrection and Locke denies this (ibid., pp. 36–7). Locke, however, would point out that the resurrection is not mainly about giving life 'to a material substance', as Stillingfleet assumes Locke to say, but to a person. Consciousness (including memory) will recall the thoughts and actions of this life, and thereby bridge the gap between death and resurrection. Although there will be a material substance at the resurrection, its identity or otherwise with the pre-mortem body is irrelevant to the identity of the person.

4.6. REPENTANCE AND MORAL MIRACLES[61]

We have seen that for Locke, personal identity is the foundation of 'all the Right and Justice of Reward and Punishment' (*Essay*, II.xxvii.18). And since personal identity is

---

[61] I thank Galen Strawson for drawing my attention to the issue of repentance. Compare Strawson, *Locke on Personal Identity* (2011b), pp. 145–9.

constituted through consciousness, just rewards and punishments too are, in the last analysis, based in consciousness. 'Punishment [is] annexed to personality, and personality to consciousness' (II.xxvii.22). This raises the question of how the Lockean theory could deal with the issue of genuine repentance as understood at the time. The notion of repentance was, of course, much discussed in early modern thought;[62] but it was only occasionally brought up in discussions of the personal identity problem. Still, the issue of repentance creates a problem for Locke's consciousness-based theory. As Galen Strawson has pointed out,[63] it would seem that I would no longer be open to punishment if I have genuinely repented, although of course I would still be conscious of my crime and thus be identical with the perpetrator in Locke's sense. And given that for Locke, 'punishment [is] annexed to personality, personality to consciousness', it would seem that, strictly speaking, on Locke's theory, I would still be open to punishment despite my repentance. It seems, then, that Locke's account is inconsistent with the notion of genuine repentance.

Locke himself does not even mention the notion of repentance in the context of his discussion of personal identity. Other thinkers of the time, however, argue that one becomes another person through repentance and so is no longer liable to punishment. According to this view, then, while 'punishment is annexed to personality', personality is not (at least not totally) dependent on consciousness. And it is because personal identity is not made dependent on consciousness that this view is not inconsistent with the notion of personality change through repentance. John Turner, of Cambridge, is a representative of this view. In Chapter 1 we encountered Turner as one of the few thinkers prior to Locke who made use of the notion of consciousness in a philosophically significant sense. In a different context, Turner points out that

a thorough Repentance, an hearty and inward sorrow and contrition for Sin, attended with an outward and visible reformation of life and manners, works such a perfect change and alteration through the whole man, that he is scarce the same person that he was before, and it doth not seem reasonable, that the Penitent, the Good, virtuous and honest man should be punished for those faults which none but the worst Sinners did commit.[64]

Thus, Turner holds that genuine 'inner' and 'outer' repentance make me a different person, and that as a result I am no longer open to punishment for my past sins. The question of whether consciousness still ascribes past sins to me does not seem to be relevant.

But what exactly is meant by 'repentance' here? There are at least two distinct relevant notions of repentance in the early modern period.[65] One is that of a sudden change of personality through a deathbed repentance by which the person is believed to be no longer subject to divine punishment. Here the change does not even have to

---

[62] Kittsteiner, *Die Entstehung des modernen Gewissens* (1995).
[63] Strawson (2011b), p. 145.
[64] Turner, *The Middle Way Betwixt Necessity and Freedom* (1683), p. 23.
[65] Kittsteiner (1995), pp. 332–56.

be the result of the conscious effort of the sinner. It is a matter of the grace of God, who can bring about a miracle of grace by changing a person (Kittsteiner, 1995, p. 345). A different notion of repentance is that of a conscious change of mind that results in a sustained good conscience that expresses itself not only in thoughts and words but also in practice. It is the latter notion of repentance that Turner has in mind. Both notions involve a change of personality, but this is not considered problematic in the case of the second notion of repentance. Here the change is thought of as gradual and as brought about by the human subject himself or herself. An essential continuity of the person is thereby retained. Regarding the notion of a sudden and miraculous change through repentance, however, some eighteenth-century philosophers argue that such a change would destroy personal identity as well as the 'moral order'.

This is what Hermann Andreas Pistorius, for instance, argues in his commentary on David Hartley's *Observations on Man*. He discusses the issue of 'moral miracles', of which the sudden change of personality through a deathbed repentance is an example.[66] Such miracles, he says, represent to us totally new persons who think and feel in a way that we could not at all have expected to believe on the basis of our past experience.[67] Such miracles would disturb the general moral and psychological order, however. As to personal identity, Pistorius writes:

No one who admits the possibility of physical miracles, can well doubt the possibility of moral ones. Whether such ever happened, or whether it be probable that God would perform such, is a different question. Philosophy seems to combat these miracles, or any forcible violation and change of the proper activity of the soul, on the ground, that the personal identity of the thinking substance which is acted upon would be thereby destroyed. The scriptures give us no instance of a miracle changing the character and way of thinking of a man immediately. When a miracle was requisite to this purpose, a physical one was always employed, as in the conversion of Paul, for instance; and this was to prevent the necessity of a moral one. The remarkable passage in Exodus, xiii.17 seems to prove, that God found it inconsistent with his wisdom to perform moral miracles. It is true we must admit, on a certain notion of divine inspiration, that God works proper psychological miracles: but I will not attempt to decide, how far the objection to moral miracles is applicable to that of inspiration. A man might be inspired by means of a psychological miracle, without having his mind altered or amended, as was the case with Balaam.[68]

---

[66] *David Hartleys Betrachtungen über den Menschen, seine Natur, seine Pflicht und Erwartungen aus dem Englischen übersetzt und mit Anmerkungen und Zusätzen begleitet*, with a commentary by Hermann Andreas Pistorius (ed.), 2 vols. (1772–73). This edition was translated into English and published in one volume: *Observations on Man... In Two Parts... Reprinted from the Author's Edition in 1749. To which are now added Notes and Additions to the Second Part... Also A Sketch of the Life and Character, and Head of the Author* (1791).
[67] 'Allein Wunder in der moralischen Welt stellen uns ganz neue Menschen vor, die auf eine solche Weise empfinden, denken, gesinnet sind und handeln, als wir es unserer innern Empfindung und der durchgängigen beständigen Erfahrung des menschlichen Geschlechts zufolge nie von ihnen erwarten oder glauben können.' Pistorius, in *David Hartleys Betrachtungen*, vol. 1, p. 404.
[68] English translation of Pistorius's edition of Hartley (1791), p. 671. The German original reads: 'An der Möglichkeit der sittlichen Wunder kan wohl niemand zweifeln, der die Möglichkeit der physischen zugestehet. Allein eine andere Frage ist es, ob dergleichen jemahls geschehen, und ob es wahrscheinlich sey, daß Gott dergleichen thun werde. Die Philosophie scheinet, sich wider diese

Pistorius does not provide much evidence for his assertion that philosophy 'would combat these miracles' on the ground that they would destroy personal identity. He cites Moses Mendelssohn's *Ueber die Empfindungen* as a source, however.[69] Mendelssohn does not specifically talk about 'moral' miracles, but he discusses and criticizes the thesis that God, 'by means of miracles', can and 'is supposed to transport me suddenly to a more blessed condition' (Mendelssohn, *Philosophical Writings*, p. 31). This issue raises the question of whether 'this altered condition' would have to be 'grounded in the present one' (ibid., p. 32). If that were not the case, then one would have to assume that 'at each passing moment, God is supposed to destroy soul and body, and create something else'. But 'as the alterations of one thing are connected with another, it can reveal itself under a thousand different shapes and yet always remain exactly the same thing' (ibid.). Presumably, Pistorius takes this to be an argument against 'moral miracles', because such miracles would not be grounded in and brought about by the previous condition and so would destroy the identity of the person. Instead of altering the person, it would be the creation of a new person.[70]

This point could be used to argue that John Turner's understanding of repentance is consistent with diachronic personal identity. Turner holds that one is 'scarce the same person' after a sustained change in inner attitude and outward practices. It could be said, however, that what we have here is not the creation of a new person, but an alteration of something that remains 'exactly the same thing' through partial

Wunder, oder gegen jede gewaltsame Unterbrechung und Veränderung der eigenen Thätigkeit der Seele auch aus dieser Ursache zu erklären, weil die persönliche Identität der denkenden Substanz, auf welche sie gewürket würden, dadurch aufgehoben würde. Man sehe den siebenden Brief unter den Briefen über die Empfindungen. Die Schrift giebt uns von Wundern, durch welche unmittelbarer Weise der Charakter und die Gemüthsart eines Menschen verändert und gleichsam umgeschaften worden, keine Beyspiele an. So oft ein Wunder zu dieser Absicht nöthig war, geschahen physische Wunder, z. B. bey der Bekehrung Pauli, und diese geschahen, damit es der sittlichen nicht bedurfte. Die merkwürdige Stelle z. B. Mosis 13, 17 scheinet zu beweisen, daß es Gott seiner Weisheit nicht gemäß finde, sittliche Wunder zu thun. Nach einer gewissen Vorstellung der göttlichen Eingebung müste man freylich annehmen, daß Gott eigentliche psychologische Wunder würke. Ich unterstehe mich nicht zu entscheiden, in wie fern gegen diese eben die Einwendung statt findet, die man gegen die sittlichen macht. Denn es könte jemand durch ein psychologisches Wunder inspirirt werden, ohne dennoch an seinem Gemüthe geändert und gebessert zu werden, wie wir an Bileam sehen.' Pistorius, *David Hartleys Betrachtungen*, vol. 1, p. 421.

[69] Mendelssohn, *Ueber die Empfindungen* (1755), English trans. in Mendelssohn, *Philosophical Writings*, ed. and transl. Dahlström (1997).

[70] In England, Joseph Priestley discussed the issue of moral miracles, without, however, relating this issue to the personal identity problem. See Priestley, *The Doctrine of the Divine Influence on the Human Mind* (1779). Priestley rejects the notion of an 'instantaneous conversion' (pp. v, 26) to which he refers as an 'internal' or 'moral miracle'. He holds 'that the agency of God upon the minds of men, though real and constant... is not *immediate* or *miraculous* (for if it were, it would be the same thing with what we do term miraculous) but always through the medium of the natural means of instruction and reformation' (p. 6). Like Locke, Priestley holds that 'a real change of character, from vice to virtue, is only to be effected in a natural, and consequently in a gradual manner' (p. 26). He emphasises that '*time* must be requisite to form any character' for the latter is 'a thing of slow growth' (p. 27).

change. The alteration is such that we are no longer subject to punishment for our past sins. Indeed, Locke's distinction between the human subject as substance, man, and person would be helpful here. Locke could argue that we have a different person but the same underlying thinking substance or the same man.

The question remains, however, whether Locke's claim that consciousness-based personal identity is the foundation of 'all the Right and Justice of Reward and Punishment' (*Essay*, II.xxvii.18) is consistent with repentance. For Locke, too, repentance is not to be understood as a 'moral miracle'—a sudden event which brings about an immediate change of personality. For him, repentance involves a conscious effort—a mental act of sorrow, as well as a change of life according to moral principles. Repentance, he says, is 'not only a sorrow for sins past, but (what is a natural consequence of such sorrow, if it be real) a turning from them into a new and contrary life' (*Reasonableness*, in *The Works* (1823), vol. 7, p. 105). It is 'a hearty sorrow for our past misdeeds and a sincere resolution and endeavour, to the utmost of our power, to conform all our actions to the law of God [for] the remainder of our lives' (ibid.). Locke also asserts that on the basis of genuine repentance we can expect 'eternal life' (ibid.). And yet, if I am still conscious of my 'past misdeeds', Locke would have to say that despite my genuine repentance I would nevertheless be subject to punishment for them, because 'punishment [is] annexed to personality, and personality to consciousness'. Thus it seems that repentance, even of the kind that Locke envisages, is not consistent with his account of personal identity in terms of consciousness. His distinction between thinking substance, man, and person does not help here. The inconsistency concerns his notion of repentance and his claim that just rewards and punishments depend only on consciousness.

Perhaps Locke could be defended here with the argument that the forensic aspect of his notion of the person must be emphasised. It is not consciousness or the ability to remember the past that is relevant, but the notion of self-concern. On this reading, Locke holds that a past act can 'affect present consciousness without being remembered'.[71] And so it could be argued that for Locke I can be concerned in an act for which I have truly repented without being open to punishment for that act.[72] Expressed differently, Locke could argue that I become a different person through repentance. And so although I can still remember the past misdeed in some way, I no longer 'appropriate' it to myself, as Locke might have put it: I no longer consider the misdeed as mine in the morally relevant sense. It is not clear, however, that this defence can succeed, as self-concern does not on its own constitute personal identity for Locke. Self-concern is based on consciousness of which it is a 'concomitant'. It remains true that 'punishment [is] annexed to personality, and personality to consciousness'. And it is this claim that would seem to be inconsistent with Locke's own understanding of repentance.

---

[71] Schechtman (1996), p. 110.
[72] This was suggested to me by Galen Strawson. See Strawson (2011b), p. 145.

4.7. THINKING MATTER AND PERSONAL IDENTITY. LOCKE AND HIS FOLLOWERS: COLLINS, VOLTAIRE, AND CUENZ

One important and influential aspect that is implied by Locke's consciousness-based account of personal identity is that it remains neutral with respect to the debate between materialist and immaterialist philosophers of the mind. Although he holds it to be the 'more probable Opinion' that thought is 'annexed' to an immaterial substance (*Essay*, II.xxvii.25), he explicitly states that he believes thinking matter to be possible (to involve no contradiction).[73] And we saw that as far as his account of personal identity is concerned, our view about the nature of the thinking substance is simply irrelevant. It is precisely this neutrality, however, that made Locke's theory of personal identity attractive to materialist inclined thinkers, as his position was seen as at least compatible with a materialist metaphysics and at the same time as immune to those anti-materialist arguments that relate to the issue of identity.

Anthony Collins—a friend and correspondent of Locke—was one of those materialist inclined philosophers, defending Locke's views on personal identity in his controversy with Samuel Clarke from 1707 to 1708.[74] Collins does not argue merely for the logical possibility of thinking matter, but goes much further and states explicitly that 'human consciousness or thinking is a mode of some generical power in matter'.[75] Clearly, then, he does not follow Locke in all aspects of his thought. Further, unlike Locke, Collins addresses the immaterialist objection, as voiced by his opponent Samuel Clarke, that if consciousness inhered in a purely material system, then one would have to make the absurd assumption that each individual material part be conscious, as the consciousness of the system must consist of the consciousnesses of the parts, so that there would be 'as many distinct Consciousnesses as there

---

[73] Locke, *Essay*, IV.iii.6. Yolton has surveyed the influence of this suggestion in eighteenth-century thought, without, however, dealing with the issue of personal identity. See Yolton, *Thinking Matter: Materialism in Eighteenth-Century Britain* (1983), and *Locke and French Materialism* (1991).

[74] All contributions to this debate by Collins and Clarke were published together after both had died: *A Letter to Mr. Dodwell... Together with A Defence of an Argument made use of in the above-mentioned Letter to Mr. Dodwell, to prove the Immateriality and Natural Immortality of the Soul. In Four Letters to the Author of Some Remarks, &c. To which is added, Some Reflections on that Part of a Book called Amyntor, which relates to the Writings of the Primitive Fathers, and the Canon of the New Testament. By Samuel Clarke.... The Sixth Edition. In this Edition are inserted The Remarks on Dr. Clarke's Letter to Mr. Dodwell, and the several Replies to the Doctor's Defences thereof* (1731). Relevant parts of the debate have recently been published by Uzgalis, 'Selections from the Clarke–Collins Correspondence', in Perry (ed.), *Personal Identity*, second edn. (2008), pp. 283–314. Compare also Uzgalis's paper in the same volume, 'Locke and Collins, Clarke and Butler, on Successive Persons', pp. 315–26. For Collins's thought in general, see O'Higgins, *Anthony Collins: The Man and His Work* (1970), and Berman, 'Anthony Collins: Aspects of his Thought and Writings', *Hermathena*, 119 (1975), 49–70. For Collins's debate with Clarke over thinking matter, see O'Higgins (1970), pp. 69–76; Ferguson, *The Philosophy of Dr. Samuel Clarke and its Critics* (1974), pp. 138–62; and Yolton (1983), pp. 39–42.

[75] Collins, *Reflections on Mr. Clark's Second Defence of his Letter to Mr. Dodwell* (1707), p. 22.

are parts in that System'.[76] Collins points out that the principle on which Clarke bases his objection—that there can be nothing in the whole which is not also in its parts—is to be rejected. For Collins, consciousness is 'a Power or Quality in Matter answering to a Mode of Motion and Figure, such as the peculiar Motion of a Clock, or Roundness' (ibid., 18). And as 'Roundness inheres in a System of Matter, without being the Sum of the Roundnesses of the Parts' (ibid.), consciousness too may inhere in a system of matter without being the sum of the consciousnesses of the parts. He concedes that 'if Consciousness inheres in a System of Matter, it must necessarily be allow'd, that the distinct Beings in that System *contribute* towards thinking, as the pieces of a Circle do towards a Circle, or as all the parts of a System of matter contribute towards the System' (ibid., 20–1; my italics), but it is not required that the 'distinct Beings in that System' have themselves the power of consciousness or that 'each part must be wholly conscious' (ibid., 24). It is only the material system as a whole to which we may ascribe the power of consciousness. This argument was also used by materialists in the second half of the century: for example, by Joseph Priestley.

Collins's leanings may be more materialist than Locke's, but his account of personal identity is, like Locke's, compatible with an agnostic position on the nature of the soul: he argues that personal identity is constituted through consciousness, and that the identity of the thinking substance, whatever its nature, is not required for personal identity.[77] It follows that personal identity is retainable if (as he assumes) the bearer of actions and consciousness is material and subject to change. For one can ascribe to oneself a past action through consciousness, although the material particles constituting that self have completely changed since the action it now recalls was performed.[78] One essential point of agreement between Locke and Collins is, then, that both hold that the identity of the underlying ontological basis of consciousness is not relevant to the identity of the person, no matter whether that basis is more likely to be immaterial (Locke) or material (Collins).

Indeed, Collins several times appeals to Locke as an authority on the issue of personal identity.[79] Like Locke, he distinguishes between the identity of the man and the identity of the person, arguing that 'the Mad Man and the sober Man are really two as distinct Persons as any two other Men in the World...and it will be thought as unjust to punish the sober Man for what the mad Man did, as to punish one Man for another's Fault, tho the Man both sober and mad is the same Man'

---

[76] Collins, *An Answer To Mr. Clarke's Third Defence of his Letter to Mr. Dodwell* (1708), p. 23.
[77] See Collins, *An Answer to Mr. Clark's Third Defence* (1708), p. 67: '*Self* or Personal Identity consists solely in Consciousness; since when I distinguish my *Self* from others, and when I attribute any past Actions to my *Self,* it is only by extending my Consciousness to them.'
[78] See Collins, *Reflections on Mr. Clark's Second Defence,* p. 29: 'by reviving the Idea of that Action, I imprint afresh the Consciousness of having done that Action, by which the Brain has as lively an Impression of Consciousness (tho it be not intirely compos'd of the same Particles) as it had the day after it did the Action.' Compare also the following passage on the same page: 'a Man may be conscious of things done by him, tho he has not one Particle of matter the same that he had at the doing of those things.'
[79] See, for example, Collins, *An Answer to Mr. Clark's Third Defence,* pp. 73, 75.

(*An Answer to Mr. Clark's Third Defence*, p. 66). And like Locke, he holds that a change of substance does not affect personal identity, just as a change of particles does not affect the identity of the man. If we hold that personal identity is constituted by consciousness, we 'may have as clear an Idea of *Personal Identity* continuing under the greatest change of Substance, as [we] may have an idea of Animal or Human *Identity,* which consisting in a continued Life, under a like continued organization of Parts, cannot be destroy'd by the greatest change or flux of particles imaginable' (ibid., p. 76).[80]

Importantly, Collins says more about the notion of consciousness and its role in constituting personal identity than do his contemporaries. Like Locke, he holds that consciousness can relate to the present[81] as well as to the past, and he emphasises that consciousness, considered at different times, is never numerically the same. He speaks of 'the impossibility of the *same Numerical Consciousness* continuing a moment in a Finite Being', insisting 'that every moment's Consciousness is a new Action' (ibid.).[82] Thus it is not the identity *of consciousness* that constitutes personal identity. Rather, consciousness itself is diverse, and personal identity is constituted through successive links of numerically distinct acts of consciousness. When Collins speaks of the 'same consciousness' (ibid.) he has in mind such a connectedness of acts of consciousness that makes me the same person over time, no matter what happens to the (material) thinking substance. Moreover, and again following Locke, he assigns a role to 'Memory extending to past Actions' in the constitution of personal identity (ibid., p. 69).

Voltaire's admiration for Locke, as expressed in his famous Letter 13 of his *Lettres philosophiques,* is well known and has been much commented on.[83] The account that Voltaire provides of personal identity, however, is less well known. There are remarks on related issues scattered in several of his writings, but the main if brief discussion is to be found in his *Traité de métaphysique* (1734).[84] Like Locke, Voltaire thinks that it

---

[80] Collins's account of the resurrection, too, is in essentially the same terms as Locke's. The identity of the resurrection-body is not required for the identity of the person at the resurrection: 'the restoring the Power of Thinking to the same (or if you please a different) Body at the Resurrection, with a Memory or Consciousness extending to past Actions, will be a raising the same Person and not a Creation of a new Person': *An Answer to Mr. Clark's Third Defence*, p. 68. For, 'if Personal Identity consists in Consciousness, or a Memory extending to past Actions, *that* will make any one as much the same Person that he was in this World, as any one is the same Person here two days together': ibid., p. 69.

[81] In *Reflections on Mr. Clark's Second Defence*, Collins says that the material subject of thought 'must at the same time know that it thinks or be conscious of its thinking' (p. 58).

[82] Uzgalis (2008) suggests that Collins differs from Locke in this respect: 'Locke and Collins', p. 322. We have seen, however, that this is Locke's view too. On the whole it seems that Uzgalis's list of Collins's 'divergences' from Locke is problematic, as he does not take into account Collins's Lockean distinction between man and person.

[83] Voltaire, *Lettres philosophiques,* ed. Lanson, third edn., 2 vols. (1924). The book was first published in English as *Letters concerning the English Nation* (1733). The French edition was published as *Lettres écrites de Londres sur les Anglois, et autres sujets* (1734). Compare Yolton (1991).

[84] Voltaire, *Traité de métaphysique* (1734), ed. Temple Patterson, second edn. (1957; first edn., 1937). The *Traité* was first published posthumously in vol. 32 of *Oeuvres complètes de Voltaire*, 70 vols. (1784–89). According to Temple Patterson, the work 'passed through three stages between 1734 and 1737' (p. vi). All references to the *Traité* are to Temple Patterson's edition.

is possible that matter may think (*Traité*, p. 35). Not surprisingly, then, Voltaire's account of personal identity is also essentially Lockean, and may also have been influenced by Collins's version of Locke's theory, as it appears that Voltaire was familiar with the controversy between Collins and Clarke by 1734.[85] As we shall see, however, his account is not very precise.

Voltaire deals with the issue of diachronic personal identity towards the end of a short chapter on the question of immortality and life after death (ibid., pp. 40–2). He argues that that which constitutes the person of Jacques and makes him, in his own eyes, the same person as the Jacques of yesterday is that he remembers the ideas he had yesterday, and that he unites, in his own understanding, his existence of yesterday with that of today. If he had lost all his memory, his past existence would seem to him to be as alien as that of another human being: he would be no more the same Jacques that he was yesterday than he is Socrates or Caesar.[86] It is important to note that Voltaire's account is in terms of memory only, rather than in terms of consciousness and memory as is the case with Locke and Collins.

Nevertheless, like Locke, Voltaire emphasises the subjective constitution of personal identity. To him, it is important what the person of Jacques is 'in his own eyes', or 'in his own understanding'. The personality and personal identity of Jacques are constituted subjectively through a particular kind of inner experience. Voltaire asks: if Jacques were to lose totally his memory through an illness but were to regain it later, say, through God's will, would that mean that the ideas that had not existed for some time would be created anew, so that a new man is being created (ibid., p. 41)? Following Locke, Voltaire employs the notions of man and person in order to deal with this issue. It is plain, however, that unlike Locke he does not distinguish clearly between these notions, and that he in fact tends to confuse them. He argues that if Jacques were to completely lose his memory through an illness, he would still remain the same *man* or human being when he recovers his memory, so there would be no creation of a new man who would be 'as different from the former as an Indian is from a European' (ibid., p. 41). What he seems to be saying is that although the personality ceased to exist with the loss of memory, the identity of the man remains, and when the same man regains his memory there is no need to speak of the creation of a new being.[87] He seems to make the identity of the person dependent on the identity of the man, however, and that would seem to contradict the thesis of the subjective constitution of personality with which he had started. Worse, he does not even speak of the human subject as a person in this context, but of the sameness of the *man*: '*Jacques* sera le même homme' (ibid., p. 41).

---

[85] See Temple Patterson's note on p. 37 in his edition of Voltaire's *Traité*.
[86] Voltaire writes: 'Ce qui constitue la personne de *Jacques*, ce qui fait que *Jacques* est soi-même, et le même qu'il était hier à ses propres yeux, c'est qu'il se ressouvient des idées qu'il avait hier, et que dans son entendement il unit son existence d'hier à celle d'aujourd'hui; car s'il avait entièrement perdu la mémoire, son existence passée lui serait aussi étrangère que celle d'un autre homme; il ne serait pas plus le *Jacques* d'hier, la même personne, qu'il ne serait *Socrate* ou *César*': *Traité*, p. 41.
[87] As Voltaire states: 'car un homme qui a entièrement perdu la mémoire dans une grande maladie, ne cesse pas d'être le même homme lorsqu'il a recouvré la mémoire': *Traité*, p. 41.

Voltaire, then, attempts to provide a Lockean account, accepting the possibility of thinking matter, but fails because he is unclear about Locke's crucial distinction between the man and the person. Voltaire himself concedes defeat in a sense, without however realizing the cause of this defeat (his confusion between man and person) when he suggests that these issues relating to personal identity are worth considering, and that he that could solve them would be 'an able man' indeed.[88]

The issue of thinking matter is the main focus of Caspar Cuenz's huge and very diffuse work *Essai d'un sisteme nouveau* (1742).[89] The Swiss philosopher announces on the title page that this 'new system' concerns the nature of spiritual beings and is 'in part founded on the principles of the celebrated Locke'. He adopts the notion of an extended soul, claiming, however, that this does not commit him to materialism (*Sisteme*, vol. 4, 195ff.). He does not discuss in any detail the issue of personal identity, but comments on the notion of person. Apart from Locke he appeals to the work of the Newtonian philosopher Willem Jacob Gravesande, Professor of Philosophy at the University of Leiden since 1734.[90] Gravesande adopts a Lockean account of personal identity in his popular *Introduction à la philosophie*,[91] emphasising the distinction between the identity of the self as person and as rational substance. He states that a person is an 'intelligent substance' that can remember its past perceptions and has an inner feeling (*sentiment intérieur*) of its present existence. This feeling and the remembering of past perceptions make up the *memory* of its past existence (pp. 36–7). And it is this memory of its past existence that constitutes an intelligent substance's identity as a person.[92] He notes that it is possible that the self as rational substance remains the same, while the self as person is no longer the same if one's memory of one's past existence has been lost.[93]

Unlike Gravesande, but like Voltaire, Cuenz focuses on the distinction between person and man. According to Cuenz, the human self is born a mere physical

---

[88] 'Ces difficultés valent bien la peine d'être proposées, et celui qui trouvera une manière sure de résoudre l'équation de cette inconnue, sera, je pense, un habile homme': ibid.

[89] Cuenz (also spelt 'Cuentz' or 'Künz'), *Essai d'un sisteme nouveau concernant la nature des êtres spirituels, fondé en partie sur les principes du célèbre Mr. Locke, philosophe anglois, dont l'auteur fait l'apologie*, 4 vols. (1742). There does not seem to be much secondary material on Cuenz, but Yolton (1991), pp. 23–4, 76–84, gives a general account of Cuenz's work and the thinking matter issue.

[90] See Yolton (1991), pp. 82–3.

[91] Gravesande, *Introduction à la philosophie, contenant la métaphysique, et la logique... Traduite du Latin* (1737). The first, Latin, edition appeared in 1736 (*Introductio ad philosophiam: Metaphysicam et logicam continens*). References to and quotations from this work relate to the 1737 French translation, which was approved by Gravesande.

[92] 'Les Metaphysiciens disent, qu'une Personne est une substance intelligente déterminée. Mais suivant eux, cette substance intelligente doit être telle, qu'outre les idées presentes, elle ait encore un tel souvenir de ses perceptions passées, qu'avec le sentiment intérieur de son existence actuelle, se trouve jointe la mémoire de son existence passée. C'est cette mémoire qui constitue proprement l'Identité d'une Personne': ibid., pp. 36–7.

[93] 'En supposant cette mémoire, une Personne est la même, en l'ôtant, la Personne est changée, quoiqu'elle soit la même par rapport à la substance. Par maladie, ou par quelque autre accident, Pierre a perdu la mémoire du passé; les idées, qu'il a presentement, ont aussi peut de relation avec celles qu'il a autrefois, qu'avec les idées que Paul a eues; & nous ne decouvrons aucune Identité entre Intelligence presente de Pierre, & son Intelligence passée. La substance cependant n'a point été changée, mais seulement la Personne': ibid., p. 37.

being that has inner and outer senses as basic mental capacities. It also has the capacity over time to become a moral being or person; that is, a being that is responsible for its actions.[94] Man is responsible for his actions not insofar as he is a physical animal being, but insofar as he is a person.[95] Cuenz links this development of the human subject from mere physical being to personhood to the development of practical reason—a development that is based on experience. In places he even identifies personality with practical reason—for example, when he speaks of 'reason or that personality through which man becomes responsible for his actions and capable of rewards and punishments'.[96] He seems to be following Pufendorf (and Locke) here, saying that personality or the human subject considered as a moral entity is superadded to the self as physical being. More precisely, he states that the person considered as a moral entity is an *ens rationis*.[97] Man's moral nature is 'relative to his personality which is a moral idea'.[98]

Regarding identity through time Cuenz argues that among the beings that God has created indivisible are those that are destined to be immortal—spiritual beings, such as the human soul. And he thinks that we have good reason to assume that such beings will always remain identical through time (*Sisteme*, vol. 3, p. 73).[99] What he does not seem to address, however, is the issue of how these indivisible spiritual beings are related to the personality of the self. Consistently with his Lockean distinction between the man and the person, he says that self-consciousness or the *sentiment intérieur* does not constitute the identity of the man. Self-consciousness or the *sentiment intérieur* cannot constitute the identity of the man because life or the living physical being of man is presupposed by self-consciousness. We could not have a *sentiment intérieur* without the man as a living physical being; the *sentiment intérieur* results from life, not vice versa.[100] Therefore, it would be absurd to claim

---

[94] Cuenz states: 'que l'home est un Tissu indéfinissable d'étendue & de puissance, un Composé de parties internes & externes; que venant au Monde, il n'est qu'un Etre purement physique, doüé de sens extérieurs & intérieurs, & d'une *capacité vuide*, au moïen de laquelle, & par le concours de ses sens extérieurs avec les intérieurs, croissant en âge & en connoissance, il devient un *Etre moral*: Il se forme en lui la Raison & ce qui en dépend, & cette *Personalité*, qui le rend responsable de ses Actions': *Essai d'un sisteme nouveau*, vol. 1, pp. 18–19.

[95] 'L'Home n'est pas responsable entant qu'Animal, mais entant que Persone' (sic), Cuenz, *Sisteme*, vol. 1, p. 19. See also ibid., vol. 2, p. xiii: 'La Personalité est l'état de l'Home fait, de l'Home intelligent, capable de Loi, & de Jugement, de récompense ou de punition, de bonheur ou de misère'.

[96] 'la Raison ou cette *Personalité*, qui rend l'Home responsable de ses Actions, & digne de récompense ou de punition, selon ses mérites ou ses démerites': ibid., vol. 1, p. 21.

[97] 'Les Etres moraux, come tout le Monde le sait, son des Etres de raison': ibid., vol. 3, p. 69.

[98] 'Je sais bien que l'Home est un Etre moral; mais ce qu'il y a de moral en lui n'est rélatif qu'a sa Personalité, qui est une idée morale, et non pas à son Existence phisique': ibid.

[99] 'Quant à ceux que Dieu a crée indivisibles, ce sont I. Ceux qu'il a déstinés à l'Immortalité.... Nous présumons avec raison, que leur *Identité* est toujours la même sans *juxta position*, *séparation*, ou *altération* quelconque. Nous ne saurions refuser une étenduë réelle à tous ces Etres Bien-Heureux, puisqu'ils ocupent un lieu, qu'ils se transportent d'un endroit dans l'autre': ibid., p. 73.

[100] Cuenz writes in response to a critic: 'Permettés moi de vous dire, que je ne comprens rien à ce langage: *Le Sentiment constitüe le Moi: Il fait l'Identité de l'Home*. Dites moi: La Vie résulte-t'elle du Sentiment, ou le Sentiment résulte-t'il de la Vie? Je ne crois pas que je vive, parce que je sens; mais que je sens parce que je vis': ibid., vol. 4, p. 276.

that this *sentiment* constitutes the identity of the man. Cuenz does not seem to say explicitly, however, that consciousness constitutes the identity of the *person*. Indeed he does not account for the notions of consciousness and self-consciousness in any detail. He notes some important aspects of these notions, however. He seems to equate the *sentiment intérieur* with 'le Sentiment de soi meme' (ibid., vol. 4, p. 275), stating that it is 'a reflex act of the soul. I feel that I am something, that I am what I am'. He argues that although the capacity of self-consciousness is an original property of the soul, in order to be able to perform such a reflex act the existence of other modifications of the soul (perceptions, thoughts) is required.[101] On the other hand, he seems to think also that we could not think and not even have sensations if we did not feel our own existence.[102] Unfortunately, he does not develop or explain this mutual relationship that he sees between self-consciousness on the one hand and thought and sensory experience on the other.

Collins, Voltaire, and Cuenz are thinkers who very clearly see a constructive role for a Lockean account of personal identity within a materialist metaphysics—even if Cuenz, for example, does not wish to commit himself explicitly to materialism. They recognize this without misreading Locke's suggestion about thinking matter as an endorsement of materialism. We noted that Locke's own theory would in principle fit as easily into a materialist as into an immaterialist theory of the mind. Nevertheless, it is obvious from the debates that followed that the various answers to the question of what constitutes personal identity depended, at least to a considerable extent, on the views adopted about the nature of the human mind. Defenders of the immateriality of the soul rejected Locke's account of personal identity precisely because it leaves open the very question of immateriality. Some eighteenth-century critics of Locke even harboured the suspicion that he chose to place personal identity in consciousness just so that he could leave open the possibility that the mind might be material.[103]

---

[101] 'Le Sentiment de soi même est, come vous dites, un Acte réfléchi de l'Ame: Je sens que je suis quelque chose; que je suis ce que je suis. Mais je crois que je ne saurois me faire cette représentation à moi même, sans quelque modification, & par consequent sans Mouvement. La capacité du sentiment de soi même est une proprieté de l'Ame': ibid., vol. 4, p. 275.

[102] 'On ne sauroit sentir, voir, ouïr, flairer etc sans la conscience de soi même': ibid., vol. 2, p. 397. See also vol. 1, pp. 36–7: 'Il est certain qu'on ne sauroit penser, sans que l'Etre, par un Acte réfléchi sur soi même, ne sente qu'il pense.'

[103] See Watts, *Philosophical Essays on Various Subjects... With Remarks on Mr. Locke's Essay on the Human Understanding* (1733; 3rd edn. 1742; reprinted, 1990), p. 302.

PART III

PROBLEMS WITH LOCKE: CRITIQUE AND DEFENCE

5

The notion of a person and the role of consciousness and memory

Although Locke's theory was taken up in a positive way, as illustrated towards the end of the previous Chapter, it aroused controversy very soon after its first publication in 1694. Indeed, it dominated the disputes over personal identity in the late seventeenth century and throughout the eighteenth century. This is true especially, but not only, of British philosophy.[1] While practically everybody who wrote on the issue positioned himself in relation to Locke's theory, the latter's influence led to a variety of responses and several quite different attempts at dealing with the issue.

In this and the following Chapter we shall look at responses that consist mainly in explicitly criticizing or defending Locke's theory. It is further testimony to Locke's importance on the topic that many of the issues that were raised in the debates about Locke's theory continue to occupy present-day philosophical discussions about personal identity.

The influence of Locke's theory is not confined to philosophical disputes: summaries appear in some of the leading encyclopaedias of the time. Thus, in the two most important British encyclopaedias of the first half of the century, the entries for 'identity' simply describe Locke's theory. John Harris's *Lexicon technicum* (1710) mainly describes Locke's account of the identity of physical objects and living bodies; it merely hints at his account of personal identity.[2] Ephraim Chambers's famous *Cyclopaedia* (1728), however, summarizes Locke's theory of personal identity quite extensively.[3] Neither Chambers nor Harris, however, engages with Locke's view in a critical or evaluative way.

Locke's theory also had a considerable impact on eighteenth-century literature—for example, in Jonathan Swift and Laurence Sterne.[4] It was satirized by the *Scriblerus*

---

[1] For an overview of eighteenth-century British responses to Locke's theory, see Thiel, *Lockes Theorie der personalen Identität* (1983), pp. 175–98. For an overview of Anglican responses to Locke's theory, see Tennant, 'The Anglican Response to Locke's Theory of Personal Identity', *Journal of the History of Ideas*, 43 (1982), 73–90.

[2] Harris, *Lexicon technicum: Or, an Universal English Dictionary of Arts and Sciences Explaining not only the Terms of Art, but the Arts themselves* (1710), vol. 2, entry 'Identity'.

[3] Chambers, *Cyclopaedia: Or, an Universal Dictionary of Arts and Sciences... The Whole intended as a Course of Antient and Modern Learning* (1728), vol. 2, p. 370.

[4] The impact of Locke's theory of personal identity on eighteenth-century literature is discussed, for example, in MacLean, *John Locke and English Literature of the Eighteenth Century* (1962); Watt, *The Rise of the Novel* (1957); Tuveson, 'Locke and the Dissolution of the Ego', *Modern Philology*, 52

Club—an association of writers such as Swift, Pope, and others.[5] The satires, first published in 1741, are aimed at perceived materialist tendencies of Lockean thought about identity and at the view that consciousness constitutes personal identity. Locke's view that personal identity is retained by consciousness through the change of our body is ridiculed, for example, as follows:

> Sir John Cutler had a pair of black worsted stockings, which his maid darn'd so often with silk, that they became at last a pair of silk stockings. Now supposing those stockings of Sir John's endued with some degree of Consciousness at every particular darning, they would have been sensible, that they were the same individual pair of stockings both before and after the darning; and this sensation would have continued in them through all the succession of darnings; and yet after the last of all, there was not perhaps one thread left of the first pair of stockings, but they were grown to be silk stockings, as was said before. (Kerby-Miller, *Memoirs*, p. 140)

The satires are written from the immaterialist point of view, affirming that there is 'an individual self-moving, self-determining principle'—in short, the soul, which guarantees identity through time. The 'same individual', the *Scriblerians* suggest, 'cannot subsist without the notion of a spiritual substance' (ibid., p. 140).

The critical attitude towards Lockean theory, if not the satirical style of writing, is shared by a majority of eighteenth-century thinkers who discuss the problem. Although some attempt to defend it,[6] most of them attack it, taking up issues discussed in the previous Chapter. We have seen that Locke's friend William Molyneux raises questions about the moral and legal aspects of Locke's consciousness-based account of personal identity, and that Edward Stillingfleet, Bishop of Worcester, bases his arguments on metaphysical and theological assumptions and attempts to tie personal identity to substantial identity. These two main types of criticism are, of course, related. Thus the relevant theological assumptions that concern the afterlife, for example, are closely linked to the issue of moral accountability. We shall see that both critique and defence are, for the most part, based on an oversimplified reading, and misrepresent Locke's complex account. Edmund Law—a follower of Locke on personal identity—is perhaps the most notable exception.

(1955), 155–74; Tuveson, *The Imagination as a Means of Grace: Locke and the Aesthetics of Romanticism* (1960); Wertz and Wertz, 'Some Correlations between Swift's Gulliver and Locke on Personal Identity', *Journal of Thought*, 10 (1975), 262–70; and Fox, *Locke and the Scriblerians: Identity and Consciousness in Early Eighteenth-Century Britain* (1988). See also Shin, 'Search for Personal Identity in Locke and Wordsworth', *Journal of English Language and Literature*, 35 (1989), 627–50.

[5] See Kerby-Miller (ed.), *Memoirs of the Extraordinary Life, Works and Discoveries of Martinus Scriblerus* (1950; reprinted, 1988). For discussions of the Scriblerians' treatment of identity, see also Erickson, 'Situations of Identity in the *Memoirs of Scriblerus*', *Modern Language Quarterly*, 26 (1965), 388–400; Lund, 'Martinus Scriblerus and the Search for the Soul', *Papers in Language and Literature*, 25 (1989), 135–50; Todd, *Imagining Monsters: Miscreations of the Self in Eighteenth-Century England* (1995), pp. 121–35.

[6] See, for example, Bold, *A Discourse on the Resurrection of the Same Body* (1705); Collins, *Reflections on Mr. Clark's Second Defence of his Letter to Mr. Dodwell* (1707); and Collins, *An Answer to Mr. Clark's Third Defence of his Letter to Mr. Dodwell* (1708).

The notion of a person and the role of consciousness and memory

Most criticisms of Locke's theory directly or indirectly concern two main issues: (1) Locke's distinction between the notions of person, man, and soul or thinking substance; (2) Locke's view that consciousness and memory constitute personal identity. Criticisms that relate to the theological, moral, and legal aspects of Locke's theory are in various ways, explicitly or implicitly, grounded in a rejection of (1) and (2). As we have seen in the previous Chapter, these two issues are closely related. Locke's consciousness-based account of personal identity is crucially linked to his distinguishing between the concepts of person, man, and soul or thinking substance. If this distinction is not accepted it is obvious that the identity of a person cannot be solely constituted through consciousness and memory, as Locke claims. Many of Locke's seventeenth- and eighteenth-century critics are aware of this. Indeed, even most of those critics who do not concern themselves specifically with that distinction and focus instead on the thesis that consciousness and memory 'make' personal identity implicitly reject (or do not grasp) that distinction. Such criticisms can therefore be met from a Lockean perspective by pointing to the importance of that very distinction, assuming that it is sound. It is more difficult to defend Locke's thesis about consciousness and personal identity against arguments that do not depend in any way on a denial of that distinction. Such arguments can be valid even if the distinction were accepted. Some critics, of course, deal critically with both the person–man–thinking substance distinction and Locke's thesis about consciousness. And among those that examine that distinction, some focus their critique on Locke's distinction between the person and the man, while others have problems with the distinction between the person and the soul or thinking substance.

In sum, it would seem that those objections to Locke would be most powerful that succeed in refuting (a) the person–man–soul or thinking substance distinction directly, or (b) the claim about consciousness and memory without ignoring or implicitly rejecting that distinction. A combination of both (a) and (b) would seem to constitute the strongest argument against Locke (present, for example, in Thomas Reid, discussed in the next Chapter).

This summary analysis is of course very general. Although it highlights the structure and nature of the most important criticisms, we need to look at the individual arguments in their contexts in order to be able to evaluate them. In this Chapter we shall first look at arguments against Locke's distinction between the man, the thinking substance or soul, and the person: the most important theological context here is the doctrine of the resurrection, as is the case in the debate between Locke and Stillingfleet discussed in the previous Chapter. We shall then turn to arguments that concern the constitutive role that Locke ascribes to consciousness and memory. These include criticisms that appeal to the significance of moral and legal issues for personal identity. The next Chapter is devoted to the two major issues that continue to be debated in connection with Locke's account of personal identity in terms of consciousness: the charge of circularity, and the argument from the transitivity of identity.

5.1. PERSON, MAN, SOUL, AND THE RESURRECTION OF THE BODY

Although the issue of Locke's distinction between the notions of person, man, and soul or thinking substance comes up in various contexts, it is put forward most frequently in debates about the afterlife and in particular about the resurrection. This is not surprising. The notions of person, man, and soul, and their relationships to each other, are central to the debates about the resurrection, as the traditional view sees the latter as a reunion of soul and body into one person. We have seen that Locke himself connects the issue of personal identity to that of the resurrection, and becomes embroiled in a debate with Edward Stillingfleet, Bishop of Worcester, over the issue. In spite of Locke's published responses to Stillingfleet, his theory of personal identity and the related distinction between person, man, and soul continued to be criticized for its alleged inconsistency with the resurrection doctrine by many theologians and philosophers after Stillingfleet. Such critics include Thomas Becconsall,[7] Samuel Parker,[8] William Lupton,[9] Winch Holdsworth,[10] Henry Felton,[11] and Robert d'Oyly.[12] These authors regard the human person as a unity of a mental and a material substance, arguing, like Stillingfleet, that the identity of the human person through time requires both the identity of the soul and that of the body. Thus they tacitly or explicitly reject Locke's distinction between man and person. Thomas Becconsall, for example, writes that 'since Man, or which is the same thing, a *humane Person*, is certainly a Being compounded of Two distinct Principles, an *animal*, and a *spiritual Principle*, a *Soul*, and a *Body*, I cannot comply with a late *Reformer* of *Humane Understanding*, that places *Personal Identity* purely in Consciousness' (Becconsall, *Resurrection*, pp. 14–15.). These critics ascribe to Locke a view that William Sherlock (but not Locke) holds: that the soul as substance alone constitutes the person, and that therefore the identity of the body is not required at

---

[7] Becconsall, *The Doctrine of a General Resurrection: Wherein the Identity of the Rising Body is asserted against the Socinians and Scepticks* (1697).

[8] See Parker, *Essays on divers weighty and curious Subjects. Particularly on Mr. Lock's and Sir William Temple's Notions* (1702); and Parker, *A Letter to Mr. Bold, occasion'd by his late Discourse concerning the Resurrection of the Same Body* (1707).

[9] Lupton, *The Resurrection of the Same Body. A Sermon preach'd before the University of Oxford* (1711).

[10] Holdsworth, *A Sermon preached before the University of Oxford... in which the Cavils, False Reasonings, and False Interpretations of Scripture of Mr. Lock and Others, against the Resurrection of the same Body are examin'd and answered* (1720); and Holdsworth, *A Defence of the Doctrine of the Resurrection of the Same Body* (1727).

[11] Felton, *The Resurrection of the same Numerical Body, and its Reunion to the same Soul; Asserted in a Sermon preached before the University of Oxford, at St. Mary's on Easter-Monday, 1725. In which Mr. Lock's Notions of Personality and Identity are confuted. And the Author of the Naked Gospel is answered* (1725).

[12] d'Oyly, *Four Dissertations* (1728), pp. 425–75.

the resurrection.[13] For them there can be the same person at the resurrection only if the soul is reunited with numerically the same body that it had in this life. As d'Oyly expresses it: 'undoubtedly to the *Identity of a Man, the Union* of the *same Soul* with the *same Body* must be necessarily requisite; unless the *Identity* of a *Compound* can be perfect and complete, without the *Union* of the *essentially constituent Parts of* it'.[14]

Several of these authors point out that they do not consider it necessary even to deal with Locke's theory of identity in any detail. Holdsworth and d'Oyly argue that it is true that in Locke the account of the resurrection depends on his new theory of personal identity, but as the latter does not require the identity of the body for the identity of the person, it should for that reason not be used in an account of the resurrection.[15] Like Stillingfleet, however, some of these critics appeal to the account of the identity of 'man' or a human being in Locke's *Essay*, arguing that that account could be used for an account of the resurrection of the same body. Locke himself points out that the body is an essential component of man; therefore, his critics argue, the body at the resurrection must be identical with the pre-mortem body, otherwise we would not have the same man as in this life.[16] According to Becconsall, 'the Identity of the animal Part must in one word consist *In a fit Construction and Organization of certain Particles of Matter, whereby one common Principle of Life is begun, continued, and the Integral Parts of the Man are perfected and maintained*' (Becconsall, *Resurrection*, p. 19).

5.1.1. 'Identity of person as apply'd to man': Felton

Of the critics listed above, Henry Felton is one who engages with Locke's account in some detail. Felton argues, against Locke, that the resurrection concerns the body, and that the debate should be about what constitutes the sameness of the body at the resurrection:

It is not enough to define what makes the same Person, if Man could be the same Person he was, without his own Body, the Question in the Resurrection is what makes the *same Body*, or whether the *same Body* shall be rais'd, and appropriated to the *same Man*, or the *same Person*, it belong'd to before. 'Tis with Respect to the *Body* alone, in which a Man *dies*, that he is said to *rise*, and therefore unless he rises in the same Body he cannot rise at all. To give him another Body is not to raise that which is dead, this is forming a new one, not raising up the old. And as far as the Body is a Constituent part of Man, as far as every Man

---

[13] See, for example, Holdsworth, *A Defence*, p. 166: 'according to Him [Locke], Men are Persons only by their Souls' (see also pp. 168ff.). Compare also Lupton, *The Resurrection of the same Body*, p. 14; Felton, *The Resurrection of the same Numerical Body*, p. 5; and d'Oyly, *Four Dissertations*, p. 428.
[14] d'Oyly, *Four Dissertations*, pp. 435–6. See also Parker, *A Letter to Mr. Bold*, p. 33; Lupton, *The Resurrection of the same Body*, pp. 15–16; Holdsworth, *A Defence*, p. 169; Felton, *The Resurrection of the same Numerical Body*, pp. 5, 9, 15, 18.
[15] Holdsworth, *A Defence*, pp. 167–8; d'Oyly, *Four Dissertations*, pp. 427–8. Parker, too, states that an analysis of Locke's theory of personal identity as such is not required. Parker, *Essays*, p. 11; Parker, *A Letter to Mr. Bold*, p. 35.
[16] Lupton, *The Resurrection of the same Body*, pp. 15–16; d'Oyly, *Four Dissertations*, p. 461.

158   *The Early Modern Subject*

in his own Body is an *Individual*, so far *another Body* makes *another Man*, and *another Man* makes *another Person*'.[17]

In some respects Felton captures Locke's position much better than do most theological critics. Like the others, he claims that for Locke 'it is indifferent what Body is united to the Soul at the Resurrection, the Body being no more than a Veil or Garment to the Soul' (ibid., p. 18). Unlike many other critics, however, he realizes that for Locke to say that the resurrection concerns the person means that the identity of the person at the resurrection is constituted through consciousness rather than by the sameness of the soul:

> The *Author* of the *Essay* has a Notion of the Resurrection of the *Dead*, without any Resurrection of the *Body*, whether the *same* or any *other*; But his Resurrection of the *Dead* is only a *Resurrection* of *Persons*, and as far as he holds the *Resurrection* of the *same Person*,'tis no more than a *Resurrection* of the *same Consciousness*'. (ibid., p. 22)

As Felton remarks quite rightly, Locke 'means the *Uniting* of the *Person*, or rather the *Consciousness* of the *Person* to some Portion of *Matter*, or *other*, *like* or *not like* the Body of Man; and this is his *Notion*... of the *Resurrection*' (ibid., p. 16). He says, correctly, that according to Locke not even the same soul is required for the resurrection: for Locke, the Person may be the same, though 'neither Body nor Soul be the same, and so for any thing the Soul signifies, Personality as well as Identity may consist in Consciousness alone'.[18]

And yet, like the other critics, Felton thinks that Locke identifies the person or personality of the self with the soul. In his view Locke believes that the person is the soul, but that the identity of the soul is constituted through consciousness. He states that Locke 'confine[s] *Personality* to the *Soul*' and 'place[s] *Identity* in *Consciousness* alone' (ibid., p. 5). For Felton, then, Locke, in order to place personal identity in consciousness alone, places personality in the soul alone; and in order to do that he distinguishes between substance, man, and person (ibid., p. 6). It is not surprising that Felton, on the basis of this reading of Locke, cannot accept the latter's account of personal identity.

As far as the distinction between the *ideas* of man, substance, and person is concerned, Felton concedes that

> it is true they are *distinct*, and we can consider *each* by it *self* in our Minds; But when these *Ideas* are apply'd to one *Subject* in which they all *meet* and are *combin'd*, however we may *abstract* and *separate* them in our *Thoughts*, we cannot *separate* them in the *Nature* and *Existence* of things. (ibid., pp. 6–7)

---

[17] Felton, *The Resurrection of the same Numerical Body*, pp. 4–5. See also pp. 17, 18: '*that* which *dies*, is to *revive*, *that* which is *laid in the Dust*, is to *rise again*; for if the *same Body* do's not *rise*, the *Man* cannot in any Sense be said to *rise again from the Dead*'; 'and when the same Body is united to the same *Soul*, then we apprehend, that the *same Person* who *died* may be said to be *risen again*'.

[18] Felton, *The Resurrection of the same Numerical Body*, second (unpaginated) page of the Dedication.

Locke's distinction applies only to our ideas or concepts, but it does not apply to things themselves.

Felton concedes further that there are (non-human) persons who may not have a body. An individual human being, however, is to be understood as a unity of a mental and a bodily substance:

> Tho' *every Substance* is not *Man*, yet *every Man* is a *Substance*; tho' *every Person* is not *Man*, yet *every Man* is a *Person*: We say, that *Man* consists of *two Substances*: one *Material*, which is the *Body*; the other *Spiritual*, which is the *Soul*; and from the *Conjunction* of *Both* results the *Person*. The *Person* of Man is not his *inward Nature alone*, but his *outward Appearance*, his *visible Body* also, that which we see, converse and transact with. (ibid., p. 7)

In this regard, Felton's thoughts are in line with Stillingfleet and Locke's other critics cited above. For Felton states: 'By *Person* then when apply'd to us, is not to be understood an *Intelligent Being* alone as *such*, but an *Intelligent Compound Being* as *Man*, which makes the *Body* a Part of the Person as much as of the *Individual*' (ibid., p. 9).

Lastly, Felton concedes to Locke that 'person' is a forensic term; but he turns this against Locke, pointing out, plausibly enough, that in legal matters in particular the person is always also regarded as a bodily being. Therefore one should not, as Felton (wrongly) believes Locke does, refer 'person' to the soul alone:

> The word *Person*, this Author tells us very truly, is a *Forensic Term*, and tho' he would refer the Meaning of it to the Soul alone, yet the Law looks upon it in a more Compound View, and takes in the Body as well as the Soul of Man. Indeed the Enquiries of the Law are upon the *Facts*, not the *Consciousness* or *Conscience* of the Offender; and by *Person* the *Law* understands the *Partys* in *Suit*, or the *Prisoner* at the *Bar*. (ibid., p. 7)

According to Felton, even if Locke were right in identifying the person with the soul, he would still be wrong in placing the identity of the person thus understood in consciousness. The identity of the soul does not depend on consciousness and is not consistent with a diversity of substances. The identity of the soul is the identity of a substance:

> If it [the soul] ceases to be the *same Substance*, or if it continues not numerically the *same*, it's *Identity* is immediately lost: whether it be *Conscious* or *not Conscious, Intelligent* or *not Intelligent*, is not the Question: The *Soul* is still the same, as long as it exists in the *Body* or out of the *Body*. That it is *Conscious*, rises from the Will and Bounty of the *Creator*; that it is the *same*, is owing to it's Continuance in that *Singularity* of it *self*, and that *Distinction* from other *Beings*, in which it was created. (ibid., p. 12)

As indicated above, however, for Felton the identity of the self as a person is a related matter but distinct from the identity of the soul:

> [It] consists in the *Principles* of *Individuation*: I say *Principles*, because there is a *Principle* of *Individuation*, which makes the *Body* one and the *same*; and there is a *Principle* of *Individuation*, which makes the *Soul* one and the *same*, and from the *Union* of these *two Individuals* arises a *third* the *Individual Person* of *Man*. (ibid., p. 15)

As not even the identity of the soul can consist in consciousness, *a fortiori* the identity of the person cannot consist in consciousness. Felton points out that if the notion of person as 'an *Intelligent Compound Being*' is accepted, it follows that Locke's '*Notion* of *Identity*' is false (ibid., p. 9). The '*Identity* of *Person* as apply'd to *Man*, either to *Body* or *Soul* or *Both*, doth not consist in *Consciousness*' (ibid., p. 11).

Felton's understanding of the resurrection was in turn criticized by a radical Deist, Jacob Ilive.[19] Ilive does not mention Locke, but he defends a view that Felton (mistakenly) ascribes to Locke—that the soul alone makes the person. Moreover, Ilive denies not only that there will be the *same* body at the resurrection, but also that the body will be resurrected at all. His aim is to 'confute this doctrine of the resurrection of the body as now taught among us' (Ilive, *Oration*, p. 14). For Ilive, 'personality must belong to the soul only, and therefore the soul will be conscious of its personality, after its disunion from the body, as well as it was before its union thereto' (ibid., p. 25). The soul, according to Ilive, is 'indivisible, immaterial, and immortal, and therefore identity and personality is the privilege of the soul only' (ibid., p. 27). This response to criticism of Locke, then, ends up not defending Locke's theory but endorsing an understanding of personal identity that Locke would have rejected just as much as he would have rejected Felton's criticism.

5.1.2. Watts on staminal particles, the resurrection, and the man–person distinction

Another theologian who comments extensively on various aspects of Locke's philosophy is Isaac Watts in his *Philosophical Essays*.[20] Watts is a self-confessed eclectic (Preface, p. v). He praises 'the Cartesian Doctrine of Spirits', but rejects much of Descartes's 'System of the Material World' (ibid.), instead following Newton. He also praises Locke, who 'has proceeded to break our philosophical Fetters' (ibid., p. vii). Locke's *Essay*, Watts maintains, contains 'many admirable Chapters', 'and many Truths in them, which are worthy of Letters of Gold' (ibid., p. viii). He disagrees with Locke on some issues (ibid., p. ix), however, and the issue of personal identity is one of them. Watts points out that he wrote the sections on Locke much earlier than the rest of the book; indeed, that he wrote them when Locke was still alive; that is, before October 1704 (*Philosophical Essays*, p. 297, footnote). Watts is also the author of a very popular *Logick* (1724), which has numerous references to Locke. His account of the resurrection is somewhat unusual, and consequently so is the perspective from which he evaluates Locke's account.

---

[19] Ilive, *The Oration spoke at Trinity-Hall in Aldersgate-street: In Answer to Dr. Felton's Two Discourses on the Resurrection of the same Body* (1738). For a summary of Ilive's religious views, see Herrick, *The Radical Rhetoric of the English Deists. The Discourse of Skepticism, 1680–1750* (1997), pp. 181–204.

[20] Watts, *Philosophical Essays on Various Subjects...With Remarks on Mr. Locke's Essay on the Human Understanding. To which is subjoined A brief Scheme of Ontology* (1733; second edn., 1734; third edn., 1742; reprint of the 1742 edition, 1990). Watts discusses the issue of the resurrection of the same body on pp. 183–95.

Watts sets up his discussion of the resurrection in the form of a debate between Locke and Stillingfleet. He gives summaries of what he takes to be Stillingfleet's and Locke's respective arguments, considers the pros and cons, and then puts forward a kind of middle way. In the end, however, his account is closer to Stillingfleet's than it is to Locke's. He emphasises that, unlike Locke, he does not distinguish between man and person.[21] In his view, Locke introduces that distinction simply as a means to extricate himself from problems for his account of personal identity (*Philosophical Essays*, p. 307). Thus Watts is aware of the importance of this distinction in Locke, but rejects it, and must for this reason alone also reject Locke's account of personal identity. For Watts, the person is soul and body united.

Watts's main argument against Locke's man–person distinction is that it corresponds neither to the nature of things, nor to ordinary language, and not even to philosophical language.[22] For example, like Felton he considers Locke's emphasis on the 'forensic' meaning of the term 'person', but argues that for the most part 'person' is not used in a forensic sense at all (ibid., pp. 307–8). He notes that in everyday usage when, for example, we refer to the men who are in one room at the same time (ibid., p. 308) we use the term 'person' not in a forensic sense at all, but simply to refer to individual human beings. More importantly, Locke's distinction has the absurd consequence that two men can be the same person or the same man two persons. Therefore, Locke's 'Opinion, if universally received, would bring in endless Confusions, wheresoever the Word *Person* was introduced' (ibid., p. 308).

Watts holds (not unlike Stillingfleet) that in an incomplete sense, the soul on its own can be regarded as the person (ibid., p. 309), but this too is of course incompatible with the Lockean account, as Watts realizes. For it implies the rejection of Locke's idea that a person is constituted by an immediate relating to one's own self through consciousness. For Watts a person cannot be something that is constituted only internally, and so is not identifiable by others. Rather, a person in a complete sense is something to which *others* can refer in an identifying way; that is, a bodily being.

When considering Locke's interpretation of the afterlife Watts states that according to Locke, God's 'Equity and Truth will discover themselves in attributing proper Recompences to *Men* or *Spirits*, considered only as *Persons*, or in their personal Identity, *i.e.* as conscious of their former Actions of Vice or Virtue' (ibid., p. 307). This seems to be a correct reading of Locke, but of course Watts rejects this view, attempting a compromise between the positions of Locke and Stillingfleet, as was indicated above (ibid., p. 188). He agrees with Locke that 'it cannot be the very same Body in all the Particles or Atoms of it which were united to the Soul in this World, that shall be raised and united to it in the Resurrection' (ibid.). He sides with

---

[21] Watts says in the context of his discussion of the resurrection that he does not observe any distinction 'between the *same Man* and the *same Person*' but he notes that 'Mr Locke makes a great Difference' between the two': Watts, *Philosophical Essays*, p. 195.

[22] 'Now I would only enquire whether such a distinction between *Man* and *Person*, is either correspondent with the Nature and Reason of Things, or with the common Language of all Men, or the accurate Expressions of true Philosophy' (ibid., p. 306).

Stillingfleet, however, when he says that it 'must be in some Sense the same Body raised which was buried, in order to answer several Expressions both of *Jesus Christ*, and of the Apostle *Paul* in their Discourses of the Resurrection' (ibid., p. 190). The apostle states that the resurrection-body is 'the same Body which died in some Respects, tho' not in all Respects' (ibid., p. 184). It is said that the resurrection-body will be '*incorruptible*', and that our bodies will be '*quickened*' and '*made like the glorious Body of Christ*' (ibid., p. 185).

Watts explains the sense in which the resurrection-body can be said to be the same as the pre-mortem body in terms of his notion of a few 'essential particles' that never change. These allow us 'justly to denominate it the same Body, and which being united to the same Soul, do render the new-raised Man the same Man and the same Person who died: For 'tis evident that a very few of the same Atoms or Particles which were laid in the Grave are sufficient for this Purpose' (ibid., p. 190). But what are these essential particles? Watts asserts that:

a new-born Infant in its Muscles and Nerves (and especially in its Bowles and Bones) has some original, essential, and constituent Tubes, Fibres or staminal Particles (if I may so call them) which remain the same and unchanged thro' all the Stages and Changes of Life in following Years, how much soever the external and fleshy Parts may be changed. (ibid.)

The nature of the 'essential staminal Particles' (ibid., p. 191) is such that they do 'not join and unite with other animal or human Bodies', 'the same staminal or constituent Particles cannot belong to the Bodies of two or more human Persons' (ibid., p. 190).

This theory of 'staminal particles', Watts states, is at least 'very probable' (ibid.). Thus, for Watts the theory is an hypothesis—a model with which we can explain the identity of the resurrection-body. Watts does not claim to know with absolute certainty precisely which particles function as constituent or 'staminal' parts, but he insists that 'these essential, constituent or staminal Particles, whatsoever they be . . . always abide the same, even when the Body is greatly enlarged by the perpetual new Interposition of additional nutritive Particles, which are in a continual Flux' (ibid.). These 'unchanging Parts . . . in union with the same Soul, are abundantly sufficient to denominate *Methuselah the Infant*, and *Methuselah the aged*, the same Person' (ibid., pp. 191–2). Thus they can also make the same person when united with the same soul at the resurrection.

Watts, then, agrees with Stillingfleet that there must be the same body in some sense at the resurrection. He does not hold that it must be the same in all respects, but his account of the person as man and his explanation of the resurrection in terms of obscure 'staminal particles' sets him clearly apart from Locke. He does not indicate what the source of his theory of staminal particles is. Materialist inclined thinkers later in the eighteenth century, however, such as Charles Bonnet and Joseph Priestley, adopt similar accounts of the resurrection, with Priestley explicitly referring to Watts.

5.1.3. The person as soul and the resurrection of the body: Lee

While defenders of the identity of the resurrection-body criticize Locke's distinction between man and person and (wrongly) accuse him of identifying the person with the soul, most of those thinkers who identify the person with the soul and thus could agree with Locke at least on this that the identity of the body is not required for the resurrection, nevertheless reject Locke's accounts both of the resurrection and personal identity. At least this criticism is based on a better understanding of Locke's own view—according to which the person is not the soul but is subjectively constituted through inner consciousness.

One notable representative of this line of criticism is Henry Lee in his *Anti-Scepticism* (1702)—a chapter-by-chapter critique of Locke's *Essay*.[23] Like Watts, Lee raises a number of critical points against Locke's theory of personal identity. In connection with the resurrection issue Lee disagrees with both Stillingfleet and Locke, arguing that the same soul is all that is required for the sameness of the human person. Thus, Lee's position is like the 'Cartesian' view of Sherlock (discussed in Chapter 1), according to whom the soul alone makes the person. Lee also adopts a standard Cartesian position on the role of the body: 'No *Part*, nor indeed the *whole* Body is any more then, than the Soul's Instrument in its Operations, does not *think*, is not *conscious* of any of its Actions' (*Anti-Scepticism*, p. 128). Thus, unlike Stillingfleet, Lee holds that the soul alone makes the person and is a complete and independent (and immaterial) substance. Unlike several other critics, however, Lee recognizes that for Locke, consciousness rather than the soul, as substance, constitutes the person. But of course he does not accept Locke's distinction between the soul, as substance, and the person.

Commenting on identity in general, Lee, like Stillingfleet, rejects Locke's notion that 'bare Existence' individuates (ibid., pp. 121–2). He (mistakenly) assumes that 'bare existence' is also the principle of diachronic identity for Locke. Indeed, Lee fails to distinguish clearly between individuation and identity through time here (ibid., pp. 121–2). Next, he argues that there are different causes of identity for different kinds of being. While this claim may sound Lockean, Lee distinguishes it from Locke's thesis that our sortal concepts or abstract ideas determine what is required for the identity of objects over time. Rather, he states that 'as the things themselves are different, so they are said to be the same with themselves at several times, for different reasons' (ibid., p. 119). Lee proceeds to argue against Locke's notions of the various kinds of beings (plants, animals, human beings). His main complaint is that Locke likens human beings too closely to other, non-human, living beings. For Locke, Lee notes, 'Man is only a certain organiz'd Machin with a *common Life*, such as Brutes and Vegetables have' (ibid., p. 123).

Now I doubt that it's insinuated here, that Vegetables have a *common life*, on purpose to make them nearer akin to Animals; and those again to have the like *common life* (with *Perception* into

---

[23] Lee, *Anti-Scepticism: Or, Notes upon each Chapter of Mr. Lock's Essay concerning Humane Understanding. With an Explication of all the Particulars of which he treats, and in the same Order. In four Books* (1702).

the bargain) to make them Cozen-Germans to Men; and so by an handsom insensible Confusion Men shall be only Vegetables a little more conveniently organiz'd; which he himself tho' in finer words do's in effect own, when he makes *Embryo's* to be Vegetables, and *Infants* Brutes. (ibid., p. 122)

For Lee, the identity of a human being does not consist in a 'common life', as Locke maintains. Rather, 'the Identity of man consists in the same Individual Spirit united to the same Body, however the several parts of that Body may have insensibly chang'd in the several successive moments and states of Life' (ibid., p. 123). And the human body, despite all the changes it undergoes through time, remains effectively the same simply 'by being *united* to the *same* Soul' (ibid.). As it performs 'much the same Functions', it remains 'the *same* Body to all the main Effects, Uses, and Purposes that a body can serve for' and may, therefore, with 'propriety of Speech' be called the same body (ibid.). The essential self, then, is the spiritual substance which functions continuously as 'the same Principle of *vital* and *intellectual* Operations'. And, as the self as person is precisely the self as spiritual substance, personal identity consists in 'the same Principle of *intellectual* Actions and Operations' (ibid., p. 121). Thus, although Lee distinguishes between person and man, to him both human and personal identity require only one and the same principle of identity; that is to say, the same soul or 'individual spirit'. This view has implications, of course, for Lee's account of the resurrection.

As indicated above, Lee, like Locke, holds that strict identity of the body (on its own) is not required for there to be the same self or person at the resurrection. Indeed, faith in the resurrection includes the hope for a body that is in some respects quite different from the one we have in this life. 'We believe the Soul is not, or ever will be, limited to the same *individual* Particles of Matter that we have daily *Specimens* of; no we hope for *better* Bodies than (so far as we can conceive) this earthly Clay can be form'd into' (ibid., p. 129). Lee rejects Locke's account of personality in terms of consciousness, however. Without the same soul, as substance, we cannot have the same person at the resurrection; indeed, if we accepted the Lockean account, we would have the creation of a new person, rather than a resurrection of the same person that lived. Locke

> thinks it can be *Consciousness* only that can make it easie to conceive the *Resurrection* of the same Person, tho' not in a *Body* exactly of the same Make and Parts that he had here; but I am much afraid, that if there was not the *same* Soul, the *same* Principle of *intellectual* Operations (which he thinks altogether needless,) that tho possibly there might be a new Creation, yet there could not be a Resurrection. That *Consciousness* or *Memory*, however impair'd, or in a manner lost, by fits of Sickness, may possibly be recover'd we have frequent Demonstrations of; but we never yet heard of any so happy or unhappy as to gain the *Consciousness* or *Memory* of what they never did, either good or ill; and therefore that *Consciousness* should be tack'd to a System of Particles without the same *thinking* Substance, we can no more conceive possible; than how two men should feel the same Pleasure or Pain in one anothers Foot. And therefore we are better contented with the Assurance of a *Resurrection*, which our own Reason and Revelation gives us, than please our selves with an *imaginary* and more than *miraculous* Creation. (ibid., p. 129)

In summary, then, Lee sides with Locke against Stillingfleet and those that follow the latter's account, in that he distinguishes between the man and the person; but the nature of this distinction in Lee differs significantly from Locke's distinction. For Lee identifies the person with the soul, and accounts for personal identity in terms of the identity of the soul as substance:

> An *intelligent finite* Being (of which only we are supposed to treat) is the *same* person, at different times, by its being or having the same *inward* or *incommunicable* Principle of all its *intellectual* Operations; but the Variety in *kind* or *degree* of these Operations do's no more alter the reason of its being the *same* at different times than a Loadstone is for its actual drawing iron oftner or seldomer, more or less ... because the *Power* or *Capacity*, the Loadstone ... has, makes it to be what it is; not the *actual* Exercise of that Power. (ibid., p. 130)

Locke, by contrast, distinguishes not only between the person and the man but also between the person and the soul, as substance. Moreover, unlike Locke, Lee accounts for the identity of the man in terms of the same soul. For Lee it is the identity of the soul or spiritual substance that turns the body to which it is united into *its* body, and it is for that reason that we may call the body the same through time, although it will have changed considerably:

> The Mind or Soul of *Man*, with all its natural Powers united to the same Body, however various that may be in the several Moments and Conditions of life, is that which denominates him the *same Man*, whether an *Embryo* or *Infant*, young or old, sick or healthy, good or bad, wise or unwise. (ibid., p. 129)

As we shall see in Chapters 7 and 8, many eighteenth-century theologians and philosophers followed Lee's essentially Cartesian line of thought, identifying the person with the soul as an (immaterial) substance and therefore rejecting the Lockean account of the person and its identity.

5.1.4. Defending Locke on the resurrection

While the reactions to Locke's understanding of the resurrection in terms of his new theory of personal identity are for the most part negative, there are also attempts at partial and complete defences of the Lockean position. Locke's contemporary and correspondent Richard Burthogge, for example, agrees with Locke that the resurrection-body need not be identical with the pre-mortem body. He differs from Locke, however, when he insists that it must have a special relation to the latter, although this does not have to be the relation of identity. According to Burthogge, it could not be just any body that becomes mine at the resurrection. He writes to Locke:

> I am much of the same opinion that you are concerning the Resurrection: the Apostle speaks of but two bodies one that is sown Another that shall be ... Only methinks the Body that SHALL BE must have a *Relation* to the body that is SOWN since as the same Apostle intimates it must be the PROPER Body. But in what PROPRIETY consists ... is as yet a mystery to me.[24]

---

[24] Burthogge's letter to Locke, 19 September 1699, in *The Correspondence of John Locke*, ed. de Beer, 8 vols. (1976–89), vol. 6, p. 685.

Burthogge, then, is indeed closer to Locke than he is to Stillingfleet and Watts, as he does not hold that the sameness of the body is in any sense required for the resurrection. He differs from both Lee and Locke, however, in that he insists on a special relationship between the pre-mortem body and the resurrection-body, thus arguing against the view that the identity of the soul (Lee) or consciousness (Locke) is sufficient for the identity of the person at the resurrection. Yet as Burthogge himself concedes, he has no answer to the question of what kind of relation is required to hold between the pre-mortem and the resurrection-body.

Some of those thinkers who, like Locke, deny the identity of the resurrection-body, sometimes cite Locke's theory of personal identity in support of their theological positions. The late seventeenth-century materialist Henry Layton, for example, explicitly endorses Locke's account of the resurrection in terms of the same consciousness:

there shall arise and accrue to the same Person the same Sensation, Perception, Understanding, Memory and Conscience that he had before in the Time of his former Life. So as mr. Locke seems to be in the right, when Fol. 183 of his said Book he teaches, That it is the same consciousness which at the resurrection makes the same person.[25]

Some of Locke's defenders, however, do not seem to do justice to Locke's theory and in particular to his person–man–soul distinction. Samuel Bold, for example, in attempting to defend Locke against Samuel Parker, states that the resurrection-body need not be identical with the pre-mortem body for there to be the same man at the resurrection, arguing that the identity of the same man at the resurrection requires only the identity of the soul and the union of this soul with a body.[26] Like many of Locke's critics, then, Bold too seems to think that to account for the resurrection in terms of the identity of the soul is to defend the Lockean position. Catherine Cockburn, arguing against Winch Holdsworth's critique of Locke, even maintains that Locke never spoke of the resurrection of the person.[27] Moreover, she holds (unlike Locke and yet attempting to defend Locke) that 'man' and 'person' are synonymous terms, and she claims it to be Locke's view that what matters at the resurrection is that there be the same man as in this life.[28]

5.1.5. Conclusion: the resurrection of the body and the immortality of the soul

It is obvious from our analyses in the previous sections that the objections to Locke's accounts of the resurrection and personal identity are based on a rejection of his

---

[25] Layton, *Observations upon a Short Treatise, Written by Mr. Timothy Manlove: Intituled, The Immortality of the Soul Asserted* (1698), p. 126.
[26] Bold, *A Discourse* (1705), pp. 18, 25, 27.
[27] Cockburn (née Trotter), *A Letter to Dr. Holdsworth . . . in which the Passages that concern Mr. Lock are chiefly considered* (1726), p. 41.
[28] Cockburn (née Trotter), *A Vindication of Mr. Locke's Christian Principles*, in Birch (ed.), *The Works of Mrs. Catherine Cockburn* (1751), vol. 1, pp. 157–378, at p. 307: 'For *men* and *persons* in common use, and Scripture language, are synonymous terms.'

concept of a person. His critics reject either Locke's distinction between the person and the man (Stillingfleet, Felton) or his distinction between the person and the soul (Lee). It appears, then, that there are three main rival positions about the nature of personhood present in these debates about the resurrection: (i) the soul is the seat of personality, or the soul is the person (Lee, Ilive); (ii) the person is the same as the man, and the man is the union of soul and body—here, sometimes the soul is said to be the person in an incomplete sense, while the man is the person in a complete sense (Stillingfleet)—(iii) the person is to be distinguished from both the soul (as substance) and the man (Locke). The anti-Lockean positions here reflect the distinction made in Chapter 1 between Scholastic (Robert South) and Cartesian (William Sherlock) notions of the person. Felton, for example, would side with South (person = man), while Lee reflects the Cartesian position of Sherlock (person = soul).

The debate about personal identity continued to be linked to the resurrection issue throughout the eighteenth century. As the issue of personal identity developed more and more into a philosophical issue in its own right, however, the question of the resurrection played a less significant role than it did in discussions of the topic in the early 1700s. The issue of the afterlife was, of course, still a major concern in much of late eighteenth-century philosophical thought about the self. With some exceptions, however, most of the available arguments for and against the identity of the body at the resurrection had been exhausted in the debates of the late seventeenth and early eighteenth centuries. There is limited scope for new philosophical arguments on that issue. For the most part the earlier arguments were simply repeated in the second half of the eighteenth century. Thomas Cooper, for example, who towards the end of the century attempted to work out a new account of the resurrection in materialist terms, cites only Locke, Stillingfleet, Watts (and the Bible) on the topic.[29] And Samuel Drew's book-length discussion of the issue early in the nineteenth century appeals to Isaac Watts's theory of 'staminal particles' from 1733.[30] However, the central philosophical issue in the debates about the identity of the resurrection-body—the Lockean distinction between person and man—continues to be discussed in present-day debates about personal identity.[31]

As is obvious from the discussion above, the issue of the immortality of the soul is closely linked to that of the resurrection of the body.[32] Both the resurrection of the body and the immortality of the soul are thought of as required for the afterlife. In Chapter 2 we saw that the *identity* of the person, as consisting of soul and body, is

---

[29] Cooper, *Tracts, Ethical, Theological and Political* (1787); reprinted in *Philosophical Writings of Thomas Cooper*, ed. Thiel, 3 vols. (2001), vol. 1, pp. 322–3; on the Bible, pp. 438–50. For details of Cooper's account, see Thiel, 'Locke and Eighteenth-Century Materialist Conceptions of Personal Identity', *The Locke Newsletter*, 29 (1998), pp. 59–83.

[30] Drew, *An Essay on the Identity and General Resurrection of the Human Body* (1809), pp. 237–64: 'The sameness of our future Bodies must be constituted by some Germ or Stamen' (p. 237), for 'that in which sameness consists must remain immovable also' (p. 247).

[31] Compare, for example, Olson, *The Human Animal: Personal Identity without Psychology* (1997). Olson favours a view known as 'animalism', identifying the person with the man as bodily being.

[32] Compare Thiel (1983), pp. 180–2.

regarded as necessary for just divine rewards or punishments in the afterlife. For these rewards and punishments can be just only if the same person who acted in this life were to be punished or rewarded for these actions in the next life. This means for the immortality of the soul, as substance, that the soul must be the *same* substance in the afterlife that it is in this life. We also noted that this 'identity'-condition of immortality is thought of as requiring the *immateriality* of the soul, as matter is subject to constant change. Indeed, most participants in the resurrection debate consider the identity and immateriality of the soul to be necessary conditions for a meaningful notion of the afterlife. Both William Sherlock and Henry Lee, who identify the person with the soul, and theologians such as Stillingfleet, Felton, and Watts, who identify the person with the man, hold that the soul must be the same and therefore be immaterial if there is to be an afterlife of the same person who lived here. In other words, independently of their differing views about the identity of the resurrection-body, they agree that there must be the same (and therefore immaterial) soul in the afterlife. We saw that for Locke, however, the immateriality of the soul is neither a necessary nor a sufficient condition of personal identity, immortality, and an afterlife. Many critics of Locke's account of personal identity focus on this point about the nature of the soul. Although there are some who agree with Locke that the immateriality of the soul is not sufficient for immortality, most traditionally inclined thinkers argue (as did Cudworth in the seventeenth century) that immateriality is at least a necessary condition of immortality and of personal identity in this life.

Obviously, then, the issue of immortality relates closely to a metaphysical issue—the nature and identity of the soul—and to the relation of that issue to that of the identity of the person. It is to a large extent precisely because the immateriality of the soul, as substance, is considered necessary for personal identity, that the Lockean view—that consciousness constitutes personal identity—is rejected. There are, however, numerous other arguments, as we shall see.

5.2. THE DEBATE ABOUT THE ROLE OF CONSCIOUSNESS AND MEMORY

There is a variety of views about personal identity from within immaterialist theory of the mind or soul, as we shall see in Chapters 7 and 8. In the present section we shall look at criticisms of Locke that focus on the role he ascribes to consciousness and memory and are based on the view that the identity of the soul or thinking substance is at least a necessary condition of personal identity. It is assumed, and often stated explicitly in this context, that the soul or thinking substance is of an immaterial nature. Strictly speaking, however, at least some of these arguments against Locke would not require the assumption of the immateriality of the soul. In most of these criticisms no clear distinction is made between consciousness and memory. And as in authors discussed above, Locke's distinctions between the man and the person, and the soul and the person, are ignored or misunderstood or rejected.

An argument typical of the critical discussions of Locke is the following. Consciousness of an action can be a consciousness that *I* performed the action only if the *substance* which performed the action is the same as the one which is now conscious of it. This is how Samuel Clarke, for example, argues against Anthony Collins's Lockean treatment of the issue; genuine consciousness that *I* did an action requires the identity of my self as substance.[33] If the thinking substance does not remain the same, then my consciousness or memory of an action is not the memory that *I* performed it, but the memory of someone else's action and not genuine self-ascription.[34] Further, for Clarke, the thinking substance can remain identical only if it is immaterial and indivisible, for material beings constantly change. According to Clarke, then, we retain our personal identity through time because we are indivisible immaterial beings.[35] Although Clarke does not seem to put it in these terms, his critique of the Lockean position implies that he regards consciousness as neither necessary nor sufficient for personal identity. It is not necessary, because personal identity is secured by the immaterial nature of the thinking substance, quite independently of consciousness and memory; it is not sufficient, because consciousness, if not genuine, may relate to other persons' actions. This type of argument is put forward in a variety of ways by a number of eighteenth-century thinkers.

Henry Felton also makes this point, however briefly, in his sermons on the resurrection of the body. First he states that the problem with Locke's account is that it does not tie consciousness to one particular subject: 'For this *Identifying Consciousness* is made, by this Writer, a thing that adheres to no one *determinate Subject*, and that which is of a desultory Nature leaping from one to another, making the same *Person distinct*, and *Another* the *same* can be no Principle of *Identity*' (*Resurrection*, p. 12). Felton says that according to Locke, 'if I once happen to find my self *Conscious* of any of the Actions of *Nestor*, then it is *Nestor* and not *I*, or *Nestor* and I together' that are the same person (ibid., pp. 16–17). He suggests, then, that *pace* Locke, consciousness is not sufficient for personal identity, as consciousness can be mistaken. He also suggests that consciousness is not necessary for identity: 'But neither our own *Existence* and *Identity*, nor the *Existence* of *things* and their *Identity*, depend upon our *Consciousness* or *Knowledge*. We are *what* we are, and they are *what* they are; the *same severally, each* in *its self,* whether we are *Conscious*, or whether we know it or no' (ibid., pp. 14–15). We remain identical through time, independently of whether or not we are conscious of our actions and identity. Felton's comment suggests a point that many other critics of Locke (including Leibniz and Butler) consider central to the issue: the distinction between what constitutes personal identity and how we know of this identity.

---

[33] Clarke, *A Fourth Defense of an Argument made use of in a Letter to Mr. Dodwell, to prove the Immateriality and Natural Immortality of the Soul* (1708), p. 56.

[34] Clarke, *A Third Defense of an Argument made use of in a Letter to Mr. Dodwell, to prove the Immateriality and Natural Immortality of the Soul. In a Letter to the Author of the Reflexions on Mr. Clark's Second Defense* (1708), p. 64.

[35] See Clarke, *Third Defense*, pp. 61–2.

170   *The Early Modern Subject*

5.2.1. Consciousness, reflection, memory, and the 'ill consequences' of Locke's theory: Lee

There is an extensive discussion of consciousness and personal identity in Henry Lee's *Anti-Scepticism* (1702). Lee argues against Locke's account of personal identity in terms of consciousness on the basis of equating person with thinking substance or soul. He also comments on the notion of consciousness itself in this context. Unlike Locke, but like many other critics of Locke, Lee thinks that consciousness is a higher-order perception or reflection: consciousness is a distinct and separate act from the act of perception to which it relates. We may find it difficult to distinguish between them because they are so closely connected to each other,[36] but acts of consciousness, Lee holds, are 'Acts of reflexion', '*repeted* Acts of the Mind' by which the mind takes notice of its own operations, such as 'Sensations, Affirmations, Denials, Doubtings, Meditations, etc' (*Anti-Scepticism*, p. 130). These successive acts of reflection or consciousness require a unity, as do the actions reflected upon by consciousness:

> But because the Mind cannot take that notice of such *different* Actions all at *once*, but must do it *successively*, therefore we conceive such Acts of Reflexion need to be *united*, as well as other *different* Operations. For I can no more at once in *one moment* remember or be conscious that I affirm'd this, deny'd that, doubted of a third Proposition, than I could affirm, deny or doubt, all at once. (ibid.)

This unity is provided by the thinking substance or mind or soul. Consciousness, for Lee, is not transferable to other minds or souls: 'no *Mind* can feel the same *Pain* or *Pleasure*, that I now have, the next moment. Thought, or Consciousness of a Thought, are inseparable and incommunicable' (ibid.). Thus, unlike Locke, he holds that there is no other unity of the self apart from that of the self as thinking substance.[37] For Lee 'it must be the *Substance*, the Spirit of which those Operations are the Modes, that must unite them' (ibid., p. 125).

The above account would seem to suggest a distinction between consciousness as an immediate relating to one's own perceptions on the one hand, and memory as a relating to actions and thoughts of the more distant past on the other. And indeed, while consciousness follows perceptions immediately and 'inseparably', memory is

---

[36] '*Consciousness*, tho it be a *distinct* Act of the Mind from *Perception*; yet it is not only *inseparable* from it, but it follows so *quick*, that it's very hard for a Man at any time to nick the *Distinction*.' Lee, *Anti-Scepticism*, p. 46.

[37] The passages cited in this paragraph are part of a continuous argument: 'And as for *Consciousness*, we reckon it nothing else but the *repeted Acts* of the Mind, by which it takes notice of its own and other Operations, its own Sensations, Affirmations, Denials, Doubtings, Meditations etc. But because the Mind cannot take that notice of such *different* Actions all at *once*, but must do it *successively*, therefore we conceive such Acts of Reflexion need to be *united*, as well as other *different* Operations. For I can no more at once in *one moment* remember or be conscious that I affirm'd this, deny'd that, doubted of a third Proposition, than I could affirm, deny or doubt, all at once. That Substance then, in which these Operations are united, is that we call our *Minds* or *Souls*; but *Consciousness* is no more that *Mind* or *Soul*, than any other Actions are . . . no *Mind* can feel the same *Pain* or *Pleasure*, that I now have, the next moment. Thought, or Consciousness of a Thought, are inseparable and incommunicable.' Lee, *Anti-Scepticism*, p. 130.

The notion of a person and the role of consciousness and memory 171

'the power of thinking again of any thing after other thoughts have interpos'd' (ibid., p. 62). Consciousness and memory are very similar, however:

> *Consciousness* is nothing else but *knowing our own Actions*, and is only different from Remembrance in this Circumstance, that whereas Remembrance is the minds taking notice or knowing its own Actions after the interruption of other thoughts, Consciousness is the Minds taking notice or knowing its own acts without the interposal of other thoughts. (ibid., p. 124)

Indeed, while not as immediate as consciousness, memory, for Lee, relates not only to actions of the distant past but also to perceptions from just a minute ago.[38] In effect, Lee blurs the distinction between consciousness and memory. This is particularly evident in his discussion of Locke on personal identity. Here he sometimes seems to hold that for Locke, memory *and* consciousness are involved in constituting personal identity (suggesting a distinction between consciousness and memory), but at other times appears to use 'consciousness' and 'memory' interchangeably.[39]

Since for Lee the unity of the self is always already provided by the soul, as substance, he argues that consciousness or memory is not necessary for personal identity. On his view I can be the same person through time although I lack the consciousness of my past: 'Suppose a person be decay'd in his Memory and Intellectuals, shall he not be reputed the *same* person for defect of *Consciousneß*?' (ibid., p. 127). The soul or 'the *same Principle* of . . . Intellectual Operations' is 'enough to denominate' him the same person (ibid.). Lee considers Locke's thought experiment of '*Castor*'s Soul in Pollux's Body, whilst asleep', but thinks it is 'a little too Romantick' (ibid., p. 47). According to Lee, 'the Soul of *one* Man can no more be in *another* Mans Body, than one Man can be *conscious* of anothers Thoughts, or feel his Pain with the Gout' (ibid.). Moreover, if, while awake, I do not remember thoughts I had while asleep, this does not turn me into two distinct persons: 'In short, a Man asleep may *perceive* or *think*, and be *conscious* of it at *that* instant, and yet not retain the Thoughts of it when *awake*; and that too, without being, to all effects and purposes, two different Persons for *want* of that Memory' (ibid.). Again, the implication is that consciousness is not necessary for personal identity. Lee sometimes expresses this by saying that the lack of consciousness or memory is not sufficient to turn me into a different person. 'For if the *want* of Memory was a sufficient reason to make *different* Persons, then the *same* Man might be an *hundred*

---

[38] This is implied by several passages. Lee states that by experience we find 'that there are a thousand Thoughts which succeed one another whilst we are awake, of which we retain not the least Memory the next hour; sometimes not the next minute'. Lee, *Anti-Scepticism*, p. 47. This would still seem to leave room for a distinction between the consciousness of the perception I am having now and the memory of a thought I had a minute ago. But Lee clearly brings consciousness and memory close together here. And, as his arguments against personal identity demonstrate, he does not assume a distinction between consciousness (or reflection) and memory in that context.

[39] See, for example, Lee, *Anti-Scepticism*, p. 127. He speaks of people who at 21 are not *conscious* of what they did as children. Clearly, he equates 'to be conscious' with 'to remember' here.

Men in the same day, by forgetting his several succeeding Thoughts within that time' (ibid.). Lee is saying here that despite of 'the *want* of Memory' I may still be the same person; and that is to say, memory is not necessary for personal identity.

Lee also suggests that consciousness is not sufficient for personal identity: '*Consciousness* alone', he says, 'do's not constitute *personal Identity*' (ibid., p. 124), because I may ascribe actions to myself through consciousness that I never did. On Locke's theory, however, 'a person ... may be everlastingly *miserable* for another persons faults, by having the Consciousness of those faulty Actions annex'd to his Soul' (ibid., p. 126). Lee does not accept Locke's escape route *via* the goodness of God, arguing that one cannot abstract God's goodness from his wisdom (ibid., p. 126).

Lastly, Lee draws attention to the '*ill consequences*' (ibid., p. 124) of Locke's position for moral and legal matters. He argues that 'if Consciousness only make a Person the *same*, and the want of it a *different* Person, then no Courts of *Humane* Judicature can be justly establish'd' (ibid., p. 127):

'For how can any Judge or Jury be certain, that a man (during the Commission of any Fact or entring into any Covenants) was sleepy or broad awake, sober or mad, sedate or passionate (for other Passions besides Anger, such as Envy, &c. are kinds of Madness for the present) sober or drunk, tenacious or forgetful? For any of these two Circumstances may so alter the State of the Case, as to denominate him a *different* person; if the want of *Consciousneß* can make him so'. (ibid.)

This point is similar to comments William Molyneux made to Locke prior to the publication of the chapter on identity (see Chapter 4 above).

5.2.2. Consciousness, drunkenness, and moral responsibility: Becconsall

We have encountered Becconsall as one of the critics of Locke's understanding of the resurrection and the man–person distinction. His discussion of the afterlife also deals with the notion of consciousness.[40] Like Lee, Becconsall points to 'ill consequences' of Locke's account of personal identity for moral accountability. One problem with Locke's theory, according to Becconsall, is that it equates *conscience* with consciousness.

It's observable Mr. Lock makes Consciousness and Conscience the same, and Conscience to consist in nothing else, but our own Opinions, of our own Actions; and pursuant to this, he affirms that in personal Identity which he makes to consist in Consciousness, is founded all the Right and Justice of Favour, Rewards and Punishment'. (*Grounds and Foundation*, p. 249)

Becconsall argues against Locke that conscience is not mere private opinion but rests 'on the unalterable measures of moral Goodness' (ibid., p. 241). The concept of conscience is much more complex than Locke's understanding of it suggests.

---

[40] Becconsall, *The Grounds and Foundation of Natural Religion, Discover'd in the Principal Branches of it, in Opposition to the Prevailing Notions of the Modern Scepticks and Latitudinarians* (1698).

The notion of a person and the role of consciousness and memory 173

Following Scholastic ideas, Becconsall considers conscience to be a complex of a number of distinct but related 'movements, or workings':

First, A Power of Retaining. *Secondly*, A Power of Animadverting, or Reflecting on past Actions. *Thirdly*, A Power of applying, and comparing them with a Law or Rule. *Fourthly*, A Power of discerning the Truth, Goodness, or Equity of the Rule, *Fifthly*, The Obligation and Authority of it, and *Lastly*, A Power of ascribing the Action to our selves, by acknowledging a Power of Acting in Conformity to this Rule; whereby the Good, or Evil, Guilt or Merit of the Action may be some way imputed to us. So that Conscience may be justly defined to be the Judgment we pass upon our own Actions, whether past, or present, as scanned and measured, by a Law. (ibid., p. 215)

Thus Locke's consciousness and memory are part of conscience but do not exhaust that notion. Becconsall thinks that Locke neglects other essential elements of conscience. Indeed, Locke's account, which bases personal identity and moral accountability in conscience understood as mere consciousness, is 'dangerous and false' (ibid., p. 250). To illustrate this, Becconsall, like Lee, takes up the issue of crimes committed in a state of drunkenness.

Becconsall puts forward three arguments against Locke's treatment of this issue. The first is that Locke's likening of drunkenness to sleep must be rejected (ibid., pp. 251–2).[41] He argues that we are not held responsible for what we have done while asleep, but are justly held responsible for crimes we have committed while drunk. States of sleep belong to our nature, but states of drunkenness are certainly not part of our nature. Rather, drunkenness points to 'a wilful neglect in human Conduct, and as such is an Act of a free Agent, and consequently the Actions that flow from it, tho' destitute of Choice and Deliberation are justly imputed' (ibid., p. 252). This is pretty much the same argument that Molyneux had put to Locke in 1693 (see Chapter 4 above).

Second, Becconsall argues that Locke misrepresents the legal practice of the day (ibid., pp. 252–4). Crimes committed in a state of drunkenness are punished not because judicatures 'cannot distinguish certainly what is real, what counterfeit', as Locke claims (*Essay*, II.xxvii.22). Rather, human judicatures deal with the outward act only and they assume that the agent is free and has knowledge of the law. 'Affected ignorance' (*Grounds and Foundation*, p. 254) is not admitted as a plea. 'Tho' he was not Master of himself, when the Fact was committed, yet he Acted by a Principle that made him Master of the cause of it; and consequently the Government may exercise a Right of Punishment' (ibid., pp. 253–4). The case of 'down-right Madness' is of course different. In such a case 'where the Mind rests under a Physical Disability, if Crimes or Mischiefs, are committed upon it, the Government only

---

[41] 'I think this Author has drawn a very unjust Parallel between Crimes committed in Sleep and Drunkenness. It's well known that Sleep is a thing entailed on us as a law, even a Law established in the frame of our Beings, and commences upon the necessities of corruptible Nature, and therefore if Mischief accidently follows, it cannot well be imputed, because it is founded in a Cause or Principle that is inseparable from Human Nature, or rather is an Appendage of the most necessary Powers of it, that set us on a level with Brutes, and consequently the Actions that flow from it cannot be imputed.' Becconsall, *Grounds and Foundation*, pp. 251–2.

enquires into the Symptoms of Madness, and upon Evidence, Acquits the reputed Criminal; and in these cases I question not, but the great Judge of all the World will do the like' (ibid., p. 255).

Third, turning to 'the proceedings of the great Day' (ibid.), Becconsall argues that these 'shall be established upon a regulated conscience' (ibid., p. 244). He concedes to Locke that 'no other Conscience can be the measure of any Man's Condemnation but his own' (ibid., p. 241). Yet 'when God puts any man on his Tryal upon the Evidence of Conscience' (ibid.), this will be 'a rectified Conscience' (ibid., p. 247); it will not be the potentially mistaken consciousness or conscience of this life. It will be 'a Conscience cleared from all Error and Mistake, Partiality or Connivance; and in a Word, a Conscience established according to the Divine Oeconomy of it' (ibid., p. 248). Indeed, there 'will not be only a new discovery of lost Idea's, Thoughts and Actions, but of their incompatibility with the Line of Duty' (ibid., p. 242). And 'consequently it is not the Plea of former Convictions, nor want of consciousness when Enormities were committed, that will be sufficient to exempt any Man from the jurisdiction of it' (ibid., pp. 244–5). Becconsall applies this to the case of drunkenness, as he seems to believe that Locke considers drunkenness an excuse in the face of divine judgement.

It's certain as long as Enormities are committed upon personal Neglects, as in the case of Drunkenness, it is not necessary the Mind should be conscious of the whole process, when actually committed. It's abundantly sufficient, if upon a representation of Circumstances we shall at last be forced to own them, or ascribe the Commission of 'em to our selves, for this will bring us under the dominion of Conscience at the last day. Certainly we may with as much force of Reason plead Exemption from the guilt of Enormities, which thro' tract of time were wiped off the Table of the Mind, as deny to account for Enormities, which when committed we were not conscious of, when it was some former Enormity had disabled us from being conscious of 'em. (ibid., p. 245)

So, for Becconsall:

no Ignorance founded in Drunkenness, will ever be admitted as a plea of Innocence, as is apparently Suggested by this Author. It's abundantly concluded, that Conscience will be Regulated according to the Divine Oeconomy of it; and that it will ascribe to its self, and yield an Assent to a great many Actions, which the present State of some Mens Consciences *either know nothing of,* or at least have caused them to be pronounced Innocent. (ibid., p. 255)

It would seem that Locke could agree with Becconsall's point about a rectified consciousness, for Locke too appeals to 'the Great Day, when every one shall receive according to his doings', when 'the secrets of all Hearts shall be laid open' (*Essay*. II. xxvii. 26). The divine sentence, Locke suggests, will be based on the consciousness we shall have at the 'Great Day', and God, he states, would not 'transfer from one to another that consciousness, which draws Reward or Punishment with it' (II. xxvii. 13). Becconsall seems to be right in his arguments against Locke concerning sleep and drunkenness and legal practice. He is clearly mistaken, however, in his belief that Locke identifies consciousness with conscience. For Locke, while conscience consists in an evaluation of one's own actions, consciousness is that which makes these

The notion of a person and the role of consciousness and memory 175

actions mine in the first place. Consciousness, for Locke, is a necessary condition of conscience, rather than identical with the latter.

5.2.3. Consciousness, 'real forgetfulness', and 'fancied memory': Watts

On the whole, Isaac Watts thinks that Locke's view about personal identity is a 'strange and novel Opinion' (*Philosophical Essays*, p. 312). He has several specific objections to Locke's account, however. We saw in our discussion of the debates about the resurrection body that Watts rejects Locke's crucial distinction between the man and the person. It is not surprising, then, that he also rejects the view that consciousness constitutes personal identity. Like Lee, he does not distinguish clearly between consciousness and memory in this context.

Watts rejects Locke's speculations about Socrates asleep and Socrates awake, for example, precisely because he equates the man with the person. He argues, *contra* Locke, that Socrates asleep and awake is the same person, although Socrates awake may not remember what Socrates asleep thought (ibid., pp. 305–6; also pp. 125–6). Locke, he says, allows that 'if *Socrates* asleep puts forth any Actions, and is not conscious of it when he awakes, sleeping and waking *Socrates* is not the same Person' (ibid., p. 305). For Watts, a man or, which is the same thing, a human person consists of an immaterial soul and a body, and the identity of this unity of soul and body through time does not depend on consciousness. Watts says:

> 'tis still the same Person, for both the Soul and Body of *Socrates* are employed in these Ideas, and that whether sleeping or waking. The Ideas of his Dreams and of his waking Thoughts, tho' they both exist in the Mind, yet both of them may be occasioned by the Motions of his Blood and Spirits, and they are the Acts or Effects of the Soul and Body united, *i.e.* of both the constituent Parts of *Socrates*. Or . . . if it were not so, and if the Soul alone were employed in Sleep, yet Mr. *Locke*'s Objection might be answered, by shewing that the Actions of Life, which belong only to the Body as their proper Principle, or only to the Soul, are generally attributed to the whole Man; 'tis the Soul of *Socrates* that philosophiz'd, and his Body wore a Gown, and yet we say 'tis the same Person, *'tis* Socrates *did them both:* So that there is no manner of Reason to suppose *Socrates* asleep to be a distinct Person from *Socrates* when he is awake, tho' the Soul alone were engaged in thinking while he was asleep, without any Operations of the Brain. (ibid., pp. 125–6)

According to Watts, then, consciousness is not necessary for personal identity, as the latter is constituted independently of consciousness. I may be the same person as in the past, even if I cannot remember what I did then (ibid., pp, 305, 307). Locke, however, mistakenly 'seems to suppose, that real Forgetfulness may make a distinct Person as well as fancied Memory may make the same' (ibid., p. 305).

Indeed, Watts argues that Locke's theory proves too much because consciousness or memory may not be veracious, and the fact that I remember an action does not by itself mean that I performed that action, as I may falsely remember things that I have not done (ibid., pp. 304–5, 306–7). Watts holds that it would be absurd to maintain that I am the same person as Socrates when I mistakenly ascribe to myself actions that Socrates did (ibid., p. 304). He refers to Locke's argument that if 'the present

176   The Early Modern Subject

Mayor of *Quinborough*' thinks he remembers that he did actions that Socrates did, then he would be the same person as Socrates (*Essay*, II.xxvii.19). Watts comments: 'But I deny this to be proper conscious Remembrance: 'Tis only a delusive Impression on the Mind or Fancy imitating the Act of Memory; 'tis a strong Belief of what is false. And can such a Frenzy be sufficient to turn two Men into one Person?' (*Philosophical Essays*, p. 304). As self-ascription of actions through consciousness or memory may mean that it is based merely on 'a strong belief of what is false', consciousness or memory cannot be sufficient to constitute personal identity.

In sum, Watts holds, like Lee, that consciousness is neither necessary nor sufficient for personal identity. He maintains that Locke himself sees these difficulties and tries to get out of them by introducing the distinction between man and person (ibid., pp. 305ff.)—which is not acceptable to Watts. 'And so [on Locke's theory] I may be the same Man that performed a hundred former Actions of Life, tho' I have entirely forgot them all; but I am not the same Person that perform'd Millions of those Actions, since I have entirely forgotten a far larger Number of my Thoughts than I can recollect' (ibid., p. 306). Watts does not seem to realize, however, that the man–person distinction is part of the reason why Locke ascribes to consciousness a constitutive role for personal identity in the first place. Locke does not first talk about identity in terms of consciousness and then decides to distinguish between the man and the person to avoid difficulties, as Watts would have us believe.

5.2.4. Actual and potential consciousness: Berkeley

George Berkeley discusses the personal identity issue in various contexts, but his discussions are very brief. Most of his few explicit comments on the issue are devoted to a critique of Locke's theory; and the main focus of his critique is Locke's thesis that consciousness constitutes personal identity. Like Lee (but unlike Watts), he bases his critique on rejecting (if only implicitly) Locke's distinction between the person and the *soul*. For Berkeley the issue of personal identity is just the issue of the identity of the soul or mental substance. His critique of Locke assumes that a person is an immaterial spiritual substance. And with this assumption it is obvious enough that Berkeley must reject Locke's view that personal identity is constituted by consciousness. But he also considers specific issues that concern Locke's theory.

Unlike Locke, Berkeley distinguishes explicitly between actual and potential consciousness—without, however, distinguishing clearly between consciousness and memory. Neither type of consciousness, Berkeley argues, can constitute personal identity. In Entry 200 of his *Philosophical Commentaries* Berkeley rejects, first, the view that personal identity consists in actual consciousness, and, second, the view that it consists in potential consciousness.[42] For if personal identity consisted in

---

[42] 'Qu: wherein consists identity of Person? not in actual consciousness, for then I'm not the same person I was this day twelvemonth, but while I think of w' I then did. Not in potential for then all persons may be the same for ought we know.' Berkeley, *Philosophical Commentaries, Generally Called the Commonplace Book*, ed. Luce (1945), no. 200.

actual consciousness, then I would be the same person as in the past only when I actually think about what I did then, which is absurd. The implication is that I am the same person without actual consciousness of past actions; that is to say, that (actual) consciousness is not necessary for personal identity.

Berkeley notes that by 'potential consciousness' he means abnormal consciousness here.[43] He suggests that if personal identity consisted in potential consciousness, then it would, in principle, be possible for everybody to remember my actions and thus to be identical with me. Berkeley's examples are drawn from Locke: if I were to ascribe Socrates's actions to myself, then, on the Lockean view, I would have to be the same person as Socrates. Berkeley believes Locke's theory to have the consequence that all persons could be identical with one another and that the term 'identity' would cease to make any sense at all. This point is similar to one of Watts's arguments. Locke's theory proves too much, as Watts argues. Like Watts, Berkeley implies that potential consciousness is not sufficient for personal identity. It may seem strange that Berkeley does not consider 'normal' or 'natural' potential consciousness. There could be a good reason for that, however. Normal potential consciousness or memory would be a consciousness or memory that is, by definition, veracious. And Berkeley would probably accept that veracious memory is sufficient (if not necessary) for personal identity.[44] But what makes such memory veracious? Normal potential consciousness is veracious because the remembered actions belong to the same spiritual substance that can now remember them—and they belong to the same substance quite independently of its ability to remember them. Thus normal potential memory does not fulfil a constitutive role for personal identity because it presupposes the identity of the soul or mental substance (= person). This may be why Berkeley does not consider 'normal' potential memory or consciousness in this context. Moreover, to say that normal potential consciousness is sufficient for personal identity would not amount even to a partial agreement with Locke, as Locke does not restrict memory to veracious memory. Berkeley himself cannot accept that potential consciousness or memory is sufficient for personal identity precisely because not all potential consciousness or memory is veracious.

5.2.5. Consciousness and self-concern: Shaftesbury

Like Berkeley, Shaftesbury deals with Locke's account of personal identity in a number of fairly brief comments scattered over several places in his writings. He does not mention Locke by name, but refers variously to the view that personal identity is constituted by consciousness or memory. As we shall see, however, Shaftesbury does not seem to grasp Locke's distinctions between consciousness and

---

[43] Berkeley, *Philosophical Commentaries*, no. 202: 'two sorts of Potential consciousness Natural & praeternatural in the last § but one I mean the latter'.
[44] This is a view ascribed to Berkeley by Flage; see 'Berkeley, Individuation, and Physical Objects', in Barber and Gracia, *Individuation and Identity in Early Modern Philosophy* (1994), pp. 133–54, at p. 135. For a similar argument, see Brown, 'Berkeley on the Unity of the Self', *Royal Institute of Philosophy Lectures*, vol. 5 (1970–71), in *Reason and Reality* (1972), pp. 64–87, at p. 84.

memory and between man and person. In short, his criticism, too, is based on a distorted view of Locke's account.

Shaftesbury's argument against the Lockean view in his *Miscellaneous Reflections* can be analysed in terms of four main steps. (1) He begins with reflections on Descartes's *cogito* argument. Here he argues that the existence of the self is already assumed in the 'I think', and cannot be deduced from the latter.[45] He agrees, however, that one's own existence is not doubtful: 'That there is something undoubtedly which thinks, our very doubt itself and scrupulous thought evinces' (ibid., p. 420). (2) The real question, then, does not concern the existence of the self but its nature and identity through time. 'But the question is, "What constitutes the 'we' or 'I'?", and "Whether the 'I' of this instant be the same with that of any instant preceding or to come?"' (ibid.). This, Shaftesbury holds, 'is not a matter so easily or hastily decided by those who are nice self-examiners or searchers after truth and certainty' (ibid.).[46] (3) Next he argues that the question of personal identity through time cannot be answered by an appeal to consciousness or memory. 'For we have nothing but memory to warrant us, and memory may be false. We may believe we have thought and reflected thus or thus, but we may be mistaken' (ibid.). Shaftesbury holds that if we accept the Lockean account, 'the same successional "we" or "I" must remain still...undecided' (ibid., p. 421). He concedes that consciousness or memory is the only evidence we have of our personal identity, but as consciousness or memory may be mistaken, we cannot be certain about our personal identity. Shaftesbury appeals to some unidentified 'metaphysicians' for this argument. 'This is what metaphysicians mean when they say "that identity can be proved only by consciousness, but that consciousness, withal, may be as well false as real in respect of what is past"' (ibid., pp. 420–1). (4) Lastly, Shaftesbury argues that the fact that the metaphysical issue of personal identity must remain undecided does not in any way affect morality and responsibility. It is not required for the issue of morality and responsibility to settle the metaphysical issue of personal identity. In matters to do with morality and practice in general we can take the identity of our own selves for granted.[47]

---

[45] Shaftesbury argues that since the '*Ego* or I...[is] established in the first part of the proposition, the *ergo*, no doubt, must hold it good in the latter': *Miscellaneous Reflections*, in *Characteristics of Men, Manners, Opinions, Times*, ed. Klein (1999), p. 420.

[46] Here is the relevant passage in full: 'in what subject that thought resides, and how that subject is continued one and the same, so as to answer constantly to the supposed train of thoughts or reflections which seem to run so harmoniously through a long course of life, with the same relation still to one single and self-same person, this is not a matter so easily or hastily decided' (ibid.).

[47] See, for example, the following passages. 'To the force of this reasoning, I confess, I must so far submit as to declare that, for my own part, I take my own being upon trust. Let others philosophize as they are able: I shall admire their strength when, upon this topic, they have refuted what able metaphysicians object and Pyrrhonists plead in their own behalf. Meanwhile, there is no impediment, hindrance, or suspension of action on account of these wonderfully refined speculations. Argument and debate go on still. Conduct is settled' (ibid., p. 421). And: 'This to me appears sufficient ground for a moralist. Nor do I ask more when I undertake to prove the reality of virtue and morals' (ibid.).

The last point is part of Shaftesbury's own, positive account of personal identity which will be discussed below in Chapter 7. Strictly speaking only step (3) of this argument relates directly to Locke's theory. Here Shaftesbury says (as do Lee and Watts) that, since memory can prove too much (Watts)—that is to say, ascribe actions to ourselves that we never did—memory is not sufficient for personal identity.[48] This point is suggested also by other passages. Thus Shaftesbury emphasises that in accounting for personal identity, we need to distinguish the inner self or character from our outward appearance. The latter is not relevant to personal identity. 'For it is not certainly by virtue of our face merely that we are ourselves. It is not we who change when our complexion or shape changes. But there is that which, being wholly metamorphosed and converted, we are thereby in reality transformed and lost' (*Soliloquy*, in *Characteristics*, p. 127). Shaftesbury then suggests that memory cannot retain identity of the inner self if the latter has changed completely.

Should an intimate friend of ours, who had endured many sicknesses and run many ill adventures while he travelled through the remotest parts of the East and hottest countries of the South, return to us so altered in his whole outward figure that, till we had for a time conversed with him, we could not know him again to be the same person, the matter would not seem so very strange nor would our concern on this account be very great. But should a like face and figure of a friend return to us with thought and humours of a strange and foreign turn, with passions, affections and opinions wholly different from anything we had formerly known, we should say, in earnest and with the greatest amazement and concern, that this was another creature and not the friend whom we once knew familiarly. Nor should we in reality attempt any renewal of acquaintance or correspondence with such a person, though perhaps he might preserve in his memory the faint marks or tokens of former transactions which had passed between us. (ibid.)

The last sentence here suggests that consciousness or memory is not sufficient for personal identity.[49] The main point of the passage as a whole, however, concerns the difference between inner and outer self. Moreover, the context of the passage concerns the 'province of philosophy'. Here Shaftesbury states: 'It is the known province of philosophy to teach us ourselves, keep us the self-same persons and so regulate our governing fancies, passions and humours as to make us comprehensible to ourselves and knowable by other features than those of a bare countenance' (ibid.).

Shaftesbury holds also that consciousness or memory is not necessary for personal identity. But again the point is made only implicitly and in passing. It appears in the context of a comment about Locke's critique of the doctrine of the pre-existence of

---

[48] For Shaftesbury's point that the Lockean view is to be rejected because memory can be false and deceptive, see also Grean, *Shaftesbury's Philosophy of Religion and Ethics: A Study in Enthusiasm* (1967), pp. 146–7; Mijuskovic, 'Hume and Shaftesbury on the Self', *Philosophical Quarterly*, 21 (1971), 324–6; Mijuskovic, *The Achilles of Rationalist Arguments* (1974), p. 107; Martin and Barresi, *Naturalization of the Soul: Self and Personal Identity in the Eighteenth Century* (2000), pp. 62–3; Winkler, '"All is Revolution in Us": Personal Identity in Shaftesbury and Hume', *Hume Studies*, 26 (2000), 3–40, at 7.
[49] See also Winkler's comment in ibid., 8.

our souls. Locke argues that the alleged pre-existence is irrelevant to ourselves as persons because we are now not conscious of that previous life and thus not concerned in it. Shaftesbury writes in *The Moralists*:

> Now to be assured that we can never be concerned in anything hereafter, we must understand perfectly what it is which concerns or engages us in anything present. We must truly know ourselves, and in what this self of ours consists. We must determine against pre-existence and give a better reason for our having never been concerned in anything before our birth than merely 'because we remember not, nor are conscious.' For in many things we have been concerned to purpose, of which we have now no memory or consciousness remaining. And thus we may happen to be again and again to perpetuity, for any reason we can show to the contrary. (*Characteristics*, pp. 253–4; Theocles speaking.)

The point that we can be concerned in things that we are not conscious of can be interpreted as implying that memory or consciousness is not necessary for personal identity.[50] But the actual point made here is about the relationship between self-concern and consciousness. Shaftesbury maintains that, *pace* Locke, self-concern does not depend on consciousness. And he assumes that self-concern presupposes identity. Thus, as we can be concerned in our past and future selves independently of consciousness, the latter is not necessary for personal identity.

In sum, then, although it is true that Shaftesbury suggests that consciousness is neither necessary nor sufficient for personal identity, he does not argue for this point explicitly and in detail. Other thinkers of the time argue this more directly and extensively.

An issue that has been somewhat neglected in discussions of Shaftesbury's understanding of personal identity is his critique of the view that bases morality on the idea of future rewards and punishments. We saw above that traditionally (and this includes Locke here) the question of future rewards and punishments plays a crucial role in the development of the personal identity issue. For Shaftesbury, however, virtue consists 'in a certain just disposition or proportionable affection of a rational creature towards the moral objects of right and wrong' (ibid., p. 177). There is 'a natural sense of right and wrong' (ibid.). If we do the good we hate or restrain from doing the ill, 'through hope merely of reward and punishment', then 'there is in this case...no virtue or goodness whatsoever' (ibid., p. 183). We do not become virtuous, 'for having only intended or aimed at it through love of the reward' (ibid., p. 188). Morality in Shaftesbury does not depend on religion and the idea of future rewards and punishments. In short, he rejects a crucial aspect of the Lockean idea of personal identity, according to which self-concern for the future relates or should relate to future rewards and punishments in the afterlife.[51]

---

[50] This is how Winkler interprets the passage; (2000), 6.

[51] Winkler holds that Shaftesbury and Locke share a sceptical outlook about personal identity (ibid., 9–10). That similarity turns out to be rather superficial, however. It is more likely that Shaftesbury's sceptical arguments relate to Bayle: see Grean (1967), pp. 16–18, 188.

5.2.6. Consciousness and the personality of infants: Roche

There are detailed critical discussions of Locke's philosophy and of some of his followers in the posthumously published work by the Abbé Roche, entitled *Traité de la nature de l'âme* (1759).[52] In metaphysics, Roche is an occasionalist, and he is sometimes labelled a 'Malebranchian' (see Yolton, 1991, p. 60). However, he is critical of some aspects of Malebranche's philosophy—for example, of the view that we know our own soul not through ideas but only through *conscience* or *sentiment intérieur*. Roche argues that if Malebranche's view of the soul's self-knowledge were true, the soul would know itself only in a confused and obscure way (*Traité* vol. 2, p. 423). That is not acceptable, he maintains, as it would mean that we know our own souls only imperfectly and that the essence of the soul remains unknown to us. In fact, the soul knows itself much better than it knows physical objects (ibid., p. 424). Roche sees no reason to deny that the soul knows itself and its essence through 'une idée distincte' (ibid.). In fact, he believes that this view is even consistent with the Malebranchian system. If the ideas of all things are in God, why should there be no idea of the soul itself? According to Roche, then, we have a *sentiment intérieur* both of the existence of our own souls and of our own thoughts, but we also have an idea of the nature or essence of the soul in general (ibid., pp. 425–7). How complete this idea is varies from person to person, depending on their education and other factors (ibid., p. 428).[53] Our distinct idea of the soul's essence is that it is an immaterial and unextended principle of thought. The soul that thinks, wills, and judges in us can only be a 'substance purement spirituelle' (ibid., p. 80).

Among Locke's followers criticized by Roche is Caspar Cuenz, whose account of personal identity was discussed in Chapter 4. Indeed, it seems that Roche often simply reads Locke through Cuenz (see Yolton, 1991, p. 77). For Roche, Locke tacitly assumes that the soul is extended in space. We have seen that Cuenz explicitly endorses this view, and there are passages in Locke that lend themselves to such an interpretation: for example, when he says in *Essay* II.xxvii.2 that finite spirits have a 'determinate time and place of beginning to exist'. Roche argues that if the soul were extended it could not have the capacity to reflect on itself (*Traité*, vol. 1, pp. 400–1). Since it does have the capacity of reflection, however, the soul cannot be extended. For the soul to be able to reflect on itself, it is required that the soul that reflects and

---

[52] Roche, *Traité de la nature de l'âme, et de l'origine des connaissances. Contre le système de M. Locke et de ses partisans*, 2 vols. (1759). According to the 'Avertissement' of the book (vol. 1, p. ix), Roche died on 22 January 1755. Not much seems to have been written about him. His critique of materialism is described by Yolton in *Locke and French Materialism* (1991), pp. 66–85, 89–90, 91n. Yolton cites a definition of person that Roche explicitly approves of (p. 77), but does not discuss the personal identity issue. There are brief references to Roche in Palmer, *Catholics and Unbelievers in Eighteenth-Century France* (1961; first edn., 1939), pp. 148, 150.

[53] Roche distinguishes between two ways of relating to our own soul (idea and *sentiment intérieur*): '1. L'idée de l'esprit en général qu'elle apperçoit distinctement en Dieu lui montre, de la maniere la plus claire, quelle est son essence; elle conçoit évidemment qu'une substance pensante ne peut être qu'immatérielle & immortelle. 2. Le sentiment intérieur par lequel elle sent ses prorpres modalités, lui apprend aussi qu'elle existe: si ce sentiment est accompagné de la réflexion, pour-lors la conviction que: l'Ame a de sa propre existence est montée à son comble': *Traité*, vol. 2, p. 430.

the soul reflected-on are one and the same thing.[54] This identity of the subject and the object of reflection, however, cannot be maintained if the soul were extended. An extended soul supposes parts that are distinct from one another. Such a soul could not reflect on itself, because the required identity of the subject and object of reflection would be destroyed. The reflecting parts or particles and those reflected upon would be distinct parts.[55]

Roche does not seem explicitly to equate French *conscience* or consciousness with reflection. In some passages, however, he suggests that consciousness is a higher-order act of perception and a kind of reflection.[56] For example, he interprets Locke's account of what it means to be a person in terms of the notion of reflection rather than that of consciousness. According to Locke, Roche maintains, children become persons only when they have reached the 'état de réfléchir' (ibid., p. 359), and an infant does not deserve to be called a person until it begins to reflect.[57] More generally speaking, on Locke's definition, people cease to be persons as soon as they become incapable of performing the mental operation of reflection (ibid., p. 366). Given that he states on the following page that for Locke personality is constituted by the 'identity of consciousness', it seems clear that Roche does not distinguish between consciousness and reflection here.[58]

Roche proceeds to list and explain five 'strange' and unacceptable 'consequences' of Locke's theory of personal identity in order to show why the theory should be rejected (ibid., pp. 368–75). All the problems listed concern the notion that consciousness constitutes personal identity. Roche does not explicitly reject Locke's man–person distinction, but it becomes clear that he does not accept it.

In drawing out the first two consequences of Locke's theory Roche in effect claims that consciousness is not sufficient for personal identity. He states that on Locke's theory it is possible that totally different beings or substances can be one and the same person.[59] This means, further, that a 'villain' who identifies himself through

---

[54] This is Roche's definition of reflection: '1. Réfléchir, c'est revenir par une espece de repli intérieur sur son propre être, sur sa propre pensée, sur sa réflexion même, qu'on veut examiner. 2. Quand l'Ame réfléchit sur elle-même, il faut nécessairement que son être soit entitativement le même que celui qui est l'objet de sa réflexion. Toutes les fois qu'un esprit agit ainsi, l'être qui apperçoit est la même chose que ce qui est apperçu; c'est la même identité d'être.' (ibid., vol. 1, p. 403).

[55] 'Par conséquent elles ne seront point le même tout, la même substance, le même être: par conséquence il n'y a aura point une véritable identité entre l'être réfléchissant & l'être réfléchi. D'où nous devons conclure en derniere analyse, que jamais l'Ame ne pourra réfléchir sur elle-même': ibid., p. 404.

[56] Roche's main discussion of personal identity is in *Traité*, vol. 1, pp. 359–75. (These sections are in the second part of the book, entitled 'De l'origine des connoissances humaines'.)

[57] 'Un enfant ne deviendroit ce qu'on appelle une *Personne*, que quand il commenceroit à réfléchir': ibid., p. 360.

[58] Roche comments that, according to Locke, 'Ce qui la [personnalité] constitue, c'est l'identité de conscience... Un être n'a-t-il pas cette identité de conscience, quand se seroit la même substance, ce ne seroit pas la même personne': ibid., p. 367.

[59] 'Des êtres distingués les uns des autres, & qui ne seroient point unis pour faire même tout, pourroient faire la même personne' (ibid., p. 368). The expression in the margin for this section is: 'Des substances totalement différentes, & qui n'auroient aucune liaison entr'elles, pouroient faire la même personne' (ibid.).

consciousness with a virtuous man could not be made accountable for his deeds.[60] Or, which is equally absurd, a saint could forget all his saintly deeds and even become identical with a villain.[61] The 'third consequence' concerns the man–person distinction. Roche argues that according to Locke's 'bizarre hypothesis' (ibid., p. 370), a man is not a person during sound sleep, for he is without consciousness during that period. And this means that the identity of the person is destroyed and reawakened every day.[62] Again this has implications for the moral and legal aspects of personal identity. On Locke's view, Roche claims, a criminal cannot be held accountable for what he did, as there is no continuous identity of his personality. The fourth and fifth consequences have to do with Roche's concern that, for Locke, animals are persons but infants are not. On Locke's theory, some animals at least would have a personality and a personal identity, for they do have memory.[63] Since a human infant, however, may not have the capacity to 'consider itself as itself, the same thinking thing in different times and places' (*Essay*, II.xxvii.9), infants are not persons for Locke.[64] This critique is also directed at Cuenz. Lockeans cannot, if they want to be consistent, ascribe personality to infants (Roche, *Traité*, vol. 1, pp. 480–3). Roche concludes that the only choice is between accepting the (absurd) consequences of Locke's account or rejecting the latter.[65] The problem with Roche's criticism is that he assumes a notion of personhood that Locke has good reasons to reject.

Roche does not develop his own view of personal identity in any detail. It is clear from his critical arguments, however, that he would base his account on the notion of the self or soul as an immaterial substance. Also, Roche cites approvingly what is obviously a Scholastic definition of 'person'. It says that by the term 'person' is meant a rational nature which subsists apart and which is not dominated by another being and not part of another being.[66] This notion of a person as an individual rational

---

[60] 'Selon ce système il pourroit arriver qu'un impie, un sacrilege, un profanateur des choses les plus saintes, se mît fortement dans l'esprit qu'il est entiérement irréprochable dans sa conduite: s'identifiant avec un homme vertueux de sa connoissance, dont toutes les actions sont une suite continuelle de bonnes oeuvres, qu'il se représentera comme étant le même être, le même *soi*, qui en différens temps & en différens lieux a fait telle ou telle action sainte: cette identité de conscience produira l'identité personnelle': ibid., pp. 369–70.
[61] 'D'un autre coté, dans les principes de la même hypothèse, il ne répugne point que l'homme vertueux, par l'effet d'une forte imagination, n'oublie tout ce qu'il a fait de bien pour s'approprier tous les attentats de l'impie dont j'ai parlé': ibid., p. 370.
[62] 'l'homme le plus raisonnable pendant son sommeil n'aura plus de part à la personnalité: car perdant ordinairement le souvenir des pensées réfléchies qui l'ont occupé pendant la veille, l'identité de conscience qu'il avoit en veillant est détruite; ce n'est plus le même *soi*.... ainsi l'identité de personne mourra & renaîtra chaque jour': ibid., pp. 371–2.
[63] 'Les animaux qui ont de la mémoire, auroient par-là la personnalité': ibid., p. 373.
[64] 'Enfin cette perfection de la personnalité ne pourra être dans les enfans: la plus simple attention suffit pour s'en convaincre. Un enfant au berceau peut-il *considérer soi-même comme le même* qui a été dans le sein de sa mere? Se rappelle-t-il le personnage qu'il y faisoit?': ibid., p. 374.
[65] 'Il faut nécessairement, ou que M. Locke admette ces conséquences, ou qu'il désavoue ses principes': ibid., p. 375.
[66] 'Par le terme *personne* on entend une nature raisonnable, qui subsiste à part, qui n'est point dominée, & qui ne fait point partie accessoire d'un autre être': ibid., p. 360. Roche cites a certain 'Ess. de Mor. Symb.T.2, p. 160' as his source for this definition. I have not been able to identify this work.

nature, subsisting separately and not dependent on any other being, comes close to Boethius's classic definition. Like Boethius, Roche links personality to the capacity to reason, not to consciousness and memory. And on this basis Roche argues that animals are not persons because they do not have a rational nature (ibid., pp. 360–1) but that human infants are persons because they have reason in a potential sense (ibid., p. 361).[67] Moreover, he points out that both the church and the law recognize children as persons. Indeed, Roche considers it relevant evidence for this that according to 'our laws', when a king dies, his son, even if he is only two days old, succeeds to the throne. In other words, the infant son is recognized as a person.[68]

In sum, then, Roche attacks Locke in two ways: (1) Locke's theory has several absurd consequences and must be rejected on that account alone; (2) there is a correct account of personhood in terms of the traditional Scholastic notion of person as an individual rational nature. Roche's criticisms of Locke are not well founded, however. His account of Locke's theory is hardly precise, as he confuses consciousness with reflection, and he does not grasp the nature of Locke's distinction between man, soul, and person. Nor is his own account of person very original, as it appeals to the old Boethian definition.

5.2.7. Ploucquet's commentary on Locke

A year after Roche's extensive critique of Locke's theory appeared as part of a comprehensive doctrine of the nature of the soul, another discussion of Locke's account of personal identity was published on the Continent—this time in Germany. Although it is much briefer and is exclusively devoted to a critique of Locke, and although most of the critical comments had been made before by others, this work is of some significance—not least as it appears to be the first, if very short, monograph on the topic.

The piece is a commentary by Gottfried Ploucquet of Tübingen.[69] The first half of the text simply quotes sections 1–19 of Locke's chapter on identity in Pierre Coste's French translation (pp. 1–13). The other half (pp. 14–36) consists of comments on each of those numbered sections. As Locke discusses personal identity from section 9 onwards, only pages 27–36 are devoted to commentary on Locke's account of personal identity.

Ploucquet begins with a comment on Locke's definition of a person. He argues (not unlike Bishop Butler, as we shall see) that given Locke's own definition of

---

[67] Roche argues that two consequences follow from the definition which he cites: (1) 'd'abord la personnalité ne se trouve point dans les animaux'; (2) 'elle est au contraire dans les enfans qui ne font que de naître': ibid., p. 360.

[68] 'Selon nos Loix, qu'un Roi vienne à mourir, son fils, n'eût-il que deux jours, lui succéde; il est unanimement reconnu pour Roi': ibid., p. 364.

[69] Ploucquet, *Examen meletematum celeberrimi anglorum philosophi, Lockii, de Personalitate* (1760).

The notion of a person and the role of consciousness and memory 185

person, it is impossible that there be personal identity in a diversity of substances.[70] Since Locke defines 'person' as 'ens intelligens & cogitans', a person must be a substance. This intelligent being or substance is necessarily one.[71] And so it simply follows from Locke's own definition of 'person' that there cannot be one person in a multiplicity of substances.[72] For Ploucquet, then, a person is a thinking substance, and personal identity is substantial identity. In short, it is the same soul, as substance, that constitutes the same person. And if Socrates and the Mogul, for example, are distinct substances, it is impossible that one can be conscious of the other's actions (ibid., p. 35). Consciousness cannot be distributed through a plurality of intelligent substances (ibid., p. 28).

Ploucquet comments on a number of issues, if only very briefly. He argues, for example, against Locke's suggestion about thinking matter (ibid., pp. 29–30), and he rejects Locke's comparison between animal identity and personal identity on the grounds that consciousness, but not animal life, relates to a unity of a thing or substance.[73] His main argument, however, is that consciousness is neither necessary nor sufficient for personal identity. This follows of course from Ploucquet's interpretation of personal identity as substantial identity, and from the fact that he does not distinguish between consciousness and memory, as his objections show.

Ploucquet argues that consciousness is not necessary for personal identity because people who do not remember their past are still the same persons as they were then. Although no one remembers being baptised as an infant, this does not mean that the adult and the infant that was baptised are not the same person.[74] Moreover, if consciousness were necessary for personal identity, then resurrected infants would not be the same persons as they had been in this life, as they would not be able to remember their past life.[75] Since they (obviously, in Ploucquet's view) are the same persons, however, consciousness cannot be necessary for personal identity.

Consciousness is not sufficient for personal identity for Ploucquet, as it is possible that I represent to myself actions that someone else performed. When this happens this does not mean that the two intelligent beings or substances constitute one person (ibid., p. 32). Something else, in addition to consciousness, is required for there to be

---

[70] 'Definitio Personalitatis a Lockio facta optime se habet, sed servata hac definitione non intelligo, quomodo una eademque personalitas distribui possit vel diffundi in pluribus substantiis': Ploucquet, *Examen*, p. 27.

[71] 'Ens intelligens necessario est Unum': ibid., p. 28.

[72] 'Plures substantias non posse constituere unam personam demonstrari potest ex ipsa Philosophi hujus definitione': ibid., p. 27.

[73] 'In conscientia sui est rei Unitas, in vita animali hoc modo descripta non est substantiae Unitas, & per consequens comparatio inter rem & non-rem male instituitur': ibid., p. 29.

[74] 'Personae identitas cadit etiam in eos, qui praeteritorum non amplius reminiscuntur. Nemo meminit se infantem esse baptizatum, e quo reminiscentiae defectu autem nemo se dicet esse diversam personam ab ea, quae fuit baptizata': ibid., p. 34.

[75] 'Si conscientia praeteritorum necessario requiritur ad constituendam Personae identitatem: infantes resurrecturi non erunt eadem personae, quae fuerunt in hac terra, quia non poterunt meminisse vitae praeteritae. Si enim adulti non meminerunt eorum, quae in infantia sunt acta; neque post resurrectionem infantes recordabuntur periodi terrestris': ibid., p. 35; on Locke's section, 15.

the same person at different points of time. It is required, for example, that the same person (= intelligent substance) *existed* at those points of time.[76]

In sum, Ploucquet lists by then well known arguments, and these are based on equally common assumptions. Like other critics of Locke, Ploucquet does not distinguish between the self as soul or immaterial substance and person, between man and person, and between consciousness and memory. Given these assumptions it is hardly surprising that he eventually rejects Locke's theory. Still, his commentary is an important publication in that it rehearses traditional arguments against Locke in Latin, and it illustrates that by 1760 Locke's account of personal identity was discussed at German universities.

5.2.8. The anonymous *Essay on Personal Identity*

Moving from French and Latin back to English, in 1769 the issue of personal identity was treated again, more extensively and comprehensively, in another monograph—an anonymous *Essay* on the topic, published in London.[77] The aim of the *Essay* is both critical and constructive: the first part is a critique of Locke's theory, according to which 'the same Consciousness be essential to, or the sole Constituent of Personal Identity' (*An Essay on Personal Identity*, pp. 9–48); the second part, to be discussed below in Chapter 8, is an 'Attempt to discover the real Constituent of Personal Identity' (ibid., pp. 49–92). Indeed, the *Essay* is significant as a first attempt to critically evaluate the debate about Locke as it existed thus far, and at the same time to establish a new theory in the light of this critical evaluation. The critical part leaves a lot to be desired, however. It mainly repeats by then well known arguments against Locke. Only in some cases does the author go beyond what has been said before, arguing that previous criticisms do not go far enough or are not powerful enough.[78] Still, the publication of a 92-page monograph on personal identity illustrates the importance of the topic in the philosophical debate at the time, and the *Essay* would have made readers aware of the extensive debate that had been conducted about Locke's theory over the decades since its first publication. Most importantly perhaps, the critical part of the *Essay* inspired a spirited and sharp defence of Locke's theory by Edmund Law—a defence that is still valuable today.

Like Ploucquet, the anonymous author begins his critical discussion with reflections on the term 'person'. He argues that the first part of Locke's definition of 'person' as a 'thinking, intelligent Being, that has reason and reflection' is 'very just' (p. 11). The second part of Locke's definition, however, which suggests that 'a person

---

[76] 'Sin autem ad personam eandem non tantum requiratur conscientia suarum actionum, sed etiam existentia sui in quibuscunque periodis; anima in utraque periodo erit eadem persona': ibid., p. 34.

[77] Anon., *An Essay on Personal Identity. In Two Parts* (1769).

[78] Kippis's review of this work in the *Monthly Review*, 40 (1769), 314–17, does not deal with the critical part at all precisely for the reason that, although it contains 'a minute confutation of Mr. Locke's scheme', 'our Author does not seem to have advanced any new objections here' (314).

can *Always* consider itself as itself, the same in different times and places' amounts, at least 'in some degree', to 'a begging of the question' (ibid.). The author argues that 'it should first... have been proved, that the same consciousness does constitute *Personal Identity*' (ibid.). According to this author, then, Locke's very definition of person assumes that consciousness constitutes the identity of a person (ibid.). It simply assumes what needs to be shown by way of argument. It is plain, however, that the charge of question-begging misses the mark. Locke's position is, as we have seen, that the concept or abstract idea of person will tell us what the criteria are for the identity of individual persons. Locke spells this out in detail. In contrast to Locke, the anonymous author assumes that a person is an immaterial soul. He declares that in his work 'the words *Soul* and *Person* will, in many cases, be synonymous, and therefore indiscriminately used' (ibid., p. 12). And since he also asserts that 'matter can by no means, in any modification, enter into the proper and essential idea of a person' (ibid.), it is plain that he equates the notion of person with that of an immaterial substance or soul.

It is not surprising, therefore, that the author holds, unlike Locke, but like Ploucquet, that there can be no change of substance without any change in personal identity (ibid., p. 44). The author's main target, however, is the role that Locke ascribes to consciousness in the constitution of personal identity. He concedes that for there to be a person there must be consciousness but argues that to say that consciousness constitutes personal identity is a different claim and that it does not follow from the former. 'Consciousness is necessary to make a man *himself to himself*, which is most certain, and readily acknowledged. But this does not prove, that the same consciousness constitutes *Personal Identity*, or that any one is not accountable for those actions of which he is not conscious' (ibid., p. 22). Consciousness, the author argues, plays no constitutive role for personal identity.

As the last quote and many other comments suggest, the author equates consciousness with memory. At least he does not distinguish clearly between the two. Like Berkeley, however, he distinguishes between actual and potential consciousness, arguing that according to Locke, actual consciousness constitutes personal identity. On this reading, Locke is committed to the claim that, 'whenever... we have not this present representation of a past action, *Personal Identity*... certainly ceases' (ibid., p. 28). And this, the author points out, is an absurd view. 'Should it then be enquired, what it is that makes a person the same today that he was when he performed any particular action yesterday; it would evidently be an absurd answer to affirm, that it is some future remembrance of that action; that our present Identity depends on what, at present, is not in existence; that we are the same today that we were yesterday; and yet, that the only thing which makes us now the same, the sole constituent of that sameness, has not, nor ever has had Being' (ibid., pp. 29–30).

Next, the author argues that Locke's theory would have to be rejected even if Locke had interpreted 'same consciousness' not in terms of actual consciousness or remembering but as a potential consciousness or memory, that is as 'a Power in the

Soul of causing that consciousness of past actions, whether exerted or not' (ibid., p. 31). Consciousness thus understood cannot constitute personal identity because there are many past thoughts and actions that are rightly considered ours but that we will never be able to remember. If one accepted Locke's theory, therefore, I could not be the same person now that I was in my infancy. 'As I believe no one was ever known *able*, in manhood, to recollect the thoughts, etc. which he had when in perfect infancy, it follows also, that no man is, nor ever was there any one, the same Person in the two states of infancy and manhood' (ibid., pp. 31–2). Moreover, the author seems to think that the ability to remember past actions would have to mean that I should be able to remember all of my past actions at any one time. Since it is evident, however, that we do not have this ability, there can be no personal identity through time if we make consciousness or memory the criterion of personal identity. 'It is impossible for the mind of man, in its present state, to conceive of many things at once: on this account, therefore, there must be innumerable past thoughts and actions that it *cannot*, at any one time, repeat; and so change must be thereby continually caused in *Personal Identity*' (ibid., p. 31).

Like Plouquet and others before him, the anonymous author can be interpreted as arguing that consciousness (as understood by him) is neither necessary nor sufficient for personal identity. It is not necessary because someone who some years ago committed a crime and no longer has any consciousness of it would nevertheless be 'accountable' for it, the crime would still be 'his action'. The author notes that Locke attempts to refute such objections by appealing to his distinction between 'man' and 'person' (ibid., p. 13). It is a consequence of Locke's theory that 'the same man, therefore, entirely losing, as he necessarily must, at different times, the consciousness of many of his past actions, becomes as many different persons' (ibid., p. 14). The author dismisses this view, stating simply: 'of the probability or propriety of this let common sense have the decision' (ibid.). It is plain that the author thinks that consciousness is not sufficient for personal identity, as he points out that if I were conscious of a crime that I have not committed, I would not be accountable for it. I do not become the person of the criminal on account of such consciousness (ibid., p. 15).

The author comments on Isaac Watts's critique of Locke in this context. He maintains that Watts 'has not shewn *wherein* lies the error of Mr. Locke's scheme; that he has only remarked upon the improbability of it and said nothing concerning its impossibility' (ibid., p. 4). Thus, he cites Watts's discussion of Locke's thought experiment about someone who 'fancied his soul to have been that of Socrates'. The author believes it follows from Watts's remarks 'that proper conscious remembrance does, in reality, constitute Personal Identity. Dr Watts, therefore, instead of refuting, does by his answer confirm Mr. Locke's general position' (ibid., p. 17). This evaluation of Watts, however, is neither fair nor sound. Watts distinguishes between genuine and false memory; genuine memory *presupposes* something else that makes it genuine. And for Watts, identity is established by means other than (genuine) memory.

5.2.9. Conclusion

We have seen in this section that a recurring critique of Locke's account is that consciousness is neither necessary nor sufficient for personal identity.[79] This is argued in variety of ways and contexts. It seems to be (not the only but certainly) the main argument in philosophical criticism of Locke's theory as far as it relates to the role that Locke ascribes to consciousness. We have also seen, however, that this critique is typically based on mistaken assumptions about Locke's theory: Lockean consciousness is identified with reflection or memory, Locke's account of the person is taken to be an account of the self as substance, and thus his distinction between soul, man, and person is not appreciated. Given these mistaken assumptions the critique does not have the devastating force the authors considered here think that it has.

One point that seems to be implied by the arguments that consciousness is not sufficient for personal identity is the following. Even if memory or consciousness were always veridical, this would not mean that consciousness constitutes personal identity; for the veracity of consciousness or memory is possible only because there is an identical soul or mind in the first place. The identity of the soul is presupposed by veridical memory and is what makes veracious memory possible. We shall see in the next Chapter that this line of argument is also relevant to the charge of circularity against Locke.

---

[79] Reid, too, at least hints at this point, in *Essays on the Intellectual Powers of Man*, ed. Brookes (2002), pp. 277–9.

6

The charge of circularity and the argument from the transitivity of identity

As indicated above, the two most prominent criticisms of Locke's account are the charge of circularity and the argument from the transitivity of identity. These are arguments, moreover, with which any account that bases personal identity on consciousness would have to deal. As far as Locke's own theory is concerned, we shall see that the charge of circularity can be rejected in a straightforward way, if Locke's text is considered carefully, while the argument from the transitivity of identity appears to pose more serious problems for his theory.

6.1. THE CHARGE OF CIRCULARITY AGAINST LOCKE

This is perhaps the most discussed objection to Locke's account of personal identity. It is argued that Locke's explanation implicitly contains what is to be explained. In other words, it is said that to account for personal identity in terms of consciousness means that personal identity is implicitly contained in this account, as consciousness always already presupposes personal identity. We have seen in Chapter 1 that in the early 1690s' debates about the trinity, Robert South rightly charges William Sherlock's notion of personality with circularity. The argument was first levelled against Locke's theory in the late 1690s. Since then it has been used many times against Locke and Lockean theories of personal identity. It was made famous by Bishop Butler in the eighteenth century, and it is still being discussed in present-day debates about the issue.[1] It is not surprising that this objection has been debated so much, for if it is valid then it would indeed be fatal to Locke's theory.

The charge of circularity against Locke is closely related to some of the arguments we have examined in the previous Chapter. Thus, those who make this charge typically do not accept Locke's distinction between the notions of person, man,

---

[1] See, for example, Wiggins, *Sameness and Substance Renewed* (2001), pp. 197ff. For other recent and influential discussions of the charge of circularity against Locke and neo-Lockean theories of personal identity, see especially Parfit, *Reasons and Persons* (1984), pp. 219–23; and McDowell, 'Reductionism and the First Person', in Dancy (ed.), *Reading Parfit* (1997), pp. 230–50, at pp. 235ff.

and soul as substance. Indeed it seems that rejecting (or ignoring) this distinction is usually the hidden basis for the charge of circularity. The charge is closely connected also to the objection, discussed above with respect to Samuel Clarke and others, that consciousness and memory are not sufficient for personal identity, as consciousness and memory may be fallacious and ascribe actions to us that we never did. As noted above, it is assumed, by contrast, that veridical consciousness and memory presuppose personal identity. Consciousness and memory cannot be veridical if I am not now the same person who committed the remembered action in the past. Thus, it seems that the objection that consciousness and memory are not sufficient for personal identity leads directly to the charge of circularity. Still, the two objections are not identical. And there are several versions of the charge of circularity against Locke.

6.1.1. Sergeant on Locke on individuation and personal identity

The earliest and one of the most detailed versions of the charge of circularity against Locke was put forward by an Aristotelian philosopher and contemporary of Locke, John Sergeant.[2] Sergeant's critique of Locke's theory of identity in his *Solid Philosophy Asserted* (1697) is part of a lengthy and careful examination of the whole of Locke's *Essay*, against the background of a Scholastic metaphysics. It is based on a similar critique of Locke's account of individuation.

Sergeant begins his discussion of individuation by making basically the same point as does Stillingfleet at about the same time. According to Sergeant, Locke confuses the external marks by which we come to know the distinction between things with what intrinsically causes this distinction, and Locke wrongly takes the former for the latter.[3] But unlike Stillingfleet, Sergeant explicitly charges Locke's account with circularity. Existence at a certain place and time presupposes individuality and therefore cannot constitute it:

'Tis evident that the Individual Thing must, (in priority of Nature or Reason) be *first* constituted such, ere it can be *capable of Existence*. Wherefore 'tis impossible that Existence,

---

[2] For literature on Sergeant's thought in general, see Bradish, 'John Sergeant, A Forgotten Critic of Descartes and Locke', *The Monist*, 39 (1929), 571–92; Yolton, 'Locke's Unpublished Marginal Replies to John Sergeant', *Journal of the History of Ideas*, 12 (1951), 528–59; Yolton, *John Locke and the Way of Ideas* (1956), pp. 76–87, 103–13; Cooney, 'John Sergeant's Criticism of Locke's Theory of Ideas', *Modern Schoolman*, 50 (1972–73), 143–58; Glauser, 'John Sergeant's Argument against Descartes and the Way of Ideas', *The Monist*, 71 (1988), 585–95; Krook, *John Sergeant and his Circle* (1993); Southgate, "Beating Down Scepticism": The Solid Philosophy of John Sergeant, 1623–1707', in Stewart (ed.), *English Philosophy in the Age of Locke* (2000), pp. 281–315. Sergeant's account of personal identity is discussed in Behan, 'Locke on Persons and Personal Identity', *Canadian Journal of Philosophy*, 9 (1979), 53–74; Thiel, 'Locke's Concept of a Person', in Brandt (ed.), *John Locke. Symposium Wolfenbüttel 1979* (1981), pp. 181–92; Thiel, *Lockes Theorie der personalen Identität* (1983); Thiel, 'Individuation', in Garber and Ayers, *The Cambridge History of Seventeenth-Century Philosophy* (1998), pp. 212–62; and Thiel, 'Personal Identity', in ibid., pp. 868–912.

[3] Sergeant says that Locke 'distinguishes not between the *Extrinsecal Marks* and *Signes* by which we may *know* the Distinction of *Individuals*, and what *Intrinsically* and Essentially constitutes or makes them *different* Things': Sergeant, *Solid Philosophy Asserted* (1697; reprinted, 1984), p. 261.

consider it how we will, can be in any manner the *Principle* of *Individuation*, the constitution of the Individuum being presupposed to it.[4]

Sergeant argues that Locke's account of individuation is circular because it assumes something to be the principle of individuation which presupposes individuality. In Sergeant's view, individuation is to be explained in analogy with the constitution of kinds or species: the latter are explained in terms of substantial forms. Substantial forms or essences are, according to Sergeant, those complexes of properties which enable beings to perform operations which are typical for their kind. And individuation, too, is said to have a formal ground; the individual character or essence is constituted by a greater number of properties than that which constitutes the kind or species: 'for, the *Species* or *Kinds* of Things are but *few*, but the *Individuums* under those Kinds are *Innumerable*; and, therefore, *more* goes to distinguish *these* from one another, than was needful to distinguish or determine the *other*'.[5] It is a being's particular set of characteristics which makes it the individual that it is. This individual character is 'the Intrinsecal or Formal *Principle of Individuation*'; that is, it 'ultimately' determines a being 'to be *This* or *That*' (ibid.). The individual character or essence is the lowest form or 'last Distinction' which completes the determination of a being as a particular. Sergeant emphasises that his theory of individuation in terms of individual essences implies that no two individuals, 'however seemingly Uniform', can have all their properties in common: there must be some intrinsic characteristics with respect to which they differ, otherwise, 'they would be *One*, and not *One*: which is a Contradiction' (ibid., p. 278). Our ideas or notions of individuals cannot capture the complete set of individuating characteristics, and 'we can never comprehend or reach all that belongs to the *Suppositum*, or *Individuum*' (ibid., p. 257). Nevertheless, we are able to distinguish between individuals on the basis of external marks such as their existence in time and space. Sergeant adds that in this sense, 'and not in making them *intrinsecally* constitute the *Individuum*, Mr. *Locke*'s Doctrin in this Point is admitted' (ibid., p. 279). Locke, obviously, could not accept this scholastic account in terms of substantial forms. We noted in Chapter 3 that Locke argues that the 'complex of accidents' relevant for individuation would have to be reduced to those of spatio-temporal location. Sergeant has no time for Locke's view that abstract ideas are relevant to the issue of identity: 'how the holding to the *Specifical Idea*, in which all the *Individuums* under it do *agree*, and which makes them *one* in Nature, should clear the Distinction of *Individuals*, is altogether inexplicable' (ibid., pp. 268–9). It is not surprising, however, that a philosopher such as Sergeant, who asserts the reality of substantial forms, can make little sense of Locke's subjectivist treatment of identity.

Although Sergeant's focus is on individuation rather than diachronic identity, he emphasises that that which individuates also determines identity over time: as long as

---

[4] Sergeant, *Solid Philosophy Asserted*, p. 260. See also Sergeant, *The Method to Science* (1696), pp. 427–8: 'their Individuation must be *presuppos'd* to Existence; and, so, cannot depend on it as on its Principle'. Compare Sergeant, *Transnatural Philosophy, or Metaphysics* (1700), pp. 112–14.

[5] Sergeant, *Solid Philosophy Asserted*, p. 257.

an individual retains its set of essential characteristics it remains the same. 'No Alteration or Defalcation of *Matter*, Quantity, or Figure, etc. makes it *Another Substance*, or *Another Thing*'; it loses its identity only through 'such a *New Form*, as makes it *unfit* for its *Primary Operation*, to which it is ordain'd, as it is a Distinct Part in Nature' (ibid., p. 270).

This point is relevant also to Sergeant's critique of Locke's account of personal identity, as his explicit focus here is again on 'individuality' rather than diachronic identity. Further, his critique has two premises. One is that he rejects Locke's distinction between the identity of the man and the identity of the person. He realizes that Locke's distinction between substance, man, and person is essential to his account of personal identity. He realizes also that his rejection of this distinction undermines Locke's theory from the start. Thus Sergeant says that he 'must forestall all his [Locke's] Subsequent Discourses by denying this Preliminary to them' (ibid., p. 262). He accounts for 'man' as a unity of soul and body in Scholastic (rather than Cartesian) terms. The soul is the form of man and adjusts to the dispositions of the bodily part. 'The *soul* [is] proportion'd to *that* Matter as its *Form*' (ibid., p. 259). He argues that it is part of the notion of a man's essence that he is an intelligent being and that therefore a man is '*Essentially* and Formally one *Person* too' (ibid., p. 262). According to Sergeant, then, the person just *is* the individual man, and the individual man is a complete substance. Indeed, he uses 'man' and 'person' synonymously, and for him there is no distinction to be made between the identity of the man and the identity of the person.

The second premise of Sergeant's critique is that unlike Locke he equates consciousness with reflection. This is clear from his concession to Locke that consciousness is inseparable from the person. He states that 'we cannot but *Reflect* on what concerns any part of our *Individuum*, which is our *Self*' (ibid., p. 266). Moreover, he explicitly rejects Locke's understanding of consciousness as an immediate and experiential relating to one's own self. For Sergeant, relating to one's own self is possible only through an act of reflection that takes place after we performed the acts on which we now reflect. 'And, I judge it impossible we should *know we know* at the same time we have that Act *only*, till *afterwards* we come to *reflect* upon it by a *new* Act; which is to know it, *not by Experience*, but *by Reflexion*' (ibid., p. 122). We can relate through immediate experience to external objects when we receive impressions from them, but we cannot relate to our thought immediately (ibid.). An act of knowledge relates only to the object of this act, not to the act of knowing itself. When we perceive an external object, then the latter is the only object of perception; we are not at the same time aware of the act of perception itself. Sergeant writes: 'I am not *conscious* I know; that is, I do not *know I know* when I have the Act of knowing.'[6] For Sergeant, to assume an immediate relating to one's own acts is to confound the distinction between direct and reflexive knowledge. Sergeant thus rejects the view, shared by Locke and Descartes, that thought is always accompanied by consciousness:

But if I be *Conscious*, or *know that I know* when I know the Object *without me*, I must by the *same* Act know what's *within me* and what's *without me both* at once; and so my Act of *Direct*

---

[6] Sergeant, *Solid Philosophy Asserted*, p. 123; see also p. 125, where Sergeant explicitly refers to Locke.

Knowledge would be *Reflex*, or rather, that *one* Act would be *both Direct* and *Reflex*, which makes it Chimerical. (ibid., pp. 123ff.)

Consciousness, then, is nothing but reflective knowledge: '*Consciousness* of any *Action* or other Accident we have now, or have had, is nothing but our *Knowldge* [*sic*] that it belong'd to us' (ibid., p. 265).

It is plain that having rejected Locke's distinctions between the man and the person and between consciousness and reflection, Sergeant will also reject Locke's view that personal identity is constituted by consciousness. Indeed, his rejection of these Lockean distinctions forms the basis of his charge of circularity against Locke. He agrees with Locke that we have no innate but only acquired knowledge. For Sergeant this means that knowledge is merely accidental to the human subject. Knowledge—including the reflective type of knowledge called consciousness—is not an essential property of the human subject—the man or person. He infers from this: 'Wherefore the Man, or that Thing which is to be the *Knower*, must have had Individuality or Personality from *other* Principles, *antecedently* to this Knowledge call'd *Consciousness*' (ibid.). A man or, which is the same thing for Sergeant, a person, is the individual it is prior to, and independently of consciousness. His view about the individuation of a man or person is that it consists in the adjustment of the soul 'to the Bodily or *Animal* Part' (ibid., p. 258). According to Sergeant 'there will be infused a Soul apt to *judge* and *discourse more perfectly*, or *leß* perfectly, according as the *Matter* requires' (ibid.). Consciousness plays no role in the individuation of the man or person understood as a unity of soul and body. Rather, consciousness relates to the self only as that substance or thing in which acts of consciousness and other types of knowledge originate; therefore, the self must be an individual prior to acts of consciousness. 'Our Person, or Individual *Self*... is the *Object* of that *Consciousness*; and *Objects* must be *antecedent* and *presupposed* to the *Acts* which are employ'd about them, because the Objects are the *Cause* of those *Acts*' (ibid., p. 267). The self as person or man is constituted independently of, and prior to, consciousness. Indeed, consciousness presupposes the individuality of the person and therefore cannot constitute it in the first place. In other words, to account for personality in terms of consciousness is circular, because to do so would always already presuppose that there be an individual self or person to which consciousness turns as its object. The person for Sergeant is the self or man who is the cause of the acts that relate to it, and therefore cannot be constituted by those acts.

This suggests that the identity of the person through time, too, is constituted prior to, and independently of consciousness, and that the Lockean account of diachronic personal identity is circular. A person or man, for Sergeant, must be constituted as identical before he can have consciousness thereof. 'It being then most evident, that a Man must *be* the same, ere he can *know* or *be Conscious* that he *is* the same' (ibid., p. 265). Thus for Sergeant, just as existence presupposes individuation, so does consciousness presuppose personal identity. It is just as circular to account for personal identity in terms of consciousness, as it is circular to account for individuation in general in terms of existence. Locke's account assumes something to be the principle of personal identity that presupposes personal identity.

6.1.2. Lee's version of the charge

There is no evidence that Henry Lee was aware of Sergeant's critique of Locke. But Lee, too, charges Locke's theory with circularity. Lee's premises for this charge differ in some respects from Sergeant's assumptions. As we have seen above, Lee's notion of the self as person is Cartesian, rather than Scholastic. He equates the person with the soul, rather than with man. Like Sergeant, however, he works with a substance-view of person, and like Sergeant he does not distinguish between consciousness and reflection (see Chapter 5 above).

Lee's formulation of the charge consists of two main steps, and it is in this respect similar to Robert South's critique of William Sherlock. First, consciousness presupposes previous mental acts to which consciousness can relate as its object. Consciousness—or, which is the same thing for Lee, reflection—must have an object, and this object can be only another mental act that exists prior to the act of consciousness or reflection. 'We cannot be *conscious* without a previous *act* of which the Mind is said to be conscious' (Lee *Anti-Scepticism*, 1702, p. 124). According to Lee, this has implications for the personal identity issue. 'Consciousness alone cannot constitute the Person the same with himself, because at least that antecedent *Act* of Sensation or Perception must be allow'd to have a share in that Composition of the Intelligent Being' (ibid., pp. 124–5).

Second, consciousness presupposes a mind or soul as that substance that has the power of consciousness and performs acts of consciousness.

> Consciousness can be only a Power, or the repeted acts of a Power; but neither Power or repeted acts of a Power can be the Thing or Substance itself that has that Power or exerts those Operations; and consequently can't be that from which a Person is denominated the *same* with himself at different times, unless we could suppose the Power to be the *Substance* of which it is the Power, or an Action to be the *Agent* itself; which is impossible. (ibid., p. 124)

Since the soul or person must be constituted prior to acts of consciousness, such acts cannot constitute its identity at different times. Actions cannot, according to Lee, unite themselves into an identical self, person or soul. '*Actions* can't *unite* themselves; it must be the *Agent* that must do that' (ibid., p. 125). This applies also to the acts of consciousness. '*Consciousneſs* alone can't unite several Acts of an Intelligent Being, without the *Substance* of which it is only the Mode and Power' (ibid.). Rather, what unites actions is the self as soul or substance itself. It is the self as soul or substance that functions as the identical source of those actions, and it is on account of it that they have a unity:

> And therefore that which must make these distinct and successive Acts of Consciousness to be the Actions of one Being, must be something distinct from the *Actions* themselves: And that must and can be nothing else but the Mind itself. And therefore 'tis *that* denominates the Person the *same* with himself at different times'. (ibid.)

For Lee, then, personal identity consists in the identity of the same soul or mental substance. Like South (arguing against Sherlock), Lee holds that consciousness presupposes, first, other mental acts to which consciousness can relate as to its objects, and second, an identical mind or soul as the source and unifying principle of mental acts, including consciousness. To explain the identity of the self in terms of consciousness is circular, because that explanation presupposes that which is to be explained.

Unlike Sergeant and other critics of Locke, Lee explicitly extends the charge of circularity from consciousness to its 'unavoidable concomitant', self-concern. Locke holds that self-concern relates not to the human subject as a thinking substance but only to our experiential self or person. Lee argues, however, that such self-concern presupposes the identity of the human subject as person or thinking substance. Locke, Lee complains, 'often noses us with saying, no man is concern'd for the same Substance, whether Material or Immaterial; only that he be himself, that shall feel the pleasure; that's true indeed, but the Question is, how that appears possible to be had without the same Substance?' (ibid., p. 129). In other words, to account for personal identity in terms of self-concern presupposes the identity of the soul as substance, although the identity of substance may not indeed be that for which we are concerned. For Lee there can be no meaningful concern for our own future if the future self is not the same substance as now.

In sum, then, Lee argues that the identity of the person (which he equates with the mind or soul) is presupposed for consciousness and self-concern to be possible; therefore consciousness cannot constitute personal identity.

6.1.3. Other versions of the charge

As indicated above, many eighteenth-century critics of Locke charged Locke's theory with circularity. Sergeant and Lee were only the first in a long line of critics to argue in this way. As our discussion of Sergeant and Lee makes clear, the charge of circularity can be made against Locke from both a Scholastic and a Cartesian perspective. Later versions of the charge are often made only in passing, and in some cases it is merely implied by other critical comments. Thus, the author of the anonymous *Essay on Personal Identity* states that consciousness provides evidence for personal identity but does not constitute it. 'Consciousness ... does not appear to be that, wherein *Personal Identity* consists; but only that, whereby we are sensible to ourselves of this Personal Identity'.[7] This does not say directly that Locke's theory is circular, but unpacking that argument will lead to the charge of circularity. We have seen that Sergeant makes a similar claim about Locke's view on individuation, arguing that existence may provide evidence for individuality but does not constitute it; rather, existence presupposes individuality. Similarly, the anonymous author's argument here assumes that personal identity is constituted prior to, and independently of, consciousness, and that therefore the latter cannot constitute it. Consciousness presupposes personal identity, and to explain personal identity in terms of consciousness is circular, because such an explanation tacitly assumes what is to be explained.

Other critics of Locke, such as the philosophers of the Common Sense school, explicitly link the claim about consciousness providing only evidence for personality

---

[7] *An Essay on Personal Identity. In Two Parts* (1769), p. 20.

to the charge of circularity. Like the author of the *Essay on Personal Identity*, Thomas Reid, for example, says that in Locke, 'personal identity is confounded with the evidence which we have of our personal identity'; Locke 'confounded the testimony with the thing testified'.[8] Moreover, Reid charges Locke with confusion between consciousness and memory, and so thinks that Locke accounts for personal identity only in terms of memory. Reid argues that precisely because memory provides only evidence for personal identity it cannot constitute the latter; otherwise it would seem that memory can produce its object, which is absurd.

To say that my remembrance that I did such a thing, or my consciousness, makes me the person who did it, is in my apprehension, an absurdity too gross to be entertained by any man who attends to the meaning of it: For it is to attribute to memory or consciousness a strange magical power of producing its object, though that object must have existed before the memory or consciousness which produced it.[9]

The 'object'—that is, personal identity—must have been constituted prior to memory, for otherwise memory could not provide evidence for it. To account for personal identity in terms of memory is circular, as memory presupposes personal identity. Reid also points out the consequences of Locke's theory for morality in this context. Consciousness of thought is transient and momentary. Therefore, 'if personal identity consisted in consciousness, it would certainly follow, that no man is the same person any two moments of his life; and as the right and justice of reward and punishment is founded on personal identity, no man could be responsible for his actions' (ibid., p. 278).

Other Common Sense philosophers, such as James Beattie, Lord Kames, and Dugald Stewart, make the charge of circularity against Locke in passing.[10] Towards the end of the century the charge continued to be repeated, but no new aspects were added. Abraham Tucker is an example of this.[11] In fact, explicit appeal is made to earlier versions of the charge. Sergeant's text seems to have been forgotten, but Thomas Morell's *Notes and Annotations on Locke on the Human Understanding* uses Lee's version of the charge.[12] And Thomas Ludlam remarks in his *Logical Tracts* that Locke's account of personal identity amounts to saying that 'personal identity consists in personal identity'.[13]

All these authors, including the Scottish Common Sense philosophers and Tucker, do not distinguish between the soul as substance and the person, thus denying

---

[8] Reid, *Essays on the Intellectual Powers of Man*, ed. Brookes (2002), pp. 277, 278. See also Reid, *Cura Prima on Common Sense*, in Marcil-LaCoste, *Claude Buffier and Thomas Reid* (1982), pp. 200–1.

[9] Reid, *Intellectual Powers* (2002), p. 277.

[10] See Beattie, *An Essay on the Nature and Immutability of Truth* (1770), p. 82; Kames, *Essays on the Principles of Morality and Natural Religion* (1779) ed. Moran (2005), p. 129; and Stewart, *Collected Works* (1854–60/1994), vol. 5, p. 60.

[11] Tucker, *The Light of Nature Pursued* (1805/1977), vol. 2, pp. 76–7.

[12] Morell, *Notes and Annotations on Locke on the Human Understanding, written by Order of the Queen* (1794), pp. 66, 68–9.

[13] Ludlam, *Logical Tracts, comprising Observations and Essays illustrative of Mr. Locke's Treatise upon the Human Understanding* (1790), p. 38.

explicitly or implicitly an important premise of Locke's account in terms of consciousness. In this respect they argue like Henry Lee. Thomas Morell, for example, again appealing to Lee, argues that 'it is much more agreeable to reason that *thinking substance and person* should be *one* and the *same* thing' (*Notes and Annotations*, p. 68). Thomas Ludlam seems to agree, and sees no reason to question one's personal identity at all. Indeed, he states that 'waiving then all debate about the essence of personal identity, a doubt concerning which the ablest physicians have long held to be the *surest* mark of lunacy' (*Logical Tracts*, p. 38).

By the late eighteenth century, both Sergeant's and Lee's versions of the charge were forgotten—except by Morell, who cites Lee. Instead, most philosophers who charged Locke's theory with circularity in the second half of the century appealed to (or were at least inspired by) Bishop Butler's critique of 1736. This may, of course, have to do with Butler's fame in other areas of philosophy. It is also true, however, that Butler's is the most succinct and clearest formulation of this charge. Reid cites Butler's critique of Locke as decisive.[14] Locke's account of personal identity 'has been censured', he writes, 'by Bishop BUTLER, in a short essay subjoined to his Analogy, with whose sentiments I perfectly agree' (*Intellectual Powers*, p. 275). Most present-day discussions of the charge of circularity against Lockean theory, too, appeal to Butler, rather than to Lee or Sergeant.

6.1.4. Butler's critique of Locke

Butler discusses personal identity in a short 'dissertation' appended to his *Analogy of Religion* (1736).[15] The issue is 'closely connected', as Butler puts it, to the book's very first chapter, entitled 'Of a Future Life' (*Works*, vol. 1, p. 316). Indeed, he points out in the first sentence of that chapter that 'strange difficulties have been raised by some concerning personal identity' (ibid., p. 17). Nevertheless, as far as Butler is concerned, personal identity is not a pressing issue, and he postpones discussion of it to the Appendix. As we shall see in Chapter 8, he takes personal identity for granted, and has no 'strange difficulties' with it. For Butler it is one of those 'subtleties' that require only 'a little' consideration (ibid., p. 317).

The dissertation 'Of Personal Identity' sets out Butler's own views on the topic, but it does so in the context of a criticism of Locke's and Collins's accounts. Here Butler restates that 'strange perplexities have been raised about the meaning of that identity or sameness of person, which is implied in the notion of our living now and hereafter, or in any two successive moments' (ibid.). He adds that, moreover, 'the solution of these difficulties hath been stranger than the difficulties themselves' (ibid.). The 'strange solution' to which he is referring is Locke's view that consciousness constitutes personal identity.

---

[14] See, for example, Stewart, *Collected Works*, vol. 5, p. 60.
[15] Butler, 'Of Personal Identity', in Gladstone (ed.), *The Works of Joseph Butler*, 2 vols. (1897), vol. 1, pp. 317–25.

The charge of circularity and the transitivity of identity

Butler's main and most important argument against Locke consists in the charge of circularity. In the process of making this charge, however, he also raises other objections to Locke's account. Like Lee and other critics, he does not accept Locke's distinction between the notions of person and thinking substance. For Butler, the question about the identity of a person concerns the identity of a thinking substance or soul. Like Ploucquet and the author of the *Essay on Personal Identity*, Butler holds that Locke's own definition of person commits him to a substance-view of persons. For Butler, Locke's statement that a person is 'a thinking intelligent being' (*Essay*, II. xxvii.9) amounts to an endorsement of a substance-view of the person 'because Being and Substance, in this place, stand for the same idea' (*Works*, vol. 1, p. 320). In places Butler seems to equate the person with the man, rather than with the soul or thinking substance. This is clear from passages in which he refers to the person as a 'living being' (ibid., pp. 323–4) or a 'living agent' (ibid., p. 321). In the last analysis, however, the personality of the living being resides in the soul or thinking substance, while 'our organized bodies are no more ourselves or part of ourselves, than any other matter around us' (ibid., p. 25).

According to Butler, there are a number of reasons why consciousness cannot constitute the identity of persons understood as thinking substances. Thus, if a person is just a thinking substance, then Locke surely is wrong to suggest that we can have the same person but different substances. The identity of a person 'cannot subsist with the diversity of substance' (ibid., p. 320). The acts of consciousness may be diverse at different points of time but 'they are consciousnesses of one and the same thing or object; of the same person, self, or living agent' (ibid., p. 321). This also means that consciousness cannot be necessary for personal identity. 'Present consciousness of past actions or feelings is not necessary to our being the same persons who performed those actions, or had those feelings' (ibid., p. 319), because personal identity is always already secured by the identity of substance.

Butler also discusses a view that he does not ascribe to Locke himself but to some of his followers—especially Anthony Collins. Collins and others, he claims, have taken Locke's position further and believe that 'personality is not a permanent but a transient thing: that it lives and dies, begins and ends continually' (ibid., p. 321). Like Lee, he points out the negative consequences of such a view for moral and legal responsibility. If a person is a transient thing, 'from hence it must follow, that it is a fallacy upon ourselves, to charge our present selves with anything we did, or to imagine our present selves interested in any thing which befell us yesterday; or that our present self will be interested in what will befall us tomorrow' (ibid., p. 322). According to Butler, although Lockeans such as Collins speak of personal identity, 'they cannot, consistently with themselves, mean, that the person is really the same' because they claim personal identity consists in something (consciousness) which does not remain the same (ibid.). Butler thinks that Lockeans do not even mean 'that the person is *really* the same, but only that he is so in a fictitious sense: in such a sense only as they assert . . . that any number of persons whatever may be the same person' (ibid.). He thus introduces the notion of personal identity as fictitious. In his case this notion is part of a critique of the Lockean view. Hume, as we shall see, will make use of the notion of fictitious identity in a more positive sense.

Butler's charge of circularity is, of course, based on his view that a person is nothing but the thinking substance or soul. Like others before and after him, he concedes that consciousness can provide evidence for the identity of our own self or person or enable us to 'ascertain' it (ibid., p. 318). He even believes that it is part of the essence of a thinking being or substance that it be endowed with consciousness. Butler's use of the term 'consciousness', however, is not consistent. In some places he suggests that consciousness relates to 'what we at present do and feel' (ibid., pp. 318–19), but in his discussion of Locke's view he reads consciousness as relating to the past only and seems to equate it with our ability to 'remember' and 'reflect upon' the past (ibid., p. 318): it is a type of 'knowledge' of the past (ibid.). Indeed, he makes a stronger claim than just to say that consciousness can provide evidence for our personal identity. Consciousness provides us with a 'proof' of our personal identity (ibid., p. 324). Although he concedes that memory is not necessarily veridical and that we can be deceived, he points out that this is a problem that applies to 'any demonstration whatever' (ibid., p. 325). 'Here we can go no further. For it is ridiculous to attempt to prove the truth of those perceptions, whose truth we cannot otherwise prove, than by other perceptions of exactly the same kind with them' (ibid., p. 325).

It is clear, then, that unlike Sergeant, Butler focuses on personal identity through time. He insists that although an intelligent being must be endowed with consciousness, and although the latter can provide evidence or even a proof of identity, it does not follow that consciousness constitutes diachronic personal identity:

But though consciousness of what is past does thus ascertain our personal identity to ourselves, yet to say, that it makes personal identity, or is necessary to our being the same persons is to say, that a person has not existed a single moment, nor done one action, but what he can remember; indeed none but what he reflects upon. (ibid., p. 318)

Butler argues that to claim that consciousness fulfils a constitutive function is to confuse what constitutes personal identity with what provides evidence for it; or in other words, it is to mistake an epistemic issue for an ontological one. As indicated above, this charge of confusing epistemology with ontology implies the charge of circularity. Butler makes this charge explicitly, however. Since, for him, consciousness or memory is a form of knowledge, and since all knowledge presupposes the truth that is known, consciousness cannot and does not produce the truths it knows. To argue that it can and does produce those truths would be to argue in a circle. And so, to argue that memory constitutes personal identity is to argue that what is known through memory, the truth of personal identity, is produced by it. But that is a circular argument: consciousness cannot constitute personal identity 'any more than knowledge, in any other case, can constitute truth, which it presupposes' (ibid., p. 318). Butler sums up his argument thus: 'One should really think it self-evident, that consciousness of personal identity presupposes, and therefore cannot constitute, personal identity' (ibid.). A person is diachronically identical 'prior to all consideration of its remembering or forgetting: since remembering or forgetting can make no alteration in the truth of past matter of fact' (ibid., p. 324).

Next, Butler argues that the source of the Lockean mistake is an inaccurate rendering of the truth that 'to be endued with consciousness is inseparable from the idea of a person, or intelligent being' (ibid., p. 318). 'For, this might be expressed inaccurately thus, that consciousness makes personality; and from hence it might be concluded to make personal identity' (ibid.). In other words, Locke and his followers have misunderstood the true claim, that wherever there is a person there is consciousness, as implying that consciousness *brings about* personality and personal identity. This analysis again confirms that Butler does not accept Locke's distinction between the soul or thinking substance and the person. For Locke would agree that that which is 'endued with consciousness' is the soul or thinking substance; and he does not claim that consciousness constitutes the identity of the thinking substance; rather, he holds that it constitutes a distinct identity: that of the human subject as a person.

Like Sergeant and Lee, then, Butler assumes that personal identity is given to us prior to, and independently of consciousness. While Sergeant equates the person with the man, Butler follows Lee in equating the person with the soul or thinking substance. And while Sergeant's version of the charge of circularity focuses on individuality and reflection, Butler's focuses on diachronic identity and memory. As indicated above, Butler's version of the charge continues to be discussed in present-day debates of personal identity concerning the 'memory criterion'. It is important to note, however, that the argument that is often ascribed to Butler in this context is not actually the argument he puts forward. Butler is typically read as making a comment about the nature of memory. Although Butler's charge of circularity against Locke concerns memory, he does not, however, make a comment about the nature of memory, as many twentieth-century commentators would have us believe.[16] Twentieth-century critics of Locke have ascribed to Butler the view that memory-claims necessarily involve personal identity-claims. Thus, in a very influential article Antony Flew suggests that Butler is arguing that all memory-claims 'carry an implicit personal identity claim about the speaker'.[17] As we have seen, however, Butler's argument is different. He argues that memory presupposes personal identity because personal identity is what is known through memory. Personal identity is presupposed by memory because it is the object of memory. Butler does not make the different claim that has been ascribed to him: namely, that it is impossible to define what it is to remember without including personal identity (see Penelhum, 1985, p. 133), and that personal identity is what makes memory possible in the first place.

6.1.5. Defending Locke against Butler

Evaluating the two main early versions of the charge by Sergeant and Butler, it is clear that they misrepresent Locke's position when they claim that for Locke,

---

[16] This was first pointed out by Penelhum, *Butler* (1985), pp. 131–3. See also Noonan, *Personal Identity* (1989), p. 68.
[17] Flew, 'Locke and the Problem of Personal Identity', *Philosophy*, 26 (1951), 53–68; reprinted in Martin and Armstrong (eds.), *Locke and Berkeley: A Collection of Critical Essays* (1968), pp. 155–78; at p. 158.

consciousness *of identity* constitutes identity. Sergeant states that Locke makes '*Personal Identity* in Man to consist in the *Consciousness* that *we are the same thinking Thing in different Times and Places*' (*Solid Philosophy*, p. 265).[18] Similarly, Butler holds that for Locke 'consciousness of personal identity' constitutes personal identity (*Works*, vol. 1, p. 318).[19] Had Locke said this, his theory would have been quite obviously circular. Locke does not hold, however, that personal identity is the object of consciousness and at the same time constituted by the latter. He does not hold that consciousness of sameness constitutes sameness; rather, he holds that consciousness of *thoughts and actions* constitutes the person and its identity over time, distinguishing the identity of the person from that of the man and that of the soul.

Locke did not publish a response to Sergeant. His marginal notes in his copy of Sergeant's book indicate, however, what his reply would have looked like: he would have appealed to his distinction between the man and the person. Locke can agree that the individuality of the self as 'man' must be presupposed for consciousness to occur; for he does not say that consciousness constitutes the identity of the human subject as man: I may have the individuality and identity of a human being independently of consciousness, but, Locke argues, I am not a person and have no personal identity without consciousness.[20] Arguing against Sergeant, he says, for example: 'A man has the individuality of a man before he has Knowledg but is not a person before he has Knowledg' (Locke, in *Solid Philosophy*, p. 265). For Locke, the man and his individuality, but not the person, are constituted independently of consciousness.[21]

Locke did not live to respond to Butler's version of the charge, but it seems clear from his notes on Sergeant how he would have responded. He would have again emphasised the importance of the distinction between person, man, and thinking substance. And as Butler equates the person with a thinking substance, he would have focused on that distinction, rather than on that between man and person. In any case, some of Locke's followers in the eighteenth century set out to defend him against Butler. The most important attempts were made by Vincent Perronet and Edmund Law.

---

[18] See also the passage cited above: 'It being then most evident, that a Man must *be* the same, ere he can *know* or *be Conscious* that he *is* the same': Sergeant, *Solid Philosophy Asserted*, p. 265. This suggests that Locke claims that consciousness of sameness constitutes sameness.

[19] Ludlam, too, suggests that for Locke consciousness of identity constitutes identity: 'But this personal identity consists in a being, which is able to consider itself as the *same* thinking *thing*, in different times and places—that is, personal identity consists in being *able* to perceive it, or in other words, personal identity consists in—personal identity': Ludlam, *Logical Tracts*, p. 38.

[20] Locke's marginal replies to Sergeant's account of identity are reproduced in the 1984 reprint edition of Sergeant, *Solid Philosophy Asserted*, pp. 265, 267. See also Thiel (1981), and Thiel (1983), pp. 49, 124–5.

[21] Nor does Locke accept Sergeant's account of the individuality of man as consisting in the soul's adjustment to the 'bodily part'. He asks: 'How will this doctrine hold in a very witty or rational man who by a knock looses his parts in the strength of his age?': Locke's manuscript note in his copy of Sergeant's *Solid Philosophy Asserted*, p. 258.

6.1.5.1. *Perronet's failed attempt at defending Locke*

Vincent Perronet published mostly on religious matters. Prior to becoming a Methodist and a friend of the Wesleys in the 1740s, however, Perronet wrote and published on philosophical issues *per se*. In 1736 he published his first *Vindication* of Locke. Its main target is Peter Browne's critique of Locke in his *The Procedure, Extent, and Limits of Human Understanding* (1728).[22] In 1740 Perronet published a critique of Hobbesian materialism.[23] It is in his *Second Vindication* of Locke (1738) that he discusses the issue of personal identity, addressing arguments put forward by Butler and Watts.[24]

One overriding issue in Perronet's philosophical writings is the nature of spirits in general and the essence of the human soul in particular. Although he vehemently rejects materialism, convinced that '*Thinking* is the *sole Act* of an *immaterial Substance*, howsoever joined or united to Matter' (First *Vindication*, p. 73), he argues that the notion of thinking matter is not a contradiction in terms. He defends Locke's position on this issue, and argues that the immateriality of the soul cannot be proved with absolute certainty (ibid., pp. 7, 62ff.; *Second Vindication*, pp. 25ff.). Moreover, he argues that spirits must exist in space, for otherwise they would not be able to act (*Second Vindication*, pp. 112–13). He shares the notion of a spatially extended soul with other followers of Locke, such as Caspar Cuenz, and with some critics of Locke, such as Samuel Clarke. Perronet defends Locke's view that the soul does not always think, and against Peter Browne he defends Locke's notion of ideas of reflection. He takes issue with Browne's view that 'Locke's ideas of reflection' are 'destructive to knowledge and religion' (First *Vindication*, p. 22), arguing that if we have an immediate consciousness of the operations of the mind (which is what Browne allows), then there is no reason to believe that we cannot have Lockean ideas of those operations (ibid., p. 37).

Most important in our context, however, is Perronet's *Second Vindication* in which he defends Locke's theory of personal identity against Butler. Perronet argues that Butler's critique is based on a misunderstanding of Locke's notion of a person. One of his first comments is 'that Dr. *Butler's Idea* of *Person* here differs from Mr. *Locke's*' (*Second Vindication*, p. 5). He concludes that 'it is by no Means surprising, if he [Butler] and Mr. *Locke* differ with regard to *Personal Identity*. Since whilst they both talk of the *same Person*, they sometimes talk of very *different* Things' (ibid., p. 23). This is certainly correct. Perronet does not seem to realize, however, that Butler's notion of person is that of an immaterial thinking substance. Rather, he focuses on Butler's use of expressions such as 'living agent' and 'living being', and

---

[22] Perronet, *A Vindication of Mr. Locke, from the Charge of giving Encouragement to Scepticism and Infidelity... In Six Dialogues* (1736).
[23] Perronet, *Some Enquiries, Chiefly Relating to Spiritual Beings: in Which the Opinions of Mr. Hobbes... Are Taken Notice of; and Wherein Likewise is Examined How Far the Supposition of an Invisible Tempter is Defensible on the Principles of Natural Reason* (1740).
[24] Perronet, *A Second Vindication of Mr. Locke, wherein his Sentiments relating to Personal Identity are clear'd up from some Mistakes of the Rev. Dr. Butler, in his Dissertation on that Subject* (1738; reprinted, with a new Introduction by John Yolton, 1991).

assumes that Butler does not distinguish, as Locke does, between the identity of the man and the identity of the person (ibid., pp. 5, 7, 24). Perronet is certainly right in saying that Locke's distinction between man and person is crucial to an understanding of his theory. We have seen above, however, that Butler equates the person with the soul or immaterial mental substance, rather than with the man. Therefore, Perronet's critique of Butler is not precise. At one point he concedes that it is not clear to him what Butler's understanding of substance is (ibid., p. 14). Yet he reads Butler as violating Locke's distinction between man and person, rather than that between (immaterial) substance and person.

In addition to not accurately presenting Butler's critique, Perronet seems to misrepresent Locke's position. When he writes approvingly about Locke's distinction between the notions of substance and person, he seems to have in mind the notion of a material substance, such as that of a man as a living bodily being. This is evident from the following comment:

Tho' we are certainly able to *discern* ourselves to be the same *Persons*, we were formerly, as Mr. *Locke* every where supposes; yet, if by *Person* be meant the same *Substance*, how will Consciousness prove to any Man, that he is the same *Person*, in this Sense; **unless** [my emphasis] by *Person*, he understands the immaterial Spirit, and that Only? But as All do not exclude every thing material out of their Idea of *Person*, it is impossible they should by *Consciousness* be able to discern, that they are the same *Persons*, in the Sense here understood. (ibid., p. 17)

Apart from the fact that Perronet speaks here only of the knowledge or 'proof' we may have of our personal identity, rather than of the constitution of personal identity which was Locke's concern, he seems to suggest that a notion of person understood as a pure immaterial substance is compatible with Locke's theory. This is confirmed by another passage in which he says that consciousness of the same person is the same as consciousness of the same substance, as long as we exclude everything material from our notion of substance. He writes: 'Tho' *He, Person*, or *Self* be certainly a *Substance*, yet Consciousness that *He* is the *same Person*, cannot, I think, be Consciousness that *He* is the *same Substance*, to any Man, who makes the Body one Part of his *Self* or *Person*'(ibid., p. 21). Here it is Perronet himself who does not observe a crucial distinction in Locke's theory—the distinction between the notion of a thinking (immaterial) substance and that of a person.[25]

Yet Perronet is correct in emphasising that 'person' in Locke does not denote '*Man*' or '*living Agent*' in general, 'but only *such* a Rational Being, as is *actually* conscious of its own Behaviour; *capable* of a Law, and *answerable* for its Actions' (ibid., p. 7). 'Person', but not 'man', is to be understood essentially in terms of consciousness. Like Locke, Perronet does not question that someone can be the same *man* independently of his consciousness of his past actions. And consciousness, he believes, is defined by Locke in terms of genuine or veridical consciousness or memory. 'Consciousness' of actions I never performed is not consciousness, but

---

[25] Given that Perronet misrepresents both Butler and Locke, I cannot concur with Yolton's praise for Perronet in his introduction to the reprint of the *Second Vindication* (1991). Yolton believes, mistakenly, that 'Perronet shows a firm understanding of what Locke is saying' (ibid., p. x).

madness (ibid., p. 125). Again, it is doubtful that Perronet captures Locke's position correctly when he suggests that for Locke consciousness is always veridical. In the last analysis, however, Perronet, like Locke, appeals to the goodness of God as that which guarantees the genuineness of consciousness (ibid., p. 21). For Perronet, the '*Goodness* of God' is the foundation of our personal identity (ibid., p. 22)

Perronet's emphasis on the distinction between man and person is more appropriately directed at Watts rather than at Butler. We have seen that for Watts, Locke's notion of the internal constitution of personal identity would preclude others from being able to relate to me as a person. In reply Perronet insists on the man/person distinction: whatever others may be able to say about my body and its identity and whatever they may infer from that about the identity of my soul, this does not concern my identity as a person—in Locke's sense of 'person'. To say something about my personality others would have to be familiar with my consciousness (ibid., pp. 121–2). Perronet concedes that it might create confusion if one were to introduce the distinction between man and person into everyday language; but this, he says, was not Locke's intention (ibid., pp. 131–2). And he is certainly right about that. Locke states that 'in the ordinary way of speaking, the same Person and the same Man, stand for one and the same thing' (*Essay*, II.xxvii.15).

6.1.5.2. *Law: the notion of a person as 'solely a creature of society'*

In Edmund Law, Locke had a much more formidable defender than in Perronet. Indeed, Law's account of Locke's theory remains one of the best to this day. Although Law does not agree with Locke on all philosophical issues ('thinking matter' is a point of disagreement), on the whole he is a self-confessed follower of Locke, whose *Works* he edited in 1777.[26] Law says that he always took 'Mr. *Locke*' for one of his 'chief guides' in philosophy.[27] In the 1720s he studied at Cambridge, where he became a Fellow of Christ's College and, in 1764, Professor of Moral Theology. He was a friend of David Hartley's and of the young William Paley's.[28] In metaphysics Law argues against the attempts by Samuel Clarke to provide an *a priori* proof of the existence of God. In this context he examines in detail the origin and nature of our ideas of space and time, arguing that space is an abstract idea in Locke's sense that has its origin in the operations of the human mind.[29] Since the idea of space originates in the human mind, all positions that operate with the assumption of the real existence of space (Newton and his followers, such as Samuel Clarke) must be rejected.

We have analysed above the first part of the anonymous *Essay on Personal Identity* (1769) and the criticism of Locke's account that it contains. The publication of this

---

[26] Law (ed.), *The Works of John Locke*, 4 vols. (1777).
[27] Law (ed.), *An Essay on the Origin of Evil by Dr. William King*, fifth edn. (1781), Preface, p. xvi.
[28] For details on Law's intellectual biography, see Stephens, 'Edmund Law and his Circle at Cambridge: Some Philosophical Activity of the 1730s', in Rogers and Tomaselli (eds.), *The Philosophical Canon in the 17th and 18th Centuries* (1996), pp. 163–73. See also Nuovo (ed.), *The Collected Works of Edmund Law*, 5 vols. (1997).
[29] Law, *An Enquiry into the Ideas of Space, Time, Immensity, and Eternity* (1734).

critique prompted Law to immediately write and publish, in the same year, a 41-page *Defence* of Locke's theory.[30] This *Defence* was reprinted in Law's own edition of Locke's *Works* (1777) and in nineteenth-century editions of Locke's *Works*, without, however, identifying its author (see Locke, *Works*, 10 vols., 1823). The critical part of the anonymous *Essay on Personal Identity* does not provide new arguments against Locke, as we have seen, but repeats those that were by then well known, such as those of Butler and Watts. This gives Law the opportunity to provide an all-out defence of Locke's position that undermines all the then known objections, including Butler's charge of circularity. Although Law's *Defence* too was at first published anonymously, it was clear even to its first readers that it 'is evidently the production of a masterly hand'.[31]

Law's strategy is not to discuss in any detail the actual objections, but to focus instead on what he considers to be the heart of all objections to Locke—the very concept of a person. Once Locke's notion of a person is clarified and correctly understood, the objections can be seen to be unsound. And indeed, we saw that most of Locke's critics reject or misunderstand either the distinction between man and person, or that between person and soul or thinking substance. As we have also seen, even some of his defenders such as Vincent Perronet tend to identify a Lockean 'person' with the notion of an immaterial thinking substance. Like Perronet, Law insists on the distinction between man and person. Unlike Perronet, however, he insists also on the distinction between person and soul, no matter whether the soul 'be a material or immaterial substance, or no substance at all' (Law, *Defence*, p. 180).

Law emphasises the 'forensic' meaning of 'person' in Locke in his opening remarks on the issue.

Now the word person, as is well observed by Mr. Locke... is properly a forensic term, and here to be used in the strict forensic sense, denoting some such quality or modification in man as denominates him a moral agent, or an accountable creature; renders him the proper subject of laws, and a true object of rewards and punishments. (ibid., pp. 179–80)

And when we apply the term to 'any man'—that is, to an individual human being—'we do not treat of him absolutely, and in gross; but under a particular relation or precision' (ibid., p. 180). Thus, when we consider an individual human being as a person we abstract from his metaphysical make-up or nature and consider only his forensic quality.

We do not comprehend or concern ourselves about the several inherent properties which accompany him in real existence, which go to the making up the whole complex notion of an active and intelligent being; but arbitrarily abstract one single quality or mode from all the rest, and view him under that distinct precision only which points out the idea above-mentioned, exclusive of every other idea that may belong to him in any other view, either as substance, quality or mode. (ibid., p. 180)

---

[30] Law, *A Defence of Mr. Locke's Opinion Concerning Personal Identity. In Answer to the First Part of a late Essay on that Subject* (1769). References to, and quotations from this work are to the reprint in Locke, *The Works* (1823; reprinted, 1963), vol. 3, pp. 177–201.

[31] Kippis's review of Law's *Defence*, *Monthly Review*, 40 (1769), 318–20, at 318.

Law proceeds to explain Lockean personal identity on the basis of this understanding of 'person'.

An inquiry after the identity of such person will be, whether at different times he is, or how he can be, and know himself to be the same in that respect, or equally subjected to the very same relations and consequent obligations which he was under formerly, and in which he still perceives himself to be involved, whenever he reflects upon himself and them. This we shall find to consist in nothing more than his becoming sensible at different times of what he had thought or done before; and being as fully convinced that he then thought or did it, as he now is of his present thoughts, acts, or existence. (ibid., pp. 180–1)

In other words, what is relevant to the self as a person—the self in the forensic sense— is whether our consciousness of the present is connected to our past consciousness. Consciousness of the present and the 'memory of a past consciousness' (Locke, *Essay*, II.xxvii.23) together constitute my identity as a person, and also make me recognize my identity as a person. Thus for Law, as for Locke himself, consciousness and memory do not merely provide evidence of personal identity, but constitute it.

Whether he now is what he was once before, in this single article of personality, can only be determined by his now being sensible of what he then thought and did... and thus again, consciousness at the same time, and by the same means, that it convinces him of this, does likewise constitute him such to all ends and purposes whatsoever. (ibid., p. 192)

Law emphasises that personal identity understood in this Lockean way is relevant to both divine and human judgements.

This distinct consciousness of our past actions, from whence arise all the ideas of merit and demerit, will most undoubtedly be regarded with the strictest exactness *in foro divino*; and indeed has its due weight *in foro humano*, whenever it can be with certainty determined: wherever this appears to be wanting, all judicial proceedings are at an end. (ibid., p. 181)

In cases in which it is possible to make out both that someone 'was incapable of knowing what he did' and 'is now under a like incapacity of recollecting it', he 'would now-a-days be acquitted from guilt in the commission' of a criminal act (ibid., p. 181). Law concedes, however, that 'such a plea has usually... small regard paid to it in courts of justice'. The reason for this consists either in

the difficulty of having this incapacity proved with the same clearness that the fact itself is established; or [in] the common maxim that one crime, or criminal disposition, is not admissible in excuse for another; as in cases of drunkenness, violent passion, killing or maiming men by mistake when one is engaged in an unlawful pursuit, &c. (ibid., pp. 181–2)

For Law, however, this is no reason to reject the Lockean theory; rather, it indicates a fault in the judicial practice. 'A kind of injustice is here indeed committed by society, which we have no reason to suppose will be admitted *in foro divino*' (ibid., p. 182). Law continues:

We must therefore conclude in general, that a person's guilt is estimated according to his past and present consciousness of the offence, and of his having been the author of it. Nor is it merely his having forgotten the thing, but his having so far lost the notion of it out of his mind, that how frequently soever, or in what forcible manner soever, it may be presented to him again, he lies under an utter incapacity of becoming sensible and satisfied that he was ever privy to it before, which is affirmed to render this thing really none of his, or wholly exculpate him when called to answer for it. (ibid., p. 183)

People 'are considered as punishable by laws, and so declared by juries, in proportion to the probability of their being conscious of the fact' (ibid.).

Although Law suggests at the beginning of his tract that to consider a human subject as a person consists in an 'arbitrary' abstraction, focusing on its forensic aspects only, he makes clear that the notion of a person understood in a forensic sense is not arbitrary but conventional. The notion of a person, he says, is 'solely a creature of society, an abstract consideration of man, necessary for the mutual benefit of him and his fellows; *i. e.* a mere forensic term' (ibid., p. 184). There are 'two grand objects which first gave birth to personality': namely 'the intent of society' and 'help to direct us in our duty'. Personality is 'a very partial confined consideration of that complex idea, substance, or being, called man' (ibid., p. 198). It is an 'abstract idea' (ibid., p. 186), to be precise, a Lockean 'mixed mode' (ibid., p. 200). Such abstract ideas are merely 'what we ourselves make them' (ibid., p. 187), and therefore 'they do not stand in need (I say) of an objective reality, or the existence of any external things in full conformity to them, since we here consider things no farther than as coming up to these original standards, settled in the minds of men' (ibid.). In short, the term does not stand for an idea of substance and so does not purport to represent an independent identical being. This reading seems to capture precisely Locke's distinction between the person and the soul as substance. And it is because 'person' is a mixed mode rather than a substance-idea that Butler's charge of circularity fails. Law says with explicit reference to Butler's dissertation: 'These ideas [mixed modes] presuppose no one being in particular, they imply nothing more than a proper subject of inquiry . . . or some such creature as is either actually endowed with it, or at least susceptible of, these specific qualities, or modes, which furnish matter for the whole tribe of abstractions daily made and preserved by such terms as usually serve to denote them' (ibid., p. 187). A thinking substance or man must exist for there to be a person, but the person or personality is a creation of the man or substance; it is not the same with the latter. Only 'in a lax, popular sense' does 'person' signify 'as much as man' (ibid., p. 189). 'But when the term is used more accurately and philosophically, it stands for one especial property of that thing or being, separated from all the rest that do or may attend it in real existence' (ibid.). The identity of a person is not the same as the identity of the human subject as man or rational agent. 'And thus sameness of person stands to denote, not what constitutes the same rational agent, though it always is predicated of such; but we consider his rationality so far only, as it makes him capable of knowing what he does and suffers, and on what account, and thereby renders him amenable to justice for his behaviour' (ibid.). Indeed 'the substance in which it [personality] is found may be perpetually varied' while the personality remains the same through consciousness (ibid., p. 196).

In an 'Appendix' to his tract Law annexes 'some observations concerning the use of the word Person' that 'a friend' had 'communicated' to him (ibid., p. 199). These observations link Law's Lockean understanding of 'person' to Cicero's account of personality. Locke's actual definition of person as 'a thinking intelligent being that has reason and reflection' is considered misleading. Indeed, 'the expression would have been more just, had he said that the word person stands for an attribute, or quality, or character of a thinking intelligent being; in the same sense as Tully uses it, Orat. Pro Syll. § 3' (ibid., p. 199). According 'to the received sense in all classical authors', the text continues, 'the word person' stands 'for a certain guise, character, quality, *i.e.* . . . a mixed mode or relation, and not a substance' (ibid., p. 200). And the 'particular quality or character' that is relevant here concerns the man 'when he is treated as an intelligent being subject to government and laws, and accountable for his actions: i.e. not the man himself, but an abstract consideration of him, for such and such particular ends' (ibid.). 'And to inquire after its identity is to inquire, not after the identity of a conscious being, but after the identity of a quality or attribute of such a conscious being' (ibid.).

Law concludes that once we have understood what 'person' means in Locke and what the question of personal identity amounts to in Locke, all the 'multitude of quibbles' which have been raised against Locke's theory (including that of circularity) can be 'most effectually prevented' (ibid., pp. 190–1). He believes that he has undermined the objections to Locke's theory. While Law seems to capture the notion of a Lockean person correctly, accounting for it in terms of a mixed mode, he overemphasises the forensic aspect of that notion. For Locke, as we have seen, purely cognitive experiences that are not relevant to accountability are relevant to making up our personality.

6.1.6. Conclusion

It seems obvious from the discussion above that the charge of circularity can be successful only if one assumes the very thing that Locke explicitly challenges: namely, that the person is an object, a man, or thinking substance, to which consciousness relates as to an already individuated and identical being. Had Locke adopted this position, the charge of circularity would indeed have struck home, just as Robert South's critique of William Sherlock did in the early 1690s. Yet unlike Sherlock—who in order to escape South's critique makes it clear that he really holds a substance-view of the person—Locke is safe from the charge of circularity precisely because he adheres to his distinction between 'man', 'thinking substance', and 'person' as representing three different ideas under which we may consider the human subject.

According to twentieth-century versions of the charge of circularity, as formulated by Antony Flew, for example, personal identity is presupposed by any genuine or veridical memory claim, and therefore, personal identity cannot be constituted by memory.[32] It is argued that I have to *know* that I was the same person in order to have veridical memory of a past action. That is why memory cannot *make* me the same person.[33] In order to respond to this objection some defenders of the Lockean

---

[32] Flew (1968), p. 158.
[33] Compare Penelhum (1985), p. 137.

position have introduced the notion of a more general type of genuine memory, called 'quasi-memory'. This type of memory is the same as our ordinary memory in all important respects but does not presuppose personal identity.[34] The notion is very controversial, however. In any case it does not seem necessary to introduce such a construct in order to defend Locke's theory against the charge of circularity. For the recent versions of the charge, too, ignore Locke's distinction of the identity of the person from that of the soul and that of the man. Moreover, Locke does not assume that memory is always veridical. Rather, to Locke, whatever it is that I ascribe to myself through consciousness or memory is part of my personality, if not part of my self as a man or a soul. Locke's theory could be vulnerable to the charge of circularity only if the distinction between person, man, and soul is rejected.[35]

One objection that Edmund Law mentions but does not discuss—since he believes he has undermined it too, simply by correcting the critics' use of the term 'person'—concerns the logic of identity: more precisely, the transitivity of identity. As we shall see, it is questionable whether Law's defence can meet that objection which he dismisses as 'egregious trifling' (*Defence*, p. 190).[36]

6.2. LOCKE AND THE TRANSITIVITY OF IDENTITY

Like the charge of circularity, the issue of the transitivity of identity continues to be discussed in present-day debates about Lockean accounts of identity.[37] This objection to Locke was first formulated by Berkeley in his dialogue *Alciphron* (1732), and was taken up by the author of the *Essay on Personal Identity* (1769) and made famous by Thomas Reid (1785). These three main historical versions of this objection differ slightly from one another.

What all three versions of the argument have in common is the claim that Locke's theory is inconsistent with the transitivity of the identity-relation. To say that identity is transitive is to say that if x is identical with y, and y is identical with z, then x must be identical with z. Against Locke it is argued that while identity is transitive, consciousness is not. Therefore, one cannot, as Locke attempts to do, account for the identity of persons in terms of consciousness. Locke's account is

---

[34] The notion of 'quasi-memory' was introduced by Shoemaker in 'Persons and their Pasts', *American Philosophical Quarterly*, 7 (1970), 269–85. See the extensive discussion of the notion in Noonan (1989), pp. 169–91. Burge has criticized this notion—in my view, decisively—in 'Memory and Persons', *The Philosophical Review*, 112 (2003), 289–337.

[35] Wiggins, for example, explicitly rejects the man–person distinction in the context of his discussion of the charge of circularity. Wiggins, *Sameness and Substance* (1980), p. 161: 'the concepts of man and person are sortally concordant'. This point is implied by comments in Wiggins (2001), pp. xiv, 234.

[36] For the impact of Law's *Defence*, see, for example, Tucker, *The Light of Nature Pursued*, vol. 7, pp. 2–3.

[37] See again Wiggins (2001), p. 197.

inconsistent with an essential characteristic of the identity-relation. Let us examine more closely the eighteenth-century versions of this objection.[38]

6.2.1. Three versions of the argument: Berkeley, the anonymous *Essay*, and Reid

This is Berkeley's formulation of the issue:

> Let us then suppose that a person hath ideas and is conscious during a certain space of time, which we will divide into three equal parts, whereof the latter terms are marked by the letters A, B, C. In the first part of time, the person gets a certain number of ideas, which are retained in A: during the second part of time, he retains one half of his old ideas, and loseth the other half, in place of which he acquires as many new ones: so that in B his ideas are half old and half new. And in the third part, we suppose him to lose the remainder of the ideas acquired in the first, and to get new ones in their stead, which are retained in C, together with those acquired in the second part of time... The persons in A and B are the same, being conscious of common ideas by supposition. The person in B is (for the same reason) one and the same with the person in C. Therefore, the person in A is the same with the person in C, by that undoubted axiom, *Quae conveniunt uni tertio conveniunt inter se*. But the person in C hath no idea in common with the person in A. Therefore personal identity doth not consist in consciousness.[39]

According to Berkeley, then, the person in C has lost the consciousness of its existence in A. On Locke's theory, this means that the persons in A and C are not identical. But the logic of identity demands that, if A = B and B = C, then A = C. Therefore, Berkeley argues, consciousness does not and cannot constitute personal identity.

---

[38] Other eighteenth-century thinkers, apart from the three discussed here, have put forward this argument. I am aware of two versions that were not, however, published in the eighteenth century. Like Reid, both account for Locke's position in terms of the notion of memory. Martin and Barresi have unearthed a manuscript of lecture notes by a student of Henry Grove. Here Grove seems to make essentially the same argument as does Berkeley. Martin and Barresi argue that Grove's version of the argument may even predate the better-known version in Berkeley. (Martin and Barresi, *Naturalization of the Soul: Self and Personal Identity in the Eighteenth Century* (2000), pp. 72–3, 184.) They do not mention Edwards, who makes the point in his early notes on 'The Mind', applying a thought experiment about fission. It is conceivable, Edwards argues, that after I (A) am annihilated, two persons (B and C) are created, both of whom have the memory of my ideas but do not know anything of each other. On the Lockean theory this would mean, absurdly, that B and C are identical because they are both identical with me (A). If B is identical with A, and A is identical with C, then B and C are identical. In Edwards's formulation: 'Can any one deny, that it is possible, after my annihilation, to create two beings in the Universe, both of them having my ideas communicated to them. With such a notion of their having had them before, after the manner of memory, and yet be ignorant one of another; and in such a case will any one say, that both these are one and the same person, as they must be, if they are both the same person with me.' Howard (ed.), *'The Mind' of Jonathan Edwards. A Reconstructed Text* (1963), p. 28.

[39] Berkeley, *Alciphron*, VII, viii, in *The Works of George Berkeley, Bishop of Cloyne*, ed. Luce and Jessop (1948–57), vol. 3, p. 299.

The author of the *Essay on Personal Identity* says about the argument from the transitivity of identity that it applies no matter whether Lockean consciousness is understood as actual or potential consciousness (*Essay*, pp. 37–8). He argues thus:

> It is self evident, that if I be now the same person that I was yesterday, and was yesterday the same person which I was the preceding day, that I am now the same person that I was that day. But, according to the scheme of the same consciousness, it is possible that the contrary of this may, nay, more than probable, that it continually will be the case. For, if I yesterday were conscious of any action I performed the day before, then, according to Mr. Locke, I was the same person yesterday that I was the preceding day. But, if I again become conscious to day of my having performed that action, yet without any remembrance of my having recollected it yesterday, I then, in consequence of that consciousness, become the same person who performed that action, but not the same who recollected it yesterday, altho' these two were the same by the supposition; which is inconsistent'. (ibid.)

This version of the argument differs from Berkeley's in three respects. First, unlike Berkeley, the author interprets Locke's 'consciousness' in terms only of memory. Second, he focuses on the memory of isolated actions. Third (and less importantly), his way of setting up the argument differs slightly from Berkeley's. He assumes a memory link between t_1 and t_2 as well as between t_1 and at t_3, but not between t_2 and t_3. He argues that on Locke's theory, if at t_2 I am conscious of the action at t_1, then at t_2 I am identical with the person at t_1. And if at t_3 I am also conscious of the action at t_1, then at t_3 I am identical with the person at t_1. But if at t_3 I do not remember having recollected the action at t_2, then at t_3 I am not identical with the person at t_2. The transitivity of identity demands, however, that at t_3 I be identical with the person at t_2, despite the lack of memory. If the persons at t_2 and t_3 are both identical with the person at t_1, then the persons at t_2 and t_3 must be identical. Therefore, Locke's theory must be rejected.

Like the author of the *Essay on Personal Identity*, Thomas Reid interprets Lockean consciousness in terms of memory.[40] And Reid too focuses on the memory of individual actions. He formulates the argument, famously, in terms of a story about a general who remembers his actions as an officer, but not what happened to him when he was a boy at school (where he was flogged 'for robbing an orchard'), although when an officer he did remember his boyhood experience. Now, on Locke's theory the officer is the same person as the boy, and the general the same person as the officer; but the general is not the same person as the boy, because there is no link of consciousness here. As Reid argues, however, it belongs to the logic of identity that if the boy and the officer, and the officer and the general, are the same person respectively, then the general and the boy are the same person. Locke's theory does not allow this, however, because 'the general's consciousness does not reach so far back as his flogging, therefore, according to Mr LOCKE's doctrine, he is not the person who was flogged'.[41]

---

[40] Stewart has pointed out that George Campbell, rather than Berkeley, is Reid's likely source for this argument. 'Reid on Locke and Personal Identity: Some lost Sources', *The Locke Newsletter*, 28 (1997), 105–16, at 109–10. Campbell does not seem to have published his version of the argument.

[41] Reid, *Intellectual Powers*, p. 276.

For all three critics Locke's theory must be rejected because identity is transitive, whereas consciousness (or memory) is not. Reid's version and the version put forward by the author of the *Essay on Personal Identity* seem problematic from the outset, because they equate consciousness with memory and because they focus on recalling isolated incidents. As M. A. Stewart has pointed out, Berkeley does not, however, hang his critique 'on the recall of isolated incidents'. Rather, he is addressing the case of a person who 'loses *all* consciousness of his previous existence'. As Stewart says, in such a case 'it *is* Locke's view that personal identity is lost'.[42] Thus it seems that Berkeley's version is the most promising one for a rebuttal of Locke's theory, as it is based on a more sympathetic reading of Locke. Still, in the debates about Locke's theory today it is mostly Reid's version that is being discussed.

6.2.2. Responses to the argument from transitivity

Many philosophers have thought about how Locke would or could have responded to this objection. There seem to be four general types of responses discussed in the literature. (1) The Day of Judgement removes the problem; (2) Locke's theory violates transitivity, but transitivity is not required for identity over time (and there are two versions of this); (3) transitivity is not a concern, as Locke's focus can be construed as personality at a particular time rather than identity over time; and (4) Locke's account is actually compatible with the transitivity of identity. There are several responses within this last category. As we shall see, responses in this category are the most promising defences of Locke.

(1) The first type of response is to say that as far as Locke is concerned, in the last analysis it is the Day of Judgement that counts for responsibility and rewards and punishments, and that on that occasion our consciousness will not miss a thing; it will be purified, so that a Reid-type case does not occur: 'The Sentence shall be justified by the consciousness all Persons shall have, that they *themselves...* are the *same*, that committed those Actions and deserve that Punishment for them' (*Essay*, II. xxvii.26). As far as this life is concerned, however, Locke clearly does not take the reliability of memory for granted, and so Reid-type cases are not only possible but are perhaps even the norm. So this response need not concern us further.

(2) Another kind of response accepts that Locke's account violates the principle of transitivity, but argues that transitivity is not required for identity through time. This type of response seems to be rare.[43] There are two versions. (a) The first is to argue that identity through time need not be a transitive relation at all. (b) The second is to claim that the transitivity of identity is not a problem for Locke, if we take into account his man–person distinction.

Argument (a) consists of two steps. The first is to state that Locke is committed 'to deny that personal identity over time is indeed a transitive relation'. The second is to claim that a denial of the transitivity of identity is not as problematic as it may at first

---

[42] Stewart (1997), 112. Compare Locke, *Essay*, II.xxvii.20, 26.
[43] Jolley proposes this response, if only tentatively, in *Locke: His Philosophical Thought* (1999), p. 121.

seem. Just as Leibniz's Law holds for synchronic identity but not for judgements of identity over time, 'it is not obviously foolish to question whether the transitivity relation holds for identity over time' (Jolley, 1999, p. 121). This is hardly convincing, however. Like reflexivity and symmetry, transitivity belongs to the very concept of identity. Indeed, it is difficult to comprehend what judgements about identity over time could mean, if the identity-relation were considered to be not transitive. Standard eighteenth-century logic, too, assumes that synchronic as well as diachronic identity is transitive. This is reflected in Berkeley's critique. At the very least, for this response to work it would be required to give a detailed account of a non-transitive notion of diachronic identity. As far as I know, proponents of this response have not developed such a notion.

(b) A second version of this response emphasises Locke's distinction between man and person. One historical suggestion to defend Locke in this way (also occasionally brought up today)[44] comes from Edmund Law whose *Defence* (1769) of Locke's account against the charge of circularity was discussed above. Law does not deal in any detail with the argument from transitivity, however, quoting and dismissing Berkeley's version of the argument. He suggests that the problem with Berkeley's objection is that he has misunderstood Locke's concept of a person. As we have seen, Law emphasises the forensic aspect of Locke's notion of person and the distinction between the latter and the notion of man (*Defence*, p. 180). Personality is 'a very partial confined consideration of that complex idea, substance, or being, called man' (ibid., p. 198). Law seems to suggest that the transitivity of identity may apply to the man but need not apply to the person.

Could Locke have argued against Reid and Berkeley by appealing to his distinction between the man and the person? Could he have argued against Reid that the general and the boy are not the same person but the same human being, and that the transitivity of identity is preserved in relation to the human subject as man but not in relation to the self as a person? Perhaps Locke would have argued in this way, but it is highly questionable that such a defence can be successful. The identity relation is supposed to obtain between the human subject as a person at different points of time. If the identity relation is transitive, then transitivity would have to apply to the identity of a person as understood by Law. Why would identity, when applied to the forensic notion of person, not be transitive? If I am allowed to make identity statements with respect to Lockean persons, then that would have to be a transitive relation.

More recently, Gideon Yaffe has defended Locke against the argument from transitivity, also focusing on Locke's technical notion of a person and its 'forensic' aspect.[45] Yaffe ascribes to Locke what he calls a 'susceptibility-to-punishment theory' of personal identity. On this reading Locke would hold that it is the appropriateness of rewards and punishments that functions as a criterion of personal identity. For

---

[44] See, for example, Forstrom, *John Locke and Personal Identity: Immortality and Bodily Resurrection in Seventeenth-Century Philosophy* (2010), p. 122.
[45] Yaffe, 'Locke on Ideas of Identity and Diversity', in Newman (ed.), *The Cambridge Companion to Locke's Essay Concerning Human Understanding* (2007), pp. 192–230.

Yaffe, Locke 'is reversing the assumed order of priority of the metaphysical and the moral' (Yaffe, 2007, p. 228). This reading is hardly compatible with Locke's text, however. For Locke, personal identity is the *foundation* of 'all the Right and Justice of Reward and Punishment' (*Essay*, II.xxvii.18). Identity, for Locke, is presupposed by appropriate rewards and punishments. Thus, the latter cannot function as criteria of the former. *Pace* Yaffe, for Locke personal identity cannot 'consist in any thing but consciousness' (*Essay*, II.xxvii.21). Moreover, even if Yaffe's interpretation were correct, it cannot be used in defending Locke against the argument from transitivity, as the relationship of just rewards or punishments is not transitive either.[46]

It would seem, then, that if Locke's theory is about a relation that is not transitive, then it is not a theory of identity. And indeed there are some who have suggested precisely that.

(3) The third type of response argues that identity through time is undeniably transitive, but that Locke does not have to worry about the argument from transitivity because his theory is not really about identity through time at all. Rather, it is about personality being constituted at any *one* time through consciousness appropriating past actions.[47] Locke's theory, according to this reading, is not about the numerical sameness of an entity through time but concerns what Marya Schechtman has called the 'characterization question'. This question 'asks which actions, experiences, beliefs, values, desires, character traits, and so on ... are to be attributed to a given person'.[48] Read in this way, Locke's theory is not affected by the issue of transitivity simply because it is not at all concerned with diachronic identity.[49]

Is this reading consistent with what Locke actually says, however? Locke explains the notion of identity in general in terms of the standard theory of diachronic identity. For him, the issue 'of identity and diversity' arises 'when considering any thing as existing at any determin'd time and place, we compare it with it self existing at another time' (*Essay*, II.xxvii.1). It is not surprising, therefore, that his critics apply this standard notion when discussing his account of the identity of persons. To argue for defence (3) then, one would have to read Locke as introducing a different, non-standard notion of identity that does not require transitivity when he turns to the special issue of personal identity and as doing so without giving his readers any hint about this. This is a very implausible reading of Locke, however, as Locke's text clearly states that he is concerned with the issue of numerical personal identity through time. It is plain that his question of whether 'the same Man would at different times make different Persons' (*Essay*, II.xxvii.20) concerns the question 'of

---

[46] This has been pointed out by Anderson, 'Susceptibility to Punishment: A Response to Yaffe', *Locke Studies*, 8 (2008), 101–6, at 104–5.
[47] See Mackie, *Problems from Locke* (1976), p. 183: 'It is therefore hardly a theory of personal identity at all, but might be better described as a theory of action appropriation.'
[48] Schechtman, *The Constitution of Selves* (1996), p. 73. Although Schechtman emphasises that she does not wish to become embroiled in 'Locke scholarship', she maintains that 'Locke's words can be seen to be addressing the characterization question instead of the reidentification question' (p. 106).
[49] Compare Schechtman (1996), p. 79.

what makes a person at time t_2 the same person as a person at time t_1'.[50] The notion of identity as employed by Locke and his contemporaries includes transitivity as an essential characteristic. This defence cannot, then, save Locke's theory from the problem of transitivity.

(4) Fourth, and perhaps most importantly, there are arguments attempting to show that Locke's theory is indeed consistent with the transitivity of identity. There are a number of different versions of such attempts—some asking for minor revisions of Locke, some asking for none.

(i) One such response is discussed (but not defended) by John Mackie and Nicholas Jolley.[51] It attempts to weaken Locke's analysis of personal identity so that the principle of transitivity is not violated. 'In response to Reid, then, we might say that though as a matter of fact the general cannot remember the flogging, he could remember it in principle, and that it is this weak construal of the 'could remember' relation which the theory needs' (Jolley, 1999, p. 121). It seems obvious, however, that to account for Locke's theory in terms of 'could remember' or potential remembering does not help in this instance. As Jolley points out (appealing to Mackie), this defence is circular. 'For the only justification that can be offered for the thesis that the general can in principle remember the flogging is that he is the same person. Thus, the defence of the theory looks circular' (ibid.). According to this defence, sameness of person is presupposed and not constituted by memory or consciousness. As even the author of the *Essay on Personal Identity* points out as early as 1769, the argument from transitivity holds no matter whether we focus on actual or potential consciousness (*Essay*, p. 38).

(ii) The usual present-day response to the argument from transitivity—at least by authors sympathetic to Locke—is that Locke's account requires only a slight revision to meet Reid's objection. This raises the question of how slight this revision really is, and whether it retains the essential characteristics of Locke's account or whether we instead end up with quite a different account. The relevant revision typically emphasises a distinction between consciousness and memory, and argues that it is consciousness rather than memory that constitutes personal identity, according to Locke. We noted above that Locke does indeed distinguish between consciousness and memory, and that it may be a problem for Reid's version of the argument from transitivity that it simply equates the two. But how is this meant to save Locke?

The suggested revision is often formulated in terms of the notion of the continuity of consciousness as distinguished from direct memory connections: It is argued that Locke could hold that 'a person at time t_2 is the same as a person at time t_1 just in case the person at time t_2 is linked by continuity' of consciousness to the person at time t_1 (Noonan, 1989, p. 10). This continuity can be accounted for in terms of the notion of 'overlapping chains' (ibid., p. 12) of direct consciousnesses, in Reid's example, from boy to officer, and from officer to general. Importantly, this would not require that the person at time t_2 can *remember* what the person at time t_1

---

[50] This is how Schechtman describes the 'reidentification question', ibid., pp. 1–2.
[51] See Mackie (1976), p. 179; and Jolley (1999), p. 121.

thought or did in order to be the same person. So, even if there is no direct memory connection from general to boy, they would still be the same person due to the continuity of consciousness. As Mackie puts it, there would be a unified mental history, and the worry about transitivity would disappear. For the general's experiences and the boy's as well as the young officer's, all belong to the same unit of consciousness (Mackie, 1976, p. 180).

Clearly, this revision, imposed on Locke under pressure from the argument from transitivity, emphasises the importance of consciousness and holds that memory or the ability to remember particular experiences is not essential to personal identity. We have seen in Chapter 4 that the notion of a continuity of consciousness is indeed emphasised by Locke himself, and that he would not simply equate consciousness with memory. Thus, it seems that Locke himself accounts for personal identity in terms of the continuity of consciousness, rather than in terms of the ability to remember past experiences, as Reid's argument would have it. Moreover, although Berkeley does not formulate his version of the objection in terms of the memory of isolated incidents, this response, it seems, can also be used against him. For although in Berkeley's construal the person at C has no conscious ideas in common with the person at A, there would have been direct connections of consciousness from A to B and from B through to C which constitute the identity of the person at A with that at C.

As we have also seen in Chapter 4, however, while it is true that Locke implies a distinction between consciousness and memory, memory is a form of consciousness, and to him, both are involved in constituting personal identity. The restoration of past consciousness as well as the bridging of gaps created by dreamless sleep, for example, can be achieved through memory. To Locke, the memory of actions even 'very remote in time' (*Essay*, II.xxvii.16) is just as important to personal identity as is the chain of consciousness relating to the present and the 'immediately preceding moment(s)' (ibid.). We noted that the importance of memory to personal identity becomes especially apparent when the practical or forensic aspect of Locke's theory is taken into account.[52] For Locke, to establish a guilty mind it would not be sufficient to point to an underlying chain of direct, overlapping consciousness-links. I must also be able to bring the actual past misdeed to mind. It must be possible that the past misdeed 'be brought home to the mind, and made present' (*Essay*, II.xxi.37).[53] But if connectedness through memory is essential to personal identity, then the problem of transitivity returns. In Reid's example, for Locke the general is not the same person as the boy, even if there is a continuity of consciousness, unless the general can recall the boy's action.

---

[52] Most philosophers who favour a Lockean account exclusively in terms of a continuity of consciousness claim that it would be able to accommodate the practical or forensic importance of Locke's theory. See Noonan (1989), p. 56; see also Winkler 'Locke on Personal Identity', *Journal of the History of Philosophy*, 29 (1991), 201–26, at 207–9. But that is precisely what is doubtful.

[53] Compare also *Essay*, II.xxvii.24. Here Locke says that for me to be the same person at different points of time, it must be possible for me 'upon recollection' to 'join' the past existence 'with that present consciousness, whereby I am now my *self*'. He also says that only those Thoughts and actions which I can 'recollect' and 'by my consciousness make my own Thought and Action' are truly mine.

Next, there are two somewhat more complex versions of the attempt to make Locke's account consistent with the transitivity of identity. As examples of these, we shall examine the readings by Kenneth Winkler and Don Garrett respectively. The former ends up demanding a modification of Locke, while the latter claims that Locke does not even require revision or amendment.

(iii) Winkler holds that Reid is right to say that the general and the schoolboy are the same person (Winkler, 1991, 207) but argues that 'this does not show that consciousness does not constitute the self... It shows only that a momentary or instantaneous consciousness does not constitute the self. Instead the constitution of the self takes place over time' (ibid.). As the general and the officer are the same person, it is true of the general that he at one time recalled some of the thoughts or actions of the schoolboy. At the moment the general is unaware of those schoolboy thoughts and actions: 'But they are nonetheless part of his self because they were appropriated by the young officer whose acts of appropriation the general cannot disown without calling his identity into question' (ibid.). Given that general and officer are identical, and the officer did recall the schoolboy experiences, the general must (given that he is identical with the officer) be able to recall the recalling of the schoolboy experience. Thus there would be sufficient psychological connectedness to save Locke's theory. 'Locke can allow Reid's general to be the schoolboy, because in taking himself to be the young officer, the general commits himself to the actions the officer appropriated' (ibid., 222).

Winkler seems to take back his proposed solution, however: 'It is one thing for the general to identify himself with the young officer, and another thing for the general to commit himself to every one of the officer's acknowledged thoughts and deeds. The general is free to judge that some of those thoughts and deeds were wrongly appropriated' (ibid.). Moreover, given that the general cannot remember the boyhood experience, he cannot, unless he wants to put an arbitrary trust into his past acts of appropriation, claim that the boyhood experiences are his and that he is the same person as the boy. Therefore, according to Winkler, Locke is forced 'to conclude that personal identity is constituted not by consciousness but by its unknown foundation' (ibid., 223)—the unknown thinking substance. It is just that Locke does not address the puzzle of 'why basis and consciousness should ever come into conflict'. It should be added that if Locke needs to be forced to move from consciousness to 'its unknown foundation', this solution of the transitivity problem can hardly count as a defence of Locke's own position, according to which personal identity is constituted solely by consciousness. It seems that Winkler ends up demanding a rather significant revision or modification of Locke's theory.

(iv) As indicated, Don Garrett has claimed that Locke does not even require revision or amendment, but that a defence against Reid is 'in fact available to Locke without amendment of his theory'.[54] Garrett argues that all that Locke needs to do in order to avoid the transitivity objection is to reject 'the view that a person P_2, existing

---

[54] Garrett, 'Locke on Personal Identity, Consciousness and "Fatal Errors"', *Philosophical Topics*, 31 (2003), 95–125, at 124.

at time t_2, is identical with a person P_1 existing at an earlier time t_1 *only if* P_2 can remember at t_2 the action or perception of P_1 at t_1' (Garrett, 2003, 109). For although Locke implies that personal identity reaches only as far as it can be 'extended' or can be 'reached' by consciousness, he does not say that the extension by consciousness of a present person into the past is always limited to what the present person can now remember. According to Garrett, Reid's general, in remembering the deed of the brave officer, also incorporates into his personal history the action of the boy, which was remembered by the brave officer, but is not remembered by the general; so there need be no conflict with the transitivity of identity. Again, on this reading, the ability to remember or recollect is not essential to Locke's account of personal identity. Garrett is of the view that 'conscious memory of an earlier perception or action also extends the history of the person to whatever *other* perceptions or actions are implicated in *sameness of consciousness* with that earlier perception or action, regardless of present ability to remember them'. Thus when the general becomes conscious of an action of the officer he becomes convinced that he is the *same self* as the officer and '*ipso facto*' becomes 'prepared to represent any of the actions' of the officer as actions performed by his own self; and this must include even actions that the officer once remembered but that the general 'cannot now specifically remember' (ibid., p. 109).[55]

Garrett argues that there are passages in the *Essay* that 'strongly suggest' that Locke in fact holds such a view. This is evident, he says, from Locke's 'pointed limitation of the two cases he discusses in which personal identity *fails* despite the identity of thinking substance or man. The first such case concerns the total permanent erasure of traces' (referring to *Essay*, II.xxvii.14)—that is, a case where there is no continuity of consciousness at all—and the second is that of alternating but entirely distinct and incommunicable consciousnesses (referring to *Essay*, II.xxvii.23). According to Garrett, 'in both of these cases, Locke suggests, there are two different persons precisely because *no* perception or action of the one person can properly be appropriated by *any* conscious memory of the other person' (Garrett, 2003, 110).[56] That is why personal identity fails in these cases. But if there was at least one perception that could be thus appropriated, then since 'remembering any *one* perception or action of a person is *ipso facto* to incorporate into one's history all of the other perceptions and actions of that same person (whether available to present consciousness or not)', we would have personal identity.

Our responses to the previous two defences of Locke indicate, however, why Don Garrett's reading too is not compatible with Locke's account. Locke's theory is not about what may be implied by the appropriation or consciousness of a particular action, but concerns the person as constituted only by consciousness (including memory) itself. Personal identity reaches as far as, and no further than what we can remember. Garrett's idea that if I can remember one past experience of a person

---

[55] Lännström, too, seems to read Locke in this way when she writes that 'you do not need to remember all of his actions to be the same person as Nestor; remembering one is enough'. Lännström, 'Locke's Account of Personal Identity: Memory as Fallible Evidence', *History of Philosophy Quarterly*, 24 (2007), 39–56, at 48.
[56] Again, Lännström seems to agree: ibid., 48–9.

I thereby appropriate, 'ipso facto', all of that person's experiences and actions, may be ingenious; but it is not Locke's, and cannot be used in a defence of Locke against Reid. The scant textual evidence that Garrett provides does not support his reading. It is true that when there is a total permanent erasure of traces, there can be no personal identity for Locke, even if there may be an identity of the man. Locke would have no reason to infer from this, however, that if only *one* experience could be remembered, this would 'extend the history of the person to whatever *other* perceptions or actions are implicated in *sameness of consciousness* with that earlier perception or action' (Garrett, 2003, 109–10). Locke says that only those thoughts and actions which I can 'recollect' and 'by my consciousness *make* my own Thought and Action' are truly mine—and, that is, are relevant in the forensic sense (my italics) (*Essay*, II. xxvii.24). For Locke, responsibility is inextricably tied to identity, and identity is inextricably tied to consciousness *and* memory.

It would seem, then, that the attempts to defend Locke's theory against the argument from the transitivity of identity have not been successful. The attempts at revising Locke's account may be commendable in many ways, but are ultimately not revisions of Locke's account, but replacements of the latter with a different theory. Locke himself does not consider the transitivity issue at all. This points to a serious weakness in his theory of personal identity based solely on the notions of consciousness and memory.

6.3. CONCLUSION

The material discussed in this and the previous two Chapters provides evidence for the extent to which Locke's theory was debated throughout the eighteenth century. Issues such as the resurrection of the body do not feature prominently in present-day debates about personal identity. Many of the questions discussed in the eighteenth-century controversy over Locke's theory, however, are still hotly debated today (for example, the role of consciousness, the charge of circularity, and the argument from the transitivity of identity). We saw that the eighteenth-century participants in the discussion about Locke on personal identity had as much difficulty in grasping the nature of Locke's account as do present-day philosophers. This applies to self-confessed followers (Voltaire) and defenders (Perronet), as well as to his critics (such as Lee, Felton, Watts, Sergeant, Butler, and Reid). Edmund Law's *Defence* comes closest to Locke's own account.

We have also seen that many of the objections to Locke can be met by pointing out the importance of adhering precisely to Locke's technical notions of 'person' and 'consciousness'. This applies, for example, to the charge of circularity and to the recurring claim that, *pace* Locke, consciousness is neither necessary nor sufficient for personal identity. It became apparent, however, that there are some objections that are difficult to deal with from within Locke's theory as it stands. These have to do with the forensic and moral aspects of his account, and in particular with the transitivity of the identity relation.

Locke's contemporaries and eighteenth-century critics realized that his theory of personal identity challenged and threatened to undermine traditional views about the resurrection of the body, life after death, and moral and legal responsibility. This explains why the perceived need to attack Locke's theory remained strong throughout the eighteenth century. Even some of the logical objections, such as the charge of circularity, were made in the interest of morality and theology, as is evident from Butler's version of that charge. Yet despite the numerous objections to Locke that were raised from a variety of perspectives, there were not only explicit 'defences' (as in Bold, Perronet, and Law) and adaptations of his theory (as in Voltaire, Collins, and Cuenz), but also independent developments based on Locke's theory, especially in the second half of the century. Moreover, there was a variety of explicitly anti-Lockean accounts of personal identity. Many thinkers who criticized Locke's account set out to provide alternative theories of personal identity, as we shall see in the next two Chapters.

PART IV

SUBJECTIVITY AND IMMATERIALIST METAPHYSICS OF THE MIND

7

The soul: human and universal

Most of the responses to Locke discussed in the previous Chapters are argued from a metaphysical standpoint about the nature of the soul: that is, from the perspective either of a materialist or an immaterialist philosophy of mind. The metaphysical positions may not always be explicitly invoked in the critical or positive responses to Locke; but (as noted above) it is plain that the various answers to the question of what constitutes personal identity through time depend to a considerable extent on the views adopted about the nature of the human mind. And here, the battle between materialist and immaterialist philosophers of the mind is of central importance.[1]

The two Chapters of this part deal with the views and arguments of a large number of thinkers who treat the issues of personal identity and self-consciousness from an immaterialist perspective. Many immaterialist thinkers argue (or assert, rather) that we know the simple, unitary, and immaterial nature of the soul through an immediate and indubitable self-consciousness or 'feeling'. Thus, the view that the soul is immaterial is certainly not unique to a 'rationalist' approach. Clearly, if it is claimed that the knowledge of the immaterial nature of soul need not be 'demonstrated' or deduced, but can be provided by an inner feeling or immediate experience, the immaterialist position is open to 'empiricists' as well as 'rationalists'—even if most philosophers who adopt empiricist lines of thought do not adopt the immaterialist view. Moreover, even when empiricists accept the notion of an immaterial soul, they tend to reflect on self-consciousness and personal identity in a way that is largely independent of their commitment to the immaterialist position. This does not, however, apply to the thinkers examined in this Chapter and the next.

There are two standard arguments in support of the immaterial nature of the mind or soul which are directly related to the questions of self-consciousness and personal identity. (1) The first concerns the unity of the self and divides into two versions which are not, however, always clearly distinguished from one another: appeal is made either (a) to the unity of the mind or soul, as substance; or (b) to the unitary nature of the *consciousness* we have of our own thoughts and minds. It is argued regarding both unities that they are not compatible with the extension of matter and with a multiplicity of material particles. In order to make these points

---

[1] I use the terms 'immaterialism' and 'immaterialist' here to refer not to the position, according to which there is no material world independently of spiritual or immaterial substance (Berkeley's position), but to the view that the human soul or mind is an immaterial substance—which is a view that Berkeley shares with many other thinkers.

about unity, some authors engage in thought experiments about fission, attempting to show that the latter is an absurd consequence of the materialist view.[2]

The second argument appeals to the issue of identity through time—we have encountered it in our examination of the seventeenth-century background: (2) the identity of the self is necessary for just divine rewards and punishments in the afterlife, for these rewards or punishments can be just only if the *same* person who acted in this life is punished or rewarded for these actions in the next life. If the soul were not immaterial, this identity required for the afterlife could not obtain (since matter constantly changes). We have seen that the Cambridge Platonist Ralph Cudworth argued in this way: to him the immateriality of the soul is not a sufficient but certainly a necessary condition of immortality. It is a necessary condition of immortality precisely because immateriality guarantees the unity and diachronic identity of the soul. If the soul were not immaterial it could not remain identical even in the course of this life.[3] A body consists of a multiplicity of material particles which do not remain the same; therefore souls, if they were material, could not remain the same throughout the course of their lives.[4] Therefore, the argument concludes, the soul cannot be material. This argument, or versions of it, is repeated over and over again in the eighteenth century. Thus in 1703 John Broughton appeals to the immateriality of the mind, equating the soul with the person when touching on the issue of personal identity, and arguing that the body is not essential to the soul.[5] And much later in the century John Whitehead, in his *Materialism Philosophically Examined* (1778), has a section on personal identity and the afterlife (pp. 72–97), arguing that both are possible only if the soul is an immaterial substance: 'we must then have recourse to a *sameness* of *substance* in our definition of *personal identity*, and as it is most obvious that the human body is no one day together the same, *i.e.* composed of the same particles; so it will follow, that if matter is supposed to think, there can be no personal identity' (p. 81).[6] Personal identity on this view requires an immaterial core of the self that is not subject to change.

Most immaterialist philosophers of the mind argue that personal identity consists in the identity of a mental substance and that the identity of a mental substance is a direct consequence of its immaterial nature; it is because of its immateriality that the

---

[2] Martin and Barresi emphasise the presence of such thought experiments in eighteenth-century debates about the soul, arguing that these 'fission examples' provide a link to present-day discussions over the question whether personal identity is what matters in survival. At the same time they point out that in the eighteenth-century genuine fission was for the most part rejected as impossible, and that such examples were used, rather, to point out an absurdity in the opposing position. Clarke (see below) is a prime example of such a strategy. See Martin and Barresi, *Naturalization of the Soul: Self and Personal Identity in the Eighteenth Century* (2000), pp. 30–48.

[3] Cudworth, *The True Intellectual System of the Universe* (1678), p. 830. See also More, *An Antidote against Atheism* (1662), in *A Collection of Several Philosophical Writings* (1662/1978), vol. 1, p. 34; Bentley, *The Folly and Unreasonableness of Atheism* (1699), p. 47; Smith, *Select Discourses* (1660), third edn. (1821), pp. 88–9.

[4] Cudworth, *True Intellectual System*, p. 46; see also p. 799.

[5] Broughton, *Psychologia: Or, An Account of the Nature of the Rational Soul* (1703), pp. 410–15.

[6] See also Price and Priestley, *A Free Discussion of the Doctrines of Materialism and Philosophical Necessity* (1778), p. 10.

mind is not subject to change and remains the same through time. For these thinkers there is no genuine problem of personal identity at all. The debates about personal identity are not, however, as clear-cut as the simple division between materialists and immaterialists might suggest. Some philosophers do not commit themselves to either the materialist or the immaterialist position. Instead they either, like some materialists, argue for consciousness or memory as a source of personal identity, or, like other materialists, they adopt a sceptical attitude towards the question of personal identity. Also, one might expect materialistically inclined philosophers to argue for the opposite view that personal identity consists in the identity of the material substrate of thought. As we have seen in the case of Collins, however, this is not necessarily the case. Rather, there is a variety of accounts of personal identity from within the materialist perspective. Similarly, there is a considerable variety of views about personal identity from within immaterialist positions about the nature of the mind. For example, although most immaterialist philosophers of the mind reject consciousness as a source of personal identity and equate personal identity with the identity of the soul, as substance, there are a number of immaterialists about the mind who distinguish between the identity of the mental substance and personal identity, recognizing, in various ways, the importance of consciousness or memory to the identity of the human subject as person. Leibniz (to be discussed in Chapter 9) is the most important and prominent representative of this position; and philosophers such as Reimarus and Mérian in the 1750s and 1760s add more subtlety and complexity to the immaterialist discussions of personal identity. Yet while there is considerable variety within the immaterialist position, innovative accounts on the basis of immaterialist understanding of the mind dwindled away in the 1760s. The last 35 years of the century do not seem to offer much that had not been said before from that perspective. By that time, immaterialists were for the most part busy warding off the increasingly powerful materialist challenge, and repeating standard immaterialist objections (as does Whitehead in his response to Priestley, cited above).

Both this Chapter and the next focus on the British debate—mostly in the first half of the eighteenth century. We have encountered many of the authors discussed here as critics of the Lockean view (such as Berkeley, Watts, Butler, and Shaftesbury) in the previous two Chapters. Their specific criticisms (such as the arguments concerning circularity and transitivity) do not necessarily depend on their immaterialist views, although some (Clarke, for example) explicitly invoke their immaterialism when criticizing Collins's Lockean view. Here we shall focus on their own, positive or constructive contributions to the debate about consciousness and personal identity, beginning with more or less standard Cartesian accounts, and moving on to more complex theories such as those of Shaftesbury, Butler, the American philosopher Jonathan Edwards, the anonymous author of the *Essay on Personal Identity*, and his critic Abraham Tucker. Also, it is in the context of an immaterialist metaphysics of the mind that more explicit and detailed accounts of the very notion of consciousness develop—in particular in Charles Mein's *Essay on Consciousness*, published anonymously in 1728.

7.1. CARTESIAN THEMES

We noted in Chapter 1 that Descartes and most of his seventeenth-century followers do not address in any detail the issue of personal identity through time. A position on personal identity is implied but not really made explicit in their immaterialist theories of the mind. An anonymous publication from the early eighteenth century, entitled *Vindiciae Mentis. An Essay of the Being and Nature of Mind* (1702), however, does make the standard immaterialist (Cartesian) position on personal identity explicit.[7] Although, to date, the author has not been identified, there are good reasons for ascribing the piece to the surgeon Thomas Emes (d. 1707).[8]

7.1.1. An English Cartesian's account of personal identity: Emes

Emes's book exemplifies accounts that do not distinguish between the immaterial soul or mind and the person. The argument runs as follows: Personal identity is the identity of an immaterial substance. Of course, the notion of man, according to this view, involves the body, but the man, the bodily being, is not the person. The body is a mere instrument and not an essential part of the self or person and so persons or minds can exist independently of bodies. Emes says: 'As my Personality must consist in my being a Mind, so my Identity, or Individuality, cannot consist in any thing whatsoever *I have belonging to me* [the body], but in what I am' (*Vindiciae Mentis*, p. 87). Although, as we have seen in Chapter 1, Descartes uses the term 'person' to refer to the individual human being as consisting of soul *and* body, he too holds that the essence of the self consists in the soul as an immaterial substance and is constituted quite independently of the body. It is just that Emes uses 'man' where Descartes would use 'person'. 'Man', Emes holds, is a 'Compound of *Mind* and *Body*', and the life of a man 'is the continuance of that Union' (ibid., p. 84). He maintains, however, following Descartes, that 'the proper Physical *Life* of the Mind is Cogitation, and whilst there is Action and Passion of *Thinking*, there is *Being*' (ibid.).

---

[7] The full title reads: *Vindiciae Mentis. An Essay of the Being and Nature of Mind: Wherein the Distinction of Mind and Body, the Substantiality, Personality, and Perfection of Mind is Asserted; and the Original of our Minds, their Present, Separate, and Future State, is freely enquir'd into, in order to a more certain Foundation for the Knowledge of God, and our Selves, and the Clearing all Doubts and Objections that have been, or may be made concerning the Immortality of our Souls. In a New Method. By a Gentleman* (1702).

[8] The 'Epistle Dedicatory' is signed 'T. E.' (p. vi). In a 1698 publication, entitled *The Atheist turn'd Deist, and the Deist turn'd Christian: Or, The Reasonableness and Union of the Natural, and the True Christian Religion*, the title-page identifies the author as 'Tho. Emes, Chirurgo-Medicus'. This book presents the same views as *Vindiciae Mentis* on all the issues that are relevant in our context. Compare, for example, the passages in *The Atheist turn'd Deist* on Descartes's *cogito* argument (pp. 3–4) and the view that the soul always thinks (pp. 9–16). See especially the passages in which the author discusses identity and life after death along the lines also present in *Vindiciae Mentis* (pp. 77–89). Often even the wording is identical or at least very similar. Moreover, the title-page of another 1698 publication, *A Dialogue between Alkali and Acid* (known to be by Emes), describes the author as 'T. E. Chirurgo-Medicus'. Thus, in what follows I will assume that Emes is the author of *Vindiciae Mentis*.

Indeed, Emes follows Descartes on many issues: he adopts Descartes's *cogito* argument for the existence of the soul (ibid., p. 11); he believes that the essence of the soul or mind consists in thinking and that the soul always thinks (ibid., pp. 33–9); and he believes that animals are just 'curious Engines' (ibid., p. 83). According to Emes, 'Mans Body', too, is 'but an Engine, tho form'd to better purposes than that of Brutes' (ibid., p. 83). And he argues, 'as for Minds, or Intelligences, which may be Actors about, or Perceivers of, or by occasion of these Machines, their Life cannot consist in Cohesion of parts, or Motion, when they have no parts to hang together, or be stirr'd; the Notion of Cogitation having no such things in it' (ibid., pp. 83–4).

Emes addresses the issue of personal identity in the context of debating life after death and 'proving the *Everlasting Duration of Thinking*' (ibid., p. 85). He argues against the 'Bodily Notion of Person' of the materialists (ibid.), again equating mind and person. Having a body or not belongs to the 'Accidents of Persons' (ibid., p. 86). Thus the mind or person can exist independently of the body. Still, his definition of person may appear to have a *prima facie* Lockean ring to it, as it is in terms of the capacity to relate to one's own self: 'A Person is that which can properly say *I*, or reflect upon *Self*, as distinct from all other Beings, and consider *Self* Abstractedly from them, as one *Individual* thing' (ibid., p. 87). It is quite obvious, however, that the central element of Emes's account of person or mind is in terms of substantiality: a person is a '*Res per se una & Intelligens*' (ibid.). For Emes, then, a person is an immaterial, thinking substance or mind.

Emes does not completely ignore one of the standard problems for immaterialist philosophers of mind – the individuation of immaterial substances – but he attempts to resolve it simply by appealing to God. He asserts that 'it must not be thought that any Two *Minds*, any more than any Two *Bodies*, are indeed exactly alike', adding that 'the manifold, or variegated Wisdom of God is to be seen in this, that he has so ordered things with an infinite Diversity (to speak laxly) that others might not easily mistake us one for another, as we cannot possibly mistake our selves' (ibid., p. 88). It is possible to suppose two minds to 'receive the same Sensations, and have exactly the same Actings of Will upon the Being and Modifications of one and the same Body; and yet the very Supposition makes them Two' (ibid., pp. 88–9). 'They are Two Agents and Two Intelligents' and they 'truly experience each his own Self Actings, and Sensations, each constituting one Numerical *Mind*, or Person; a variable, yet the same *Mind*, or Cogitation' (ibid., p. 89).

Personal identity through time is unproblematic, according to Emes. Persons, understood as immaterial substances, 'remain Individually, and Numerically the same while they have a Being' (ibid., p. 87). Their diachronic identity is implied by their immaterial nature. This nature includes the constant activity of thought. It follows that, in regard to personal identity:

there can be no such thing, unless the *Being* of *Mind* continues without any Cessation. Whatever alterations may be in a Thing, and however it may differ from what it was, or be like another, there must be some Ground or Basis still the same, unchanged, or else the Thing would not be the Thing, nor this Thing this Thing. (ibid., pp. 89–90)

Thus there can be no personal identity if thought ceases to exist. For 'Continual uninterrupted Thinking' is 'an Essential Property' of the mind (ibid., p. 90). If thought ceases to exist, there is no mind, no person, and, consequently no personal identity. For as long as the mind exists, however, there is personal identity. Identity, for Emes, is not constituted through the capacity to relate to past and present thoughts and actions, but is guaranteed by the immaterial thinking nature of the mind or person. Indeed, he does not even consider the question of whether consciousness could play any constitutive role for personal identity.

As persons 'may be supposed to cease', however, Emes states that his argument does not prove the immortality of souls or persons (ibid., pp. 90–1). Immateriality is not a sufficient ground for immortality (ibid., p. 91), but it is clear that the cessation of life in matter does not necessarily bring along the end of 'the Life of the Mind, *viz.* Thinking' (ibid., p. 91). Thus immortality is at least possible on account of the immateriality of the soul. And any future rewards or punishments must relate to the mind or person; for 'Minds, not Bodies, sin or obey; Wills, not Blood and Bones, can be Righteous, or Wicked' (ibid., p. 94). Emes says that he challenges the materialists 'and all men besides, to make out the *Personal Identity*, or sameness of a Saint, or a Sinner, to be possible by any thing but the Mind, and its incessant duration' (ibid.). 'The Creature that *is*, may be changed in whatever is not essential, but if its essential Properties be chang'd, the change must be cessation of Being' (ibid.). 'If a Thing be chang'd, the thing must be the same in some respects, that it may possibly be changed in others' (ibid., p. 95). This general principle—that the notion of change presupposes the notion of an identical subject that undergoes change—is certainly correct. Plainly, however, this principle does not show that that subject has to be a mind, let alone an immaterial one, as Emes assumes.

Although Emes's treatise illustrates nicely the Cartesian treatment of the personal identity issue, it seems not to have had much of an impact itself, apart that is, from it being criticized in an 88-page pamphlet by the materialist Henry Layton.[9] For Layton, experience and observation show that a separate immaterial soul is not required for a human being to function as a rational being. The hope for immortality relates to the resurrection of man as a bodily being.[10]

7.1.2. Consciousness as an 'external imaginary denomination', and identity: Clarke

Samuel Clarke's position on personal identity is in many respects very similar to that of Thomas Emes in *Vindiciae Mentis*. Clarke comments on the issue of personal identity and related issues, such as the resurrection and the notion of consciousness, mainly in his controversy with Anthony Collins about the natural immortality of the

---

[9] Layton, *Observations upon a Treatise intituled Vindiciae Mentis* (1702). The piece was reissued in a posthumous collection of Layton's writings, *A Search after Souls*, 2 vols. (1706). Compare Ball, *The Soul Sleepers: Christian Mortalism from Wycliffe to Priestley* (2008), pp. 197–200.

[10] For a discussion of Layton's 'mortalism', see Ball (2008), pp. 131–5.

soul and related matters (1707–1708).[11] Like Emes, Clarke does not distinguish between personal identity and the identity of the soul, as substance because, as in Emes's standard Cartesian account, for Clarke the personality of the self is the soul or mind. Unlike Descartes and most of his followers, however, Clarke holds that although the soul is immaterial and indivisible, it is extended in space.[12] To many, this notion of an extended but immaterial soul is self-contradictory. Clarke argues, however, that the extended soul, as he understands it, does not have parts, and so is not in any sense material. Moreover, his notion of the extended soul or person does not affect his account of the identity of the soul. Like Emes and other Cartesians, Clarke believes that the identity of the soul or person is guaranteed *a priori* on account of its immaterial nature. Importantly, however, quite unlike Emes, he considers the question of whether consciousness plays a role in personal identity in some detail.

---

[11] For Clarke's philosophy as a whole, see, for example, Kurze, *Die Metaphysik des Samuel Clarke* (1929); Ferguson, *The Philosophy of Samuel Clarke and its Critics* (1974). For his debate with Collins over thinking matter, see Ferguson, pp. 138–62, and Yolton, *Thinking Matter: Materialism in Eighteenth-Century Britain* (1983), pp. 39–42. Clarke's account of personal identity is referred to mostly in larger contexts, but is very rarely discussed or analysed in detail. See, for example, Martin and Barresi (2000), pp. 34–6 (fission), 51–2, 55, 57–60 (consciousness, thinking matter, personal identity). Uzgalis focuses on Clarke's view that it is impossible to transfer properties from one substance to another: 'Locke and Collins, Clarke and Butler, on Successive Persons', in Perry (ed.), *Personal Identity* (2008), pp. 315–26. As far as I know, the most detailed discussion is Ducharme's 'Personal Identity in Samuel Clarke', *Journal of the History of Philosophy*, 24 (1986), 359–83. Ducharme is concerned with shedding light on Clarke's moral epistemology, and argues that its starting point is the knowledge of one's own identity. He also argues that Clarke anticipates Butler's account of personal identity in several respects (370, 373), and in particular he emphasises that Clarke anticipates the charge of circularity against Lockean accounts of personal identity (377, 378): 'the historical credit on this is best returned to Dr. Clarke' (378). As is obvious from the previous Chapter, however, the charge of circularity against Locke was first made as early as 1697, by Sergeant in his *Solid Philosophy Asserted* (pp. 265–7). More importantly, in his account of Clarke, quite unlike Clarke himself, Ducharme confuses 'individuation' with 'discernment' (361), applying present-day treatments of the issue to Clarke. Ducharme's modern, epistemological use of 'individuation' (366) is clearly inadequate for an account of Clarke's understanding of the notion. For Clarke, individuation and identity (which Ducharme does not clearly distinguish from one another) are constituted *a priori* and quite independently of any 'discernment'. For a general discussion of this issue, not related to Clarke, see Thiel, '"Epistemologism" and Early Modern Theories of Individuation and Identity', *British Journal for the History of Philosophy*, 5 (1997b), 353–72. Lastly, Ducharme misleadingly likens some of Clarke's arguments to Kant's transcendental arguments about identity, while he neglects the relationship of Clarke's account of personal identity to that of Leibniz—who is mentioned only very briefly, and mostly in footnotes (Ducharme, 1986, 366, 370, 372).

[12] For an account of Clarke's notion of the soul as extended in space, see Vailati, 'Clarke's Extended Soul', *Journal of the History of Philosophy*, 31 (1993), 387–403. See also Vailati, *Leibniz and Clarke: A Study of Their Correspondence* (1997), pp. 53–77. Henry More, the Cambridge Platonist, also holds that the soul is immaterial but extended. Not unlike More, Clarke argues that the soul could only act where it is substantially, and since the soul acts on the body (as Clarke assumed it does), the soul must be substantially present where at least a part of the body is (in a part of the brain, the sensorium). Vailati (1993) argues that Clarke's view of the soul as both extended and as essentially unitary is not as problematic as his critics thought; but he concedes that Clarke himself did not succeed in rebuffing his critics who charged his account with inconsistency (402).

The soul: human and universal 231

In the debate with Collins, Clarke makes extensive use of the notion of consciousness, but he does not examine it as a separate object of enquiry in its own right. He says simply that 'Every Man feels and knows by experience what Consciousness is, better than any Man can explain it ... And it is not at all necessary to define more particularly what *it is*'.[13] Nevertheless, like Collins, Clarke assumes that consciousness is a form of relating to one's own self. He also indicates that it is to be distinguished from memory, for he says that consciousness, 'in the most strict and exact Sense of the Word, signifies neither a *Capacity* of *Thinking*, nor yet *Actual Thinking*, but the *Reflex Act, by which I know that I think, and that my Thoughts and Actions are my own and not Anothers*' (ibid., p. 4). At the same time he makes use of 'consciousness' in contexts when 'memory' would be more appropriate (as we shall see). In any case, for Clarke, consciousness, in the strict and narrow sense of the term, is a mental act through which I relate to my own thoughts and to my own self as the subject of those thoughts. Moreover, the notion of a 'Reflex Act' suggests that Clarke thinks of consciousness as a higher-order act of perception. But what role, if any, does consciousness play for personal identity?

Clarke's position is that the soul's or person's identity through time exists prior to any 'reflex acts' of consciousness. As indicated in Chapter 5, he argues against Collins's Lockean view that consciousness or memory constitutes personal identity. Indeed, he says that the consciousness of an action can be a consciousness that *I* performed the action only if the substance which performed the action is the same as the one which is now conscious of that action. Genuine consciousness that *I* did an action requires the identity of my own self through time: 'the *individual numerical Consciousness*, which identifies the Person, is that Perception, by which the Person is sensible, that his *Past Acts of Thinking* were his *own Thoughts* and not *anothers;* which *Perception,* in the same continued Being, is a *true Memory*, and can be *true* in that one numerical Being only'.[14] The diachronic identity of the self or soul or mental substance is a necessary condition for genuine memory to be possible. As Clarke argues, if the thinking substance has changed, then my memory of an action is not the memory that *I* did the action, but the memory of someone else's action and not genuine self-ascription. Using the terminology of consciousness instead of memory, Clarke says that 'it is a manifest Contradiction, that the *Consciousness* of its being done by *Me,* by *my own Individual Self* in particular, should continue in me after my whole substance is changed'.[15] Not unlike Butler in his critique of Locke, it seems, Clarke argues that consciousness or memory presupposes personal identity and thus cannot constitute it. If consciousness or memory were to constitute personal identity, then, Clarke argues, people might 'by a false *Consciousness*... *imagine* themselves to have *done* what they never did' (*A Fourth Defense*, p. 59). If personal identity

---

[13] Clarke, *A Second Defense of an Argument made use of in a Letter to Mr. Dodwell* (1707), p. 26.
[14] Clarke, *A Fourth Defense of an Argument made use of in a Letter to Mr. Dodwel, to prove the Immateriality and Natural Immortality of the Soul* (1708), p. 56.
[15] Clarke, *A Third Defense of an Argument made use of in a Letter to Mr. Dodwel, to prove the Immateriality and Natural Immortality of the Soul* (1708), p. 64.

may be constituted by such a 'false consciousness' (as would be the case on Collins's Lockean theory), then 'all Mankind, it seems, are nothing but a Dream'. Clarke adds, addressing Collins: 'Unless rather your Opinion it self be a Dream; as I presume, it will be found to be, by every Man whose Reason is awake' (ibid., p. 54).

Again, not unlike Butler a little later, Clarke charges Collins and Locke with accounting for personal identity merely in an 'imaginary' (Clarke) or 'fictitious' (Butler) sense.[16] Collins makes '*Individual Personality* to be a mere *external imaginary Denomination*, and nothing at all in reality' (*A Third Defense*, p. 65). For, 'if a Man at forty years of Age, has nothing of the same Substance in him, neither material nor immaterial, that he had at twenty', then the only way in which 'he may be called the *same Person*' is 'by a mere *external imaginary denomination*' (ibid.) such as consciousness, but he is not in reality the same person.

> For, the continued Addition or exciting of a *like Consciousness* in the new acquired parts, after the manner you [Collins] suppose; is nothing but a Deception and Delusion under the Form of Memory; making the Man to seem to himself to be Conscious of having done That, which really was not done by Him, but by Another. (ibid., p. 66)

On this basis Clarke also argues that the Lockean account creates problems for an understanding of the resurrection (ibid., pp. 87–92). Like Locke and Collins, he emphasises the importance of personal identity to responsibility and just rewards and punishments, saying that 'the Justice of all Reward and Punishment manifestly depends' on personal identity (ibid., p. 91). As Collins's theory cannot account for real personal identity, however, it makes just rewards and punishments and the resurrection 'inconceivable and impossible' (ibid., p. 91). If thinking inheres 'in a loose and fleeting System of Matter', it

> perishes utterly at the Dissolution of the Body; then the restoring the Power of *Thinking* to the same Body *at the Resurrection*, will not be a Raising again of the *same Individual Person*; but it will be as truly a *Creation* of a *new Person*, as the Addition of the like Power of *Thinking* to a new Body *Now*, would be the *Creation* of a *new Man*. (ibid., p. 88)

So, for Clarke personal identity obtains when there is identity of the self as soul or mental substance, and there can be no personal identity without substantial identity. Further, Clarke argues that the self or person or mental substance can remain identical only if it is of an immaterial and indivisible nature, for material beings constantly change. Clarke argues that Collins's materialist version of Locke's account leads to absurdities:

> For if the Brain or Spirits be the Subject of Consciousness; and the Parts of the Brain or Spirits be (as they certainly are, whatever Question may be made concerning any original *Solid Stamina* of the Body), in perpetual flux and change; it will follow that That Consciousness, by which I *not only Remember* that certain Things were done many Years since, but also *am Conscious that they were done by Me, by the very same Individual Conscious Being* who now

---

[16] This particular link between Clarke and Butler was first pointed out by Ducharme (1986), 373.

remembers them; it will follow, I say, that That Consciousness is transferred from one Subject to another; that is to say, that it is a real Quality which subsists without inhering in any Subject at all. (*A Second Defense*, 1707, p. 16)

Thus, for Clarke, genuine consciousness that *I* did an action requires the identity of my self as substance, and it is required further that this substance is not material. For diachronic personal identity and genuine memory to be possible, the self or soul or person must be of an indivisible and immaterial nature.[17]

Moreover, Clarke makes use of some of the standard arguments against materialism cited above, including thought experiments about fission.[18] He presents the unity or 'individuality' of the soul as an argument, 'why a System of Matter cannot think' (ibid., p. 31). If a system of matter could think, then every part of that system would have to be conscious—which, he claims, is absurd, as it would destroy the unity and individuality of the thinking being. He argues that any mental activity requires a unitary mind: mental activity involves consciousness, and consciousness is 'an individual Power' that must inhere in an individual, unitary substance. In short, if the soul were material it would be divisible and would make the substantial unity required by the unity of consciousness impossible; therefore the soul must be immaterial. Thus, although Clarke states that we cannot define or explain consciousness beyond what is evident to us about it through inner experience, he asserts that we do know 'what it *is not*, viz. that it is not a Multitude of distinct and separate Consciousnesses', but an 'Individual Power'; and to know this is sufficient 'to prove that it does not and cannot inhere in a Being, that consists of a Multitude of separate and distinct Parts'.[19] As Clarke emphasises:

Every Imagination, every Volition, and every Thought is the Imagination, Will, and Thought, of that Whole Thinking Substance, which I call *I my self*. And if this One Substance (which we usually stile the *Soul* or *Mind*) has no Parts, that can *Act* separately, it may as well be conceived to have none, that can *Exist* separately; and so, to be absolutely *Indivisible*.[20]

For Clarke, then, a genuine problem of personal identity does not arise: an immaterial, indivisible mind or soul or person is not subject to change, and so the question of how much it may change and still retain its identity does not arise either. Rather, the identity of the self is guaranteed *a priori*, and obtains independently of my becoming conscious of thoughts and actions. As Clarke declares, 'if the Soul be, as We believe, a *permanent indivisible Immaterial Substance*, then all these Difficulties

---

[17] Ducharme thinks that Clarke's argument here is a Kantian 'transcendental type of argument': (1986), 374, 380. But that reading is clearly false. For Kant, not every argument that concerns *a priori* conditions is transcendental. 'Transcendental', rather, refers to a meta-theory of the *a priori*. Indeed, Clarke's type of argument which aims to prove the immateriality of the soul, as substance, is the object of detailed criticism by Kant in the section on 'Rational Psychology' of the Transcendental Dialectic in the *Critique of Pure Reason*.

[18] For a description of these, compare Martin and Barresi (2000), pp. 33–8.

[19] Clarke, *A Second Defense*, p. 26. Materialist critics of Clarke such as Collins reject the principle that an individual power must inhere in an individual being. For Clarke's argument against materialism from the unity of the mind, see also Vailati (1993), 391–6; and Mijuskovic, *The Achilles of Rationalist Arguments* (1974), p. 82.

[20] Clarke, *A Third Defense*, pp. 61–2.

[that he identifies in Collins's account] vanish of Themselves' (*A Third Defense*, p. 91). In this regard he is at one with Leibniz, but unlike Leibniz he does not allow for a notion of moral or personal identity as dependent on, but distinct from, the identity of the self as immaterial soul or substance.

7.1.3. The unity of consciousness and the 'moral man': Grove

Henry Grove—a dissenting minister and a contemporary of Isaac Watts at the Moorfields Academy in London—is critical of some aspects of Clarke's philosophy, but as far as the issues of consciousness and identity and related topics are concerned he follows Clarke's lead for the most part. His comments on the relevant issues are scattered over various writings, however, and their context and emphases differ in several respects from Clarke.[21] He comments more than does Clarke on related moral issues, and although mostly critical of Locke he accepts aspects of Locke's account that are relevant to accountability. Grove discusses the unity of consciousness, accounts for the relation of consciousness to conscience, and considers issues to do with imputability, identity through time, and related questions concerning the immortality of the soul and the resurrection of the body.[22]

In an early work, Grove provides an argument for the immateriality of the soul from the unity of consciousness,[23] appealing to Clarke's arguments and 'thankfully' making 'use of his assistance' (*Works*, vol. 3, p. 175). Like Clarke, Grove holds that 'thinking or consciousness' is 'a numerical quality, perfectly simple and uncompounded' (ibid., p. 213). That is to say that, unlike matter it does not consist of parts. Since consciousness is 'a simple individual thing', it 'cannot be made up of partial *consciousnesses*, and for that reason can never have its abode in a system of *matter*, where it cannot be supposed to exist, unless compounded' (ibid., p. 217). Grove explains:

No one *consciousness* can be compounded of two or more several *consciousnesses*. For in case several *consciousnesses* may unite into one, either their union destroys their distinction, or it doth not. If it doth, I desire to know how this general *consciousness* subsists. After no other manner than a whole, constituted of several parts, can exist without these parts, or a universal exist without particulars. If on the other hand these partial *consciousnesses* after they are united together, remain distinct, how can they be one? In no other way than a multitude of sands make one heap; for so a parcel of *consciousnesses* thrown together would be a heap of *consciousnesses*, not one *consciousness*. (ibid., pp. 213–14)

---

[21] Henry Grove, *Ethical and Theological Writings*, ed. Sell, 6 vols. (2000); vols. 1–4, reprint of *The Works of the Reverend and Learned Mr. Henry Grove, of Taunton, containing all the Sermons, Discourses, and Tracts published in his Life-Time*, 4 vols. (1747); vols. 5–6, reprint of Grove's *A System of Moral Philosophy*, ed. Amory, 2 vols., second edition (1749). References to vols. 1–4 are to *Works*.

[22] My attention was first drawn to Grove by Martin's and Barresi's (2000) account, pp. 38, 70–3, in which they refer to unpublished lecture notes on pneumatology by one of Grove's students, but not to any of Grove's published writings which contain discussions of the listed issues.

[23] Grove, 'An Essay towards a Demonstration of the Soul's Immateriality' (1718), in *Works*, vol. 3, pp. 171–237.

Although Grove believes that the nature of consciousness as an 'individual quality' is evidenced by everybody's own inner experience if they would only consult it (ibid., p. 215), he attempts to convince his readers by presenting a thought experiment about fission. Again, the purpose of engaging in this kind of thought experiment is to make plain the implausibility of the materialist view and show that only an immaterial soul can account for the unity of consciousness. Thus, if it is argued 'that *consciousness* is made up of partial *consciousnesses*', then this can only mean that '*consciousness* inheres in a Being that hath parts, and that each part hath its share of the *consciousness*' (ibid., p. 214).

Now let us suppose these parts removed at a considerable distance from one another: *consciousness* being an inherent quality, their separation would annihilate their *thinking*, but each must still have its piece of *thought*. But then these pieces of *consciousness* thus disjoined can no more make one *consciousness* than the *consciousnesses* lodged in the heads of several men can make one. (ibid.)

How, Grove asks next, could these separated *consciousnesses* be brought together again? They would gain nothing in terms of unity by their spatial contiguity. For 'each part can be *conscious* only for itself; it cannot share in the *consciousness* of the rest' (ibid., p. 215). There would be no 'common *consciousness*, that may run through all, and, like a band, tie them together'. And yet, Grove argues, 'such common *consciousness* is necessary to constitute all these parts one *thinking conscious* Being' (ibid.).

Apparently Grove uses 'consciousness' synonymously with 'thinking' in this argument for immateriality. For him, however, thinking and consciousness are not simply identical. Rather, he conceives of consciousness as the 'primary quality' of thought (ibid., p. 217). Thought is understood very broadly as including not only reasoning but also feelings of pleasure and pain. It is defined in terms of consciousness:

Thought is an operation that **involves in it** [my emphasis] a consciousness of itself. So that when a person is said *to think*, the meaning is, he perceives, or is conscious of something that passes within him. (ibid., p. 187)

This formulation clearly suggests a notion of consciousness as an inherent reflexivity of thought itself, rather than a second-order act of perception. Here, his position would seem to differ significantly from Clarke's. Grove does not, however, elaborate on this aspect of consciousness. Rather, he focuses on other features—that consciousness provides an 'infallible assurance' that 'we ourselves do think and reason, feel pleasure or pain' (ibid., p. 199), and that it is to be distinguished from 'a distinct knowledge' of thought (ibid., p. 191).

Elsewhere, in his *System of Moral Philosophy*, Grove explains consciousness by distinguishing it from conscience:

Consciousness is confined to the actions of the mind, being nothing else but that knowledge of itself, which is inseparable from every thought and voluntary motion of the Soul. *Conscience* extends to all human Actions *bodily* as well as *mental*. *Consciousness* is the knowledge of the

Existence, *Conscience* of the *moral Nature* of Actions; *Consciousness* is a province of *Metaphysicks*, *Conscience* of *Morality*. (*System*, vol. 1 (ed. Sell, vol. 5), pp. 5–6)

The comments on consciousness in this quotation are not entirely consistent, though. At first, consciousness is said to relate only to 'actions of the mind', but then is implied to be knowledge of the existence of all of one's own actions. And indeed, such knowledge is required for conscience to fulfil its function of judging past and present actions with respect to moral principles. In his account of conscience Grove follows the traditional account in terms of three main parts. The first part is conscience as moral principle, the second is testimony (knowledge of our actions), and the third is the judgement of these actions with respect to those principles. He does not use 'consciousness' for the second part—testimony—but he does use 'syneidesis' which is often translated as 'consciousness', and which he translates as 'a knowledge of the Fact' (*System*, vol. 1, p. 10). Conscience also involves, Grove claims, 'a sense or consciousness not to be suppressed of his being the *free author* of his actions, and justly *accountable* for the good or evil which is in them' (ibid., p. 187). Like Locke in this respect, he holds that 'no man is answerable for any more than his own actions; for these he is rewarded and punished' (ibid., p. 238). He even explicitly appeals to Locke's notion of *moral man*—arguing, like Locke, that we are not accountable for actions we have committed 'unknowingly'; that is, without being conscious of what we were doing. Thus, as in Locke, rationality and freedom, as well as consciousness, are relevant to the imputability of actions.

The actions which it is the office of Virtue to regulate, are such only which we term *human*, that is, such as proceed from men as rational and free agents, or, in one word considered as *Men*... The actions of a *fool* or lunatick are *actiones hominis, non humanae*, actions of the *natural*, not of the *moral* man, as Mr. *Locke* somewhere calls him. To which let me add all those actions that are done by persons having their Reason, but unknowingly, and without observing that they do them. (ibid., p. 132)

Grove addresses the related issue of diachronic personal identity in his discussion of the afterlife.[24] He rejects the 'mortalist' position, arguing that only the body dies and the soul continues to exist. If both soul and body were annihilated and then brought to life again, this would lead to problems of identity and therefore of divine justice.

And, indeed, if we strictly examine the notion of the *utter extinction* of the Being, and its *reproduction* after a certain interval of time, it will be highly absurd to Reason; for after it hath once ceased to exist, the same *individual, thinking Being* can never exist more. A new one may be produced exactly like the former, and so may a *thousand* more; but that will not make them all to be the same Being; as it would do, for the same reason as any one of them may be the same with *that* which had an end put to its existence, some time ago; whether a longer or a shorter, makes no difference. After there hath been a gap, or separating space of time, nothing

---

[24] Grove, 'Some Thoughts concerning the Proofs of a Future State from Reason' (1730), in *Works*, vol. 3, pp. 239–483.

can possibly unite the Being existing before, and that which exists after, into *one*. (*Works*, vol. 3, pp. 368–9)

Therefore, if the soul died with the body, the resurrection 'would not be barely *refitting up the body*, that it might be united to *the same conscious principle*, with which it was in union before... but *producing another conscious principle*', and this 'would constitute it a *distinct individual agent*, having no interest in the good or bad conduct of that other; though perhaps it resembles it as nearly as one Being can another' (ibid., p. 369).[25] The resurrection of the body is secondary with respect to the afterlife, 'for the body is not the whole Being, nor immortalized for its own sake, but as belonging to a composition, one part of which is immortal by the priviledge of its nature'.[26] It is clear, then, that Grove, like Clarke, adopts the Cartesian view about the soul–body relationship: 'the soul is the man, not the body; this is but the instrument by which it acts, the house in which it dwells, the medium by which it receives impressions from surrounding objects' (ibid., p. 163).[27]

7.1.4. The importance of personal pronouns for the issue of personal identity: Watts

Like Clarke and Grove, Watts follows the Cartesian tradition in many respects.[28] As we have seen in Chapter 5, Watts basically and explicitly accepts 'the Cartesian Doctrine of Spirit' (*Philosophical Essays*, p. v) and agrees with Descartes's position on 'the Nature of the Mind' (ibid., p. 119). He believes that the soul always thinks, and is immaterial (ibid., p. 116) and naturally immortal (ibid., p. 131), and he rejects Clarke's view (which he ascribes to Locke) that the soul is extended in space.[29] Nevertheless, his treatment of personal identity differs significantly from a straightforward Cartesian view.

According to Watts, the soul, as substance, can be regarded as the person in an incomplete sense (ibid., p. 309). Unlike Emes in *Vindiciae Mentis*, however, he does not identify the soul with the person. For Watts, 'person', in 'a complete sense' of the term, refers to the soul and body united. He points out that, *pace* Locke, 'person' is often used, if not most frequently, without any forensic sense: 'We say, *There were*

---

[25] In this context, Grove appeals to Lucretius's comment 'that if time should gather together our materials after death, and, after they were reduced into the same situation, life should be superadded, yet would not that signify any thing to us; any more than it does, what Beings had been composed of the same stuff before we were born': *Works*, vol. 3, p. 370. Compare Lucretius, *De rerum natura*, bk. III. See also the discussion of Lucretius in Chapters 2 and 3 above.
[26] Grove, 'The Evidence for Our Saviour's Resurrection considered: with the Improvement of this Important Doctrine. In three Sermons' (1730), in *Works*, vol. 1, pp. 359–465, at p. 174.
[27] Grove, 'A Discourse concerning Saving Faith' (1736), in *Works*, vol. 3, pp. 1–170, at p. 163.
[28] Watts, *Philosophical Essays on Various Subjects... With Remarks on Mr. Locke's Essay on the Human Understanding. To which is subjoined A brief Scheme of Ontology* (1733; third edn., 1742; reprinted, 1990).
[29] Watts, *Philosophical Essays*: 'if Minds were extended, why may not two created Minds be in the same Place, and penetrate each other as well as he [Locke] supposes God the infinite Mind to penetrate all Minds and Bodies whatsoever?' (p. 295).

five Persons present in the Room at such a Time, or *I had but one Person with me, &c*' (ibid., p. 308). For Watts, then, 'person' is used—and rightly used—in such a way that it includes a reference to the body. He insists, however, that personal identity through time implies that the soul is an immaterial substance, and that without an immaterial soul there could be no personal identity: 'the Word *Person* implies one thinking Being, one intelligent Substance, which is always the same whether it be or be not conscious and mindful of its own Actions in different Times and Places' (ibid., p. 301). Again, 'in a complete sense', however, personal identity consists in 'the same Spirit united to the same Body, that is, in short, *the same Man;* Person and Man are here the same' (ibid., p. 309).[30] Thus, Watts disagrees with both Locke and Emes by identifying the person with the man, and the identity of the person with that of the man.

Given his understanding of 'person' it is not surprising that Watts rejects the Lockean view according to which a person is constituted only internally, through consciousness and memory. Instead, for Watts, rather, the human person is a being that is identifiable by others. In order to make plausible his view of the person (and of personal identity) he emphasises the importance of ordinary language, and in particular the use of personal pronouns and their objects of reference. He argues that a term such as 'consciousness' relates only to personal pronouns in the first person singular; but that one must also regard 'you' and 'he' as pronouns that refer to a person: 'Let us consider a little. The words *Self* and *Consciousness of Self* refer only to the Pronoun *I;* but are not the Pronouns *Thou* and *He* personal Pronouns as well as *I?*' (ibid., p. 300). The ordinary use of pronouns suggests, to Watts, that the person is a bodily being.

Watts concludes that consciousness which is a relating merely to one's own inner self cannot determine personality and personal identity. It is through our bodies that others identify us. Indeed, people are justified to infer the identity of the soul from that of the body: 'They know his Body to be the same; and according to the Laws of Nature, they justly infer his soul must be the same also.'[31] At the same time Watts argues against the view that restricts the notion of the person to the body, pointing out that he is 'considering the Word *Person* rather in a philosophical than a meer vulgar Sense' (ibid., p. 308). For 'there are some Modes of vulgar Expression, wherein the Idea of *Personality* seems confin'd to the Body of Man: And thus we say, *A very tall Person*, or *a very comely Person*' (ibid.). At other times, 'the same Mode of speaking is used, with regard merely to the Qualities of the Mind in Union with the Body, as when by long Sickness or old Age the Memory or reasoning Powers are impair'd, we say of our Neighbour, *He is quite another Person than he was*' (ibid., p. 309). Watts emphasises that his business is to consider personality 'rather in its

---

[30] If one focuses on 'person' in an incomplete sense, then it can be said that the identity of the person is that of the thinking substance: 'the same Person in an *incompleat Sense,* is the same intelligent Substance, or the same conscious Mind or Spirit' (ibid., p. 309).

[31] Ibid., p. 301; see also p. 312: 'By their senses they know his Body is the same; and they know that without a Miracle his Soul must be the same too, because 'tis contrary to the Laws of Nature for a new Soul to be united to that Body.'

philosophical Signification', but since the 'philosophical signification' includes the body, it 'is by no means so very different from the mere usual Meaning of it in common Life, as Mr. *Locke's* Account of it is' (ibid.). To my knowledge, no one before Watts noted the importance of language to the issue of personal identity. His idea does not, however, seem to have been taken up by other eighteenth-century philosophers.

It follows from Watts's account of the person that the identity of a person requires both the identity of the soul and that of the body. As regards the identity of the human body, he gives two answers. One of these he also uses in the context of his discussion of the resurrection, examined in Chapter 5. He argues that it is 'most highly probable, that there are some original Particles of an animal Body, which continue from its Birth to its Death, through all the gradual and successive Changes of other Particles, which may be sufficient to pronounce it the same Body' (ibid., p. 310). In the second half of the century the materialist Joseph Priestley, appealing explicitly to Watts, adopted this idea of essential 'staminal' parts of the body that are not subject to change and thus guarantee the identity of the body.[32] Watts's other answer to the question of human bodily identity appeals to Locke's account of the identity of the man. He argues that even 'if there should be no such unchanging Particles in the Body of Man' (ibid.) we can still account for the identity of the body through the change of particles: 'In the same current Course of animal Life the Body may be called *the same*, according to the common Laws of Nature, continuing the same animal Life and slow and successive Changes of the Particles of Matter, while Man abides in this World' (ibid.). As regards the identity of the soul, Watts gives the standard immaterialist account: the soul's identity is guaranteed by its immaterial nature. As a unitary being that does not consist of parts it remains the same for as long as it exists (ibid., pp. 310–11). Since the soul is immaterial and unextended, 'it is impossible that any Part of the Substance of it can be changed or diminished, without destroying the whole; because 'tis so uniform and simple a Being, 'tis a conscious and active Power subsisting by itself. It has no Parts, and cannot but exist or cease to exist in the whole or at once' (ibid., pp. 310–11). In sum then, 'this is the true notion of the Sameness of Man as relating to this World only; (*viz.*) That the same successive Body changing itself by Degrees, according to the Laws of animal Life, and united to the same conscious Mind, must make the same Man' (ibid., p. 299). Thus, in his account of the same human body in this life he does not appeal to unchanging essential 'staminal' particles that are relevant to his discussion of the resurrection.

Watts concedes that consciousness or memory is important to personal identity; he argues, however, that this does not concern the ontological issue of identity, but merely an epistemological question. This distinction is present in other authors, of course, as we have seen in the discussion of the critics of Locke. To Watts, neither amnesia nor false memory (when we ascribe actions to ourselves that we never did) affects our personal identity. Watts asks:

---

[32] Compare the chapter on the resurrection in Watts, *Philosophical Essays*, esp. pp. 190–5.

But supposing that *Frenzy* should so far impose upon one Man as to make him fancy himself conscious of the former Actions of another Man, or that *Forgetfulness* should make him unconscious of his own past Actions; how could he know and be assured that he was the same Person who performed his own Actions, or that he was not the same Person who perform'd the Actions of another? (ibid., p. 11)

Clearly, for Watts the question about amnesia is one about the knowledge we may have of our own identity, and not about the nature of personal identity itself. He presents two answers to this question. One simply says that this sort of thing does not happen that often, and that for that reason it should not concern us greatly. In this rather weak response he appeals to the goodness of God: 'for the common Affairs of human Life, God has in general ordained that Persons should be sufficiently conscious of their own Personality and Sameness with themselves' (ibid., p. 311). The second response again appeals to the bodily nature of the human person: if such things (amnesia, false memory) were to happen, then personal identity can be established through witnesses;

If thro' any Disorder of Nature a Man should lose or change the true Idea of *himself* and his own Actions, or falsely ascribe the Actions and Personality of *another* Man to himself, and should say, *I did this*, or *I did not that*, contrary to plain Truth and Fact, there are generally Witnesses enough among his fellow Creatures who are not thus disordered in their Minds, to assure him *Thou didst not* or *Thou didst* according to plain Fact and the Truth of Things: and they are able to make effectual Proof to him, if he be capable of receiving it, that *He* is the *same Person* with his former self, and that *He* is not *another Person*, or that *He* is the same Man and not another. (ibid., pp. 311–12)

Not unlike Leibniz, as we shall see, Watts emphasises that personal identity can be confirmed externally, through identification of the same body. Although personal identity is not the same as bodily identity, bodily identity allows us to infer personal identity. When we are concerned not with the 'common affairs of human life', but with 'Matters of great or final Importance', however, Watts again appeals to God, for 'the Equity and Goodness of God will take care to prevent that one Man shall not be rewarded for Actions which he never did... God the Judge of all will effectually secure this Matter in all his final Recompences of Mankind' (ibid., p. 312). Watts draws attention to the fact that he is actually in agreement with Locke here. His resorting to the goodness of God means, however, that the problem of personal identity remains philosophically undecided, and his account, for all its implicit and explicit critique of Locke's theory, has little advantage over the latter in this regard.

7.2. THE UNIVERSAL SOUL AND HUMAN PERSONAL IDENTITY: SHAFTESBURY

It may seem odd to some readers of Shaftesbury that the latter is dealt with in a Chapter on the immaterialist philosophy of mind. It has been argued that Shaftesbury is not committed to the notion of a simple, immaterial soul, and it is certainly true that his account of personal identity differs from the standard Cartesian one, as represented by *Vindiciae Mentis*, and as modified by the other thinkers discussed so far in this Chapter. Still, as we shall argue, the view that the soul is a simple and immaterial substance forms an essential part of Shaftesbury's account of personal identity.

As in many other immaterialist philosophers of mind, the issue of personal identity does not feature prominently in Shaftesbury's writings. There is no section or chapter devoted to the issue; rather, there are a few comments scattered over various places and in a variety of contexts. Some of these remarks are critical of Locke's theory, and these have been discussed in Chapter 5. Some scholars, however, believe that Shaftesbury makes an important constructive contribution to the eighteenth-century debate about personal identity. Indeed, some see him as providing a link between Locke and Hume on that issue.[33] The most important passages concerning personal identity in Shaftesbury's *Characteristics* appear in the dialogue *The Moralists, a Philosophical Rhapsody, being a Recital of Certain Conversations on Natural and Moral Subjects* (first published separately in 1709), and in the *Miscellaneous Reflections* (especially 'Miscellany IV'). *The Moralists* is a dialogue between Theocles and a sceptic, Philocles. Traditionally it has been assumed that Theocles represents Shaftesbury's own philosophy.[34] We shall address this issue further below, but our analysis assumes that in relation to the issue of personal identity, Theocles speaks for Shaftesbury himself.

We have seen above that Shaftesbury argues against Locke that even if the metaphysical issue of personal identity cannot be decided, this does not matter for morality and action, because I can 'take my own being upon trust' (*Characteristics*, 'Miscellany IV', p. 421).[35] This means that we assume our own personal identity independently of philosophical argument, and, Shaftesbury holds, this assumption is sufficient as a starting point for proving 'the reality of virtue and morals' (ibid.).[36] Clearly, there is an obvious 'ethical orientation' in Shaftesbury's account, and it is obvious that he appeals to 'ethics or practice' in his account of personal identity. We shall argue, however, that this appeal to ethics does not mean that Shaftesbury 'renounces metaphysics' and that there is an important metaphysical side to his discussion of personal identity.[37] Shaftesbury rejects materialist metaphysics, arguing that on the basis of materialism one could not account for personal identity. Of course, anti-materialism does not necessarily involve a commitment to the view that

---

[33] In different ways respectively, Mijuskovic and Winkler link Shaftesbury's account of personal identity to that of Hume: Mijuskovic (1974), pp. 105, 107, 110; Winkler, '"All is Revolution in Us": Personal Identity in Shaftesbury and Hume', *Hume Studies*, 26 (2000), 5–6. On the question of Shaftesbury's relevance to Hume on personal identity, see Chapter 12, 'Hume and the belief in personal identity'.
[34] See, for example, Weiser, *Shaftesbury und das Deutsche Geistesleben* (1916), p. 101.
[35] Unless stated otherwise, all references (including page numbers) to Shaftesbury's *Characteristics* (first published in 1711) are to *Characteristics of Men, Manners, Opinions, Times*, ed. Klein (1999).
[36] Winkler (2000), has pointed out that Hume adopts a similar position (8, 14).
[37] The quotations are from Winkler (2000), 5.

there are immaterial mental substances, but in Shaftesbury, anti-materialism is linked to an immaterialist view of the mind.

Shaftesbury's main discussion of the unity and identity of the person functions as part of a larger metaphysical argument about the unity of nature and a universal mind in part III, section 1, of *The Moralists*. The issue is prepared, however, in part II, section 4.[38] Indeed, his discussion of personal identity can be said to be a digression from that larger issue. In the relevant sections of *The Moralists*, Theocles attempts to present what is essentially a cosmological proof for the existence of a (divine) universal mind. This notion of a universal mind or soul testifies to the influence that the Cambridge Platonists, and in particular Ralph Cudworth's *The True Intellectual System of the Universe* (1678), had on Shaftesbury.[39] It is important to keep in mind that the discussion of personal identity occurs in this context.

Theocles's argument can be analysed into seven steps. (1) It begins with an appeal to the idea of order and proportion: 'Nothing surely is more strongly imprinted on our minds or more closely interwoven with our souls than the idea or sense of order and proportion' (*The Moralists*, pt. II, sect. 4, p. 273). (2) Next there is the inference from the idea of order to that of design: 'whatever things have order, the same have unity of design' (ibid., p. 274). (3) This idea implies the notion of a whole or totality to which the parts belong in an ordered way. For to say that things have unity of design means that they 'concur in one, are parts constituent of one whole or are, in themselves, entire systems. Such is a tree, with all its branches, an animal, with all its members, an edifice, with all its exterior and interior ornaments' (ibid.). It is noteworthy that step (3) does not consist in an inference to a God as that being that has 'designed' the order, but to the idea of systematicity or totality in individual beings that we encounter in nature. The next step (4) is, again, not an inference to a designer God. Rather, it is that the individual being that exhibits 'order and proportion' must itself be part of a larger order or system, and this larger order in turn must belong to an even larger whole, until we arrive at the universe. 'Neither man nor any other animal, though ever so complete a system of parts as to all within, can be allowed in the same manner complete as to all without, but *must be considered as having a further relation* [my italics] abroad to the system of his kind. So even this system of his kind to the animal system, this to the world, our earth, and this again to the bigger world and to the universe' (ibid.). In the last analysis, then, not only are all things related to one another (ibid., p. 275), they are also united parts of a whole: 'All things in this world are united. For as the branch is united with the tree, so is the tree as immediately with the earth, air, and water which feed it' (ibid., p. 274). There is a

---

[38] Shaftesbury, *Characteristics*, pp. 272–88; and there are similar passages in *Philosophical Regimen*, in Rand (ed.), *The Life, Unpublished Letters, and Philosophical Regimen of Anthony, Earl of Shaftesbury* (1900).

[39] For a brief account of Cudworth's influence on Shaftesbury, see Passmore, *Ralph Cudworth: An Interpretation* (1951), pp. 96–100. For Shaftesbury and the Cambridge Platonists more generally, see Grossklaus, *Natürliche Religion und Aufgeklärte Gesellschaft. Shaftesburys Verhältnis zu den Cambridge Platonists* (2000). See also Cassirer, *The Platonic Renaissance in England*, trans. Pettegrove (1953). Shaftesbury's first publication, in 1698, was an edition of Whichcote's *Select Sermons*.

The soul: human and universal 243

union of things, 'thus evidently demonstrable, by such numerous and powerful instances of mutual correspondency and relation, from the minutest ranks and orders of beings to the remotest spheres' (ibid., p. 275). The argument does not stop here. We have arrived at the notion of the unity of all things, but we still need the notion of a principle that provides this unity, and that is step (5). It leads us, at last, to the notion of an active mind behind the 'system of the universe' (to borrow a phrase from Cudworth)—to the recognition of a universal mind as that which provides the unity of 'all things'. The unity of all things is not achieved by the various things themselves but by a uniting principle, the universal mind:

> Now having recognized this uniform consistent fabric, and owned the universal system, we must of consequence acknowledge a universal mind which no ingenious man can be tempted to disown except through the imagination of disorder in the universe, its seat. (ibid., p. 276)

There follows a sceptical interjection by Philocles and a discussion of Philocles with Theocles about nature. The issue of an active, universal mind is taken up again in part III, section 1, of *The Moralists*. Here, Theocles takes up the argument about the universe as a whole and the need for an active mind as a principle that brings about the unitary nature of the whole. He repeats that the universe is 'one entire thing' and that 'all hangs together as of a piece' (pt. III, sect. 1, p. 299). And 'if it may indeed be said of the world that "it is simply one", there should be something belonging to it which makes it one' (ibid.). When Philocles asks 'As how?', he provides an opportunity for Theocles (step 6) to illustrate his view about the universal mind by way of explaining the unity of individual beings within the universe, such as trees and individual human beings. It is here, as part of this illustrative point about the universal mind, that Theocles introduces the issue of personal identity. He responds to Philocles's question: 'No otherwise than as you may observe in everything' (ibid.). As far as our topic is concerned, this is the most important step in the argument. It introduces a discussion of the individuality and identity of plants and human beings in order to illustrate and make plausible the idea of a universal mind that creates unity in nature.

Thus, Theocles says about the individuation and diachronic identity of trees:

> Wherever there was such a sympathizing of parts as we saw here in our real tree [as opposed to an artificial tree composed of wax], wherever there was such a plain concurrence in one common end, and to the support, nourishment, and propagation of so fair a form, we could not be mistaken in saying there was a peculiar nature belonging to this form, and common to it with others of the same kind. By virtue of this, our tree is a real tree, lives, flourishes, and is still one and the same even when by vegetation and change of substance not one particle in it remains the same. (ibid., p. 300)

In other words, the 'peculiar nature' of the tree guarantees its diachronic identity. Theocles then moves from the tree to the human self. It is important to keep in mind that the purpose of this discussion, too, is to illustrate and make plausible the notion of a universal mind as the principle of the unity and systematicity of the universe: 'Leaving therefore these trees ... let us examine this thing of personality between you and me, and consider how you, Philocles, are you, and I am myself' (ibid.). That there is a special relatedness among the parts that make up a human being is said to be obvious from experience: 'For that there is a sympathy of parts in these figures of ours other than in those of marble formed by Phidias and Praxiteles, sense, I believe, will teach us' (ibid.). The experientially accessible parts out of which human beings are made are, however, changeable. The matter out of which we are composed changes constantly. That stuff 'of which we are composed', Theocles states, 'wears out in seven or at the longest in twice seven years'. This, 'the meanest anatomist can tell us' (ibid.). Still, we remain the same person despite the total change of material particles. Obviously, however, this identity of our person cannot lie 'in the stuff itself or any part of it': 'For when that is wholly spent, and not one particle of it left, we are ourselves still as much as before' (ibid.). Thus, it is clear that there is personal identity and that it survives the change in the matter of which we are composed. Clearly, Shaftesbury here employs the standard anti-materialist argument from identity—the kind of argument that we have seen is present in Cudworth. If the essential self were a material thing, then there could be no identity of the self through time, as matter constantly changes.[40] Philocles interjects, saying that whatever philosophers think they are, 'for the rest of mankind' he affirms that 'few are so long themselves as half seven years' (ibid.).[41] Theocles appears even to concede this, and adds that this is particularly the case in someone 'whose contrary vices set him at odds so often with himself' (ibid., p. 301). Yet, he adds, 'when he comes to suffer or be punished for those vices, he finds himself... still one and the same' (ibid.). As we have seen, this point that we must assume personal identity for moral purposes is also made in Shaftesbury's critique of Locke (*Characteristics*, 'Miscellany IV', pp. 420–1).[42] The unity and identity of the self are demanded by morality.[43] In *The Moralists*, however, the argument does not stop there. Here, Theocles/Shaftesbury develops a view about the nature of the self or mind. Theocles asserts:

You see... there is a strange simplicity in this 'you' and 'me', that in reality they should be still one and the same, when neither one atom of body, one passion, nor one thought remains the same. (pt. III, sect. i, p. 301)

---

[40] Compare the passage in pt. II, sect. 1: 'All is revolution in us. We are no more the self-same matter or system of matter from one day to another. What succession there may be hereafter we know not since even now we live by succession, and only perish and are renewed. It is in vain we flatter ourselves with the assurance of our interest's ending with a certain shape or form. What interested us at first in it we know not, any more than how we have since held on, and continue still concerned in such an assemblage of fleeting particles' (p. 254).

[41] Note that this opposition between philosophers or metaphysicians and 'the rest of mankind' also appears in Hume's discussion of personal identity. See the Chapters on Hume below.

[42] The importance of the will to personal identity is hinted at in 'Soliloquy', where Shaftesbury addresses the reader, saying that the purpose of the treatise 'is to gain him a will and ensure him a certain resolution by which he shall know where to find himself, be sure of his own meaning and design and, as to all his desires, opinions and inclinations, be warranted one and the same person today as yesterday and tomorrow as today': *Characteristics*, 'Soliloquy', p. 84. Shaftesbury does not, however, develop the point in this context.

[43] Weiser makes this point (1916), p. 102: 'Die Einheit des Bewußtseins... wird bei Shaftesbury zu einer sittlichen Forderung.'

Theocles argues that there is obviously a diachronic identity of the self and that this can be accounted for only on the basis of a simple nature that binds the various changing parts and thoughts together. Matter does not have this feature of simplicity, and it follows that the self or mind cannot be material. In this context Theocles rejects the notion of individual essential particles (Watts's 'stamina') that are unchangeable and would thus guarantee the identity of the whole: 'And, for that poor endeavour of making out this sameness or identity of being from self-same matter or particle of matter, supposed to remain with us when all besides is changed, this is by so much the more contemptible as that matter itself is not really capable of such simplicity' (pt. III, sect. 1, p. 301).[44]

It may seem that when Shaftesbury accounts for the diachronic identity of the self, he accounts for it in terms of the Lockean theory of man (rather than person), for he emphasises the ordered structure of the self, that all parts have a 'common end'; and he appears to liken his account of self-identity to that of the identity of organic beings such as trees. We have noted the analogy between tree-identity and the identity of the human self in Shaftesbury. If the economy of the parts of the self is still the same, then the person or self is still the same (ibid., pp. 299–300).[45] In the last analysis, however, Shaftesbury emphasises that the parts require a uniting principle without which they could not form such a unity. The self is a unity by virtue of 'a principle which joins certain parts, and which thinks and acts consonantly for the use and purpose of those parts' (ibid., p. 303). Thus, Shaftesbury does not really adopt Locke's account of the identity of man (as that of a 'living organized body') for his account of the identity of the person. Unlike Locke, he argues that the principle that joins the parts of the person together into a unity is the mind—a being that is characterized by simplicity: 'This simple principle, by which they are really one, live, act and have a nature peculiar to themselves' (ibid., p. 301). Quite unlike Locke, Shaftesbury falls back on the notion of a simple mind as that which guarantees personal identity through time.

Moreover, Shaftesbury holds that the mind that creates our unity is a substance. Indeed, he even has the sceptic Philocles concede to Theocles: 'Truly... as accidental as my life may be or as random that humour is which governs it, I know nothing, after all, so real and substantial as myself. Therefore, if there be that thing you call substance, I take it for granted I am one' (ibid., p. 302). According to Theocles, this substance is not only of a simple, uncompounded (immaterial) nature; it is also essentially active. The mind 'is something which acts upon a body and has something passive under it and subject to it... it superintends and manages

---

[44] For Shaftesbury's discussion of his argument against materialism, see also Grean, *Shaftesbury's Philosophy of Religion and Ethics. A Study in Enthusiasm* (1967), pp. 146–7.

[45] For this idea of the 'economical self', see Shaftesbury's posthumously published *Philosophical Regimen*, in Rand (1900): 'What else but order, agreement, sympathy, unity, subserviency of inferior things to superior, proper affections of subjects making them to operate correspondingly towards a general good, a conversion of everything into use, a renovation of all things by changes and successions; nothing idle, nothing vacant, nothing superfluous, nothing abrupt' (p. 19). For a discussion of this in the *Regimen*, see Uehlein, *Kosmos und Subjektivität. Lord Shaftesburys Philosophical Regimen* (1976), pp. 133–59.

its own imaginations, appearances, fancies, correcting, working and modelling these as it finds good and adorning and accomplishing the best it can this composite order of body and understanding' (ibid.). In short, the mind is 'the governing part' (ibid.).

After this digression into the nature of the human mind as that which guarantees personal identity, Shaftesbury returns to his main business: the universal mind (step 7). Theocles holds that given that there is a simple substance in every human being that constitutes its unity and identity, how shall we 'at the same time overlook this in the whole, and deny the great general One of the world?' (ibid., p. 301).

Theocles proceeds as follows (ibid., p. 302): If Philocles were to argue that there cannot be a universal One or that its existence cannot be proven philosophically, then he would have also to accept that there cannot be a personal One either—indeed 'that there cannot be any such particular one as yourself' (ibid.). That there is a personal One is, however, obvious: 'But that there is actually a one as this latter, your own mind, it is hoped, may satisfy you' (ibid.). If we accept a mind as a governing principle in human beings, then we have no reason to reject a mind or governing principle that provides the unity and systematicity of the universe: a 'uniting principle in nature' (ibid., p. 303). Our own unity and identity, rather, just imitates the unity and identity of the universe. Theocles is convinced that our own self is 'a real self drawn out and copied from another principal and original self, the great one of the world', and 'to this general mind each particular one must have relation, as being of like substance... alike active on body, original to motion and order, alike simple, uncompounded and individual' (ibid., p. 304). 'So that it cannot surely but seem natural that the particular mind should seek its happiness in conformity with the general one and endeavour to resemble it in its highest simplicity and excellence' (ibid.).[46]

It seems, then, that Shaftesbury's account of personal identity is very much in terms of the notion of an immaterial, active mind, and even part of a metaphysics of a universal mind. The statement that Shaftesbury 'renounces metaphysics' in his treatment of personal identity does not seem to be well warranted at all. Of course, this 'metaphysical reading' can only be accepted if there are good reasons for ascribing Theocles's utterances about the simplicity of the mind to Shaftesbury, as we have done in the analysis above. As it has been argued that Theocles's statements about the simplicity of the human mind do not express Shaftesbury's own opinion,[47] we need to address the arguments against ascribing Theocles's view to Shaftesbury.

---

[46] In *Philosophical Regimen* too, Shaftesbury relates the individual human mind to the world mind. The human mind which is the principle of unity of parts is said to be part of a larger whole: Rand (1900), pp. 138–9. Even the wording is similar to what Shaftesbury has Theocles say in *The Moralists*: 'And the particular mind, what?– Part of this general mind, of a piece with it, of like substance... alike active on body, original to motion and order; alike simple, uncompounded, ONE, *individual*': Rand (1900), p. 139. And again: 'Consider, then, what am I? what is this self? a part of this general mind, governing a part of this general body, itself and body both, governed by the universal governing mind, which, if it willingly be, it is the same as to govern with it. It is one with it, partakes of it, and is in the highest sense related to it': ibid.

[47] Winkler (2000), 12–13.

One argument is that the 'dialogue form of *The Moralists*' is an 'obstacle to associating Shaftesbury with Theocles' (Winkler, 2000, 12). This is not, however, very convincing. A few pages prior to the discussion of identity, Theocles defends Shaftesbury's *Inquiry concerning Virtue* (*Characteristics*, pp. 265–72), which is not in dialogue form. More importantly, it seems to be uncontroversial that Theocles's version of the design argument and his view that nature must be governed by a universal mind represent Shaftesbury's position. We have seen that the discussion of personal identity and the claim about the simplicity of the self are part of that larger metaphysical argument. There is no reason to believe that Shaftesbury accepts the argument about a universal mind but not the supporting argument about the simplicity of individual human minds. A second argument is that 'the premise Theocles uses to defend his hypothesis falls far short of its conclusion' (Winkler, 12). Even if that were the case, however, it is not obvious that this would necessarily speak against identifying Theocles's position about the simplicity of the self with that of Shaftesbury. Third, it is argued that 'some of Shaftesbury's arguments against Locke run counter' (ibid., 13) to the view that the mind is a simple substance. However, Shaftesbury's main critique of Locke—that consciousness or memory is neither necessary nor sufficient for personal identity—is perfectly consistent with the view that the self is a simple thing. Indeed, Shaftesbury's version of this critique even requires an immaterial core of the self, given that he rules out that the self be all of a material nature. Lastly, it is argued that 'the highly integrated identity Shaftesbury is seeking is not strangely simple but richly articulated: it would be altogether lost if our founding commitments were to shift' (ibid., 13). For immaterialists, however, richness in articulation is no argument against the simplicity of the core. The integration of a multiplicity of parts, on this view, requires a unifying principle that cannot itself be one of the parts to be unified. It cannot itself be characterized by multiplicity if its function is to unify. This point, then, does not speak against ascribing to Shaftesbury Theocles's view that the soul is of a simple and non-material nature.[48]

Perhaps the most important consideration is the one mentioned in response to the first argument. If we ascribe to Shaftesbury Theocles's argument for a universal mind (and this seems uncontroversial), then we must also ascribe to him the argument for a simple non-material human soul, as the latter argument forms part of the former. There can be no doubt about Shaftesbury's 'ethical orientation' in philosophical matters (see Winkler, 2000, 5), and it is plain that this also affects his treatment of the issue of personal identity. The identity of the self is required for agency and morality, and whatever the metaphysical truth about identity, we can take our identity on trust insofar as practice and morality are concerned. At the same time, however, we must not ignore the metaphysical aspects of Shaftesbury's account—which include his immanent theism, the notion of a universal mind, and the view that individual human minds are of a simple, non-material nature. To ignore Shaftesbury's metaphysical commitments would also mean to neglect the impact that the Cambridge Platonists had on his thought.

---

[48] In fact, Winkler (2000), 13, concedes that this consideration is not decisive.

8

Relating to the soul, pure thought, original sin, and the afterlife

8.1. ON RELATING TO ONE'S OWN SOUL

The authors discussed in the previous Chapters say very little about how we relate to our own minds or souls, but this is not the case with those thinkers who take up Malebranchian ideas. We have seen in Chapter 1 that Malebranche distinguishes between the knowledge of external objects via ideas that represent them and the knowledge we have of our own souls via an immediate consciousness or *conscience* or *sentiment intérieur*.

8.1.1. Consciousness versus reflection: Norris, Browne, and Berkeley

The notion that we know our own souls only through an immediate relating to our own selves, and not through the mediation of ideas, was taken up by British thinkers early in the eighteenth century. The Malebranchian John Norris, for example, argues that I 'have no Ideal Knowledge of my Soul' (and its operations), but merely an 'inward Sense and Consciousness of it'.[1] Like Malebranche, Norris distinguishes between perception 'in the way of Idea' and perception 'in the way of sentiment': 'Perception in the way of Idea, is when we perceive something that is without us... Perception in the way of Sentiment is that inward feeling which we have of our selves, and of the different Manner of our Being, as when we are in Pleasure or in Pain' (ibid., p. 124). Norris links consciousness to feeling and sentiment, thereby expressing the immediacy of consciousness. Yet although he rejects the notion of an 'Ideal Knowledge' of one's own soul, he seems to accept reflection as a distinct form of relating to one's own self—for example, when he distinguishes between 'direct' and 'reflex' thought. Norris says that in the 'reflex way of thinking... the Mind retiring as it were from all Ideas turns its view as I may say inwards, and in a very wonderful manner considers what passes there'.[2]

---

[1] Norris, *An Essay towards the Theory of the Ideal or Intelligible World* (1704), vol. 2, p. 111.
[2] Ibid., pp. 120–1. On p. 120 Norris states that in reflection 'there seems to be a kind of return of the Mind upon it self' and that in reflection the mind 'terminates upon it self, or is its own Object.'

Norris does not, however, equate the 'reflex way of thinking' with consciousness or 'perception by sentiment'. Rather, he characterizes reflection as an explicit 'return of the mind upon itself' and links it to the notion of contemplation and attentive observation (ibid., pp. 120–1). This does not mean that he adopts a Lockean notion of reflection as a source of simple ideas. Indeed, Norris does not explain what precisely the distinction is between consciousness and reflex thought, but there are passages which hint at what his views are about this: thought as such is accompanied by an immediate consciousness; and through reflexion we learn what types of mental acts we perform; reflection already relates to conscious material: "'Tis by Reflexion that we come to learn what the several Acts of thought are which we are conscious of in our selves' (ibid., pp. 123–4). The problem for Norris's Malebranchianism is that this view appears to be closer to Locke's position than to Malebranche's account of self-knowledge, according to which there is only one way of relating to the self—namely, through consciousness or 'perception by sentiment'.

Without adopting a Malebranchian metaphysics, Peter Browne, Bishop of Cork, explicitly rejects the Lockean notion of reflection as a source of simple ideas of our mental operations, arguing that we have only an immediate consciousness of the latter.[3] The context of his discussion is his attempt at providing an epistemological 'foundation' of his view that we know God and 'all things supernatural' not directly but only by analogy; that is, 'by the Mediation and Substitution of those Ideas we have of our selves, and of all other things of Nature' (Browne, *Procedure*, pp. 1–2). In short, the aim is 'to clearly and distinctly apprehend where mere *Knowledge* ends, and *Faith* begins' (ibid., p. 3).

According to Browne, our cognitive faculties can be reduced to our five external senses, imagination, and reason (ibid., p. 53). 'Our five senses...are, however, the only *Source* and Inlets of those Ideas, which are the intire *Groundwork* of all our Knowledge both Human and Divine' (ibid., p. 55). There is no space for inner sense or reflection as a source of simple ideas. Mental operations are not given to us in the form of representative ideas, but only through immediate consciousness. Although Browne is mostly concerned with rejecting the notion of reflective ideas of mental operations, in some passages he also rejects the view that we have an idea of our own self as the subject of these operations. 'The Eye of the Mind...cannot take a view either of its own Substance or Essence, or of its own Properties or Qualities by any *Reflex* Act.'[4] Although he firmly believes in the existence of an immaterial soul, he holds that 'we have not even the least *Direct Idea* or Perception of the purely spiritual Part of us'; indeed, 'we are forced to argue and infer its very *Existence* from

---

[3] Browne, *The Procedure, Extent, and Limits of Human Understanding* (1728), pp. 64–72, 222–30. See also Browne, *Things Divine and Supernatural conceived by Analogy with Things Natural and Human* (1733), pp. 23–31.

[4] Browne, *Procedure*, pp. 96–7. Thus it is misleading to suggest, as Michael and Michael do, that Browne's *apprehensio simplex* is reflection: 'Corporeal Ideas in Seventeenth Century Psychology', *Journal of the History of Ideas*, 50 (1989), 31–48, at 47. Like consciousness, the *apprehensio simplex* is intuitive knowledge. See Browne, *Procedure*, p. 393.

our Observation only of such Operations as we conclude could not proceed from mere Matter' (ibid., p. 97). There seem to be two main arguments in Browne against representative ideas of reflection. One is that the operations of thinking, remembering, and so on, are obviously in the mind already, and it makes no sense to assume that they are represented to us by another mental item such as an idea. To assume ideas of reflection would mean that

we should have no Perception or even Consciousness of the Operations *Themselves*; but of those Characters only and Representations of them, which would stand in the Mind instead of the Operations... And since there neither is nor can be an *Idea* of what is *Itself* actually in the Mind already, those Operations can be perceived no other way than by a *Self-consciousness*. (ibid., p. 96; see also pp. 412–14)

The other argument against ideas of mental operations is based on the close union of the mind with the body. We cannot 'form to our selves any *Original* and *Purely Intellectual* Ideas of the Nature and workings of our own Mind', because even 'the most abstracted and exalted Operations of the Human Mind are Actions of both Matter and Spirit in Essential Union' (*Things Divine and Supernatural*, p. 23). As this quotation indicates, the close bond between mind and body also speaks against a reflective idea of the mind itself. 'As we cannot form one Thought of our Spirit, otherwise than as it is in conjunction with the Body; so neither can we conceive any of its Operations but as performed together with bodily Organs' (*Procedure*, p. 97).

For Browne, then, *willing, thinking, remembering,* and so on, are not simple ideas of those operations but '*Complex Conceptions* which we form to our selves from that immediate internal Consciousness we have of the Mind's different Manner of *Acting* or *Operating*' (*Things Divine*, pp. 23–4). He emphasises, however, that consciousness relates not only to the operations themselves, but via the latter also to our cognitive faculties.[5] And although he rejects the notion of a reflective idea of our own mind or soul, he claims we are assured through consciousness of our own existence as experiencing subjects. Indeed, the very notion of existence is in part derived 'from the Consciousness of our own Existence' (ibid., p. 283).

Browne does not say that consciousness is the only way in which we can relate to our own selves. Rather, he often refers to other, mediate forms of self-relation; for example, when he suggests that we can 'look into' ourselves (*Procedure*, p. 64) and speaks of 'man' and 'the Observation of what passes within him' (ibid., p. 229). Indeed, he appeals to this kind of introspection as an argument in favour of his position, as such inner observation would show that we cannot find in our mind 'any Idea of *Thinking* or *Willing* intirely separate and abstracted from any thing to be thought of or willed' (ibid., p. 64; see also p. 229). Although Browne would insist that this kind of introspection is not to be equated with Lockean reflection (a source of simple ideas), it must be understood as a kind of 'Reflex act' which is different from consciousness.

---

[5] We know 'by an immediate Consciousness of what passes within' us that we have 'a Faculty of *Reason* and Understanding as well as of *Sensitive Perception*': Browne, *Procedure*, p. 225.

But how does Browne account for consciousness? In some respects, Browne's conception of consciousness appears to be very similar to Locke's. For Browne, as for Locke, consciousness is an immediate relating to one's own self and likened to intuition. 'We have an immediate feeling or *Consciousness* of what is transacted in our Mind', Browne says (ibid., p. 222), and on account of its immediacy, consciousness is 'a Sort of *Intuition*' (ibid., p. 230) and is characterized by absolute certainty (ibid., p. 224). Moreover as we have seen in Chapter 4, for Locke too, consciousness is not a source of ideas. Lastly, consciousness for Browne, as for Locke, is not 'original'; it presupposes the existence of mental operations to which it relates, as well as objects to which these operations relate. In this sense, ideas of sensation are always presupposed by consciousness: 'we cannot think, or be conscious of thinking, 'till we have some Idea or Semblance of an Object to think upon; and without our Senses, we could not have one internal Idea or Semblance of any thing without us' (ibid., p. 55).[6] It remains unclear, however, whether Browne conceives of consciousness as a first-order inherent reflexivity that belongs to thought itself, or as a higher-order act of perception. On the one hand Browne so emphatically distinguishes consciousness from any 'Reflex Act' that one would expect him to regard consciousness as an element of thought itself. On the other hand, he equates consciousness with an act of 'internal sensation' which suggests that consciousness is a distinct, higher-order act of perception (ibid., pp. 223, 224).

Berkeley takes up Malebranchian ideas about self-knowledge. How do we know about the self or soul or person, according to Berkeley, and what do we know about it? Like Norris and Browne, Berkeley claims that we are not able to acquire 'ideas' of our own souls.[7] The only mode of knowing one's own self is through consciousness which does not generate ideas: 'There are two supreme classes of things, body, and soul. By the help of sense we know the extended thing... but the sentient, percipient, thinking thing we know by a certain internal consciousness' ('conscientia quadam interna').[8] Like Browne, Berkeley regards knowledge by consciousness as an immediate or intuitive form of knowledge.[9] Occasionally he makes use of the term 'reflection', but when he does, this term does not denote a form of self-relation

---

[6] See also Browne, *Procedure*, p. 67: 'all the Operations of the Mind necessarily presuppose Ideas of Sensation as prior Materials for them to work upon'; 'the pure Intellect could have no Notion or Consciousness of any one of its Operations, without some precedent Idea in the Imagination to work upon'. Compare also *Procedure*, p. 223: 'we can have no Consciousness of any of the Powers of our Minds before they actually operate', and in turn 'their first Operations must necessarily be upon Ideas of Sensation'. See also *Procedure*, pp. 412–14.

[7] Berkeley, *A Treatise concerning the Principles of Human Knowledge* (1710), § 135, in *The Works of George Berkeley, Bishop of Cloyne*, ed. Luce and Jessop, 9 vols. (1948–57), vol. 2, pp. 1–113, at p. 103.

[8] Berkeley, *De Motu*, § 21, in *Works*, vol. 4, pp. 9–52, at pp. 15–16, 36. For a discussion of Berkeley's view of self-knowledge, see, for example, Lloyd, 'The Self in Berkeley's Philosophy', in *Essays on Berkeley: A Tercentennial Celebration*, ed. Foster and Robinson (1985), pp. 187–209, esp. pp. 199ff.

[9] Berkeley, *Three Dialogues between Hylas and Philonous*, Third Dialogue, in *Works*, vol. 2, pp. 163–263, at p. 232: 'My own mind and my own ideas I have an immediate knowledge of.'

which differs from that of consciousness or 'immediate intuition'.[10] Although Berkeley does not accept Malebranche's doctrine of a vision of ideas in God, and although he at one point criticizes Malebranche's distinction between knowledge by idea and knowledge by consciousness,[11] he too argues that as far as the self as spirit or soul is concerned, it is 'manifestly impossible there should be any such *idea* [of spirit]'.[12] For Berkeley we cannot have an idea of spirit because the spirit is an active being, and ideas are passive or 'inert'.[13] We do, however, have what Berkeley calls a *notion* of spirit 'that is, we understand the meaning of the word' (ibid., § 140, p. 105) and so are able to speak about it.[14] He characterizes this knowledge of the meaning of the 'terms *I* and *myself*' by the terminology of consciousness. This is suggested by the passage quoted above in which Berkeley says that 'the sentient, percipient, thinking thing we know by a certain internal consciousness'.[15] Thus, the notion of self or person or mind we can and do have is possible only through an immediate relating to one's own self in the form of consciousness. According to Berkeley, consciousness does not seem to play a role in personal identity, but unlike Norris and Browne he does comment on the issue, if not very extensively (as we shall see below). The theme of relating to one's own self through consciousness, however, is taken up in an anonymously published work on the topic.

[10] Ibid., p. 233. For Berkeley's use of the terminology of reflection, see, for example, *Principles*, § 89, in *Works*, vol. 2, p. 80: 'We comprehend our own existence by inward feeling or reflexion'. See also *Three Dialogues between Hylas and Philonous*, in *Works*, vol. 2, pp. 232–3. I am not convinced by Brown's reading, according to which Berkeley does not believe that the self is immediately known: Brown, 'Berkeley on the Unity of the Self', in *Royal Institute of Philosophy Lectures* (1972), vol. 5, pp. 64–87, at pp. 66–9. Brown bases his reading on the ascription to Berkeley of two senses of reflexion—one immediate, the other mediate. There is, however, no evidence for ascribing such different uses of 'reflexion' to Berkeley. On this point I am in agreement with Mijuskovic, who reads Berkeley as saying that the knowledge we have of our own self is not inferential but immediate and intuitive: Mijuskovic, *The Achilles of Rationalist Arguments* (1974), p. 103.
[11] See, for example, Berkeley, *Philosophical Commentaries* no. 888: 'De Vries will have it we know the Mind [as we do Hunger not by Idea but sense or] Conscientia. So will Malebranch. This is a vain distinction.' In *Philosophical Commentaries* no. 230 he states: 'Absurd that men should know the soul by idea ideas being inert, thoughtless, hence Malebranch confuted.' This latter remark is puzzling, as Malebranche agrees that we do not know the soul 'by idea': *Philosophical Commentaries, Generally Called the Commonplace Book*, ed. Luce (1945).
[12] Berkeley, *Principles of Human Knowledge*, § 135, in *Works*, vol. 2, p. 103.
[13] Berkeley, *Philosophical Commentaries*, p. 230. Compare Lloyd (1985), pp. 201–2. For a different account, see Bettcher, 'Berkeley on Self-Consciousness', in *New Interpretations of Berkeley's Thought*, ed. Daniel (2008), pp. 197–220.
[14] Compare Winkler, *Berkeley: An Interpretation* (1989), pp. 281–2.
[15] See also *Three Dialogues between Hylas and Philonous*, in *Works*, vol. 2, p. 233: 'I know or am conscious of my own being.' Berlioz holds that there is an important difference between Malebranche's *sentiment intérieur* and Berkeley's consciousness. Unlike Malebranche, he claims, Berkeley does not believe that the spirit can be *known* independently of its ideas (although Berkeley does not *identify* the soul or spirit with its ideas). Berlioz does not, however, provide convincing evidence for this reading. See Berlioz , 'L'esprit comme principe individuel chez G. Berkeley', in Cazzaniga and Zarka (eds.), *L'Individu dans la pensée moderne* (1995), pp. 391–403, at p. 397. For a detailed account of the relationship between Berkeley's and Malebranche's notions of the self, see Fritz, 'Berkeley's Self: its Origin in Malebranche', *Journal of the History of Ideas*, 15 (1954), 554–72.

8.1.2. Consciousness as the 'basis and foundation of all knowledge whatsoever': the *Essay on Consciousness*

As mentioned in the Introduction, the *Essay on Consciousness*, published anonymously in 1728, is the first extensive early modern treatment of consciousness as such.[16] The author himself is very much aware of this, even stating that his work is 'the very first Essay' on the topic, and thus a 'Work or Performance which is wholly new in its kind' (p. 143; see also p. 195). Although the author's claims to originality may have some substance, we shall see that his ideas about the human soul (which are relevant to his account of consciousness) are for the most part rather traditional. For a long time the authorship of the *Essay* remained a mystery, but as noted in the Introduction, it has recently been shown that a certain Charles Mein—a London customs officer and a friend of William Congreve—is the author.[17] In what follows I shall therefore refer to Mein as the author of the *Essay on Consciousness*.

Mein emphasises that he finds it 'a little surprising that They, who have search'd and ransack'd every nook and corner of the Mind, for *Ideas*... should never once happen to *Stumble* upon *Consciousness*' (ibid., p. 195). Mein himself thinks that the notion of consciousness is central to any investigation about the nature and extent of knowledge. Consciousness, he claims, 'is indeed the Basis and Foundation of all Knowledge whatsoever' (ibid., p. 147; see also p. 177). In accounting for consciousness, Mein proposes an observational method. He takes his 'Rise and Beginning from what is most plain and obvious, and occurs at first View to every one's Observation' (ibid., p. 144). On the basis of such observation he provides the following 'Definition, or rather short and summary Description' of consciousness. It 'is that inward Sense and Knowledge which the Mind hath of its own Being and Existence, and of whatever passes within itself, in the Use and Exercise of any of its Faculties or Powers' (ibid., pp. 144–5).

Consciousness is understood, then, as a relating to one's own self in two ways. It relates to one's own mental acts and to one's own self or subject which performs those acts. The two objects of consciousness are distinct but closely connected. The mind is conscious of its acts of perceiving and thinking as its *own* acts; that is, it is conscious that it is itself the subject of these acts. The mind is '*Conscious* of them [mental acts] as its *own* Acts, or knows that it is *it self* (its own actual Being) which *Thinks, Perceives*, &c'. (ibid., p. 145). Also, it knows 'at the same time' that it is 'endued with such and such Powers, as a Power of *Imagining*, a Power of *Remembering*,

---

[16] The *Essay on Consciousness* was published as an appendix (pp. 141–231) to a work entitled *Two Dissertations concerning Sense, and the Imagination. With an Essay on Consciousness* (1728). Brandt has published a modern edition and German translation of the Essay, with an introduction and notes: Pseudo-Mayne, *Über das Bewußtsein 1728* (1983).

[17] Buickerood, '*Two Dissertations concerning Sense, and the Imagination. With an Essay on Consciousness* (1728): A Study in Attribution', *1650–1850: Ideas, Aesthetics, and Inquiries in the Early Modern Era*, 7 (2002), 51–86. See also Buickerood, '"The whole exercise of reason": Charles Mein's Account of Rationality', *Journal of the History of Ideas*, 63 (2002), 639–58. Buickerood shows that Mein is also the author of *An Essay concerning Rational Notions* (1733). On this, see also Brandt's introduction to Pseudo-Mayne, *Über das Bewußtsein 1728* (1983), pp. xi–xii, xliv.

&c' (ibid.). Moreover 'in being *conscious* of its own Acts, the Mind perceives their several Natures; that is to say, it knows the precise and exact Manner of its own Acting and Operating' (ibid.). At the very outset, then, Mein claims that a great deal is known through mere consciousness—not only the existence of the mental acts and that of our own self as the subject of these acts, but also the nature of the acts that we do perform. Moreover, he maintains that we are conscious of our mental powers and faculties (ibid., p. 203), including the 'Power of acting with Choice and Preference'; that is, the will (ibid., p. 205). Finally, Mein holds that the notion of consciousness can be used to prove the freedom of the will (ibid., pp. 205–14) as well as the immateriality (ibid., pp. 214–21) and immortality of the soul (ibid., pp. 223–5).

Several times Mein emphasises the immediacy of consciousness: 'The *Mind's Consciousness* of all its Acts, of what kind soever, does immediately accompany, and, as it were, closely adhere to them.'[18] And it is because consciousness 'is the *Mind's immediate Perception of itself*' that it is 'in the highest degree Certain' (ibid., p. 177): it is 'impossible' that it 'should be deceived or imposed on' (ibid.). On the basis of its immediacy, consciousness is distinguished from reflection. Unlike reflection, consciousness does not require attention or application. Consciousness, Mein says, does not '*judge* or *reflect*', but 'barely *perceives*... and exposes to the Mind's View its Thoughts and other Acts' (ibid., p. 174). Whereas consciousness necessarily accompanies all perceptions and is not 'capable of being exerted, as the Mind's other Faculties and Powers are' (ibid., pp. 173–4), this is not true of reflection: our acts of thinking are not automatically accompanied by reflection, for that would be a 'Hindrance and Impediment to such Acts'.[19]

In spite of its immediacy, however, consciousness is said by Mein to be an act of perception or representation (ibid., p. 174) distinct from the acts to which it relates—a higher-order perception: '*Thinking*, the *Consciousness* of it, and the *Perception* of This, tho' each of them be a several Act, and quite distinct from the other, are *simultaneous*.'[20] The simultaneity and immediacy of consciousness in relation to its objects mean that there is not 'the least Interval or Space of Time interceding between its *acting*, and the *Conscious Sense* or *Perception* which it has of it' (ibid., p. 175).[21] Indeed, the higher-order nature of consciousness is used in an argument for the unity of the self and its immaterial nature. The self

---

[18] *Essay on Consciousness*, p. 175. Mein says that no other perception is 'so truly and thoroughly Intimate, or so immediately present to the Mind, and so much, as I may say, within itself, or so near and close to it, and as it were of a piece with it, as This [consciousness] is' (pp. 149–50).

[19] Ibid., p. 206. See Hume, *A Treatise of Human Nature*, ed. Selby-Bigge (1978), p. xix, for a similar point.

[20] *Essay on Consciousness*, p. 214; see also p. 215: 'first, there is the Act of *thinking*; next the *Consciousness* of it; and then succeeds the *Perception* of This'.

[21] In the piece to which the *Essay on Consciousness* is appended—*Two Dissertations concerning Sense and the Imagination*—Mein distinguishes between two kinds of reflection: an explicit '*After-Consideration* and *Reflection*' that is required for 'a thorough and exact Knowledge and Understanding of almost every thing we are capable of Conceiving or Apprehending', and a kind of reflection 'which necessarily accompanies every Act of *Understanding*, or Operation of *Thinking*'

in its several Acts of *thinking*, and being *conscious*... cannot be supposed or imagined, to *think*, in one part; to be *conscious of thinking*, in another; and to *perceive* that *Consciousness*, in a Third. For such a Supposal would quite destroy the very Notion of *Self*, which implies (or nothing does) *absolute Indivisibleness*, or the most strict and *indissoluble Unity*. (ibid., p. 214)[22]

Why does Mein say that consciousness fulfils a foundational role for knowledge? His argument here is that the very notion of an object (of possible knowledge) for which he also uses the term 'appearance' is due to consciousness. For in order to be able to acquire knowledge of something, the latter (whatever it may be) must first of all be present to consciousness. 'Whatever the mind is employed about in the Exercise of any of its Faculties, it is *conscious* of it, as its Object.' That is to say, it is something that 'appears' to it. No matter whether the object is external or internal, the mind must be conscious of its 'Appearance' (ibid., p. 146). I must be conscious of 'my own *Perception*, and of the Appearance to which it refers' in order to be able 'to consider or regard any thing'.[23] In this sense, then, 'the Notion of Object... is entirely owing to *Consciousness*', and it follows from this that '*Consciousness* is indeed the Basis and Foundation of all Knowledge' (ibid., pp. 146–7). Further, as this notion of consciousness involves a distinction between the self as the 'Perceiver' and 'the Thing perceived', it follows for Mein that the very concept of an object 'is undoubtedly Intellectual' (ibid., p. 147). Moreover, he claims that consciousness is essentially intellectual, as the knowledge of one's own existence, acts, and powers is a '*Rational* or *Intellectual Knowledge*' (ibid., p. 166). The intellect or understanding is thought of as a faculty that unites our acts and powers (ibid., pp. 167–8).

These almost Kantian sounding formulations about consciousness, appearance, and concepts of the understanding lead Mein to a consideration of the self as an object of consciousness. '*Self*, or one's own Being', Mein states, is not only the subject of consciousness—that which performs acts of consciousness—but also the 'Principal and most proper Object' of consciousness (ibid., p. 148). '*Self* is likewise the Subject, as well as the Object of *Consciousness*', he maintains (ibid., p. 149). We saw above that the consciousness of mental acts involves the consciousness that we are the subject or self that performs these acts: 'it is impossible to be Conscious of any Act whatever, without being sensible of, or perceiving one's *Self* to be that which Does it' (ibid., p. 148). Mein emphasises, however, that we could not have a consciousness of self without having performed other mental acts. In this sense, consciousness of self is

---

(pp. 97, 98). This kind of reflection seems to be the same as consciousness insofar as it relates to mental activity, but not, as Buickerood has pointed out, to consciousness insofar as it provides us with the notion of an object: Buickerood (2002), 656.

[22] Buickerood's (2002) formulation that for Mein 'consciousness is a property of all thought' (656) can be misleading here, as it suggests the notion of consciousness as an inherent reflexivity, rather than as a higher order act of perception.

[23] Here is the relevant passage in full (pp. 146–7): 'The Notion of Object... is entirely owing to *Consciousness*; it being plainly impossible that I should be able to consider or regard any thing, as having such an Appearance to me in my Act of perceiving it, (which is the true and proper Notion of an Object) any otherwise than by being *conscious* of my own *Perception*, and of the Appearance to which it refers.'

not 'original' but dependent on the existence of other mental acts: 'we are conscious of ourselves only from our Acting, or because we act' (ibid.).[24] Still, as the existence of one's own self is implied by the consciousness of our acts, there is no need for a proof of one's own existence. Against Descartes, Mein argues that 'he could not know or be assured that he Thought, without being *Conscious* of *Himself*, as that Being or Thing which had Thought' (ibid., p. 180). Descartes 'certainly knew that he Existed, before ever he sought for a medium to prove it by' (ibid.).

Importantly, Mein does not identify soul with self. The soul is a self only insofar as it is conscious of itself. 'The Mind or Soul, tho' it be truly one's Self, yet is it so far only so, as it is Conscious, and merely upon that account' (ibid., p. 149). This is reminiscent of Locke's distinction between the soul, as substance, and the person or 'personal self' which is constituted by consciousness. Mein does not use the terminology of personality here, but he may implicitly appeal to Locke when he says that we may still have the same soul when we are not conscious ('thro' Phrenzy, or other Disorder') but not the same self. 'So that *Consciousness* denominates *Self*, and *Self* may rightly be defined, *That which is Conscious*' (ibid.). Since the self is constituted through consciousness, however, it is not the same as the soul, as substance (ibid., pp. 157–8): the self, understood in this way, is not 'reducible to any kind of Being or Existence yet taken Notice of' (ibid., p. 157). Mein does not discuss the issue of personal identity, however, and refers only in passing to the moral dimension of consciousness and its relation to conscience, 'that Judge within a Man, which tries and censures his Actions' (ibid., p. 230). Conscience, Mein argues, in line with the traditional *conscientia* theorem, presupposes a knowledge or consciousness of the actions to be judged. It therefore 'appeals to our *Consciousness* of the Knowledge ... we have of such Actions' (ibid., pp. 161–2). Memory is also relevant here. It is not the same as consciousness but requires consciousness (ibid., p. 201). It is, moreover, of a 'purely *spiritual Nature*', which is why 'the *Soul* will always retain the *Memory* of its *Conscious Acts*, and they will never be defaced or obliterated' (ibid., p. 220). After death, Mein asserts, our conscious acts will be remembered by us in such a way that they 'will appear as plain and conspicuous, or rather more fresh and lively, than during the Soul's Continuance and Abode in the Body' (ibid., p. 221).

Apart from Mein's questionable metaphysical claims that he bases on his understanding of consciousness, there would seem to be problems with his very notion of consciousness as such. We have seen that according to Mein, consciousness is inner-directed—a relating to one's 'own Being and Existence, and of whatever passes within itself' (ibid., p. 144). We have also seen that there is a sense in which object-related acts depend on this inner-directed consciousness, as the very concept of an object depends on consciousness. And yet there seems to be a sense in which the outer-directed consciousness has priority over consciousness as a relating to one's own self when Mein says that the consciousness of self presupposes other mental acts: 'we are conscious of ourselves only from our Acting, or because we act, and

---

[24] See also the following passage (pp. 195–6): 'the Mind's Consciousness of it self and of its own Powers depends on its Acting; and to be *Self-conscious* is nothing else but being *sensible* of one's self as that which acts and hath a Power of Acting'.

Self-Consciousness must of course depend thereon for its Existence' (ibid., p. 148). It has been argued by one of the few commentators on this text—Manfred Frank—that Mein's account of consciousness is circular here: for on the one hand, he holds that the consciousness of objects depends on self-consciousness; and on the other hand he believes that self-consciousness depends on other, object-related acts of consciousness.[25] It is not certain, however, that we do have a vicious circle here. First, it is not obvious that 'our Acting' must be understood as being outer-directed. Mein does not say or imply that those mental acts of which we are conscious, and through which we become conscious of our own self or 'being', must be outer-directed. Second, even if we do assume that 'our acting' is related to external objects, it seems that what Mein wants to say is that the object-related consciousness and self-relating consciousness are mutually dependent on each other. We cannot have one without the other. Thus, immediately after having said that 'we are conscious of ourselves only from our Acting', Mein hastens to add: 'yet it is impossible to be Conscious of any Act whatever, without being sensible of, or perceiving one's *Self* to be that which Does it. And it is this Sense or Perception of *Self*, which constitutes the true Nature of any Act considered as *Conscious*, and as I may say, gives a Sanction to it' (*Essay on Consciousness*, pp. 148–9). Moreover, Mein does not claim that a self-relating consciousness occurs only after we have had consciousness of other objects; rather, as noted above, he believes that the two are simultaneous:

The Mind, for instance, in *Thinking*, is *sensible* of the *Act* or *Operation*, of its *Thought*, or what it thinks; and of the Object thought on, or Subject Matter of it; and knows also that it is *Itself* which *thinks*, and hath a Power of thinking; and moreover hath a *Perception* of its *Consciousness*, or inward Sense and Knowledge of all These, at one and the very same instant of time. (ibid., pp. 175–6; see also pp. 214, 215)

Both the object-directed consciousness and the inner-directed consciousness (relating to the 'actings' as well as to the subject of the actings) are always involved when we think at all. We cannot have self-consciousness without also having a consciousness of an object of thought (be the object external or internal); and at the same time we cannot have a consciousness of an object without also being conscious of our own self. Mein seems to hold, then, that there is a mutual dependence and interaction between the consciousness of objects and self-consciousness. His claim seems to be that both are involved in all acts of thought. To claim this, however, does not seem to involve any circularity.

This is not to say that there are no problems with Mein's account. One is that he does not make the relation of mutual dependence explicit, let alone explain it in any detail. And he does not assign any special epistemological status to this interrelatedness of consciousness of objects and consciousness of the self. Moreover, Mein's account clearly leads to the old problem of an infinite regress, for he conceives of consciousness in terms of a higher-order act of perception, and also maintains that all mental acts are accompanied by consciousness (it 'is perpetually present to our Minds' (ibid., pp. 179–80)). We have seen that Hobbes raises the issue in his objections to Descartes, and Leibniz in his critique of Locke. Mein explicitly

---

[25] Frank (ed.), *Selbstbewusstseinstheorien von Fichte bis Sartre* (1991), p. 444.

addresses this issue: he holds that we are conscious of all our mental acts and are always conscious of our consciousness of our mental acts, but maintains that it does not follow that there should be any further acts of consciousness beyond this second level. He says:

> But farther than This, or beyond a *Sense* of *Consciousness*, there is no proceeding. For admitting a *Perception* of a *Sense* of *Consciousness*, that is, in other Words, a *Perception* of a *Perception*, of a *Perception* (for all *Consciousness* is unquestionably *Perception*, and nothing else) the Progress might as well be *in infinitum*; which therefore cannot be admitted, as being absurd and impossible. (ibid., p. 165)

Mein notes that an infinite regress of acts of consciousness is not acceptable; therefore he maintains that there are no further acts of consciousness beyond the consciousness of consciousness. He does not show, however, how on his account the problem can be avoided. Since, on his view, consciousness is a separate mental act, and acts of consciousness accompany all our mental acts, it follows that the consciousness of consciousness must in turn be accompanied by another act of consciousness, and so on, *ad infinitum*.

8.2. BERKELEIAN THEMES

We have examined Berkeley's account of relating to one's own soul, and his critical comments on Locke's theory of personal identity—in particular his version of the argument from transitivity. Some of his remarks on the issue, however, go beyond criticizing Locke, and advance his own positive account. This account is similar in many respects to the Cartesian view presented in Emes's *Vindiciae Mentis*. Although it is more complex than the latter, the notion of the human soul or person as an immaterial substance is also at the core of Berkeley's account.

8.2.1. The person as 'the concrete of the will and understanding': Berkeley

It is well known that in early, posthumously published writings Berkeley toys with a different notion of the soul or self or person. In *Philosophical Commentaries* he considers what is today called the 'bundle view' of the self. Here, he states: 'Mind is a congeries of perceptions. Take away perceptions and you take away the mind put the perceptions and you put the mind.'[26] This view seems to be very similar to the view of the mind that is usually ascribed to Hume. Even in *Philosophical Commentaries*, however, Berkeley is not really committed to a bundle view. Rather, he seems to be torn between two positions: the 'congeries', or bundle view, and the unity-picture of the self.[27] By the time he completed *A Treatise Concerning the Principles of*

---

[26] Berkeley, *Philosophical Commentaries*, no. 580. Compare also nos. 637–9, 614–15. In no. 577 Berkeley states: 'The very existence of Ideas constitutes the soul.'
[27] Compare *Philosophical Commentaries*, nos. 713, 848.

Human Knowledge he had abandoned the bundle view of the self completely in favour of the view of the self as a unitary substance.

According to Berkeley's published writings, the self is an active being, and cannot be a mere collection of ideas but must be an immaterial spiritual substance.[28] This is evident from several passages in *Principles* and *Three Dialogues*. He states that 'this perceiving, active being is what I call *mind, spirit, soul* or *myself*' (*Principles*, § 2); and in *Principles* § 139 he declares that this mind, spirit, soul, or self is a substance: 'What I am myself, that which I denote by the term I, is the same with what is meant by *soul* or *spiritual substance*.'[29] Also, like Descartes and Thomas Emes in *Vindiciae Mentis*, Berkeley holds that the soul always thinks (*Principles*, § 98): the existence of a spirit 'consists... in perceiving ideas and thinking' (*Principles*, § 139). Berkeley very rarely makes use of the term 'person' in the writings published during his lifetime. In the early *Philosophical Commentaries* he uses 'person' more often; but he later drops the term, and mostly uses 'mind' or 'spirit' instead. And even when he does use 'person' in *Philosophical Commentaries*, the term denotes the immaterial thinking substance. 'Person' is clearly used synonymously with 'spirit', when Berkeley says in entry no. 24 that only persons exist.[30] In other writings, too, Berkeley suggests that persons are immaterial spiritual substances. In *Siris* (1744), for example, he states that 'personality is the individual centre of the soul or mind, which is a monad so far forth as he is a person' (ibid., § 346), and: 'the person or mind of all created beings seemeth alone indivisible and to partake most of unity' (ibid., § 347).[31] Thus, in contrast to Locke, and like Emes in *Vindiciae Mentis*, Berkeley does not distinguish between the soul as immaterial substance and the self as person.[32] This is different from both the Cartesian and the Scholastic notion of a person which in different ways respectively account for personhood in terms of a mind–body unity. As Berkeley rejects mind–body dualism and the notion of an independently existing material substance, the issue of mind–body unity and interaction does not arise for him in the way it does for the Cartesians.

Berkeley does, however, distinguish between two essential features within the mind, soul, or person: He holds that the 'Concrete of the Will & Understanding' constitutes the 'person' or 'mind'.[33] This suggests that will and understanding are distinct characteristics of the person or mind. The distinction between will and understanding does not, of course, undermine the unity and substantiality of the mind or person.

---

[28] Berkeley, *Principles*, § 139, *Works*, vol. 2, pp. 104–5. See also *Principles*, § 2, *Works*, vol. 2, pp. 41–2; and *Three Dialogues between Hylas and Philonous*, in *Works*, vol. 2, p. 231.

[29] Compare also *Three Dialogues between Hylas and Philonous*: 'The mind, spirit or soul, is that indivisible unextended thing, which thinks, acts, and perceives': *Works*, vol. 2, p. 231.

[30] 'Nothing properly but persons i.e. conscious things do exist, all other things are not so much existences as manners of yᵉ existence of persons': *Philosophical Commentaries*, no. 24. Compare that passage with *Principles*, § 7: 'there is not any other substance than *spirit*, or that which perceives'.

[31] Mijuskovic (1974), p. 84, drew my attention to these passages. *Siris* is in *Works*, vol. 5.

[32] Mijuskovic (1974), p. 103, asserts that there is an 'awareness' in Berkeley 'of the difference between soul and person', but he does not elaborate on this claim.

[33] Berkeley, *Philosophical Commentaries*, no. 713: 'The Concrete of the Will & Understanding I must call Mind not person.'

Understanding and will are merely two different respects under which we may consider the self or spiritual substance: 'A spirit is one simple, undivided, active being: as it perceives ideas, it is called *understanding*, and as it produces or otherwise operates about them, it is called the *will*.'[34] He clearly emphasises the activity of the self or mind, however, arguing that the active mental substance is the seat of personality.

As to the issue of diachronic self-identity, Berkeley distinguishes between the identity of substances and that of perceptions or non-substances. For him, the identity of the self as a person or spiritual substance is guaranteed by its immaterial nature. The identity of mental substances is, indeed, the only real identity of individuals that exists; for, according to Berkeley's metaphysics, immaterial spirits are the only individual beings that are substances. Since there can be no material substances (see again, *Philosophical Commentaries*, no. 24: only persons really exist), the identity of individuals that are not persons is reduced to certain relations among perceptions: here there is no numerical identity at all, but only qualitative identity, 'identity' in the sense of perfect equality.[35] Moreover, actions and thoughts have 'divers beginnings, & endings' and may be 'frequently interrupted' (*Philosophical Commentaries*, no. 194). This would seem to lead to a problem raised by Locke's account: namely, that we could ascribe actions or thoughts to ourselves that we never did or had. Berkeley's solution is to account for thoughts and volitions in terms of their corresponding faculties, understanding, and will: 'Doctrine of Identity best explain'd by Takeing the Will for Volitions, the Understanding for Ideas. The difficulty of Consciousness of w^t are never acted etc solv'd thereby' (ibid., no. 681). In the last analysis this means, of course, that actions and thoughts are accounted for in terms of the spiritual substance that has brought them about. The 'Concrete of the Will & Understanding' just is the mind or person or spiritual substance (ibid., no. 713). All actions are the actions of a substance: there are no free-floating perceptions or actions.

Thus, no matter whether we consider the mind or person as will (see ibid., nos. 478a, 194) or as understanding—that is, as thinking or acting—our personal identity is secured by the spiritual substance that thinks or acts. For Berkeley, action-attribution is justified by reference to the fact that the actions in question were willed by the person or mind. 'Men impute their actions to themselves because they will'd them & that not out of ignorance but whereas they knew the consequences, of them whether good or bad' (ibid., no. 157). It is quite true, then, as some commentators have pointed out, that Berkeley emphasises the self as active being, but it would be misleading to suggest that in his treatment of personal identity he

---

[34] Berkeley, *Principles*, § 27; see also *Philosophical Commentaries*, no. 848.

[35] See *Philosophical Commentaries*, no. 192: 'No identity other than perfect likeness in any individuals besides persons.' This note has the plus sign in Berkeley's manuscript. The standard view, going back to Luce, *Berkeley and Malebranche* (1934), pp. 187–8, that this sign always marks notes that Berkeley decided not to use or was at least hesitant about, has been challenged by Belfrage: 'A New Approach to Berkeley's *Philosophical Notebooks*', in *Essays on the Philosophy of George Berkeley*, ed. Sosa (1987), pp. 217–30.

appeals in any significant way to 'conduct or practice'.[36] The latter is relevant, but what is important to Berkeley's understanding of personal identity is that 'conduct or practice' issues from an immaterial spiritual substance, and that it is the latter that constitutes our personal identity. His account of personal identity is in terms of the notion of a continuously thinking and active immaterial spiritual soul or substance. Therefore, from his perspective there is no *problem* of personal identity through time that needs to be solved.[37]

It follows that consciousness or memory does not play any constitutive role in Berkeley's understanding of personal identity. It has been argued, however, that for Berkeley 'a veracious memory is a sufficient . . . condition for judging that one is the same person that formerly was conscious of a certain idea'.[38] The point being made here concerns our 'judging' of identity, not what constitutes identity itself; and as such that thesis would seem to be quite compatible with our interpretation. If we examine what constitutes personal identity, rather than our knowledge of it, we would have to ask what is required for memory to be veracious according to Berkeley. The answer seems obvious enough. For there to be veracious memory, the identity of the person or mental substance at t_1 (when one 'was conscious of a certain idea') and at t_2 (when one remembers that one was conscious of that idea at t_1) must be presupposed. This implies that consciousness or memory plays no *constitutive* role for personal identity.

A question that has not been discussed much in relation to Berkeley relates to the afterlife. He certainly believes that his immaterialist philosophy constitutes a defence of Christianity, and so one would think he needs to address this issue. The immortality and identity of the soul is not a problem for him, of course, as these are guaranteed by the soul's assumed immaterial nature. But how does the doctrine of bodily resurrection square with his immaterialist metaphysics? In places, he uses the old argument from an analogy with nature, appealing to the seed metaphor.[39] But it seems that his view is really a version of the view according to which sameness of the human body in this life and at the resurrection is due to the mind or soul. He holds

---

[36] Winkler, "'All is Revolution in Us': Personal Identity in Shaftesbury and Hume', *Hume Studies*, 26 (2000), 3–40, at 8, 33. To be fair, Winkler does not elaborate on this point here but merely mentions Berkeley, relating him to Shaftesbury, to whom he ascribes a similar appeal to 'conduct or practice'. Other commentators have emphasised the notion of the active self in Berkeley. See, for example, Berlioz (1995), pp. 397: 'Plus que la conscience, c'est l'expérience des volitions, de activité, du projet qui caractérise le sujet ou l'esprit pour Berkeley.' There is no doubt that the will is important to Berkeley, but I am not convinced that it has any priority over the cognitive side of the self. After all, it is the concrete of will *and* understanding that constitutes the mind or person for Berkeley. 'The Concrete of the Will & Understanding I must call Mind not person': *Philosophical Commentaries*, no. 713.

[37] This conforms to Luce's reading in *The Dialectic of Immaterialism* (1963), pp. 180–1, where he states that Berkeley accepts 'the continuing active mind as the percipient subject and the seat of personal identity'.

[38] Flage, 'Berkeley, Individuation, and Physical Objects', in Barber and Gracia, *Individuation and Identity in Early Modern Philosophy* (1994), pp. 133–54, at p. 135. A similar point is made by Brown (1972), p. 84.

[39] This is analysed in detail by Hight, 'Berkeley and Bodily Resurrection', *Journal of the History of Philosophy*, 45 (2007), 443–58. Compare Berkeley, *Works*, vol. 7, pp. 106–8.

that the difficulties with the resurrection disappear once we adhere to the principles of his immaterialist metaphysics and abandon the notion of an independently existing material substance.

> Take away this *material substance*, about the identity whereof all the dispute is, and mean by *body* what every plain ordinary person means by that word, to wit, that which is immediately seen and felt, which is only a combination of sensible qualities, or ideas: and then their most unanswerable objections come to nothing. (*Principles of Human Knowledge*, § 95)

There is no reason, then, why a 'combination of sensible qualities' cannot reappear at the resurrection in a manner sufficiently similar to the pre-mortem ones.[40] Since these are ideas belonging to a mind or soul whose identity is not in question they can count as *my* body—the same that I had before.

8.2.2. Personal identity and original sin: Edwards

Theological issues as well as Berkeleian metaphysical themes play a central role in the account of personal identity by Jonathan Edwards—one of the most eminent American philosophers of the eighteenth century.

We have seen in Chapter 4 that Locke's new account of personal identity is connected to his rejection of the doctrine of original sin. For Locke, we can be held responsible only for actions that we can ascribe to ourselves through consciousness. He states that 'though all die in Adam, yet none are truly punished but for their own deeds'.[41] Jonathan Edwards sets out to defend the doctrine of original sin in a huge tome entitled *The Great Christian Doctrine of Original Sin defended*.[42] He does not put forward objections to Locke's theory, and in places even refers approvingly to aspects of the latter,[43] but he develops an alternative account of personal

---

[40] Compare Hight (2007), 453–5. As he points out, Berkeley does not attempt to prove the resurrection doctrine but merely aims to show that it is reasonable (448).

[41] Locke, *Reasonableness of Christianity*, in *Works* (1823), vol. 7, p. 8.

[42] Edwards, *The Great Christian Doctrine of Original Sin defended; Evidences of its Truth produced, and Arguments to the Contrary answered* (1758), in Holbrook (ed.), *The Works of Jonathan Edwards*, vol. 3 (1970). For his account of original sin, see, for example, Holbrook, 'Jonathan Edwards on Self-Identity and Original Sin', *The Eighteenth Century: Theory and Interpretation*, 25 (1984), 45–63; Yarbrough, 'The Beginning of Time: Jonathan Edwards's Original Sin', in Derounian-Stodola (ed.), *Early American Literature and Culture* (1992), pp. 149–64; Daniel, *The Philosophy of Jonathan Edwards* (1994), pp. 130–51.

[43] In his early, posthumously published notes on 'The Mind', however, Edwards does critically engage with aspects of Locke's account. He rejects the view that personal identity consists in the identity of consciousness, 'if, by sameness of consciousness, be meant, having the same ideas hereafter, that I have now, with a notion or apprehension that I had had them before', for 'it is possible... for God to annihilate me, and after my annihilation to create another being that shall have the same ideas in his mind that I have ... and yet I be in no way concerned in it, having no reason to fear what that being shall suffer, or to hope for what he shall enjoy': *'The Mind' of Jonathan Edwards: A Reconstructed Text*, ed. Howard (1963), pp. 27–8. We noted in Chapter 6 that Edwards also puts forward a version of the argument from transitivity against Locke, employing a thought experiment about fission. Elsewhere in the notes Edwards argues that the identity of consciousness can be reduced to the identity of substance or spirit. 'Well might Mr. Locke say, that, Identity of *person* consisted in identity of consciousness; for he might have said that identity of *spirit*, too,

identity—one that requires divine agency and is consistent with the doctrine of original sin.[44] In spite of its very obvious theological orientation, Edwards's account has been discussed in the context of twentieth-century debates.[45]

In order to defend the doctrine of original sin, Edwards needs to explain how Adam's posterity can be guilty for actions they did not perform and of which they may have no knowledge whatsoever. Such questions of imputation are obviously linked to the issue of personal identity. Edwards begins by seemingly conceding to Locke that sameness of consciousness 'is one thing essential' to personal identity (*Works*, vol. 3, p. 398). In the last analysis, however, consciousness does not seem to play an essential role at all in his account. First, for Edwards, continuity of consciousness cannot exist on its own, but 'depends wholly on a law of nature'; that is, 'on the sovereign will and agency of God' (ibid., p. 399). It is 'evident', he maintains, 'that the communication or continuance of the same consciousness and memory to any subject, through successive parts of duration, depends wholly on a divine establishment' (ibid., p. 398). 'There would be no necessity, that the remembrance and ideas of what is past should continue to exist, but by an arbitrary constitution of the Creator' (ibid., pp. 398–9). It is God who gives the soul such a nature that it will retain the ideas and consciousness it once had (ibid., p. 399). Consequently, personal identity and accountability also depend on God: 'personal identity and so the derivation of the pollution and guilt of past sins in the same person, depends on an arbitrary divine constitution' (ibid., p. 399).

Second, this also applies, Edwards holds, if, like many critics of Locke, we 'suppose sameness of substance requisite' for personal identity (ibid.). For Edwards, the identity of substances, too, is dependent on God, so that it does not matter whether we follow Locke or his critics on this issue: 'even this oneness of created substances, existing at different times, is merely *dependent* identity; dependent on the pleasure and sovereign constitution of him who worketh all in all' (ibid., p. 400). It makes no difference, then, if we reject the Lockean position and argue that it is the nature of the soul that retains sameness of consciousness. As Edwards points out, 'then let it be remembered, who it is, gives the soul this nature' (ibid., p. 399). For

---

consisted in the same consciousness; for a mind or spirit is nothing else but consciousness and what is included in it. The same consciousness is, to all intents and purposes, individually, the very same spirit or substance; as much as the same particle of matter can be the same with itself at different times' (ibid., p. 52). As we shall see, however, Edwards ends up arguing that appealing to the notion of (created) substance does not help in accounting for personal identity either.

[44] Given these features of Edwards's account, it can hardly be said that 'the spirit of his approach is Lockean', as Helm claims. See Helm, 'A Forensic Dilemma: John Locke and Jonathan Edwards on Personal Identity', in Helm and Crisp (eds.), *Jonathan Edwards: Philosophical Theologian* (2003), pp. 45–59, at p. 49. But Helm's account of Locke, too, is problematic. Thus he confuses the notions of person and soul when he asserts that for Locke 'soul' is 'a forensic notion' (p. 46), maintains that Locke conflates consciousness with self-consciousness (p. 47), and interprets Locke's account of personal identity in terms of the notion of 'immanent causation' (p. 48). See also Helm's earlier 'John Locke and Jonathan Edwards. A Reconsideration', *Journal of the History of Philosophy*, 7 (1969), 51–61.

[45] See, for example, Chisholm, *Person and Object: A Metaphysical Study* (1976), pp. 138–44.

Edwards, neither consciousness nor substance has an 'absolute independent identity' (ibid., p. 400).

As in Berkeley, the reasoning behind Edwards's account is reminiscent of Malebranche's metaphysics, according to which created things do not have any causal efficacy themselves.[46] Every present existence is dependent existence, Edwards argues, and is therefore an effect, dependent on a cause. This cause must be 'either the *antecedent existence* of the same substance, or else the *power of the Creator*' (ibid.). He holds that as antecedent existence has to be ruled out, it is the 'power of the creator' that brings about continuity of existence. Antecedent existence is ruled out as a cause for the following reasons: (1) 'what existed the last moment' was 'no active cause, but wholly a passive thing'; (2) 'no cause can produce effects in a *time* and *place* on which itself is *not*'. And since, 'in point of time, what is *past* entirely ceases, when *present* existence begins', it follows that 'the present existence of this, or any other created substance' cannot be the effect of the antecedent existence of the same substance (ibid.). The continued existence of consciousness, substance, person, and so on, is therefore due to the 'immediate continued creation of God'; that is, to 'his creating those things out of nothing at each moment of their existence' (ibid., p. 401). Independently of God, there is no diachronic identity of anything; for 'what exists at this moment, by this power, is a *new effect*; and simply and absolutely considered, not the same with any past existence' (ibid., p. 402). Therefore:

there is no identity or oneness in the case, but what depends on the *arbitrary* constitution of the Creator; who by his wise sovereign establishment so unites these successive new effects, that he *treats them as one*, by communicating to them like properties, relations, and circumstances; and so, leads us to regard and treat them as one. (ibid., pp. 402–3)[47]

It is only because God treats the series of new effects as being part of the same being that we are led to regard them in the same way and ascribe identity to something that 'simply and absolutely considered' would not be identical. This does not mean,

---

[46] The Berkeleian aspects of Edwards's metaphysical views are discussed in Lyttle, 'Jonathan Edwards on Personal Identity', *Early American Literature*, 7 (1972), 163–71; and Hoopes, *Consciousness in New England: From Puritanism and Ideas to Psychoanalysis and Semiotic* (1989), pp. 64–94. Lyttle even suspects that Edwards 'ran the danger of pantheism', as Edwards suggests that 'the universal mind of God is the ground of the creature's consciousness' (p. 166). Both Lyttle and Hoopes refer to Edwards's posthumously published notes on 'The Mind' for their accounts of his general metaphysics.

[47] Helm reconstructs Edwards's position in terms of the twentieth-century theory of temporal parts or four-dimensionalism, in 'Jonathan Edwards and the Doctrine of Temporal Parts', *Archiv für Geschichte der Philosophie*, 61 (1979), 37–51. On the modern theory of temporal parts I am responsible for past actions even though I am not strictly identical with the 'person-stage' who committed the crime. Rather, all that is required are certain relations and a qualitative identity between me now and the earlier 'person-stage' (45). See also Helm (2003), pp. 51, 55–7. One difference between Edwards and the modern theory is, of course, that the latter appeals to the 'powers and forces of matter' rather than to God (p. 51). Moreover, Edwards does not seem to deny diachronic numerical identity; rather, he is saying that it is constituted by divine agency. We have seen that some writers ascribe four-dimensionalism even to Locke's account. While not engaging with such interpretations, Helm would disagree, and holds that 'Locke is an endurantist' (p. 51). It seems that there is a strong tendency, however, to view the whole complex history of these issues in terms of one currently favoured position in metaphysics.

however, that numerical identity of persons is merely fictional or unreal, according to Edwards. Rather, his claim that identity is constituted by divine agency means that it 'depends wholly on a law of nature' (ibid., p. 399).

As for Edwards any unity is due to divine constitution, there is no problem with the idea that Adam and his posterity may be constituted as a unity in some respects. Just as the identity of an individual person is dependent on divine establishment, so is the unity between Adam and his posterity. The creator has constituted a unity between Adam and his posterity, so that 'Adam and his posterity are viewed as one' (ibid., p. 404). This does not apply, however, to the relationships among other individual human beings. They are not so united. 'By reason of the established union between Adam and his posterity, the case is far otherwise between him and them, than it is between distinct parts or individuals of Adam's race; betwixt whom is apparently no such constituted union: as between children and other ancestors' (ibid., p. 408).[48] As in Edwards's view God has established a unity only *in a certain respect* between Adam and his posterity, he does not claim that I am identical with the person of Adam. He is concerned with individual personal identity through time when he argues that neither consciousness nor the notion of self as substance can account for it and that divine agency is required. As far as imputation and responsibility are concerned, however, it seems that we do not have to treat distinct existences as belonging to an identical person.[49] Adam's sin can be imputed to us even though we are not thought of as identical with Adam; all that is required is the unity established in some respect by God. Thus for Edwards personal identity is not a necessary condition of imputation, although it is for Locke (and for most people).[50]

Even in the eighteenth century, Edwards's account of original sin was considered problematic, to put it mildly. Charles Chauncy thought it was 'as wild a conceit of a vain imagination as ever published to the world'.[51] Edwards's theory of personal identity also raises many questions, even if we were to accept his theological assumptions and aims. For example, what degree of similarity is required for making a unity of distinct existences? That is to say, to what extent precisely do the 'properties, relations, and circumstances', communicated to the 'successive new effects' (ibid., pp. 402–3), have to be like earlier ones so that the successive effects can be treated as parts of one being?

---

[48] Helm shows, in arguing against Chisholm's interpretation of Edwards, that there needs to be 'a certain fitness in the relation between A and B' so that God treat A and B as a unity: Helm (1979), 47. As Helm points out, the 'relation between Adam and his posterity is such that they can be regarded as a moral unity for certain purposes' (48). Compare Chisholm (1976), pp. 139–40.

[49] Helm suggests that treating Adam and his posterity as a unity in certain respects is treating Adam in a 'sense identical with his posterity': (1979), 49.

[50] Edwards's appeal to God in his account of personal identity is very different from Locke's appeal to the 'goodness of God' and the 'Great Day when all the secrets shall be laid open' (*Essay*, II. xxvii.22). In Locke these appeals refer to a purified consciousness that relates to our own deeds only, and for Locke 'no one shall be made to answer for what he knows nothing of' (*Essay*, II.xxvii.22).

[51] Chauncy, *Five Dissertations on the Scripture-Account of the Fall, and its Consequences* (1785), p. 135. Discussed in Holbrook (1984), 58ff.

8.3. THE SENSES OF IDENTITY: BUTLER'S EPISTEMOLOGY AND METAPHYSICS OF PERSONAL IDENTITY AND THE FUTURE LIFE

Butler's famous charge of circularity against Locke, examined above, is based in his own particular positive view about the nature of personal identity. Butler's own account is not very detailed, but several features can be identified—some (but not all) of which are shared by other immaterialist thinkers discussed in this and the previous Chapters. Butler deals with the topic in the opening chapter ('Of a Future Life') of his *Analogy of Religion* (1736) and in a short dissertation appended to the book that concerns specifically the identity issue.[52] Clearly, for Butler the future life is the main issue in this context. He complains that personal identity 'has been explained so by some, as to render the inquiry concerning a future life of no consequence at all to us' (*Analogy*, p. 317). Indeed, he points out that the enquiry into personal identity is of importance above all, because 'identity or sameness of person' is 'implied in the notion of our living now and hereafter' (ibid.). If our account of personal identity had the result that we would neither comprehend nor be concerned for a future life, there would have to be something wrong with that account.[53] Butler reports that the 'Dissertation' on personal identity had at first been part of the chapter 'Of a Future Life' (see ibid., p. 316, 'Advertisement'). Accordingly, this chapter refers to the issue of personal identity in the very first sentence (ibid., p. 17). It should be noted here that Butler is certainly wrong in suggesting that Locke and his followers deal with personal identity in such a way so 'as to render the inquiry concerning a future life of no consequence at all to us'. As we have seen, the notion of a future life is an essential component of Locke's account of personal identity.

Butler begins the 'Dissertation' with the claim that personal identity is so fundamental that it cannot be defined. Indeed, he maintains that 'all attempts to define' it 'would but perplex it' (ibid., p. 317). The same is true, he says, of other relations such as 'similitude, or equality' (ibid.). While personal identity cannot be defined, he asserts that it is not difficult to ascertain it, for 'upon comparing the consciousness of one's self, or one's own existence, in any two moments, there... immediately arises to the mind the idea of personal identity' (ibid.). Moreover, this comparison of our own self-consciousness at any two points of time not only provides us with the *idea* of personal identity, 'but also shows us the identity of ourselves in those two moments' (ibid., p. 318). Thus, the act of comparing the consciousness of our own existence at any two points of time provides 'immediate' evidence for the fact that we are the same persons at these points of time. Our own personal identity is a matter of intuitive certainty, and there is no need to provide a theory of it. Butler's point here is, however, epistemological. For, as was evident in his critique of Locke,

---

[52] All references to Butler's *Analogy of Religion* and the Dissertation on personal identity appended to it (both 1736) are to the first volume in *The Works of Joseph Butler*, ed. Gladstone, 3 vols. (1897).

[53] For this point, see also Penelhum, *Butler* (The Arguments of Philosophers) (1985), p. 130.

for Butler consciousness and the comparing of consciousnesses at different points of time play no role in constituting personal identity itself. The mental activity of comparing consciousness can only provide evidence for our own personal identity. Personal identity is constituted independently of consciousness: 'present consciousness of past actions or feelings is not necessary to our being the same persons who performed those actions, or had those feelings' (ibid., p. 319).

Why does Butler think that 'all attempts to define' personal identity 'would but perplex it'? And what does the confusion consist in, according to Butler? He does not seem to attempt to show or argue that attempts to define personal identity would necessarily lead to confusions. What he does, though, is point out alleged confusions in some (Lockean) accounts of personal identity. His criticism of Locke and Collins, discussed above, is part of this argument, as he charges them with confusing that which provides evidence for personal identity with that which constitutes personal identity.

As to the notion of person, Butler identifies the person with the soul, as immaterial substance, and assigns a merely instrumental role to the body: our bodies 'are not part of ourselves' (ibid., p. 27).[54] Like other immaterialists he deduces the notion of person or self or soul as a simple and indivisible substance from the unity of consciousness: 'since consciousness is a single and indivisible power, it should seem that the subject in which it resides must be so too' (ibid., pp. 24–5). He explicitly appeals to Clarke's argument against Collins here:

In like manner it has been argued . . . that since the perception or consciousness, which we have of our own existence, is indivisible, so as that it is a contradiction to suppose one part of it should be here and the other there; the perceptive power, or the power of consciousness, is indivisible too; and consequently the subject in which it resides; i.e. the conscious being. (ibid., p. 25)

Given that Butler bases his discussion of personal identity in a Cartesian metaphysics of the soul as a simple, immaterial substance, it is not surprising that he argues that we have no reason to believe that death will destroy the essential self or soul. For Butler, death is just another, if more radical, change that man undergoes but can survive (ibid., p. 20).[55] As the body is not part of our self, its destruction is not our destruction (ibid., p. 27). The self, as soul, is not affected by this change and remains the same. Although the afterlife that Butler envisages is a bodily one,[56] the identity of the self in this life and the future life depends on the identity of the self as a soul or immaterial mental substance. What does it mean, however, to say that something—a being such as the soul—remains the same?

As to the notion of identity, Butler adopts an old distinction between two senses of identity which proved to be immensely influential in subsequent discussions: a

---

[54] 'Upon the whole then, our organs of sense and our limbs are certainly instruments, which the living persons ourselves make use of to perceive and move with: there is not any probability, that they are any more': Butler, *Analogy*, p. 31.
[55] For this, compare also Penelhum (1985), p. 128.
[56] See the discussion in ibid., pp. 118ff.

distinction between identity 'in a loose and popular sense', and identity 'in a strict and philosophical' sense (ibid., p. 320). He explains that identity in the loose and popular sense allows for change, but that identity in the strict sense does not. According to Butler, then, plants and vegetables do not, strictly speaking, remain the same individuals through time. We may call a tree the same at different points of time for 'all the purposes of property and uses of common life', although the tree at t_2 does not have any one particle left of the tree at t_1; but in the strict and philosophical sense, trees do not have identity through time because they are subject to change. 'In a loose and popular sense then, the life and the organization and the plant are justly said to be the same, notwithstanding the perpetual change of parts' (ibid., p. 320); but in the strict sense there would be no identity. Butler next applies the distinction between the two senses of identity to the issue of personal identity. Sameness or identity is used in the strict and philosophical sense when applied to persons: 'The identity of these, therefore, cannot subsist with diversity of substance' (ibid.). Personal identity, then, in Butler's view, does not allow for change in the self or person. Since he also maintains that the self or person is just an immaterial mental substance that is not subject to change, there arises no problem of personal identity from his perspective.

It is plain, however, that Butler's account raises a number of questions. Apart from all the usual problems associated with a Cartesian, substance-dualist account of the self (such as individuation and interaction), Butler's notion of identity that precludes change is highly problematic. Are there any such beings at all that remain identical in this 'strict' sense? For Butler, adopting the strict notion of identity means that he has to introduce the notion of an unchanging substance to rescue the notion of personal identity. Later in the century, philosophers who took over the notion of strict identity but did not believe that there are substances which are not subject to change, ended up having to deny that identity through time exists at all (Thomas Cooper). There is, however, no reason to adopt either extreme. It would seem, rather, that the very notion of identity through time requires the notion of change, just as much as the notion of change requires that of identity. The question that philosophers struggle with to this day is just how much a being may change and yet retain its identity. The very examination of this question is undermined, however, when identity is defined in such way as to preclude any change at all.

Although Butler's account is problematic, his epistemological point about the intuitive certainty we have of our own identity is, of course, compatible with both his thesis about the indefinability of personal identity and his Cartesian metaphysics of the self. There is, however, no necessary connection between his epistemology and his metaphysics of personal identity. Obviously, we do not require a Cartesian metaphysics of the self in order to argue that we have a 'certain conviction, which necessarily and every moment rises within us, when we turn our thoughts upon ourselves, when we reflect upon what is past, and look forward upon what is to come' (ibid., p. 323). Butler says that this intuitive knowledge of our own identity is part of our 'natural sense of things' (ibid.). He appeals to a common sense view about personal identity that seems to be connected with his idea that personal identity cannot be defined. And this common sense position would even be compatible with a sceptical attitude about the metaphysics of the self. The common sense position about identity, as debated later in the century, requires no commitment to an immaterialist metaphysics, although it may of course be linked to it. In any case, the common sense position is certainly and naturally linked to the practical and ethical dimensions of personal identity. We have seen that Shaftesbury, for example, believed both that we can take our personal identity 'on trust', and that personal identity plays an important role in determining our actions. Butler, too, emphasises those features of personal identity when he points out the practical implications of the view that personal identity is not part of the natural sense of things. We would not determine our actions with a view to the future if we did not believe that we remain the same persons, and this relates to this life as much as it does to the future life: 'Nor is it possible for a person in his wits to alter his conduct, with regard to his health or affairs, from a suspicion, that, though he should live tomorrow, he should not, however, be the same person he is to-day' (ibid., p. 323; see also p. 322).

8.4. 'PURE THOUGHT' AND IDENTITY: THE ANONYMOUS *ESSAY ON PERSONAL IDENTITY*, AND TUCKER'S CRITIQUE

Moral implications of our understanding of personal identity are also emphasised in the anonymous *Essay on Personal Identity* (1769). In the previous Chapter we examined the first part of this *Essay* that deals with Locke (pp. 9–48) and Edmund Law's treatment of it in his *Defence* of Locke. The second part is entitled 'An Attempt to discover the real Constituent of Personal Identity' (pp. 49–92). Obviously, in terms of pure chronology, this *Essay* belongs firmly to the second half of the century, but in terms of its form and content it is connected to the immaterialist thinkers discussed in this Chapter. Like Butler, and indeed like Locke, the author emphasises that the issue of personal identity is of moral significance. The consequences of a mistaken account of personal identity, he says, 'will either be directly contradictory to common sense and reason, or absolutely repugnant to what are deemed established principles of divine, as well as human justice and equity' (*Essay*, p. 6). In more general terms, he declares that the 'whole rationale of man's creation as a moral agent' depends on the 'individuation of persons' (ibid., p. 48). Indeed, he begins his account by linking the notion of person to that of moral agency. 'Person', he says, is considered 'as signifying an universal idea, applicable to moral agents in general' (ibid., p. 11). He emphasises, therefore, the importance of considering the notion of person 'more peculiarly... in the light of a moral agent; or as deserving reward or punishment' (ibid., p. 12).

Underlying this idea of moral agency, however, is the metaphysical concept of a person as an immaterial substance or soul. Indeed, the author argues explicitly against Watts's view, according to which 'the complete sense of *Person*' is 'the same Spirit united to the same Body' (ibid., p. 10). Instead, like Butler, he adopts the Cartesian position in this respect, stating that 'Body is not an essential part of the idea to which it [the term 'person'] is applied' (ibid., p. 10). 'Matter', he maintains, 'can by no means, in any modification, enter into the proper and essential idea of a person' (ibid., p. 12). Moreover, he declares that in his *Essay* 'the words *Soul* and *Person* will, in many cases, be synonymous, and therefore indiscriminately used' (ibid.). In fact, the author uses 'spiritual identity' synonymously with 'personal identity' (ibid., p. 68).

As the person is identified with the immaterial soul or mental substance, one would here expect the standard Cartesian account of diachronic personal identity: namely, that it is guaranteed by the identity of the soul, as substance, and that the latter identity is guaranteed simply by the immaterial nature of the soul. The anonymous author does not, however, adopt this position. Rather, what constitutes personal identity, according to this author, 'must be some distinguishing, incommunicable property or affection' of the soul or person (ibid., p. 48). This property or affection, he says, is 'thought as such'. Thus, despite his critique of Locke's theory there is a Lockean element in his account when he says that just as the identity of animate beings does not consist in the identity of substance, but in life, so the identity of the person (or soul, as substance) does not consist in substantial identity either but in the 'life' of that substance. Unlike Locke, however, he does not focus on the notion of consciousness, but on 'thought as such'. The author argues that the 'sole constituent of any thing must be essential to it'. Therefore, we must look for the constituent of personal identity 'in *Thought, as such*; an uninterrupted continuation of which is evidently distinguishing and incommunicable' (ibid., p. 51). This view, although different from the standard Cartesian view about identity, makes use of a distinctive Cartesian position about the nature of the soul—a position that Locke rejects: that the soul's essence consists in thought and that the soul always thinks. The 'life' of the soul or person consists in thought, the author says, and therefore the person's identity consists in 'thought as such'. The 'Identity of all living or animate Beings whatever consists not merely in the Identity of substance, but in the Identity of the life of that substance; for no living thing whatever can be living, and therefore can be the same, any longer than it has life' (ibid., p. 55), 'and, consequently', the identity of a person or soul 'is determined in the same manner by thought, its essential life' (ibid.).

The author holds that the idea that personal identity consists in the identity of the mental substance is acceptable if the notion of substance is interpreted in terms of 'pure thought'. He cites Watts as saying that personal identity consists in the identity of substance, but suggests that Watts's 'substance' should be read as 'pure thought' (ibid., p. 56): 'Even, therefore, according to the supposition of Dr. Watts, *Personal Identity* does properly consist in an uninterrupted continuation of thought' (ibid., pp. 57–8). He emphasises, however, that personal identity must not be said to consist merely in the *power* of thought (ibid., pp. 59–60). 'Thought as such' or 'pure thought' refers to thinking in general but not in the sense of a faculty or power of thought. It refers to thought in a generic sense: some mental activity (= thought) which, whatever its actual manifestation, (intellectual thought, desiring, remembering etc.) is always going on at any time. When this author speaks of 'thought as such' he has in mind the uninterrupted flow of actual thought, but abstracting from the various particular types of thought in which we are able to engage. He emphasises that the notion of 'thought as such' is opposed not only to the notion of a mere 'power of thought', but also to the notion of any particular thought or kind of thought as constituting personal identity:

> It must be observed, that it is not a particular thought, or kind of thought, which constitutes *Personal Identity*, but only thought in general; that is, present *Personal Identity* is not determined by a present thought, considered as versant about any particular object, but considered as part of a general idea, as thought, and nothing else. The case, therefore, being thus, *Personal Identity* is not constituted by something diverse and changing, but simple and uniform. (ibid., p. 86)

This argument is implicitly directed against Lockean accounts—here understood as claiming that consciousness is a particular kind of *thought* that constitutes personal identity. For this author, personal identity consists not in any particular thought or type of thought (including consciousness) but in the uninterrupted continuation of thought or the 'life' of the soul. 'It is manifest', he thinks, 'that *Personal Identity* must be constituted and determined by an uninterrupted continuation of thought' (ibid., p. 55). Of course, as noted above, the author endorses the view that the soul does in fact always think, citing approvingly Watts's critique of Locke on this issue (ibid., p. 61). Thought is essential to the soul, and is always present throughout its existence (ibid., p. 67): 'if thought at any time be essential to it, it must always be essential' (ibid.). Moreover, 'if it be essential to the soul to think always, it is manifest that the Being of a soul or person, as the same, depends upon its continual thinking' (ibid., p. 61).

We have seen that the author equates the soul with the person. Since he believes that the body is not essential to the person it is not surprising that he emphasises that we must distinguish sharply between the person and the man. He insists on the distinction in the context of discussing an anonymous work entitled *De natura rerum dissertatio* (pp. 70–81).[57] The author of the *Dissertatio* argues against the view that personal identity consists 'in the sameness of material substance, or of the organization: for it is notorious, our corporeal substance is constantly changing: it is also possible, that two bodies may be modified or organized exactly alike'.[58] Here the anonymous author of the *Essay* could agree; but he cannot agree when the author of the *Dissertatio* conceives of a person not as a simple substance either but as a moral or modal being: 'Our perplexity on this subject' of personal identity 'arises from the

---

[57] *De natura rerum dissertatio* (1757). I have not been able to locate a copy of this work. It is summarized in English in *Monthly Review*, 30 (1764), 536–49. The author of the *Essay on Personal Identity*, too, refers only to this summary.

[58] *De natura rerum dissertatio* as described in *Monthly Review*, 30 (1764), 541.

errour of supposing the person of an individual, a simple and uncompounded Being; whereas it is compounded of a multiplicity of physical, metaphysical, and moral qualities and relations; the combination of which is its essence, and determines its identity'.[59] Like Edmund Law in his defence of Locke, the author of the *Dissertatio* likens personal identity to the identity of 'political characters and institutions', 'the essence of which consists of the combination of their constituent parts, and the several relations in which they stand to other Beings of the same, or of a different kind'.[60] The author of the *Essay*, however, thinks that this view of the person as a compound of various types of qualities confounds the man with the person: moral qualities and relations, he argues, belong to the man, not to the person (p. 80). He suggests that the *Dissertatio*'s notion of qualities be reduced to that of metaphysical qualities and relations, for these can be interpreted in terms of modes of *thought*, and then we would have an acceptable account of personal identity:

This author's *physical* and *moral* qualities and relations, therefore, are entirely foreign to the Identity of Person, properly so called, and so treated in this dispute. There remain, then, only his *metaphysical* qualities and relations; and, if he would chuse to consider *Personal Identity* on a continuation of them, we have no objection; since it is evident that these metaphysical qualities can, in the present case mean only different modes of thought. (ibid.)

The account of personal identity in the anonymous *Essay* provoked some criticism in the eighteenth century—in particular by Abraham Tucker.[61] We have encountered Tucker as one of many authors who charged Locke's theory with circularity. Tucker studied at Oxford, but does not seem to have communicated with other philosophers while writing his books. His philosophy combines an experiential or observational approach, and detailed analyses of individual issues with bizarre metaphysical speculations.[62] As far as the anonymous *Essay*'s account of identity in terms of the 'uninterrupted continuation of thought' (*Essay*, p. 55) is concerned, Tucker sees it as just another version of Lockean theory. Like Clarke, Butler, and many others, Tucker insists that personal identity must consist in the identity of substance, and he argues that the latter is presupposed by the 'continuation of thought' and so cannot be constituted by it. He questions the author's assumption that 'the soul always thinks', but argues that even if we were to accept this assumption, it is difficult to see how the 'continuation of thought' can constitute the individuality and identity of a person.[63] 'Thought as such'—or as Tucker says, 'thought in general'—is what all human beings have in common, and it therefore cannot account for the individuality

---

[59] Quoted in the anonymous *Essay*, 78–9; *De natura rerum dissertatio*, as described in *Monthly Review*, 30 (1746), 541.

[60] *De natura rerum dissertatio* as described in *Monthly Review*, 30 (1764), 542.

[61] Tucker, *The Light of Nature Pursued*, 7 vols., second edn. (1805; reprinted, 1977). Vols. 1–4 were first published in 1768, and vols. 5–7 were published in 1778, four years after Tucker died. He published his volumes under the pseudonym 'Edward Search', and in the eighteenth century he was often referred to by that name.

[62] Compare Thiel, 'Abraham Tucker', in Holzhey and Mudroch (eds.), *Grundriss der Geschichte der Philosophie. Die Philosophie des 18. Jahrhunderts. Band 1: Grossbritannien und Nordamerika, Niederlande* (2004), pp. 411–14.

[63] Tucker, *The Light of Nature Pursued*, vol. 7, pp. 5–14.

of distinct persons. Assuming, then, that 'our thinking constitutes us persons', the question remains: 'what constitutes us as different persons?' (*The Light of Nature Pursued*, vol. 7, p. 7). Tucker answers: 'Surely not our thinking, for in that respect we are exactly the same' (ibid.). How are we meant to 'distinguish one continuation from another?', he asks, 'for there are multitudes of them in the world, and there may be a continuation of thought in general imagined, where there is a change of the subject wherein the thought at different times is found' (ibid., p. 6). The notion of numerically distinct continuations of thought presupposes that we consider them 'as the thoughts of so many persons, each distinguished from the rest in some other respect than that of their thinking' (ibid., p. 7). In other words, there must be numerical distinctness of persons prior to ascribing to them distinct continuations of thought. As Tucker points out:

Thus you see the same objection actually lies against the continuation, as I had supposed lying against consciousness... For the idea of person must precede that of continuation: so it is no help to tell me I may find my personality by my continuation, because I must settle my idea of personality before I can make use of the explanation. (ibid., pp. 7–8)[64]

Moreover, he makes use of Lucretius's comment on identity (discussed above) in order to rebut the anonymous author's account. Lucretius holds that if after death our matter were to be brought back together exactly as it is now, that afterlife would be of no concern to us if we had lost all memory of our previous life (*De rerum natura*, III, pp. 847–51). Tucker interprets Lucretius (without quoting the passage) as denying that there 'would be the same soul' in the afterlife (*Light of Nature*, vol. 7, p. 12), and he believes that this argument can be applied to the account of the anonymous *Essay*. If God 'should work a resurrection of my atoms, and set them a thinking again', we would have 'a new continuation of thought, another person, not me, nor anywise affecting me' (ibid., p. 14). Clearly, this argument assumes that the soul could not continue to think apart from the body. We shall see that this is indeed Tucker's view.

As indicated, Tucker's own account of personal identity is very much in terms of the traditional notion of an immaterial mental substance or soul, and he himself counts himself as 'orthodox' in this regard (ibid., vol. 3, p. 111). He makes use of arguments from Clarke and others to the effect that the unities of consciousness and of self are incompatible with materialism, and that the notion of a life after death requires that of an immaterial mental substance (ibid., pp. 68–75). 'I humbly conceive it necessary', he writes, 'to place identity of the person in that of the substance, and its essence in the faculty of perceptivity' (ibid., vol. 7, p. 17). 'Perceptivity' is the essence of the mental substance or soul, as solidity is the essence of matter (ibid.). The unity of the self that is required for perception cannot be provided by a material system. 'I have no notion of one Self to see, another to hear, another to smell, and so on'; rather, 'it is the same *I*, the same *Self*, that see the one and feel the other', and this suggests 'that this Self' must be 'something distinct from

---

[64] Compare Tucker's similar comment on Locke in *The Light of Nature Pursued*, vol. 3, p. 77.

the nerves and organs'.[65] Tucker's account goes beyond repeating traditional arguments, however, in that he appeals to our use of personal pronouns to make his point. This is reminiscent of Watts, of course, but in Watts the appeal to our ordinary use of personal pronouns is designed to show that the body is an essential element of the person. This is not the case with Tucker, who assumes that 'the grammatical meaning' of personal pronouns 'points out the true origin of our ideas primarily annexed to them' (*Light of Nature*, vol. 7, p. 24). And personal pronouns are used, he argues, 'to distinguish some one person from all the rest'; that is, they apply 'to one particular percipient; which term includes the idea of substance' (ibid., p. 18). The person, 'which perceives and acts upon all occasions, seems the thing expressed by the word I in its grammatical sense: for it is the same I who see and hear and push and speak and pay bills, although the parts of my body respectively concerned herein are various' (ibid., p. 25). Tucker thinks that everybody 'apprehends the word I to signify a true individual without parts, when he uses it in his common discourses, how little soever he may reflect upon his so doing' (ibid.). The necessary unity of the self, then, is expressed by our use of personal pronouns.

Given Tucker's account of person in terms of a unitary, immaterial substance, it is not surprising that he assigns no constitutive role to consciousness, which is 'only a power or property of some Being'. If it were constitutive of identity, then 'a man loses his existence or personality every time he loses his consciousness, by falling fast asleep' (ibid., vol. 3, p. 76). At best, consciousness can function as 'evidence to us of our identity, for scenes that we remember convince us of our being the very persons present at them' (ibid.). Like Butler, then, Tucker emphasises the distinction between what constitutes identity and what provides evidence for identity. It is assumed that we remain the same individual spiritual substance throughout all changes of consciousness or the material compositions of our body: 'we are possessed of an existence and identity of which we cannot even in imagination divest ourselves' (ibid., p. 84). The mind has a 'distinct existence and individuality', and is 'another species of substance, essentially distinct from body, and which we call Spirit' (ibid., p. 92).[66]

Tucker deviates from immaterialist 'orthodoxy' in some important respects, however, due to empiricist tendencies in his thought. For all his critique of Locke on specific issues, he appeals to Locke's observational approach, stating that he stands

---

[65] Tucker, *Man in Quest of Himself: Or A Defence of the Individuality of the Human Mind, or Self* (1763)—published under the pseudonym 'Cuthbert Comment'—in Parr (ed.), *Metaphysical Tracts by English Philosophers of the Eighteenth Century* (1837; reprinted, 1974), pp. 171–210, at pp. 198–9. Tucker refers to these passages in *The Light of Nature Pursued*, vol. 7, p. 24.

[66] Martin and Barresi state that according to Tucker, the spirit when attaching itself to different bodies 'would become different persons': *Naturalization of the Soul. Self and Personal Identity in the Eighteenth Century* (2000) p. 118. I am not convinced that this is Tucker's view. See, for example, the following passage in *The Light of Nature Pursued*, vol. 3, p. 374. Spirits, Tucker says, 'have a personality annexed from which they cannot be divested without losing their existence. I have been a child and am now a man; I have been in joys and in troubles; I may imagine myself transformed into a lion, a sheep, or an ostrich, inhabiting the vehicular state, or wholly disengaged from matter and mingled among similar spirits: yet in all these changes I should still continue to be myself, for from the moment I began to exist I must have been myself, and must remain so until I cease to be at all.'

'indebted to Mr. Locke for, having learned from him which way to direct my observation and how to make use of what I observe' (ibid., vol. 1, p. xviii). This appeal to experience and observation leads him to ascribe a more important role to the body than does the standard Cartesian account. Although we can infer the 'perpetual duration' of the mind from its 'individuality and distinct existence' (ibid., vol. 3, p. 110), and although 'personality belongs in property to spirit alone' and 'body has none of its own, but assumes a borrowed personality from the particular spirit whereto it is vitally united' (ibid., vol. 5, p. 560), the body is nevertheless essential to make spiritual action possible. On its own, the mind or spirit has only a 'bare capacity' to perceive and act; actual perception or action, even reasoning, remembering, and so on, 'requires an organization' and 'organs of reflection' (ibid., vol. 3, p. 113). Thus Tucker ends up distinguishing between two notions of mind: (1) one is that of a 'pure uncompounded spirit endowed with perceptivity and activity'; and (2) the other is that of 'this same spirit together with so much of its organization as is concerned in the business of thinking and reflection, which must be a compound consisting chiefly of corporeal parts'—this latter notion being what 'is commonly called the human soul' (ibid., p. 115). Only in the former sense, then, is the mind 'perpetual, unperishable and unchangeable' (ibid., p. 117).

This leads Tucker to leave experience and observation behind and engage in various bizarre speculations about the afterlife. He assumes, for example, 'what no one can disprove': namely, 'that the spirit, upon quitting her present mansion, does not go out naked, nor entirely disengaged from matter', but carries with it 'a fine vehicle for the habitation of the spirit' (ibid., p. 322). This 'vehicular state' is, however, only temporary. The 'vehicular people', Tucker thinks, 'on the disruption of their vehicles', enter a 'mundane soul', a unity or 'ocean' of all spirits (ibid., p. 375) where they remain, nevertheless, as a 'host of distinct spirits' (ibid.). This provides Tucker with the opportunity for further abstruse speculations about how pure spirits can act and communicate, given that he argued previously that actual perception and action require bodily organization (ibid., pp. 377ff.). It is best to leave Tucker here.

8.5. CONCLUSION

We have seen in this and the previous Chapter that among British immaterialist philosophers of the soul or mind there is considerable variety as far as the issue of personal identity is concerned. Most immaterialists are in agreement with their opponents that moral agency and responsibility are significant aspects of human personal identity. There are, however, several versions of a Cartesian account of personal identity (Emes, Clarke, Grove). Moreover, there is Watts's emphasis on the body and his rather modern comments on the use of ordinary language, Shaftesbury's account in terms of a universal soul or mind, new reflections on the nature of relating to one's own self through consciousness (Browne, Berkeley, Mein), and reconsiderations of relevant theological issues (Edwards) and of the very notion of identity as unanalysable and thus not definable (Butler). There is also our anonymous author who insists that the person is an immaterial mental substance but that its identity is to be accounted for in terms of 'pure thought' or 'thought as such', and finally there are Tucker's speculations insisting on the notion that personal identity consists in the identity of substance.

It is plain, though, that the most original and complex account of personal identity argued from within an immaterialist point of view comes from Germany, with Leibniz's discussion of the issue forming the basis of quite a different debate in the first half of the eighteenth century.

PART V

SUBSTANCE, APPERCEPTION, AND IDENTITY: LEIBNIZ, WOLFF, AND BEYOND

9

Individuation and identity, apperception and consciousness in Leibniz and Wolff

There can be no doubt that Leibniz is the most important early critic of Locke, including of the latter's account of personal identity. He is also the most prominent thinker among those (described above) who, unlike others such as the author of *Vindiciae Mentis*, accept the notion of an immaterial mental substance or soul, but distinguish between the identity of a mental substance and personal identity. Leibniz's critique of Locke is so closely linked to his own, positive account of personal identity that the two cannot be usefully separated from one another. His views and arguments concerning personal identity were taken up, at least to a considerable extent, by Christian Wolff, the leading metaphysician in eighteenth-century Germany. Wolff was for a long time, and wrongly, seen as a mere systematizer of Leibniz's philosophy—a view expressed in the misleading notion of a 'Leibniz–Wolffian system', used even in the eighteenth century. Certainly, Leibniz and Wolff did not consider themselves as part of such an alliance—which is not surprising, on account of the many significant differences between their respective philosophies.[1] Still, as far as our topics are concerned there are several positive connections, as we shall see. The debate about the Wolffian philosophy which dominated Germany in the middle of the eighteenth century meant that a basically Leibnizian position was of central importance prior to the impact of Lockean theory and to the development of materialist accounts in Germany in the 1770s. As far as the second half of the century is concerned, the German debate about self-consciousness and personal identity is much less self-contained than it may appear to be in the first half of the century. Even here, however, Lockean theory of personal identity serves as a foil for the discussions of the issue, as is evidenced by Leibniz's account. We shall see in the next two Chapters that there was a development of thought on the issues of self-consciousness and personal identity even within the framework of Leibnizian or Wolffian thought. While the Leibnizian account is of importance in its own right, the critics of Wolff were of particular importance in moving the debate forward in important ways.

---

[1] Compare, for example, Antognazza, *Leibniz: An Intellectual Biography* (2009), pp. 474–6; and Rutherford, 'Idealism Declined. Leibniz and Christian Wolff', in Lodge (ed.), *Leibniz and His Correspondents* (2004), pp. 214–37.

Leibniz had worked out his own theory of self-identity and of identity in general independently of Locke and well before he wrote the *Nouveaux essais sur l'entendement humain* (1705) against Locke, and, indeed, even well before the first edition of Locke's *Essay* was published.[2] And there are similarities as well as significant differences between Leibniz's and Locke's accounts of self-identity, as we shall see. Unlike many other writers who commented on personal identity at the time, Leibniz offers a detailed theory of individuation and identity in general; and his account of the specific issue of personal identity is linked to this general account of identity. The individual substance, or 'monad', as he calls it in his later writings, is a main focus of his philosophical thinking. It appears that his interest in the individual originates in the Scholastic disputes over the principle of individuation which he studied in his early years. His first publication was a student dissertation on that topic. In his later works he writes in support of individual human immortality and against philosophers such as Spinoza and the 'Neo-Cartesians' (such as Malebranche), whose theories Leibniz takes to be incompatible with immortality.[3] His other target is atomism—a position that he adopted himself for a short time. He attempts to 'rehabilitate' substantial forms, but in a way that is compatible with the Christian doctrine of human immortality.

9.1. LEIBNIZ ON INDIVIDUATION AND IDENTITY

The method and terminology of his early dissertation, *Disputatio metaphysica de principio individui* (1663), written in Leipzig under the supervision of Jakob Thomasius, are still very Scholastic in character. Leibniz carefully distinguishes between the *principium cognoscendi* and the *principium essendi*, and he states that his subject is the real or 'physical' principle of individuation in all created substances.[4] He reviews various traditional answers to the problem of individuation, and lists authors who held those views. His own position is that of Suárez.[5] As we have seen in the

---

[2] Leibniz, *Nouveaux essais sur l'entendement humain*, in *Sämtliche Schriften und. Briefe*, ed. Deutsche Akademie der Wissenschaften zu Berlin, VI.6, ed. Robinet and Schepers (1962). Translations are from Leibniz, *New Essays on Human Understanding*, transl. and ed. Remnant and Bennett (1981), which follows the same pagination.

[3] See 'Considerations sur la doctrine d'un Esprit Universel Unique' (1702): 'Some discerning people have believed and still believe today, that there is only one single spirit, which is universal and animates the whole universe and all its parts... Spinoza, who recognizes only one single substance, is not far from the doctrine of a single universal spirit, and even the Neo-Cartesians, who hold that only God acts, affirm it, seemingly unawares': *Die Philosophischen Schriften von Gottfried Wilhelm Leibniz*, ed. Gerhardt (1875–90; reprinted, 1978), vol. 6, pp. 529–30; Leibniz, *Philosophical Papers and Letters*, ed. and transl. Loemker (1969), p. 554.

[4] *Philosophische Schriften*, vol. 4, pp. 15–26, at p. 17.

[5] The Suárezian character of Leibniz's view on individuation has been emphasised by a number of scholars. See especially McCullough, 'Leibniz and Traditional Philosophy', *Studia Leibnitiana*, 10 (1978), 254–70; and *Leibniz on Individuals and Individuation* (1996), esp. pp. 90–121, 187. McCullough also points out, however, that Leibniz moves beyond Suárez (p. 142). Compare Robinet, 'Suárez im Werk von Leibniz', *Studia Leibnitiana*, 13 (1981), 76–96. Robinet adopts a more sceptical view than do most scholars about Suárez's influence on Leibniz. He points out that

Introduction, Suárez's position is that in all created substances it is the very *entity* of a thing (the intrinsic principles that compose it) that makes it the individual it is. A being does not require anything over and above its own entity for its individuation. That which individuates 'cannot be distinguished from the entity itself'. Thus composite beings such as men which consist of 'matter and form united' (*Disputationes metaphysicae*, V.6.1) are individuated 'by this matter and this form united to each other' (ibid., V.6.15). Like Suárez, Leibniz rejects the Scotist position, according to which an individual emerges through negation from a real universal, and the theory which identifies existence as the principle of individuation. He argues that existence cannot be the principle of individuation, because existence and essence cannot be separated from one another (*Philosophische Schriften*, vol. 4, p. 22). He concedes, however, that if existence is said to differ from essence only in thought ('solum ratione'), then that position coincides with his own view (ibid., p. 21). We have seen that Suárez, too, holds that 'existence' can be interpreted in such a way that the 'existential' theory of individuation coincides with his own solution.

Leibniz's main target, however, is the Scotist position (ibid., pp. 22–6). In fact, he spends more time examining and rejecting the Scotist theory than he does explaining his own view. For the Scotists there is a formal cause of individuation, which is explained in analogy to specification: just as the species emerges from the genus through the specific difference, so the individual emerges from the species through the individual difference, or 'haecceitas'. Leibniz's response is in terms of the nominalist tradition: he rejects the real existence of genus and species (ibid., p. 24); and once natural kinds are rejected the Scotist account no longer makes sense. Leibniz links his own position explicitly to the nominalist tradition (such as Petrus Aureolus, Durandus), to Suárez, and to his university teacher Daniel Stahl (ibid., p. 18). Like Suárez he identifies the 'entity' as the positive ground of individuation: 'Every individual is individuated by its whole entity' (ibid.). As in Suárez, the 'whole entity' can be interpreted as the two intrinsic causes of being: matter and form. What brings about a being's individuality, according to Leibniz, is not just one of its component parts (form or matter), but all the constituents which make up its entity. Leibniz provides a syllogistic argument to support his position: he says that that which constitutes a thing also makes it numerically one; and since a thing is intrinsically constituted by its entity, it follows that each thing is one by its own entity. The major premise is derived from the principle that oneness does not add any reality to being (ibid.). Leibniz's early adherence to nominalism is also expressed in a preface (1670) to an edition of Marius Nizolius's *De veris principiis et vera ratione philosophandi contra pseudophilosophos libri IV* (first published in 1553). Here Leibniz states that according to the nominalists, 'everything in the world can be explained without any reference to universals and real forms', adding that 'nothing is truer than this opinion'.[6]

---

among the thousands of authors whom Leibniz quotes extensively and in detail, Suárez is rarely mentioned. Bartha links Leibniz's account of the nature of individual substance to Duns Scotus, whose view Leibniz rejects in the early dissertation. Bartha, 'Substantial Form and the Nature of Individual Substance', *Studia Leibnitiana*, 25, 1 (1993), 43–54.

[6] *Philosophische Schriften*, vol. 4, p. 158; Leibniz, *Philosophical Papers* (1969), p.128.

Leibniz's later theory of individual substances, which is central to his metaphysics as a whole, develops from his early dissertation on the Scholastic disputes over the *principium individuationis*.[7] He later abandons Scholastic terminology and method, and thinks that the traditional search for an individuating principle is superfluous. Nevertheless, he continues to believe that the works of 'deeper Scholastics, such as Suárez... sometimes contain substantial discussions, for instance... of the principle of individuation' (*Nouveaux essais*, IV.viii.9).[8] Leibniz's early position on individuation has several essential features in common with his later theory. First, there is the sharp distinction between what is relevant for the evidence or knowledge of individuality and what constitutes individuality in reality. Second, there is the insistence that individuality must have an intrinsic ground. Third, there is the nominalist emphasis on the priority of the individual over the universal. Fourth, there is the view that there are not different causes of individuality for different kinds of being. And fifth, there is Leibniz's later notion of 'complete being' or of 'complete entity', which is reminiscent of the Suárezian notion of the 'whole entity' which Leibniz uses in the early dissertation; it certainly develops from the earlier concept.[9] Although there are common features, however, the later theory is not simply identical with the early Suárezian doctrine.

As indicated, Leibniz was led to regard the whole debate over the *principium individuationis* as superfluous. This is implied by his famous principle of the identity of indiscernibles. Leibniz states this principle in many places. In the *Discours de métaphysique* (1686) he formulates it thus: 'It is not true that two substances are completely alike, differing only numerically.'[10] In his *Fourth Paper* to Samuel Clarke (1716) he says: 'There is no such thing as two individuals indiscernible from each other.'[11] This is to say that no two substances have all their characteristics in common; there must be at least one property which they do not share. It also means

---

[7] Mugnai retraces the intermediate steps in the development of Leibniz's thought on this issue. See Mugnai, 'Leibniz on Individuation: From the Early Years to the "Discourse" and Beyond', in *Studia Leibnitiana*, 33 (2001), 36–54. As Mugnai notes (38–40), in the *Confessio philosophi* of 1672–73 Leibniz assigns place and time a central role in individuation: *Sämtliche Schriften*, A VI.3, p. 147; see also Cover and O'Leary-Hawthorne, *Substance and Individuation in Leibniz* (1999), pp. 60–1. Clearly, this view is at odds with both Leibniz's earlier and later accounts. It cannot be said, however, that this view is characterized by 'novelty' and constitutes a 'departure from scholastic doctrines', as Mugnai claims (39). As is evident even from our sketch in the Introduction above, this view was an option within the context of Scholastic debates. See, for example, Keckermann, *Scientiae metaphysicae compendiosum systema* (1614), vol. 1, cols. 2016–17.

[8] Thus, Mugnai's statement that the mature Leibniz treats 'the scholastic disputes concerning individuation' with 'quite an air of dismissal' is too strong: Mugnai (2001), 37.

[9] Leibniz, *Discours de métaphysique* (1686), sect. 8. See also his letter to Arnauld, 30 April 1687, in *Philosophische Schriften*, vol. 2, pp. 101–2; *The Leibniz–Arnauld Correspondence*, ed. and transl. Mason (1967), pp. 127–8. Compare McCullough (1978), 260.

[10] Leibniz, *Discours de métaphysique*, sect. 9. See also Leibniz, *Monadologie* (1714), sect. 9. An early formulation of this principle is in Leibniz's *Meditatio de principio individui* (1676), in *De Summa Rerum. Metaphysical Papers 1675–1676*, transl. and ed. Parkinson (*The Yale Leibniz*, ed. Garber and Sleigh) (1992), pp. 50–3.

[11] *Philosophische Schriften*, vol. 7, p. 372; Leibniz, *The Leibniz-Clarke Correspondence*, ed. Alexander, p. 36.

that, 'to suppose two things indiscernible, is to suppose the same thing under two names':[12] If I refer to two items as having all their properties in common, I am in fact referring to one and the same thing, only under different names. Leibniz offers both *a priori* and *a posteriori* arguments for his principle. The *a priori* argument is that the identity of indiscernibles follows from the principle of sufficient reason. Leibniz concedes that the 'supposition of two indiscernibles' is 'possible in abstract terms'; that is, it is logically possible that two substances are exactly alike, 'but it is not consistent with the order of things, nor with the divine wisdom, by which nothing is admitted without reason'; for if there were two indiscernibles, then 'God and nature would act without reason, in ordering the one otherwise than the other'.[13] There must therefore be an intrinsic difference between things which accounts for their numerical diversity.[14] Leibniz regards the principle of the identity of indiscernibles as central to his philosophical system as a whole; he holds that together with the principle of sufficient reason it would 'change the state of metaphysics', making it 'real and demonstrative; whereas before it did generally consist in empty words'.[15] The *a posteriori* argument is that, as a matter of fact, two things are never found to be exactly alike. This is not offered as a proof of the principle, but as an argument which shows that the principle is confirmed by experience; and Leibniz gives numerous examples. In his *Fourth Paper* to Clarke he writes:

There is no such thing as two individuals indiscernible from each other. An ingenious gentleman of my acquaintance, discoursing with me, in the presence of Her Electoral Highness the Princess Sophia, in the garden of Herrenhausen; thought he could find two leaves perfectly alike. The Princess defied him to do it, and he ran all over the garden a long time to look for some; but it was to no purpose. Two drops of water, or milk, viewed with a microscope, will appear distinguishable from each other.[16]

In some passages Leibniz suggests that his principle is a more general application of Aquinas's view that angels or 'separate intelligences' do not only differ numerically, and that each angel constitutes a distinct kind—a 'lowest species'.[17] Clearly, Leibniz's position implies a rejection of Aquinas's view that 'designated matter' is the

---

[12] Leibniz's *Fourth Paper* to Clarke: *Philosophische Schriften*, vol. 7, p. 372; Leibniz, *Leibniz-Clarke Correspondence*, p. 37.
[13] Leibniz's *Fifth Paper* to Clarke: *Philosophische Schriften*, vol. 7, p. 394; Leibniz, *Leibniz-Clarke Correspondence*, p. 61.
[14] See also *Primae veritates*: Leibniz, *Opuscules et fragments inédits*, ed. Couturat (1903), pp. 518ff.; Leibniz, *Philosophical Papers* (1969), p. 268: 'It follows also [from the principle of sufficient reason] that *there cannot be two individual things in nature which differ only numerically*. For surely it must be possible to give a reason why they are different, and this must be sought in some differences within themselves... Never are two eggs, two leaves, or two blades of grass in a garden to be found exactly similar to each other.'
[15] Leibniz's *Fourth Paper* to Clarke: *Philosophische Schriften*, vol. 7, p. 372; Leibniz, *Leibniz-Clarke Correspondence*, p. 37.
[16] Leibniz's *Fourth Paper* to Clarke: *Philosophische Schriften*, vol. 7, p. 372; Leibniz, *Leibniz-Clarke Correspondence*, p. 36. See also *Nouveaux essais*, II.xxvii.3.
[17] Leibniz, *Discours de métaphysique*, sect. 9. *Primae veritates*: Leibniz, *Opuscules*, p. 520; Leibniz, *Philosophical Papers* (1969), p. 268. See also Leibniz's 'Remarques sur la Lettre de M. Arnaud': *Philosophische Schriften*, vol. 2, p. 42; *The Leibniz–Arnauld Correspondence*, p. 45.

principle of individuation in material things.¹⁸ Yet, like Aquinas's angels, Leibniz's individual substances differ from each other essentially as well as numerically; all the attributes of an individual substance belong to it essentially. Individual substances each have their own natures or essences by which they are individuated. As just indicated, Leibniz makes use of the terms 'complete being' and 'complete entity' which replace the earlier Suárezian notion of 'whole entity'. Indeed, Leibniz uses 'individual substance' synonymously with 'complete being'. He states: 'The nature of an individual substance or complete being is to have such a complete notion as to include and entail all the predicates of the subject that notion is attributed to.'¹⁹ That is to say, the intrinsic nature or complete notion of an individual substance contains all its properties.²⁰ The individual is a being which is completely determined. This is not to say that an individual may not appear undetermined to us. Leibniz recognizes that we may not be able to grasp the intrinsic nature or complete notion of a substance.

When Leibniz says that no two things differ only numerically, he means that they do not 'differ from one another in respect of place and time alone'.²¹ Leibniz accepts that the spatio-temporal position of things is in some cases a useful means for us to mark individuals off from one another; but like Stillingfleet and Sergeant he argues against Locke that we should distinguish between what constitutes individuality and distinctness in the thing itself and what serves as a mark or sign by which we discover the individuality and distinctness of things: 'In addition to the difference of time or of place there must always be an internal *principle of distinction*.'²² Thus, although

---

[18] Compare the discussion of Aquinas in the Introduction above.

[19] Leibniz, *Discours de métaphysique*, sect. 8.

[20] Sleigh distinguishes between what he calls 'superintrinsicalness' and 'superessentialism'. Superintrinsicalness is the thesis that 'every individual has all its properties intrinsically', and superessentialism is the doctrine 'that each individual substance has all its properties essentially' (necessarily): Sleigh, *Leibniz and Arnauld: A Commentary on Their Correspondence* (1990), pp. 51, 57. He argues that the former does not imply the latter, and that Leibniz is committed to superintrinsicalness, but rejects superessentialism (58, 67–72). Thus, the superessentialist account of the connection between the concept of Adam and the property of having posterity would be that 'necessarily, the complete individual concept of Adam includes the property of having posterity' (59–60). God could not have brought it about that Adam existed and yet lacked posterity. According to Sleigh, Leibniz holds that 'the complete individual concept of Adam includes the property of having posterity' is *contingent*; that is, dependent on the will of God. For a critical discussion of Sleigh, see Cover and O'Leary-Hawthorne (1999), pp. 128–31. For further discussion of the notion of 'complete concept', see Bella, *The Science of the Individual: Leibniz's Ontology of Individual Substance* (2005).

[21] Leibniz, *Opuscules*, p. 8; Leibniz, *Philosophical Writings*, ed. Parkinson (1934; reprinted, 1973), p. 133. Note that this formulation does not exclude place and time from the properties that individuate a substance. Indeed, elsewhere Leibniz states explicitly that the complete concept of an individual includes the 'individual circumstances of time, place, etc': Leibniz to Arnauld, *Philosophische Schriften*, vol. 2, p. 49; compare also ibid., p. 56. As Mugnai puts it, the circumstances of time and place are 'internalized' in the complete concept: Mugnai (2001), 54. At the same time, of course, place and time can function as the basis of *discerning* the differences between individuals. Thus, when Leibniz writes against Locke that 'time and place do not constitute the core of identity and diversity' (*Nouveaux essais*, II.xxvii.1), he is not saying that they play no role at all in individuation.

[22] *Nouveaux essais*, II.xxvii.1.

Leibniz himself refers to his principle as that of the identity of *indiscernibles*, which could suggest that he thinks of it as an epistemic principle,[23] he clearly keeps the metaphysical and epistemological issues separate. Locke's argument that for atoms spatio-temporal location must be postulated as the only 'principle of distinction' which holds in all cases, would not have impressed Leibniz. Rather, he employs the principle of the identity of indiscernibles as an argument against the atomist hypothesis itself. If atomism were true, Leibniz argues, then one would indeed have to accept that there are things which differ only numerically; but this cannot be accepted, because it would violate the principle of the identity of indiscernibles; and this principle must be valid, since it can be deduced *a priori* from the principle of sufficient reason. Leibniz points out in many places that the principle of the identity of indiscernibles 'overthrows the whole of purely corpuscularian philosophy'.[24] Against Locke he writes:

If there were atoms, i.e. perfectly hard and perfectly unalterable bodies which were incapable of internal change and could differ from one another only in size and shape, it is obvious that since they could have the same size and shape they would then be indistinguishable in themselves and discernible only by means of external denominations with no internal foundation; which is contrary to the greatest principles of reason.[25]

Leibniz argues that this mistaken assumption—that there are things which differ only numerically—brought about philosophers' 'perplexities about what they called the *principle of individuation*'.[26] For Leibniz there is no need to search for such a principle, since it can be demonstrated that nature simply never makes two things exactly alike. Every individual is individual by itself—that is, by its intrinsic nature. Things differ from each other by virtue of their individual essences.

So far, Leibniz's theory of individuation in terms of his principle of the identity of indiscernibles appears to be merely a more elaborate version of his early account of individuation in terms of the Suárezian notion of 'whole entity'. It seems merely to make explicit certain implications of the early Suárezian version of the theory. One difference between Leibniz's later theory and both his own early account of individuation and the Scholastic doctrines is the new emphasis on the essential relatedness of all individual substances to one another. Although each substance is 'independent of everything else apart from God',[27] he argues that every substance is related to all other substances: every substance mirrors the whole universe, 'expressing it in its own way, somewhat as the same town is variously represented according to the different

---

[23] Leibniz's *Fourth Paper* to Clarke: *Philosophische Schriften*, vol. 7, p. 372; Leibniz, *Leibniz-Clarke Correspondence*, p. 37.
[24] Leibniz, *Opuscules*, p. 8; Leibniz, *Philosophical Writings*, p. 133.
[25] *Nouveaux essais*, II.xxvii.3. For Leibniz's rejection of atomism, see also his letter to Arnauld of 30 April 1687: *Philosophische Schriften*, vol. 2, pp. 96–9; *The Leibniz–Arnauld Correspondence*, pp. 120–4.
[26] Leibniz's *Fifth Paper* to Clarke: *Philosophische Schriften*, vol. 7, p. 395; Leibniz, *Leibniz-Clarke Correspondence*, pp. 62–3.
[27] Leibniz, *Discours de métaphysique*, sect. 14.

positions of an observer'.²⁸ Each substance mirrors the whole universe from its own particular perspective. Leibniz emphasises the 'connexion or adaptation of all created things with each, and of each with all the rest'.²⁹ In *Nouveaux essais* he says (now in contrast to thinkers such as Sergeant and Stillingfleet): 'In metaphysical strictness there is no wholly extrinsic denomination, because of the real connections amongst all things.'³⁰ One could say that since it belongs to the intrinsic nature of the individual substance that it is essentially connected to all other substances, Leibniz's metaphysics of individuality is in terms of the interrelatedness of all things. We have seen that Spinoza, too, accounts for individuality in terms of the relationship of individuals to the totality of which they are part. In Spinoza, of course, those individuals are not substances. Nevertheless, despite all the differences in their metaphysical systems, the idea of the essential interconnectedness of all individuals is one which Leibniz's and Spinoza's accounts of individuality have in common.

Another difference between Leibniz's early and later theory is the latter's focus on the issue of identity through time which is not present in the 1663 account. As to this issue, he is concerned mainly with the special problem of personal identity (see the next section). It may seem that his principle of the identity of indiscernibles implies that a substance is identical with itself at different points of time only if it has exactly the same properties at those points of time. This would be such a strict notion of identity through time, however, that it would rule out change altogether—a problem that we encountered above in our discussion of Butler. Leibniz recognizes, of course, that things are subject to change. So, how can a substance, on Leibniz's principles, be said to remain identical through time and partial change? The answer is that within Leibniz's metaphysics, this is not a problem. Since the intrinsic nature or 'complete notion' of a substance contains all its actions and properties, it contains properties not only of the present, but also of the past and of the future. All the changes which a substance undergoes are necessarily part of its nature. Everything that will ever happen to any substance is contained all along in its intrinsic nature or complete notion: everything that will ever happen to a substance is predetermined. It follows that the identity of a substance through time is included in its complete notion: 'Everything occurs in every substance as a consequence of the first state which God bestowed upon it when he created it, and, extraordinary concourse excepted, his ordinary concourse consists only of preserving the substance itself in conformity with its preceding state and the changes that it bears.'³¹ Thus, each individual substance's

---

[28] Ibid., sect. 9.
[29] Leibniz, *Monadologie*, sect. 56.
[30] Leibniz, *Nouveaux essais*, II.xxv.5. See also *Nouveaux essais*, II.xxv.10: 'there is no term which is so absolute or so detached that it does not involve relations and is not such that a complete analysis of it would lead to other things and indeed to all other things'. McCullough has argued that according to Leibniz, only relations as universals or concepts of the mind are ideal; universals or concepts of the mind are founded in the properties of substances. And these properties are 'one and all relational': McCullough (1978), esp. 37–8; see also McCullough (1996), pp. 172–6. For a somewhat different account, see Mugnai (2001), 47–9.
[31] Letter to Arnauld, 30 April 1687: *Philosophische Schriften*, vol. 2, pp. 91–2; *The Leibniz–Arnauld Correspondence*, p. 115.

identity over time is guaranteed *a priori*, because the substance's different states at different points of time are, by definition, nothing but states of one and the same unfolding individual nature. Leibniz again emphasises that this *a priori* ground of identity must not be confused with our *a posteriori* ways of discovering this identity. In the case of human souls, inner experience can provide *a posteriori* evidence for identity.[32]

Leibniz later develops this doctrine of the 'complete notion' of a substance into his theory of monads (from *c.*1695 onwards). This theory constitutes a third important difference between his later and his early account of individuality. According to the theory of monads, what makes something remain numerically the same individual is 'an enduring principle of life which I call "monad"'.[33] Monads are immaterial, simple, indivisible 'atoms of substance'—soul-like beings. Human souls are merely a special kind of monad; in fact, all things are in the last result composed of monads: 'The monad... is nothing but a simple substance which enters into compounds.'[34] Leibniz regards monads as the only true substances—the 'sources of action' and the principles or 'forms' of genuine unity and identity.[35] As he writes in the *Système nouveau*:

> I perceived that it is impossible to find *the principles of a true unity* in matter alone... since everything in it is but a collection or accumulation of parts *ad infinitum*. Now a multiplicity can be real only if it is made up of *true unities* which come from elsewhere and are altogether different from mathematical points... Therefore, to find these *real unities*, I was constrained to have recourse to what might be called a *real* or *animated point* or to an atom of substance which must embrace some element of form or of activity in order to make a complete being... I found then that their nature consists of force and that from this there follows something analogous to feeling and to appetite; and that therefore it was necessary to form a conception of them resembling our ordinary notion of *souls*... I saw that... these souls must be indivisible like our mind.[36]

---

[32] See Leibniz's 'Remarques sur la Lettre de M. Arnaud': *Philosophische Schriften*, vol. 2, p. 43; *The Leibniz–Arnauld Correspondence*, pp. 46–7. For further discussion of Leibniz's notion of individual substance, see Hacking, 'Individual Substance', in Frankfurt (ed.), *Leibniz: A Collection of Critical Essays* (1972), pp. 137–53; Woolhouse, 'The Nature of an Individual Substance', in Hooker (ed.), *Leibniz: Critical and Interpretive Essays* (1982), pp. 45–64; Mates, *The Philosophy of Leibniz: Metaphysics and Language* (1986), pp. 138–44; Wilson, *Leibniz's Metaphysics: A Historical and Comparative Study* (1989), pp. 88–98; Brown, *Leibniz and Strawson: A New Essay in Descriptive Metaphysics* (1990), chap. 2; Bartha (1993), 43–54; Cover and O'Leary-Hawthorne (1999); McCullough (1996); di Bella (2005).

[33] Leibniz, *Nouveaux essais*, II.xxvii.4.

[34] Leibniz, *Monadologie*, sect. 1.

[35] There is a debate over the question of whether Leibniz is a 'realist' or an 'idealist', or holds a position that is compatible with aspects of both those readings. On the idealist reading, Leibniz holds that only minds and ideas exist and that the world of matter is mere appearance; the realist interpretation says that for Leibniz there is a real world of animals and material aggregates. Whatever the correct label may be, it is clear that for Leibniz even if all monads are essentially linked to body, monads themselves are not part of matter. See also the comment on Garber in the footnote below. For detailed discussions of these issues, see Phemister, *Leibniz and the Natural World: Activity, Passivity and Coporeal Substances in Leibniz's Philosophy* (2005); Hartz, *Leibniz's Final System: Monads, Matter and Animals* (2007).

[36] *Philosophische Schriften*, vol. 4, pp. 478–9; Leibniz, *Philosophical Writings*, pp. 116–17.

Monads constitute the real or objective identity of any being: there is only one single 'principle' which constitutes real identity in plants, animals, and human beings alike: the 'indivisible spirit' that 'animates them'.[37] Without being united to a true substance or soul or monad, organic bodies would only have 'apparent identity'; an organic body can be said to be genuinely identical only if we assume that it is united to a monad.[38] Leibniz distinguishes sharply between this genuine identity and what he calls 'accidental unity' or 'apparent identity'. This distinction is also present in writings of the mid-1680s—that is, prior to the theory of monads.[39] In the correspondence with Arnauld (1686–88), Leibniz argues that genuine unity and identity are due to mind-like substances, whereas artefacts and other 'entities through aggregation', such as a society, are unified entities only in the sense that they are 'entities of reason'.[40] For example, we conceive of a society 'as a single thing' because there are 'connexions between the constituents'. These unities 'are made complete only by thoughts and appearances', however.[41] They are not unified by an intrinsic principle of unity. Thus:

> a marble tile is not a single complete substance, no more than would be the water in a pool with all the fish included, even if all the water with all these fish were frozen; or a flock of sheep, even though these sheep should be bound together to such an extent that they could walk only at the same pace and that one could not be touched without all the others crying out. There is as much difference between a substance and such an entity as there is between a man and a community, such as a people, army, society or college, which are moral entities, where something imaginary exists, dependent on the fabrication of our minds.[42]

---

[37] Leibniz, *Nouveaux essais*, II.xxvii.4.

[38] Leibniz, *Nouveaux essais*, II.xxvii.4–6.

[39] Garber argues that in the *Discours de métaphysique* (1686) and in the correspondence with Arnauld, Leibniz's notion of the unities that constitute the real entities of the physical world differs from that of his later theory of monads: Garber, 'Leibniz and the Foundations of Physics: The Middle Years', in Okruhlik and Brown (eds.), *The Natural Philosophy of Leibniz* (1985), pp. 27–130; see also Garber, 'Soul and Mind: Life and Thought in the Seventeenth Century', in Garber and Ayers (eds.), *The Cambridge History of Seventeenth-Century Philosophy* (1998), pp. 759–95. According to the theory of monads, bodies are aggregates of monads (incorporeal substances); but in the correspondence with Arnauld, for example, Leibniz's view is that *corporeal* substances are the real entities of the physical world. And corporeal substances are to be understood 'in analogy to human beings, a mind or something mindlike (a substantial form), connected with a body': Garber (1985), 35. These unities are the ultimate building blocks that ground bodies, not the incorporeal substances themselves. As Garber concedes, however, the individuality and identity of these corporeal substances are said by Leibniz to be constituted by the mind-like component. As Garber says: 'This principle of individuation seems to be an extension of what might be considered a simple-minded Cartesian principle of individuation for persons (same mind, same person) to the wider domain of corporeal substances, soul-like entities united to bodies' (58–9).

[40] Letter to Arnauld, 30 April 1687: *Philosophische Schriften*, vol. 2, pp. 96–7; *The Leibniz–Arnauld Correspondence*, p. 121.

[41] Letter to Arnauld, 30 April 1687: *Philosophische Schriften*, vol. 2, pp. 100–1; *The Leibniz–Arnauld Correspondence*, p. 126.

[42] Letter to Arnauld, 28 November/8 December 1686: *Philosophische Schriften*, vol. 2, p. 76; *The Leibniz–Arnauld Correspondence*, p. 94. See also Letter to Arnauld, 30 April 1687: *Philosophische Schriften*, vol. 2, p. 101; *The Leibniz–Arnauld Correspondence*, p. 126.

Leibniz emphasises that even these 'entities through aggregation', such as artefacts and a society, presuppose genuine units or mind-like substances; for

what constitutes the essence of an entity through aggregation is only a state of being of its constituent entities; for example, what constitutes the essence of an army is only a state of being of the constituent men. This state of being therefore presupposes a substance whose essence is not a state of being of another substance.

The multiplicity that is involved in an aggregate presupposes genuine units which make up the aggregate: 'The plural presupposes the singular, and where there is no entity, still less will there be many entities.'[43] Unlike his early dissertation on the principle of individuation, Leibniz's mature metaphysics holds that individuality is due to a soul-like immaterial being.[44]

It is not surprising that Leibniz barely mentions Locke's thesis that our sortal concepts provide criteria of numerical identity through time. Within Leibniz's metaphysics of identity there is no room for a discussion of this thesis, and Leibniz dismisses it as being merely about 'the signification of words', saying that what is at issue is the real ground of identity.[45] Leibniz's view that individuality requires complete determination and individual essence is reminiscent of the realist Scholastic notion of the individual form or 'haecceitas'. As is the case with his early account, however, Leibniz's mature theory is much closer to a Suárezian or nominalist theory about individuation than it is to Scotist and Thomist versions of realism. The late as well as the early Leibniz rejects the view that individuals emerge from real universals (or natural kinds) through a process of specification and individuation. According to both the early and the late Leibniz, individuals are individuals by themselves. The individuality of substances is given immediately with their being. As he points out to Arnauld: 'What is not truly *one* entity is not truly one *entity* either.'[46]

9.2. LEIBNIZ ON PERSONAL IDENTITY

We have noted that Leibniz's later theory focuses on the issue of identity through time—a focus which is not present in the 1663 account—and that here he seems to be concerned mainly with the problem of personal identity. As indicated above, there are some similarities between Leibniz's and Locke's accounts of self-identity. For

---

[43] Letter to Arnauld, 30 April 1687: *Philosophische Schriften*, vol. 2, p. 97; *The Leibniz–Arnauld Correspondence*, p. 121, last two quotes.
[44] For a detailed discussion of Leibniz on aggregates, see Hartz (2007).
[45] Leibniz, *Nouveaux essais*, II.xxvii.28–9.
[46] Letter to Arnauld, 30 April 1687: *Philosophische Schriften*, vol. 2, p. 97; *The Leibniz–Arnauld Correspondence*, p. 121. For different accounts of the relationship between Leibniz's early and mature theories of individuation, see McCullough, 'Leibniz on Individuals and Individuation: How the Mature Philosophy Resolves Problems of the Earliest Philosophy', in Heinekamp (ed.), *Leibniz. Tradition und Aktualität. V. Internationaler Leibniz-Kongress. Vorträge* (1988); McCullough (1996), pp. 133–55; di Bella (2005).

example, Leibniz too distinguishes between substantial and personal identity. In the last analysis, however, the differences between Leibniz and Locke on this issue are more significant than the similarities.

Although in many places Leibniz emphasises that on his view the soul is never without a body,[47] it is clear that he regards the soul as the real self. And for him, human souls are, like all monads, immaterial substances.[48] Unlike other monads, they have rationality and the ability to attain knowledge of moral truths and of their own essence. Their identity over time is, however, just like that of other substances, secured by their intrinsic nature or 'complete notion'. Leibniz maintains that everything that is to happen to the self 'is already included virtually in his nature or notion, just as the properties of a circle are included in its definition'.[49] Thus, 'there is in the soul of Alexander for all time traces of everything that happened to him, and marks of everything that will happen to him'.[50] And this is what distinguishes his soul from all others and guarantees its identity through time. In *Nouveaux essais* Leibniz explains this interrelation of 'marks' and 'traces' that constitutes identity in terms of his doctrine of 'minute perceptions'—that is, unconscious states of the soul: 'These insensible perceptions also indicate and constitute the same individual, who is characterized by the vestiges or expressions which the perceptions preserve from the individual's former states, thereby connecting these with his present state.'[51] It follows that for Leibniz the identity of the self, as soul, does not require that we are conscious of those 'traces' or 'perceptions' and their interconnection.[52] He consistently treats the problem of self-identity in the same way as he treats identity in general, distinguishing between the *a priori* ground of self-identity and the *a posteriori* criteria for discovering self-identity: the *a priori* ground of my identity lies 'in the complete concept of me which makes what is called myself, which is the basis of the connexion between all my different states and of which God had perfect knowledge from all eternity'.[53] Consciousness or 'my subjective experience' merely convinces me '*a posteriori* of this identity'.[54] The real identity—the identity of the soul—is constituted independently of consciousness. Consequently, Leibniz points out against Locke that consciousness of past states of the mind merely makes 'the real identity appear'.[55]

This point can be illustrated by Leibniz's objection to Locke's theory which is based on a 'duplicate-world' thought experiment (*Nouveaux essais*, II.xxvii.23). Suppose there is a world 'in another region of the universe' which is 'in no way sensibly different from this sphere of earth on which we live, and inhabited by men each of

[47] See, for example, Leibniz, *Nouveaux essais*, Preface: *Philosophische Schriften*, vol. 5, p. 50; Leibniz, *New Essays on Human Understanding* (1981), p. 58.
[48] For the last two points see *Nouveaux essais*, II.xxvii.14.
[49] Leibniz, *Discours de métaphysique*, sect. 13.
[50] Ibid., sect. 8.
[51] Leibniz, *Nouveaux essais*, Preface: *Philosophische Schriften*, vol. 5, p. 48; Leibniz, *New Essays*, p. 55.
[52] Compare *Nouveaux essais*, II.xxvii.14.
[53] 'Remarques sur la Lettre de M. Arnaud': *Philosophische Schriften*, vol. 2, p. 43; *The Leibniz–Arnauld Correspondence*, p. 47.
[54] Ibid., p. 46.
[55] *Nouveaux essais*, II.xxvii.14.

whom differs sensibly in no way from his counterpart among us'. On Leibniz's general theory of identity there must be a difference between originals and duplicates 'in their insensible constitutions', in addition to their numerical difference. He holds that if we accept Locke's theory we cannot distinguish between the original person and a duplicate-person, since the thought experiment supposes that their states of consciousness are not distinguishable. Thus, Locke's theory would have the absurd consequence that original and duplicate are one and the same person.

Like Locke, however, Leibniz seems to ascribe to consciousness a constitutive function after all, for he says that consciousness constitutes the identity of the human subject as *person*. And by 'person' he means the self as a moral entity: as persons we are members of the 'moral world or City of God, the most noble part of the universe'.[56] Not unlike Locke, so it seems, Leibniz bases moral or personal identity on consciousness, for he argues that human subjects retain their personality or moral quality through a 'recollection, consciousness or power to know what they are, upon which depends the whole of their morality, penalties and punishments'.[57] Leibniz distinguishes, then, between the metaphysical identity of the self (as immaterial substance) and the moral identity of the self (as person) which is constituted by consciousness: 'The intelligent soul that knows what it is, and is capable of pronouncing this *me* which says so much, not only remains the same metaphysically... but it also remains morally the same and constitutes the same personality. For it is the memory and knowledge of this *me* that makes it liable to punishment and reward.'[58]

Also, Leibniz links the notion of consciousness-based personality to that of life after death. Like Cudworth and Locke, he argues against the view that the future life is merely a state of 'perpetual subsistence'.[59] The future life requires personal as well as substantial identity; that is, it requires that 'the soul possesses consciousness or is familiar in itself with what every man calls "my self". This renders it susceptible of moral qualities, and of reward and punishment... immortality without memory would be useless'.[60] In the writings prior to *Nouveaux essais* Leibniz holds that substantial identity is always and necessarily accompanied by personal identity; that is, we always and necessarily retain a memory of our past actions.[61] He seems

---

[56] Leibniz, *Discours de métaphysique*, sect. 36.
[57] Letter to Arnauld, 9 October 1687: *Philosophische Schriften*, vol. 2, p. 125; *The Leibniz–Arnauld Correspondence*, p. 160. This notion of a person as moral quality is reminiscent of Valla's notion of *persona*. Leibniz explicitly refers to Valla's treatment of *persona*, in Leibniz, *Textes inédits d'après les manuscrits de la bibliothèque provinciale de Hanovre*, ed. Grua (1948), vol. 2, pp. 558–9.
[58] Leibniz, *Discours de métaphysique*, sect. 34. See also *Nouveaux essais*, II.xxvii.9. On the distinction between moral and metaphysical identity in Leibniz, see also Scheffler, 'Leibniz on Personal Identity and Moral Personality', *Studia Leibnitiana*, 8 (1976), 219–40; and Wilson, 'Leibniz: Self-Consciousness and Immortality in the Paris Notes and After', *Archiv für Geschichte der Philosophie*, 58 (1976), 335–52.
[59] Leibniz, *Discours de métaphysique*, sect. 34.
[60] Letter to Arnauld, 4/14 July 1686: *Philosophische Schriften*, vol. 2, p. 57; *The Leibniz–Arnauld Correspondence*, p. 64.
[61] For a detailed discussion of the relationship between Leibniz's early and later writings on this issue, see Wilson (1976).

simply to assume that our memory will not fail us, because if it did there would be no personal identity and no just divine judgement. He says that human souls or minds '*must* keep their personality and their moral qualities in order that the city of God lose no one', and that it is '*necessary* that they be free from those upheavals in the universe which would make them totally unrecognizable to themselves, and would turn them, morally speaking, into another person'.[62] According to Leibniz, then, consciousness or inner experience constitutes personal identity *a posteriori*; but *that* consciousness does so and that it always *correctly* ascribes past actions to the self is a necessity. Leibniz does not seem to be disturbed by the common fact of forgetfulness and by cases of amnesia. Even in the preface to *Nouveaux essais* he says of human souls that they 'are *destined* always to preserve the *persona* [*le personnage*] which they have been given in the city of God, and hence to retain their memories, so that they may be more susceptible of punishments and rewards'.[63] In the chapter on identity in *Nouveaux essais*, however, he does take into account issues such as amnesia and incorrect memory, arguing that these issues do not affect what he calls immediate memory or consciousness; that is, consciousness of immediately preceding states: 'The consciousness or reflection which accompanies inner activity ... cannot naturally deceive us.'[64] And he indicates that this immediate connection between conscious states is all that is required for personal identity: 'To discover one's own moral identity unaided, it is sufficient that between one state and a neighbouring ... one there be a mediating bond of consciousness.'[65] Just as substantial or 'real' identity is secured by the 'liaison' of minute perceptions, Leibniz seems to suggest, personal identity is preserved by the 'liaison' of immediate memories from one moment to the next. Here he appears to adopt a connected consciousness view of personal or moral identity. As we have seen in previous Chapters, this is a view that is present in Locke and Collins—although in Locke, memory also plays a crucial role.

Leibniz recognizes, however, that 'we can be deceived by a memory across an interval'.[66] And his discussion of the issue of amnesia shows that his theory differs markedly from Locke's account of personal identity. For here he argues that consciousness is not necessary for personal identity: the identity of the self as person can also be established by the testimony of others. Leibniz explicitly rejects Locke's idea that moral or personal identity is based solely on inner consciousness:

> Thus, if an illness had interrupted the continuity of my bond of consciousness, so that I did not know how I had arrived at my present state even though I could remember things further back, the testimony of others could fill in the gap in my recollection. I could even be punished on this testimony if I had done some deliberate wrong during an interval which this illness had made me forget a short time later. And if I forgot my whole past, and needed to have myself

---

[62] Letter to Arnauld, 9 October 1687: *Philosophische Schriften*, vol. 2, p. 125; *The Leibniz–Arnauld Correspondence*, p. 160 (my italics).
[63] Leibniz, *Nouveaux essais*, Preface: *Philosophische Schriften*, vol. 5, p. 51; Leibniz, *New Essays*, p. 58 (first italics mine).
[64] Leibniz, *Nouveaux essais*, II.xxvii.13.
[65] Leibniz, *Nouveaux essais*, II.xxvii.9.
[66] Leibniz, *Nouveaux essais*, II.xxvii.13.

taught all over again, even my name and how to read and write, I could still learn from others about my life during my preceding state; and, similarly, I would have retained my rights without having to be divided into two persons and made to inherit from myself. All this is enough to maintain the moral identity which makes the same person.[67]

These remarks are quite consistent, however, with his statement, in the same section, that consciousness does constitute moral or personal identity. For he does not say *tout court* that consciousness establishes personal identity; he says that consciousness does so 'when accompanied by truth'; that is, when the self-ascription of actions through consciousness is a correct, truthful ascription of actions.[68] He realizes, of course, that the testimony of others is not an absolutely reliable basis for action-ascription either, as there may be cases where others conspire to deceive me so that the external evidence turns out to be just as false as the internal evidence of consciousness might turn out to be. Leibniz finally resorts to God: for 'in relation to God, whose social bond with us is the cardinal point of morality, error cannot occur'.[69] He rejects, however, Locke's idea that the divine judgement is just because we shall have a purified consciousness which is free from error. Even human courts of law do not have to rely on the evidence of a person's consciousness, and may refer to the evidence of eyewitnesses to establish the personal identity of the accused. The omniscient God does not have to rely on either individual consciousness or on the testimony of others, for the knowledge 'of that just Judge who is never deceived' is sufficient on its own.[70] The truth about action-ascription lies in the intrinsic nature or 'complete notion' of the human subject as substance which is known to God.

Here lies the most fundamental difference between Leibniz and Locke. For Locke it is a real possibility that there be personal identity without substantial identity, or in Leibniz's terminology, 'that this apparent identity could be preserved in the absence of any real identity'.[71] To Leibniz, however, this would 'disrupt the order of things for no reason, and would divorce what can become before our awareness from the truth—the truth which is preserved by insensible perceptions'.[72] According to the 'order of things', Leibniz argues, real identity must be presupposed by apparent identity. Thus, although he does not equate personal with substantial identity, he holds that the former depends on the latter. Whereas Locke argues for keeping personal and substantial identity separate, Leibniz maintains what is

---

[67] Leibniz, *Nouveaux essais*, II.xxvii.9.
[68] Vailati, too, emphasises the importance of the phrase 'when accompanied by truth' in this context: Vailati, 'Leibniz's Theory of Personal Identity in the New Essays', *Studia Leibnitiana*, 17 (1985), 41–3.
[69] Leibniz, *Nouveaux essais*, II.xxvii.9.
[70] Leibniz, *Nouveaux essais*, II.xxvii.22.
[71] Leibniz, *Nouveaux essais*, II.xxvii.9.
[72] Leibniz, *Nouveaux essais*, II.xxvii.18. For different accounts of the relationship between Leibniz's and Locke's theories of personal identity, see Curley, 'Leibniz on Locke on Personal Identity', in Hooker (1982), pp. 302–26; Jolley, *Leibniz and Locke: A Study of the New Essays On Human Understanding* (1984); and Wilson (1989), pp. 232–49. Book-length treatments of Leibniz's account of individuation, such as those by McCullough and Cover and O'Leary-Hawthorne cited above, do not address the special issue of personal identity.

assumed by the Cartesians: namely, that the (personal) identity required for morality can be preserved only by the metaphysical identity of the self as immaterial soul.

One could raise a number of questions in relation to points of detail in Leibniz's account. Some have been raised along the way in the analysis above. One issue that relates to his theory as a whole, and has been debated in recent decades, is the question of whether Leibniz's theory of personal identity is incoherent.[73] Thus, Margaret Wilson has claimed that Leibniz holds both (1) 'I am a particular immaterial substance', and (2) 'It is [logically or] metaphysically possible that I continue as an identical self-consciousness and identical self, independently of this particular substance', arguing that there is a *prima facie* incoherence in the conjunction of (1) and (2) (Wilson, 1976, 346). 'How can it be, from a logical or metaphysical point of view, that I cease to be the substance I am now identical with, and yet continue to exist?'(ibid., 347). As should be obvious from the account given above, on our reading of Leibniz there is no such inconsistency. It is true that the conjunction of (1) and (2) is incoherent, but Leibniz does not hold both (1) and (2): he subscribes to (1) but not to (2). For Leibniz, personal identity cannot be retained if there is no metaphysical or 'real' identity. If he did accept the possibility of personal identity without metaphysical identity, his account would collapse into Lockean theory; but there is no reason to believe that Leibniz is committed to this, let alone that he explicitly subscribes to it.[74]

It may be argued that although Leibniz can be rescued from the charge of inconsistency, his problem is that he subscribes to (1) at all. We have noted above that for Leibniz, finite monads do not exist apart from a body, but also that he is committed to the existence of immaterial mental substances that constitute the real or essential self in human beings. Unlike Locke, he is committed to the view that there is an immaterial core of the self which provides the basis for personal identity to be possible at all.[75] Obviously it can be argued that the notion of an immaterial mental substance is a deeply problematic notion on which to base an account of human personal identity, and that in this respect at least, Leibniz's account is no better off than traditional Cartesian views of the self. In the seventeenth and eighteenth centuries, however, the notion of an immaterial soul was of course a very common starting point for any treatment of the self, and this commitment to the soul as immaterial substance is

---

[73] The relevant literature includes the following: Wilson (1976), esp. 346–7; Scheffler (1976); Jolley (1984), esp. pp. 136–9; Vailati (1985), 36–43; Mates (1986), p. 145; Curley (1982); Bobro, 'Is Leibniz's Theory of Personal Identity Coherent?', *The Leibniz Review*, 9 (1999), 117–29; and Bobro, *Self and Substance in Leibniz* (2004), pp. 39–59.

[74] Bobro has analysed the debate about this issue in some detail, so there is no need to rehearse all the pros and cons here. He too argues against the ascription of (2) to Leibniz: 'Leibniz never countenances the logical possibility of an individual retaining personal identity over time while undergoing change in substantial identity': Bobro (1999), 126; Bobro (2004), p. 55.

[75] In his examination of the metaphysical presuppositions of Leibniz's account of man or human being, Leinkauf has documented in detail that the notion of an immaterial, spiritual substance is one of these presuppositions. For Leibniz, 'the unity of the substance or monad is the ontological root of being human' ('Diese... Einheit der Substanz oder Monade ist die *ontologische* Wurzel des Mensch-Seins'). See Leinkauf, 'Substanz, Individuum und Person. Anthropologie und ihre metaphysischen und geisttheoretischen Voraussetzungen im Werk von Leibniz', *Internationale Zeitschrift für Philosophie*, 1 (1999), 24–45, at 33.

Individuation and identity, apperception and consciousness   295

something that he has in common with all other philosophers that are dealt with in this and the two previous Chapters. That commitment is, indeed, what unites the thinkers discussed in these Chapters, however they may differ in other respects.

9.3. PROBLEMS WITH LEIBNIZ: APPERCEPTION AND CONSCIOUSNESS

Even accepting the commitment to a notion of the soul as a simple, immaterial substance or monad as a basis for Leibniz's account, however, there is another issue that affects his account of personal (rather than metaphysical) identity as a whole. This has to do with the notion of consciousness that he employs when he accounts for personal identity as distinct from metaphysical identity. We have seen that for Leibniz, consciousness is not the only means by which personal or moral identity can be established. Nevertheless, he does say that 'consciousness or the sense of *I* proves moral or personal identity' (*Nouveaux essais*, II.xxvii.9). But what is meant by consciousness here? In *Nouveaux essais* Leibniz employs several terms for consciousness (French 'conscience', 'consciosité', 'conscienciosité'). He also makes use of other notions that concern a relating to one's own self in this context: 'the sense of *I*' ('le sentiment du *moy*') in the passage just quoted, 'reflection' (ibid.), 'consciousness or reflection' (ibid., II.xxvii.13), 'immediate memory' (ibid.), and 'apperception' (ibid., II.xxvii.14). What is meant by these various notions? Do they refer to the same or different ways of relating to one's own self, and, if the latter, how are they related to one another? As the notion of personal or moral identity includes the notion of relating to one's own self, Leibniz would need a clear account of the ways in which one can relate to one's own self. We have seen that Locke's notion of consciousness is that of an immediate relating to thoughts and actions, and that he distinguishes consciousness from other types of relating to one's own self such as reflection and memory, for example. What is Leibniz's understanding of relating to one's own self? We shall begin with an examination of the famous and immensely influential notion of apperception that Leibniz introduces into the philosophical terminology.

Leibniz first introduces the term 'l'apperception' in *Nouveaux essais*. There is, however, no agreement among commentators as to how Leibniz's notion of apperception should be understood. Some passages clearly suggest that Leibniz uses 'l'apperception' synonymously with consciousness ('la conscience'). For example, in a famous passage from section four of *Principes de la nature et de la grâce, fondés en raison* (1714) he defines 'perception' and 'apperception' as follows:

It is well to distinguish between *perception,* which is the inner state of the monad representing external things, and *apperception,* which is *consciousness* ['conscience'], or the reflective knowledge of this inner state, and which is not given to all souls, nor at all times to the same soul.[76]

---

[76] Leibniz, *Principes de la nature et de la grâce, fondés en raison,* § 4, in *Philosophische Schriften,* vol. 6, pp. 598–606, at p. 600. The translation is by Morris and Parkinson, in *Leibniz: Philosophical Writings* (1934/1973), p. 197.

Similarly, in the *Monadologie* (also 1714) Leibniz states: 'The passing state, which involves and represents a plurality within the unity or simple substance, is nothing other than what is called *perception*, which must be carefully distinguished from apperception or consciousness ('la conscience').'[77] These passages suggest a higher-order understanding of consciousness. In order to be conscious of this table in front of me, it is required that I have a perception of the table as well as a second-order mental state that relates to that perception. Consciousness is not an element of all perceptions as such. A mind that perceives a table represents that table, but this representation does not necessarily involve consciousness. Further evidence for a higher-order reading of Leibnizian consciousness is provided by the connection in the quotation above between consciousness and 'reflective knowledge'. In *Nouveaux essais*, too, Leibniz links consciousness to reflection when he speaks of 'the consciousness or reflection which accompanies inner activity'.[78]

In these passages, 'l'apperception' is explained in terms of 'la conscience'; and 'la conscience' is understood as 'knowledge' of inner states or perceptions and 'inner activity';[79] and this in turn is accounted for in terms of reflection or 'reflective knowledge'. Next, he explains consciousness, apperception, and reflection in the same way: through the notion of attention ('l'attention', 'prendre garde'). Attention turns what Leibniz calls 'insensible' or 'minute' perceptions into apperceived ones.[80] He also suggests that apperception or consciousness relates to the past only, and thus involves a form of memory. He states that 'the consciousness or reflection which accompanies inner activity' is immediate memory or 'the memory of what was taking place immediately before'.[81]

---

[77] The French original reads: 'L'état passager qui enveloppe et represente une multitude dans l'unité, ou dans la substance simple, n'est autre chose que ce qu'on appelle la PERCEPTION, qu'on doit distinguer de l'appreception ou de la conscience': *Monadologie*, sect. 14, in *Principes de la nature et de la grâce, fondés en raison. Principes de la philosophie ou Monadologie*, ed. Robinet (1954). The translation is from Morris and Parkinson (1934/1973).
[78] 'la conscience ou la reflexion, qui accompagne l'action interne': *Nouveaux essais*, II.xxvii.13.
[79] Gennaro holds that Leibniz does not equate apperception with consciousness, and believes that for Leibniz there are 'unconscious apperceptions'. The latter would include (unconscious) second-order thoughts directed at first-order thoughts. See Gennaro, 'Leibniz on Consciousness and Self-Consciousness', in Gennaro and Huenemann (eds.), *New Essays on the Rationalists* (1999), pp. 353–71, at pp. 354, 356. Gennaro appeals to Rescher for this reading. See Rescher, *Leibniz: An Introduction to his Philosophy* (1979), p. 127. While it may well be true in principle that higher-order thoughts or perceptions need not be conscious, the question is, where does *Leibniz* speak of 'minute' or 'unconscious' apperception? The infinite regress passage to which Gennaro refers here (*Nouveaux essais*, II.i.19, quoted below) does not make use of, or appeal to, such a notion. It is plain that any interpretation of this passage needs to take into account the Lockean context. Leibniz argues against Locke's view that perceptions are essentially conscious, and assumes—wrongly—that Locke, in making this claim, applies a higher-order understanding of consciousness.
[80] Leibniz, *Nouveaux essais*, Preface: *Philosophische Schriften*, vol. 5, p. 47; Robinet and Schepers (1962), p. 53. On this point see McRae, *Leibniz: Perception, Apperception and Thought* (1976), p. 35. McRae draws attention to a passage from the preface to *Nouveaux essais* in which Leibniz says that 'la reflexion n'est autre chose qu'une attention à ce qui est en nous': Preface, *Philosophische Schriften*, vol. 5, p. 45; Robinet and Schepers (1962), p. 51.
[81] 'Le souvenir present ou immediat, ou le souvenir de ce qui se passoit immediatement auparavant c'est à dire la conscience ou la reflexion qui accompagne l'action interne, ne sauroit tromper naturellement': *Nouveaux Essais*, II.xxvii.13. Compare also the following passages.

Further, some passages suggest that apperception can denote *self*-consciousness. This seems to be the case particularly in Leibniz's discussion of personal identity. It is the consciousness of self, rather than (as Locke would have it) just the consciousness of thoughts and actions that constitutes moral or personal identity. As indicated above, Leibniz speaks of the 'consciousness or the sense of I' (*Nouveaux essais*, II. xxvii.9) in this context. And when dealing explicitly with the knowledge of the existence of one's own self, he accounts for it in terms of apperception (*Nouveaux essais*, IV.ix.2). He does not, however, seem to distinguish explicitly between the consciousness of perceptions and the consciousness of self.[82] Possibly he assumes that the latter is entailed by the former, but in *Nouveaux essais* he states that the apperception of one's own existence is 'immediate' in the sense that in this case 'nothing comes between the understanding and its object' (ibid.). Unlike Locke, Leibniz also holds that apperception or reflection reaches not only mental operations but also the nature of the self as a simple, spiritual substance.[83] Some commentators even maintain that apperception in Leibniz just *is* a form of self-consciousness—rather than a relating to perceptions. These interpretations are aided by the fact that their proponents simply translate Leibniz's 'l'aperception' and 'la conscience' as self-consciousness.[84] The texts cited above, however, do not allow for a simple identification of consciousness or apperception with self-consciousness.

'Conscientia est nostrarum actionum memoria': *Textes inédits* (1948), vol. 1, p. 181. 'Conscientia est reflexio in actionem, seu memoria actionis nostrae ita ut cogitemus nostram esse': *Opuscules*, p. 495. Memory is, clearly, a second-order mental act. It is a 'perception of one's own perceptions' as Leibniz states in an early note: *Definitiones Cogitationesque Metaphysicae* (*Sämtliche Schriften*, A VI.4, p. 1394). It should be noted, however, that 'mémoire' and 'souvenir' are not identical in Leibniz. For a detailed study of Leibniz's various notions of memory, see the classic study by Naert, *Mémoire et conscience de soi selon Leibniz* (1961), esp. pp. 51ff. In some passages Leibniz distinguishes explicity between memory (mémoire) as the storage of earlier perceptions and the act of recollecting (reminiscence) prior perceptions (*Nouveaux essais*, I.i.5). Elsewhere he speaks of the 'memory or knowledge of this I' (*Discours de métaphysique*, sect. 34), thus linking memory to self-knowledge. It is not clear, however, if the quoted passage from *Nouveaux essais*, II.xxvii.13, is meant to say that self-knowledge is required by immediate memory (souvenir).

[82] Commentators have, of course, distinguished between different types of apperception and then ascribed such distinctions to Leibniz. Thus, Gennaro distinguishes not only between unconscious and conscious perceptions but also between three types of self-consciousness, all of which he also finds in Leibniz. He concedes, however, that Leibniz is not always 'very clear' about which type of apperception he has in mind. See Gennaro (1999), pp. 359–60.

[83] 'Cette reflexion ne se borne pas aux seules operations de l'esprit... elle va jusqu'à l'esprit luy même, et c'est en s'appercevant de luy, que nous nous appercevons de la substance': *Echantillon de reflexions sur le II. livre* (of Locke's *Essay*), in *Sämtliche Schriften*, VI.6, p. 14. See also *Principes de la nature et de la grâce*, ed. Robinet, sect. 5, p. 41. Elsewhere Leibniz claims that the fact that we have an idea of substance 'comes from the fact that we, who are substances, have an internal sense of it in ourselves': *Philosophische Schriften*, vol. 3, p. 247. See also Leibniz, *Nouveaux essais*: 'It is my opinion that reflection enables us to find the idea of substance within ourselves, who are substances' ('Je suis d'opinion que la reflexion suffit pour trouver l'idée de la substance en nous mêmes, qui sommes des substances': *Nouveaux essais*, I.iii.18.

[84] Rescher (1979), p. 119; Cramer, 'Einfachheit, Perzeption und Apperzeption. Überlegungen zu Leibniz' Theorie der Substanz als Subjekt', in Cristin (ed.), *Leibniz und die Frage nach der Subjektivität* (*Studia Leibnitiana Sonderheft*, 22) (1994), pp. 19–45, at p. 34. Cramer accepts that for Leibniz apperception is an 'epistemic act' that is distinct from mere perception (p. 34). He

Rather, the texts indicate that for Leibniz the relation to oneself via apperception (or consciousness) is, like reflection, a higher-order mental act, 'actio in se ipsum'— an act that may relate to perceptions as well as to the subject who has those perceptions.[85] This does not mean that he would equate consciousness or apperception with reflection *simpliciter*.[86] Some forms of reflection involve reason and the knowledge of necessary truths. But although Leibniz may not use 'reflection' in precisely the same sense in all contexts, he assumes that 'consciousness', 'reflection', and 'apperception' are terms that stand for essentially the same type of relating to one's own self in the sense that they all denote higher-order mental acts.[87] We have seen that for Locke, consciousness is a type of intuition and an essential quality of thought itself, and as such is to be distinguished from what he calls 'reflection' or inner sense. For Locke, reflection, but not consciousness, is a higher-order mental act. Leibniz does not seem even to consider the notion of consciousness as an essential quality of thought itself. This is obvious from his critique of Locke in *Nouveaux essais* (II.i.19)—referred to briefly above, in the chapter on Locke. Here, Leibniz takes Locke's statement that thinking consists in being conscious that one

argues, however, that this epistemic act is not a relating to perceptions, but a 'mental activity of a totally different kind'. Apperception 'acquaints with perceptions as perceptions of that entity which performs the act of apperception' ('Apperzeption... macht... mit Perzeptionen als Perzeptionen *derjenigen Entität* bekannt... welche den Aktus der Apperzeption vollzieht', or, in a slightly different formulation, 'Apperzeption vermittelt Bekanntschaft mit Perzeptionen als den Perzeptionen derjenigen Entität, deren Perzeptionen sie sind': p. 35). These formulations clearly suggest, however, that Cramer too thinks that a relating to perceptions is necessarily involved in self-consciousness. What is not so clear is exactly how, on this reading of Leibniz, apperception is meant to 'acquaint' us with perceptions as our own perceptions, if not by a higher-order mental activity. In short, what exactly is (in Leibniz!) this 'epistemic act' by which we become acquainted with our own self as the subject of perceptions?

[85] *Textes inédits*, vol. 1, p. 300.

[86] McRae (1976), chap. 3, holds that because he links apperception to reflection, Leibniz would attribute apperception only to rational souls. But this is a highly controversial reading. For the link between apperception and reflection, see McRae (1976), p. 33.

[87] Kulstad argues that there are two distinct and clearly defined concepts of reflection in Leibniz: *Leibniz on Apperception, Consciousness, and Reflection* (1991), pp. 148ff. This would allow us to ascribe to Leibniz a clear distinction between reflection and apperception (or consciousness, assuming the sameness of apperception and consciousness). According to Kulstad, Leibniz distinguishes between '*simple* or *mere* reflection' on the one hand, and '*focused* reflection' or reflection proper on the other: pp. 23–7; see also pp. 167–8. Kulstad would concede that both simple and focused reflection involve a second-level perception—and both involve attention. But he says that 'only one [focused reflection] involves a focusing of the mind's attention on what may properly said to be in us, that is the self and its operations'. He adds that 'one can be conscious without focusing one's attention in this way, hence without reflecting in this way' (p. 24), and this would be what he calls 'simple reflection'. *Simple* reflection involves attention to *external* objects or, as Kulstad says, 'in some passages', to the sense-images which are different from operations *about* such images (p. 24). Following his reading, then, it could be argued that only simple reflection, but not focused reflection, is to be understood in terms of apperception or consciousness. While I accept that Leibnizian consciousness is not to be equated with reflection *simpliciter*, Kulstad provides no convincing evidence for the claim that his own talk of focused and simple reflection corresponds to a distinction in Leibniz. For a detailed discussion of Kulstad's interpretation, see Thiel, 'Leibniz and the Concept of Apperception', in *Archiv für Geschichte der Philosophie*, 76 (1994), 195–209, esp. 207–8.

thinks to be saying that thought is always accompanied by reflection. It is clear from Leibniz's critique of Locke that his understanding of Lockean 'consciousness' is in terms of reflection—a higher-order mental act. He translates Locke's 'being conscious' (of thoughts) as 's'apercevoir de', but then makes use of the terminology of reflection and says:

> it is impossible that we should always reflect explicitly on all our thoughts; for if we did, the mind would reflect on each reflection, *ad infinitum*, without ever being able to move on to a new thought. For example, in being aware of ['en m'appercevant de'] some present feeling, I should have always to think that I think about that feeling, and further to think that I think of thinking about it, and so on *ad infinitum*. It must be that I stop reflecting on all these reflections, and that eventually some thought is allowed to occur without being thought about; otherwise I would dwell for ever on the same thing.[88]

As a critique of Locke, this argument makes sense only if it is assumed that consciousness is, like reflection, a higher-order mental act.

It is sometimes claimed that Leibniz intends the 'or' in 'consciousness or the reflective knowledge of this inner state' to be read in the exclusive sense, but there is no evidence to support this claim. Leibniz nowhere distinguishes explicitly between apperception and reflection; and there are no passages suggesting that the latter, but not the former, is a higher-order mental act. Indeed, there are passages which appear to preclude such a distinction. For example, in the Preface to *Nouveaux essais* Leibniz says that 'at every moment there is in us an infinity of perceptions, unaccompanied by awareness ['sans apperception'] or reflection; *that is,* of alterations in the soul itself of which we are unaware ['dont nous ne nous appercevons pas']'.[89] Further, it is often argued that, at an 'ontological level', Leibniz distinguishes between apperception in animal souls and apperception in rational souls, and only in the latter is apperception linked to reflection.[90] Even assuming that this is the case, it does

---

[88] The French original reads: 'il n'est pas possible que nous reflechissions tousjours expressement sur toutes nos pensées; autrement l'Esprit feroit reflexion sur chaque reflexion à l'infini sans pouvoir jamais passer à une nouvelle pensée. Par exemple, en m'appercevant de quelque sentiment present, je devrois tousjours penser que j'y pense, et penser encor que je pense d'y penser, et ainsi à l'infini. Mais il faut bien que je cesse de reflechir sur toutes ces reflexions et qu'il y ait enfin quelque pensée qu'on laisse passer sans y penser; autrement on demeureroit tousjours sur la même chose': *Nouveaux essais*, II.i.19.

[89] *Nouveaux essais*, ed. Robinet and Schepers (1962), p. 53 (my italics). The orginal reads: 'il y a à tout moment une infinité de perceptions en nous, mais sans apperception et sans reflexion, c'est à dire des changements dans l'ame même, dont nous ne nous appercevons pas.'

[90] See, for example, Schüßler, who speaks of Leibniz's 'twofold application of the concept of apperception' ('doppelte Anwendung des Apperzeptionsbegriffs'). Schüßler, *Leibniz' Auffassung des menschlichen Verstandes (intellectus). Eine Untersuchung zum Standpunktwechsel zwischen 'systeme commun' und 'systeme nouveau' und dem Versuch ihrer Vermittlung* (1992), p. 106. Perler argues that Leibniz distinguishes between non-conceptual apperception (which applies to animals) and conceptual apperception (which applies to human souls and involves a consciousness of self). The distinction itself makes perfect sense, of course, but the problem is that Leibniz nowhere draws such a distinction. See Perler, 'Graduelle oder Kategorische Unterschiede? Leibniz über das Verhältnis von Tieren und Menschen', in Barke, Wernstedt, and Breger (eds.), *Leibniz neu denken* (*Studia Leibnitiana Sonderhefte*, 38) (2009), pp. 76–95, at pp. 87–8, 94–5.

not affect the reading of apperception as a higher-order mental act. The texts indicate that Leibinz thinks of both apperception and reflection as higher-order mental acts.

While several (perhaps most) commentators would seem to accept an interpretation of Leibnizian consciousness in terms of a higher-order mental act, there are some who prefer a first-order interpretation.[91] We have noted that defenders of a higher-order account of consciousness can avoid the infinite-regress issue that Leibniz invokes against Locke by rejecting the thesis that all mental states are conscious. This is, of course, Leibniz's position. We have seen that his account of the identity of the self, as soul, appeals to the notion of 'insensible perceptions' or unconscious states. We have also noted, however, that rejecting the Lockean thesis raises the question of how the conscious can arise from the unconscious. This would seem to be a problem for Leibniz in particular, as he states explicitly in some passages that 'noticeable [conscious] perceptions arise *by degrees* [my italics] from ones that are too minute to be noticed' (*Nouveaux essais*, p. 57). How can consciousness develop 'by degrees' from something that is totally unconscious, however? The passage could be read as suggesting that all perceptions, even minute ones, are conscious to some degree; but that would clearly go against Leibniz's stated view that *not* all perceptions are conscious.[92] More importantly in the present context is that the claim made in the quoted passage would seem to be inconsistent with a higher-order account of consciousness. It contains a special application of Leibniz's principle of continuity—the principle that 'nature never makes leaps' or that 'all natural change is produced by degrees'.[93] The higher-order account of consciousness, however, does not seem to allow for such a gradual development, but assumes that it consists solely in a second-order mental activity directed at selected perceptions and that a perception cannot be more or less conscious.[94] It is because of this apparent inconsistency of the higher-order account with the principle of continuity that some have argued in favour of a first-order interpretation of Leibnizian consciousness.[95] In short: if only a first-order

---

[91] Gennaro and Simmons, for example, adopt a higher-order reading of Leibniz's notion of consciousness. See Gennaro (1999), esp. pp. 355–7; Simmons, 'Changing the Cartesian Mind: Leibniz on Sensation, Representation and Consciousnesss', *Philosophical Review*, 110 (2001), 31–75, at 53–6. Kulstad's reading too is in terms of a higher-order interpretation of Leibnizian apperception. See Kulstad (1991), pp. 23–4, 39, 146.

[92] Simmons has pointed out that this passage must not be read as stating that more conscious perceptions come from less conscious ones—precisely for the reason that otherwise it would imply that all perceptions are conscious to some degree: Simmons (2001), 45. Commentators, including Simmons, have worked hard at attempting to reconstruct the degree conception of consciousness hinted at in the quotation in such a way so as to make it consistent with Leibniz's denial of the thesis that all perceptions are conscious to some degree: Simmons (2001), 57–61. Some scholars (a minority) are prepared to read Leibniz as saying that all perceptions *are* conscious to some degree, but, as noted, this would be a blatant contradiction to Leibniz's stated view about unconscious perceptions. Furth presents the minority view in 'Monadology', in Frankfurt (ed.), *Leibniz: A Collection of Critical Essays* (1972), pp. 99–136.

[93] *Monadologie*, sect. 13: *Philosophische Schriften*, vol. 6, pp. 607–23; *Philosophical Papers* (1969), pp. 643–53.

[94] Compare Simmons (2001), 57.

[95] See Jorgensen, 'The Principle of Continuity and Leibniz's Theory of Consciousness', *Journal of the History of Philosophy*, 47 (2009), 223–48. Jorgensen argues that for Leibniz consciousness reduces 'to some level of perceptual distinctness'. On this basis, he argues that Leibniz's suggestion that

account can avoid inconsistency in Leibniz, then we must try to reconstruct his text in terms of such an account. The problem is that the texts cited above speak overwhelmingly in favour of a higher-order interpretation.[96] We may still argue, of course, that Leibniz *should have* advanced a first-level account of consciousness—but that is a different matter.

On the whole, although Leibniz points out the difference between unconscious perceptions and conscious perceptions or perceptions which are apperceived, and although he employs numerous terms for relating to one's own self (apperception, consciousness, reflection, memory, 'sense of *I*', and so on), he does not draw any clear distinctions between different ways of relating to one's own self. And this affects his account of personal identity which makes use of notions such as consciousness, reflection, memory, sense of *I*, and so on. It remains unclear exactly what kind of self-relation is involved in personal or moral identity.

9.4. LEIBNIZ AND WOLFF

Leibniz's impact will be evident in several of the subsequent sections and Chapters, but a few general comments are in order at this point. As was indicated in the Introduction, in the eighteenth century the interest in the traditional Scholastic problem of individuation in general was not as strong as that in the special issue of personal identity. Very often, philosophers and theologians discussed individuation and identity in general merely as a preliminary to an examination of the problem of

---

consciousness 'comes in degrees' can be made consistent with his denial that all perceptions are conscious to some degree. Compare also Poser, who holds that distinctness is the 'criterion of apperception'. For Poser, 'distinct perceptions are apperceptions which are always accompanied...by self-consciousness'. Although this formulation suggests a distinction between apperception and self-consciousness, Poser follows Cramer (see above) by saying that in apperception we become aware of our own self as the perceiving subject: Poser, 'Innere Prinzipien und Hierarchie der Monaden', in Busche (ed.), *Gottfried Wilhelm Leibniz: Monadologie (Klassiker auslegen,* 34) (2008), pp. 81–94, at pp. 89–90. As Simmons has pointed out, however, distinctness and consciousness cannot be the same thing in Leibniz. Rather, distinctness is the reason why a perception gets noticed by a second-order perception: Simmons (2001), 53, 56–9.

[96] Jorgensen's interpretation of Leibniz's 'consciousness' proceeds to a considerable extent by appealing to analogies with continuities in other areas (mathematics, physics). Of course, he also analyses (some of) Leibniz's statements about consciousness in support of his reading. I am not convinced, however, that the passages selected need to be interpreted in the way that Jorgensen suggests. The passages from the Preface in *Nouveaux essais,* for example, where Leibniz says that insensible perceptions are not strong enough 'to attract attention', do not in any obvious way support Jorgensen's first-level reading in terms of 'perceptual distinctness'. He even seems to concede that his interpretation may be controversial. It is plain that the passages can be read as saying that only once attention is directed at minute perceptions can they become conscious. It is not at all clear that it is Leibniz's view that attention and memory 'result from' consciousness, as Jorgensen suggests. Rather, as was indicated above, he seems to be saying that attention is what turns minute perceptions into perceived ones. Jorgensen does not consider the infinite regress passage in *Nouveaux essais.*

personal identity (for example, Butler and Reid). As far as Leibniz's account of personal identity is concerned, it does not seem to have had much of a direct impact in the first half of the eighteenth century. Obviously, this has to do with the fact that his most detailed treatment of that topic is in *Nouveaux essais*; and although *Nouveaux essais* was completed in 1705 it was not published until 1765. On the other hand, as was noted above, Leibniz had worked out his conception of self-identity and of identity well before he wrote *Nouveaux essais sur l'entendement humain*. As indicated, in Germany, Christian Wolff adopted a largely Leibnizian account of the identity of persons, even if he did not deal with the issue in much detail. And because of the dominance of Wolffian philosophy at German universities up to the 1770s, a largely Leibnizian account of the person and personal identity prevailed as part of that Wolffian influence. Also, Wolff further developed the notion of apperception. It is due to Wolff's discussion of that notion that it became of central importance in subsequent discussions prior to Kant. And Kant himself adopted the term 'apperception' for his own, quite different, account of self-consciousness.

Leibniz's principle of the identity of indiscernibles had a considerable impact on eighteenth-century metaphysical debates (and even today). Again, some of Leibniz's own writings in which he discusses his principle belong to the eighteenth century. I have mentioned the late publication of *Nouveaux essais*. Further, the relevant papers of the correspondence with Samuel Clarke are from 1716. Wolff adopts Leibniz's principle, and is full of praise of it.[97] And because Wolff's philosophy had a large following, Leibniz's principle was widely accepted by German metaphysicians in the first half of the eighteenth century. There were critics of the principle, however. Christian August Crusius, for example, insisted that the identity or diversity of substances is a matter which can only be determined *a posteriori*.[98] Later in the century, Johann Heinrich Lambert rejected the notion that numerical diversity between substances precludes qualitative identity.[99] In the English-speaking world, Leibniz's principle was known through his correspondence with Samuel Clarke which was first published in English and French in 1717.[100] In France too, it was mainly through the publication of the correspondence with Clarke that Leibniz's principle became known (and also widely accepted).[101] Clarke himself rejects Leibniz's view that it is against the order of nature that there be two substances which are 'exactly alike'. He argues that 'there is no impossibility for God to make two drops of

---

[97] Wolff, *Deutsche Metaphysik*, §§ 586–90. Wolff's work Typically referred to as *Deutsche Metaphysik* is entitled *Vernünfftige Gedancken von Gott, der Welt und der Seele des Menschen, auch allen Dingen überhaupt*, ed. Charles A. Corr, facsimile of Halle, 1751, *Gesammelte Werke*, pt. 1, vol. 2 (Hildesheim, 1983). The first edition was dated 1720 but in fact appeared late in 1719; see Corr's Introduction.

[98] Crusius, *Entwurf der nothwendigen Vernunft-Wahrheiten* (1745), §§ 383–4.

[99] Lambert, *Anlage zur Architectonic* (1771), vol. 1, §129.

[100] *A Collection of Papers, which passed between the late learned Mr. Leibnitz, and Dr. Clarke, in the Years 1715 and 1716, relating to the Principles of Natural Philosophy and Religion* (1717).

[101] For the impact of Leibniz's correspondence with Clarke in France, see Barber, *Leibniz in France. From Arnauld to Voltaire. A Study in French Reactions to Leibnizianism, 1670–1760* (1955), pp. 94–7.

water exactly alike. And if he should make them exactly alike, yet they would never the more become one and the same drop of water, because they were alike... Two things, by being exactly alike, do not cease to be two'.[102]

Apart from praising Leibniz's principle of the identity of indiscernibles, Wolff has little to say about the problems of individuation and identity in general. Like Leibniz, he accounts for individuality in terms of the notion of 'complete determination'.[103] He states that 'something becomes an individual thing by being determined in everything that belongs to it internally as well as in that which belongs to it externally in relation to other things'.[104] Also like Leibniz, he distinguishes between the *a priori* proof of the principle of the identity of indiscernibles and the experiential confirmation of that principle. Again, like Leibniz, he derives the principle of identity from the principle of sufficient reason which he invokes as an ontological principle.[105] Moreover, he invokes a metaphysical distinction between simple and compounded things in his account of individuation: Wolff says that while simple things differ from each other through their internal states, compounded things differ from each other through the manner in which they are compounded.[106]

In contrast to his brief remarks on individuation and identity, Wolff's analysis of consciousness and self-consciousness is fairly detailed.[107] He deals with the latter issues in his *Deutsche Metaphysik* (1720), as well as in his later *Psychologia empirica* (1732) and *Psychologia rationalis* (1734). Leibniz had coined the French

---

[102] Clarke, *Fourth Reply* to Leibniz: *Philosophische Schriften*, vol. 7, p. 382; Leibniz, *Leibniz-Clarke Correspondence*, p. 46.

[103] Wolff, *Deutsche Metaphysik*, §§ 17, 180. See also Wolff, *Philosophia prima, sive Ontologia* (1736), §§ 227–9. For a discussion of Wolff's account of individuation, see Gracia 'Christian Wolff on Individuation', *History of Philosophy Quarterly*, 10 (1993), 147–64. Gracia does not take into account Wolff's *Deutsche Metaphysik*, however, and he does not discuss Leibniz in this context. For a critical discussion of Gracia, see Thiel, '"Epistemologism" and Early Modern Debates about Individuation and Identity', *British Journal for the History of Philosophy*, 5 (1997b), 353–72.

[104] 'Hierdurch wird etwas zu einem einzelnen Dinge, weil es so wohl in allem dem, was es in sich hat, als in dem, was ihm äusserlich in Ansehung anderer Dinge zufället, determiniret ist': Wolff, *Vernünftige Gedanken von den Kräften des menschlichen Verstandes* (1713), in Arndt (ed.), *Gesammelte Werke* (1978), pt. 1, vol. 1. The quote is from chap. 1, § 27.

[105] Wolff, *Deutsche Metaphysik*, §§ 30–1. See also the *Discursus praeliminaris*, in which he distinguishes between the reasons of things and our knowledge of these reasons which may not be complete: Wolff, *Discursus praeliminaris de philosophia in genere*, in *Gesammelte Werke*, ed. École (1983), pt. 2, vol. 1.1, § 5.

[106] Wolff, *Deutsche Metaphysik*, §§ 588, 592.

[107] While the literature on Leibniz's account of apperception is considerable both in extent and quality, Wolff's account of apperception has only occasionally been discussed in detail by philosophers and historians of ideas, and mostly in broader contexts. There is even less on his account of diachronic personal identity. Brief descriptions of Wolff's view on apperception are in Sommer, *Grundzüge einer Geschichte der Deutschen Psychologie und Ästhetik von Wolff-Baumgarten bis Kant-Schiller* (1892), pp. 7, 16–18; Dessoir, *Geschichte der Neueren Deutschen Psychologie* (1902), pp. 72–3; Salomon, *Zu den Begriffen der Perzeption und Apperzeption von Leibniz bis Kant* (1902), pp. 43–6; and Grau, *Die Entwicklung des Bewußtseinsbegriffes im XVII. und XVIII. Jahrhundert* (1916), pp. 188–94. There are, however, some more detailed recent discussions of aspects of Wolff's analysis to which I refer in the notes below.

'l'aperception', but hardly used the Latinized version of the term.[108] It was Wolff who introduced the latter into the philosophical debates.[109] And, as indicated above, it was through Wolff's immense influence on eighteenth-century German philosophy that the term became standard philosophical currency not only in the metaphysical debates on the human soul, but also in the developing discipline of empirical psychology and in epistemological discussions. Wolff defines the human soul as a simple substance which is characterized by one unitary power: the power to represent the universe.[110] He also accounts for the soul in terms of consciousness, however, describing the soul as a thing or substance which is conscious of itself and of other things.[111] His analysis of consciousness does not include a discussion of personal identity. He comments on the latter issue in a related but different context, when discussing the differences between the souls of animals and of human beings and the question of the immortality of the human soul at the end of the fifth chapter of the *Deutsche Metaphysik* (§§ 921–7). The notions of consciousness and personal identity are, however, linked in Wolff. His comments on personal identity make use of the notion of consciousness, but he focuses on aspects of the notion that do not occur in his analysis of the consciousness of objects and self-consciousness. In his comments on personal identity, the possibility of self-consciousness is taken for granted. The relevant distinction here is between the consciousness of past and present perceptions on the one hand, and the consciousness of one's own diachronic identity on the other. As his discussion of personal identity presupposes the notion of self-consciousness, we begin with his analysis of the latter.

9.5. WOLFF ON CONSCIOUSNESS, SELF-CONSCIOUSNESS, AND APPERCEPTION

Like Leibniz, Wolff links the notion of apperception to consciousness ('Bewustseyn' or 'conscientia'), appealing explicitly to Leibniz's 'l'apperception' and to Descartes's

---

[108] Leibniz uses the Latin 'apperceptio' in a letter to Des Bosses of 11 July 1706: *Philosophische Schriften*, vol. 2, p. 311. I owe this reference to Busche, 'Apperzeption und Intellekt', *Allgemeine Zeitschrift für Philosophie*, 19 (1994), 53–63. Thümmig appears in print with a Latin version of Leibniz's notion ('adperceptio') prior to Wolff's relevant publications: Thümmig, *Institutiones philosophiae Wolfianae* (1725–26); reprinted in Wolff, *Gesammelte Werke*, pt. 3, vol. 19 (1982). Compare Wunderlich, *Kant und die Bewußtseinstheorien des 18. Jahrhunderts* (2005), p. 36.
[109] Wolff, *Psychologia empirica*, in *Gesammelte Werke*, pt. 2, vol. 5, facsimile of Frankfurt 1738 edn., ed. École (1968), § 25.
[110] Wolff, *Psychologia rationalis*, in *Gesammelte Werke*, pt. 2, vol. 6, facsimile of Frankfurt 1740 edn., ed. École (1972), § 63, p. 42; see § 53, p. 35. See *Deutsche Metaphysik*, §§ 744, 755–6, 256, pp. 464, 469, 143–4.
[111] Wolff, *Deutsche Metaphysik*, §§ 192–4, pp. 107–8; *Psychologia empirica*, §§ 11, 20–2, pp. 9, 15–16; *Psychologia rationalis*, § 10, pp. 9–10. Wolff emphasises, however, that, unlike the Cartesians he does not claim that consciousness is the essence of the soul and that 'nichts in der Seele seyn könte, dessen sie sich nicht bewust wäre': *Deutsche Metaphysik*, § 193.

'conscientia'.[112] In Wolff, however, 'consciousness' is broader than 'apperception': it can denote a relation to external objects as well as to one's own ideas or thoughts. 'Apperception', by contrast, always denotes a relation to our own perceptions.[113] But what precisely is the object of inner-directed consciousness or apperception? Wolff sometimes implies that consciousness accompanies thoughts or perceptions.[114] In his *Psychologia empirica* he even explicitly defines apperception as that mental act through which we become conscious of our own perceptions.[115] Like Leibniz, Wolff appears to conceive of apperception as a higher-order mental act directed at perceptions. Explicitly appealing to Descartes, he defines thought in terms of consciousness. All thought, he holds, involves both perception—the representation of an object—and apperception as the consciousness of that perception.[116] So, in one sense, inner-directed consciousness or apperception relates to our own thoughts, feelings, or perceptions in general. Moreover, 'apperception' is analysed differently in *Psychologia empirica* and *Psychologia rationalis* respectively. While the former describes apperception as the mental act by which the soul becomes conscious of its perceptions, the latter emphasises the need for further analysis. Here, Wolff argues that consciousness consists in the act of distinguishing between the partial perceptions that compose a whole perception. The soul is conscious of its own activity when it is conscious of the modifications that occur in it and is able to distinguish between them.[117]

---

[112] 'Apperceptionis nomine utitur *Leibnitius*: coincidit autem cum conscientia, quem terminum in praesenti negotio *Cartesius* adhibet': *Psychologia empirica*, § 25.

[113] 'Menti tribuitur *Apperceptio*, quatenus perceptionis suae sibi conscia est': *Psychologia empirica*, § 25.

[114] Compare *Deutsche Metaphysik*, § 735, where Wolff paraphrases 'that we are conscious' (daß wir uns bewust sind) as 'that we know what we think or that our thoughts are accompanied by consciousness' (daß wir wissen, was wir gedencken oder ... [daß] unsere Gedancken ein Bewustseyn mit sich bringen). See also §§ 194–5.

[115] 'Actus prior, quo fit repraesentatio, est perceptio [§ 24]; actus posterior, quo mens sibi conscia est repraesentationis, vocatur apperceptio'; *Psychologia empirica*, § 48. This formulation would suggest, as Wunderlich has pointed out, that (inner-directed) consciousness and apperception are not simply identical, but that apperception is that mental act through which a representation becomes a conscious representation: Wunderlich, 'Christian Wolff über Bewußtsein, Apperzeption und Selbstbewußtsein', in Stolzenberg and Rudolph (eds.), *Christian Wolff und die Europäische Aufklärung* (2007), vol. 2, pp. 367–75, at pp. 370–1.

[116] 'Cogitare dicimur, quando nobis conscii sumus eorum, quae in nobis contingunt, & quae nobis tanquam extra nos repraesentantur. *Cogitatio* igitur est actus animae, quo sibi sui rerumque aliarum extra se conscia est': *Psychologia empirica*, § 23. Wolff refers to Descartes, *Principia philosophiae*, 1, 9: 'omnis cogitatio et perceptionem [§ 24] & apperceptionem involvit': *Psychologia empirica*, § 26.

[117] *Psychologia rationalis*, §§ 10, 12. For the difference between *Psychologia rationalis* and *Psychologia empirica* in this respect, see the discussions in Wunderlich (2007), pp. 368–9; and Fabbianelli, 'Tatsachen des Bewußtseins und 'nexus rerum' in Christian Wolffs Psychologie', in Stolzenberg and Rudolph (2007), vol. 2, pp. 355–66, at pp. 356–8. Fabianelli casts the difference between the two approaches in terms of a distinction between 'form' and 'content'. The account in *Psychologia empirica* provides a 'formal definition' of apperception, according to which the soul is conscious of itself in so far as it is conscious of its own perceptions—independently of the partial peceptions that make up each perception; *Psychologia rationalis* gives a 'contentful' account of apperception, as apperception is here said to be connected to the multiplicity of perceived objects

There is, however, another sense of inner-directed consciousness in Wolff: as a relating to the self or subject as that thing or being which thinks and is conscious— and for this he does not seem to use the terminology of *apperceptio*. The latter notion does, of course, involve a relating to one's own self in the sense that it is a mental act through which we become conscious of perceptions as *our own* perceptions. His analysis of self-consciousness is not in terms of *apperception*, however. In *Deutsche Metaphysik* he several times states that 'we are conscious of ourselves and of other things'.[118] Clearly, the term 'ourselves' is here to be understood as analogous to 'other things'. According to Wolff, it is simply an empirical fact that we are conscious of our own self and of other things. It appears that he implies a distinction between the notion of self-consciousness invoked here and the notion of an explicit knowledge of our own existence. The latter he derives syllogistically in the opening section of the *Deutsche Metaphysik*, entitled 'How we know that we exist'. The certainty of our own existence is said to rest on syllogistic demonstration (§§ 5–7). This is how Wolff formulates the syllogism: 'Whoever is conscious of himself and of other things, exists. We are conscious of ourselves and of other things. Therefore, we exist' (ibid., § 6).[119] He ascribes considerable importance to this syllogistic self-knowledge, parading it as a model of a proof that leads to the highest certainty (ibid., §§ 4, 8–9).[120] The minor premise invokes a relating to one's own self, however: namely, a *consciousness* of one's own self that is different and more fundamental than the explicit knowledge of one's own existence which is supposed to be derived by way of syllogistic argumentation. Indeed, the statement that 'we are conscious of ourselves and other things' also appears as the first sentence in the first chapter of the *Deutsche Metaphysik*. This statement, he says, is based on immediate experience and is indubitable (ibid., §§ 5, 7).[121] Also, it is suggested by the minor premise (and the first sentence of the *Deutsche Metaphysik*) that

(p. 357). Wunderlich emphasises, rightly, that the act of distinguishing, according to the account in *Psychologia rationalis*, does not relate to things or objects but to perceptions (p. 369). See also Wunderlich, *Kant und die Bewußtseinstheorien des 18. Jahrhunderts* (2005), pp. 25–31.

[118] *Deutsche Metaphysik*, § 5. Compare also § 730. Elsewhere Wolff states that 'the soul is conscious of itself and what passes in it' (die Seele ... [ist] sich ihrer und was in ihr vorgehet, bewust). *Der Vernünfftigen Gedancken von Gott, der Welt und der Seele des Menschen, auch allen Dingen überhaupt, Anderer Theil, bestehend in ausführlichen Anmerckungen*, in Wolff, *Gesammelte Werke*, pt. 1, vol. 3, ed. Corr (1983), § 263.
[119] See also *Psychologia empirica*, § 16.
[120] For a discussion of Wolff's argument here, see Blackwell, 'Christian Wolff's Doctrine of the Soul', *Journal of the History of Ideas*, 22 (1961), 339–54, esp. 340–3. Compare also Corr, 'Cartesian Themes in Wolff's German Metaphysics', in *Christian Wolff 1679–1754. Interpretationen zu seiner Philosophie und deren Wirkung*, ed. Schneiders (1983), pp. 113–20, esp. pp. 117–18; Euler, 'Bewußtsein–Seele–Geist. Untersuchungen zur Transformation des Cartesischen "Cogito" in der Psychologie Christian Wolffs', in Rudolph and Goubet (eds.), *Die Psychologie Christian Wolffs* (2004), pp. 11–50, at pp. 15–19; Stolzenberg '"Wie wir erkennen, daß wir sind." Überlegungen zu Wolff's Beweis des Satzes "Ich bin" im ersten Kapitel der *Deutschen Metaphysik*', in Madonna (ed.), *Macht und Bescheidenheit der Vernunft. Beiträge zur Philosophie Christian Wolffs. Gedenkband für Hans Werner Arndt* (2005), pp. 123–31; and Madonna, 'Die Erkenntnis der Existenz in der Philosophie von Christian Wolff', ibid., pp. 133–50. Madonna argues that Wolff uses the syllogistic argumentation primarily for didactic reasons (p. 141).
[121] See also *Vernünftige Gedanken von den Kräften des menschlichen Verstandes*, chapter 5, § 1. Werner Euler has pointed out that Wolff combines two criteria by reference to which that statement

being conscious of our own self is correlated, somehow, to being conscious of objects or 'other things'.[122] The claim with which the *Deutsche Metaphysik* begins expresses the experiential fact that consciousness is both inner-directed and outer-directed.[123] This is restated in chapter 3—the 'empirical' part of Wolff's psychology here (ibid., § 192). He does not explain the relation between the inner- and outer-directed forms of consciousness in detail until chapter five—the 'rational' part of his psychology in the *Deutsche Metaphysik*. At first it seems (§ 728) that he intends to deal with the two forms of consciousness separately—first with the consciousness of objects (§ 729), and then with the consciousness of our own self (§ 730). As will become apparent, however, the two accounts are just two aspects of one argument.

Indeed, Wolff does not regard the consciousness of our own self as an independent (or 'original') act: it is necessarily linked and even dependent on certain other mental activities. This is implied in his analysis of our consciousness of objects which reveals the way in which the consciousness of self and that of objects are correlated according to Wolff.[124] His first step in this analysis is to argue that it is part of our consciousness of objects that we *distinguish* objects from one another.[125] Unless we distinguish objects from one another, we may have a chaotic assemblage of ideas, but no determinate consciousness of particular things. As he says, 'all our thoughts would be obscure' (ibid., § 731). His second step is to say that in distinguishing objects from one another we become conscious of our own activity of distinguishing and, thereby, of ourselves, as distinct from the objects of which we are conscious. So he argues (1) that to be conscious of an object is to distinguish it from other objects; and (2) that in distinguishing objects from one another we become conscious of ourselves as distinct

becomes certain: inner empirical observation, and the principle of non-contradiction. Moreover, Euler notes that the reference to 'other things' is directed at Cartesian 'idealism'. See Euler (2004), pp. 12–14.

[122] Wundt notes that in the first edition of *Deutsche Metaphysik* Wolff defines the soul as a thing that is conscious. Only in later editions does Wolff's definition include the relation to 'other things'. See Wundt, *Die Deutsche Schulphilosophie im Zeitalter der Aufklärung* (1945), p. 165.

[123] For a distinction between inner and outer experience in Wolff, see *Deutsche Metaphysik*, § 251, and *Philosophia rationalis sive logica* (1740), in Wolff, *Gesammelte Werke*, pt. 2, vol. 1.2, ed. École (1983), §§ 30, 31, where he distinguishes between inner sense and outer sense. Compare Grau (1916), pp. 186–7. Wolff does not seem to comment on the relationship between inner sense and consciousness, however. It is not clear, then, whether or not he would distinguish between inner sense and (inner-directed) consciousness. Elsewhere he appears to identify self-consciousness even with self-knowledge: 'Wer sich seiner bewust ist und dessen, was er thut, der erkennet sich: denn eben dadurch erkennen wir uns, daß wir uns unser und der Würckungen unserer Seele bewust seyn': *Deutsche Metaphysik*, § 979.

[124] For the following argument, see Wolff, *Deutsche Metaphysik*, §§ 729–34. See also Thiel, 'Between Wolff and Kant: Mérian's Theory of Apperception', *Journal of the History of Philosophy*, 34 (1996), 213–32; Thiel, 'Zum Verhältnis von Gegenstandsbewußtsein und Selbstbewußtsein bei Wolff und seinen Kritikern', in Stolzenberg and Rudolph (eds.), *Christian Wolff und die Europäische Aufklärung* (2007b), vol. 2, pp. 377–90.

[125] Wolff says that 'we are conscious of things when we distinguish them from one another' (wir ... [sind] uns alsdenn der Dinge bewust ... wenn wir sie voneinander unterscheiden): *Deutsche Metaphysik*, § 729. We noted in the Introduction that the general idea that consciousness is linked to the act of distinguishing goes back to Aristotle. See Schmitt, 'Synästhesie im Urteil aristotelischer Philosophie', in Adler and Zeuch (eds.), *Synästhesie. Interferenz-Transfer-Synthese der Sinne* (2002), pp. 122–30.

from the objects of which we are conscious. It seems, then, that for Wolff the consciousness of our own self is doubly derivative: it depends on the consciousness of objects, and on the consciousness of our mental act of distinguishing that is involved in the consciousness of objects. Without a consciousness of external things we could not become conscious of ourselves, for without the consciousness of objects we could not distinguish ourselves from other things. If we were not conscious of external things there would be no mental act of distinguishing of which we could become conscious, and therefore we could not become conscious of ourselves (ibid., § 731). We are conscious of the act of distinguishing, and as a result of becoming conscious of this activity we become conscious of our own soul or self. There are other passages which suggest that self-consciousness requires only the consciousness of mental activities; but here too, self-consciousness is linked to the act of distinguishing ourselves from other objects.[126] In short, Wolff seems to be a proponent of the position that self-consciousness is dependent on and derived from the consciousness of objects—and this is indeed how his account is often interpreted.[127]

The relation between the consciousness of objects and the consciousness of one's own self is not, however, as one-sided as it may at first seem. While Wolff holds that without the consciousness of external things we could not become conscious of ourselves, his argument also implies (3) that, conversely, we could not be conscious of objects without being conscious of our own self: the consciousness of objects cannot be had without (and thus requires) self-consciousness. He argues that in being conscious of objects we are conscious of our mental act of distinguishing and thereby of our own self. His argument that an act of distinguishing is involved in the consciousness of objects implies the claim that in distinguishing objects from one another, we (necessarily) become conscious of ourselves as distinct from the objects of which we are conscious. We cannot have a consciousness of objects that does not involve a consciousness of our own self. Or, expressed differently, if there is no consciousness of our own self there can be no consciousness of objects either. For Wolff to say that the mental act of distinguishing is always involved in the consciousness of objects implies that the latter also always and necessarily involves self-consciousness. He assumes that the act of distinguishing necessarily brings along a consciousness of this act, and, thereby, also of the subject of that act. We cannot choose to become or not to become conscious of our own self in the process of becoming conscious of objects. If we are conscious of objects, the consciousness of our own self is always already involved.[128] It is true that the relating to external things

---

[126] *Deutsche Metaphysik*, § 730: 'For if we do not think of the *acts* of the soul... and *thereby* distinguish ourselves from the *things* which we think, then we are not conscious of ourselves either' (Denn wenn wir an die *Würckungen* der Seele nicht gedencken... und uns *dadurch* von denen *Dingen*, die wir gedencken, unterscheiden; so sind wir uns auch unserer nicht bewust (my italics)). Compare also *Psychologia rationalis*, § 12.

[127] See for example, Henrich, 'Die Anfänge der Theorie des Subjekts', in Honneth, McCarthy, Offe, and Wellmer (eds.), *Zwischenbetrachtungen. Im Prozeß der Aufklärung. Jürgen Habermas zum 60. Geburtstag* (1989), pp. 106–70, at p. 139.

[128] Thus he says in *Deutsche Metaphysik*, § 730, that we are conscious of ourselves when we notice the difference or distinctness between ourselves and other things, and hastens to add that this

has priority in the sense that without a multiplicity of other things, the act of distinguishing would be impossible, and consequently there would be neither consciousness of objects nor consciousness of our own self. As Wolff says, 'for if we do not think of the acts of the soul and thereby distinguish ourselves from the things of which we think, then we are not conscious of ourselves either' (ibid., § 730). Nevertheless, he assumes a double relation of consciousness to both the subject and the object of consciousness.[129]

Thus, Wolff's analysis is that there can be no self-consciousness without consciousness of objects, and no consciousness of objects without self-consciousness. It suggests, then, that self-consciousness and the consciousness of objects are mutually dependent on each other. Wolff appears to be opposed both to the position according to which self-consciousness is to be derived empirically from the consciousness of objects and to the other extreme according to which the consciousness of our own self has absolute primacy.

Wolff's next step (4) is to conclude that reflection (or 'Überdencken', as he translates 'reflexio')—understood not as Lockean inner sense, but as the act of comparing a multiplicity of ideas—is required for consciousness to be possible. For to distinguish objects from one another, we have to compare them. To compare a multiplicity of things or ideas and to distinguish them from each other is to reflect: 'That is why it is clear that consciousness requires reflection' (ibid., § 733). Like Leibniz, Wolff links reflection to attention—the faculty of relating to particular thoughts in such a way that these thoughts become clearer than other thoughts. Reflection is nothing but the continued attention directed at particular thoughts.[130] Next (5), he points out that in addition to reflection, memory is required for consciousness, for in order to compare ideas we must be able to remember them and know that we have had them before (ibid., § 734). Lastly (6), the fact that consciousness requires reflection and memory means, moreover, that consciousness has its own temporal duration: time is required for consciousness to be possible (ibid., § 736).

---

noticing is immediately given with the consciousness of other things: 'Dieser Unterscheid aber zeiget sich so gleich, so bald wir uns der anderen Dinge bewust sind'. That is, consciousness of objects is directly or immediately (and necessarily) linked to the noticing of the distinctness between self and other things; that is, to self-consciousness.

[129] Here my reading differs somewhat from that of Wunderlich, who holds that self-consciousness for Wolff is not directly involved in the consciousness of perceptions or objects, but that the latter needs to be made explicit to result in self-consciousness. Wolff, according to Wunderlich, has in mind only a 'possible self-consciousness': Wunderlich (2007), p. 372. In support of his reading he claims that there are passages in Wolff (*Deutsche Metaphysik*, § 730) that suggest we can have a consciousness of objects without self-consciousness. I read the relevant passages differently. What Wolff seems to be saying, rather, is that if there were no relating to our own activities there would be no self-consciousness. But such a relating is, as Wolff has argued, always involved in the consciousness of objects. To be conscious of objects involves the act of distinguishing ourselves from objects. We would not be conscious of our own self only in the case that 'wir nicht die Würckungen unserer Seele, und dadurch den Unterschied unserer von dem, was wir gedencken, uns vorgestellet haben': *Deutsche Metaphysik*, § 730.

[130] *Deutsche Metaphysik*, § 272; *Psychologia empirica*, § 257.

It appears that the notion of self-consciousness invoked in this analysis is different from that of apperception: the latter is a consciousness of perceptions, while the former is likened to the consciousness of objects. We are conscious of our own self as a distinct entity or thing. The most important feature of his analysis is, however, the above-mentioned relationship of mutual dependence between self-consciousness and the consciousness of objects. This means that neither consciousness of self nor consciousness of objects is 'original'. Both are always already involved when we are conscious of anything. According to Wolff, consciousness always and necessarily involves a double relation, (1) to the subject of consciousness, and (2) to 'other things' as objects of consciousness. And this double relation is mediated, he suggests, through the mental act of distinguishing. Consciousness, to Wolff, is always already related to a subject as well as to an object. This analysis also shows that the notion of self-consciousness is a central philosophical issue for Wolff. To him, the question about our knowledge of the external world cannot even be formulated consistently without bringing into play the notion of self-consciousness.

One potential problem for this reading is that it may seem to be inconsistent with the larger structure of Wolff's philosophical system. Thus, appealing to the fact that in Wolff cosmology precedes psychology, it could be argued that this indicates that the question of self-consciousness is secondary for him.[131] Originally and primarily, the soul should be seen as belonging and relating to the world or cosmos. The latter context has systematic priority over the consciousness the soul may have of itself. On this account, Wolff's psychology presupposes his cosmology and ontology. And one of his reasons for structuring his metaphysics in this way is, on this reading, precisely that the relating to the world or to objects in general is presupposed by his account of the soul. In short, the priority he ascribes to cosmology over psychology is grounded in the priority he ascribes to the relating to the external world over that to one's own self. Now it is true, of course, that in Wolff, *rational* psychology at least is preceded by cosmology. However, the logical relationship between ontology, cosmology, logic, and psychology is more complex than the external order may suggest.[132] Moreover, it is doubtful that the fact that cosmology precedes rational psychology is directly relevant to the specific issues of consciousness and self-consciousness. Rather, the ordering of the various philosophical disciplines would seem to be an issue distinct from the concrete analyses of the latter. Further, although consciousness and self-consciousness are discussed only in the context of Wolff's psychologies, they are of course involved in *all* thought, including thought about the world or cosmos; and in this sense at least, Wolff's reflections on those issues are more fundamental than his cosmology.

It is important to emphasise that Wolff's statement that 'we are conscious of ourselves and of other things' is not meant to be an abstract 'definition' of thought

---

[131] See, for example, Klemme, *Kants Philosophie des Subjekts* (1996), p. 18.

[132] For a discussion of this, see, for example, Rey, 'Ontologie et psychologie dans la pensée de Christian Wolff: la raison de l'actualisation', in Rudolph and Goubet (2004), pp. 99–118; Goubet, 'In welchem Sinne ist die Wolffsche Psychologie als Fundament zu verstehen? Zum vermeintlichen Zirkel zwischen Psychologie und Logik', ibid., pp. 51–60; and Arnaud, 'Où commence la 'Métaphysique allemande' de Christian Wolff?', ibid., pp. 61–73.

but a description of an immediate experiential fact. Thus the thesis about the relationship between self-consciousness and the consciousness of objects is not just implied by his analysis of consciousness but is also stated explicitly—not as an *a priori* principle, but as an empirical fact—when he says that it is an immediate and 'indubitable experience' ('ungezweifelte Wahrheit', *Deutsche Metaphysik*, § 7) that we are 'conscious of ourselves and of other things'.[133] The relation of mutual dependence is not made explicit here when the mere fact of consciousness of self and of objects is noted, but it suggests that both exist together. And even when describing the empirical fact Wolff clearly wishes to avoid ascribing priority to either self-consciousness or the consciousness of objects. His analysis and explanation of consciousness in part 5 of *Deutsche Metaphysik* that we examined concerns the possibility of what he described earlier. Here he attempts to explain the interrelatedness of the consciousness of self and the consciousness of objects by way of reconstructing the possibility of both in terms of the mental act of distinguishing. It remains true, however, that the starting point is an empirical or phenomenological fact that is described in the first sentence of his *Deutsche Metaphysik*: 'we are conscious of ourselves and of other things'. Thus, he even seems to assign a special status to the interrelatedness of the two forms of consciousness, appealing to it at the outset of his work, and proceeding to elaborate on this in the opening paragraphs of the 'rational' part of his psychology in the same book.[134]

It remains true, however, that his remarks on consciousness are made against the background assumption that the 'subject' of consciousness is an immaterial soul or mental substance, and that consciousness is essentially a type of perception—a higher-order mental act. Nevertheless, the Wolffian understanding of apperception is adopted and sometimes modified in many subsequent discussions—even by authors who reject Wolffian philosophy as a whole and tend towards a materialist analysis of the mind. This is true, for example, of philosophers such as Charles Bonnet, who was important to the developing discipline of empirical psychology in the second half of the century.[135]

9.6. WOLFF ON CONSCIOUSNESS, PERSONAL IDENTITY, AND IMMORTALITY

Wolff's notion of self-consciousness discussed in the previous section concerns an immediate relating to one's own present self as the subject of thought. In his analysis

---

[133] See also the following passages in which Wolff states as a fact that we are conscious both of our own self and of other things: 'Wir sind uns unser und anderer Dinge bewust, daran kann niemand zweifeln, der nicht seiner Sinnen vollständig beraubet ist': *Deutsche Metaphysik*, § 1. See also *Deutsche Metaphysik*, § 5: 'wir erfahren unwidersprechlich, daß wir uns unserer und anderer Dinge selbst bewust sind'.
[134] This aspect is relevant even to post-Kantian accounts of consciousness—notably in Reinhold. See the discussion in Thiel (2007b), pp. 385–8.
[135] We shall examine Bonnet's analysis in *The Enlightened Subject* (in preparation).

of that notion he does not consider the issue of consciousness as relating to the past and/or future. The notions of time and memory are invoked, but only as requirements for the activity of distinguishing that is involved in consciousness. The issue of relating to one's own past is discussed elsewhere in Wolff, however, when he discusses the issues of personality and the identity of persons. These latter issues appear in the context of Wolff's argument for the immortality of human souls and the mortality of animal souls at the end of the fifth chapter of the *Deutsche Metaphysik* (§§ 921–7). Indeed, identity through time, consciousness, and the concept of a person, are all linked in Wolff. This may sound rather like a Lockean mix, but as we shall see, Wolff's account is anti-Lockean in the last analysis.

As indicated, in his discussion of immortality and identity Wolff takes for granted the notion of self-consciousness: he takes for granted that it is possible for human beings to relate to their own selves in this way. He holds that animal souls, too, have self-consciousness in some sense: animals, too, are conscious of themselves and of what they feel; they know that they see, hear, and feel.[136] Moreover, they have a memory of past perceptions (ibid., § 870). According to Wolff, animals have souls, and these are, like human souls, simple things and thus indestructible—divine intervention excepted (ibid., § 921). They lack reason (ibid., § 870) and language, however—the latter being required for the use of reason (ibid., § 868)—which means that they are not able to recognize themselves as the same beings that existed at an earlier point of time. Animals do not know that they are now the same beings who at an earlier point of time existed in this or that state (ibid., § 923). And to Wolff, this means that although they have souls, they are not persons. For persons are defined by Wolff as beings that are conscious that they are now the same beings as those who at an earlier point of time existed in this or that state. Human beings are beings that are capable of such consciousness of their own identity through time; therefore, they are persons. Animals are not capable of such consciousness, and hence they are not persons.[137]

Like both Locke and Leibniz, Wolff links personality to morality, which is why he also uses the expression 'individuum morale' for 'person' (*Psychologia rationalis*, § 741). The moral nature of persons has to do precisely with their ability to recognize themselves as identical through time. Persons are beings that are responsible for their

---

[136] See *Deutsche Metaphysik*, § 794: 'so kan man auch begreiffen, daß die Thiere sich ihrer und dessen, was sie empfinden, müssen bewust seyn, das ist, ein Thier weiß es, daß es siehet, oder höret, oder fühlet etc.'

[137] In *Deutsche Metaphysik* Wolff says: 'Da man nun eine *Person* nennet ein Ding, das sich bewust ist, es sey eben dasjenige, was vorher in diesem oder jenem Zustande gewesen; so sind die Thiere auch keine Personen: hingegen weil die Menschen sich bewust sind, daß sie eben diejenigen sind, die voher in diesem oder jenem Zustande gewesen; so sind sie Personen': *Deutsche Metaphysik*, § 924. See also Wolff, *Psychologia rationalis*, § 741, p. 660: '*Persona* dicitur ens, quod memoriam sui conservat, hoc est, meminit, se esse idem illud ens, quod ante in hoc vel isto fuit statu. Dicitur etiam *Individuum morale*'. Here Wolff argues that his notion of person does not contradict the Scholastic notion of person as 'suppositum intelligens'. For a self that remembers its own past self is an intelligent individuum; that is, an individual substance. In § 743 follows the argument that human beings are persons: 'Quia homo memoriam sui habet... quod experientia obvia unicuique manifestum; *homo persona est*.'

Individuation and identity, apperception and consciousness 313

past actions, as they are able to recognize their identity with the being that performed those actions in the past. Wolff argues that we are persons or moral beings because of the consciousness or memory we have *of our identity through time*.[138] It is important to note that despite its emphasis on consciousness and memory, his account is not Lockean. Locke's view is that consciousness of thoughts and actions constitutes personality and personal identity; but Wolff holds that the consciousness *of identity* makes us persons. Like Leibniz, but unlike Locke, he believes the identity of the soul, as mental substance, must be presupposed for there to be personal or moral identity.

As indicated, Wolff, like others before him (notably Leibniz), links his account of personality to that of immortality. We have noted that for Wolff both animal and human souls are naturally indestructible. To Wolff, however, only human souls are immortal, because human souls, but not animal souls, are persons; and they are persons, as we have seen, because of their ability to be conscious of their own diachronic identity. The soul of man is of such a nature that it recognizes its identity with the being that was in this or that state in the past (that is, its nature is such that it constitutes a person). Now, since we have no reason to believe that after the death of the body the human soul will lose this ability to be conscious of its identity through time, the soul will be a person after the death of the body. And to say this is to say that it is immortal: 'For what is indestructible is immortal if it always retains its personality' (*Deutsche Metaphysik*, § 926). Although indestructibility (and thereby the natural permanence) of the soul, as substance, are required for immortality, they are not sufficient for immortality; rather, it is the permanence of the soul, *as a person*, that makes it immortal. As animals are not persons, their souls are not immortal.[139] This is reminiscent of Leibniz of course: he too argues, as we have seen, that the metaphysical identity (relating to the soul, as substance) is a necessary but not a sufficient condition of moral identity (relating to the self as a person).

Wolff does not enter into any detail about the question of how we arrive at the consciousness of our own diachronic identity. He suggests, however, that it is implied by the memory of past experiences: the soul is not only conscious of itself and of what passes in itself, but its present state is also always linked to its past states, and memory assures us that we have formerly been in those states. He seems to suggest, then, that it is through memory that we arrive at the consciousness of our

---

[138] Wolff, *Deutsche Metaphysik*, § 924, p. 570. See also *Psychologia rationalis*, §§ 741, 743, pp. 660–1.
[139] See *Deutsche Metaphysik*, § 926: 'In dem Zustande deutlicher Gedancken ist nicht allein die Seele ihrer [§ 730] und dessen, was sie gedencket, bewust [§ 729], sondern der gegenwärtige Zustand bringet auch jederzeit etwas von dem vergangenen hervor [§ 238] und das Gedächtniß versichert uns, daß wir uns vorhin in demselben befunden [§ 249]. Da nun die Seele des Menschen erkennet, sie sey eben diejenige, die vorher in diesem Zustande gewesen, und demnach den Zustand ihrer Person auch nach dem Tode des Leibes behält [§ 924]; so ist sie *unsterblich*. Denn das unverweßliche ist *unsterblich*, wenn es den Zustand einer Person beständig behält'. Wolff accounts for the consciousness of one's own diachronic identity also in terms of the notion of 'memoria sui': *Psychologia rationalis*, § 743. See also *Psychologia rationalis*, § 742. Wolff argues that the soul retains a memory of itself (memoria sui) after death. Hence, the soul after death is an 'individum morale', a person: '*anima immortalis post mortem idem individuum morale permanere debet, seu statum personalitatis conservet opus est*' (p. 661).

own identity in our present and past states. We saw that some of Locke's critics appeal to the notion that memory presupposes identity and therefore cannot constitute it. Wolff does not make this point explicitly, but he seems to appeal implicitly to the view that memory of the past presupposes diachronic personal identity, when he links the consciousness of diachronic identity to the memory of past states.[140]

Again, there are seeming similarities to the Lockean position, as Wolff emphasises a connection of consciousness or a psychological connectedness between the premortem and the post-mortem states. For Locke, however, consciousness is *constitutive* of personal identity in the afterlife, and independent of the identity of the soul, as substance. This is not true of Wolff. Although he distinguishes the permanence of the soul (indestructibility) from the permanence of the self, as person (immortality), the latter requires the former. Immortality (retaining one's own personality after death) presupposes the permanence or indestructibility and thus the identity of the soul, as substance. Wolff follows Leibniz, rather than Locke. He distinguishes between the identity of human subject as soul and the identity of the subject as a person, but argues that the latter cannot exist without the former. The identity of the soul, as substance (metaphysical identity), is a necessary condition (but not a sufficient one) of the identity of the self as person (personal or moral identity). This, as we have seen, is not the Lockean position.

The view that it is the consciousness of our own diachronic identity that makes us persons was propagated in the eighteenth-century by many of Wolff's followers—mostly in the context of discussions of immortality. Wolff's philosophy, presented in many large tomes, prompted some of his followers to produce abridged versions of his thought: for example, in the form of dictionaries. The Latin dictionary by Friedrich Christian Baumeister and the German dictionary by Heinrich Adam Meißner provide summaries of Wolff's views on a large variety of philosophical issues, including the issue of identity. Indeed, both Baumeister and Meißner repeat the accounts of the notion of person in *Deutsche Metaphysik* and *Psychologia rationalis*.[141] It is not surprising, then, that a Wolffian understanding of consciousness and personal identity (and thereby aspects at least of Leibnizian thought on these matters) dominated the scene in mid eighteenth-century Germany.

---

[140] This is evident from the first few lines quoted in the previous note (*Deutsche Metaphysik*, § 926): 'In dem Zustande deutlicher Gedanken ist nicht allein die Seele ihrer [§ 730] und dessen, was sie gedencket, bewust [§ 729], sondern der gegenwärtige Zustand bringet auch jederzeit etwas von dem vergangenen hervor [§ 238] und das Gedächtniß versichert uns, daß wir uns vorhin in demselben befunden [§ 249]. Da nun die Seele des Menschen erkennt, sie sey eben diejenige, die vorher in diesem Zustande gewesen, und demnach den Zustand ihrer Person auch nach dem Tode des Leibes behält [§ 924]; so ist sie *unsterblich*.'

[141] Meißner, *Philosophisches Lexicon, darinnen die Erklärungen und Beschreibungen aus des... hochberühmten Welt-Weisen Herrn Christian Wolffens sämmtlichen teutschen Schrifften seines Philosophischen Systematis sorgfältig zusammen getragen* (1737; reprinted, 1970), p. 431. Baumeister, *Philosophia recens controversa complexa definitiones theoremata et quaestiones nostra aetate in controversiam vocatas* (1741), p. 158.

10

Beyond Leibniz and Wolff: from immortality to the necessary 'unity of the subject'

It was not only abridgements and summaries of Wolff's writings that contributed to the spread of his philosophy on the continent, as his own works—especially the German volumes—also became immensely influential. There were twelve editions of the *Deutsche Metaphysik* during Wolff's lifetime, the book was translated into Dutch in 1767, and as early as 1745 the first part of *Psychologia empirica* appeared in a French version, thereby apparently introducing the very term 'psychologie' into the French language.[1] Wolff's philosophy was taught at many German universities; indeed by 1735, 112 professorships at German universities and gymnasia were held by committed Wolffians.[2]

As many Wolffians more or less repeated what Wolff had said before them, there would be no point in going through all of his followers' works in which his accounts of identity and consciousness are simply restated with only slight if any modification. Instead, in this Chapter we shall look at followers who explain, modify, or elaborate on Wolff's theory to some significant extent. These include strict Wolffians such as Israel Gottlieb Canz, as well as thinkers who are critical of other aspects of Wolff's philosophy but nevertheless adopt and elaborate on the Wolffian notions of identity and consciousness. In the next Chapter we shall examine the arguments of Wolff's critics. Some of these, such as Jean-Bernard Mérian, develop their own independent positions on these issues precisely through their critique of Wolffian views and arguments. The issue of personal identity is dealt with mostly in the context of a discussion of the doctrine of immortality in the first section of this Chapter. While Wolff's followers adopt his notion of personhood in terms of the consciousness of one's own diachronic identity, there are philosophical developments within the Wolffian school in relation to this idea. We shall look at this in the second section of the present Chapter, focusing especially on Hermann Samuel Reimarus's argument that we could have no perceptions at all without tacitly appealing to our diachronic identity. It was Wolff's critics in particular, however,

---

[1] *Redenkundige bedenkingen over God, de wereld, en de menschelyke ziele...doar Christian Wolff*, 2 vols. (1767–68); *Psychologie ou Traité sur l'ame, contenant les connoissances, que nous en donne l'experience. Par M. Wolf* (1745/1998).
[2] See Ludovici, *Ausführlicher Entwurf einer vollständigen Historie der Wolffischen Philosophie, zum Gebrauche seiner Zuhörer* (1737), §§ 469–84.

who moved the debate forward in most important ways. These will be discussed in the next Chapter. The above-mentioned Jean-Bernard Mérian is of special significance in this regard, as he introduced the notion of a 'pre-existing' or 'original' apperception as a necessary condition of thought.

10.1. WOLFFIAN ACCOUNTS OF IMMORTALITY AND IDENTITY

Most Wolffians do not seem to regard the issue of personal identity as a particularly pressing philosophical problem in its own right. Like Wolff, they take the diachronic identity of the soul for granted and adopt his notion of a person as a being that is conscious of its own diachronic identity. Therefore, personal identity is discussed for the most part rather briefly and within other contexts, such as the doctrine of immortality. Indeed, all the authors discussed in this section, from Canz and Poley to more independent thinkers such as August Friedrich Müller and Georg Friedrich Meier, are committed to a notion of the soul as immaterial substance. They reject, however, what Meier calls the 'Cartesian proof' of immortality. This is said to proceed as follows: (1) the simplicity of the soul is deduced from the notion of thought in general; (2) the souls's indestructibility from its simplicity; and (3) its immortality from its indestructibility[3]. Wolffians regard it as one of Leibniz's and Wolff's achievements to have replaced the 'Cartesian proof' with a more subtle account.[4]

10.1.1. Leibnizian 'footprints' and identity: Canz, Poley, and von Creuz

Israel Gottlieb Canz's discussion is of importance, as it reduces the Wolffian account of immortality to three basic elements and elaborates on these in more detail than does Wolff.[5] The three elements are: (1) that the soul is indestructible; (2) that the soul continues to exist as a 'spirit'; and (3) that the soul will be conscious of its identity with its pre-mortem being; that is, that it will retain its personality (Canz, *Beweiß*, pp. 15–16). Like Wolff, Canz emphasises the third element as the most important feature of the state of the soul after death.[6] The notion of divine rewards and punishment in the afterlife would not make sense, he notes, without the continuation of one's personality (the consciousness of one's own identity). For 'what is punishment worth if the punished being does not know that it was him who

---

[3] Meier, *Gedancken von dem Zustande der Seele nach dem Tode*, third edn. (1762), p. 35.
[4] As is obvious from our Chapter on the seventeenth-century background, however, this critique of the 'Cartesian' view of immortality is by no means unique to Leibniz and Wolff.
[5] Canz, *Uberzeugender Beweiß aus der Vernunft von der Unsterblichkeit sowohl der Menschen Seelen insgemein, als besonders der Kinder-Seelen*, second edn. (1744).
[6] Canz's pupil Gottfried Ploucquet restates this view in his *Principia de substantiis et phaenomenis* (1764), §§ 498–512, pp. 322–7. For Canz and Ploucquet in general, see Aner, *Gottfried Ploucquets Leben und Lehren* (1909), pp. 5–7. For Ploucquet's metaphysics and psychology, see Aner (1909), pp. 40–63.

committed a crime?'⁷ Canz argues—explicitly appealing to Wolff and Leibniz as authorities—that to prove the indestrucibility of the soul is not sufficient for a proof of its immortality (ibid., p. 16). Like Wolff, he holds that the soul is a simple substance; and like earlier immaterialist thinkers (not just Wolffians), he argues that this simplicity is not consistent with materiality. Moreover, if the soul were material it could not remain identical through time. And if the soul did not remain the same through successive thoughts we would not only have different thoughts every moment but would also become a different thinking being every few hours. And this would mean that I would not be able to know tomorrow what I have thought today (ibid., pp. 45–7). For 'two thinking and distinct beings cannot look into each other's hearts'.⁸ As a material being cannot remain identical through time, it is impossible that the soul be material (ibid., p. 48). Canz applies, but does not discuss, the old distinction between a strict and a loose sense of identity to which, as we have seen, Bishop Butler attaches considerable importance. The latter sense of identity is relevant to an account of the identity of the body; for strictly or philosophically speaking, the body does not remain identical through time (ibid., p. 53). It is clear, then, that for Canz, as for Wolff, the indestructibility of the soul, as simple substance, is a necessary (but not a sufficient) condition of its immortality.

Next, Canz looks at what he calls 'spirituality' as a requirement for immortality. This concerns the continued (everlasting) existence of an intelligent being—a feature that Wolff does not seem to discuss as a distinct issue. For Wolff, continued existence is implied by the soul's indestructibility. Canz, however, emphasises that the spirituality of the soul involves self-consciousness: the question of whether the soul remains a spirit after death is the question of whether it is conscious of itself in its postmortem state.⁹ Canz maintains that self-consciousness is 'the most essential' attribute of the soul.¹⁰ Moreover, applying Wolff's ideas he argues that the soul's self-consciousness involves an act of distinguishing itself from all other things. Thus, Canz's claim that the soul will be conscious after death means that it will continue to distinguish itself from other things (ibid., p. 179). This leads up to the third element of immortality. Canz goes into more detail than does Wolff about this main feature of immortality—that the soul retains its personality; that is, has a consciousness of its identity with the soul as it existed in this life. He explains the possibility and indeed plausibility of such a consciousness by way of appealing to various Leibnizian and Wolffian doctrines.

---

[7] Canz, *Beweiß*, pp. 15–16: 'Würde sie [the soul] nichts mehr von dem jetzigen Zustand wissen: fürwahr, so würde alle Belohnung und Bestrafung vergebens seyn. Was soll eine Belohnung, wann einer weder vor jetzo weißt, noch jemahl erfahren kan, warum sie ihm zugedacht werde? Was taugt eine Strafe, wann der Gestrafte nicht weißt: ob er jemahl etwas verbrochen habe?'
[8] Canz, *Beweiß*, p. 46: 'Zwey denkende, und unterschiedene Wesen aber können einander nicht in das Herze sehen.'
[9] Canz, *Beweiß*, p. 13: 'ob sie noch um sich selbsten, nach dem Tod, wisse'.
[10] Canz, *Beweiß*, p. 283: 'Das wesentlichste, das eigentlichste was der Seelen zustehet, der Grund worauf alle Würkungen des Verstandes ankommen, ist daß wir um uns selber wissen. Ohne dieses Bewußtseyn heissen alle unsere Verstandeswürkungen so viel als nichts. Nun aber ist das Bewußtseyn unserer Seele ein Vermögen, welches schlechterdinges nicht vom Leibe des Menschen abhänget.'

Canz begins by asserting that 'everything that, at all times, distinguishes itself from all other things in the world, is identical and always the same thing'.[11] Consciousness or the act of distinguishing one's own self from other things is not sufficient, however, for the consciousness of diachronic identity. Canz argues that when the soul in its post-mortem state distinguishes itself from other things, it will necessarily be *reminded* of its pre-mortem life in which it also considered itself a creature which has its own individual nature and is distinct from all other things.[12] In short, Canz appeals to memory. It is memory rather than mere self-consciousness that provides me with the consciousness of my own diachronic identity; for the fact that I now distinguish myself from other things does not necessarily include a consciousness of my diachronic identity. A being *A* in the pre-mortem state may distinguish itself from other things, and a being *B* may distinguish itself from other things in the post-mortem state. It does not follow from this that *B* thinks of itself as identical with *A*. Canz argues that the consciousness of diachronic identity is not brought about by the act of distinguishing alone but requires a memory of past experiences. In this context he appeals to the claim, made by critics of Locke and suggested but not made explicitly by Wolff, that memory presupposes identity. The consciousness that the soul has of its own diachronic identity is involved in the memory it has of its past actions. And Canz assumes that my present memory of a past experience presupposes that I am the same self who had the experience in the past. It is through memory, then, that I acquire the knowledge or consciousness of my identity and thereby retain my personality.[13] On this basis, Canz argues with respect to the afterlife that it is through memory that we will come to know of the identity of the post-mortem self

---

[11] Canz, *Beweiß*, pp. 181–2: 'Diese Handlung, wenn sich die Seele in jenem Leben von allen anderen Sachen unterscheiden wird, ist ein besonderes Exempel, welches unter einer allgemeinen Wahrheit stehet, die also lautet: Alles, was sich von allen Dingen in der Welt, zu allen Zeiten unterscheidet, das ist einerley, und immer eben dieselbige Sache: Denn die vorhergehende Zeit die ich A nennen will, worinnen es sich unterscheidet, und die nachfolgende, deren wir den Namen B geben wollen, kan mit einander verwechselt werden, ohne daß nach der Verwechslung etwas anders, als zuvor, herauskomme, nemlich eben dieselbe Sache, eben das Geschöpfe, welches sich von allen andern unterscheidet.'

[12] Canz, *Beweiß*, p. 182: 'Woferne die Seele, sage ich, sich über das nach dem Tode besinnet, daß sie sich von allen übrigen unzerstörlichen Dingen unterscheiden könne, und eben dieselbe immer sey: so muß ihr nothwendig eben dasselbige Exempel einfallen, welches ihr in diesem Leben begegnet, da sie sich gleichfalls als ein Geschöpfe angesehen, welches seine eigene und besondere Natur unter allen anderen habe. Mithin erinnert sie sich des gegenwärtigen Lebens. Sie erkennet also aus dem schon angeführten Grunde, daß sie eben das in diesem Leben auch gethan, was sie zu solcher Zeit in dem zukünftigen würklich thut, nemlich, daß sie sich als unterschieden von allen Dingen ansiehet.'

[13] Canz, *Beweiß*, pp. 177–8: 'Wer in der Ewigkeit glückselig ist, der kommt in natürlicher Ordnung der Gedanken auf diese allgemeine Wahrheit: Keine Glückseligkeit wird von Gott ungefähr verhänget, sondern hat ihren Grund in dem vormaligen Zustande dessen, welchen das Glück betrifft. Nun stehe ich, Seele, dißmal in der höchsten Glückseligkeit, deren ich nur fähig seyn mag. Also muß ich vorher etwas gewesen seyn, welches Gott vermocht, mir diese unendliche Gnade zuzutheilen. *Hier kömmt es endlich bey der Seele auf eine Erinnerung dessen, was mit ihr in diesem Leben vorgeloffen, an.* **Dadurch** *erkennet sie, sie sey eben dieselbige, welche in diesem Leben so oder so gehandelt*' (my italics and bold).

or soul with that of the pre-mortem self or soul, or, in other words, that we retain our personality in the afterlife.

Lastly, Canz attempts to explain the possibility of such identity-involving memory by referring to the notion of traces that past experiences leave in the soul—a thesis that is reminiscent of Leibniz's minute perceptions. Since the post-mortem soul, as a simple and indestructible being, is identical with the pre-mortem soul, it retains in itself 'the footprints of the thoughts of this life to eternity' (ibid., p. 183).[14] The thoughts of this life are connected with those of the afterlife and allow the soul to become conscious of itself as the same being that had those thoughts in the pre-mortem life. As Canz puts it, these 'footprints' give the soul occasion to reflect that it has formerly existed in a different state, that its present state is grounded in the former, and that it always remains the same subject to which those states belong (ibid., p. 184).[15] As is obvious from the analysis above, Canz's account of personal identity presupposes both the simplicity and indestructibility of the soul and the existence of such traces or 'footprints' that past experiences leave in the soul.

Heinrich Engelhard Poley applies the Leibnizian notion of traces to the issue of personal identity in his notes to his German translation of Locke's *Essay*, published in 1757; that is, prior to the publication of Leibniz's *Nouveaux essais*.[16] In his comments Poley variously appeals to both Wolff and Canz.[17] He discusses the issue, raised by Locke's theory, of whether we can be conscious of actions as done by us which we have not in fact done. He maintains that this is possible only in people who suffer from some disease of the brain. Normal people, while awake, cannot represent to themselves actions as done by themselves that they have not in fact done. According to Poley, this follows from the principle of sufficient reason. On the basis of that principle we know that we are awake and are not dreaming.[18] Our dream experiences

---

[14] Canz, *Beweiß*, p. 183: '...die Fußtapfen derer Gedanken dieses Lebens in und an sich, mit in die Ewigkeit hinaus'.

[15] These footprints bring about that the soul 'durch Ueberlegung, und vermittelst allgemeiner Wahrheiten, öfters darauf fiele, sie habe ehmals in einem anderen Zustande gelebet, alles was ihr jetzo widerfahre, sey in dem vorigen gegründet, sie aber sey und bleibe immer einerley, und eben dieselbige': Canz, *Beweiß*, p. 184. 'Woraus denn erscheinet, daß in allewege die Seele nach dem Tode erkennen werde, sie sey keine andere Person, als welche sie in diesem Leben gewesen': ibid.

[16] Poley, *Herrn Johann Lockens Versuch vom Menschlichen Verstande. Aus dem Englischen übersetzt und mit Anmerkungen versehen* (1757).

[17] For example, Poley appeals to Canz's use of the distinction between strict and loose identity: Poley, *Lockens Versuch*, pp. 333–4.

[18] 'Das ist nur bey solchen elenden Personen möglich, denen das Gehirne durch eine hitzige Krankheit, oder einen andern Zufall verrücket ist. Nur diese können sich, auch wenn sie wachen, etwas, als von ihnen gethan vorstellen; ungeachtet sie es niemals gethan, noch von einen andern wirkenden Wesen bewerkstelliget worden ist. Die Ursache ist, weil eine solche Vorstellung sodann an Klarheit alle die Vorstellungen übertrifft, oder wenigstens ihnen gleich kömmt, welche zu ihrem Gegenstande solche Dinge haben, die wirklich außer uns vorhanden sind. Denn da sind sinnlichen Empfindungen, im Absehen auf eine solche Vorstellung oder Einbildung, so schwach, als es irgend eine im Traume ist; und also geben solche Personen in der That wachende Träumer ab. Wäre dem Verfasser der allgemeine Satz des zureichenden Grundes bekannt gewesen; wäre er auch, da er uns zuerst die vergesellschafteten Begriffe entdecket, auf das Gesetz der Einbildungskraft gekommen; und hätte er einen deutlichern Begriff von dem Bewußtseyn gehabt: so würde er nicht von dem Bewußteyn vormaliger Thaten so zweifelhaft geredet haben': Poley, *Lockens Versuch*, p. 342.

may not be consistent with the principle of sufficient reason, but in our waking state everything that happens has a sufficient reason.[19] Appealing to Wolff and what he calls 'the law of the imagination', Poley says that no sensation can reappear in our soul unless some present sensation contains a part of it or has at least in common with it the place, time, or other circumstances—otherwise there would be no sufficient reason why our soul should reproduce this rather than another past sensation. We need not be concerned, therefore, that we could be conscious of a past action that we never committed. This would be inconsistent with the nature of the soul; indeed, it would be inconsistent with the nature and order of things in general. For an action that we have never committed could not have left any traces in our soul, and therefore no present sensation can have anything in common with it, and therefore the imagination is not capable of reproducing such a representation of that action as committed by us. Therefore, we cannot become conscious of such an action. To be conscious of a past action it is required that we are aware of the main circumstances that accompanied and brought about that action—and especially of the sufficient reason why we did that action, and how we did it. That is to say, we must be conscious that at the time we were awake and not dreaming. None of this can happen, however, with regard to an action that we never committed. Therefore, there cannot be a consciousness of such an action.[20]

Poley's argument, however, shows at best that I can have no *genuine* consciousness or memory of actions that I have not done—which is not a lot, given that genuine memory would have to be defined in terms of remembering actions that one has in

---

[19] 'Denn vermöge des Satzes des zureichenden Grundes wissen wir es gewiß, daß wir wachen und nicht träumen; folglich kann auch nicht in wachendem Zustande, so wie im Traume, eine solche Vorstellung möglich seyn, die keine wirklich geschehene That zum Gegenstande hat. Im Traume geschiehet alles durch einen Sprung, und ohne einen zureichenden Grund': Poley, *Lockens Versuch*, p. 342.

[20] 'Ganz anders hingegen verhält es sich, wenn wir wachen. Da hat alles seinen zureichenden Grund, wir mögen thun, was wir wollen... Vermöge des Gesetzes der Einbildungskraft, das sich auf einer so unumstößlichen Erfahrung gründet, kann keine vormalige Empfindung in unserer Seele wieder zum Vorscheine kommen, dafern nicht eine gegenwärtige sinnliche Empfindung einen Theil davon enthält, oder etwas mit ihr der Zeit, oder den Orte nach, oder in andern Umständen gemein hat. Denn es würde sonst kein zureichender Grund vorhanden seyn, warum unsere Seele vielmehr diese als eine andere alte Empfindung hervorbringen sollte. S. des Herrn von Wolf Psychol. Empir. Par. 117 und die Psychol. Rat par. 123.124': Poley, *Lockens Versuch*, p. 343. 'Dergestalt dürfen wir uns nicht bei Herrn Locken besorgen, daß wir uns vielleicht einer vormaligen That bewußt seyn könnten, die wir gleichwohl niemals unternommen hätten. Dieß würde offenbar mit der Natur der Seele, ja mit der Natur und Ordnung der Dinge streiten. Denn da eine That, die wir niemals unternommen, keine Spuren einer Empfindung in unserer Seele hat zurück lassen können; und keine gegenwärtige Empfindung mit derselben etwas gemein haben kann: so ist auch die Einbildungskraft niemals vermögend, eine solche That, als von uns geschehen, wieder hervorzubringen; folglich werden wir auch niemals zu einem Bewußtseyn derselben gelangen können. Wenn wir uns einer vormahligen Handlung bewußt seyn sollen; so müssen wir uns auch, wo nicht aller, doch der vornehmsten Umstände, welche die Unternehmung und Bewerkstelligung derselben begleitet haben, und insonderheit des zureichenden Grundes bewußt seyn, warum wir sie unternommen, und wie sie von uns bewerkstelliget worden ist. Wir müssen uns bewußt seyn, daß wir zur selbigen Zeit gewachet, und nicht geträumet haben. Aber all dieses kann in unsern Seelen bey einer nie geschehenen That nicht vorgehen; folglich ist ein Bewußtseyn derselben gar nicht möglich': Poley, *Lockens Versuch*, pp. 343–4.

fact done. Poley asserts that all my waking consciousness or memory must be genuine unless I am mentally diseased. That assertion is based on an application of Leibniz's principle of sufficient reason as a metaphysical principle and on other assumptions of Wolffian philosophy, such as assumptions about the nature of the imagination. In short, Poley's argument requires rather heavy metaphysical baggage as a means of attempting to refute Locke.

Even a critic of central aspects of Wolffian Metaphysics, however, such as Friedrich Carl Casimir von Creuz, appears to adopt an essentially Wolffian account of immortality and personal identity.[21] Von Creuz differs from Wolff and other traditional immaterialist thinkers by claiming that the soul is neither a simple nor a compound thing, but something in between (a 'Mittelding', *Versuch über die Seele*, vol. 1, pt. 1, p. 41). He agrees with the traditional view that the soul is indivisible and indestructible, but argues that it does not follow from this that it is simple (ibid., pp. 41–8). The soul is a unitary entity but consists of parts. These parts, however, cannot exist without one another; they coexist necessarily—and this is to say that the soul cannot be divided (ibid., p. 48).[22] The details of von Creuz's arguments for the soul as a 'Mittelding' that is neither compound nor simple need not concern us here, as they do not affect his essentially Wolffian argument for immortality and identity. As we shall see below, he is critical of Wolff's account of self-consciousness—making comments of considerable importance in this context. His argument for immortality and identity, however, is based on the view that he shares with Wolff and the Wolffians: namely, that the soul is indivisible and indestructible, and so not material.

Von Creuz's arguments are similar but not identical to those of Canz (ibid., pt. II). He argues that three things are required for immortality: (1) that the soul continues to exist forever; (2) that it always remains conscious of itself and of other things; (3) that 'consequently', it 'remembers the past' and remembers that it is the same soul as the one that existed before death separated it from the body.[23] Von Creuz's thesis (1) assumes the indestructibility of the soul—the first thesis in Canz. Indestructibility, he argues, implies continued existence (assuming God does not intervene). Thesis (2) corresponds to Canz's second thesis about self-consciousness;

---

[21] von Creuz, *Versuch über die Seele*, 2 vols. (1754). For von Creuz's philosophy in general, see Eleutheropulos, *Friedrich Carl Casimir von Creuz's Erkenntnistheorie* (1895).

[22] von Creuz, *Versuch*, vol. 1, pt. 1, pp. 47–8: 'Dieses Mittelding hat mit dem Einfachen gemein, daß es nur eine Kraft haben, und folglich auch des Bewußtseyns fähig seyn kann...; ferner daß es nicht anders als auf einmal entstehen, und nicht anders als auf einmal untergehen kann, wenn anders dessen Vernichtigung möglich ist: Denn ein Ding, das aus Theilen besteht, die ohne einander unmöglich existiren können; folglich jederzeit nothwendig coexistiren, ist also auch nothwendig untheilbar; dahingegen ein jedes Zusammengesetztes, weil es aus vor sich bestehenden Dingen bestehet, jederzeit an und vor sich (absolute) theilbar seyn muß.' Early critics of von Creuz's view of the soul include Hase, *De anima humana non medii generis inter simplicem et compositam substantiam* (1756).

[23] von Creuz writes: 'Es wird zur Unsterblichkeit unsrer Seele mehr nicht erfordert, als daß solche (1) Ohne Ende fortdaure; (2) Sich ihrer und anderer Dinge außer ihr *beständig* bewußt bleibe, und *folglich* (3) Sich auch des Vergangenen und ihrer selbst, daß sie dieselbige Seele sey, welche der Tod von dem Körper, den sie in diesem Weltraume gehabt, getrennet, erinnere': von Creuz, *Versuch*, vol. 2, 'Vorbericht', unpaginated, leaf 5, verso (my italics).

and likewise, von Creuz's thesis (3) corresponds to Canz's third thesis about the consciousness of diachronic identity. Von Creuz, however, makes more explicit than does Canz the connection between the consciousness of self and memory and how the two result in the consciousness of our own diachronic identity. Consciousness, according to von Creuz, is intimately connected to remembering. The self that remains conscious also remembers its past, and this means that it becomes (or at least can become) conscious of its identity through time. This is how it retains its personality after death. The soul's future state after death is related to its present state in this life, and it will remember that it is the same soul that played certain roles in this life while it was attached to its body.[24] According to von Creuz, then, consciousness of self, memory of past experiences, and the consciousness of one's own diachronic identity (retaining the personality) are required for immortality, in addition to the continued existence of the soul as substance. On this basis von Creuz distinguishes explicitly between metaphysical and moral immortality, thus highlighting ideas that are present in both Wolff and Leibniz. Metaphysical immortality refers to the continued existence of the soul as substance. Moral immortality means that the soul does not merely continue to exist, as substance, but also retains its personality.[25]

10.1.2. Lockean leanings: Müller and Meier

It is an indication of the powerful impact of the Wolffian account of immortality that philosophers who were otherwise critical of Wolffian philosophy as a whole, including those even more critical than von Creuz, still adopted its account of immortality and identity. An example of this is August Friedrich Müller—a pupil of Wolff's critic Andreas Rüdiger, and strongly influenced by Locke.[26] In his *Einleitung in die Philosophischen Wissenschaften*, first published in 1728, he holds that although we cannot know the soul's 'inner substance' and are able only to describe it in terms of its faculties which we infer from their experientially known effects (mental operations) (*Einleitung*, vol. 1, p. 825), we can still know that soul is a simple and incorporeal, and therefore indestructible ('unverweßliche') substance.[27]

---

[24] 'Ihr künftiger Zustand nach dem Tode hat allemal eine Beziehung auf ihren gegenwärtigen Zustand in diesem Leben...so ist dieses allemal ihr ordentlicher Zustand, daß sie in dem Zusammenhange ihrer Gedanken bleibt, und sich erinnert und erinnern muß, daß sie dieselbige Seele sey, die in einem ihr eigenthümlich gewesenen Körper in dieser Welt oder in diesem Leben gewisse komische und gewisse tragische Rollen gespielet hat': von Creuz, *Versuch*, vol. 2, p. 92.

[25] Creuz writes: 'so wird auch kein Zweifel mehr übrig bleiben, daß unsere Seele nicht nur metaphysisch; sondern auch moralisch unsterblich sey; oder, daß sie nicht nur schlechtweg fortdaure; sondern auch den Stand ihrer Persönlichkeit behalte': von Creuz, *Versuch*, vol. 2, p. 92.

[26] Müller, *Einleitung in die Philosophischen Wissenschaften*, 3 vols. (1728; second edn., 1733).

[27] 'So viel aber kan doch aus dem beweiß des vorhergehenden §. noch nützlich geschlosssen werden, daß ein geist seiner natur nach unverweßlich sey. Denn die verwesung ist nichts anders, als eine natürliche auflösung einer aus den elementen zusammengesezten substanz, und also eines cörpers in seine einfachen principia...Nun aber ist ein geist eine nicht etwa aus den elementen zusammengesezte, sondern denen elementen entgegengesezte einfache substanz': Müller, *Einleitung*, vol. 2, p. 828.

Müller does not accept Wolff's account of consciousness. He deals with this issue only very briefly, however. He represents Wolff as maintaining that to be conscious of one's own self is an essential feature of human reason. It is not clear that Wolff actually says this, but this is how Müller interprets Wolff's statement that we are conscious of ourselves and of other things. Müller maintains that to be conscious of one's own self is not fundamental or essential, as it depends on an inner sensation ('innerliche empfindung') which presupposes further ideas. To be conscious of one's own self is to have an idea of one's own self. Since, as Müller claims, all our ideas derive from sensations, the soul, when it has an idea of itself and its operations, would have to have a sensation of itself and its operations.[28] Müller clearly argues along empiricist lines here, but his account of self-consciousness is very unclear. In the end he seems to equate (self-)consciousness with inner sense. Locke, by contrast, distinguishes between the two, as we have seen.

Very much like Leibniz, Wolff, and von Creuz, however, Müller emphasises the importance of moral identity to a meaningful notion of immortality and life after death. Unlike Wolff in the relevant sections discussed above, Müller points out that as being indestructible is an attribute of all simple substances (including material atoms),[29] it needs to be shown also that God created the human soul for eternal duration (ibid., p. 831). For from the (alleged) fact that human souls are naturally indestructible, it does not follow that they are also everlasting. They could be annihilated by the will of the creator (ibid., pp. 830–1). That is why eternal duration, or everlasting existence, is a second, distinct feature of immortality. Yet even eternal duration or continued everlasting existence is not sufficient for immortality. It is required, further, that the soul retains its 'moral nature'; that is, its personal identity. Müller's formulation appears to be more Lockean than Wolffian in places: for example, when he speaks of a memory merely of past actions, not of the consciousness of identity. On the other hand, he also says that in addition to the indestructibility and everlasting existence of the soul, the latter's identity, as substance, is required for immortality, claiming that *this* means it will retain its 'moral nature'. For if it will be the same soul as in this life it will be conscious of its own self and of its own past actions, and this means it is capable of a moral state of happiness or

---

[28] 'Der Herr HoffR. Wolff nennet diese wirckung des menschlichen verstandes, sich seiner selbst bewust seyn, und suchet darinnen den grund und das wesen der vernunft. Doch ist dieses sich seiner selbst bewust seyn allererst eine wirckung der innerlichen empfindung, die die seele durch ihre innerlichen sinne von sich selbst und ihren idéen hat. Denn eben dadurch ist die seele sich ihrer selbst bewust, weil sie sich selbst, und ihre wirckungen, in sich selbst zu empfinden fähig ist: indem, sich seiner bewust seyn, nichts anders heissen kan, als eine idée von sich selber haben; alle idéen aber aus den empfindungen der sinne entspringen, und also, wenn die seele eine idée von sich selber und ihren eigenen wirckungen haben, d.i. sich ihrer selbst bewust seyn soll, sie nothwendig vermittelst innerlicher sinne eine empfindung ihrer selbst und ihrer wirckungen in ihr selber haben muß': Müller, *Einleitung*, vol. 1, p. 176.

[29] 'Jedoch ist hierbey zu erwegen, daß diese erwiesene unverweßlichkeit noch lange nicht die idée der unsterblichkeit ausmache, die den menschlichen seelen zukomme. Denn die blosse unverweßlichkeit ist, vermöge der vorhergehenden demonstration, allen einfachen substanzen, und also auch den seelen der bestien, ja so gar auch den elementen...gemein': Müller, *Einleitung*, vol. 1, p. 830.

misery.[30] Thus, although Müller's emphasis on memory may sound Lockean, it is clear that his account is along Leibnizian and Wolffian lines. For Müller, the soul's simple and incorporeal nature is a necessary condition of its identity through time. He even believes that the soul's moral nature (its identity through time) can be derived from its indestructibility;[31] and, moreover, that memory of past actions *requires* the diachronic identity of the soul. We saw that Locke does not think of immortality and personal identity as necessarily linked to simplicity and immateriality.

A thinker who starts from a Wolffian standpoint, but whose Lockean leanings are stronger than Müller's, is Georg Friedrich Meier. Meier, too, considers personal identity in the context of the immortality issue.[32] Here he argues, among other things, that there is no *a priori* proof of the immortality of the soul.[33] His attitude towards the issue is much more sceptical than that of the Wolffians. As indicated above, he is with the Wolffians, however, in rejecting the traditional argument for immortality which he calls the old 'Cartesian' proof of immortality (*Gedancken*, p. 35). These days, he states, philosophers have a subtler notion of immortality—one that includes thoughts about the state of the soul after its death (ibid., p. 36), such as its moral nature or personal identity. Thus immortality would require that one is conscious of oneself and of other things after death, otherwise one would not be

---

[30] 'Ferner ist auch zur rechten idée der unsterbligkeit der seele noch nicht genug, daß sie ewig fortdaure: sondern es wird auch noch über dieses erfordert, daß sie in der ihr bevorstehenden ewigkeit noch eben dieselbe sey, die sie in dieser zeitligkeit gewesen, folglich ihre völlige moralische natur behalte, und also ihrer selbst, ihrer im leben begangenen thaten, sich bewust, auch eines moralischen zustandes der freude und traurigkeit fähig, und solchergestalt im stande der seligkeit oder unseligkeit sey. Derowegen muß zu völliger darthuung der unsterbligkeit der menschlichen seele, über die unverweßligkeit derselben, noch zweyerley erwiesen werden: erstlich ihre unvergängligkeit oder ewige dauer, zum andern der in solcher ewigkeit ihr bevorstehende stand der seligkeit oder unseligkeit, dessen sie sich bewust seyn werde': Müller, *Einleitung*, vol. 1, p. 831.

[31] 'Was erstlich ihre moralische natur, und daß sie dieselbe auch im stande ihrer absonderung von dem leibe behalten werde, anlanget, so lässet sich dieselbe zur genüge aus ihrer unverweßligkeit erweisen. Denn da allen von ihren leibern abgesonderten seelen, weil sie unverweßlich sind, ihre wesentliche kräfte, nemlich der vernünftige verstand, wille, und innerliche empfindung, und also ihre ganze moralische natur, übrig bleiben. Und weil, in betrachtung solcher ihrer moralischen natur, die menschlichen seelen ihren eigenen, von ihren cörpern independenten zweck, nemlich ihre glückseligkeit haben...auf welchen zweck ihre ganze moralische natur abgerichtet ist, und nach welchem sie also schon in diesem leben unabläßlich streben: so muß nothwendig den menschlichen seelen, zugleich mit ihrer moralischen natur, dieser ihr eigene und von dem cörper independente zweck übrig bleiben, so daß sie solches zweckes entweder theilhaftig seyn müssen, oder nicht, und sie also im stande ihrer absonderung von ihren leibern in einem entweder seligen oder unseligen stande müssen seyn können': Müller, *Einleitung*, vol. 1, pp. 831–2.

[32] Meier, *Gedancken von dem Zustande der Seele nach dem Tode*, third edn. (1762).

[33] For Meier's philosophy of religion, see Gawlick, 'G. F. Meiers Stellung in der Religionsphilosophie der deutschen Aufklärung', in Hinske (ed.), *Zentren der Aufklärung I: Halle: Aufklärung und Pietismus* (1989), pp. 157–76; and Dierse, 'Nachträge zu G. F. Meiers Religionsphilosophie', in Kreimendahl (ed.), *Aufklärung und Skepsis. Festschrift für Günter Gawlick* (1995), pp. 33–46. For general accounts of Meier, see Schaffrath, *Die Philosophie des Georg Friedrich Meier. Ein Beitrag zur Geschichte der Aufklärungsphilosophie* (1940); and Schenk, *Leben und Werk des Halleschen Aufklärers Georg Friedrich Meier* (1994).

capable of happiness and misery.³⁴ Moreover, to prove the immortality of the soul one would need to prove also that (1) the soul remembers in its future state that it is the same entity as in this life, and (2) that it remembers its own actions from this life. Meier reports, following Wolff, that recent philosophers call this feature of immortality the personality of the soul. He emphasises, like Wolff, that it is an essential element of immortality, for without it the notion of rewards and punishments in the future state would not make sense. Rewards and punishments cease to be rewards and punishments if one does not remember the actions on account of which one receives rewards and punishments.³⁵ He states that both the memory of past actions and the consciousness of diachronic identity are involved, rather than following the Lockean idea that memory and consciousness of past actions constitute the diachronic identity of the human subject as a person.

Although Meier believes that these features are required for immortality, he holds that one cannot prove that they will in fact be part of the condition of the soul after death. He differs from the Wolffians in other respects as well. While he believes that the soul is a simple substance, he does not believe that it follows that a materialist cannot believe in the immortality of the soul. For Meier, therefore, belief in immortality does not require that one refute materialism (*Gedancken*, pp. 52–3, 75–9). He argues against Canz in particular that one can be a materialist and still believe in immortality (ibid., p. 188). Here he seems to be of the same view as Locke: the materiality of the soul is consistent with an afterlife (ibid., p. 189). As to the personality of the soul after death, Meier is sceptical that it can be proved (ibid., pp. 140–4). He thinks it is more natural and hence more probable that the soul will remember its former life than that it will not be able to remember it. We must assume that after death the soul will receive ideas that are similar to the ones it had in this life, otherwise there would be a gap in the development of its ideas. Therefore, it would seem more natural that the soul will recall its former life.³⁶ Still, it is not inconsistent with the nature of the soul that it may forget its former state.³⁷ So,

---

³⁴ To prove the immortality of the soul includes the argument, 'daß sie sich ihrer selbst und anderer Dinge, in dem zukünftigen Leben, wenigstens wechselweise bewust seyn werde. Ohne diesem Bewustseyn, würde sie keiner Straffen und Belohnung fähig seyn, als welche aufhören dergleichen zu seyn, wenn man sie nicht mit einem Bewustseyn empfindet': Meier, *Gedancken*, p. 49.
³⁵ 'Daß die Seele in ihrem zukünftigen Zustande sich auch erinnern werde, daß sie eben diejenige sey, die sie in diesem Leben gewesen, und daß sie sich auch erinnere, was sie gethan habe. Dieses Stück nennen die neuern Weltweisen die Persönlichkeit der Seele nach dem Tode; und wenn man annimmt, daß wir, die Belohnungen und Straffen unser gegenwärtigen Handlungen, nach dem Tode erst recht zu erwarten haben: so ist es ein nothwendiges Stück des Zustandes der Seele nach dem Tode. Man muß ja wissen, warum man belohnt oder bestraft wird, weil der Lohn und die Straffe aufhören dergleichen zu seyn, wenn man die Handlungen nicht weiß, um welcher willen man sie empfängt': Meier, *Gedancken*, pp. 49–50.
³⁶ One needs to assume 'daß die Seele nach dem Tode Vorstellungen bekommen werde, die den gegenwärtigen ähnlich sind, weil sonst in der Entwicklung ihrer Begriffe ein Sprung geschehen müste: so müste die Seele ihre Natur ganz ablegen, das Gesetz der Einbildungskraft müste von Gott widerrufen werden, wenn die Seele ihrer selbst ganz vergessen sollte': Meier, *Gedancken*, p. 143.
³⁷ 'das gänzliche Vergessen des vorhergehenden Zustandes, [ist] der Natur der Seele nicht zuwider': Meier, *Gedancken*, p. 143.

fulfilment of these conditions after death cannot be proved, and so it remains uncertain whether the soul will retain its personality after death.[38] Again Meier argues against Canz in particular, saying that it is not sufficient to prove that the soul will retain its power of representation; for even if it did retain the latter it would not follow that the soul will also retain its power of consciousness (ibid., p. 191). Consciousness requires a higher degree of representation than do obscure thoughts. So one would have to prove that the soul's power of representation will be of the same degree as in this life;[39] but it is doubtful that this can be done.

What is Meier's understanding of consciousness? He makes use of the Wolffian notion of consciousness when arguing against the Lockean thesis about thinking matter.[40] He even makes use of the terminology of apperception, stating that consciousness or apperception consists in the act of distinguishing between representations and between the objects that are being represented.[41] A thought is not a mere representation of an object; it also contains the representation of the distinctness of this object from other objects (that is to say, consciousness is not an essential feature of representation). A representation ('Vorstellung') becomes a thought only when it is accompanied by consciousness; we have to represent its distinctness for it to become a thought.[42] Moreover, when we consider our own self we notice the mental operation of thinking. Meier accepts—with Wolff, it seems—that we infer

---

[38] 'Wenigstens ist es alsdenn viel natürlicher, daß die Seele sich des vorhergehenden Lebens nach dem Tode erinnere, als daß sie desselben gantz vergessen solte, das natürlichere aber ist jederzeit wahrscheinlicher, als dasjenige, was nicht so natürlich ist. Allein die angeführten Bedingungen können, aus der Vernunft nicht demonstrirt werden, und es bleibt also ungewiß, ob die Seele nach dem Tode ihre Persönlichkeit behalten werde': Meier, *Gedancken*, pp. 143–4.

[39] Zum 'Bewustsein [wird] ein grösserer Grad der Vorstellungskraft erfodert, als zu den dunklen Begriffen. Wer also beweisen will, daß die Seele nach dem Tode sich ihrer bewust sey, und die Kraft dazu im Tode behalten werde, der muß nicht blos erweisen, daß sie ihre Kraft behalte, sondern daß sie auch den Grad der Kraft behalte, den sie vorher besessen hat': Meier, *Gedancken*, p. 191.

[40] Meier, *Beweis: daß keine Materie denken könne*, second edn. (1751).

[41] 'Das Bewustseyn (apperceptio, conscium esse) besteht darin, wenn man die Vorstellungen und die Gegenstände derselben von einander unterscheidet; oder wenn man nicht nur die Sache sich vorstelt, sondern auch dasjenige, wodurch sie von andern Sachen verschieden ist. Ein Gedancke muß demnach nicht aus einer blossen Vorstellung des Gegenstandes, der Sache an welche man denckt, bestehen; sondern die Vorstellung des Unterschiedes dieses Gegenstandes muß noch hinzukommen': Meier, *Beweis*, pp. 74–5. See also Meier's *Auszug aus der Vernunftlehre* (1760; first edn., 1752) (a text used by Kant for his lectures): 'Wir sind uns unserer Vorstellungen und unserer Erkenntnisse bewust (conscium esse, adpercipere) in so ferne wir sie und ihren Gegenstand von andern Vorstellungen und Sachen unterscheiden. Das Bewußtseyn ist eine doppelte Vorstellung: eine Vorstellung des Gegenstandes, und eine Vorstellung seines Unterschiedes von andern. Das Bewußtseyn verhält sich wie das Licht in der Körperwelt, welches uns den Unterschied der Körper entdeckt': § 13, p. 11.

[42] 'Eine Vorstellung wird nicht eher zu einem Gedancken, bis das Bewustseyn dazu komt, wir müssen uns ihren Unterschied vorstellen, wir müssen erkennen, daß sie eben diese Vorstellung und keine andere ist. Das Bewustseyn hat eine grosse Aehnlichkeit mit dem Lichte in der Körperwelt. Mittern in einer stockfinstern Nacht sind alle um uns befindlichen Körper unsichtbar, wir können keinen von dem andern unterscheiden, das blaue das grüne alles siehet einerley aus, denn wir sehen gar nichts. Die Sonne geht auf, und ihre malerischen Strahlen erleuchten den gantzen Gesichtscreys. Wir erblicken die Körper und unterscheiden sie von ein ander. Das Bewustseyn ist das Licht der Seele, oder vielmehr die Quelle dieses Lichts': Meier, *Beweis*, pp. 75–6.

our own existence from our thoughts. According to Meier, Descartes's 'I think' is indeed the first certain truth that we know. I infer my own existence, and also that there are other things outside me from the *cogito*. Although like Wolff, Meier does account for consciousness in terms of the capacity to distinguish, which would suggest an essential link between self-consciousness and the consciousness of objects, he seems to ascribe primacy to the relating to one's own self. Prior to knowing other things, Meier argues, I know that I think and therefore exist.[43] According to Wolff, by contrast, we cannot be conscious of our own selves without also relating to other things.

10.1.3. Wolffian accounts of immortality and the four main theses of rational psychology

The end of the eighteenth century was a time to review the various theories of immortality that had been developed thus far. Georg Samuel Francke, who published such an overview, praises the Wolffian accounts for having identified these three elements as essential to immortality: (1) the *indestructibility* of the soul; (2) the continued existence of the soul as a spiritual or intelligent being—its *spirituality*—(3) the soul's *personality*, that is, the soul's ability in its post-mortem state to recognize its identity with the soul of the pre-mortem state.[44] Francke's summary seems fair, but it omits the role that memory and self-consciousness (as distinct from the consciousness of diachronic identity) play in Wolff and in those who adopt and modify Wolff's account. Francke agrees with the view that he ascribes to Wolff and the Wolffians: namely, that thesis (3), about the personality of the soul, is the most important feature of immortality (*Uebersicht*, p. 6). He suggests that our notion of immortality and future happiness would be seriously weakened without that aspect; for what we hope for is the continuation of our personality. The hope for future happiness is seriously weakened if we have reason to think that we will have no consciousness of our diachronic identity in the post-mortem state. Francke claims that there is general agreement (not just among Wolffians) about this.[45] According to Francke, the disagreements concern the question of whether theses (1) and (2) are required for the continuation of our personality to be possible:

---

[43] 'Wenn ich mich gantz allein betrachte, und an kein anderes Ding ausser mir dencke, so werde ich gewahr, und ich fühle es in mir selbst auf die allerunleugbarste Weise, daß ich dencke. Alle diejenigen, welche aus der Metaphysick die Entstehungsart aller unserer Erkenntnis gelernt haben, die wissen, daß Cartesius Recht hat, wenn er sagt: der Erfahrungssatz: ich denke, sey die erste gewisse Wahrheit, die wir erkennen. Daraus schliesse ich, daß ich würcklich vorhanden bin, und daraus schliesse ich ferner, daß auch andere Dinge ausser mir vorhanden sind. Ehe ich also mit Gewisheit wissen kan, daß etwas ausser mir vorhanden sey, muß ich schon wissen, daß ich würcklich vorhanden bin. Mein Daseyn schliesse ich aus meinen Gedancken. Daß ich dencke, ist demnach das erste, was ich von mir weis, und was ich dencken kan und muß, ehe ich noch an irgends eine Sache ausser mir dencke': Meier, *Beweis*, pp. 80–1.

[44] Francke, *Versuch einer kurzen historisch-kritischen Uebersicht der Lehren und Meinungen unserer vornehmsten neuen Weltweisen von der Unsterblichkeit der menschlichen Seele* (1796), p. 2.

[45] There is almost universal agreement, he says: 'daß die Fortdauer unsrer Persönlichkeit gerade das sey, was wir wünschen, was wir hoffen, was wir bestätigt haben möchten, oder daß sie der

do indestructibility and spirituality have to be proved first? This has been an issue, he says, especially since Locke argued that immortality does not require the immateriality of the soul (ibid., p. 7). Francke himself thinks that the notion of a continuation of personality requires either the idea of the immateriality of the soul or, at least, the notion that the materiality of the soul is as doubtful as its immateriality. According to Francke, an endorsement of materialism would not be compatible with the notion of a continuation of personality (ibid., pp. 8–9). As indicated above, Wolff himself emphatically maintains that (1) and (2) are necessary conditions of (3) and, therefore, of immortality.

Francke's summary account of Wolffian theory is of course post-Kantian, but it is worth noting that the Wolffian accounts of the soul and its immortality from Canz onwards correspond to Kant's reconstruction of the main theses of rational psychology in terms of four 'paralogisms'. We saw that the Wolffian view of immortality involves claims about the substantiality of the soul (first paralogism, *Critique of Pure Reason*, A 348), about its simple and indestructible nature (second paralogism, A 351), about its personality, conceived of in terms of the consciousness of identity (third paralogism, A 361), and about its distinctness from other things, its spirituality, or, as Kant puts it, its 'ideality' (fourth paralogism, A 366–7).

10.2. WOLFFIAN ACCOUNTS OF CONSCIOUSNESS, THE UNITY OF THE SOUL, AND PERSONAL IDENTITY

Some independent Wolffians—Hermann Samuel Reimarus in particular—develop thoughts about personal identity that are present neither in Wolff nor in Wolff's followers discussed so far, linking diachronic identity and consciousness in a new way. One point made in this context relates to the unity of the soul. It is that thought requires the activity of comparing and distinguishing, and that this in turn requires a unitary subject, and indeed a simple (immaterial) substance. This is not an entirely new idea, but Reimarus adds another thesis.[46] We have seen that for Locke, consciousness and memory bring about personal identity, and that others (Butler, for example) argue that identity must be presupposed for memory and thus cannot be constituted by it. For Reimarus, diachronic identity is presupposed not just by memory but also by the consciousness we have of the present. This argument is made explicitly only by Reimarus himself, but it is anticipated to some extent in briefer comments by earlier Wolffian philosophers.

Hauptpunct sey, worauf es bey den Beweisen für die Unsterblichkeit der Seele ankomme': Francke, *Uebersicht*, p. 7.

[46] We noted in Chapter 2 that many philosophers arguing against materialism—such as Ralph Cudworth in the seventeenth century—believe that immateriality is required by the unity of the soul. The Wolffians, however, give a more detailed account of why unity is required for thought to be possible in the first place.

10.2.1. The necessary 'unity of the subject': Winckler, Knutzen, and Mendelssohn

According to Johann Heinrich Winckler, for example, every thought involves three basic elements: at least two distinct ideas or representations (*Vorstellungen*), and the act of distinguishing between those ideas.[47] Moreover, it is required that the subject who forms these ideas and distinguishes between them be one and the same. If there is to be a thought, the various ideas must be present in one and the same being—a being that is conscious of the distinctness of those ideas. Clearly, this argument relates only to the notion that the unity and simplicity of the thinking being are required for consciousness of ideas. Winckler seems only to hint at the idea that diachronic identity of the subject is also required. He states at one point that a being who has different ideas and the consciousness of their distinctness, but who cannot, while engaged in those mental activities, remain the same, could not think.[48] He does not, however, seem to explain or elaborate on this issue.

Kant's teacher Martin Knutzen makes a similar comment about the necessary unity of the thinking subject, but has more to say about it than does Winckler.[49] Like Wolff, Knutzen points to the experiential fact that we are conscious of ourselves and of other things.[50] And like Wolff, he argues that the consciousness of self depends on the act of distinguishing ourselves from other things.[51] Knutzen goes beyond Wolff's argument, however, in that he argues that the act of distinguishing (by implication, the act of consciousness) requires the 'unity of the subject' in a twofold sense: first, the unity of the subject in which the representations or ideas of things exist, for without such a unity the act of distinguishing between them would not be possible; second, the unity of the (active) subject as that which performs the act of comparing. So, to distinguish things it is required that one and the same thinking subject represents several things, and that these representations are compared by one and

---

[47] Winckler, *Institutiones philosophiae Wolfianae* (1735), §§ 317–19. Excerpts translated in Francke, *Uebersicht*, pp. 30–6, with comments by Francke on the necessary unity of consciousness (pp. 32–3).

[48] 'Ein Wesen nun...welches sich nicht zwey verschiedene Dinge zugleich vorstellen, und indem es das thut, und dazu den Unterschied zwischen beyden bemerkt, Eins und dasselbe bleiben oder Ein und dasselbe Wesen behalten kann, kann nicht denken': quoted after Francke, *Uebersicht*, pp. 33–4. See also Winckler, *Die Frage, ob die Seelen der Thiere Verstand haben* (1742), pp. 94–6.

[49] Knutzen, *De humanae mentis individua natura sive immaterialitate* (1742). An authorised German translation by Georg Heinrich Püschel appeared two years later: *Philosophische Abhandlung von der immateriellen Natur der Seele, darinnen theils überhaupt erwiesen wird, daß die Materie nicht dencken könne und daß die Seele uncörperlich sey, theils die vornehmsten Einwürffe der Materialisten deutlich beantwortet werden. Aus dem Lateinischen übersetzet* (1744).

[50] 'Die Erfahrung überzeuget uns mit unumstößlicher Gewissheit, daß sich in uns etwas befinde, welches so wie seiner selbst, also auch verschiedener Vorstellungen von anderen Dingen, ja der Dinge selbst sich bewußt ist': Knutzen, *Philosophische Abhandlung*, § 1, p. 1.

[51] 'Eine ermunterte Aufmerksamkeit, wird uns mit rührender Klarheit überzeugen, daß wir alsdann unserer selbst uns bewußt sind, wann wir uns von anderen Sachen unterscheiden': Knutzen, *Philosophische Abhandlung*, § 2, p. 9. Knutzen explicitly refers to Wolff and Rüdiger's *Herrn Christian Wolffens Meinung von dem Wesen der Seele und eines Geistes überhaupt; und D. Andreas Rüdigers Gegen-Meinung* (1727; reprinted, 2008) in this context.

the same subject.[52] Knutzen's main aim here is, however, to show that materiality is not compatible with this unitary subject. For Knutzen, the unity required for holding various representations together is the unity of an immaterial substance: the unity of the thinking subject is the unity of a *res cogitans*.[53] Thus, Knutzen's argument is part of the traditional anti-materialist strategy and must not, as sometimes happens, be misunderstood as an 'anticipation' of Kant.[54] Moreover, Knutzen does not discuss diachronic personal identity in this context.

In comparison with the Wolffians discussed so far, Moses Mendelssohn is a much better known thinker working in the Wolffian tradition of metaphysics. He too does not address the issue of diachronic personal identity in any detail, not regarding the issue as particularly problematic at all. He occasionally comments on the topic in larger contexts. For example, he makes remarks on the topic when arguing for the immortality of the human soul in his *Phädon* (1767).[55] The Wolffian nature of his reflections on the mind is beyond doubt. He takes over Wolff's understanding of the soul when he speaks of it, literally in Wolffian terms, as of a simple, incorporeal being who is conscious of its own being and of other things.[56] All our ideas, he argues, must be united in one substance. Otherwise we could not engage in mental activities such as remembering, comparing, and thinking; and we could not remain the same person through time if our ideas were dispersed over various thinking beings and were not connected into the unity of one thinking substance.[57] This substance cannot consist of parts; that is, it must be of a simple nature, for otherwise we would require another activity of combining and comparing to make a whole of

---

[52] 'Die Einheit des Subjekts in welchem die Vorstellungen der unterschiedlichen Sachen zugleich sich finden müßen, wenn anders die Unterscheidung derselben, oder das Anschauen des Unterscheides soll zur Würklichkeit gelangen': Knutzen, *Philosophische Abhandlung*, § 3, p. 16. See also § 3, p. 18: 'Die Einheit des Subjekts, von welchem die Zusammenhaltung der Vorstellungen unternommen wird.'

[53] Carl has argued that this is the view Kant held in the 1770s. He does not mention Knutzen in this context, however. See Carl, *Der Schweigende Kant. Die Entwürfe zu einer Deduktion der Kategorien vor 1781* (1989), pp. 92, 96–8, 101–2. In 1775 Kant states: 'Die Bedingung aller apperception ist die Einheit des denkenden subiects': *Reflexion* 4675, in Kant, *Gesammelte Schriften*, vol. 17, p. 651. Carl argues that 'the unity of the thinking subject' is to be understood ontologically here: Carl (1989), p. 92.

[54] On this see Wunderlich, 'Kant's Second Paralogism in Context', in Lefèvre (ed.), *Between Leibniz, Newton, and Kant* (2001), pp. 175–88; and Wunderlich, *Kant und die Bewußtseinstheorien des 18. Jahrhunderts* (2005), pp. 47–9. See also Thiel, 'Kant's Notion of Self-Consciousness in Context', in Gerhardt, Horstmann, and Schumacher (eds.), *Kant und die Berliner Aufklärung* (2001), vol. 2, pp. 468–76.

[55] In his overview of theories of immortality Francke links Winckler's argument to Mendelssohn's in *Phädon oder über die Unsterblichkeit der Seele* (1767): Francke, *Uebersicht*, p. 34.

[56] He speaks of 'Beschaffenheiten des einfachen, unkörperlichen Wesens, das sich in ihnen seiner selbst und anderer Dinge bewußt ist': Mendelssohn, *Phädon*, ed. Bourel (1979), pp. 108–9. He ascribes such an incorporal nature to both animal souls ('sinnlich empfindende Naturen') and thinking beings ('denkende Naturen').

[57] 'Wir würden weder uns erinnern, noch überlegen, noch vergleichen, noch denken können, ja wir würden nicht einmal die Person seyn, die wir vor einem Augenblick gewesen, wenn unsere Begriffe unter vielen vertheilet und nicht irgendwo zusammen in ihrer genauesten Verbindung anzutreffen wären. Wir müssen also wenigstens eine Substanz annehmen, die alle Begriffe der Bestandtheile vereiniget': Mendelssohn, *Phädon*, p. 96.

the parts. The thinking substance must also be unextended simply because, for Mendelssohn, extended beings are divisible and thus consist of parts.[58] This simple substance that unites all our ideas is called the soul (*Phädon*, p. 97).

Like Winckler and Knutzen, then, Mendelssohn goes beyond the standard immaterialist argument, according to which the soul must be an immaterial substance because a multiplicity of material entities cannot constitute a unitary thinking being. Rather, he appeals to our various cognitive capacities and argues that they could not be exercised the way they are if they did not belong to a unitary and simple substance. Elsewhere, in an earlier work, Mendelssohn again emphasises that it must be possible for us to combine concepts, for otherwise we could not exercise our cognitive capacities: 'Memory, insight into the future, and capacity to infer. On what do these capacities rest more than on the combination of our concepts, the foregoing ones with the present ones, and the latter with the future ones? If one cancels the combination, how can those concepts persist?'[59]

This combination of our concepts, Mendelssohn suggests, points not just to a unitary being, but to a diachronically identical being. Only insofar as alterations (including changing representations) are connected to one another, can there be one being that remains the same through these changes:

As long as the alterations of one thing are connected with another, it can reveal itself under a thousand different shapes and yet always remain exactly the same thing. The same insect becomes in various transformations a worm, a larva, and a beetle; the same plant was seed, becomes a bud, and sprouts up into a tree. Why? In each condition lay the basic formation of the developing shape. In the worm already, indeed, in the egg itself was the image of the future beetle and, wrapped up in the seed, the mature tree was to be found. (Mendelssohn, *Empfindungen*; ed. Dahlström, p. 32)

Mendelssohn does not, however, discuss in any detail the relationship between our faculty of thought or consciousness and diachronic personal identity.[60]

---

[58] The text continues from the passage quoted in the previous note: 'und diese Substanz wird sie aus Theilen zusammengesetzt seyn können?—Unmöglich, sonst brauchen wir wieder ein Zusammennehmen und Gegeneinanderhalten, damit aus den Theilen ein Ganzes werde, und wir kommen wiederum dahin, wo wir ausgegangen sind. Sie wird also einfach seyn? Nothwendig. Auch unausgedehnt? Denn das Ausgedehnte ist theilbar, und das Theilbare nicht einfach: Richtig!': Mendelssohn, *Phädon*, pp. 96–7.

[59] Mendelssohn, *Über die Empfindungen* (1755), in *Gesammelte Schriften*, ed. Bamberger (1929/1971), vol. 1, p. 70; quoted from 'On Sentiments', Letter 7, in Mendelssohn, *Philosophical Writings*, transl. and ed. Dahlström (1997), p. 33.

[60] Klemme has argued that Markus Herz, a correspondent of Kant's, appeals to Mendelssohn when he argues that relations between things or ideas are not simply given to us but result from an activity of the subject. Herz, *Betrachtungen aus der spekulativen Weltweisheit* (1771/1990), p. 40. See Klemme, *Kants Philosophie des Subjekts* (1996), pp. 510, 519. Compare Wunderlich (2005), p. 60. Like Knutzen, however, Herz conceives of the unity of the subject as a simple substance. As Herz's account is closely linked to Kant, we shall look at it in more detail in *The Enlightened Subject* (in preparation).

10.2.2. From unity to identity: Eberhard and Reimarus

Johann August Eberhard provides more detailed arguments on these matters than do Winckler, Knutzen, and Mendelssohn, linking what he takes to be the main cognitive faculty—the faculty of representation—to diachronic personal identity. He was educated in the Wolffian tradition, and later became one of the most important early critics of Kant, maintaining that Kant's views were derived from Leibniz. Eberhard's most important work, *Allgemeine Theorie des Denkens und Empfindens*, however, was published before Kant's *Critiques* appeared.[61] The book consists largely of Leibnizian and Wolffian principles. He argues that the soul is a simple, immaterial substance, and consists of one basic and unitary power or faculty ('Grundkraft' or 'Urkraft'): the faculty of representation. Thought ('Denken') and sensation or feeling ('Empfinden'), for example, are just different modifications of the one *Grundkraft*: one is active (thought), the other passive (sensation, feeling) (*Allgemeine Theorie*, p. 33). Eberhard appeals to this *Grundkraft* in his discussion of personal identity. He also comments on the issues of self-consciousness and personal identity in his later *Kurzer Abriß der Metaphysik* (1794)—here in the context of an account of immortality (*Abriß*, 171–3), very much like Wolff and the Wolffians discussed so far. In the *Allgemeine Theorie*, however, Eberhard discusses the issues of self-consciousness and personal identity primarily in the context of general epistemological and metaphysical considerations. His formulations, unfortunately, are not always as precise as they might be, and they suggest that he tends to confound epistemological and metaphysical matters. Nevertheless, the fact that he places personal identity more in the context of epistemology and general metaphysics rather than in that of the more specific immortality issue, constitutes a significant difference between his account and that of earlier Wolffians.

Like other Wolffians, such as von Creuz for example, Eberhard adopts Leibniz's distinction between the real identity of the soul, as substance, and its moral or personal identity (*Abriß*, pp. 172–3). Eberhard says that the soul's 'personality or moral identity' consists in the fact that it remembers its former states, arguing that it will retain such memory in the afterlife.[62] The identity of the self or soul, as substance, requires the uninterrupted, permanent connection of all its states, including 'obscure' or unconscious perceptions (Leibniz's minute perceptions). When we are not conscious of this connection, there is still the identity of the soul, as substance, but no personality or moral identity. Thus, like Leibniz, Wolff, and others, Eberhard regards the metaphysical identity of the soul as a necessary but not a sufficient condition of its personal identity. And although he thinks it is 'natural' for the soul to retain its personality or moral identity as well as its metaphysical identity after death, he suggests that it is logically possible (involves no contradiction) that the

---

[61] Eberhard, *Allgemeine Theorie des Denkens und Empfindens. Eine Abhandlung, welche den von der Königl. Akademie der Wissenschaften in Berlin auf das Jahr 1776 ausgesetzten Preis erhalten hat.* (1776).

[62] 'Wenn die Seele ewig lebt: so ist es natürlich, daß sie sich ihres vorigen Zustandes erinnere, worin ihre Persönlichkeit oder moralische Identität bestehet': Eberhard, *Abriß* p. 172.

soul may have metaphysical but no moral personal identity. For it involves no contradiction to say that the soul will not remember its former state.[63]

The epistemological and metaphysical considerations concerning personal identity in the *Allgemeine Theorie* are linked to the issue of the simplicity of the soul. Eberhard appeals to the notion that we necessarily think of our own souls as unitary and identical through time. He infers from this necessity of thought that the self or soul *is* a unitary and diachronically identical substance. This is precisely the kind of move from thought to being that Kant, of course, criticizes and rejects in his *Critique of Pure Reason*. Moreover, Eberhard claims not merely that the simplicity of the soul's nature can be inferred from the necessity to *think* of the self as unitary, but also that in addition, it is a matter of *feeling*; that is, that we feel both the unitary nature of the soul and its identity through time.[64]

His arguments about the simplicity and diachronic identity appeal to the notion mentioned above of a single, unitary *Grundkraft* of the soul. At times he appears to appeal to such a *Grundkraft* when arguing for the simplicity and diachronic identity of the soul. At other times, however, it seems that his arguments about simplicity and identity are designed to show that there is such a *Grundkraft*. Without the latter, he claims, there would be no diachronic identity. This argument simply takes the diachronic identity of the soul for granted.

Regarding the question of unity, Eberhard states that as a mattter of fact, a thinking being *thinks* of itself as the sole subject of all the changes it undergoes, of all its thoughts, sensations, and so on. He argues that this would not be possible, if the thinking being were not in fact a unitary thing, and asserts that if all those changes belonged to a multiplicity of subjects, the thinking being would not be able to *think* of itself as a unitary thing. He also relates this to the issue of the *Grundkraft*. The thinking being would not be able to think of itself as unitary if all its changes were due to a multiplicity of distinct powers that are independent of a fundamental *Grundkraft* of the soul. One power would not know of the changes that other powers have brought about if they were not all modifications of one universal *Ur-* or *Grundkraft*. Due to this *Grundkraft* the thinking being *is* one, and through it alone it is also able to *think* of itself as one.[65] In the later *Abriß* Eberhard adds an

---

[63] 'Die Identität unseres Ichs oder die Fortdauer der Substanz unserer Seele, erfodert den ununterbrochenen Zusammenhang aller ihrer Veränderungen, also die stätige Verbindung aller Zustände. Dieser Verbindung sind wir uns aber nicht allemal bewußt, denn die Zustände hangen auch durch dunkele oder unbemerkte Vorstellungen zusammen. In diesem Falle ist die physische Identität der Substanz der Seele ohne moralische Identität; denn diese besteht in dem Bewußtseyn der Zwischenvorstellungen, wodurch die Zustände verbunden sind, oder in dem deutlichen Erinnern': Eberhard, *Abriß*, pp. 172-3.

[64] 'Man kann diesem Beweise durch die Aufmerksamkeit auf unser Bewußtseyn noch mehr Evidenz geben. Wir fühlen nämlich, daß unsere Seele nicht nur Eines sondern auch beständig Dieselbige sey': Eberhard, *Allgemeine Theorie*, p. 23.

[65] 'Zu dem erstern gehört, daß sich das Wesen, welches in uns denkt, als das alleinige Subjekt, aller seiner Veränderungen, seines Denkens, Empfindens, Handelns, Leidens u.s.w. vorstelle. Dies kann nicht geschehen, wofern es nicht Eines ist, das den Grund aller dieser unzertrennlichen und in Einem zusammenkommenden Bestimmungen enthält. So wenig nun dies möglich wäre, wenn diese verschiedenen Bestimmungen in vielerley Subjekte vertheilt wären, ohne wenigstens zuletzt in ein

appeal to an argument that Martin Knutzen and others had proposed. He appeals to Rousseau's critique of Helvetius as a source for this argument: a multiplicity of thoughts can be represented as one, and the individual thoughts can be distinguished from one another only in a simple substance. Distinguishing requires comparing, and both these activities are involved in the forming of propositions and inferences. The activity of comparing, in turn, requires that the thoughts compared belong to one and the same substance. Our very ability to form propositions or judgements and inferences points to the fact that the soul is a unitary entity. For Eberhard this means that the soul must be a simple entity.[66] He does not argue for this in any detail, however, but merely appeals to Rousseau as an authority here.[67]

Eberhard's treatment of the diachronic identity of the self or soul is similar to his account of the soul's unity and simplicity. As a matter of fact, the soul thinks of itself as identical through time. It could not do this without a *Grundkraft*. Moreover, the soul could not *be* identical through time if it did not have this *Grundkraft*.[68] We recognize our own self-identity through consciousness. In order to be able to think of itself as identical through time, the soul must think of itself as the subject of all the changes of which it is conscious.[69] This consciousness of identity requires a unitary *Grundkraft*, though. If there were several independent powers of the soul, the soul could not think of itself as the unitary and identical subject of all the changes it undergoes. For in that case power *a*, for example, may not notice the changes that were brought about by powers *b*, *c*, and *d*. We would not be able to recognize that we are the same person at different points of time. Experience, however, confirms that we think of ourselves as identical, and so we must assume the existence of a unitary

Einziges zusammen gesammlet zu werden; eben so wenig würde es erfolgen, wenn alle diese Veränderungen des Denkens, Empfindens u.s.w. in verschiedenen von einander und von Einer ersten Urkraft unabhängigen Kräften sich endigten. Die Kraft a würde nichts von dem wissen, was durch die Kraft b wirklich wird, die Kraft b würde nichts von den Veränderungen wissen, die durch die Kräfte a, c, etc hervorgebracht werden, sie würden sich also nicht als Eins denken können, so lange sie nicht die Modifikationen Einer allgemeinen Urkraft x wären, in die sich alles auflöset, alles vereinigt, aus der sich alles erklären läßt, und die dadurch, daß sie der Ursprung aller Veränderungen ist, zum festesten Naturbande wird, wodurch ein Ding Eins ist, und das weder durch die Kraft der Natur noch der Allmacht kann getrennt werden': Eberhard, *Allgemeine Theorie*, pp. 23–5.

[66] 'Das Viele kann nur in dem Einfachen sowohl als Eins vorgestellt, als auch voneinander verschieden werden; denn zu dem Unterscheiden gehört Vergleichen. Unterscheiden, Urtheilen und Schließen sind also nur in einer einzigen Substanz, also in keinem zusammengesetzten Dinge möglich. Aus dem Urtheilen und Schließen hat am faßlichsten die Immaterialität der Seele bewiesen, J. J. Rousseau Rem. sur le Livre d'Helvetius de l'Esprit. In den Suppl. zu seinen Werken T. III, S. 103.104': Eberhard, *Abriß*, p. 167.

[67] We shall look at Rousseau's own account of these issues in *The Enlightened Subject* (in preparation).

[68] 'Ohne diese innige und wesentliche Einfachheit der Urkraft kann sich hiernächst auch die Seele nicht als Ebendasselbige Wesen die ganze Dauer ihres Daseyns hindurch denken. Die Seele kann nicht das nämliche Ich, ebendieselbige Person bleiben, ohne die genaueste Einfachheit ihrer Kraft': Eberhard, *Allgemeine Theorie*, p. 25.

[69] 'Um diese Identität ihrer selbst zu erkennen, muß sie sich als das Subjekt aller der Veränderungen denken, deren sie sich bis auf den gegenwärtigen Augenblick bewußt ist': Eberhard, *Allgemeine Theorie*, p. 25.

Grundkraft.⁷⁰ Clearly, Eberhard's argument simply assumes the diachronic identity of the soul. He argues that the fact that there is such diachronic identity means that there must be a unitary *Grundkraft*, for without it there could be no diachronic identity of the self.

Eberhard concedes that madness is a condition that involves mistaking one's own identity for someone else's.⁷¹ For Eberhard, however, such cases just confirm his account, rather than constitute counter-examples to it. They show that only a simple, unitary *Grundkraft* can guarantee that we are able to recognize our diachronic personal identity—which is what all normal people are in fact able to do. He is not really concerned with the question of what constitutes identity through time. Rather, he takes the latter for granted, and asks what is involved in our actual recognition of our own selves as identical through time, arguing that the *Grundkraft* or faculty of representation is required for such recognition of identity. Eberhard does not argue that consciousness as such, even of the present, requires diachronic personal identity. This argument is developed from within a Wolffian context by Hermann Samuel Reimarus.

Although Reimarus appeals to Leibniz and Wolff in many places, he was a much more independent thinker than the Wolffians discussed so far. Regarding the issues of self-consciousness and personal identity, he starts from a Wolffian position, but his argument takes him beyond the standard Wolffian view about these matters. Reimarus's works had a considerable impact in the second half of the century, and he was cited by such diverse thinkers as Ernst Platner, Dietrich Tiedemann, and Karl Spazier. The work that is most relevant in the present context is his *Die Vornehmsten Wahrheiten der natürlichen Religion*, which was first published in 1754,⁷² well before Eberhard's main work we have just discussed. Like Eberhard, Reimarus discusses the issue of the identity of the self or soul (he does not use the term 'person' here)

---

⁷⁰ 'Man sieht daher leicht, daß es bloß das Bewußtseyn der Stätigkeit in unsern Vorstellungen ist, wodurch unsere Seele ihre numerische Identität anerkennet, und sich davon versichert, daß sie noch immer als dasselbige Ich oder moralische Individuum fortdaure. Es wird vor der Hand genug, nur im Allgemeinen anzugeben, warum dieses ohne die Einfachheit der Kraft in der Seele nicht zu erhalten stehe. Es muß sich nämlich bald finden, daß, wofern verschiedene Veränderungen in der Seele aus verschiedenen abgesonderten Kräften ihren Ursprung nehmen, das Bewußtseyn von dem allgemeinen Zusammenhange und dem stätigen Fortfließen dieser Veränderungen unmöglich in der Seele wird Statt haben. Wenn eine Veränderung durch eine Kraft erfolgt: so wird das eine Begebenheit seyn, die außerhalb dieser Kraft nicht bemerkt wird, wobey also das allgemeine Band, wodurch alle Vorstellungen der Seele zu einer Kraft vereinigt werden, und also die Anerkennung der persönlichen Identität nicht bestehen kann': Eberhard, *Allgemeine Theorie*, pp. 26–7.

⁷¹ 'Wenn daher ein Mensch durch eine Verrückung, die nicht ohne Beyspiel ist, sich für andern hielte, als er vor einigen Jahren gewesen ist: so würde er auch glauben, daß nicht seine gegenwärtige Substanz die Gedanken und Empfindungen gehabt, oder die Handlungen vorgenommen habe, die er vor dem Zeitpunkte seiner Umwandlung gehabt oder vorgenommen hat. Ein solcher Zufall läßt sich durch nichts anders erklären, als dadurch, daß in einer solchen Seele gewisse Vorstellungen dergestalt sind ausgelöscht worden, daß der Uebergang aus dem einen Zustand in den andern zerstört, und das Band, wodurch sie zusammenhalten, gänzlich zerrissen worden': Eberhard, *Allgemeine Theorie*, pp. 25–6.

⁷² References are to Reimarus, *Die Vornehmsten Wahrheiten der natürlichen Religion*, third edn. (1766; facsimile ed. Gawlick, 1985). Gawlick's introduction provides an excellent overview of Reimarus's thought and its impact.

not mainly in the context of a discussion of the afterlife. His main treatment of the issue is in more general terms, in a chapter entitled 'On Man'.[73]

At first there seems to be nothing special about Reimarus's account. Like Wolff, he takes for granted that we are conscious of ourselves and of other things, even using the same wording as Wolff.[74] The nature of the self, he claims, is accessible through 'inner sensation' or introspection.[75] The soul is a substance—a being that persists through change (*Wahrheiten*, p. 446), and it has the faculty of consciousness—the latter relating to the soul's own states. Moreover, it is an indivisible, simple, and immaterial substance (ibid., pp. 459, 461). Reimarus argues that the materialist cannot explain the consciousness which the soul has of its own identity through time.[76] Independently of our consciousness we are not able to say about any part of our body that it remains the same through time (ibid., p. 462). Although man consists of soul and body, the soul is that which is conscious in us and constitutes the essence of man.[77] We are the same human beings at different points of time on account of the identity of our soul (ibid., p. 446). The soul knows itself inwardly as one and the same thing in its various states.

Reimarus argues that the body belongs to our own self only insofar as consciousness is linked to it. If this link via consciousness is lacking, then we do not count the body or parts of the body as part of our own self.[78] Also, like all immaterialist philosophers of the mind, Reimarus argues that physical bodies, as such, do not remain identical through time (ibid., pp. 434ff.). This also applies to the human body (ibid., p. 438).[79] Moreover, it is a fact, he claims, that people regard themselves as

---

[73] The chapter is entitled 'Von dem Menschen an sich, insonderheit nach der Seele, betrachtet' (pp. 430–91).

[74] See, for example: 'weil wir uns unser selbst und anderer Dinge ausser uns bewußt sind': Reimarus, *Wahrheiten*, p. 440; and 'Es ist uns aber keine Wahrheit auf der Welt klärer, offenbarer und gewisser, als daß wir uns unser selbst, und anderer Dinge ausser uns, bewußt sind': p. 444.

[75] Reimarus speaks of 'die innere klare Empfindung und das Bewußtseyn dessen, was in uns vorgeht': Reimarus, *Wahrheiten*, p. 432.

[76] 'Allein, sie [the materialists] mögen für eine Beschaffenheit des Körpers annehmen, welche sie wollen, so werden sie sich nicht darinn als ein Wesen erkennen, das sich bey seinen Veränderungen bewußt ist eins und dasselbe zu seyn': Reimarus, *Wahrheiten*, p. 448.

[77] 'Wir eignen uns eine Seele zu, so ferne wir empfinden, denken, wollen, oder mit einem Worte, uns bewußt sind. Weil nun unser einzelnes besonderes Wesen, oder unser Ich, hauptsächlich auf den Theil ankömmt, der sich in uns bewußt ist, so machet die Seele auch vornehmlich den Menschen aus': Reimarus, *Wahrheiten*, p. 445.

[78] 'Ein jeder unterscheidet sein Ich, von fremden Dingen ausser sich, durch ein Gefühl in einem gewissen Körper. So weit diese Empfindung zu jeder Zeit geht, so weit rechnet er das wirkliche zu sich selbst und seinem einzelen Wesen... Weil wir uns demnach, durch die Empfindung, welche man auch ueberhaupt das Gefühl nennet, in vielen Theilen eines gewissen Körpers auf mancherley Weise bewußt sind, so erkennen wir so ferne, den ganzen Körper, bis an die äusserste Haut, gegenwärtig, für unser Ich, für uns selbst': Reimarus, *Wahrheiten*, pp. 432–3.

[79] 'So bald es ausser den Schranken unsers Gefühles ist, und wir uns darinn nicht mehr bewußt sind, so bald höret es auf, ein Theil von uns selbst zu seyn; wir wissen und bekümmern uns nicht, wo es hin kömmt... Folglich ist allein unsere Empfindung oder Bewußtseyn ein gegenwärtiges Merkmaal der einzelnen Theile des Körpers, der unser Ich ausmachet': Reimarus, *Wahrheiten*, p. 438.

Beyond Leibniz and Wolff 337

identical at different points of time but not on account of their bodies.[80] We know the bodily parts only insofar as we have a consciousness of them. We consider ourselves as identical through time on account of that being that is conscious in us.[81] Reimarus argues that the self that has feelings and desires at present is at the same time conscious that he is the very same being who some months or years ago did this, saw that, and so on. He infers from this *consciousness* of identity that that being in us that is conscious does in fact remain the same through all the changes in the body.[82] In other words, he infers the real identity of the self from the consciousness of our own identity. We *regard* ourselves as diachronically identical conscious beings; therefore, as thinking, conscious beings we *do* remain the same through time. Obviously, however, this does not follow at all. I may regard myself as identical through time, and yet may be mistaken about this. Like Eberhard then, Reimarus appears to counfound epistemological considerations with ontological or metaphysical ones.

So far there seems to be nothing significantly new about Reimarus's account of consciousness and identity. He seems to follow more or less the standard Wolffian lines of thought. As indicated, however, there is one argument in Reimarus about the connection between consciousness and identity that seems to constitute an advance over the standard Wolffian argument.

Reimarus does not give a detailed analysis of consciousness and self-consciousness. Like Wolff, he links consciousness to the capacity of distinguishing ourselves from other things. Unlike Wolff, however, he attempts to show that consciousness, even of the present, can exist only in a being that remains identical through change and is conscious of its identity.[83] Of course, this argument is linked in Reimarus to his immaterialist view of the mind, but it seems to be a distinctive argument for personal identity and, as such, to be independent of any commitment to an immaterialist view of the mind.[84] The structure of his argument is as follows. (1) In order to be conscious of a (present) thing, we must distinguish it from other things. (2) We can distinguish it from other things only if we relate it to its kind or species; that is, to

---

[80] '...da ein jeder Mensch, in dem Verlaufe vieler Jahre, sich für einen und eben denselben Menschen hält. Gewiß nicht nach seinen körperlichen Theilen': Reimarus, *Wahrheiten*, p. 440.

[81] 'Niemand kennet und hält sich also in seiner Dauer für einen und denselben Menschen, der er vorhin war, nach seinem Körper, sondern wegen des Wesens, das sich in ihm bewußt ist': Reimarus, *Wahrheiten*, p. 441.

[82] 'Und daraus ist auch offenbar, daß dasjenige Wesen in uns, welches sich bewußt ist, bey aller übrigen Ebbe und Fluth des Körpers, oder bey allen abwechselnden Begebenheiten, fortdaure': Reimarus, *Wahrheiten*, p. 441.

[83] It could be argued that Reimarus's thesis is implied by Wolff's own analysis. We saw that for Wolff, reflection and memory are required for consciousness; but for reflection and memory to play their respective roles, surely, the identity of the subject to which the act of reflection and the acts reflected on belong, must be one and the same being. The point is that Wolff does not seem to argue in this way. Moreover, unlike Reimarus, Wolff does not claim, implicitly or explicitly, that a *consciousness* of diachronic identity is required for consciousness of the present.

[84] 'Wenn man sich auch nur deutlich vorstellet, was das Bewußtseyn heiße und in sich halte, so kann man leicht erkennen, daß das Bewußtseyn nicht Statt finde, als in einem fortdaurenden einzelnen Wesen, welches unter mancherley Veränderungen eins und dasselbe bleibt': Reimarus, *Wahrheiten*, p. 441.

similar things of which we have been conscious previously and to which we have given a common name and which we have learned to distinguish from one another.[85] (3) Therefore, our consciousness of present things requires that we are beings who have persisted through several changes and states and who know that they are the same beings that have previously been in states similar to their present ones.[86] If we were not thus diachronically identical and conscious of our identity, we could not engage in the activities of distinguishing and relating that are involved in our being conscious of the present. We could not, however implicitly, relate to previous conscious states of our own self. It is not required, Reimarus argues, that we have a distinct memory of our previous states. An indistinct ('undeutliche') memory of our previous experience suffices for us to be conscious of it now (ibid., pp. 442–3).

Reimarus explains this idea further by arguing that if the self had no diachronic identity, and other, similar individual entities would take its place one after the other, then what happened to an earlier entity in this sequence would be of no relevance to the self that exists now (ibid., p. 443). The latter could not, from its experience, recall occurrences similar to present ones; that is to say, it could not distinguish these from others, and this in turn would mean that it could not be conscious of them. It could not be conscious of what it sees at the present moment (ibid., p. 443). If that being that has a conscious sensation now were not the very same thing that previously had similar conscious sensations, it could not have that present consciousness. Everything that such a being perceives would be a completely new experience. Without diachronic identity and a memory of the past, it could not compare present with earlier sensations. It could be conscious neither of external things nor even of its own self (ibid., p. 444). Thus, according to Reimarus, the actual consciousness we have of our own self, of our present inner states, and of external objects, provides evidence for the fact that we are diachronically identical conscious beings. We could not have such a consciousness if we were not identical through time. This, then, is the essence of Reimarus's argument: we know as an experiential fact that we are at present conscious of our own self and of other things, and a necessary condition of such consciousness is that we are beings that remain identical through time.[87]

Reimarus's argument can be summarized as follows (ibid., pp. 444–5). (1) We are conscious of ourselves and of outer things—an experiential fact. (2) We cannot at present be conscious without remembering past states of our own self. (3) It follows that that being that is conscious in us remains the same through change and is the

---

[85] 'Wir kennen und unterscheiden aber ein Ding nicht eher, als wenn wir es zu seiner eigenen Art oder Gattung hinrechnen, das ist, zu den ähnlichen Dingen, deren wir uns vormals in unserm Leben bewußt gewesen sind, und die wir mit einem gemeinen Namen zu bezeichnen und unterscheiden gelernet haben': Reimarus, *Wahrheiten*, p. 442.

[86] 'Es ist also kein einziges gegenwärtiges Bewußtseyn möglich, als in einem Wesen, das schon unter verschiedenen Veränderungen und Zustande fortgedauret hat, und auch weis, daß es eben dasselbe sey, welches vorhin mehrmals in einem ähnlichen Zustande gewesen': Reimarus, *Wahrheiten*, p. 442.

[87] Clearly, as stated, the argument shows only that diachronic identity is required, not that a consciousness of this identity is required.

same that has thought, willed, and so on, at previous times. Of course, premise (2) is formulated in a way that assumes that memory presupposes diachronic identity.[88]

As indicated above, Reimarus's arguments were appealed to by various subsequent thinkers. One of the most important of these is Dietrich Tiedemann.

10.2.3. Consciousness and 'complete' identity: Tiedemann

Although the title of Tiedemann's main work—*Untersuchungen über den Menschen*—suggests a general anthropology, it is really a doctrine of the soul: an experiential 'psychological system', as he says.[89] Tiedemann's starting point is 'the Leibnizian–Wolffian system', as he concedes, but he also points out that he differs in many respects from that system (*Untersuchungen*, vol. 1, Preface, pp. xxiii–xxiv). He certainly follows Wolff in that he regards the faculty of representation as the main faculty of the soul from which all other faculties are to be derived. Like Eberhard, Tiedemann refers to the faculty of representation as the *Grundkraft* of the soul.[90] He differs from Leibniz and Wolff in his account of the nature of the soul. Like Leibniz and Wolff, he explicitly and at length argues against materialism, rejecting Locke's suggestion of thinking matter (ibid., vol. 2, pt. 2, pp. 35–129). He also rejects the view, however, that the soul is a simple and unextended substance. For Tiedemann (as for Samuel Clarke), the soul is incorporeal but extended: it must be extended in order to be able to interact with the body.[91] In his account of the workings of the mind, he follows the theory of the association of ideas.[92] He appeals to Bonnet, Irwing, Meiners, Locke, and Hume, and elsewhere also to David Hartley. His account of the imagination and memory is in terms of the association of ideas.[93] Like Bonnet and Hartley his theory of the workings of the mind tends towards materialism, but he does not wish to adopt materialism.

---

[88] There is a brief summary of this argument for personal identity in *Wahrheiten*, pp. 694–6. Here the argument is used as a basis of Reimarus's discussion of immortality.

[89] Tiedemann, *Untersuchungen über den Menschen*. 3 vols. (1777–78). He speaks of 'Seelen-Lehre und Menschen-Kenntniß' (vol. 1, Vorrede, p. xii), but it is clear that he focuses on the 'Seelen-Lehre', as he is concerned mainly with the 'Entwickelung der Seelen-Kräfte' (vol. 1, Vorrede, p. xxv). The term 'psychological system' is used in the Vorrede of vol. 1, p. xxviii. Tiedemann emphasises his experiential method in the following remark: 'In den einzelnen Untersuchungen habe ich mich immer bemüht, die allgemeinen Sätze mit bestimmten Erfahrungen zu begleiten...Erstlich um die allgemeinen Sätze dadurch zugleich mit bestimmten Beweisen zu versehen': Tiedemann, *Untersuchungen*, vol. 1, Vorrede, p. xxxiv.

[90] Tiedemann, *Untersuchungen*, vol. 1, Vorrede, p. xxiii; see also *Erstes Hauptstück* in vol. 1, which is entitled 'Von der Grund-Kraft der Seele', pp. 1–22.

[91] Tiedemann, *Untersuchungen*, vol. 2, p. 111: soul and body could not interact if the soul was simple; pp. 113–14: simple souls could not be individuated; against Locke: pp. 94–6. Locke's suggestion is a mere conjecture ('Vermutung').

[92] See in particular the long seventh chapter in the first volume entitled 'Von den Ideen-Reihen': Tiedemann, *Untersuchungen*, vol. 1, pp. 177–274.

[93] 'Einbildungskraft und Gedächtnis sind...nichts als, verschiedene Arten schon gehabter Vorstellungen, vermöge der Ideen-Association, zu erneuern': Tiedemann, *Untersuchungen*, Vorrede, vol. 1, p. xxvi. The accounts of thinkers such as Bonnet, Irwing, Meiners, and so on, will be discussed in *The Enlightened Subject* (in preparation).

340   *The Early Modern Subject*

As far as self-consciousness is concerned, Tiedemann rejects Wolff's account of consciousness in terms of the ability to distinguish. He argues that it is the function of judgement to distinguish an idea or representation ('Vorstellung') from another idea; and judgement is not the same as consciousness.[94] Although Tiedemann explicitly rejects materialism, his own positive account of consciousness is similar to accounts presented by materialist thinkers.[95] His account of personal identity, however, is in terms of an immaterialist understanding of the soul or self. Indeed, he deals with personal identity in the chapter in which he criticizes materialism (ibid., vol. 2, pp. 66–70; the whole chapter is pp. 35–129), pointing out the negative consequences of a materialist view of the mind for personal identity. He argues that the materialist 'proofs' are not what they are said to be: irrefutable, and based on immediate experience (ibid., vol. 1, p. 66). He gives a list of objections to materialist conceptions of the mind, and first on the list is an objection relating to personal identity. In this context, Tiedemann explicitly appeals to Reimarus.

Tiedemann states that as a matter of fact, we have a consciousness that we are the very same beings that in the past performed certain actions and suffered certain 'fates'.[96] And like Reimarus and Eberhard, he seems to argue that this consciousness of identity is evidence for the actual identity of the self or person. Tiedemann disagrees with Reimarus, however, in that he emphasises that his argument is not based on the idea that we are conscious of our own *complete* identity; it is an illusion to think that we have a consciousness of our complete identity through time. As a matter of fact, Tiedemann claims, we do not have such a consciousness, arguing that it is not even required that we are conscious of all aspects of our past life in order to be conscious of our diachronic identity.[97] He insists that we know through experience 'with complete conviction' that it was us and not another person who 10, 20, or more years ago was at a particular place living in such-and-such circumstances.[98] In the years that pass between certain events in our life, we suffer many changes. If these were so comprehensive that nothing remained of us from the earlier parts of our life,

---

[94] 'das Unterscheiden einer Vorstellung von der andern, in welchem sie das Bewußtseyn bestehen lassen [Footnote: 'Wolf in seiner Metaphysik'], kommt eigentlich dem Urtheile zu, und Bewußtseyn ist nicht Urtheil': Tiedemann, *Untersuchungen*, vol. 1, p. 53.

[95] Therefore, his views on that issue need to be discussed in the context of materialist positions on self-consciousness. This material will be examined in *The Enlightened Subject* (in preparation).

[96] 'Wir sind uns bewußt, daß wir seit vielen Jahren noch eben diejenigen sind, die ehemals gewiße Handlungen verrichteten, und gewiße Schicksale erfuhren': Tiedemann, *Untersuchungen*, vol. 2, p. 67.

[97] 'Wir sind uns bewußt, daß wir seit vielen Jahren noch eben diejenigen sind, die ehemals gewisse Handlungen verrichteten, und gewisse Schicksale erfuhren [*Footnote: 'Reimarus natürl. Religion. Abh. VI. Para 2 sqq. gebraucht diesen Beweis gleichfalls, aber auf eine etwas andere Art']. Falsch, sagt man, dies Bewußtseyn einer vollkommenen Identität haben wir nicht, und wir betrügen uns selbst, wenn wir es zu haben glauben [**Footnote: 'Meiners vermischte Schriften, Band II']. Falsch, sage ich auch; denn auf das Bewußtseyn einer vollkommenen Identität baue ich hier nichts; nur das wünschte ich mir...' (continued in next note): Tiedemann, *Untersuchungen*, vol. 2, p. 67.

[98] 'nur das wünschte ich mir nach allen Erfahrungen eingeräumt, daß wir mit vollkommener Ueberzeugung wißen, daß wir selbst, und keine andern Persohnen [*sic*] es waren, die vor zehn, zwanzig, oder mehr Jahren an dem und dem Orte waren, mit den und den Gegenständen sich beschäftigten; unter solchen Umständen lebten': Tiedemann, *Untersuchungen*, vol. 2, pp. 67–8.

it would be impossible to convince ourselves that it was us who did this or that in the past. In short, it would be impossible for us to remember our earlier years and believe 'with complete conviction' that we are the same person who did this or that in the past, if there were no core self that would remain the same through all the changes.[99] This core self, Tiedemann holds, cannot be our body, for the body is subject to constant change. 'It follows that that being in us which knows all these things and which always remains unchanged and the same is distinct from the body and its organisation.'[100]

In short, like others before him, Tiedemann infers the real identity of the self or person from the consciousness we have of our identity; but his argument differs from that of his predecessors in that he concedes that experience shows that we are not in fact conscious of our complete identity. Nevertheless, he argues that we could not even have the limited identity-consciousness we in fact do have if there were not an underlying, immaterial core of the self that is not subject to change. This is, of course, the problematic step in his argument. Our identity-consciousness could simply be mistaken; that is, nothing about the real nature or the real identity of the self can be inferred from the fact that we have a consciousness of our own diachronic identity. Tiedemann, however, infers from our actual identity-consciousness both that there is an immaterial core of the self, and that this part of the self remains identical through time, as it is not subject to change. Tiedemann emphasises the importance of memory to the *consciousness* of our own identity (which he also terms 'consciousness of personality'): he says that this consciousness comes and goes with memory.[101] Although his account may sound Lockean because of the emphasis on consciousness and memory, it is of course not Lockean at all, because, as we have

---

[99] 'In der Reihe von Jahren, die zwischen gewißen Begebenheiten unsers Lebens verfloßen sind, sind in und an uns große Veränderungen vorgegangen; wären diese so allgemein, daß an uns von unsern ehemahligen Theilen nichts übrig geblieben wäre: so könnten wir uns unmöglich überzeugen, daß wir selbst es sind, die ehemals dies oder jenes vornahmen, wie könnte diese Ueberzeugung fortdauern, wenn all diejenigen Theile von uns, in denen und durch die wir sie hatten, verlohren gegangen sind?': Tiedemann, *Untersuchungen*, vol. 2, p. 68.

[100] 'Es ist also unmöglich, daß wir uns an unsere vorigen Jahre erinnern, und mit vollkommener Ueberzeugung wißen können, daß wir diejenigen sind, die vormahls dies oder jenes thaten, wenn nicht in uns etwas ist, das unter allen unsern Veränderungen immer unverändert fortdauert. Nun aber ist dies nicht unser Körper': Tiedemann, *Untersuchungen*, vol. 2, p. 69. See also: 'und wir erinnern uns doch der Dinge, die vor 20, 30, und mehr Jahren mit uns vorgegangen sind; wißen ganz genau, daß sie mit uns selbst, nicht mit einer andern fremden Persohn sich zugetragen haben, wißen dies so fest, als ob es erst heute geschehen wäre? Es folgt also, daß das Wesen in uns, welches dies alles weiß, immer unverändert dasselbe bleibt, das ist, daß es von dem Körper und seiner Organisation verschieden ist': Tiedemann, *Untersuchungen*, vol. 2, p. 70.

[101] In the Appendix to vol. 2 (which has its own pagination) Tiedemann says: 'Bewußtseyn der Personalität hängt doch wol offenbahr vom Gedächtniße ab, weil es mit ihm vergeht und entsteht': Tiedemann, *Untersuchungen*, Appendix to vol. 2, p. 37. 'Das unerhörte Gefühl der Individualität...dürfte doch wohl am Ende nichts weiter als das Bewußtseyn der Personalität unter einem neuen Nahmen seyn. Denn wenn ich weiß, daß ich noch dieselbe Persohn bin: so weiß ich auch nothwendig, daß ich noch daßelbe Individuum bin': Tiedemann, *Untersuchungen*, Appendix to vol. 2, pp. 37–8. This quote shows that for Tiedemann, the consciousness of personality is the same as the consciousness of one's own diachronic identity.

seen, unlike Locke, Tiedemann believes that the consciousness of personal identity proves the reality of an incorporeal and diachronically identical self.

The distinctive feature of Tiedemann's account consists in his explicit concession to the empiricist position—also shared by some materialists—that we do not have a consciousness of a 'complete' identity of our own selves. He holds, however, that it is not even required for his argument that we have such a consciousness. All that is required is the consciousness of our identity in respect to particular actions or circumstances. Therefore, an account of identity in terms of consciousness is possible, even if we do not have and cannot have a consciousness of our 'complete' diachronic identity. For the consciousness of identity in relation to particular circumstances and actions is sufficient, according to Tiedemann, to convince us that there must be an incorporeal self that remains the same through all change.

11

From the critique of Wolffian apperception to the idea of the 'pre-existence' of self-consciousness

Few of Wolff's critics address the issue of personal identity when dealing with his metaphysics, but this is perhaps not surprising, since Wolff himself does not provide a detailed account of personal identity. And we have seen that those of his followers who developed new ideas about identity from within the Wolffian system did not seem to regard the issue as central or especially pressing. Moreover, as was indicated above, by the time Leibniz's most extensive treatment of personal identity was published in *Nouveaux essais* (1765), the debate about personal identity was well under way with Locke as its central focus. Thus, although the impact of the 'Leibnizian–Wolffian system', especially in Germany, was immense, and although their views on the issues were taken up and developed further (Eberhard, Reimarus), there seem to be no major debates focusing on Leibniz's and Wolff's account of personal identity. There was, however, considerable discussion of Wolff's account of consciousness and self-consciousness; and in this context non-Wolffian views about personal identity were also proposed, if not always explicitly, as part of a critique of Leibniz and Wolff. Therefore, the main focus of this Chapter is the issue of self-consciousness. The most important anti-Wolffian thinker in this regard is Jean-Bernard Mérian, who will be discussed in the final section of this Chapter.

11.1. THE PRIMACY OF CONSCIOUSNESS: RÜDIGER AND CRUSIUS *CONTRA* WOLFF AND KLOSSE

Wolff's account of consciousness and self-consciousness in *Deutsche Metaphysik* was debated even in the 1720s, well before his Latin Rational and Empirical Psychologies appeared. In 1723 Daniel Strähler published a critical commentary on Wolff's *Deutsche Metaphysik*, covering the latter's chapters 1–3, without, however, focusing on issues that are relevant in the present context.[1] The most important early critic is

---

[1] Strähler, *Prüfung der Vernünftigen Gedancken des Herrn Hoff-Rath Wolffes von Gott, der Welt und der Seele des Menschen, auch allen Dingen überhaupt*, 2 vols. (1723; reprinted, 1999).

Andreas Rüdiger, who was influenced by Locke and especially by the eclectic philosopher Christian Thomasius. By the time Rüdiger's critique of Wolff appeared in 1727 he had already worked out his own alternative system, presented in many publications. He rejects the doctrine of pre-established harmony with which Wolff attempts to solve the mind–body problem, and argues for the system of physical influx. He is a proponent of the doctrine of the extended soul, and on this basis is sometimes accused of tending towards materialism. Through his pupil A. F. Hoffmann he influenced other critics of Wolff, such as Christian August Crusius, and via Crusius Rüdiger may have been an important influence on Kant.[2] Rüdiger's notion of the extended soul appears to have impressed Tetens in the 1770s, and his critique of the Wolffian understanding of consciousness reappears in later critics of Wolff such as Crusius and Jean-Bernard Mérian. In short, Rüdiger's anti-Wolffian philosophy is of considerable importance in the German eighteenth-century context. Rüdiger's critique of Wolff deals exclusively with the fifth part of the *Deutsche Metaphysik*—the rational part of Wolff's German psychology which includes the analysis of consciousness.[3] Wolff himself did not respond to Rüdiger, but the latter's critique was examined and rejected, for example, by Johann Gottlieb Klosse, who belonged to a group of Wolffians who called themselves *Alethophile*.[4]

Rüdiger does not address the issue of personal identity in any detail, but he discusses Wolff's understanding of 'person' and his account of immortality.[5] He maintains that Wolff's account implies that animals are persons, and as that would make animals immortal, it is a view that must be rejected. According to Rüdiger, Wolff defines 'person' in terms of consciousness, and as animal souls are, for Wolff, conscious of their sensations, Wolff would be committed to the view that animals are persons, even though he explicitly rejects this view (*Gegen-Meinung*, p. 321). Klosse defends Wolff by noting that for the latter, animals are not persons because they are not conscious of their own *diachronic identity*.[6] And it seems clear that Klosse has a point. Rüdiger misrepresents Wolff's position. Wolff does not say simply that human beings are persons because they are conscious of perceptions. Rather, he says that they are persons because they are conscious of their *diachronic identity*, emphasising that animals, by contrast, are conscious of their present sensations (*Deutsche Metaphysik*, § 794) but not of their diachronic identity. It would seem, then, that Klosse is right in saying that Wolff is not committed to the view that animals are persons.

---

[2] Schepers, *Andreas Rüdigers Methodologie und ihre Voraussetzungen* (1959) (on Rüdiger and Kant, pp. 9, 71–2, 123). For other general accounts of Rüdiger, see Wundt, *Die deutsche Schulmetaphysik des 17. Jahrhunderts* (1939), pp. 82–98; Dessoir, *Geschichte der Neueren Deutschen Psychologie* (1902), pp. 98–101; Leinsle, *Reformversuche Protestantischer Metaphysik im Zeitalter des Rationalismus* (1988), pp. 206–26; Albrecht's Preface to the reprint of Rüdiger's critique of Wolff (see next footnote).
[3] Andreas Rüdiger, *Herrn Christian Wolffens Meinung von dem Wesen der Seele und eines Geistes überhaupt; und D. Andreas Rüdigers Gegen-Meinung* (1727); reprinted, with a Preface by Albrecht (2008); hereafter *Gegen-Meinung*.
[4] Klosse, *Hieronymi Aletophili Erinnerungen auf die Gegen-Meinung der Meinung Herrn Hof-Rath Wolffens Von dem Wesen der Seele und eines Geistes überhaupt* (1729). Sometimes a certain Adolf le Fevre is mentioned as a co-author. The translator of Locke's *Essay*, Heinrich Engelhard Poley, discussed above, also belonged to the *Alethophile*.
[5] Rüdiger, *Gegen-Meinung*, pp. 319–35 (commenting on Wolff's *Deutsche Metaphysik*, §§ 922–7).
[6] 'Ein anders ist, sich bewust seyn, daß man *ietzo* ist: ein anders, daß man *vor diesem* gewesen. Jenes gehöret vor die Thiere, nicht dieses, E. sind sie nicht Personen': Klosse, *Erinnerungen*, p. 114.

On the other hand, Wolff concedes that animals too have memory of past sensations (ibid., § 870), but he does not seem to accept that such a memory would involve a consciousness of their diachronic identity. Clearly, if Wolff did accept the latter, then Rüdiger's criticism would seem to be correct, for then animals would fit Wolff's account of a person. We have seen, however, that Wolff suggests that the ability to recognize one's own diachronic identity involves more than just consciousness and the memory of sensations; it also involves the use of reason and the use of language (ibid., §§ 868–70). As animals do not have the latter, and no reason in the sense that human beings do, they are not able to recognize their diachronic identity, and so they are not persons. Klosse defends Wolff against Rüdiger precisely along these lines, stating that the 'intellect' is required for the recognition of identity.[7] It is questionable, however, whether Wolff's position is really consistent; for even the very basic memory that Wolff ascribes to animals seems to require an implicit recognition of their own identity and thus the status of personhood as defined by Wolff himself. Rüdiger holds that animals do not even have a consciousness of their present sensations, as even that would involve the capacity to abstract and the use of language (*Gegen-Meinung*, pp. 106–7).

Rüdiger sees himself as defending the traditional Scholastic definition of person as 'suppositum intelligens' against Wolff's account in terms of consciousness (ibid., pp. 321–2). He is concerned that on Wolff's account, a newborn baby could not be a person, as it has no consciousness of its previous state in the mother's womb. Klosse responds to this rather weakly by asserting that we can infer from the baby's behaviour that it must have some awareness of its previous state, and that at the very least, one cannot prove that it does not have such a consciousness.[8] A basic disagreement between Wolff and Klosse (and other defenders) on the one hand, and Rüdiger on the other, concerns the question of whether the body is required for personhood. Rüdiger again sides with what he considers to be the Scholastic account by assuming that soul and body are both required for human personhood, while Wolff and his defenders believe that the seat of personality is the soul, and that the soul when separated from the body is a person.[9]

In his critique of Wolff's account of the nature of consciousness Rüdiger seems to equate consciousness with inner sense (ibid., p. 106). This is not due to an influence of Locke, as Max Wundt thinks (*Schulmetaphysik*, pp. 84–6), but of Christian Thomasius. We have seen that Locke implies a distinction between consciousness

---

[7] 'Denn sich seines vorigen Zustandes bewust seyn, fliest ex intellectu & memoria, der erste mangelt den Thieren': Klosse, *Erinnerungen*, p. 114.

[8] '*Objicitur:* Ein Kind ist seines vorigen Zustandes im Mutter-Leibe nicht bewust. *Resp.* Es ist sich dessen bewust, denn im Mutter-Leibe hat es durch den Mund Nahrung bekommen, das weiß es, darum sperret es wieder den Mund auf. Zum wenigsten kan man nicht erweisen, daß es sich dessen nicht bewust, wenn jenes argument irgend auch auf die bestias könte appliciret werden': Klosse, *Erinnerungen*, pp. 114–15.

[9] 'Es ist nicht absurde, daß ein Geist ohne Leib und im Leibe ein Person sey, nam propter quod aliquid est tale, illud magis est tale. Der Leib participiret von der Persönlichkeit der Seele': Klosse, *Erinnerungen*, p. 115. On this particular issue at least this debate corresponds to the controversy between Sherlock and South, discussed in Chapter 1. Like Wolff, Sherlock adopts the view that the soul is the person, while South argues that the body too is required for human personality.

and inner sense or reflection. Thomasius does not discuss consciousness in any detail, but he refers to the Cartesian notion of *conscientia* in the non-moral sense which he interprets in terms of inner sensation. Thus he speaks of an inner sense ('innere Empfindligkeit') that one has of one's own thoughts; and this inner sense or *conscientia* is said to consist in thinking that one thinks.[10] What remains entirely unclear in Thomasius is the nature of this inner sense or consciousness; for example, he does not address the question of whether consciousness is a separate mental act or is part of the act of thinking itself (but he seems to be committed to the former idea). Nevertheless, the notion of consciousness as inner sensation was taken up by various philosophers who were influenced by Thomasius, including Rüdiger, August Friedrich Müller (see the previous Chapter), and Crusius (see below).

On the basis of this understanding of consciousness as inner sense, Rüdiger discusses and rejects Wolff's view that consciousness requires comparison and an act of distinguishing. According to Rüdiger, Wolff simply fails to show that consciousness of objects depends on an act of distinguishing. Our act of distinguishing cannot be the *cause* of consciousness, because in order to be able to distinguish between two things we must be conscious of them in the first place (*Gegen-Meinung*, p. 4). Further, Rüdiger argues that, even if Wolff's point was merely that distinguishing is a *criterion* of consciousness, it would have to be rejected; for, as a matter of fact, we are conscious of many things without distinguishing between them (ibid., p. 5). Having criticized the claim that our consciousness of objects depends on an act of distinguishing, Rüdiger also rejects the argument that *self*-consciousness depends on an act of distinguishing ourselves from other things. To Rüdiger, self-consciousness requires only the consciousness of our own mental activities (ibid., p. 9). He adds that even if the soul existed alone, with no world, so that it could not distinguish between itself and other things, it would still be conscious of itself and its existence (ibid., pp. 7–8). In other words, we are conscious of ourselves independently of any act of distinguishing between ourselves and other things. Rüdiger does not elaborate on the notion of self-consciousness in this context,[11] but as he holds that self-consciousness requires some other mental activity, it is clear that he does not believe in a direct or immediate consciousness of one's own self.

Klosse argues against Rüdiger's claim (that an act of distinguishing cannot be the cause of consciousness) as follows. It is one thing to distinguish between things with which one is already familiar (and, that is, of which one is conscious), and quite

---

[10] See, for example, Thomasius, *Einleitung zu der Vernunftlehre* (1691), where he speaks of 'eine innerliche Empfindligkeit' of thought (§ 22, p. 102). He says that 'bestehet diese Empfindligkeit in nichts anders, als daß ich bedencke, daß ich gedencke, oder nach dem *Stylo* der Cartesianer, in *conscientia*' (ibid., § 29, pp. 104–5). He emphasises that the *innere Empfindligkeit* is much more subtle than those *Empfindligkeiten* that are due to the movements of the body (ibid., p. 104), but it is still called a sense or *Empfindligkeit* although *conscientia* is a *thinking* that one thinks. Thinking is defined by Thomasius as an internal speech ('innerliche Rede'), ibid., § 22, p. 102. In inner sense one is 'mitwissend... was er gedenckt' (ibid., § 32, p. 105).

[11] For Rüdiger's account of inner sense, see Schepers (1959), pp. 50–9.

another thing to distinguish between things one has never seen before. According to Klosse, when children encounter things for the first time they always have to distinguish between them, without being conscious of them prior to the act of distinguishing.[12] Klosse obviously confuses consciousness with knowledge, however. For Rüdiger's argument is not that I have to be familiar with, or have knowledge of, something in order to be able to distinguish it from other things; rather, what Rüdiger seems to be saying is that I need to have some basic awareness of an entity before I can relate it to, or distinguish it from other things. In his example, although children may have never seen gold or silver before, when they distinguish gold and silver for the first time they need to be aware of them in order to relate them to one another and to state that they are distinct. Klosse is right, however, in thinking that Rüdiger's critique of Wolff has problems. *Pace* Rüdiger, Wolff's account need not be read as stating that acts of distinguishing are the cause or a criterion of consciousness. Rather, it could be read as stating that the *ability* to distinguish is always involved in the consciousness of objects, and that that ability functions as a necessary condition of the consciousness of objects. This view is hinted at but not developed in Klosse's response to Rüdiger's thought experiment concerning a man who is born without any external senses and who suddenly acquires the sense of hearing and hears the beating of a hammer ('Hammerschlag'). Rüdiger says that that person would be conscious of that sound and yet not be able to distinguish it from anything. Klosse responds by saying that the soul must have had some thoughts prior to that sensation of hearing, and that it would distinguish its present sensation from those thoughts it had prior to it. In that sense, having a present sensation or feeling involves distinguishing it from previous perceptions.[13]

Christian August Crusius's discussion of consciousness and related issues can be found in two of his main works: *Entwurf der nothwendigen Vernunft-Wahrheiten* (1745), and *Weg zur Gewißheit und Zuverlässigkeit der menschlichen Erkenntnis* (1747). We have noted his criticism of Leibniz's principle of the identity of the indiscernibles (*Entwurf*, §§ 383–5), but he does not seem to discuss the issue of personal identity through time. He elaborates, however, on the critique of Wolff's account of consciousness along the lines of Rüdiger and August Friedrich Müller. Like Rüdiger's, Crusius's thoughts about the soul belong to the Thomasian

---

[12] 'Ich kan bekannte Sachen unterscheiden und auch unbekannte. Ein Mensch, der sein Lebtage weder Gold noch Silber gesehen, noch davon gehöret hätte, würde dennoch es aufs erste mal von einander unterscheiden, und das Gold nicht vor das Silber & vice versa halten. Die Kinder müssen alle Dinge das erste mal von einander unterscheiden, ohne sich derer zuvor bewust zu seyn': Klosse, *Erinnerungen*, pp. 19–20.

[13] 'Das gegebene Exempel von den Menschen, der gar keine Sinnen gehabt von Geburth an ist uns nicht zuwider. Denn wenn er plötzlich das Gehör bekäme, und einen Hammerschlag hörte, da meynt der Herr D. würde er sich dieses ersten Hammerschlagss bewust seyn, ohne ihn von etwas unterscheiden zu können. *Resp.* Die Seele dieses Menschen müste doch zuvor Gedancken gehabt haben, und von denselben unterscheidet er gegenwärtige Empfindung. Ja wer weiß, ob er gar wüste, wie ihm widerführe: zumahl nicht glaublich, daß in einem Leibe ohne Sinnen eine Seele wohnt. Das Gefühle mangelt niemahlen durch den gantzen Leib einem lebendigen Menschen': Klosse, *Erinnerungen*, p. 20.

tradition,[14] and he adopts from Rüdiger the notion of the soul as non-material but extended (ibid., p. 836).

Crusius emphasises the importance of the notion of consciousness. Consciousness, he says, adds something new and important to the mere representation (*Vorstellung*) of an object. Through consciousness we have a representation of the thought itself that represents the object. For Crusius it follows from this that consciousness requires a distinct mental capacity ('eine besondere Grund-Kraft') that makes consciousness possible.[15] He rejects accounts according to which any idea of some degree of vividness is accompanied by consciousness, but he argues especially against Wolff's notion of consciousness—against those, that is, 'who derive consciousness from the distinction of concepts' (ibid., p. 863). His argument against Wolff is mostly like Rüdiger's: we need to be conscious of things in order to be able to distinguish between them; therefore, we cannot account for consciousness in terms of the capacity to distinguish between things. Crusius thinks that Wolff and others have been misled by the fact that consciousness and the distinguishing between things always occur together. He differs from Rüdiger by emphasising that the primacy of consciousness is not temporal but metaphysical. Rüdiger's formulations suggest a temporal order, but Crusius states explicitly that consciousness is prior according to the order of nature ('der Natur nach'). He also maintains, however, like Rüdiger, that consciousness is one of the effective causes of the act of distinguishing. The latter requires consciousness as well as the capacity to abstract.[16]

Like Rüdiger's pupil August Friedrich Müller, Crusius follows Thomasius in linking consciousness to inner sense ('innerliche Empfindung'). Again, however, it does not seem to be clear what exactly the relationship is between *innerliche Empfindung* and consciousness. Sometimes it seems that Crusius simply equates inner sense with consciousness, while other times he suggests that we become conscious of our thoughts through inner sense. He says, for example, that it is 'through inner sensations that we become conscious of ourselves, our thoughts and

---

[14] For Crusius in general, see Krieger, *Geist, Welt und Gott bei Christian August Crusius* (1993). See also Grau, *Die Entwicklung des Bewusstseinsbegriffes im XVII. und XVIII. Jahrhundert* (1916), pp. 222–6.

[15] 'Ferner verdienet insonderheit das Bewustseyn viel Aufmercksamkeit. Denn dadurch kömmt zu der Action, wodurch ein Object vorgestellet wird, etwas hinzu, welches in der Vorstellung des Objects gar nicht enthalten ist. Durch das Bewußtseyn haben wir von unsern Gedanken selbst eine Vorstellung.... Man wird dahero zugeben müssen, daß das Bewußtseyn eine besondere Grund-Kraft erfordere, wodurch es möglich ist': Crusius, *Entwurf*, pp. 862–3.

[16] 'Eben so wenig kann man denenjenigen Recht geben, welche das Bewustseyn aus der Unterscheidung der Begriffe herleiten. Sie haben sich dadurch verführen lassen, daß sie gefunden, daß das Bewustseyn und die Unterscheidung allezeit beysammen sind. Allein wir sind uns der Dinge nicht darum bewust, weil wir sie unterscheiden, sondern darum können wir sie allererst unterscheiden, weil wir uns bewust sind. Das Bewustseyn ist der Natur nach eher als das Unterscheiden, und ist eine von den wirckenden Ursachen des Unterscheidens....Wenn wir sagen, wir unterscheiden Dinge, so heißt dieses so viel, als wir sind uns des Unterschiedes derselben bewust. Daher das Unterscheiden allererst durch die Abstractions-Kraft, und die Kraft des Bewustseyns, möglich wird': Crusius, *Entwurf*, pp. 863–4.

state of mind'.[17] Here he seems to be saying that inner sense is precisely that special mental capacity that we must assume for consciousness to be possible. Elsewhere, however, he identifies inner sense with the faculty of consciousness itself: inner sense is defined as the *Kraft des Bewußtseyns*,[18] and Crusius suggests that inner sensation (consciousness) may require not just one but several basic mental capacities or *Grundkräfte*. He does not seem to elaborate on this, however (*Weg zur Gewißheit*, p. 155).

Crusius does not say much about the consciousness of one's own self, but he comments on Descartes's *cogito* argument for the knowledge we have of our own existence. Crusius suggests that the argument should read: *I am conscious that I think, therefore I am* (and not simply *I think therefore I am*). In order to be able to infer my own existence from the existence of my thoughts I have to presuppose the existence of my thoughts, and this I can do because I know them through inner sense or consciousness (he equates the two in this context). For Crusius, then, there is no immediate or 'original' consciousness of one's own self; the latter consciousness is to be derived from the consciousness we have of our own ideas. Consciousness relates directly only to thoughts and ideas, not to the self.[19] He does not seem to consider that the consciousness of thoughts as mine already involves or presupposes the existence of a self that has thoughts and cannot therefore be established in the first place through an inference drawn from the consciousness of thoughts.

11.2. ON WOLFFIAN SELF-CONSCIOUSNESS: HOLLMANN AND VON CREUZ

We have seen that even a critic of Wolff such as G. F. Meier accepts that we infer the existence of our own self from our thoughts. Samuel Christian Hollmann—the first Professor of Philosophy at the University of Göttingen—relates the Cartesian *cogito* and the notion of consciousness to the question about of the nature of the mind.[20] Hollmann differs from Wolff in many respects, but does not criticize Wolff explicitly on all those points of disagreement, and he takes over much of the Wolffian conceptual framework. He critically engages with the theory of the pre-established

---

[17] 'Durch dieselben [innerliche Empfindungen] sind wir uns unserer selbst, unserer Gedanken, und unseres Gemüths-Zustandes, bewust': Crusius, *Entwurf*, p. 825.

[18] 'Die *innerliche Empfindung* ist, wodurch wir etwas empfinden, welches wir uns als in unserer Seele vorstellen. Sie ist also die *Kraft des Bewußtseyns*': Crusius, *Weg zur Gewißheit*, p. 113.

[19] 'Durch die *innerliche Empfindung* aber werden wir uns desjenigen bewust, was in unserer Seele vorgehet. Wenn die Frage ist, woher wir wissen, daß wir sind: So antwortet zwar Cartesius darauf, *ich denke; darum bin ich*. Es sollte aber heissen: *ich bin mir bewust, daß ich denke; darum bin ich*. Wenn man also unsere Existenz aus der Existenz unserer Gedanken schlüssen will: So muß man erst die Existenz unserer Gedanken selbst aus einer Empfindung, nehmlich aus der innerlichen Empfindung oder dem Bewustseyn derselben voraus setzen': Crusius, *Entwurf*, p. 29.

[20] The most detailed account of Hollmann is the article by Cramer, 'Die Stunde der Philosophie. Über Göttingens ersten Philosophen und die philosophische Theorielage der Gründungszeit', in Stackelberg (ed.), *Zur Geistigen Situation der Zeit der Göttinger Universitätsgründung 1737* (1988), pp. 101–43. See also Wundt (1939), pp. 205–7, 290–1.

350   *The Early Modern Subject*

harmony, arguing (as do others) that the theory is inconsistent with human freedom.[21] His concern with the *cogito* is not the nature of relating to one's own self, but the question of whether the *cogito* can function as a first principle. Hollmann seems to take for granted that the Cartesian *cogito* is to be read as an inference, and to accept this understanding of the *cogito*. As long as 'principium' (principle) is understood merely in terms of beginning—that is, 'first' in a temporal sense—then it must be granted that Descartes's *cogito* is indeed the first principle of all human knowledge, as it would be absurd to concern oneself with the knowledge of other things while one considers one's own existence doubtful.[22] Most people, he says, see no reason to doubt their own existence and tacitly presuppose the latter, but for all those who may think there is reason to doubt their existence, Descartes's argument can be used to convince them otherwise. In both cases it is the first 'fundamental truth of all human cognition' ('Grundwahrheit aller Menschlichen Kenntnisse', ibid., p. 3). Regrettably, so Hollmann thinks, Descartes is misled by the ambiguity of the word 'principium', and ascribes to the *cogito* a foundational function as well, claiming that it is a first truth in the sense that other truths can be deduced from it. Descartes regards it as a first principle in a logical and metaphysical sense, and as such it must be rejected as false.[23] It is plain from these remarks that like Rüdiger, Hollmann does not adopt the notion of an immediate consciousness of one's own self. Rather, as he states explicitly elsewhere, we are immediately conscious only of representations. Thought does not only involve representing something, but also, at the same time, the consciousness of that representation. Hollmann terms this relating to one's own thought variously 'inner sense', 'apperception', 'immediate reflexion', and 'logical' *conscientia* (as opposed to 'moral' *conscientia* or conscience).[24] As is clear from his comments on

---

[21] See, for example, Hollmann, *Gedancken von der Beschaffenheit der menschlichen Erkäntnüß, und den Quellen der Welt-Weißheit* (1737), pp. 61–3.

[22] Hollmann, *Zufällige Gedanken über verschiedene wichtige Materien*, vol. 6 (1776), pp. 2–3: 'Wenn man man unter dem Nahmen des Principii nemlich nichts anders, als den bloßen Anfang einer vorkommenden Sache, versteht, welches man denn, mehrerer Kürze und Deutlichkeit halber, gar wohl den Grammatischen, und Physischen, Verstand des Worts nennen könnte, (als wenn man von dem principio einer Rede, eines Jahrs, Monaths, oder Tages, einer Reise, u.s.w. redet): so kann man dem Cartesianischen Satz nicht absprechen, daß er, nicht allein von der Philosophie, sondern von allen Menschlichen Kentnißen, das primum principium abgebe, und abgeben müße: da es ja höchst thöricht und unvernünftig seyn würde, um die Kenntniß anderer Dinge um und neben sich in der Welt sich zu bekümmern, wenn man von sich selbst, und seiner eignen Existenz, noch nicht einmahl dergestalt überzeugt wäre, daß man weiter daran nicht die geringste Ursache zu zweifeln fünde'.

[23] Hollmann, *Zufällige Gedanken*, vol. 6, p. 4: 'Und hiemit ändert sich die ganze Scene, mit diesem so berüchtigten Cartesianischen Principio, mit einmahl: und nun ist es nicht mehr so viel, als ein bloßes Initium cognitionis humanae, oder ein Principium im Grammatischen und Physikalischen Verstand, sondern wird nun ein Principium cognoscendi im Logicalischen und Metaphysischen Verstande, der von jenem ersten Himmelweit unterschieden ist; und zugleich ein falscher Grundsatz des ganzen Cartesianischen Lehrgebäudes, wie zu andern Zeit und an andern Orten mit mehrern ist erwiesen worden'.

[24] Hollmann, *Philosophia rationalis, quae Logica vulgo dicitur, multum aucta et emendata. Paullo Uberioris in Universam Philosophiam Introductionis* (1746), pt. 1, pp. 91–2. 'Immo non res solum ipsas, quas cogitamus, repraesentare nobis hoc modo possumus; sed ad ipsam quoque hanc illarum repraesentationem, in nobis factam, animum iterum advertere, idemque & in hac denuo facere,

the *cogito*, the inner sense or consciousness of representations is the basis for our knowledge that there is a thinking being in us that has those representations and is conscious of them.[25] Not unlike Leibniz, then, Hollmann uses several terms for relating to one's own thoughts, but without examining in any detail the nature of this operation. He seems to assume, however, that it is a distinct, higher-order mental activity—a 'reflex act'.

Although Hollmann accepts a version of the *cogito* argument and takes over a largely Cartesian notion of 'logical' *conscientia*, he is critical of other aspects of Cartesian metaphysics. For example, he does not accept that the soul knows itself better than it knows other things. Rather, the soul is largely ignorant of its own nature.[26] Hollmann's notion of consciousness, as discussed above, is relevant here. For it involves the notion that we do not have any direct or immediate consciousness even of our own existence as the subject of thought. We infer our existence as thinking beings from the consciousness we have of mental operations and states. As we cannot imagine how the body could be the cause of these operations we infer the existence of the soul as a substance that is distinct from the body. Now, since the soul's existence is inferred from the inner experience of certain states and operations, it is clear that the soul does not have any *a priori* knowledge of its own existence (see also Cramer (1988), p. 119). This means that the soul knows its own *nature*, too, only through inferences drawn from its operations: the soul must be an immaterial substance so that it can function as the cause of those operations (ibid., p. 121). Moreover, the soul has no knowledge at all of other aspects of its nature. For example, it does not know (*a priori* or *a posteriori*) where it is located in the body; and although we must assume a unity of soul and body, the soul does not know wherein this unity consists and how soul and body can interact. The soul does not even know how it manages to have sensations.

Like Wolff and his followers, however, Hollmann holds that the soul can know that it exists and that it is an immaterial substance. The agnostic aspects of Hollmann's position mentioned above are quite compatible, then, with his explicit rejection of materialism.[27] Like other thinkers before him, in rejecting materialism

---

possumus, &c: id quod nonnulli reflexionem, sensu intransitivo, seu actum cogitandi reflexum, alii recentius apperceptionem, alii iterum conscientiam logicam, appellare solent. Logica vero haec conscientia dicitur, ne cum morali, de qua suo loco, temere confundatur'. For the use of inner sense as synonymous with reflexion and apperception, see ibid., 99–100 where Hollmann appeals approvingly to Locke's definition of inner sense in *An Essay Concerning Human Understanding*, ed. Nidditch (1975), II.i.4.

[25] See Hollmann, *Institutiones pneumatologiae et theologiae naturalis Paulo Uberioris in Universam Philosophiam Introductionis Tomo III* (1741), pp. 99–100.

[26] Hollmann, *Dissertatio prior de stupendo naturae mysterio, anima humana sibi ipsi ignota* (1722; another edition, 1750). Hollmann says: 'ignorantia crassa est, qua mens nostra in sua ipsius cognitione laborat' (p. 8). Quoted from Cramer (1988), p. 118. Cramer discusses this dissertation in some detail on pp. 118–25. The claim concerning our ignorance about the soul is also stated in other writings, however. See, for example, Hollmann, *Ueberzeugender Vortrag von Gott und der Schrifft* (1733), pp. 183–5; and Hollmann, *Der Zerstreuer* (1737), pp. 241–8.

[27] Cramer points out that Hollmann nevertheless takes materialism seriously as an option, and encourages his readers to consider the materialist option: Cramer (1988), pp. 130–6.

he appeals to the nature of consciousness. He argues that the nature of consciousness is incompatible with the complex nature of material beings. For Hollmann, as for other immaterialist metaphysicians of the mind, relating to one's own representations cannot be reduced to a material process in the brain. He employs the standard immaterialist arguments. The unity of the thinking subject or soul would not be possible if the thinking substance were material. If the thinking substance were material, then different parts of the soul would be responsible for different kinds of mental operations (such as the representation of objects, and the consciousness of such representations), and the unity of the soul could not be guaranteed.[28] It is important to emphasise that Hollmann does not speak of a direct consciousness of the self or subject—consistently with his reflections on consciousness discussed above. It is misleading, therefore, to ascribe to him the view that consciousness of the self as the *subject* of representations plays a role in his critique of materialism.[29] As indicated above, like Leibniz, Hollmann does not even distinguish clearly between different ways of relating to one's own self, equating consciousness with inner sense, apperception, and reflection.

Friedrich Carl Casimir von Creuz discusses the nature of self-consciousness in more detail than does Hollmann. As we saw in the previous Chapter, von Creuz follows Wolff on the issue of immortality and identity. He criticizes and rejects Wolff's account of self-consciousness, however. His critique differs significantly from that of earlier critics such as Rüdiger, Müller, and Crusius. Unlike the latter, he takes his criticism an important step further, and argues (in some passages at least) for the possibility of a self-consciousness that is independent of the consciousness of outer things and of the act of distinguishing ourselves from other things. Unfortunately, however, von Creuz's account is not as clear as it might be.

Von Creuz begins with a critique of the Wolffian definition of thought—which says that thought is a representation that is connected with consciousness. He rejects this view, arguing that it may well be true that a representation requires consciousness, but that it does not follow that consciousness requires representation. There can be consciousness without representation. It is possible for us to be conscious of our own selves without thinking of anything outside us. According to von Creuz, then, it is quite true that while we distinguish our own selves from other things, we are conscious of our own selves; but it does not follow that we have to distinguish ourselves from outer things in order to become conscious of our own selves.[30]

---

[28] See Hollmann, *Institutiones pneumatologiae et theologiae naturalis*, pp. 71–83.

[29] Here my reading differs from that of Cramer, who reconstructs Hollmann's argument in terms of a notion of self-consciousness understood as an immediate consciousness of one's own self as the *subject* of representations: Cramer (1988), pp. 138–40. The passages Cramer cites do not seem to justify the ascription of such a notion to Hollmann. As far as I can see, Hollmann speaks of a direct consciousness only of representations, not of the subject of representations. It seems that Cramer ascribes a (post-)Kantian idea of self-consciousness to Hollmann, and indeed he hints at a link between Hollman and Kant (p. 143).

[30] 'Einen Gedanken eine mit einem Bewußtseyn verknüpfte Vorstellung zu nennen, dieses macht die Sache nicht aus. Wo eine Vorstellung ist, da muß wohl ein Bewußtseyn seyn... nicht aber umgekehrt, indem ein Bewußtseyn, in gewissem Verstande, Statt findet ohne Vorstellung. Wenn wir der Dinge außer uns bewußt werden, so sagen wir, daß solche die Vorwürfe oder Objecte

Consciousness is said by von Creuz to be a continuation ('Fortsetzung') of our existence, even to *constitute* our existence.[31] The soul has within itself the power to produce thought, and, that is, consciousness. The evidence for this is experience ('ein gewisses unleugbares inneres Gefühl'; *Versuch*, vol. 1, p. 89).

Von Creuz argues that a thinking being must, as soon as it exists, become conscious of its own self. Without such a primary or primitive self-consciousness it could not even attempt to become conscious of itself and of other things.[32] His account may seem to be circular here. He seems to be saying that we require self-consciousness to become conscious of our own selves. On the other hand, he may imply a distinction between a primitive self-consciousness that is simply given with the soul's existence and a consciousness of one's own self that is involved in the consciousness of objects. And he may want to say that the latter cannot be had without primitive self-consciousness. His thesis seems to be that self-consciousness cannot be separated from the existence of a being that is able to have consciousness of other things, and through the latter become conscious of its own self. As he provides no detailed analysis of the various types of consciousness to which he appeals, however, the precise meaning of this thesis remains unclear.

Also, although he seems to be saying in the passages referred to above that self-consciousness does not require a relating to other things, he seems to link consciousness and the ability to distinguish more closely in other passages (ibid., vol. 1, pt. 1, pp. 111–12). For example, he says that although it is true that we can think of our own selves without thinking of other things, all that follows from that is that when we introspect we find more in ourselves than just the consciousness of other things (ibid., p. 111). Consciousness consists in distinguishing (a) our own self from other things, and (b) that which is distinct in our own minds; that is, the multiplicity of

unseres Bewußtseyns seyn, und nennen diese Objecte Vorstellungen. Allein können wir uns nicht mit uns selbst beschäfftigen, und unserer bewußt seyn, ohne an etwas außer uns zu gedencken? Wenn wir uns von Dingen außer uns unterscheiden; so sind wir freylich uns unserer bewußt; allein daraus folgt nicht, daß wir uns nothwendig von Dingen außer uns unterscheiden müßten, wenn wir unserer bewußt seyn wollten. Wir können in uns selbst so viel zu unterscheiden finden, als zu unserem Bewußtseyn erfordert wird': von Creuz, *Versuch über die Seele*, 2. vols. (1754), vol. 1, pt. 1, p. 90.

[31] 'Indessen kann doch unser Bewußtseyn nicht allein darinnen bestehen, daß wir etwas in uns, oder uns von etwas außer uns unterscheiden. Das Bewußtseyn ist eigentlich eine Fortsetzung unserer Existenz... ja es macht unsere ganze Existenz in gewissem Verstand aus. Was ist nun eigentlich ein Gedanke? das Bewußtseyn ist von ihm, wie ich gesagt, nicht zu trennen; das Bewußtseyn ist eine Fortsetzung unserer Existenz. Es ist also ein Gedanke eine jede innere Wirkung der Seele, woraus sich ihre Fortdauer erklären, oder der Grund anzeigen läßt, warum sie fortdauret': von Creuz, *Versuch*, vol. 1, pt. 1, p. 91.

[32] 'Aus dem unmittelbar vorhergehenden erhellet also genugsam, daß ein Ding, welches eine Kraft hat, Gedanken, das ist, ein Bewußtseyn herfür zu bringen; sich auch, so bald es existirt, seiner selbst bewußt seyn müßte; und es wäre schlechterdings nicht zu begreifen, wie es, ohne sich seiner selbst bewußt zu seyn, sich bemühen könne, seiner selbst und anderer Dinge bewußt zu werden. Das Bewußtseyn seiner selbst läßt sich also von der Kraft eines Dings, ein solches Bewußtseyn herfür zu bringen, nicht trennen, obgleich ein solches Ding in einer beständigen Bemühung seyn kann, sich seiner selbst und anderer Dinge bewußt zu bleiben, auch immer mehrerer Dinge bewußt zu werden, und also auch das Bewußtseyn seiner selbst immer zu erneuern und zu vervielfältigen': von Creuz, *Versuch*, vol. 1, pt. 1, p. 96.

thoughts and feelings ('was in uns vorgeht'; ibid., p. 112).[33] Consciousness, he argues here, is necessarily connected with the consciousness of other things but not identical with such consciousness; consciousness of self involves more than the consciousness of objects.[34] Unlike his claims discussed in the previous paragraph, this thesis is consistent with the position taken by Wolff, who argues for a necessary connection between self-consciousness and the consciousness of other things.

Again, von Creuz's comments on the issue of consciousness and self-consciousness are lacking in clarity. One reason for this is obviously that he does not elaborate on the notion of a primary or primitive self-consciousness in much detail. He merely hints at the thesis that self-consciousness, insofar as it is simply given with the soul's existence, functions as a necessary condition of other forms of consciousness, but does not make it explicit, and certainly does not develop the idea; and it seems to be inconsistent with other passages in which he maintains that self-consciousness requires the consciousness of other things. Unlike Wolff, he does not attempt to explain self-consciousness and the consciousness of objects in terms of a mutual dependence.

The notion of self-consciousness plays a more central role in the thought of two independent thinkers who develop their position through a critique of Wolffian philosophy.

11.3. SELF-CONSCIOUSNESS AND THE BODY: SULZER

Early in the nineteenth century, Gottlob Ernst Schulze—known today mainly as a critic of Kant and Reinhold—begins his *Psychische Anthropologie* with a chapter on consciousness and self-consciousness. Here, he mentions two eighteenth-century authors whose contributions to the topic he considers especially important: Jean-Bernard Mérian (1723–1807) and Johann Georg Sulzer (1720–79).[35]

It may be somewhat surprising that in the heyday of German Idealism, after Kant and Fichte, these two thinkers are selected for special mention on this topic. Both are little known today, even to historians of the philosophy of mind. Sulzer's main work is,

---

[33] 'Denn eines Dings bewußt seyn, heißt: dasselbe von andern unterscheiden. Ich sehe wenigstens nicht, wie man von dem Bewußtseyn die Handlung der Seele, wenn sie eines von dem andern unterscheidet, trennen könne. Es ist zwar wahr, daß wir an uns allein denken können, ohne an andere Dinge außer uns zu denken; allein es folgt daraus nichts weiter, als daß in uns selbst auch etwas mehreres, als das Bewußtseyn anderer Dinge anzutreffen sey. Wir unterscheiden freylich auch in uns etwas von dem andern; dieses ist aber vielmehr ein Beweis, daß unser Bewußtseyn darinnen bestehe, daß wir uns von andern und das, was in uns selbst verschieden ist, in sich unterscheiden, so weit es dem Wesen unserer Seele nach möglich ist': von Creuz, *Versuch*, vol. 1, pt. 1, p. 111.

[34] 'Es ist aber dessen ungeachtet nicht zu leugnen, daß zum Bewustseyn noch etwas mehreres, als das bloße Unterscheiden eines von dem andern erfordert werde, und daß auch das Bewußtseyn unserer selbst mit dem Bewußtseyn anderer Dinge nicht gänzlich einerley, obgleich ersteres mit letzterem allemal nothwendig verknüpft sey': von Creuz, *Versuch*, vol. 1, pt. 1, p. 112.

[35] 'Viele gute Beobachtungen über den Inhalt des Selbstbewußtseyns und über den Einfluß der Helligkeit desselben aufs Leben, sind enthalten in einer Abhandlung *Mérian's* Ueber die Apperception, in der Histoire de l'Acad. R. de Berlin Tom. V (deutsch in Hißmann's Magazin für die Philosophie B. 1) und in einem Aufsatze *Sulzer's*, Von dem Bewußtseyn, in dessen vermischten Schriften B. 1': Schulze, *Psychische Anthropologie* (1816), p. 20; third edn. (1826), p. 33.

moreover, in aesthetics.[36] As a matter of fact, however, Schulze has a point. Sulzer and Mérian are philosophers who, like him, favour an empirical approach in philosophy and contribute to an important aspect in empirical psychology. Mentioning Sulzer and Mérian in one breath makes sense for other reasons as well, as they have several things in common. Both were Swiss thinkers of almost the same age, both were based at the *Académie Royale des Sciences et Belles-Lettres* in Berlin from 1750 onwards, and both published philosophical papers in the Yearbooks of the Academy. Philosophically, both came from a Wolffian background which, however, they transcended in different ways respectively. Both were influenced also by British philosophy, and although their outlook was anti-sceptical, they were both interested in Hume and were involved in translations of Hume's writings into German (Sulzer) and French (Mérian).[37] As is evident from Schulze's comment, both of them published papers on the notion of consciousness or apperception that were taken up in subsequent empirically and psychologically oriented philosophy. In the case of Mérian, at least, there may be even a link to Kant, as we shall see below.

There are, however, also important differences between Mérian and Sulzer. In general Mérian is clearly more critical of Wolff than is Sulzer, and he provides a more detailed and precise analysis of the conceptual distinctions relevant to the issue of apperception than does Sulzer. For example, Mérian, unlike Sulzer, carefully distinguishes between apperception as self-consciousness and apperception as a consciousness of ideas. Moreover, Sulzer focuses more than does Mérian on the 'influence' that consciousness as understood by him has on other aspects of our mental life; that is, on the application of the notion of consciousness to our thinking about practical matters. Although Sulzer's comments on consciousness are meant to be part of what he calls a 'physics of the soul' ('Physik der Seele'), a systematic body of knowledge which would allow us to enter into the 'inner soul', ultimately the aim of this 'physics' is practical application.[38] For example, he expresses the hope that his analyses may provide principles of the art of resisting 'the tyranny of the passions'.[39] Still, in spite of this practical orientation his claims are relevant to the 'establishing of a proper system' ('Festsetzung eines richtigen Systems'; ibid., p. 199). He does not always present detailed argumentation for his views, but in some cases at least his arguments can be reconstructed on the basis of the texts and the philosophical context of the time. We shall see that in the last analysis there are problems concerning the consistency of his conception of consciousness with other, related philosophical claims central to his thought.

---

[36] Sulzer, *Allgemeine Theorie der Schönen Künste*, 2 vols. (1771–74); fourth edn., enlarged, with supplements by Blanckenburg, 4 vols. (1796–98).
[37] Zart is correct in stating that 'Sulzer war zuerst Wolffianer und wurde später Eklektiker; aber alle seine Schriften verrathen vielfach den Einfluss der Engländer': Zart, *Einfluss der englischen Philosophen seit Bacon auf die deutsche Philosophie des 18. Jahrhunderts* (1881), pp. 105–6. Zart's thesis, however, that the 'Einfluss der Engländer' constitutes merely a slight modification of Sulzer's 'essential Wolffianism', is questionable. Compare Zart (1881), p. 111.
[38] Sulzer, 'Von dem Bewußtseyn und seinem Einflusse auf unsre Urtheile', in Sulzer, *Vermischte Philosophische Schriften*, vol. 1 (1773), pp. 199–224 (abbr. 'Bewußtseyn'), p. 199.
[39] 'der Tyrannei der Leidenschaften': Sulzer, 'Erklärung eines psychologisch paradoxen Satzes', in Sulzer, *Vermischte Philosophische Schriften*, vol. 1 (1773), pp. 99–121, at p. 100.

Mérian published his articles on the notion of apperception in the Yearbooks of the Academy in 1751. This is much earlier than Sulzer's main essay on the topic 'Of Consciousness' that Schulze cites—even considering that he presented it to the Academy ten years prior to its first, French, publication.[40] Sulzer does not seem to refer to Mérian's treatment of the topic, however, and as Mérian's analysis is more detailed and points to future developments more than does Sulzer's, we shall look at Sulzer first, before turning to Mérian.

11.3.1. Sulzer on consciousness and self-consciousness

Sulzer's comments on consciousness are scattered over a number of his writings,[41] but the most important text is the essay cited by Schulze. Here Sulzer defines consciousness as follows:

Philosophers understand by the word consciousness [apperceptio] that action of the mind, by which we distinguish our own being from the ideas we are employed about and [by which] we therefore know what we do and what occurs in us and around us.[42]

In spite of its brevity this definition is quite rich, but is not as clear as it might be. Sulzer's suggestion that he is merely reporting what 'philosophers' mean by consciousness points to the fact that he is not concerned with presenting an entirely new understanding of the notion but is happy to follow tradition. The latter is obviously that of Wolff and his school, though his terminology is not the same as Wolff's. We have seen that Wolff does not equate consciousness with apperception; apperception relates to one's own perceptions, while consciousness may relate also to external things. Sulzer, by contrast, does equate consciousness with apperception—which is obvious from the original French title of the essay which uses 'l'apperception' rather than 'la conscience'. Elsewhere he relates apperception to Descartes and Latin 'conscientia'.[43] By referring to both Descartes and Leibniz in this context, Sulzer clearly appeals to Wolff's definition of apperception in his *Psychologia empirica* (§ 25).

---

[40] Sulzer's 'Bewußtseyn' (see footnote 38 above) was first published in French, entitled 'Sur l'apperception, et son influence sur nos jugemens', in *Histoire de l'academie royale des sciences et belles-lettres. Année 1764* (1766), pp. 415–34. Sulzer states in a note on p. 415 that it has been ten years since he presented this Mémoire to the Academy.

[41] Most of the relevant writings are collected in Sulzer, *Vermischte Philosophische Schriften*, 2 vols. (1773–81; reprinted, 1974). Vol. 2 was published posthumously, and was edited by Blanckenburg. Vol. 1 consists of German translations of Sulzer's contributions to the Yearbooks of the Berlin Academy. Vol 2, entitled *Vermischte Schriften*, has a biography by Blanckenburg and contains philosophical as well as non-philosophical essays.

[42] 'Die Philosophen verstehen durch das Wort Bewußtseyn (apperceptio) diejenige Handlung des Geistes, wodurch wir unser Wesen von den Ideen, welche uns beschäfftigen, unterscheiden, und also deutlich wissen, was wir thun und was in uns und um uns vorgeht': Sulzer, 'Bewußtseyn', p. 200.

[43] Sulzer, 'Gedanken über einige Eigenschaften der Seele', in *Vermischte Philosophische Schriften*, vol. 1, p. 351. Here Sulzer says that apperception is that which 'Descartes calls consciousness'. See also ibid., p. 367.

At first it seems that Sulzer restricts consciousness to a relating to one's own self, for he says that 'consciousness is that act of the mind by which we distinguish our own being from the ideas we are employed about'. He certainly adopts the Wolffian account of consciousness in terms of the act of distinguishing. This act, however, seems to concern only one's own self and one's own ideas, as noted. He adds, however, that through this act of distinguishing between our own being and our ideas we know (1) about our actions ('what we do'), (2) what we passively experience ('what occurs in us'), and (3) what happens 'around us'; that is, external, non-subjective events and objects. It is not obvious how we should learn about external events and objects by distinguishing between our own being or self and our ideas. Sulzer's notion of representation can help to clarify this, however. Here his position differs significantly from that of Wolff. For Wolff there is only one main mental faculty—the faculty of representation—but Sulzer argues that there are two fundamentally distinct faculties of the mind: representation ('Vorstellen') and feeling ('Empfinden'). For Sulzer, a representation ('Vorstellung') does not involve a relating to our own self, but only to that 'what occurs around us'. A representation is essentially object- or outer-directed. Sulzer describes the faculty of representation as the faculty by which we can come 'to know the qualities of things'.[44] With respect to representations 'we are conscious of a thing that we consider to be distinct from our own selves'.[45] In feeling ('Empfinden'), however, as when we feel pain, the soul is 'solely concerned with its own self'; 'we feel only our own self'.[46] Sulzer concedes that usually the soul exercises both faculties 'at the same time' ('zugleich'), but one still can, and indeed must, distinguish between the two faculties.[47] We shall return to the issue of how Sulzer's notion of consciousness relates to his distinction between representing (Vorstellung) and feeling (Empfinden), but in the present context the relevant point is that an outer- or object-directed relation of consciousness is always already implied by his concept of representation. Sulzer adopts an essentially Wolffian notion of consciousness without, however, arguing for it in the way that Wolff does. For Sulzer, as for Wolff, consciousness is characterized by a twofold relating to one's own self (the self and its ideas or representations) and—via these representations—to objects. Although he does not explain this, to him, two acts of distinguishing must be involved in consciousness: (1) between the self and its ideas;

[44] 'Anmerkungen über den verschiedenen Zustand, worinn sich die Seele bey Ausübung ihrer Hauptvermögen, nämlich des Vermögens, sich etwas vorzustellen und des Vermögens zu empfinden, befindet': Sulzer, *Vermischte Philosophische Schriften*, vol. 1, p. 225.
[45] Sulzer, *Allgemeine Theorie der Schönen Künste*, vol. 4, p. 408.
[46] Sulzer, 'Anmerkungen über den verschiedenen Zustand', in *Vermischte Philosophische Schriften*, vol. 1, p. 229; *Allgemeine Theorie*, vol. 4, p. 408.
[47] Sulzer, 'Anmerkungen über den verschiedenen Zustand', in *Vermischte Philosophische Schriften*, vol. 1, p. 225. Sulzer's distinction between *Vorstellen* and *Empfinden* had a considerable impact on subsequent psychological writing in the eighteenth century. Hissmann, for example, takes over this distinction, explicitly appealing to Sulzer as an authority on this: Hissmann, *Psychologische Versuche* (1777), pp. 106–7. He does not seem to accept Sulzer's idea that feeling relates to the self, and representation only to objects.

(2) between what is 'in us' and that which is 'around us'.[48] Sulzer expresses this thought explicitly in the following passage: 'Consciousness therefore presupposes on the one hand the clear idea of our own self and of what one does, while on the other hand the understanding is employed about some other thing that it regards as external to itself and as independent of its being.'[49] It is not clear what one is to make of the notion of presupposition that Sulzer makes use of here. According to his own definition, consciousness is that by which we distinguish the self from its ideas in the first place, which does not seem consistent with the idea that consciousness 'presupposes' the idea of the self. Moreover, the passage suggests that Sulzer thinks of the relating to one's own self through consciousness in terms of the notion of representation. He speaks of the 'clear idea of our own self' and, a little later, of the 'representation of our own self' ('Vorstellung von uns selbst', 'Bewußtseyn', p. 201). We shall have to look at the question of how this is compatible with Sulzer's official distinction between Vorstellen (representation) and Empfinden (feeling), according to which it is essential to a representation that it relates to something other than the self, while feeling is purely self-relating. How can Sulzer say that the consciousness of one's own self is a representation? Perhaps it is just a matter of terminological imprecision. Even if we were to accept this, there are other problems, as we shall see. Before turning to these, however, we need to look at an aspect of Sulzer's notion of self-consciousness which distinguishes his account from that of Wolff and his followers, as well as that of many of their critics.

11.3.2. Sulzer on self-consciousness and the body

If Sulzer was a materialist it would hardly be surprising that he links self-consciousness to our physical existence. Sulzer does the latter, while explicitly rejecting materialism. As far as his account of consciousness in terms of the act of distinguishing is concerned, he largely follows Wolff rather than his critics. His account is also Wolffian in that he accepts that a relating to objects is involved in self-consciousness. He distinguishes himself from both Wolff and most of his critics, however, by insisting that self-consciousness involves a relating to one's own body. According to Sulzer, self-consciousness requires not only the consciousness of objects but also (1) the existence of external, physical objects, and (2) the bodily nature of our own being. He states that

the soul feels itself only through the body and a certain effect that other bodies have on the nervous system, and that it does not have an absolute idea of itself because it can feel itself only

---

[48] Moreover, like Wolff, Sulzer links consciousness to attention. Attention makes possible the act of distinguishing that characterizes consciousness: Sulzer, 'Zergliederung des Begriffs der Vernunft', in *Vermischte Philosophische Schriften*, vol. 1, p. 253. Sulzer also comments on the causes of attention. Different causes bring about different kinds of attention.

[49] 'Das Bewußtseyn setzet also auf der einen Seite die klare Idee von sich selbst, und von dem, was man thut, voraus, da sich indessen auf der andern Seite der Verstand noch mit irgend einer andern Sache beschäfftiget, welche er als ausser sich und von seinem Wesen unabhängig betrachtet': Sulzer, 'Bewußtseyn', p. 201.

when it compares itself with other things. Without the material world, then, the soul would be nothing but a dead power which would remain in an eternal state of inactivity.[50]

Sulzer does not argue in any detail for his thesis that 'the soul can have no clear representations and no consciousness of its own existence without the help of the bodily organs'.[51] It is easy to see, however, why he maintains this. Like any mental activity, self-consciousness requires representations of other things.[52] Without the latter the self would not be able to *distinguish* itself from other things. And we can have representations of other things only through our bodily organs. Therefore, self-consciousness too is dependent on the existence of bodily organs, and Sulzer can say that we acquire the idea that we have of our own self 'vermittelst der Sinne'—by means of the senses ('Bewußtseyn', p. 201). This means, clearly, that the idea or representation of one's own self or soul cannot be acquired by an act of reflection that relates only to the soul itself. The mediation of the senses and thereby of one's own body is required. Our body ('which we also call our own self'), says Sulzer, is 'constantly' and 'essentially connected with our own existence'.[53] The 'act of self-consciousness'[54], as he puts it, presupposes the existence of the body, and relates to it.

We saw above that Leibniz too insists that the soul is never without a body, but in Leibniz this claim is part of a general metaphysical doctrine. The argument in Sulzer is empirically based, and relates to the very possibility of self-consciousness. Wolff's position, by contrast, clearly implies that self-consciousness is not dependent on the existence of one's own body. According to Wolff, the soul is conscious of itself and of what it thinks when it is in a 'state of distinct thoughts', and the soul can be in such a state, even when after death it is without a body.[55]

---

[50] 'daß die Seele sich nicht anders als vermittelst des Körpers und einer gewissen Wirkung, welche andere Körper auf das Nervensystem haben, empfinde; und daß sie keine absolute Idee von sich selbst habe, weil sie sich nicht anders empfinden kann, als wenn sie sich mit andern Dingen vergleicht. Die Seele würde also ohne die materialische Welt nichts anders als eine todte Kraft seyn, die in einer ewigen Unwirksamkeit bleiben würde': Sulzer, 'Bewußtseyn', pp. 202–3. See also Sulzer, 'Ueber die Unsterblichkeit der Seele', in *Vermischte Philosophische Schriften*, vol. 2 (1781), p. 1: 'Es scheint, wirklich, als ob man es, wie eine Thatsache, annehmen müsse, daß die Seele nichts empfinden, nichts wahrnehmen, und sich keine klare Vorstellungen, so gar von ihrer eigenen Existenz nicht, als durch die Vermittelung des Körpers, machen könne. Wenn sie dieses Werkzeuges ihrer Kenntnisse beraubt wäre: so würde sie, Trotz ihrer Immaterialität, ein Wesen ohne Leben seyn'.

[51] 'die Seele ohne die Beyhülfe der körperlichen Organen keine klaren Vorstellungen, und kein Bewußtsein ihres Daseyns haben kann': Sulzer, 'Gedanken über einige Eigenschaften der Seele', in *Vermischte Philosophische Schriften*, vol. 1, p. 373.

[52] The activity of the soul 'presupposes clear representations, and if we are lacking the latter, the soul is naturally inactive because it lacks matter or objects about which it could be employed' ('setzt also klare Vorstellungen voraus; und wenn diese uns mangeln, so ist sie natürlicher Weise unwirksam, weil es ihr an Materie, oder an Gegenständen fehlt, mit welchen sie sich beschäfftigen könnte'): Sulzer, 'Gedanken über einige Eigenschaften der Seele', in *Vermischte Philosophische Schriften*, vol. 1, p. 352.

[53] 'beständig und ... wesentlich mit unsrer Existenz verbunden': Sulzer, 'Bewußtseyn', pp. 201–2.

[54] 'Aktus des Selbstbewußtseyns': Sulzer, 'Gedanken über einige Eigenschaften der Seele', *Vermischte Philosophische Schriften*, vol. 1, p. 366.

[55] 'In dem Zustande deutlicher Gedanken ist ... die Seele ihrer und dessen, was sie gedencket, bewust': Wolff, *Deutsche Metaphysik*, § 926. 'In dem Untergange des Leibes ... [ist] gar kein Grund vorhanden, warum sie etwas verlieren sollte, was sie bereits hat' (ibid., § 925). 'Und demnach

Sulzer's account of self-consciousness does not prevent him from believing that the soul and its powers or faculties could exist without the body ('Bewußtseyn', p. 222).[56] For the soul can exist without consciousness. Although we know of the active nature of the soul through self-consciousness or feeling (which depends on the body), its activity does not require consciousness. Here, Sulzer follows Leibniz and Wolff: the soul can be active without being conscious of its activity. He argues 'that the activity of our soul is independent of apperception or that which Descartes calls consciousness'.[57] The existence of the soul and its powers is not dependent on the body and does not necessarily involve consciousness and self-consciousness ('Gedanken', Vermischte Philosophische Schriften, vol. 1, pp. 367–8). It is important to note, however, that in Sulzer, self-consciousness is not a consciousness merely of one's own existence; rather, it is a concrete, empirical consciousness that relates to the body as well as to the spatio-temporal location of the bodily self. In this context Sulzer speaks of a more or less 'complete idea' we can have of our own self.

Sulzer distinguishes between a complete idea of one's own self and an abstract, empty 'representation of our existence in general' ('Vorstellung von unserem Daseyn überhaupt', 'Bewußtseyn', p. 222). In the last analysis, this distinction is a gradual one. We can have no absolutely complete idea of our own self, but only more or less incomplete ideas. The more incomplete the idea, the more it approaches the abstract idea merely of our existence. Sulzer's argument can be reconstructed as follows. (1) All ideas of individual beings are incomplete (ibid., p. 206); (2) the idea of our own self is an idea of an individual being (ibid., p. 207). Therefore, the idea of our own self is incomplete. Sulzer's argument for (1) is that an individual entity is determined not only by what constitutes its inner being, but also by its relations to other things. And so a complete idea of an individual would have to include an infinite number of things which determine the individual according to all its relations (ibid., p. 206); therefore it is impossible for us to have a complete idea of a single individual being (ibid., p. 207). 'Now one must note that the idea we have of our own self, which belongs to consciousness, must necessarily be incomplete, as it is the idea of an individual. We never grasp all the determinations which constitute our individuality.'[58]

---

verbleibet sie nicht allein in dem Zustande deutlicher Gedancken, sondern erhält auch noch darinnen grössere Klarheit und Deutlichkeit': ibid., § 925.

[56] See also 'Gedanken über einige Eigenschaften der Seele', where Sulzer says that the soul is an active being ('thätiges Wesen'), which has 'powers in itself independently of the effects of the material world' ('unabhängig von den Einwirkungen der materiellen Welt, in sich selbst Kräfte besitzt, vermittels derer sie sich bestrebt, die empfangenen Ideen durch neue Verhältnisse einzuschränken, und dadurch ihren eigenen Zustand zu verändern': Vermischte Philosophische Schriften, vol. 1, p. 354.

[57] 'daß die Thätigkeit unsrer Seele von der Apperception, oder von dem was Descartes Bewußtseyn nennt, unabhängig ist, und daß die Seele ihre Energie haben kann, wenn sie sich auch gar keiner Empfindung bewußt ist': Sulzer, 'Gedanken über einige Eigenschaften der Seele', Vermischte Philosophische Schriften, vol. 1, p. 351.

[58] 'Nun muß man bemerken, daß die Idee von uns selbst, welche zum Bewußtseyn gehöret, da es die Idee von einem Individuo ist, nothwendig sehr unvollständig seyn muß. Wir sehen uns

Sulzer attempts to show, by way of examples, that the idea of our own self can become so incomplete that it almost changes into a general concept (ibid., p. 208). When someone awakes after having fainted during an accident, he may perceive what people around him say but not be able to relate this to himself. Sulzer says that this means that this person has no knowledge of his 'outer state', that he 'does not know where he is', and that he lacks the idea of the place where he is situated. The knowledge of one's 'outer state', however, is part of self-consciousness. This example illustrates Sulzer's view that self-consciousness does not relate merely to my existence as a thinking being, but also to my body and its spatio-temporal location (ibid., pp. 209–10). Without such a consciousness, 'our whole life would be a constant dream' (ibid., p. 222).[59]

11.3.3. Sulzer on the consciousness of the unity and identity of the self

Sulzer's conception of self-consciousness also relates to the issue of the unity and diachronic identity of the human subject. Like other thinkers of the time who tend towards an empiricist approach, he wants to dissociate himself from materialism, maintaining that the unity and indivisibility of the soul is evidenced immediately through self-consciousness. He simply asserts that 'all men will agree that we feel our own self in no other way but as a single indivisible being', and that when it is active we do not have 'any idea of compoundedness or multiplicity'.[60] Experience or 'inner feeling' ('innere Empfindung'), he claims, bears witness ('Zeugniß der Erfahrung'; ibid., p. 364) to the unity and indivisibility of the human subject. This feeling allows us to infer that the soul is of a unitary and indivisible nature. In this context Sulzer uses 'self-consciousness' ('Selbstbewußtsein'), 'feeling of self' ('Selbstempfindung' and 'Selbstgefühl'), and even 'apperception', interchangeably.[61] This is worth noting, as elsewhere he speaks of an idea or representation of the self, and distinguishes, as we have seen, between representation (Vorstellung) and feeling (Empfindung). This again hints at the issue of how Sulzer's conception of consciousness relates to this distinction. We shall address that issue in the next section.

---

selbst niemals mit allen den Bestimmungen, welche unsre Individualität ausmachen': Sulzer, 'Bewußtseyn', p. 207.

[59] Later empiricist thinkers, tending towards materialism, appeal to Sulzer's notion that the consciousness of one's own physical spatio-temporal location is important to an understanding of self-consciousness. Hissmann, for example, explicitly refers to Sulzer in this context. He takes up Sulzer's idea of the incompleteness of self-consciousness. See Hissmann, *Psychologische Versuche*, p. 112. For a discussion of this, see Thiel, 'Varieties of Inner Sense. Two Pre-Kantian Theories', *Archiv für Geschichte der Philosophie*, 79 (1997a), 58–79.

[60] 'Denn alle Menschen werden darinnen einig seyn, daß wir unser Selbst nicht anders empfinden, als wie ein einziges untheilbares Wesen, und wenn dasselbe selbststhätig wirkt, wir keine Idee von Zusammensetzung und Vielheit dabey haben': Sulzer, 'Gedanken über einige Eigenschaften der Seele', in *Vermischte Philosophische Schriften*, vol. 1, p. 364.

[61] For example, Sulzer speaks of a faculty ('Vermögen') to perceive one's own being ('sein eigenes Daseyn wahrzunehmen': Sulzer, 'Gedanken über einige Eigenschaften der Seele', in *Vermischte Philosophische Schriften*, p. 365. Sulzer uses 'Aktus des Selbstbewußtseyns' (p. 366), and, obviously as a synonym, 'Aktus des Selbstempfindens' (p. 367). He also uses 'Apperzeption' in the same sense (p. 367). For a discussion of the eighteenth-century notion of *Selbstgefühl*, see Thiel (1997a).

Sulzer's argument, which infers the indivisibility and immateriality of the soul from a feeling of unity and indivisibility that (allegedly) all human beings have, is, of course, highly problematic. Materialists of the time were not impressed.[62] It also raises questions about the consistency of Sulzer's thought. We have seen that for Sulzer, self-consciousness depends on the body, on the 'Wirksamkeit der körperlichen Organen' (ibid., p. 365). Given that the body is always involved in the feeling of our own self, it is not at all obvious that this feeling can relate to, and provide direct evidence of, an immaterial being in us. Later materialists adopt Sulzer's account of the essential relation that consciousness has to the body, but reject— with good reason, it seems—the claim that such a feeling of self can provide evidence of the immateriality of the soul.

According to Sulzer, however, materialism cannot deal satisfactorily with the issue of diachronic identity. 'According to the system of the materialists, during a state of unconsciousness [Ohnmacht] the soul is totally inactive, it does not exist.'[63] Therefore, when the soul awakes from such a state, the soul is being created anew; and this means that this soul is not the same soul that existed before.[64] In dealing with this alleged problem for materialism, Sulzer appeals again to self-consciousness. He maintains that this consequence of materialism 'contradicts our feeling of self' which 'testifies' indubitably that we would be the same being—the same self as before.[65] Memory presupposes the existence of earlier ideas ('vorhergegangene Ideen'), and thus, Sulzer asserts, the 'consciousness of our continued existence' ('Bewußtseyn unserer Fortdauer'; *Gedanken*, p. 372). It may seem that by linking the issue of diachronic personal identity to the notion of consciousness, Sulzer appeals to Lockean theory;[66] but as is the case with Wolff, there is only a seeming similarity here to Locke's account. According to the latter, consciousness and

---

[62] Hissmann, for example, vehemently rejects Sulzer's critique of materialism, citing the latter's view that matter is inactive and passive: Hissmann, 'Falsche Voraussetzungen; falsche Folgerungen', in *Psychologische Versuche*, p. 271.

[63] 'Nach dem System des Materialisten ist die Seele während einer tiefen Ohnmacht ganz nichtthätig...sie ist gar nicht': Sulzer, 'Gedanken über einige Eigenschaften der Seele', in *Vermischte Philosophische Schriften*, vol. 1, p. 369.

[64] 'Demnach, wenn der Mensch aus der tiefen Ohnmacht wieder zu sich kommt, wird also die Seele von neuen [sic] hervorgebracht': Sulzer, 'Gedanken über einige Eigenschaften der Seele', in *Vermischte Philosophische Schriften*, vol. 1, p. 369. 'So ist die Seele, welche aus diesen neuerweckten Bewegungen itzt resultirt, ein von neuem hervorgebrachtes Wesen': Sulzer, 'Gedanken über einige Eigenschaften der Seele', in *Vermischte Philosophische Schriften*, vol. 1, p. 370.

[65] 'Nun aber ist dieses unserm Selbstgefühl gänzlich zuwider, welches uns unwidersprechlich bezeugt, daß wir nach der Ohnmacht noch das nämliche Wesen, das nämliche Selbst sind, das wir vorher waren': Sulzer, 'Gedanken über einige Eigenschaften der Seele', in *Vermischte Philosophische Schriften*, vol. 1, p. 370.

[66] Meiners relates Sulzer's account to Locke's theory of personal identity: Meiners, *Vermischte Philosophische Schriften* (1775–76), vol. 2, p. 38. Without mentioning the seeming similarity to Locke, Platner recommends Sulzer's discussion of the 'consciousness of personality' ('Bewußtsein der Persönlichkeit'). See Platner, *Philosophische Aphorismen nebst einigen Anleitungen zur Philosophischen Geschichte* (1793), I, § 122, p. 77.

memory constitute personal identity, but for Sulzer it is consciousness of continued existence that makes genuine memory possible in the first place. He does not seem to deal with the concept of a person, but we have seen that Wolff accounts for personhood in terms of the consciousnesss of one's diachronic identity. This conforms to Sulzer's claims about the 'Bewußtseyn der Fortdauer'.

In explaining how this feeling of identity is possible across states of unconsciousness, Sulzer appeals to his conception of 'obscure ideas' which clearly derives from Leibniz's 'minute perceptions'.[67] These remain during the unconscious existence of the soul, and continue to influence the self. According to Sulzer, then, there is a psychological continuity of the self, underlying our conscious life, and it is this continuity that makes the consciousness of identity possible. Even in deep sleep, Sulzer maintains, we retain not only those obscure ideas but also the faculty of memory and other capacities—even 'moral sentiments', and 'concepts and dispositions' ('moralische Gesinnungen', 'Begriffe und Anlagen', 'Gedanken', p. 373).[68]

11.3.4. Sulzer and Herder: self-consciousness and the distinction between representation (*Vorstellung*) and feeling (*Empfindung*)

Early in his career, Johann Gottfried Herder—better known as a critic of Kant and a philosopher of history—mounted a critique of Sulzer's distinction between representation and feeling, eventually published in 1778 as *Vom Erkennen und Empfinden der menschlichen Seele*.[69] Marion Heinz has shown that Herder's critique is concerned, among other things, with the relation between self-consciousness and the consciousness of objects implied by Sulzer's account. In Sulzer the distinction between representation and feeling is so stark that he is even led to speak of 'two souls in man' that are responsible for the two faculties respectively ('Anmerkungen über den verschiedenen Zustand', in *Vermischte Philosophische Schriften*, vol. 1, p. 225). As noted above, for Sulzer, representation relates to external objects only; and here the soul does not notice itself. Feeling, or *Empfindung*, however, relates to the self only,

---

[67] Thus, I am not convinced by Wunderlich's suggestion that Sulzer anticipates the 'Kantian idea' here, that there could be a principle of connection in consciousness itself ('daß im Bewusstsein selbst ein Prinzip der Verbindung liegen koennte', Wunderlich, *Kant und die Bewußtseinstheorien des 18. Jahrhunderts* (2005), p. 221.

[68] 'Dieses also beweist offenbar, daß die Seele während der Schlafsucht nicht vernichtet ist, weil dasselbe Gedächtniß, und dieselben Fertigkeiten der Seele und andere Dinge mehr, welche ohne die Seele, in der sie sind, nicht hätten fortdauern können, während dieser scheinbaren Nichtthätigkeit existirt und also gewirkt haben': Sulzer, 'Gedanken über einige Eigenschaften der Seele', in *Vermischte Philosophische Schriften*, vol. 1, p. 372.

[69] There are three versions of this essay—of 1774, 1775, and 1778—in Herder, *Sämmtliche Werke*, ed. Suphan (1877–1913; reprinted, 1967), vol. 8, pp. 165–333; also in Herder, *Werke*. *Vol. 2: Herder und die Anthropologie der Aufklärung*, ed. Proß (1987), pp. 543–724. Heinz provides a detailed analysis of these writings and gives an account of their importance to the development of Herder's thought: Heinz, *Sensualistischer Idealismus. Untersuchungen zur Erkenntnistheorie des jungen Herder* (1994), pp. 108–73. Here we are concerned only with Herder's critique of Sulzer and Heinz's analysis thereof. Herder's own account of consciousness will be discussed in *The Enlightened Subject* (in preparation).

and here the soul does not notice external objects. Marion Heinz demonstrates that Herder takes up this distinction—modifying it, however, and arguing against Sulzer that the representation of an object is mediated through the subject and the representation of the subject is mediated through the object (Heinz 1994, pp. 119–21). To Herder, the soul feels itself when it represents other things, and the soul engages in a form of representing when it feels itself.

Herder seems to have a point. More importantly in the present context, however, is that Sulzer himself seems to undermine his own distinction between object-related representation and subject-related feeling by adopting an essentially Wolffian conception of consciousness. We have seen that in some passages Sulzer speaks of an idea or a representation of the self; that is, of a representation that does not relate to something that is distinct from the soul or self.[70] Even if this is a matter merely of imprecise formulation, there is an obvious problem once we take into account his conception of consciousness. We have seen in Section 3.1 that like Wolff, Sulzer holds that consciousness is always related both to the self and other things. This is not, however, in any obvious way consistent with Sulzer's strict distinction between representation and feeling, where representation relates *only* to external things and feelings *only* to the self. According to his own notion of consciousness, both representation and feeling must relate in some way both to the self as subject and to other things. Perhaps it could be argued that Sulzer's notion of degrees of consciousness could solve this problem. Sulzer could say that in representing other things we do relate to our own self, but only in a weak, barely noticeable form. Some of his formulations would seem to suggest such a reading, for example, when he says that the more we focus on an external object the less we feel the self (rather than not at all).[71] Similarly, he seems to be saying that feeling involves the representation of an object, but only weakly so.[72] Maybe he wants to say that in representing other things we have at least the abstract, empty consciousness of the mere existence of our own self. He does not, however, appeal to such ideas when he contrasts representation and feeling. Moreover, other formulations suggest a strict separation

---

[70] Sulzer makes use of the notion of feeling (Empfindung, Gefühl) also in order to explain what is involved in having ideas. 'Das innere...Gefühl bringt unmittelbar das Vermögen, Ideen zu haben, hervor. Eine Idee haben, die dem Geiste gegenwärtig sey, heißt nichts anders, als, empfinden, daß man in dem gegenwärtigen Augenblicke auf eine gewisse bestimmte Art afficirt wird': 'Zergliederung der Vernunft', p. 248. On the notion of inner feeling (inneres Gefühl), see also Hissmann, *Psychologische Versuche*, p. 106.

[71] Sulzer, *Allgemeine Theorie der Schönen Künste*, vol. 4, p. 408. The following passage suggests that self-consciousness is a matter of degree: 'Je stärker wir unsre Aufmerksamkeit auf die Beschaffenheit des Gegenstandes richten, je mehr vergessen wir uns selbst': p. 408.

[72] For example, Sulzer says 'daß die Seele bey der Empfindung bloß ihren eigenen Zustand *deutlich* gewahr wird, und daß sie den Gegenstand, der diesen Zustand hervorbringt, *kaum* bemerket': *Vermischte Philosophische Schriften*, vol. 1, pp. 230–1; my italics. Compare also his comments on dreaming: here, 'die Empfindung unser selbst sehr schwach'; 'das, was wir sind, und was wir thun, nur sehr verworren und schwach empfinden'; 'Zergliederung der Vernunft', p. 256. 'Denn alsdann empfinden wir unsre eignen Kräfte nicht, und folglich geben wir ihnen auch nicht die Richtung; wir haben weder Absichten noch Endzwecke': p. 256.

of representation from feeling. When Sulzer speaks of reflection or 'Nachdenken'—the most intensive form of representing—he says that during such an activity nothing occurs in the body that could give rise to the idea of our own self.[73] And he says in the same context about feeling that during this activity one does not feel the object but *only* one's own self.[74] Only feeling, it seems, is connected with a consciousness of self.[75] This stark contrast between feeling and representing is clearly not compatible with Sulzer's Wolffian understanding of consciousness as relating both to the self and the objects. This issue does not, in any direct way, affect Sulzer's other contributions to the debates about consciousness, such as his influential idea of self-consciousness and embodiment. In order to make his account consistent, however, he would have to give up either his essentially Wolffian conception of consciousness or his stark opposition between object-related *Vorstellen* and subject-related *Empfinden*. The combination of the two positions undermines his account of representation and feeling, and that is precisely that aspect of his thought that is generally considered to be his most innovative contribution to philosophy.[76] His Wolffian notion of consciousness, then, has implications which point to problems with central claims in his philosophy—claims that are directed *against* Wolff.

11.4. TOWARDS KANT? MÉRIAN ON APPERCEPTION AND IDENTITY

Although, like most of the philosophers discussed in this Chapter, Jean-Bernard Mérian is not much discussed today, he is clearly the most important pre-Kantian critic of Wolff to have written on the issue of self-consciousness.[77] Like Sulzer a

---

[73] 'Während des Nachdenkens geht in dem Körper nichts vor, das die Idee von uns selbst in uns erwecken könnte; alles ist da vollkommen stille und ruhig': 'Anmerkungen über den verschiedenen Zustand', in *Vermischte Philosophische Schriften*, vol. 1, p. 232.

[74] 'bey der Empfindung ist die Seele *bloß* mit sich selbst beschäfftiget': 'Anmerkungen über den verschiedenen Zustand', in *Vermischte Philosophische Schriften*, vol. 1, pp. 229–30; my italics.

[75] Compare also Sulzer's distinction between 'speculative' and 'practical' ideas. The former 'are not accompanied by any consideration of our own self' ('werden von gar keiner Rücksicht auf uns selbst begleitet'); we cannot be aware of practical ideas, however, 'without the feeling of our own self which accompanies their representation'; (praktische Ideen) 'sind dergestalt in uns, daß wir sie nicht anders als mit der Empfindung unser selbst, welche ihre Vorstellung begleitet, gewahr werden': 'Anmerkungen über den verschiedenen Zustand', in *Vermischte Philosophische Schriften*, vol. 1, p. 234.

[76] For the historical importance of Sulzer's account of *Empfinden*, see, for example, Palme, *J. G. Sulzers Psychologie und die Anfänge der Dreivermögenslehre* (1905), p. 34. See also Heinz (1994), p. 114.

[77] Harnack, *Geschichte der Königlich Preussischen Akademie der Wissenschaften zu Berlin*, 3 vols. (1900), vol. 1, pp. 454–7, gives a short overview of Mérian's thought. There are a few brief discussions of specific topics. For example, Altmann provides a description of Mérian's critique of the principle of the identity of indiscernibles, in *Moses Mendelssohns Frühschriften zur Metaphysik* (1969), pp. 70–2. Markovits discusses Mérian's views about the Molyneux problem: 'Diderot, Mérian et l'Aveugle', in J.-B. Mérian, *Sur le problème de Molyneux* (1984), pp. 193–281. Dessoir (1902), pp. 195–6, gives a brief description of Mérian's psychology. Beck, *Early German Philosophy. Kant and his Predecessors* (1969), pp. 315–16, has one sentence about Mérian's philosophy, in which he states that Mérian 'anticipated Kant in criticizing Leibniz for seeing sensations as confused thoughts

member of the *Académie Royale des Sciences et des Belles-Lettres* in Berlin from 1750, he became director of the Class for Belles-Lettres in 1771, and permanent Secretary of the Academy from 1797.[78] Mérian's general philosophical position is a self-conscious eclecticism. Among his philosophical papers are two on apperception, two on identity, a paper about Leibniz and Locke on thought and sensation, a discourse on metaphysics, a paper on the notion of moral sense, and a series of seven papers on the Molyneux problem.[79] His treatment of the issue of apperception is both critical and constructive. It is critical in that it analyses and argues against the Wolffian account of apperception, and it is constructive in that it proposes an alternative account based on a different method of dealing with the problem. The two papers on the topic date from 1749 (published in 1751), and they are Mérian's first contributions to the Berlin Academy's *Mémoires*.[80] They had a wider circulation than most of his other writings, since in 1778 a German translation of them was published by Michael Hissmann in the first volume of his *Magazin für die Philosophie und ihre Geschichte*.[81] In the late eighteenth and early nineteenth centuries some of

and Locke for transforming thoughts into sensations'. The same point was made earlier by Dessoir (p. 424). Henrich mentions, but does not discuss, the French version of Mérian's first paper on apperception. See the endnotes to his article 'Die Identität des Subjekts in der transzendentalen Deduktion', in Oberer and Seel (eds.), *Kant: Probleme, Analysen, Kritik* (1988), p. 64. See also the English translation: 'The Identity of the Subject in the Transcendental Deduction', in Schaper and Vossenkuhl (eds.), *Reading Kant: New Perspectives on Transcendental Arguments and Critical Philosophy* (1989), p. 280. Recently there have been more extensive discussions of various aspects of Mérian's philosophy. On apperception, see Thiel, 'Between Wolff and Kant: Mérian's Theory of Apperception', *Journal of the History of Philosophy*, 34 (1996), 213–32. See also Häseler, 'Johann Bernhard Mérian: ein Schweizer Philosoph an der Berliner Akademie', in Fontius and Holzhey (eds.), *Schweizer im Berlin des 18. Jahrhunderts* (1996), pp. 217–30. Baertschi, 'La conception de la conscience developpée par Mérian', in *Schweizer im Berlin des 18. Jahrhunderts* (1996), pp. 231–48. Laursen, 'Swiss Anti-skeptics in Berlin', in *Schweizer im Berlin des 18. Jahrhunderts* (1996), pp. 261–81. Laursen and Popkin, 'Hume in the Prussian Academy: Jean-Bernard Mérian's "On the Phenomenalism of David Hume"', *Hume Studies*, 23 (1997), 153–91. Frank and Wunderlich take up the discussion on apperception from Thiel (1996). See Frank, *Selbstgefühl* (2002), pp. 85–7, 154–70; and Wunderlich (2005), pp. 101–7.

[78] For more detailed biographical information about Mérian, see Ancillon, 'Éloge historique de J. B. Mérian', in *Abhandlungen der Königlichen Akademie der Wissenschaften zu Berlin, Historische Einleitung* (1810), pp. 52–90; Prantl's entry on Mérian in *Allgemeine Deutsche Biographie* (1885), vol. 21, pp. 428–30; and Harnack, *Geschichte*, vol. 1, pp. 454–7.

[79] There is a modern edition of the papers on the Molyneux problem: J.-B. Mérian (1984). For Mérian's papers on apperception, see the notes below. For details of his other publications, see Harnack (1900), vol. 3, pp. 185–6.

[80] Mérian, 'Mémoire sur l'apperception de sa propre existence', in *Histoire de l'académie royale des sciences et belles lettres. Année 1749* (1751), pp. 416–41; hereafter, Mérian (1749*a*). In the same volume of the *Histoire*: Mérian, 'Mémoire sur l'apperception considerée relativement aux idées, ou, sur l'existence des idées dans l'âme', pp. 442–77; hereafter, Mérian (1749*b*).

[81] Mérian, 'Ueber die Apperzeption seiner eignen Existenz', in *Magazin für die Philosophie und ihre Geschichte. Aus den Jahrbüchern der Akademien angelegt*, ed. Hissmann, vol. 1 (1778), pp. 89–132. In the same volume: Mérian, 'Ueber die Apperzeption in Rücksicht auf die Ideen, oder auf die Existenz der Ideen in der Seele', pp. 133–94. Another paper that was translated into German is Mérian's 'Parallèle de deux principes de psychologie', *Histoire de l'académie royale des sciences et belles lettres. Année 1757* (1759), pp. 375–91. It appeared in vol. 6 of Hissmann's *Magazin* (1783), pp. 175–204, as 'Parallel der beiden Prinzipien der Psychologie, der Empfindungs- und Vorstellungskraft'.

the arguments in these papers were discussed, for example, by Tetens in his influential *Philosophische Versuche*, and by Platner, Schulze, Maine de Biran, and Victor Cousin.[82]

As noted above, Mérian was strongly influenced by empiricist thought; he even translated Hume's philosophical writings into French.[83] Although he was critical of some aspects of the empiricist tradition,[84] he explicitly committed himself to an empiricist method when dealing with the notion of apperception. He argues against the 'synthetic' method in philosophy, which begins with arbitrary definitions and proceeds by demonstrating propositions on the basis of these definitions. Mérian says that this synthetic method can result only in an 'ideal science'; that is, in a science such as mathematics that concerns itself only with ideas and does not make any claims about real existence outside the understanding. According to Mérian, the proper method of acquiring knowledge of reality is the analysis of experience.[85] He argues that failure to distinguish between the real and the merely ideal in our knowledge is the source of many errors in philosophy, citing Spinoza as an example of this confusion. Although his method is synthetic, Spinoza makes claims about real existence. Yet these claims are not justified, for in employing the synthetic method he merely explicates propositions he has adopted without foundation. To confuse the ideal and the real in this way, Mérian suggests, is to commit a 'paralogism'—adding that 'one encounters this paralogism in many systems'(Mérian, 1749b, p. 444). He insists that his own account of apperception belongs to a science that concerns itself with reality (a 'science réelle') and consequently must be based on a 'collection of observations which experience gives us' (Mérian, 1749a, p. 418). The faculties of the human soul define themselves through their application; therefore, in order to know what apperception is, one needs only to have apperceived and reflected on what has passed in one's own mind. We shall see that in the course of his argument, however, Mérian transcends his official, purely empiricist approach.

---

[82] Tetens, *Philosophische Versuche über die menschliche Natur und ihre Entwicklung*, 2 vols. (1777; reprinted, 1979); hereafter *Versuche*. Platner, *Philosophische Aphorismen*, § 141n. Schulze, *Psychische Anthropologie*, § 14. Biran, *Commentaires et marginalia: dix-huitième siècle*, in *Oeuvres de Maine de Biran*, vol. 11–12, ed. Baertschi (1993). Cousin, *Premiers essais de philosophie*, third edn. (1855), pp. 109–23.

[83] Hume, *Essais philosophiques sur l'entendement humain*, 2 vols. (1758). This translation has a preface by Formey. Mérian translated two more volumes, and a fifth volume was translated by Robinet. The five volumes were published as *Oeuvres philosophiques de Mr. D. Hume* (1758–60).

[84] He rejects, for example, Hume's extreme scepticism. See Mérian's 'Sur le phénoménisme de David Hume', in *Mémoires de l'académie royale des sciences et belles-lettres depuis l'avènement de Frédéric Guillaume II au thrône* (1793), pp. 417–37. There is a recent edition of this paper, edited by Laursen and Popkin, in *Hume Studies*, 23 (1997), 163–77. The same issue has an English translation of the paper by Briscoe, entitled 'On the Phenomenalism of David Hume' (178–91).

[85] Mérian (1749b), pp. 442–3. For the methodological debate over analysis and synthesis in the seventeenth and eighteenth centuries, see Schepers (1959), pp. 18–27; Tonelli, 'Analysis and Synthesis in XVIIIth Century Philosophy Prior to Kant', *Archiv für Begriffsgeschichte*, 20 (1976), 178–213; Engfer, *Philosophie als Analysis. Studien zur Entwicklung philosophischer Analysiskonzeptionen unter dem Einfluß mathematischer Methodenmodelle im 17. und frühen 18. Jahrhundert* (1982).

11.4.1. Mérian on personal identity

Mérian deals with the issue of personal identity in a later article entitled *Sur l'identité numérique*.[86] His treatment of this issue is much less original than is his account of apperception, but it appeals to his earlier work on apperception, as he regards this notion as central to personal identity. He argues against what he calls 'arbitrary definitions' of the term 'person', as such definitions may have problematic consequences (ibid., pp. 471–2). He rejects what he takes to be the Lockean definition of person in terms of memory. If we define 'person' in terms of memory then it would seem to follow that I am not accountable for actions that I have forgotten because, on this account, I am no longer the same person as the person who committed those actions. Mérian thinks that this is the absurd result of Lockean theory—a theory based on a play of words and an arbitrary definition of 'person'.[87] However, he distinguishes—following Leibniz—between the real or 'physical' identity and the moral identity of the self or person. The same person in terms of real or 'physical' identity is simply 'the same self continued in the same being'. The same person in terms of moral identity is the same self continued in an intelligent being that takes an interest in its own self and is capable of feeling pleasure and pain and whose free actions merit reward or punishment.[88] Mérian's notion of moral identity is consistent with Locke's account of person as a 'forensic term', but significantly, unlike Locke, he does not regard memory as essential to moral identity.

But what, on Mérian's view, constitutes personal identity? What is meant by his notion of real identity in terms of 'the same self continued in the same being'? What guarantees moral identity? Although he rejects memory in this context, still his account is in terms of a psychological criterion; of a continuous consciousness or 'feeling' ('sentiment') of self; a feeling of our own being which remains invariable during all the changes we undergo. Mérian asserts that this feeling of self accompanies all our thoughts[89] and is inseparable from the understanding. It is essential to the soul. This feeling links my present existence to my past existence, and thus functions as the basis of my moral identity. The interest we take in our own individual selves derives from this feeling. Without it, Mérian argues, there could

---

[86] Mérian, 'Sur l'identité numérique', in *Histoire de l'academie royale des sciences et belles-lettres. Année 1755* (1757), pp. 461–75 (personal identity is discussed from p. 469 onwards). He also has an article criticizing Leibniz's principle of the identity of the indiscernibles, but he does not, in that context, discuss personal identity. See Mérian, 'Sur le principe des indiscernables', in *Histoire de l'academie royale des sciences et belles-lettres. Année 1754* (1756), pp. 383–98. Mérian's main point seems to be that Leibniz's principle contradicts experience.

[87] 'Votre assertion n'est fondée que sur un jeu de mots, & sur une définition arbitraire': Mérian, 'Sur l'identité', p. 472.

[88] 'La même personne dans le sens physique est le même *moi* continué dans le même être: dans le sens moral c'est le même *moi* continué dans une Intelligence qui prend interêt à son Individu, qui est capable de sentir le plaisir & la douleur, & qui par conséquent a pû mériter & démeriter par ses actions libres': Mérian, 'Sur l'identité', p. 472.

[89] 'c'est le sentiment de notre propre être, qui demeuroit invariable, pendant que tout changeoit autour de nous, de ce *Moi* pensant, qui est comme une toile permanente où la Nature vient peindre ses variétés': Mérian, 'Sur l'identité', p. 463. See also ibid., p. 469: 'ce sentiment du *Soi*, qui accompagne toutes les pensées et qui semble être le caractere indélébile des Intelligences'.

be no memory, no thought at all, and probably even no soul.[90] In short, he postulates a feeling that is essential to the self or soul, and which constantly relates to the latter. For as long as I feel my existence, my personality remains the same, quite independently of memory.[91] It is not immediately obvious, however, how, according to Mérian, the feeling of my present existence can constitute my diachronic identity as a person. Perhaps he can be construed as saying that since this feeling is always present it provides a continuous chain of consciousness from moment to moment. In this way it could be said to constitute diachronic identity and make possible other forms of relating to the self (such as memory).

In the last analysis, however, Mérian does not appear to ascribe any constitutive role to self-consciousness. Rather, he asserts that the reason that self-consciousness can exist and play any role in our mental life at all is that it is based in a simple, thinking substance. In defining the soul as an immaterial thinking substance, he suggests, we free ourselves of all the difficulties that Locke and others have raised about personal identity. And since the feeling of self is essential to the soul, the personality exists for as long as the substance exists to which self-consciousness or the *sentiment du soi* is intimately connected. Therefore, there is no reason to doubt that I will be the same person after my death—both in a 'physical' and in a moral sense.[92]

Thus, 'the same self continued in the same being' is a simple thinking being or substance. As such it has a continued existence and remains the same during the whole course of its existence ('Sur l'identité', p. 469). This is the real basis of personal identity. The same self or soul that was joined to a particular perception ten years ago and is today joined to a different perception, reunifies these perceptions in my person, even if I have forgotten the first one or have forgotten both of them. In order to be myself, it is not necessary that I have the history of my whole life present to mind.[93]

---

[90] 'Je ne connais qu'une chose dans mon ame qui paroisse lui être essentielle; c'est le sentiment de *Moi*, inséparable de mon intelligence; toutes les autres perceptions son sujetes à la vicissitude . . . s'il y a quelque chose de certain, c'est assurément que je suis *Moi même*: c'est par là que mon existence présente se lie à mon existence passée: de là cet interêt personel que je prends à mon propre Individu, & que je repands, dans une juste mesure, sur les choses qui m'environnent. Sans ce sentiment point de réminiscence, point de pensée, & probablement point d'ame': Mérian, 'Sur l'identité', p. 470.

[91] '*Cajus* en délire, & *Cajus* dans son bon sens ne sont que deux façons d'être du meme *Cajus*, comme *Cajus* éveillé & Cajus faisant des rêves: il est puni comme etre sensible, pour une action qu'il a commise comme être libre: sa personalité est inaltérable aussi long-tems qu'il sent son existence': Mérian, 'Sur l'identité', p. 475.

[92] 'Nous nous sommes délivrés de toutes ces discussions, en définissant notre ame un être immatériel pensant. Si le sentiment du *Soi* lui est essentiel, la personalité subsistera aussi long-tems que la substance à qui elle est intimément unie . . . s'il est vrai que je suis aujourdhui la même personne que je fus hier, ou que j'étois il y a dix ans; je n'ai pas plus de raison de douter que je ne sois après ma mort, tant dans le sens physique que dans le sens moral, la personne que je suis durant le cours de ma vie': Mérian, 'Sur l'identité', p. 471.

[93] 'Ce *moi*, qui étoit joint à une perception, il y a dix ans, & qui aujourdhui est joint à une autre, les reuniroit dans ma personne, quand même j'aurois oublié la premiere, ou quand je les aurois oubliées toutes deux. . . . Pour être *moi même*, faut il que j'aye toujours l'histoire de ma vie devant moi?': Mérian, 'Sur l'identité', p. 472.

In a much later paper Mérian briefly deals with what he takes to be David Hume's account of the self.[94] He says that according to Hume, 'subject and substance' are

> terms empty of meaning, pure creatures of reason, that is to say phenomena, or the succession or accumulation of phenomena [perceptions], that it pleases us to name improperly with these fine names. Finally, what am I myself, my self, my person, what am I if not such an accumulation, which coexists with other accumulations, which succeed each other, as I succeed to what I call myself? I do not know myself under any other aspect: I am a phenomenon like everyone. ('Phénoménisme', p. 180)

Mérian notes that Hume admits that there are 'fictitious subjects', but that he introduces these only 'in order to use them as props and supports' (ibid., p. 188).

Not unlike Isaac Watts much earlier, Mérian appeals to the use of pronouns in his account of the self. 'What is the meaning in your mind [he asks Hume] and your mouth of these personal pronouns which you cannot prevent yourself from continually using, and without which you would not know either to think or to express your thoughts, *me, I, we*, etc?' (ibid., p. 190). The use of these pronouns suggests that we regard ourselves as persons. They express forms of thinking that we cannot avoid using, and that suggest that we are more than just instable 'phenomena' or, at best, 'fictitious subjects'. These forms of thought are inescapable: 'You cannot detach yourself from these forms of thinking, speaking, acting. They are stronger than you, and indicate that these forms are, so to speak, rooted in some principle that constitutes you, and that you [Hume] believe is abusively called your mind, your soul, your intelligence' (ibid.). Without these forms of thought, expressed by personal pronouns, 'you would not know how to understand nor make yourself understood. You try in vain; you will never succeed in denying yourself to yourself' (ibid.). Those 'forms of thought' suggest to us the notion of a subject beyond that of a mere fiction:

> *Thought* presuppposes the *thinker*, fiction someone or something who pretends; as painting presupposes a painter ... as a quality or faculty, a being, a subject that possesses this quality or faculty. It is necessary then ... to stop in the last instance at something stable, without which you would think or speak wildly. (ibid., p. 189)

Hume–at least as Mérian reconstructs him—could of course agree that the notion of a stable subject or thinker is a necessity of thought, but argue that nothing corresponds to the notion in reality. Mérian, by contrast, asserts that the necessity to think a subject reveals the reality of such a subject. The stability required is that of a soul as substance. A 'collection, a bundle, or so to speak, a wad of phenomena' requires a self or subject as a link.

> And it is this, with your permission, I would call myself or my person [ibid., pp. 186–7] ... a permanent thing, or if I dare say it, a subject, a substance. It is always there ... in what one calls

---

[94] Mérian, 'Sur le phénoménisme de David Hume', in *Mémoires de l'académie royale des sciences et belles-lettres depuis l'avènement de Frédéric Guillaume II au thrône* (1793), pp. 417–37. Quotations are from Briscoe's translation of this paper, entitled 'On the Phenomenalism of David Hume', *Hume Studies*, 23 (1997), 178–91.

loss of mind, in delirium itself, it does not entirely evaporate nor become unable to return and reinstall itself: which would assure it at least a certain identity, a basis of continuity, and could even make it presume or hope for its perpetuity. (ibid., p. 187)

Mérian asks what the self is relative to perceptions or phenomena. His answer is: 'The thing, the being, the subject, the substance that experiences them' (ibid., p. 186).

The formulations quoted from his paper on Hume commit Mérian to a substance-view of the self, but they do not seem to commit him to the view that the self is a simple and immaterial substance. In the earlier paper on numerical identity, however, he clearly maintains the simplicity of the soul or mental substance. And elsewhere he explicitly rejects materialist accounts of the soul. He argues that the materialist error consists in confounding the sensible being with some of its particular sensations and in confounding a state of the soul with the soul itself.[95] The claim that the soul is extended or solid is, he suggests, based on our sensing extension or solidity. But this sensation or the state of having this sensation must not be taken for the soul itself. He says:

If I am a sensation, what kind of sensation am I? If I am a heap of sensations, what kind of heap am I? The same reasoning which says that I am extended or solid could equally well lead me to say that I am the white, the black, warm or cold, hard or soft, or all of these together. These are nothing but sensations that I feel. They are not my self. I cannot cease to be I. But of all those things there is none that I could not cast off.[96]

It appears, then, that Mérian ties personal identity to the identity of a (simple, immaterial) thinking substance. He seems to agree with Leibniz and the Cartesians, at least in this, that there is an individual, immaterial substance which continues to exist. He regards self-consciousness or the feeling of existence as important in this context, but only insofar as it is an essential property of a simple thinking substance. It is the latter which in the last analysis constitutes diachronic personal identity. In the paper on identity he does not analyse the notion of self-consciousness itself in any detail, but he does so in his papers on apperception. And, importantly, his argument about self-consciousness or apperception in these papers does not depend on his belief in an immaterial, simple substance.

---

[95] Mérian, *Parallèle de deux principes de psychologie*, in Hissmann's translation of 1783, pp. 194–5.

[96] Mérian, *Parallèle*, in Hissmann (1783): 'Der Irrthum des Materialismus liegt darinnen, daß das empfindende Wesen mit einigen seiner partikulären Sensationen, und daß ein Zustand der Seele mit der Seele selbst verwechselt wird. Wenn ich eine Sensation bin; was soll ich für eine seyn? Wenn ich ein Haufen von Sensationen bin; was für ein Haufen? Man kann mit eben so viel Grund sagen, ich sey das Weiße oder das Schwarze, das Warme oder das Kalte, das Harte oder das Weiche, oder das alles zusammen; als man sagen kann, ich sey das Ausgedehnte oder das Solide. Das sind lauter Sensationen, die ich empfinde. Es ist nicht mein Ich. Ich kann nicht aufhören Ich zu seyn. Von allen jenen Dingen aber ist kein einziges, was ich nicht ablegen könnte': pp. 194–5.

11.4.2. Mérian on 'original apperception' as a necessary condition of thought

As noted above, Mérian distinguishes carefully between the apperception of self and the apperception of ideas.[97] The apperception of self or self-consciousness is 'the apperception of our own existence' or, as he sometimes says, 'the *conscium sui*' (Mérian, 1749*a*, p. 419). He points out that metaphysicians have not regarded apperception understood as self-consciousness as a topic worthy of detailed attention, but himself emphasises both the importance and the difficulty of the issue (ibid., pp. 440–1). It is plain that his conception of self-consciousness as the consciousness of one's own existence differs markedly from Sulzer's notion of self-consciousness. The latter relates to the concrete physical being, located in a particular situation in space and time, not to mere existence as such.

In his critique of Wolff, Mérian translates 'Bewustseyn' as 'l'apperception' (ibid., pp. 437–9), demonstrating that for him 'l'apperception' has a broader sense that includes Wolff's 'Bewustseyn'.[98] He concedes that we distinguish between different objects of consciousness and that we distinguish between objects and ourselves. He argues, however, that it does not follow that consciousness or apperception depends on the faculty of distinguishing. It could be the case that apperception and the faculty of distinguishing co-exist in the same way as the movements of the planets and my present thoughts co-exist, without one being dependent on the other. He does believe that there is a relation of dependence, but that it is the opposite of the one Wolff has in mind: he holds that apperception is prior to our distinguishing things, rather than *vice versa*, arguing that we can distinguish things from one another only if we are conscious of them or have apperceived them. For how can we compare ideas or things unless we are conscious of them? And since reflection involves comparison, reflection, too, depends on apperception, rather than *vice versa*.

We have seen that prior to Mérian, other critics of Wolff, such as Andreas Rüdiger, argued similarly against the Wolffian understanding of consciousness. Rüdiger does not examine self-consciousness, however. Mérian's argument against Wolff is directed against the view that our consciousness of objects depends on reflection and the capacity to distinguish, and it is part of a larger analysis of self-consciousness. As we shall see, he argues that self-consciousness is immediate and is quite independent of other mental activities. He thereby distinguishes himself from Rüdiger as well as from Wolff. For Rüdiger, self-consciousness requires that we are conscious of our mental activities, but for Mérian, self-consciousness is not at all dependent on other forms of consciousness.

According to Mérian there are only two possible answers to the question of how I know my existence: I either know it mediately (through reason or reflection) or

---

[97] See Mérian (1749*a*), p. 419; and Mérian (1749*b*), p. 445.

[98] Since Mérian adopts this broad notion of apperception, he sometimes speaks of the apperception of external objects. This usage of 'apperception', however, is not consistent with his official account of what apperception relates to: he states explicitly that apperception relates only to our own self, to our ideas, and to our actions: Mérian (1749*b*), p. 419. To be consistent, Mérian would have to say that apperception relates to our *ideas* of external objects.

immediately (through apperception). No one would want to claim, he thinks, that we derive the knowledge of our own existence from imagination or memory (ibid., p. 419). He believes that the notion of mediate self-knowledge is present in the Cartesian *cogito* argument. He deals with this argument as it is presented not by Descartes, but by Wolff—namely, in an explicitly syllogistic form[99]—and reconstructs it as follows. Whatever thinks, exists. I think. Therefore, I exist. Mérian agrees with Wolff that the certainty of our own existence is the highest certainty we can have; but he rejects the latter's idea that this certainty rests on syllogistic demonstration. He argues, for example, that the minor premise already contains the conclusion. To think is nothing else but to exist under a certain modification. In other words, 'I think' is equivalent to 'I exist thinking'.[100]

In more general terms Mérian contends that *no* reflection or reasoning can teach me that I exist (ibid., pp. 432ff.): the *conscium sui* cannot be derived from reflection.[101] In order to reflect I need to return to what has passed in my own soul. Now, if reflection were to teach me my existence it could do so only immediately or mediately. However, it cannot do this immediately if that perception to which reflection turns does not itself contain the *conscium sui*. The knowledge of my own existence cannot be derived from a thought that is not accompanied by the *conscium sui*. Mérian argues that even supposing that reflection can somehow produce knowledge of my existence, it would have to be conceded that this existence was already known to me prior to that act of reflection. He illustrates his point as follows. Suppose the soul has a thought *A* which is not accompanied by the *conscium sui*. In this case the immediate act of reflection would be nothing but the act of remembering *A* (without the *conscium sui*). In other words, immediate reflection on past thoughts cannot generate the *conscium sui*, if these thoughts do not already contain it.

---

[99] Mérian (1749*a*), pp. 420–3. For Wolff's syllogistic argument for the existence of the self, see Chapter 9 above and the comments on *Deutsche Metaphysik*, §§ 5–7. See also *Psychologia empirica*, § 16. Mérian alludes to the importance which Wolff ascribes to this syllogistic self-knowledge. He says that the argument has been paraded as a model of a proof that leads to the highest certainty: Mérian (1749*a*), p. 422; compare *Deutsche Metaphysik*, §§ 4, 8–9.

[100] Leibniz and Kant also make this point. For Leibniz, see *Nouveaux essais sur l'entendement humain*, IV.vii.7; *Die Philosophischen Schriften von Gottfried Wilhelm Leibniz*, ed. Gerhardt, vol. 5 (1882), p. 391. Kant says in the *Critique of Pure Reason*: 'what is referred to as the Cartesian inference, *cogito ergo sum*, is really a tautology, since the *cogito* (*sum cogitans*) asserts my existence immediately' (A 355); see also B 422n. (References to Kant's *Critique of Pure Reason* are to the standard first and second edition paginations—hereafter A and B respectively. Other references are to *Gesammelte Schriften* (1900ff.), abbreviated as AA and cited by volume and page number.) Of course, this account in terms of a 'tautology' is problematic. It assumes that the 'sum' in '(ego) sum cogitans' concerns existence when in fact it is used as the copula joining the predicate to the subject in a sentence. For a detailed discussion of this, see Brands, '*Cogito ergo sum*'. *Interpretationen von Kant bis Nietzsche* (1982), pp. 81ff., 92–4.

[101] Frank is critical of my reading here, and claims that Mérian does not use 'reflection' in the sense of turning back to one's own self, but rather in Wolff's sense as 'Überdenken' or thinking and comparing in general: Frank, *Selbstgefühl* (2002), pp. 158, 165. It is true, of course, that Mérian uses 'reflection' in more than one sense, but the passages cited here clearly indicate that he has in mind a mediate form of relating to one's own self. Frank himself seems to concede that Mérian makes use of this notion as well as of the Wolffian notion of reflection as 'Überdenken': Frank (2002), pp. 165, 167. See also Wunderlich (2005), p. 103.

If the act of reflection contains the *conscium sui*, then it does so only because it was already contained in the thought that is the object of reflection. Mérian says:

> If, however, the formula of apperception were this: *I apperceive A*, then the formula of immediate reflection would be: *I have apperceived A*, because that selfhood ['egoïté'] which is contained in the formula of reflection is merely a copy of that selfhood which is contained in the formula of apperception—in a word, because immediate reflection is nothing but the memory of the apperceived object. (ibid., p. 433)

According to Mérian, then, immediate reflection on its own cannot produce the *conscium sui*.

He further argues that the *conscium sui* cannot be produced mediately through reflection; for this mediate production of the *conscium sui* would presuppose a certain relation between the self and the thought *A*. But since we have supposed *A* to be separate from the *conscium sui*, the transition to the *conscium sui* is cut off (ibid., p. 433). Without assuming a prior relation between the thought *A* and the *conscium sui*, reflection can never arrive at the latter. The mental act of reflection presupposes a certain relation between the self and its thoughts—for if there were no such prior relation between the self and its thoughts, the self could not *turn* to its thoughts in the reflective mode. I always already know that I exist when I think, see, remember, and so on. What I know through reflection are the notions of my mental faculties, including those of apperception, memory, judgement, and so on. These notions arise through the connection of the *conscium sui* with my other thoughts. If these thoughts did exist without the 'co-apperception' of my own self, I should never have these notions, and could not know that it is I who sees, hears, remembers, reasons, and so on (ibid.).

Mérian holds that since we do not arrive at the knowledge of our own existence through reasoning, reflection, or any other mediate way, we may infer that we know our own existence immediately; that is, through apperception (ibid., p. 434). Since the thesis about mediate knowledge is false, the thesis about immediate apperception of one's own self must be true. Mérian maintains that apperception itself, however, is not immediately known: apperception cannot become an object of apperception. He argues that if it were possible that I apperceive my own apperceiving, my own self would have to be duplicated. I should have to be at once myself and someone else. I should have to apperceive through my apperceiving self. Further, the notion of apperceiving one's own apperception leads to an infinite regress. I should have to be able to apperceive an idea and at the same time apperceive my apperception, and also to apperceive my apperception of my first apperception, and so on. Thus the apperceiving being would be not only duplicated, but multiplied *ad infinitum* (ibid., p. 417). He stresses that the fact that one cannot apperceive one's apperception does not mean that one cannot apperceive oneself or one's own existence, for apperceiving one's own existence does not presuppose the duplication of the apperceiving being. One does not apperceive oneself insofar as one apperceives, but insofar as one exists. The being which apperceives, say, images, does not apperceive an image of its own apperception. Nevertheless it apperceives itself, independently of the images it apperceives (ibid., p. 435).

Mérian's account of apperception, as analysed so far, raises the following question. Is the *conscium sui* (a) a feeling of my existence which is separate from all my other feelings and sensations, or is it (b) a feeling of my existence that is an element inherent in each particular sensation? Mérian's answer is that the *conscium sui* (the apperception of one's own existence) is not only independent of, but also logically prior to, all other thought. His argument that everything one apperceives (perceptions, actions) is 'accompanied by the ad-apperception or co-apperception of one's own existence' (Mérian, 1749*b*, p. 446) is of course consistent with both (a) and (b)—depending on how one understands the term 'accompany'. Mérian's explicit distinction, however, between ideas in the mind and one's own existence as two distinct objects of apperception clearly indicates that he regards the apperception of one's own existence as an independent act (ibid., p. 445). More importantly, he makes it plain that the consciousness or apperception of one's own self is not only an independent act, but prior to all other thoughts: he says it is the 'first act' of a thinking being, and speaks of the 'pre-existence of the *conscium sui*' (Mérian, 1749*a*, p. 434). This notion of 'pre-existence' is not to be understood in terms of a temporal priority. He argues that the *conscium sui* is a *necessary* condition of all thought as such: it is presupposed by all other cognitions, and no particular thought could exist without it. For any given thought it can be shown that it cannot exist without the 'pre-existence of the *conscium sui*'. The *conscium sui* is absolutely fundamental; it 'is presupposed by all other knowledge and cannot be subordinate to any prior thought' (ibid.). Mérian argues that 'the apperception of oneself is the first act and an essential act of an intelligent being, as intelligent being, considering that it is presupposed by all cognitions, while it alone does not presuppose anything' (ibid.). He rejects the counter-argument that I require a particular thought to awaken the *conscium sui* in the first place, and that therefore the *conscium sui* is not fundamental. This argument must be rejected, according to Mérian, because whichever thought we take to be the one that is to awaken self-consciousness, for it to be a thought at all it must presuppose the *conscium sui*. It is impossible to identify any thought that could ground the *conscium sui*. We revolve around the *conscium sui* as in a circle; it is always already involved when we think at all. This is why he explicitly speaks of the 'original apperception' ('l'apperception primitive') of our own existence (ibid., 432–3). The consciousness of our own existence is an 'original apperception' that is necessary to all thought as such.

It follows, as Mérian points out, that '*only* [my italics] the apperception of oneself is necessary and essential' to a thinking being; all other thoughts it may have are accidental to it (ibid., 434). He holds that it is possible to conceive of a thinking being that apperceives only itself, but that it is not possible to conceive of a thinking being that apperceives only the sun, for example, but not its own existence. If I had no ideas, no mental faculties of reflection, imagination, memory, and so on, I should still be a thinking being, for I should still have an 'original' self-consciousness. If, however, I had no consciousness of self I should cease to be a thinking being (ibid., 434–5). According to Mérian, the idea of a thinking being that does not apperceive itself is abstruse and self-contradictory. This distinguishes his position from those of both Wolff and Rüdiger and other critics of Wolff. Against Wolff, he argues that one's own existence is not known through reason and reflection; the *conscium sui* is always presupposed by any attempt to demonstrate the existence of one's own self. Rüdiger holds that we are not conscious of ourselves if we are not conscious of our mental activities (*Gegen-Meinung*, p. 9), and he implies that we can be conscious of mental activities without being conscious of our own existence. Mérian, by contrast, argues that the consciousness of self is not subordinate to the consciousness of mental activities, and that it is 'originally' and necessarily involved in the consciousness we have of our thoughts.

In arguing for the 'pre-existence' and necessity of self-consciousness Mérian clearly goes beyond his own official empiricist approach to the issue of apperception and his critique of Wolff. For the notion of its logical priority and necessity is not, of course, an object of inner-directed observation; rather, it is the result of his reflection on what makes the objects of introspection (thoughts and feelings), as well as the very act of introspection, possible. The 'originality' or 'pre-existence' of self-consciousness is to be understood in terms of a universal and necessary condition of thought in general. This function that Mérian ascribes to the 'original apperception' of ourselves appears to point towards a Kantian understanding of that notion.

11.4.3. Beyond Mérian

As indicated, German philosophers in the second half of the eighteenth century were undoubtedly aware of Mérian's work, and took it seriously (see references to Platner, Maine de Biran, and others, above).[102] It is significant in itself that Michael Hissmann—who was himself interested in the issue of self-consciousness—published German translations of Mérian's two papers on apperception in the first volume of his *Magazin* in 1778. Hissmann states in the preface (p. 4) that the purpose of the *Magazin* is to make generally available 'the most valuable pieces' that were published in the Academy's large quarto-size Yearbooks. For the latter, he points out, are for the most part available 'only in the richest public libraries'; here one can browse through the huge tomes, but cannot study the 'treasures' they contain in any detail.

Even before the German translation of Mérian's essays on apperception appeared, arguments about consciousness as a necessary condition of thought could be found in authors working against the background of Wolffian philosophy. Of course, it is not always clear whether Mérian was an influence here. Thus, Gottfried Ploucquet—a pupil of the Wolffian thinker Israel Gottlieb Canz whose account of immortality and identity we discussed above—seems to adopt the view that prior to any other thought or observation the self is 'revealed' or 'manifest' to itself.[103] Ploucquet does not seem to

---

[102] According to Frank, it is of special importance that a philosopher such as Maine de Biran took up Mérian's ideas about apperception. See Frank (2002), pp. 86–7, 156–8, 160–1. Compare Maine de Biran, *Rapports des sciences naturelles avec la psychologie et autres écrits sur la psychologie*, in Maine de Biran, *Oeuvres*, vol. 8, ed. Baertschi (1986), p. 568.

[103] Ploucquet, *Principia de substantiis et phaenomenis* (1764), p. 6: 'Primum, quod in me observo, & sine quo nihil amplius observare possum, est Manifestatio mei ipsius. Ex hac manifestatione debet

refer to Mérian, however, and it is doubtful that he was even aware of his essays on apperception. Moreover, Ploucquet thinks the 'manifestation of one's own self' is due to an absolute principle, the soul as substance.[104]

Johann Heinrich Lambert, too, does not refer to Mérian's essays; indeed, he does not even provide any detailed conceptual analysis of consciousness. His remarks about consciousness in his *Neues Organon* (1764) are important, however, because Lambert too turns away from psychological considerations of consciousness to epistemological ones.[105] According to Lambert, consciousness is a necessary condition of conceptual thought in general.[106] Sensations as such do not give rise to concepts: we acquire concepts of things only by directing our attention to our sensations and thus becoming conscious of them. For Lambert, consciousness is a fundamental 'postulate' or principle: it is a postulate for thought in general because 'in thinking beings no clear sensation, representation, concept etc would be possible without consciousness' (*Neues Organon*, 1990, vol. 1, p. 386). While this understanding of consciousness as an essential element of thought was not new (it is present in Locke), Lambert's shift towards epistemological considerations was significant in the largely psychology-based context of the 1760s and 1770s in Germany. In Lambert's writings, however, there seems to be no discussion of self-consciousness and personal identity.

A year before the German translations of Mérian's essays on apperception appeared, Johann Nicolas Tetens discussed Mérian in his *Philosophische Versuche* (vol. 1, pp. 46–7). Tetens's own views about consciousness are of importance in their own right, and will be discussed elsewhere.[107] His reference to Mérian may be of further significance, since we know that Kant carefully read Tetens early in 1778.[108] As far as I know, there is no decisive evidence as to whether or not Kant had read Mérian's papers on apperception. He probably knew of Mérian as a member of the Berlin Academy, and it is probable that he was at least aware of the existence of Mérian's first paper on apperception, for he would have noticed Tetens's discussion of Mérian in the first part of the *Versuche*. The letter to Marcus Herz which mentions his reading of Tetens, dates from April 1778. Since this was when Kant was studying the psychology of the day, he may well have turned to Mérian's papers when their

---

intelligi omne id, quod in me peragitur'. Wunderlich has drawn my attention to this and other similar passages in Ploucquet. See Wunderlich (2005), p. 68.

[104] On this, see Wunderlich (2005), p. 68.

[105] For this issue in post-Wolffian discussions of apperception, see also Salomon, *Zu den Begriffen der Perzeption und Apperzeption von Leibniz bis Kant* (1902).

[106] Lambert, *Neues Organon, oder Gedanken über die Erforschung und Bezeichnung des Wahren*, 2 vols. (1764), ed. Schenk (1990), vol. 1, p. 7.

[107] Thiel, *The Enlightened Subject* (in preparation).

[108] Kant had a high regard for Tetens. See his letters to Herz from April 1778 and May 1781 (AA 10: 232, 270), and the letter to Garve of 7 August 1783 (AA 10: 341). Kant made marginal notes on pp. 19 and 131 in vol. 1 of his copy of Tetens's *Versuche* (see *Reflexionen*, 4847 and 4848, in AA 18: 5). At the same time, he was very critical of Tetens's psychological approach to philosophical problems (compare *Reflexionen*, 4900 and 4901, in AA 18: 23). For an account of the general relationship between Kant's and Tetens's philosophies, see Carl, *Der schweigende Kant. Die Entwürfe zu einer Deduktion der Kategorien vor 1781* (1989), pp. 115–26.

German translations appeared in 1778. He could of course have read the original French versions on first publication by the Berlin Academy in the middle of the century; but until the 1770s, Kant was apparently not much interested in the topic of self-consciousness.[109]

There are a number of ways in which Mérian's account of apperception is quite clearly removed from Kant's understanding of the problem in the *Critique of Pure Reason*. The most obvious difference consists in Mérian's appeal to an empiricist methodology. Related to this is the fact that he does not explicitly distinguish between 'empirical' and what Kant calls 'pure' or 'transcendental' apperception. Further, his discussion of apperception is certainly not part of a deduction of pure concepts of the understanding. Lastly, he does not challenge the traditional notion of the self or soul. For him, as we have seen in the section on Mérian on personal identity, the self of apperception appears to be a soul or mental substance. Thus, our claim is not that Mérian 'anticipated' Kant's theory. Rather, it is that despite the differences mentioned above, Mérian's account of apperception is closer to a Kantian understanding of pure apperception than other contemporary accounts of self-consciousness (such as Wolff's, for example), and may even have been an inspiration to Kant.

First, there is the basic point that according to Mérian, apperception relates to the self as subject, not just to ideas and mental acts. He argues that the consciousness that accompanies our ideas presupposes the 'co-apperception' of the self that has these ideas and is conscious of them: consciousness of ideas presupposes consciousness of self (Mérian, 1749*a*, p. 433; and Mérian, 1749*b*, p. 445). This apperception of the I is not, however, the same as knowledge of the nature of the I. Mérian argues that what is given through the *conscium sui* or 'Selbstbewußtseyn', as the 1778 German translation renders it, is my existence or 'Daseyn'. Consciousness of self does not constitute knowledge of my nature or the manner of my existence. This concurs with what Kant says about pure or transcendental apperception.

Second, as shown above, Mérian holds that apperception or self-consciousness is an independent 'first' or 'original' act—the term 'first' expressing a logical rather than a temporal priority. He believes that apperception or self-consciousness makes possible, and is presupposed by, all other thought and knowledge. He argues quite explicitly that apperception is absolutely fundamental; it is presupposed by all other thought and knowledge, and it does not itself presuppose anything (Mérian, 1749*a*, p. 434; in Hissmann, *Magazin*, vol. 1, p. 119). This can be linked to Kant's thesis that apperception is the 'radical faculty of all our knowledge' (A 114). Moreover, the 'pre-existence' of the *conscium sui* or apperception is linked to the necessity of thought in general, as we have seen. As indicated above, despite his appeal to an empiricist methodology, Mérian in the end reflects on the necessary conditions of thought, arguing that apperception or self-consciousness is necessary to all thinking beings as such. The 1778 German translation of his first paper on apperception even uses the phrase 'ursprüngliche Apperzeption' (original

---

[109] See Brandt, 'Rousseau und Kants "Ich denke"', *Kant-Forschungen*, 5 (1994), 1–18, at 2–6.

apperception; see Mérian in Hissmann, *Magazin*, vol. 1, p. 117). This phrase reappears in Kant's *Critique* (A 117; compare A 108 and B 132). Apart from Mérian's paper there does not seem to be any other printed text prior to Kant in which the phrase 'ursprüngliche Apperzeption' appears.

Third, although Mérian believes that the self is a mental substance or soul, he does not infer this belief from his account of 'original apperception'. Conversely, his arguments concerning the original apperception of one's own existence do not depend in any way on his belief that the self is a mental substance or soul.[110] By giving an account of self-consciousness that is independent of any metaphysical commitment to the nature of the soul, he distinguishes himself significantly from other thinkers of the time—especially, but not only, Wolffians such as Eberhard and Reimarus. The fact that he appeals to the notion of the self as soul or substance in other papers, and even in one passage of the first paper on apperception (Mérian, 1749*a*, p. 436; in Hissmann, *Magazin*, vol. 1, pp. 122–3), must not mislead us. In that passage he makes use of the notion of substance only in order to highlight the difference between thoughts and various mental operations on the one hand, and the self or subject that has those thoughts and performs those operations on the other. In his papers on apperception at least he conceives of the self only in terms of a subject of thought. Indeed, he explicitly distinguishes himself from philosophers who wish 'to define this self which one apperceives' (Mérian, 1749*a*, p. 440; in Hissmann, *Magazin*, vol. 1, p. 130). The main point is that nothing he says about apperception or self commits Mérian to the view that the self of 'original apperception' is a mental substance or soul. Wolfgang Carl has argued that Kant did not discover the paralogisms of pure reason until 1780, and that to do so he required a notion of apperception which does not depend on the notion of self as mental substance.[111] In my view such a notion is present in Mérian.

It remains true, of course, that there are several crucial differences between Kant's and Mérian's accounts of apperception—some of which are listed above. Further, Mérian himself later rejected Kant's philosophy in a contribution to the Academy's *Memoires* of 1797, defending the principles of empiricist philosophy. Nevertheless, he has praise for the general design of Kant's critical philosophy, which, he says, isolates our various mental faculties and assigns to each its precise import.[112] In any case, his 1797 opinion of Kant's philosophy is quite irrelevant to the question of whether his earlier writings on apperception have any bearing on Kant's account of that notion. It should be clear from what has been said above that they have such a

---

[110] Wunderlich seems to disagree with this interpretation, arguing that Mérian's thesis about the 'pre-existence' of apperception *results* from his account of what he takes to be the essential property of a soul or mental substance: Wunderlich (2005), p. 105. This is not, however, how Mérian argues. While it is true that he believes that the soul is a substance with certain properties, his argument about the 'pre-existence' of apperception relates to what is required for thought and reflection to be possible.

[111] See Carl (1989), pp. 116–18.

[112] Mérian, 'Parallèle historique de nos deux philosophies nationales', in *Mémoires de l'académie royale des sciences et belles-lettres depuis l'avènement de Frédéric Guillaume II au thrône, Classe de philosophie spéculative* (1797), pp. 53–96, esp. pp. 53–6. Compare Harnack (1900), vol. 1, pp. 455–7.

bearing.[113] On the other hand, our claim is not of course that Mérian was the only thinker who was important to Kant's thought about consciousness and identity. David Hume was, as is well known, perhaps the most important philosopher in this regard.

Also, we have noted several times that both Sulzer and Mérian themselves were influenced by British philosophy and that they had a strong interest in David Hume's thought, even though they both rejected central tenets of the latter. Indeed, it is now time to turn to David Hume and to consider one of the most discussed early eighteenth-century accounts of personal identity.

---

[113] It will be shown in *The Enlightened Subject* (in preparation) that the accounts of more independent thinkers in the second half of the eighteenth century that have been linked to Kant (such as Tetens and Rousseau) do not have as much in common with Kant's position as does Mérian's theory of self-consciousness.

PART VI

BUNDLES AND SELVES: HUME IN CONTEXT

12
Hume and the belief in personal identity

Like Locke's discussion of personal identity, Hume's treatment of the topic continues to engage philosophers and scholars—partly because of its philosophical importance, but also because of difficult questions concerning the interpretation of his text. Many passages in Hume's discussion are very opaque, and the nature of his theory is still a matter of dispute among scholars. Moreover, it is not just present-day commentators who find his account problematic. One eighteenth-century critic exclaimed in exasperation: 'When he [Hume] treats... of personal identity... he expresseth himself so strangely, that his words either have no meaning, or imply a contradiction.'[1]

Clearly, 'Hume on personal identity' is not exactly a neglected topic in philosophical scholarship. In fact, the literature on this subject is vast.[2] Most (but not all) commentators, however, look at Hume's discussion in isolation from its eighteenth-century context. This is perhaps not surprising, for his account seems to be so radical, and it is formulated 'so strangely' that it may seem to bear no relation to other discussions of the time. But of course, it does. As we have seen, by the time Hume published the first two books of his *A Treatise of Human Nature* in 1739 (Book III and an Appendix were published in 1740), the issue had been much debated by philosophers—and it continued to be discussed after Hume—mostly with a critical stance towards his account.

We shall argue that Hume's position and that of some of his Scottish critics on the issues of self-consciousness and personal identity are closer than is assumed by most commentators, despite all the undeniable differences that will be highlighted

---

[1] Beattie, *An Essay on the Nature and Immutability of Truth* (1770), p. 263.
[2] Among the most important pieces in the literature are series of articles by Penelhum, McIntyre, Ainslie, Winkler, Strawson, and Garrett, including Penelhum, 'Hume on Personal Identity', *Philosophical Review*, 64 (1955), 571–89; McIntyre, 'Personal Identity and the Passions', *Journal of the History of Philosophy*, 27 (1989), 545–57; Ainslie, 'Hume on Personal Identity', in Radcliffe (ed.), *A Companion to Hume* (2008), pp. 140–56; Winkler, '"All is Revolution in Us": Personal Identity in Shaftesbury and Hume', *Hume Studies*, 26 (2000), 3–40; Garrett, 'Difficult Times for Humean Identity?', *Philosophical Studies*, 146 (2009), 435–43; and Strawson, 'Hume on Himself', in Egonsson, Josefsson, Petersson, and Rønnow-Rasmussen (eds.), *Exploring Practical Philosophy: From Action to Values* (2001), pp. 69–94. In addition there are the relevant chapters in Stroud, *Hume* (1977), pp. 118–40; Garrett, *Cognition and Commitment* (1997); and Allison, *Custom and Reason in Hume* (2008). Recent book-length studies of various aspects of Hume's account of the self include Strawson, *The Evident Connexion: Hume on Personal Identity* (2011a); Pitson, *Hume's Philosophy of the Self* (2002); Baxter, *Hume's Difficulty: Time and Identity in the Treatise* (2008); and Wilson, *Body, Mind and Self in Hume's Critical Realism* (2008).

below. In this Chapter we shall begin with an outline of our reading of Hume's theory, relating it to earlier positions and raising some problems of interpretation. In the next Chapter we shall discuss objections to Hume's account by some of his Scottish contemporaries, generally known as Scottish Common Sense philosophers: thinkers such as James Beattie, Thomas Reid, and others, focusing on Hume's kinsman Henry Home, Lord Kames. It will become apparent that some of Kames's arguments can help to illuminate Hume's position.[3]

When Hume wrote about personal identity in the *Treatise of Human Nature*, he was very much aware of the earlier debates about this issue. For example, he says that 'the nature of *personal identity*... has become so great a question in philosophy, especially of late years in *England*, where all the abstruser sciences are study'd with a peculiar ardour and application'.[4] Hume does not give names of particular thinkers, and he does not explicitly refer to particular debates. The main players, however, can be identified easily enough. Like most eighteenth-century discussions, Hume's treatment of the topic is strongly influenced by Locke, even if his own account turns out to be quite different in several crucial respects.[5]

As we have seen in earlier Chapters, Locke's theory aroused controversy very soon after its first publication in 1694; and it dominated the disputes over personal identity in the eighteenth century. It is clear that Hume, too, worked out his own arguments against the background of Locke's account and the debates about Locke's theory 'of late years in *England*'. The most important and influential of these debates was the controversy between Anthony Collins and Samuel Clarke (discussed above), which took place between 1706 and 1708 but was republished many times prior to the appearance of Hume's *Treatise*. We saw that while Collins's leanings are more materialist than Locke's, his account of personal identity is Lockean insofar as it, too, appeals to a psychological criterion of personal identity, rather than to the identity of the thinking substance, whatever its nature.[6] Samuel Clarke, by contrast, defends the view that the human soul is an immaterial and indivisible substance, arguing that personal identity is based in the immaterial nature of the soul, and rejecting Collins's Lockean account of personal identity in terms of consciousness.[7] As we saw, this view was defended, also against Locke and Collins, by Joseph Butler in his dissertation 'Of Personal Identity' of 1736. Hume sent Butler a copy of his *Treatise* after the first two

---

[3] We shall look at the Common Sense philosophers' own account of personal identity and self-consciousness in *The Enlightened Subject* (in preparation).

[4] David Hume, *A Treatise of Human Nature*, ed. Selby-Bigge, revised by Nidditch (1978), p. 259. I have also used the recent edition of the *Treatise* by Norton and Norton (2000) which has the Selby-Bigge pagination in the margins.

[5] Hall has provided textual evidence for the considerable extent to which Hume's account is related to Locke's. See Hall, 'Hume's Use of Locke on Identity', *The Locke Newsletter*, 5 (1974), 56–75.

[6] Collins, *An Answer to Mr. Clarke's Third Defence of his Letter to Mr. Dodwell* (1708), p. 67.

[7] See Clarke, *A Third Defence of an Argument made use of in a Letter to Mr. Dodwel, to prove the Immateriality and Natural Immortality of the Soul. In a Letter to the Author of the Reflexions on Mr. Clark's Second Defence* (1708), pp. 61–2: 'Every Imagination, every Volition, and every Thought; is the Imagination, Will, and Thought, of that Whole Thinking Substance, which I call *I my Self*. And if this One Substance (which we usually stile the *Soul* or *Mind*) has no Parts, that can Act separately, it may as well be conceived to have none, that can *Exist* separately; and so, to be absolutely *Indivisible*.'

volumes had appeared in 1739. Insofar as his account of personal identity involves a critique of traditional views, it relates to positions such as Clarke's and, as we shall see, Butler's in particular.[8] There are other authors who may be relevant to Hume in this context. There are passages in Shaftesbury, Bayle, and Claude Buffier, for example, which can be related to various aspects of Hume's account of identity, as we shall see. It remains true, however, that Locke and the discussions about Locke's theory form the most important part of the background against which Hume thought and wrote about personal identity.

12.1. THE 'NATURAL PROPENSION' TO BELIEVE IN PERSONAL IDENTITY

Hume's section entitled 'Of Personal Identity' appears towards the end of the first Book of the *Treatise* which deals with the understanding. In this section Hume implicitly and sometimes explicitly appeals to arguments he makes in earlier parts of the book, and he also refers to issues discussed in Book II ('Of the Passions'). Clearly, his account is meant to be an integral part of his 'science of human nature'. We shall comment later on the relevance of Book II to his account of personal identity. Other important sections include I.iv.5 on the immateriality of the soul, preceding the one on personal identity, and section I.iv.2, in which he discusses the identity of objects—an issue that reappears in the section on personal identity. It should be noted at the outset that in I.iv.6 Hume equates the question of personal identity with that of the identity of the mind (*Treatise*, pp. 259, 260)—but unlike Locke, he does not distinguish here between the mind or soul and the person.

As indicated, even Hume's contemporaries did not regard the section on personal identity as an easy read. At least the section is very clearly structured. It can be divided into three main parts: (1) Hume begins with a brief critique of a traditional view about personal identity—the view that is argued for by philosophers such as Butler (ibid., pp. 251–2). (2) Then, again quite briefly, he points out what we can know about the self or person or mind on the basis of inner experience or introspection (ibid., pp. 252–3). (3) The third part is the most extensive, complex, and, at least from Hume's point of view, the most important part of the section (ibid., pp. 253–63). Here Hume attempts to explain why we tend to ascribe identity to ourselves, although introspection provides no evidence for such identity.

---

[8] The importance of the Clarke–Collins controversy, and especially of Collins to Hume's philosophy in general, has been emphasised in the literature from more than one perspective. For Hume and Collins in general, see Russell, 'Hume's *Treatise* and the Clarke–Collins Controversy', *Hume Studies*, 21 (1995), 95–115, esp. 102–6; and McIntyre, 'Hume: Second Newton of the Moral Sciences', *Hume Studies*, 20 (1994), 3–18, esp. 4, 8, 10–15. Russell and McIntyre agree on the importance of Collins for Hume, but Russell rejects McIntyre's claim about Hume's Newtonianism. For Russell, Hume is, rather, the second Hobbes of the moral sciences: Russell (1995), 109, 113–15. See also Russell's recent *The Riddle of Hume's Treatise: Skepticism, Naturalism, and Irreligion* (2008), pp. 188–92.

Regarding the first part, it is important to be clear about the view that Hume attacks here. His description is very brief, but it would seem obvious that his target is not a rationalist position, as is sometimes maintained—if by 'rationalist' is meant the view that we are assured of our own personal identity on the basis of *a priori* reasoning or proof.[9] Rather, he attacks the view that we have an immediate inner experience or feeling of our own simplicity and diachronic identity, and that for that reason, no proof of personal identity is required. The view rejected by Hume is, in his own words, that 'we are every moment intimately conscious of what we call our SELF; that we feel its existence and its continuance in existence; and are certain, beyond the evidence of a demonstration, both of its perfect identity and simplicity' (ibid., p. 251).

In short, our inner *experience* 'is pleaded for' by the proponents of this position (ibid.). The view that we are certain of our own self's simplicity and identity on the basis of immediate inner experience or feeling was not uncommon in the eighteenth century, and was expressed by many philosophers before and after Hume—including some of his Scottish critics.[10] It was also the view of Butler, who seems to have been the most likely target for Hume here.[11] In 'Of Personal Identity' (1736) Butler says that 'upon comparing the consciousnesses of one's self, or one's own existence, in any two moments, there ... *immediately arises to the mind the idea of personal identity*' (my italics).[12] He speaks of our conviction of our own personal identity as of '*that certain conviction, which necessarily and every moment rises within us, when we turn our thoughts upon ourselves*' (my italics). This is part of our 'natural sense of things'.[13] Therefore, 'it is ridiculous to attempt to prove the truth of those perceptions, whose truth we can no otherwise prove, than by other perceptions of exactly the same kind with them'.[14]

It is also clear from the introductory paragraph of the section that Hume is concerned with two issues: the simplicity (and indivisibility) of the self, and its identity through time. The main focus of his discussion in the section is on identity. He leaves simplicity aside in the following paragraphs, and does not return

---

[9] Thus Mijuskovic, for example, states that it is 'the rationalist's conception that Hume is concerned to challenge'—a conception which includes the view 'that the immateriality, simplicity, and unity of the soul can be *demonstrated*' (my italics): Mijuskovic, 'Hume and Shaftesbury on the Self', *Philosophical Quarterly*, 21 (1971), 324–6, at 328. In fact, Hume is concerned only with thinkers that Mijuskovic calls 'intuitional rationalists' (328). See also Mijuskovic, *The Achilles of Rationalist Arguments* (1974), p. 109.

[10] See the discussion in Thiel, 'Varieties of Inner Sense. Two Pre-Kantian Theories, *Archiv für Geschichte der Philosophie*, 79 (1997a), 58–79, at 76.

[11] Ainslie suggests that Locke may have been Hume's target, because Locke is of the view that 'self-awareness is omnipresent': Ainslie, 'Hume's Reflections on the Identity and Simplicity of Mind', *Philosophy and Phenomenological Research*, 62 (2001), 557–78, at 559. See also Ainslie (2008), pp. 143–4. It is true that Locke says that we are always aware of the existence of our own self whenever we think, perceive, or do anything. As we have seen, however, in Locke, self-awareness of existence does not include a consciousness of the nature of the self. We are not aware that its nature is simple and we are not conscious of its identity (rather, we are conscious of thoughts and actions and thereby construct our identity as persons). Thus, it seems unlikely that Locke's view was Hume's target.

[12] *The Works of Joseph Butler*, ed. Gladstone, 3 vols. (1898), vol. 1, p. 317.

[13] Ibid., p. 323.

[14] Ibid., p. 325.

to the issue until the penultimate paragraph of the section, suggesting briefly that it should be dealt with in analogy to the question of why we ascribe identity to the mind (ibid., p. 263). Moreover, the issue of the simplicity and indivisibility of the human soul as substance is dealt with in the previous section I.iv.5 (ibid., p. 242). There, certain 'theologians' are Hume's target. Clearly, section I.iv.5 on immateriality prepares the section on personal identity: if we have no idea of a mental substance, as is argued in section five, then how does our belief arise that we exist as one and the same thing through time?[15]

In his critique of the traditional view Hume focuses on the alleged experiential basis for this position. He makes a point of appealing to the same source as the proponents of the view he rejects, arguing that the latter cannot be justified by experience. Rather, if we appeal to experience, he argues, we must reject this view: the 'very experience, which is pleaded' for it contradicts the metaphysicians' assertions. As is to be expected, he makes use of his theory of ideas in this context. We have no idea of the self, 'after the manner it is here explain'd' because there is no impression from which such an idea could be derived. An impression that could give rise to such an idea of the self would have to 'continue invariably the same, thro' the whole course of our lives' (ibid., p. 251). For on the metaphysicians' view, the self or person is something that does 'continue invariably the same'. As experiential evidence shows, however, 'there is no impression constant and invariable', and we have no idea of the self '*after the manner it is here explain'd*' (my italics) (ibid., p. 251). Moreover, Hume points to a principle that he has emphasised elsewhere in the *Treatise*: namely, that all our perceptions 'are distinguishable, and separable from each other ... and may exist separately, and have no need of any thing to support their existence' (ibid., p. 252). According to Hume, then, there is no idea of a simple and identical self as understood and explained by the position he attacks.

Clearly, Hume's argument in the second part, concerning what we can know about our own minds, is based on his critique of the traditional view. Like the philosophers he criticizes, he appeals to inner experience, but argues that the latter—rather than providing us with evidence for an identical self—presents us only with a multiplicty of different perceptions. As Hume says in a famous and much quoted passage, in inner experience or introspection: 'I always stumble on some particular perception or other, of heat or cold, light or shade, love or hatred, pain or pleasure. I never can catch *myself* at any time without a perception, and never can observe any thing but the perception' (ibid., p. 252). Were my perceptions to be removed, I would be insensible of myself; that is to say, there would be no experiential evidence for my existence, and in this sense I 'may truly be said not to exist' (ibid.). When I introspect I can identify only a variety of distinct perceptions, thoughts, feelings, and so on. There is no experiential evidence of a simple soul or mind that remains the same through time. And so, all we can say on the basis of introspection is that the mind is 'nothing but a bundle or collection of different perceptions, which succeed

---

[15] For section I.iv.5 and its importance to Reid's understanding of Hume's position, see Falkenstein, 'Hume and Reid on the Simplicity of the Soul', *Hume Studies*, 21 (1995), 25–45. For the relationship between I.iv.5 and 6, see 26.

each other with an inconceivable rapidity, and are in a perpetual flux and movement' (ibid., p. 252).[16]

For this reason, Hume holds that 'they are the successive perceptions only, that constitute the mind'; and that 'there is properly... no *identity* [of the mind] ... [at] different [times]' (ibid., p. 253). The view he expresses here has become known as the 'bundle theory' of the self or mind—a view that continues to be debated in different versions today. Moreover, it is clear from this passage that, for Hume at least, the bundle view of the self has implications for the issue of personal identity: the person or mind has no identity through time if it is just a bundle of perceptions. This view is shared by Hume's contemporaries and critics, as we shall see. What is, however, not as obvious from this passage, contrary to what is often assumed, is that Hume adopts the bundle theory as a position that represents an ontological truth about the nature of the mind. This question will be discussed in more detail in the next Chapter. We should note here, however, that all he is saying in this passage is that the bundle view is what inner experience or introspection suggests to us about the mind or person.

Turning, then, to the third and most extensive part of the section, where Hume attempts to explain why we tend to ascribe identity to the mind, although there seems to be no experiential evidence to support this belief. Importantly, Hume recognizes that despite the evidence of inner observation, we nevertheless, as a matter of fact, do ascribe identity to the self. Indeed, he claims that we have a 'natural propension' (ibid., p. 253) to believe in the simplicity and identity of our own selves. He then introduces what he regards as the main question to be answered about personal identity: what gives rise to this propension? The remainder of the section is devoted to answering this question, focusing, as was indicated above, on the issue of identity rather than simplicity. At the outset of this part Hume emphasises that the issue of identity of the mind should be explained analogously to the issue of why we ascribe identity to plants, vegetables, animals, artefacts, and other physical objects (ibid.), and he devotes a large part of the section to the latter issue (ibid., pp. 253–8). He does not take up the question of personal identity again until page 259. His treatment of this is quite short—eight paragraphs at the end of the section. As he himself emphasises, however, the account of identity in general is important to his account of personal identity. His account here is linked to his discussion of identity in earlier sections in the *Treatise*, especially to I.iv.2 (ibid., pp. 189–90; 199–210).

12.2. TIME, CHANGE, AND IDENTITY

We have seen in previous Chapters that many eighteenth-century philosophers—no matter whether or not they believe in the immateriality of the soul—worked with a notion of identity that precludes change. Hume seems to adopt this notion when he

---

[16] See also *Treatise*, p. 207, where Hume speaks of the mind as 'a connected heap of perceptions'.

says that identity is 'apply'd in its strictest sense to constant and unchangeable objects' (ibid., I.i.5, p. 14). In the section on personal identity too, he maintains that the idea of identity is the 'idea of an object, that remains invariable and uninterrupted thro' a suppos'd variation of time' (ibid., p. 253). The first passage suggests the old distinction between a strict and a 'loose and popular sense' of identity which is present in Butler. Hume calls the strict sense of identity 'perfect identity'.[17] In adopting an account of identity that precludes change, however, his discussion is in this respect fraught with the same sort of problems that we encountered in other philosophers of the time. As several commentators have pointed out, given his notion of identity as precluding change, there is nothing to which this notion is applicable.[18] Indeed, it can be said that this is the main problem with Hume's account: it is based on a notion of identity that precludes even partial change.

Hume emphasises—rightly, it would seem—that in order to understand the notion of diachronic identity we must 'have recourse to the idea of time or duration' (ibid., p. 200). The idea, however, expressed in the quotation above, that perfect identity applies to an unchanging object 'thro' a *suppos'd* variation of time' (my italics), may seem puzzling. Hume explains this, however, in an earlier section of the *Treatise* (ibid., I.ii.3). Here he argues that 'the idea of time ... [is] deriv'd from the succession of our perceptions of every kind' (ibid., pp. 34–5). Indeed, without the succession of perceptions we would have no idea of time at all: 'time cannot make its appearance to the mind, either alone, or attended with a steady unchangeable object, but is always discover'd by some *perceivable* succession of changeable objects' (ibid., p. 35). And since 'there is a continual succession or perceptions in our mind', the idea of time is 'for ever present with us' (ibid., p. 65). As far as unchanging objects are concerned, however, it follows, according to Hume, that the idea of time cannot be applied to them 'without a fiction' (ibid., p. 37)—but note that he is talking about the *idea* of time. Due to the invariableness of such an object we do not in respect of it have a succession of different perceptions. Therefore, the idea of a perfectly identical object requires 'a suppos'd variation of time' (ibid., p. 253) or 'fictitious duration' (ibid., p. 65).[19] Hume illustrates this notion of a 'fictitious duration' by way of example:

When we consider a stedfast object at five-a'-clock, and regard the same at six; we are apt to apply to it that idea [the idea of time] in the same manner *as if* every moment were distinguish'd by a different position, or an alteration of the object. The first and second appearances of the object, being compar'd with the succession of our perceptions, seem equally remov'd *as if* [my italics] the object had really chang'd [or as if we had experienced change]. (ibid., p. 65)

---

[17] Hume says that when we ascribe perfect identity to an object, we 'regard it as invariable': *Treatise*, p. 254.

[18] See, for example, Noonan, *Hume on Knowledge* (1999), p. 205.

[19] See Hume, *Treatise*, pp. 200–1: "tis only by a fiction of the imagination, by which the unchangeable object is suppos'd to participate of the changes of the co-existent objects, and in particular of that of our perceptions'.

The above analysis of time and fictitious duration assumes the notion of perfectly identical objects. But what if there is no empirical evidence for the perfect identity of an object? Given his notion of identity, a perception of a perfectly identical object would have to be not only 'invariable' but also 'uninterrupted'.[20] The ideas of 'invariableness and uninterruptedness' would require corresponding impressions (ibid., p. 251). While some of our perceptions may seem invariable at least, they are, however, often interrupted (ibid., p. 202). On the basis of our experience, then, we would not, strictly speaking, be entitled to ascribe identity to an object, given the disrupted nature of our perceptions. Hume does not deny that such an object may have identity. He is concerned only with the requirements for justifying our *ascription* of perfect identity to it, arguing that these are not met. He recognizes, however, that we nevertheless tend to ascribe identity to an object of which we have only interrupted perceptions. He then attempts to explain what makes us attribute identity to objects that do not meet the requirements of both invariableness and uninterruptedness of perception, and he does this at length in I.iv.2 (ibid., pp. 201–5), and more briefly in the section on personal identity. We ascribe identity to an object when the successive perceptions are closely related to one another in certain ways. The disposition of the mind when viewing an object that 'preserves a perfect identity' is that 'we suppose the change to lie only in the time' (ibid., p. 203). A succession of closely related objects places the mind in the same disposition and 'is consider'd with the same smooth and uninterrupted progress of the imagination, as attends the view of the same invariable object' (ibid., p. 204). 'The thought', Hume says, 'slides along the succession with equal facility, as if it consider'd only one object; and therefore confounds the succession with the identity' (ibid.).[21]

12.3. CONFOUNDING IDENTITY WITH DIVERSITY: HUME, SHAFTESBURY, AND BUFFIER

The relation that is mainly responsible for our confounding diversity with identity, is that of resemblance (ibid., pp. 202–3)—which is, of course, one of Hume's principles of association through which ideas are connected in the imagination. He emphasises that resemblance is involved in two ways in this 'very natural' mistake

---

[20] Identity through time involves 'the *invariableness* and *uninterruptedness* of any object, thro' a suppos'd variation of time, by which the mind can trace it in the different periods of its existence, without any break of the view, and without being oblig'd to form the idea of multiplicity or number': ibid., p. 201.

[21] As Allison has pointed out, there is a problem for Hume's account here that also affects his discussion of personal identity. If we never experience an uninterrupted and invariable object, 'how could the imagination ever confuse these two "experiences"?': Allison (2008), p. 297, see also p. 241. As noted above, however, the more fundamental problem with Hume's account is his assumption that partial change is incompatible with identity in the strict sense.

of confounding difference with identity: (1) the resemblance of the perceptions; and (2) the resemblance 'which the act of the mind in surveying a succession of resembling objects bears to that in surveying an identical object' (ibid., p. 205, footnote).

In the section on personal identity he explains how it comes about that 'in our common way of thinking' we tend to confound identity with diversity (with a 'succession of related objects') by focusing on the second type of resemblance: that between 'the action of the imagination, by which we consider the uninterrupted and invariable object, and that by which we reflect on the succession of related objects' (ibid., pp. 253–4). 'This resemblance', Hume says, 'is the cause of the confusion and mistake, and makes us substitute the notion of identity, instead of that of related objects' (ibid., p. 254). Our propension to ascribe identity where empirical evidence suggests diversity 'is so great' that our imagination creates the notion that there is something that underlies the succession of related objects and binds them together into a unitary and identical entity. As Hume says, 'we are apt to imagine something unknown and mysterious, connecting the parts, beside their relation' (ibid., p. 254).

Some scholars have made much of the fact that at this point Hume inserts a footnote in which he refers to Shaftesbury, and says:

If the reader is desirous to see how a great genius may be influenc'd by these seemingly trivial principles of the imagination, as well as the mere vulgar, let him read my Lord *Shaftesbury's* reasonings concerning the uniting principle of the universe, and the identity of plants and animals. See his *Moralists: or, Philosophical rhapsody.* (ibid., p. 254)

It has been suggested that Shaftesbury is of special importance to Hume's account of personal identity, and even that 'Hume's views of the self follow the Earl of Shaftesbury's...analyses'—indeed, that 'Hume in fact follows the identical train of reasoning taken up by...Shaftesbury', and that in the note 'Hume is praising Shaftesbury, not criticizing him'.[22] This assessment is not convincing, however. Hume's note does not even relate to the specific issue of personal identity. It is plain that the purpose of the footnote is neither to commend nor to condemn or criticize Shaftesbury. It is meant merely to illustrate the point that this tendency of the imagination to invent an underlying something that connects the related parts into a unity is as common in philosophers as it is in ordinary people (see also ibid., pp. 259, 262). This qualifies Hume's earlier remark in the same paragraph that philosophical reflection can correct our mistake, but that our common way of thinking cannot rid itself of it. Even someone as distinguished as Shaftesbury commits this mistake, and he does so even when he is philosophizing.

---

[22] See Mijuskovic (1971), esp. 324, 326, 331; see also Mijuskovic (1974), pp. 105–12. For a critical discussion of Mijuskovic's reading, see Corcoran, 'Do we have a Shaftesburean Self in the *Treatise*?', *Philosophical Quarterly*, 23 (1973), 67–72. Winkler holds that Shaftesbury is important to an understanding of Hume's comments on personal identity in the Appendix to Book III. See Winkler (2000), 5, 24ff. On this, see the relevant footnote below. For Shaftesbury's own views on identity and for his critical comments on Locke, see Chapters 5 and 7 above.

Why does Hume say that our ascribing identity to our own selves is a 'mistake'? It is a mistake just because we cannot 'justify our notion of identity' here (ibid., p. 255); and we cannot justify it because in experience we cannot 'find any thing invariable and uninterrupted' (ibid.). Again, what is at issue is our ascription of identity and the question of whether it can be justified given the empirical evidence.

Hume next considers examples of identity-ascriptions that lack justification. He has already explained one feature of why we tend to ascribe identity without experiential evidence. The close relation of parts 'produces an association of ideas, and an easy transition of the imagination from one to another' (ibid., p. 255). This is so similar to 'that action of the imagination, by which we consider the uninterrupted and invariable object' (ibid., pp. 253–4) that we tend to ascribe identity although we cannot really justify such an ascription. In the discussion of particular cases or examples of unjustified identity-ascriptions, Hume focuses on another aspect of his explanation: namely, on the *kinds of relations* of parts that produce such an association of ideas that lead us to ascribe identity. His examples are a 'mass of matter', artefacts (such as ships), vegetables or plants, and animals (oak tree, man) (ibid., pp. 255–8). Most of these examples are discussed in earlier accounts of identity—notably in Hobbes and Locke. Hume is not merely repeating these, however; rather, he is using them to explain the types of relation between parts that lead the imagination to attribute identity. Regarding a mass of matter of which 'the parts are contiguous and connected' (ibid., p. 255), Hume argues that the imagination would still ascribe identity to the mass when only a very small part is lost, or when the change of parts occurs '*gradually* and *insensibly*'. Strictly speaking, of course, this kind of change 'absolutely destroys the identity of the whole' (ibid., p. 256). In the case of artefacts such as a ship, 'of which a considerable part has been chang'd by frequent reparations', there is a 'common end, in which the parts conspire, [and which] is the same under all their variations' (ibid., p. 257). It is this common end that 'affords an easy transition of the imagination from one situation of the body to another' (ibid.). In the case of animals and vegetables there is also a common end of the parts, and in addition 'a *sympathy* of the parts to their *common end*'. That is to say, here, the parts also have 'a mutual dependance on, and connexion with each other'—'a reciprocal relation of cause and effect in all their actions and operations' (ibid.). The effect of this 'strong... relation' is that although vegetables and animals within very few years 'endure a *total* change, yet we still attribute identity to them, while their form, size, and substance are entirely alter'd' (ibid.). Hume uses Locke's examples of the oak tree and a man, considered as bodily organisms. Towards the end of his discussion of examples he emphasises the difference between specific and numerical identity which, he says, are often confused with one another (ibid., pp. 257–8). He gives the example of a church that has been completely rebuilt, and where only the relation to the inhabitants is the same—a case of specific identity or resemblance, not of numerical identity. He concludes this discussion by considering objects such as rivers, which 'are in their nature changeable and inconstant'. In relation to these 'we admit of a more sudden transition', and still call them the same (ibid., p. 258).

Hume's analysis of the identity of objects has striking similarities, in some respects, with Claude Buffier's earlier account in his *Traité des premières véritez*

(1724).[23] Some commentators have contended for an influence of Buffier on Hume, without, however, dealing with the issue of identity.[24] The matter does not seem to have been established decisively, however. Some of the Scottish Common Sense philosophers (such as Reid) explicitly mention Buffier in their later writings; and indeed Buffier seems to anticipate several of their positions, though it remains true that Hume's relation to Buffier is unclear. What is absolutely clear is that Buffier's account, in a chapter entitled 'De l'identité et de la diversité' (*Traité*, pt. 2, pp. 198–205), is in parts very similar to Hume's analysis of the identity of physical objects, and may well have been an inspiration for Hume. Thus Buffier argues that similarity is often confused with identity (ibid., p. 200), and that 'by resemblance...two things are said to be the *same*, when one succeeds the other by an imperceptible, but still real change'.[25] Buffier refers approvingly to Bayle, who argued that Spinoza's failure to distinguish between the identity of resemblance (specific identity) and the identity of substance (numerical identity) is the foundation of his whole system, which postulates that there is the same substance in all beings (ibid., p. 201). Even Buffier's examples (the ship, the river, the same human body; ibid., p. 200) reappear in Hume. As indicated above, however, these were also used prior to Buffier, and must be regarded as standard by Hume's time. Also, apart from some brief and dismissive comments on Locke's account (ibid., p 201; pt. 3, pp. 264–5) which he considers 'strange', Buffier has little to say on personal identity, and so he is unlikely to have impressed Hume on that issue.

12.4. 'THE IDENTITY WHICH WE ASCRIBE TO THE MIND OF MAN'

Hume at last returns to the issue of personal identity (*Treatise*, pp. 259–62)—to his account, that is, of what it is that makes us attribute identity to the mind, although inner experience suggests that it is a 'compounded and changeable' thing (ibid., p. 259).[26] First, he emphasises again the importance of the analogy between the

---

[23] Buffier, *Traité des premières véritez, et de la source de nos jugemens* (1724). Towards the end of the century an English translation was published entitled *First Truths, and the Origin of our Opinions explained* (1780).

[24] See the references in Jones, *Hume's Sentiments* (1982), pp. 196, 204; Laird, *Hume's Philosophy* (1967), p. 71. For Buffier, see especially Wilkins, *A Study of the Works of Claude Buffier* (Studies on Voltaire, 66) (1969). Wilkins does not discuss Hume. See also Hutchison, *Locke in France* (1991).

[25] Buffier, *First Truths*, p. 168. The original reads: 'Par la resemblance, deux choses sont dites aussi *la même*, quand l'une succéde à l'autre avec un changement imperceptible, bien que très-réel': Buffier, *Traité des premières véritez*, pt. 2, pp. 199–200.

[26] Ainslie argues that these 'positive portions of the Section, in which Hume offers a psychological mechanism for the generation of the belief in mental simplicity and identity, are meant to deal with the beliefs of philosophers who are observing their minds, not the beliefs of those inhabiting common life': Ainslie (2001), 563; see also 565. I am not convinced by this reading. Hume analyses and explains, as he says, a 'natural propension' that we all have to ascribe identity to our own minds: *Treatise*, p. 253. He attempts to explain universal beliefs in terms of his philosophy,

identity we ascribe to plants, animals, and artefacts on the one hand, and the identity we ascribe to the self or mind on the other (ibid.). 'The identity, which we ascribe to the mind of man, is only a fictitious one, and of a like kind with that which we ascribe to vegetables and animal bodies. It... must proceed from a like operation of the imagination upon like objects' (ibid.).

Second, he repeats that (1) 'every distinct perception, which enters into the composition of the mind, is a distinct existence', and that (2) 'the understanding never observes any real connexion among objects' (ibid., pp. 259–60). These are the two principles which he 'cannot render consistent' when he critically reflects on his account of personal identity in the Appendix of 1740 (ibid., p. 636). Further, quotation (2) is followed by: 'even the union of cause and effect, when strictly examin'd, resolves itself into a customary association of ideas' (ibid., p. 260). As we shall see, this comment too relates to his self-doubts discussed in the Appendix.

Third, Hume says in the section on identity in Book I that it 'evidently follows' from (1) and (2) 'that identity is nothing really belonging to these different perceptions, and uniting them together; but it is merely a quality, which we attribute to them, because of the union of their ideas in the imagination' (ibid.).

Fourth, he reminds the reader of his earlier argument that there are three basic 'uniting principles', according to which the imagination associates ideas: contiguity in space and time, resemblance, and causation. The belief in personal identity is due to such principles of connection: 'our notions of personal identity, proceed entirely from the smooth and uninterrupted progress of the thought along a train of connected ideas, according to the principles above-explained' (ibid.).

Fifth, he asks which of three relations are responsible for the 'smooth progress of thought'. He says that contiguity is not relevant here; but he does not explain why. It should be obvious, however, from I.iv.5, where he argues that at least some perceptions cannot be said to exist anywhere in space; which makes the principle of contiguity useless for unifying our perceptions. Causality and resemblance are the important principles, according to Hume. And in both cases memory plays a major role (ibid.).

Sixth, Hume considers resemblance and memory. Memory, he says, is 'a faculty, by which we raise up the images of past perceptions' (ibid.). Images resemble their objects. And 'the frequent placing of these resembling perceptions in the chain of thought, convey[s] the imagination more easily from one link to another, and make[s] the whole seem like the continuance of one object' (ibid., p. 261). Memory fulfils an important function here because it 'contributes to its [identity's] production, by producing the relation of resemblance among the perceptions' (ibid.).

Seventh, he discusses causation and memory. Causality seems to be more important than resemblance in this context. He emphasises elsewhere that in general the relation of cause and effect produces the strongest connection in the imagination

---

but he is not concerned with 'beliefs of philosophers' in particular. For a detailed discussion of Ainslie's reading on this point, see Pitson (2002), pp. 76–9. See also Baxter (2008), pp. 79–80.

(ibid., p. 11). And here he says that 'the true idea of the human mind, is to consider it as a system of different perceptions or different existences, which are link'd together by the relation of cause and effect, and mutually produce, destroy, influence, and modify each other' (ibid., p. 261).[27] Hume thinks that the soul or mind or person can properly be compared to a 'republic or commonwealth': 'in like manner the same person may vary his character and disposition, as well as his impressions and ideas, without losing his identity' (ibid.). And memory is 'the source of personal identity' in the sense that it alone acquaints us with the succession of our perceptions. Without memory we would have no notion of causation, 'nor consequently of that chain of causes and effects, which constitute our self or person' (ibid., p. 262). Once we have acquired the notion of causation through memory, we can extend the chain of ideas and, therefore, the identity of our persons 'beyond our memory' (ibid.). Thus 'memory does not so much *produce* as *discover* personal identity, by shewing us the relation of cause and effect among our different perceptions' (ibid.). In what is probably a critical remark directed at Locke, Hume rejects the view that 'memory produces entirely our personal identity'. If we adopted the Lockean view we could not explain why we can 'extend our identity beyond our memory' (ibid.). Moreover, the causal connections among the perceptions lead the imagination to 'feign' an identical self to which those distinct but causally related perceptions belong.[28] Therefore, Hume says that 'the identity, which we ascribe to the mind of man, is only a fictitious one' (ibid., p. 259).

In sum, then, Hume argues that the belief in a single persisting or identical mind or self is due to the imagination (ibid., p. 260), which connects ideas in accordance with certain general principles. The most important connecting principle in this context is causality (ibid., p. 261): it is the causal connection of our perceptions in particular which leads the imagination to construct the belief in an identical self. The notion of causality is, in turn, linked to memory. According to Hume, memory can be said to be a source of personal identity—first, because it alone acquaints us with the succession of our perceptions and provides instances of resembling perceptions; and, second, because without memory we would have no notion of causation, 'nor consequently of that chain of causes and effects, which constitute our self or person' (ibid., p. 262). Once we have acquired the notion of causality through memory, we can extend the chain of ideas, and that is the identity of our persons, 'beyond our memory' (ibid.). Lastly, as was the case with identity ascriptions to objects, the imagination tends to come up with the notion of an entity to which all the experienced perceptions belong as their bearer.

---

[27] Some have argued against the use of the 'bundle' metaphor for Hume's account of the self, preferring the terminology of systematicity to which Hume appeals in this passage. See, for example, Pitson (2002), p. 22; Allison (2008) pp. 295–6; Swain, 'Personal Identity and the Skeptical System of Philosophy', in Traiger (ed.), *The Blackwell Guide to Hume's Treatise* (2006), pp, 133–50, at p. 135. Nevertheless, Pitson and Allison at least continue to use the more common 'bundle' metaphor as well.

[28] Of course, the importance of a causal relationship among perceptions in Hume's discussion of personal identity has been emphasised by several other commentators. See, for example, Winkler (2000), 3–40, esp. 16–18; Pitson (2002), pp. 22–3.

12.5. HUME AND LOCKEAN THEORY

This outline of Hume's argument is not complete, but as far as it goes it closely follows the text in the section on personal identity. And we can see even on its basis how Hume's account relates to Lockean theory. Like Locke and Collins, Hume rejects the view which bases personal identity on the idea of an immaterial thinking substance; moreover, like them, he emphasises the importance of consciousness and memory in explaining personal identity. In Hume, memory fulfils a different function, however. In the Lockean account, consciousness and memory are said to constitute our real personal identity through time. In Hume, memory is crucial insofar as it makes us aware of our past perceptions, helps us to discover resemblances and causal connections among them, and thus aids the imagination in creating the fictitious belief in our personal identity. Here, Butler provides a link between the Lockean accounts and Hume's account. Clearly, Butler's own positive account of personal identity would be acceptable neither to Hume nor to the Lockeans. What is of interest here, rather, is Butler's reading of Locke and Collins. We have seen that according to Butler, 'they do not, mean, that the person is *really* the same, but only that he is so in a fictitious sense: in such a sense only as they assert... that any number of persons whatever, may be the same person'.[29] Butler, of course, rejects this idea. For him, personal identity must be real, and to him this means that it must be based in an immaterial thinking substance or soul. Clarke makes a similar point against Collins, saying that the latter makes '*Individual Personality* to be a mere *external imaginary Denomination*, and nothing at all in reality'.[30] While Collins and Locke would have rejected Butler's and Clarke's reading of their accounts, Hume adopts the notion of a fictitious identity and argues that it makes sense to account for personal identity in this way, and, moreover, that he can explain how this fictitious belief arises.

Our outline of the argument, however, has neglected a crucial aspect of Hume's account to which we shall turn presently. This will be relevant to our discussion of how Hume's account relates to the discussions of personal identity by some of the Scottish Common Sense philosophers. It is expressed in a couple of passages suggesting that the section 'Of Personal Identity' deals with only one of two important features of the issue. Hume says that 'we must distinguish betwixt personal identity, as it regards our thought or imagination, and as it regards our passions or the concern we take in ourselves. The first is our present subject' (*Treatise*, p. 253): that is, here, in Book I. The other passage hints at a positive relation between

---

[29] Butler's dissertation, 'Of Personal Identity', in Gladstone (ed.), *The Works of Joseph Butler*, 2 vols. (1897), vol. 1, p. 322.

[30] Clarke, *A Third Defence of an Argument made use of in a Letter to Mr. Dodwell*, in *A Letter to Mr. Dodwell... Together with A Defence of An Argument made use of in the above-mentioned Letter to Mr. Dodwell, to prove the Immateriality and Natural Immortality of the Soul. In Four Letters to the Author of Some Remarks, &c.... The Sixth Edition. In this Edition are inserted The Remarks on Dr. Clarke's Letter to Mr. Dodwell, and the several Replies to the Doctor's Defences thereof* (1731), p. 290.

the two features of personal identity. When emphasising the importance of the causal relations among our perceptions to the creation of the belief in identity, Hume says that our identity with regard to the passions 'serves to corroborate that with regard to the imagination, by... giving us a present concern for our past and future pains and pleasures' (ibid., p. 261)—for example, by making us aware of the causal connection among our perceptions. Elsewhere he emphasises that there are causal relations among our passions: 'Our passions are found by experience to have a mutual connexion with and dependance on each other' (ibid., p. 195). He believes that our identity with regard to the passions strengthens the imagination in constructing the idea of an identical self, because the former makes the causal relations between our perceptions apparent (ibid., p. 261). In other words, the causal connections among our passions provide support for our belief in the causal connections between our perceptions in general, and they thereby 'corroborate' the fictitious identity of the imagination.

This distinction between personal identity as it regards the imagination, and personal identity as it relates to the issue of self-concern and the emotional aspect of human nature, again reflects the Lockean background of Hume's discussion. We have seen that Locke explains the moral importance of personal identity by stating that the consciousness of perceptions is always accompanied by self-concern. In Locke, the metaphysical or 'speculative' discussion of personal identity and the 'practical' account in terms of self-concern and moral and legal considerations belong together. Hume does not wish to separate these, but his explanation in Book I of how we come to have the belief in personal identity cannot at the same time deal with the issue of self-concern. Therefore, one would perhaps expect Hume to deal with personal identity 'as it regards our passions or the concern we take in ourselves' in Book II of the *Treatise*. There is no section on personal identity, however—no discussion of the issue in Book II. There are not, as some have suggested, two distinct theories of personal identity in Hume.[31] He nowhere speaks of a second theory of personal identity that has a separate task from the 'first' theory. All he is saying is

---

[31] McIntyre, for example, speaks of a separate theory of personal identity in Book II of the *Treatise* that has its own, distinct task. See McIntyre (1989), 545–57, at 547. Other scholars endorsing the two-theories view include Purviance, 'The Moral Self and the Indirect Passions', *Hume Studies*, 23 (1997), 195–212, at 200–1; and Martin and Barresi, *Naturalization of the Soul: Self and Personal Identity in the Eighteenth Century* (2000), pp. 84–5. As Hume does not deal explicitly with personal identity in Book II and only very occasionally mentions the issue there, some have attempted to reconstruct a second theory of personal identity from various passages in which Hume discusses such aspects of selfhood as the passions, character, and so on. See again McIntyre (1989), 545–57, at 553–7. See also Wilson, 'Substance and Self in Locke and Hume', in Barber and Gracia (eds.), *Individuation and Identity in Early Modern Philosophy* (1994), p. 183. Wilson argues that for Hume 'the issue of personal identity *cannot* be resolved without turning to our passions and the concern we take in ourselves' (pp. 177–8); see also Wilson (2008), pp. 353ff. Other scholars have expressed scepticism about this approach. Penelhum, for example, argues that despite the importance of Book II, 'the psychological work of establishing the belief in self-identity is primarily the work of the understanding and the imagination': 'The Self of Book 1 and the Selves of Book 2', *Hume Studies*, 18 (1992), 281–91, at 283. Penelhum is sceptical, therefore, about 'mining' Book II for Hume's theory of the self (288). Waxman, too, argues for the primacy of personal identity as it regards the imagination, *Hume's Theory of Consciousness* (1994), p. 224.

that when accounting for personal identity we must distinguish two related aspects of the issue, and that only one of them is under consideration in Book I. The other is implied by his account of the passions, but does not require another 'theory'. In Hume, then, there is one account of personal identity, but personal identity has two features. As indicated, the second feature is crucial to his account and must not be neglected in discussions of his view about personal identity.[32] We shall return to this issue in more detail below.

12.6. HUME'S APPENDIX

Another important aspect of Hume's discussion of personal identity which we have not yet discussed concerns a section in the *Treatise* that has puzzled generations of scholars and has led to many ingenious analyses and arguments about what Hume might be saying there. This is, of course, the Appendix which he published with Book III of the *Treatise* in November 1740.[33] This includes three-and-a-half pages (in the Selby-Bigge edition) in which Hume reflects on his discussion of personal identity in Book I (ibid., pp. 633–6). It is clear from his letter to Hutcheson of 16 March 1740 that he had some revisions for the Appendix ready by early 1740 at the very latest.[34] In this letter, his comments on the issue of simple ideas correspond to the discussion of the topic in the Appendix (ibid., p. 637) which follows the comments on personal identity. Thus, the comments on personal identity may have been drafted by that time as well, though it seems impossible to provide a precise dating of these comments.[35]

---

[32] Some commentary, however, ignores the importance of the second ('passionate') feature of personal identity altogether. See, for example, Garrett (1997). The book's section on personal identity (pp. 163–6) deals with the Book I account and the Appendix, but without discussing the relevance of Book II in this context. See also Noonan (1999), in which the section on 'The Self and Personal Identity', pp. 187–211, does not even mention the fact that Hume distinguishes between the two features of personal identity. Baxter, too, in his book on Hume on identity, does not consider the importance of Book II to Hume's theory. He cites some relevant passages from the second Book of the *Treatise*, addressing the question of consistency, but does not seem to think that Book II is relevant to Hume's overall account of personal identity. See Baxter (2008), pp. 73–4, 77.

[33] Some scholars, however, simply avoid dealing with the Appendix. See, for example, Noonan's chapter on 'The Self and Personal Identity', in Noonan (1999), pp. 187–211. Noonan mentions the Appendix briefly, saying simply that Hume provides us with no clue about how to read the comments on personal identity, and notes that 'Hume scholars will doubtless continue to speculate' about what Hume meant (p. 210).

[34] *The Letters of David Hume*, Greig (ed.), 2 vols. (1932), vol. 1, pp. 38–40. The comments on the issue of simple ideas are on p. 39.

[35] I am grateful to M. A. Stewart for drawing my attention to these connections concerning the composition of the Appendix. Hume's letter of 16 March, cited in Greig (1932), also refers to a 'conversation' (p. 39) he had with Hutcheson about matters relating to the Appendix. Raynor argues that 'it is probable' that Hutcheson voiced criticisms of Hume's bundle theory of the self at that meeting, and that Hume's second thoughts about the self 'may have been occasioned' by Hutcheson: Raynor, 'Hume and Berkeley's *Three Dialogues*', in Stewart (ed.), *Studies in the Philosophy of the Scottish Enlightenment* (1990), pp. 231–50; at p. 238. But this is, of course, speculation. Moreover, as will be seen below, the bundle theory of the self is not rejected by Hume in the

Hume and the belief in personal identity   399

As indicated, there are numerous interpretations of Hume's reflections on his earlier account of personal identity; indeed, virtually every reader of Hume seems to have his or her own interpretation of those reflections.[36] What does Hume say? He says that the account in Book I is 'very defective' (ibid., p. 635), that it contains 'a considerable mistake' (ibid., p. 623), 'contradictions' (ibid., pp. 633, 636), 'absurdities' (ibid., p. 633), and worse still, that he does not 'know how to correct' his 'former opinions' (ibid., p. 633). He even concedes that 'this difficulty is too hard for my understanding' (ibid., p. 636). He never again discusses the personal identity problem explicitly in any of his published writings.[37]

Hume begins with a review of the argument that led him 'to deny the strict and proper identity and simplicity of a self or thinking being' (ibid., p. 633). He does not seem to reject anything in that argument. He says that his account becomes 'defective' only when it proceeds 'to explain the principle of connexion, which binds them [the perceptions that constitute the mind] together, and makes us attribute to them a real simplicity and identity' (ibid., p. 635). Before explaining this, however, he reviews his explanation of the connecting principle, insofar as it has 'a promising aspect' (ibid.). Here he restates his view that 'thought alone finds personal identity, when reflecting on the train of past perceptions' (ibid.). This seems promising, as it is consistent with what 'most philosophers' think. Hume clearly equates the view of 'most philosophers' with that of Locke—the view 'that personal identity *arises* from consciousness', where consciousness is understood as 'a reflected thought or perception' (ibid.). He then returns to the problem: all his 'hopes vanish', he says, 'when I come to explain the principles, that unite our successive perceptions in our thought or consciousness' (ibid., pp. 635–6). Thought has to do with ideas, and it is the imagination that unites ideas according to the principles of association. It is clear, then, what constitutes a problem for Hume in his account in Book I: it is his attempt to explain how the particular connecting principle of the imagination he has identified in Book I gives rise to the belief in an identical self. This is also clear from the earlier quotation in which he says that his account is 'defective' with respect to that principle of connection which '*makes us attribute*' (my italics) identity to the self (ibid., p. 635).[38] We have seen that according to Book I,

---

Appendix. So, if Hutcheson had voiced criticism of the bundle theory to Hume, the latter did not take this up for the Appendix.

[36] This is not to say that the various interpretations cannot be divided into groups of similar readings. Indeed, there are several such groupings. Apart from Garrett's (1997) very useful typology of 'theories of Hume's second thoughts', pp. 167–80, there are somewhat different groupings in Baxter (2008), pp. 77–80; Ainslie (2008), pp. 148–51; and Ellis, 'The Contents of Hume's Appendix and the Source of his Despair', in *Hume Studies*, 32 (2006), 195–231, at 199–200. A future development might be that we hear of 'theories of theories of Hume's second thoughts'.

[37] Hume's *Abstract* of the *Treatise* briefly mentions the issue but was published in the spring of 1740, prior to the Appendix. What Hume says elsewhere about immortality, for example, does not apply in any direct way to his treatment of personal identity in Book I of the *Treatise*. See the comments in the note below on attempts to trace Hume's utterances about the self after the Appendix.

[38] On this point we seem to be in agreement with scholars such as Winkler (2000), 18–20, 23–4, 30, but in disagreement with Strawson, Garrett, and Allison, for example. Strawson argues that the issue of the Appendix is *not* the Book I account of how we come to have the belief in personal

the main principle of connection that is responsible for the ascription of identity to the self is causality. Hume realizes that the causal connection among perceptions cannot fulfil the role that he had assigned to it in the section 'Of Personal Identity'. He realizes, quite rightly, that pointing to causal connections among perceptions does not explain how we derive the belief in an identical self. It is not clear how their causal connectedness should bring about the idea of a unitary and identical self to which they all belong. Perceptions that are part of the idea of my own self may be causally related to perceptions that I do not attribute to myself at all. While causality is a principle of association and can and does connect ideas in the imagination, it is not clear that the awareness of causal connections among perceptions would give rise to the belief in a unitary and identical self. There may be causally related perceptions of which one belongs to my idea of myself, whereas the other does not.[39] Hume says

identity: Strawson (2001), pp. 83–5. Rather, for Strawson the problem is about the 'evident fact that there is a real unity (not imagination generated) and connection among our successive perceptions' (p. 84). It is 'a problem about what sort of unity or connection can account for the operations of the mind' in accordance with the principles of association of ideas (p. 83). Allison argues that Hume's worry concerns the fictional nature he assigned to the belief in personal identity, and not the adequacy of his genetic account. According to Allison, if the worry were about the latter it would concern merely a 'matter of detail', and it would not be clear 'why it would be of such a concern to Hume': Allison (2008), p. 307. Strawson, too, describes this issue as 'a problem of detail': Strawson (2011a), pp. 117, 129, 135–8. As noted above, however, Hume says explicitly that his self-doubts are about 'what makes us attribute' identity to the self. Nothing in the Appendix seems to suggest that Hume no longer believes that 'feigning' is involved in the construction of the belief in personal identity. Moreover, as we have seen, the main part of the Book I discussion is concerned precisely with how we come to believe in personal identity (and Strawson, for one, agrees that Hume's 'principal aim in "Of personal identity" is . . . to give a psychological explanation of how it is that we come to believe in a continuing single self': Strawson (2011a), p. 71). On our interpretation, then, Hume's second thoughts relate to what he considers to be of prime importance in the Book I account. Also, this interpretation squares well with Hume's account of what would be a solution to his problem. If it was known what the self is beyond the perceptions, then it would be easy to explain how our belief comes about; indeed, the belief would not require explanation, as in this speculative situation we would know that the belief has a basis in reality. Winkler notes, rightly, that the footnote in *Treatise*, p. 636, points to p. 260 of the *Treatise*, where Hume introduces resemblance and causation as the principles of connection that give rise to the belief in personal identity. He concludes, correctly, 'that what troubled Hume in the Appendix is not his metaphysics of the person, but his scientific explanation of attributions of personal identity': Winkler (2000), 18–19. For a detailed discussion of the Appendix footnote, see Ellis (2006), 201–8.

[39] According to Winkler, Shaftesbury is relevant to Hume's argument in the Appendix: Winkler (2000), 3–40. Winkler argues that Hume realized that he made the same mistake as did Shaftesbury, whom he has portrayed as 'a victim of trivial propensities of the imagination' (24). Winkler says: 'If I think of myself as one because of the kind of causal relations Hume follows Shaftesbury in pointing to, why don't I think of tree-and-vine as one, or of cone-and-crossbill, or of mulch-and-worm? Hume tells us in the Appendix that causation cannot unite successive perceptions in our thought or consciousness. I think these Shaftesburian texts point to the reason why. Causation cannot explain why we unite perceptions we call a mind or person because it is equally present when we experience little or no inclination to unify, much less an inclination to think of the unified complex as simple and strictly identical' (25). But Hume refers to Shaftesbury in I.iv.6, not in the Appendix, and the footnote on Shaftesbury in I.iv.6 (see above) does not even refer to the specific issue of personal identity. To suggest that Hume had a fresh look at Shaftesbury on unity in general, and then realized the problem in his account of personal identity through time, seems to be entirely speculative. For a critique of the view that causal connections among our perceptions can lead to the

that he could solve his personal identity problem only if he could give up at least one of two principles of his epistemology: (1) that all perceptions are distinct existences; and (2) that the mind never perceives any real connection among distinct existences. If he could give up (2), then we would be able to tell which perceptions belong to the same self. If not all perceptions were distinct existences (1), we could tell which belong to the one mind and not to the other. Thus, the problem with his account in terms of a causal connection would disappear if he could give up either (1) or (2).[40] He cannot give up these principles, however, as they are fundamental principles of his philosophy of human nature.

Given that Hume rejects his own account, can we forget about his theory of personal identity altogether? The answer is a resounding 'no'. Hume does not reject everything he says about personal identity in Book I. Indeed, most of what he says there is not affected by his self-doubts. These concern only one particular issue—an important one, to be sure, especially from Hume's point of view—but they do not concern his other comments about the self and its identity. Hume thinks that he cannot, consistently with some basic principles of his philosophy, explain how the fictitious belief in self-identity arises. This is an important issue for Hume, so his distress is understandable. It remains true, however, that other aspects of his discussion are not targeted in the Appendix. He still believes all of the following:

(i) Belief in an identical thinking *substance* cannot be justified.
(ii) Inner experience and observation reveal only collections or *bundles of perceptions*.
(iii) We nevertheless have a *natural propension* to ascribe identity to the self.
(iv) This ascription of identity commonly involves a *fiction* of the imagination.
(v) We need to distinguish between personal identity as it regards *the imagination*, and personal identity 'as it regards *our passions or the concern we take in ourselves*'.

None of the claims (i) through to (v) are challenged by Hume in the Appendix. What is challenged is his earlier explanation of how the ascription of identity comes about. A substantial part, then, of the Book I account remains in place as far as Hume is

---

idea of one mind, see also Stroud (1977), pp. 125–6. But Stroud does not seem to think that this was Hume's problem in the Appendix. Stroud thinks that Hume sensed a problem of circularity in his account: Stroud (1977), pp. 138–40. On the issue of circularity, see comments below.

[40] Green argues that for Hume there is an 'inconsistency between these principles and his attempt to explain the idea of a temporary extended self': 'The Idea of a Momentary Self and Hume's Theory of Personal Identity', *British Journal for the History of Philosophy*, 7 (1999), 103–22. The principles are inconsistent with the explanation of such an idea, 'because they rule out the only two ways that perceptions could be genuinely united' (120). Green concedes, however, that his reading is 'mainly speculation' (121). He ties this reading to the view that Hume thought he had to explain how the idea of a temporally extended self is generated by repeated ideas of a momentary self (121). According to Green, Hume's problem was that he did not diagnose the roots of his problem: the distinction between the idea of a momentary self that comes with every perception a person has, and what those perceptions represent (121). Green also concedes that Hume does not explicitly state the attributes of an idea of a momentary self (122).

concerned. He is neither wholly dissatisfied with his Book I treatment, nor is he dissatisfied with the whole section on personal identity.[41]

12.7. THE *ABSTRACT*

Several months prior to the publication of the Appendix, early in 1740, Hume published (anonymously) a pamphlet entitled *An Abstract of a Book lately Published; entituled, A Treatise of Human Nature, &c. wherein the Chief Argument of that Book is farther Illustrated and Explained.*[42] The purpose of this pamphlet is to promote the *Treatise* and defend it against criticism. Since we know that some comments for the Appendix were ready by early 1740 (see above), it is probable that composition of the Appendix and the *Abstract* overlapped—at least to some extent.[43]

The *Abstract* includes a very brief account of themes discussed in the chapter on personal identity (1740 edn., pp. 24–5; Norton and Norton edn., p. 414). Hume may well have penned his second thoughts on the issue prior to, or concurrently with, composing the *Abstract*, although it is not surprising that it does not refer in any way to these, considering the purpose of the pamphlet. In any case, what Hume says in the *Abstract* seems to be consistent with the second thoughts in the Appendix. The *Abstract* does not even refer to the question of how we come to believe in our personal identity—which is, as we saw, what the Appendix is about. The *Abstract* focuses instead on features of the Book I account that the Appendix leaves intact. It emphasises 'that the soul, *as far as we can conceive it* [my italics], is nothing but a system or train of different perceptions, those of heat and cold, love and anger, thoughts and sensations; all united together, but without any perfect simplicity or identity' (ibid.). He then critically refers to Descartes's view that thought in general is the essence of the mind. For Hume it is only 'our several particular perceptions, that compose the mind. I say, *compose* the mind, not *belong* to it. The mind is not a substance, in which the perceptions inhere' (ibid., p. 25). The notion of the mind as a substance is an 'unintelligible' one (ibid.)—a point that Hume makes in *Treatise* I.iv.5. 'We have no idea of substance of any kind, since we have no impression of any substance either material or spiritual. We *know* [my italics]

---

[41] Thus, Noonan's (1999) assertion, in *Hume on Knowledge*—that in the Appendix Hume 'is *wholly* [my italics] dissatisfied with his treatment of the topic in the main body of the *Treatise*' (p. 187)—is false.

[42] Keynes and Sraffa (eds.), *An Abstract of A Treatise of Human Nature 1740: A Pamphlet hitherto unknown by David Hume* (1938; reprinted, 1990). Quotations from Norton and Norton (eds.), *A Treatise of Human Nature* (2000), pp. 403–17. For the time of the *Abstract*'s original publication, see Hume's letter to Francis Hutcheson of 4 March 1740, in *Letters*, vol. 1, pp. 37–8.

[43] I am grateful to M. A. Stewart for drawing my attention to points of detail in this context. In a letter to Hutcheson of 4 March 1740 Hume says that he 'sent up the Abstract' to London after a review of the *Treatise*, an 'Article with regard to my Book' (*Letters*, p. 38), had been published in *The History of the Works of the Learned*. This was the issue containing book news up to November–December 1739, so would not have appeared until January 1740. As Stewart points out, it is likely that Hume composed the *Abstract* around December 1739.

nothing but particular qualities and perceptions... So our *idea* [my italics] of any mind is only that of particular perceptions, without the notion of any thing we call substance, either simple or compound' (ibid.).

In the *Abstract*, then, Hume emphasises only two points from the account in Book I: belief in an identical thinking *substance* cannot be justified, and inner experience and observation reveal only collections or *bundles of perceptions*. These points are not challenged by his second thoughts in the Appendix, and so, again, there is no inconsistency here between the *Abstract* and the Appendix. The *Abstract* neither mentions his claim that we nevertheless have a *propension* to ascribe identity to the self, nor considers his Book I explanation of how this propension comes about. In the *Abstract* he simply does not refer to the main point of his second thoughts about personal identity.

12.8. HUME ON CONSCIOUSNESS AND REFLECTION

As we have seen, Hume variously makes use of the notion of consciousness both in the Appendix and the Book I account of personal identity. What is his notion of consciousness? Not much has been written on this important question. The problem is that there is no section or chapter on the topic in Hume—indeed, no discussion at all of consciousness. Hume applies a certain conception of consciousness in his discussion of personal identity and elsewhere without, however, explaining it in any detail. When scholars refer to his 'theory of consciousness', they typically refer to his entire 'philosophy of mind', assuming that 'consciousness' simply means 'mind or thought in general'.[44] Although there are passages in which he seems to use 'consciousness' in this sense[45], this is not the notion of consciousness that he mainly employs and is relevant to his dicussion of personal identity. In the above-cited passage from the Appendix Hume states, rather, that 'consciousness is nothing but a reflected thought or perception' (*Treatise*, p. 635). This is his only explicit statement about what consciousness is, and it seems to account for it in terms of reflection. We have seen that according to Hume 'the thought alone finds personal identity, when *reflecting* [my italics] on the train of past perceptions (ibid.)'.[46] He suggests here, however, that this can be interpreted in terms of consciousness, given that consciousness is to be understood as a 'reflected thought or perception'. Other passages seem to confirm this understanding of 'consciousness'. For example, he says that ideas 'make their

---

[44] See, for example, Grau, *Die Entwicklung des Bewusstseinsbegriffe im XVII. und XVIII. Jahrhundert* (1916), p. 113; Waxman (1994).

[45] See, for example, *Treatise*, p. 1, where Hume speaks of 'our thought or consciousness'. In *An Enquiry Concerning Human Understanding* (abbr. *Enquiry* 1) Hume says that 'the only proper object of hatred or vengeance is a person or creature, *endowed with thought and consciousness*' (*Enquiries Concerning Human Understanding and Concerning the Principles of Morals*, ed. Selby-Bigge, third edn. (1975), p. 98; my italics). Compare also Hume's essay 'On the Immortality of the Soul', in which he refers to 'consciousness, or that system of thought': *Essays Moral, Political and Literary* (1963), p. 598.

[46] See also *Treatise*, p. 260, where Hume says that identity is a quality which we attribute to different perceptions, 'because of the union of their ideas in the imagination, when we *reflect* [my italics] upon them'.

passage into the mind' through the 'common channels of sensation or reflection', a little later referring to 'consciousness and sensation', and obviously using 'consciousness' and 'reflection' synonymously (ibid., pp. 157–8). Although his use of consciousness as 'reflected thought or perception' may not amount exactly to the same thing as what the synonymous use of 'consciousness' and 'reflection' suggests, it appears from these passages that for Hume, consciousness is to be understood in terms of reflection. If consciousness is understood in this way, then it seems clear that to Hume, consciousness is, like reflection, a form of relating to one's own self. But is it the same as reflection? And what is reflection, according to Hume?

As in other thinkers we have considered above, in Hume reflection involves an explicit turning to one's own self or perceptions. For example, he asks us to turn our attention to what we feel or observe 'when we reflect on any of those sensations or movements' (*Enquiry* 1, p. 18). In his discussion of personal identity, too, Hume appeals several times to what we discover about ourselves through reflection; that is, through observing our own mental operations. That I 'never can perceive this *self* without some one or more perceptions', nor can 'perceive any thing else but the perceptions', is what I discover 'when I turn my reflexion on *myself*' (*Treatise*, p. 634). In reflection, our own perceptions become the objects of attention and observation. Reflection, then, is a special kind of *perception*—a higher-order perception that has other perceptions as its object. Moreover, Hume assumes that reflection can relate to past perceptions as well as to present ones. The imagination constructs personal identity, as we have seen, 'when reflecting on the train of past perceptions' (ibid., p. 635).

However, would Hume simply identify reflection with consciousness? As we have seen in thinkers such as Arnauld, use of the terminology of *reflexio* in accounting for consciousness does not necessarily mean that the two notions are identical. *Reflexio* may merely indicate that both concepts denote a relating to one's own self, but they may still be different kinds of self-relation. And indeed, several passages suggest that Hume implies a distinction between consciousness and reflection. As is obvious from the passages cited earlier, he characterizes reflection as an explicit turning of the mind's attention to its own perceptions. By contrast, he often describes consciousness as an immediate relation of oneself to oneself: for example, when he says that perceptions are 'immediately present to us by consciousness' (ibid., p. 212). It is through consciousness, but not through reflection, that operations of the mind are 'most intimately present to us' (*Enquiry* 1, p. 13). Unlike reflection, moreover, consciousnesss always accompanies our perceptions. For Hume, 'all actions and sensations of the mind are known to us by consciousness' (*Treatise*, p. 190).[47] Thus, 'consciousness' denotes an immediate and constant presence to my own self throughout my waking life. Indeed, Hume links the language of immediacy and intimacy of presence many times to the notion of consciousness (but not to that of

---

[47] This is also implied in the following statement: 'When my perceptions are remov'd for any time, as by sound sleep; so long am I insensible of myself, and may truly be said not to exist': *Treatise*, p. 252.

reflection)[48]; for instance, when referring to 'that succession of related ideas and impressions, of which we have an intimate memory and consciousness' (ibid., p. 277).[49]

The terminology of *feeling* that Hume uses occasionally for consciousness points to the same kind of immediate self-relation. For example, he speaks of the 'sentiment or consciousness' (*Enquiry* 1, p. 67) or of an 'inward sentiment or consciousness' (ibid., p. 66).[50] Other passages too suggest a difference between consciousness and reflection in Hume (ibid., p. 92).[51] According to Hume, consciousness, in contradistinction to all forms of reflection, is the most basic or fundamental self-relation. The immediate grasp of our own mental operations which consciousness affords is accompanied by absolute certainty: 'The only existences, of which we are certain, are perceptions, which being immediately present to us by consciousness, command our strongest assent' (*Treatise*, p. 212). It is clearly the immediacy of the self-relation through consciousness which Hume thinks is responsible for the fact that 'consciousness never deceives'—is absolutely certain (*Enquiry* 1, p. 66).[52]

Because of its immediacy and certainty, consciousness seems to be seen by Hume as a basis for reflection. He holds that 'what is really distinct to the immediate perception may be distinguished by reflexion' (ibid., p. 14). He points out, however, that despite the fact that our mental operations are immediately present to us by consciousness, distinguishing and examining them by reflection is not an easy task. Mere consciousness does not seem to him to be of great help here. 'It is remarkable concerning the operations of the mind', he says, 'that, though most intimately present to us, yet whenever they become the object of reflexion they seem involved in obscurity; nor can the eye readily find those lines and boundaries, which discriminate and distinguish them' (ibid., p. 13).[53] Obviously, then, the absolute certainty that is distinctive of the self-relation *via* consciousness does not, according to Hume, extend to other forms of self-relation such as reflection. In making these points, he clearly implies a distinction between consciousness and reflection.[54]

---

[48] As far as I know, there is only one exception: Hume, *Treatise*, p. 240: 'whatever we feel internally by reflection'.

[49] See also Hume, *Treatise*, pp. 317–18, 320, 329, 339–40, 354.

[50] For the notions of sentiment and feeling in Hume, see Brissenden, '"Sentiment": Some Uses of the Word in the Writings of David Hume', in Brissenden (ed.), *Studies in the Eighteenth Century* (1968), pp. 89–107, at pp. 91–3 and 96–100. On p. 399 of the *Treatise*, Hume speaks of the '*internal impression we feel and are conscious of, when we knowingly give rise to any new motion of our body, or new perception of our mind.*'

[51] Noxon holds that a notion of 'reflexive consciousness' is implied by Hume's account of memory; yet he makes the not uncommon mistake of identifying this 'reflexive consciousness' with Locke's 'reflection': 'Senses of Identity in Hume's Treatise', *Dialogue*, 8 (1969), 367–84, esp. 379.

[52] See also Hume, *Treatise*, pp. 190, 212. Here, Hume is in agreement with Locke, Browne, and Charles Mein, the author of the *Essay on Consciousness*.

[53] See also *Enquiry* 1, p. 60: 'But the finer sentiments of the mind, the operations of the understanding, the various agitations of the passions, though really in themselves distinct, easily escape us, when *surveyed by reflection*' (my italics).

[54] Bricke, too, points out that Hume accepts the possibility of 'introspective mishaps', and that he denies this possibility on what Bricke calls the 'level of mere awareness'. Bricke ascribes to Hume a distinction between 'awareness' and 'introspective judgement': Bricke, *Hume's Philosophy of Mind*

Although Hume implies this distinction, however, it is not clear whether he thinks of consciousness as an inherent quality of thought itself or as a higher-order perception of a different kind. Some passages suggest that to Hume consciousness is, like reflection, a higher-order perception. The feature of 'immediacy' alone does not necessarily mean that consciousness is thought of as an inherent quality of thought itself, as we have seen. Moreover, when Hume speaks, for example, of the 'impression or consciousness' (*Treatise*, p. 318) and the 'immediate feeling or perception' (ibid., p. 305), he seems to suggest that like reflection, consciousness is a higher-order perception of other perceptions. If it is true that to Hume, consciousness is, like reflection, a higher-order perception, then his account raises the old problem of an infinite regress of consciousness, since he also claims that '*all* actions and sensations of the mind' (my italics) are accompanied by consciousness.

More important in the present context, however, is Hume's distinction between consciousness as affording immediate and absolute certainty on the one hand, and reflection as not characterized by such immediacy and certainty on the other. For it is through consciousness that we are immediately aware and certain of the existence of individual perceptions, but it is on the basis of inner observation or reflection that we judge the mind to be 'nothing but' a bundle of perceptions. Hume believes that 'consciousness never deceives', but he leaves open the possibility that our introspective judgement may not represent the true nature of things.

This point is important—not least because the target of most of Hume's early critics is the 'bundle of perceptions' view of the mind or self. That is to say, these critics realize at least that the bundle view of the self is not affected by Hume's second thoughts in the Appendix. They do not suppose, rightly, that Hume changed his mind about that, and they thus feel free to target that position and its perceived implication for the issue of personal identity.

(1980), p. 125. Garrett, arguing against Baxter's (2008) view in *Hume's Difficulty* that 'consciousness's ideas represent the past pereceptions as they are' (p. 69), also appears to accept a distinction between consciousness and reflection in Hume. Garrett's statement that for Hume consciousness is 'an immediate awareness involved in *having* a perception' suggests that he ascribes a first-order understanding of consciousness to Hume: Garrett (2009), 439–40. As noted below, however, it is not obvious that Hume does adopt such a view.

13

Hume and the bundle view of the self

The Scottish Common Sense philosophers, such as Beattie, Reid, and Stewart, all deal with the problem of personal identity, and they reject both Locke's and Hume's accounts of the issue.[1] Very roughly speaking, their own view is that there are certain fundamental principles which we have to take for granted and accept as true. These principles require no argument or proof; they are immediately and intuitively known and consented to by all mankind. They are part of human 'common sense'. Personal identity is said to be one of these Common Sense principles. Thus Reid states that 'another first principle is our own personal identity and continued existence'. 'This we know immediately, and not by reasoning'. Everybody has an 'immediate and irresistible conviction' of his own identity.[2]

13.1. CRITIQUE OF THE BUNDLE VIEW OF THE SELF: BEATTIE'S AND REID'S OBJECTIONS TO HUME'S ACCOUNT

It is not surprising, then, that Reid and company have little patience with Hume's tortuous analysis of personal identity. In fact, Beattie says about Hume that 'it is not necessary' that he should 'examine his arguments' about personal identity, 'because the point in question is *self-evident*, and therefore all reasoning on the other side *un*philosophical and irrational'.[3] Nevertheless, he does comment on the implications of Hume's position for morality and religion. We have seen that the identity of the self is regarded by most philosophers of the time as presupposed by the Christian dogma of immortality as well as by our everyday concern for the future. Beattie refers to these issues in his critique of Hume's 'bundle' account of the mind:

If I were to believe, with Mr Hume, and some others, that my mind is perpetually changing, so as to become every different moment a different thing, the remembrance of past, or the

---

[1] We shall deal with their positive theories of personal identity in more detail in *The Enlightened Subject* (in preparation). Here we are concerned with their critique of Hume which requires only a preliminary account of their own positions on personal identity.
[2] Reid, *Essays on the Intellectual Powers of Man*, ed. Brookes (2002), p. 476. Compare also the following statement: 'I take it for granted that all the thoughts I am conscious of, or remember, are the thoughts of one and the same thinking principle, which I call *myself*, or my *mind*': ibid., p. 42.
[3] Beattie, *An Essay on the Nature and Immutability of Truth* (1770), p. 80.

anticipation of future good or evil, could give me neither pleasure or pain; yea, though I were to believe, that cruel death would overtake me within an hour, I should be no more concerned, than if I were told that a certain elephant, three thousand years hence, would be sacrificed on the top of Mount Atlas. To a man who doubts the individuality or identity of his own mind, virtue, truth, religion, good and evil, hope and fear, are absolutely nothing.[4]

In short, Hume's view, that the self is nothing but a succession of different perceptions, undermines morality and religion. Beattie's critique implies that he believes that Hume makes an ontological claim, reducing the self to perceptions, and that he denies the existence of a self underlying the perceptions. This is also Reid's reading of Hume and the basis of his critique. Reid says that according to Hume, 'I am ... that succession of related ideas and impressions of which I have the intimate memory and consciousness' (*Intellectual Powers*, p. 473). He continues:

But who is the *I* that has this memory and consciousness of a succession of ideas and impressions? Why, it is nothing but that succession itself... This succession of ideas and impressions, not only remembers and is conscious, but... it judges, reasons, affirms, denies; nay... it eats and drinks, and is sometimes merry, and sometimes sad. If these things can be ascribed to a succession of ideas and impressions, in a consistency with common sense, I should be very glad to know what is nonsense. (ibid., pp. 473–4)

Reid charges Hume with nothing less than having 'annihilated', as he says, 'even his own mind' (ibid., p. 470).[5] Unlike Beattie in the earlier quotation, he does not focus here on the implications of Hume's account for morality, but on the need for a real self, distinct from perceptions, for a subject of thought and experience that allows us to account for mental activity in general.[6] Elsewhere, however, Reid too comments on morality: 'If one set of ideas makes a covenant, another breaks it, and a third is punished for it, there is reason to think that justice is no natural virtue in this system.'[7] This comment assumes that the bundle view destroys personal identity on which morality and responsibility depend.

We have seen in previous Chapters that views about the nature of the mind have implications for the position that is adopted about personal identity—and views about the nature of personal identity depend on whether we adopt a materialist or an immaterialist position about the nature of the mind. Similarly, the bundle view as

---

[4] Beattie, *An Essay*, pp. 75–6.

[5] Of course, it was not only the Common Sense philosophers who made this criticism. Compare the following passage in a letter from George L. Scott to Lord Monboddo, 3 April 1773: 'Our friend Hume, strikes out even his own spirit, and leaves nothing but Ideas!': quoted in Raynor, 'Hume and Berkeley's *Three Dialogues*', in Stewart (ed.), *Studies in the Philosophy of the Scottish Enlightenment* (1990), p. 249. Stewart has shown that in Edinburgh 'Hume was being read ... as a Berkeleyan, or Berkeley as a Humean': Stewart, 'Berkeley and the Rankenian Club', in Berman (ed.), *George Berkeley: Essays and Replies* (1986), pp. 25–45, at p. 40. Stewart points out that a certain George Wallace argued that Hume's account of the self is inconsistent with his alleged immaterialism (p. 41). The reference is to Wallace, *A System of the Principles of the Laws of Scotland* (1760), p. 42.

[6] See also Reid, *An Inquiry into the Human Mind: on the Principles of Common Sense*, ed. Brookes (2000), pp. 32–3.

[7] Reid, *Inquiry*, p. 35. See also the comments by Grave in *The Scottish Philosophy of Common Sense* (1960), pp. 201–3.

such is not a view about personal identity, but one that is regarded as having implications for the issue of identity, as is obvious from the comments by Beattie and Reid. The bundle view about the mind or self as understood here includes the 'no owner' view of the self: the self just *is* experiences or perceptions, which can and do exist without a subject that experiences or perceives. There is no subject or self apart from the perceptions; there are only perceptions but no perceivers. And Hume himself seems to think that this view has implications for personal identity. If the mind or self is 'nothing but a bundle or collection of different perceptions', then there is 'properly no ... *identity*' of the self through time (*Treatise*, pp. 252–3). Hume's critics, such as Beattie and Reid, agree. The bundle view 'annihilates' the self and thereby its identity and moral accountability and concern for the future. Hume recognizes the fact, however, that we nevertheless have a belief in personal identity, and he attempts to explain how this comes about.

The criticisms levelled against the bundle view here are similar to those proposed by immaterialist philosophers of the mind against materialists. We have seen that immaterialist philosophers of the mind, such as Ralph Cudworth, accuse materialists of destroying the self, reducing it to a '*Heap* of *Substances*',[8] thereby making impossible the personal identity, immortality, and moral responsibility of the self.[9] The bundle view that Beattie, Reid, and many present-day writers ascribe to Hume is not identical with the materialist position, however.[10] It denies the existence and even necessity of any owner or subject of experience—even that of a material one. The materialist position leaves open the possibility for a material owner or subject of experience that retains its identity through time—even if eighteenth-century materialists, as a matter of fact, have difficulties accounting for identity.[11] Moreover, it makes a difference whether one claims the self to be a system of material parts (or, negatively, a 'heap of substances') or a collection of perceptions—where the ontological nature of the latter may remain undetermined. Also, a 'heap of substances' suggests a multitude of subjects, but not that there is no subject at all, which is what Hume's bundle view seems to maintain. It is important to emphasise the difference between the 'Humean' bundle view and the materialist position when considering the historical context. For it has been claimed that Hume's bundle view has certain 'predecessors' which may have inspired him to adopt such a view.

---

[8] Cudworth, *The True Intellectual System of the Universe* (1678), p. 830, where he emphasises that the self must be 'one Single Substance'.

[9] We shall deal in detail with eighteenth-century materialist accounts of identity, and Reid's critique, in *The Enlightened Subject* (in preparation). Reid says of Priestley's materialism too, that it annihilates the self, personal identity, and the afterlife. See the (untitled) review of Priestley's edition of Hartley in *Monthly Review*, 53 (1775–76), 380–90, at 382. For Reid's authorship, see Raynor (1990), pp. 231–50, at pp. 249–50.

[10] Some have contended for a materialist reading of Hume (see notes on Wright, Strawson, and Buckle below). It is plain, however, that Hume does not appeal to a materialist account of the mind in the section on personal identity.

[11] See Thiel, 'Locke and Eighteenth-Century Materialist Conceptions of Personal Identity', *The Locke Newsletter*, 29 (1998a), 59–83.

13.2. VARIETIES OF THE BUNDLE VIEW. 'ANTICIPATIONS' OF THE HUMEAN POSITION: HUTCHESON, BAYLE, BERKELEY, RÉGIS, BOULAINVILLER, AND DESCHAMPS

Hume emphasises that what he says about the mind as a bundle of perceptions is 'peculiar to himself' (*Abstract*, p. 24; Norton and Norton, p. 414). Some commentators have argued, however, that there were 'anticipations' of Hume's view of the mind in the seventeenth and eighteenth centuries.[12] In this section we shall examine the alleged anticipations. For example, even Cudworth's discussion, cited above, of the view that the self is a '*Heap of Substances*' may seem to refer to a Humean bundle view. In fact, however, his critique is aimed at a *materialist* theory of the mind and its alleged consequences. We have seen that Anthony Collins tends towards materialism but adopts a largely Lockean view about personal identity; and the Lockean view is not a bundle theory of the self. Butler, Clarke, and the Scriblerians attack a materialistically inclined version of Locke's account—not the kind of bundle view of the self that is ascribed to Hume.[13]

Francis Hutcheson too, in a passage from *A System of Moral Philosophy* in which he seems to be rejecting the bundle theory, is in fact dealing with materialist accounts of the mind. Hutcheson does not cite anyone who actually holds the bundle view, nor does he debate it there. His comment appears in the context of a discussion of the possibility of a future life. He puts forward the standard anti-materialist argument that the unity of consciousness is not consistent with a material system, and he cites Aristotle, Clarke, and Baxter in support of his position here.[14] In another, much earlier passage, however, Hutcheson seems to debate the bundle view. It appears in a letter from 1727, in which he cites and rejects the view that the mind is 'only a system of perceptions'. This is all, however, that is said about the view, and it is not certain from this expression what precisely the view is and how it is argued for. He seems to be addressing a view that extends Berkeley's analysis of body or material substances to the mind. He complains that the addressee, William Mace,

---

[12] In a very enlightening and important article that we have cited several times already, Raynor argues that 'the bundle theory of the self was being debated' by Cudworth, Bayle, Hutcheson, and Berkeley, and satirized by the Scriblerians in *Memoirs of Martinus Scriblerus*. He also holds that Collins advocated 'something like the bundle theory'. Raynor (1990), pp. 231–50, at p. 237.

[13] Kerby-Miller (ed.), *Memoirs of the Extraordinary Life, Works, and Discoveries of Martinus Scriblerus* (1950), pp. 138, 140.

[14] Hutcheson says: 'The opinion [of a future life] is natural to mankind, and what their Creator has designed they should entertain.' Tis confirmed not a little by arguments which shew the subject of thought, reason, and affections not to be a divisible system of distinct substances, as every part of matter is. The simplicity and unity of consciousness could not result from modes dispersed and inherent in an aggregate of different bodies in distinct places*. Nor is the activity of the soul consistent with the passiveness of matter. (*This argument from our consciousness of the unity of the perceiver and agent, in all that multitude of sensations, judgements, affections, desires, is well urged by Aristotle *de Anima*, I. i. and by Dr. Sam. Clarke. See also Mr. Baxter's ingenious book on this subject).': Hutcheson, *A System of Moral Philosophy* (1755), vol. 1, p. 200.

has 'fallen into' a certain 'scheme of thinking', and 'not only by our Dr. Berkly's books, and by some of the old academics, but by frequent conversation with some few speculative friends in Dublin'. Not unlike Beattie and Reid, however, Hutcheson argues that this view is incompabtible with the 'unity of person', suggesting that it does indeed annihilate the mind, personal identity, and self-concern and the possibility of a future life.[15] As he argues elsewhere, the qualities of the self that we experience rather point to an immaterial or spirtual substance as the bearer of those qualities.[16] His target, then, is materialism, not a Humean bundle view of the self.

Pierre Bayle, however, criticizing Leibniz, seems to argue that 'it is impossible to understand how a multitude of perceptions can exist in an indivisible substance'.[17] Indeed, Bayle says that Leibniz's theory

> would be more comprehensible if we supposed that man's soul is not a spirit but rather a legion of spirits, each of which has its functions that begin and end precisely as demanded by the changes that occur in the human body ... But then the soul of man would no longer be a substance. It would be a *being by aggregation*, a heap or collection of substances, just like material beings. We are seeking here for a single being that may form at one time joy, at another grief, and so on. We are not looking for several beings, one of whom produces hope, and another dispair, and so on.[18]

It may seem that Bayle 'dangled' the bundle theory of the self 'in front of Leibniz as a necessary but unpalatable option'.[19] What Bayle is in fact dangling in front of Leibniz, however, is the idea of a multiplicity of perceiving subjects, not that of a

---

[15] Hutcheson's letter to William Mace, 6 September 1727: 'I was well apprized of the scheme of thinking you are fallen into, not only by our Dr. Berkly's books, and by some of the old academics, but by frequent conversation with some new speculative friends in Dublin. As to your notion of our mind as only a system of perceptions, I imagine you'll find that every one has an immediate simple perception of *self*, to which all his other perceptions are some way connected, otherwise I cannot conceive how I could be any way affected with pleasure or pain from any past action, affection, or perception, or have any present uneasiness or concern about any future event or perception; or how there could be any unity of person, or any desire of future happiness or aversion of misery. My past perceptions or future ones are not my present, but would be as distinct as your perceptions are from mine: that it is otherwise I believe everyone is conscious': *The European Magazine, and London Review*, 14 (September 1788), 158. The passage is quoted in part by Raynor (1990), p. 237. *The European Magazine* gives no further information about this letter, except for stating that Mace was a 'Professor at Gresham College' and that this letter was 'never before printed'.

[16] Hutcheson says that there is a special kind of perceptions, 'when we are conscious of knowledge, goodness, faith, integrity, friendliness, contempt of sensual pleasures, publick spirit. These we feel to be the immediate qualities of this *self*, the personal excellencies in which all its true dignity consists, as its baseness would consist in the contrary dispositions. We know these qualities, and their names, as well as we do the sensible ones: we feel that these have no relation to the body, or its parts, dimensions, spaces, figures. *Nature* thus intimates to us a spirit distinct from the body over which it presides, in regulating its motions, as clearly as it intimates the difference of our bodies from external objects. Nay it intimates a greater difference, or disparity of substance; as all the qualities of the soul are quite disparate and of a different kind from those of matter; and 'tis only by their qualities that substances are known': *Moral Philosophy*, pp. 201–2.

[17] Raynor (1990), p. 246.

[18] Bayle, *Dictionnaire historique et critique* (1697), entry 'Rorarius', quoted from Bayle, *Historical and Critical Dictionary: Selections*, ed. Popkin (1965), p. 252.

[19] Raynor (1990), p. 237.

bundle of subjectless perceptions. The view he is considering here is like the materialist position, as Bayle himself points out. While this is similar to the bundle theory, it is not identical with it.[20]

We noted in Chapter 8 that Berkeley considers the bundle view in his early notebooks. Here he states that 'mind is a congeries of perceptions. Take away perceptions and you take away the mind, put the perceptions and you put the mind'.[21] We saw also, however, that there is no unitary account of the self in the notebooks. Rather, Berkeley seems to be torn between two positions: the 'congeries' view and the unity picture of the self (*Philosophical Commentaries*, no. 581). Berkeley considers the bundle view, but in the end rejects it. It is unlikely that Hume would have been aware of Berkeley's early comments. It has been pointed out, however, that Berkeley also considers the bundle view in print.[22] The very brief passage appears in the 1734 version of Berkeley's *Three Dialogues between Hylas and Philonous*. Here Hylas questions whether Philonous can claim there is a spiritual substance or soul, given that he concedes that we have no idea of it.[23] Hylas then proposes the bundle view to Philonous, as a proposed *reductio* of immaterialism. Hylas says that 'in consequence of your own principles, it should follow that you are only a system of floating ideas, without any substance to support them' (ibid., p. 233). Philonous responds with the well-known Berkeleyan view that although we can have no idea of such a substance, 'we have a *notion* of spiritual substance' (ibid.). Now, can we discern in these passages 'the inspiration of Hume's bundle theory of the self'? Did Hume 'realize that he was adopting what Berkeley had shied away from accepting?'[24] In our view it seems highly unlikely that Hume should have been inspired by such a brief statement of a view that Berkeley rejects. It is, of course, possible that the passage did have an impact on Hume, even if there is no evidence in support of this thesis.

Other writers have maintained that there are French versions of the Humean bundle view. However, most of the contenders—such as Condillac and Rousseau[25]—are post Hume's *Treatise*. More important in the present context are

---

[20] As Raynor reports, in *Theodicy* Leibniz insists against Bayle 'that he could not understand the difficulty which Bayle had raised, because "everyone who recognizes immaterial and indivisible substances also attributes to them a multitude of simultaneous perceptions"; and he added... that "it is no proof of the impossibility of a matter merely to say that one cannot understand this thing or that"': Raynor (1990), p. 247. Bayle appears to have favoured the view that the soul is an indivisible and immaterial substance; compare Mijuskovic, *The Achilles of Rationalist Arguments* (1974), pp. 41–2.

[21] Berkeley, *Philosophical Commentaries, Generally Called the Commonplace Book*, ed. Luce (1945), no. 580. See also no. 577: 'The very existence of Ideas constitutes the soul'; and compare nos. 637–9 and 614–15.

[22] Raynor (1990), pp. 235–9.

[23] *The Works of George Berkeley, Bishop of Cloyne*, ed. Luce and Jessop, 9 vols. (1948–57), vol. 2, p. 232.

[24] Ibid., pp. 236–7. For a different account of the relationship between Hume and Berkeley on this issue, see Bettcher, 'Berkeley and Hume on the Self and Self-Consciousness', in *Topics in Early Modern Philosophy of Mind*, ed. Miller (2009), pp. 195–224.

[25] Davies, *'Conscience' as Consciousness: The Idea of Self-Awareness in French Philosophical Writing from Descartes to Diderot* (1990), pp. 79–84. We shall deal with Condillac and Rousseau in *The Enlightened Subject* (in preparation), arguing against the ascription of the bundle view to their accounts of the self.

philosophers who may have inspired Hume with their thoughts about the nature of the self.

It has been argued, for example, that the Cartesian Pierre-Sylvain Régis, in his *Système de philosophie* (1690), 'anticipates' the Humean bundle theory of the mind.[26] We noted in Chapter 1 that Régis extends Descartes's notion of a single universal material substance to the mental sphere.[27] The relevant claim in the present context is that for Régis, individual minds are 'bundles of qualities' in the universal mental substance. The view is that Régis 'suggests' that 'individual minds consist of their thoughts' only, and that this 'anticipates Hume's analysis of the mind' (Lennon, 1994, p. 27). It is true that Régis is quite explicit about individual minds being modal, rather than substantial beings.[28] The thesis that his account amounts to an anticipation of a Humean bundle theory is nevertheless questionable. As we saw in Chapter 1, Régis distinguishes explicitly between 'esprit' ('spirit' or 'mind') and 'âme' ('soul'). In Régis, 'spirit' denotes thinking substance in general, while 'soul' denotes an *individual* or particular spirit. The important point for Régis is that a soul is essentially related to an organic body.[29] This notion of the soul seems a far cry from any 'anticipation' of a Humean bundle analysis of the mind. A soul is constituted, says Régis, through the spirit's relation to an organic body, not by its thoughts. There seems to be no evidence at all, then, for the claim that Régis holds a bundle theory of the self or soul; rather, there is evidence that he does not hold such a position.

There were other French thinkers closer to Hume's time, however, who seem to have endorsed a straightforward bundle theory of the self: in particular, Henry de Boulainviller (also known as Henri Comte de Boulainvilliers), and Léger-Marie Deschamps. Deschamps's main work was published posthumously, so no suggestion has been made that he could have influenced Hume; but such a claim has been made about Boulainviller. So we shall look at Boulainviller first, before turning to Deschamps, to see whether his account constitutes at least a 'French parallel' to the Humean bundle theory.

---

[26] Lennon, 'The Problem of Individuation among Cartesians', in Barber and Gracia (eds.), *Individuation and Identity in Early Modern Philosophy: Descartes to Kant* (1994), pp. 13–39; on Régis, pp. 24–30. For a more detailed discussion of Régis, and Lennon's interpretation of Régis, see Thiel, '"Epistemologism" and Early Modern Debates about Individuation and Identity', *British Journal for the History of Philosophy*, 5 (1997b), 353–72, esp. 357–61.

[27] Régis, *Système de philosophie contenant la logique, la métaphysique, la physique, et la morale*, 3 vols. (1690). All references are to vol. 1, and translations are mine unless indicated otherwise. For Régis, see also the comments in Chapter 1.

[28] Israel has pointed out that Régis, despite seeking to provide a Cartesian refutation of Spinoza, in fact 'occasionally lurches perilously close to Spinoza's stance': Israel, *Radical Enlightenment: Philosophy and the Making of Modernity 1650–1750* (2001), p. 492. Israel does not, however, discuss the issue of the self.

[29] 'par *Ame* je n'entendray pas l'esprit considéré en luy-même & selon son estre absolu, selon lequel il est une substance qui pense, mais j'entendray seulement le rapport que l'esprit a au corps organique avec lequel il est uni; d'où il s'ensuit que l'ame prise abstractivement ne sera autre chose Que l'union de l'esprit avec un corps organique': Régis, *Système*, p. 113.

Boulainviller's *Essai de métaphysique* was completed in 1712, but published posthumously in 1731.[30] His remarks on the self and its unity and identity are expressed in the context of an exposition of Spinoza.[31] This has to be taken into account when evaluating his comments on the self. For it has been claimed that the latter constitute 'an adumbration' of Hume's analysis of the mind, and that 'it is possible' that 'a reading of Boulainviller... may have contributed' to Hume's notion of the mind as a bundle of perceptions.[32] It is possible, of course, but there is no positive evidence to support the notion of an influence of Boulainviller on Hume. Moreover, it is doubtful that Boulainviller even proposes a Humean bundle theory of the self.

It has been argued, however, that Boulainviller 'states quite explicitly that the self and its states are identical, that I, the subject of my ideas, am not to be distinguished from the ideas themselves'.[33] And indeed, it seems that there are a number of passages supporting this 'Humean' reading of Boulainviller. For example, he speaks of 'that assemblage of modes of thought and extension that constitute my present self', he argues that 'the human soul... has no other reality except that which it derives from ideas', and he states that 'the spirit exists only through the succession and chain of its ideas and its perceptions.'[34] Once these and other passages are read in context, however, they provide no evidence for a Humean bundle view. Instead, they indicate that not unlike Spinoza, Boulainviller holds that individual beings such as the human self exist, but are modal beings rather than substantial beings. He holds that there is only one substance—the absolute—which must not be confused with the modal existence of individual beings ('Essai', p. 114). Moreover, he claims that the mind could not exist as a mere substrate or bearer of properties: it cannot exist without its attributes.

And so, when Boulainviller says that the being and properties of an individual entity are the same thing, 'considered in different respects', all he is saying is that a

---

[30] The full title of Boulainviller's 'Essai' is 'Essai de métaphysique dans les principes de B... de Sp...' It was published as part of a collection, *Réfutation des erreurs de Benoît de Spinosa*, edited by Nicolas Lenglet Dufresnoy, and published in Amsterdam in 1731—though on the title-page, 'Bruxelles' is falsely declared to be the place of publication: see Israel (2001), p. 570. Boulainviller's 'Essai' is not at all a refutation of Spinoza, however. I have used the edition of the 'Essai' published in his *Oeuvres philosophiques*, ed. Simon (1973–75), vol. 1, pp. 83–212.

[31] Of course, my claim is not that Boulainviller is simply a Spinozist. There are several important differences between them: see Simon's Introduction to his edition of Boulainviller's *Oeuvres* (1973–75), pp. xii; xiv–xv. For Boulainviller and Spinozism, see also Israel (2001), pp. 565–74.

[32] Davies (1990), pp. 78–80. Davies does not relate Boulainviller's comments on the self to the Spinozistic context.

[33] Davies (1990), p. 78.

[34] '...l'assemblage des modalités de pensée et d'étendue qui constitue le moi présent': 'Essai', in Simon (1973–75), vol. 1, pp. 153–4. '... l'âme humaine... n'a d'autre réalité que celle qu'elle tire des idées': ibid., p. 179. '... l'esprit n'existant que par la suite et l'enchaînement des ses idées et de ses perceptions': ibid., p. 159. Davies also gives the following passage as evidence for her reading: 'Chaque idée occupe tout le fond du sujet pensant et je puis m'assurer que ce qui pense en moi au moment que j'écris, ceci n'est point différent de mon idée présente': ibid., p. 97. See Davies (1990), p. 79.

particular entity must exist in a certain manner.[35] A being can exist only in those modes or forms that are proper to it.[36] One cannot assume, for example, that a body exists but is neither in a state of motion nor in a state of rest (ibid.). Boulainviller holds, however, that we are ignorant of the ultimate nature of both our mind and body. We know our being only through its attributes.[37] Indeed, this *is* a view that Boulainviller seems to share with Hume: the essence of the mind cannot be known; all we know of it are its perceptions. This is not the same, however, as claiming that there is no self or subject apart from the perceptions. And given his scepticism about knowledge of real essence, it is not surprising that Boulainviller does not commit himself to any view about the ultimate nature of the mind—not even the view that it consists in a bundle of perceptions.

All we can know about the self, according to Boulainviller, is that it is a modal being that participates in the two attributes of the absolute. The self or the 'individu personnel' is a unity of body and mind, considered as a modal being, not as a unity of substances (ibid., pp. 152–3). It is true that he rejects the Cartesian idea of a 'master of the house who says *I*',[38] but he also, consistently with this critique, speaks of a feeling we have of our own self and its unity: a *sentiment intime*. According to Boulainviller, it is precisely the unity of our being as consisting of spirit and body which *results* in this feeling that we have of our own self as unitary.[39] Boulainviller does not seem to explain how exactly this feeling of self comes about, but it is clearly based in the reality of our unitary self. In short, Boulainviller's position too is a far cry from a Humean bundle theory of the self.

Léger-Marie Deschamps is said to subscribe to a Humean bundle theory in his main, posthumously published work *La vérité, ou le vrai système*.[40] There is no chapter in this work that deals with the self; rather, Deschamps's comments on the

---

[35] 'les êtres particuliers ne sont point le sujet de leurs propriétés, mais...leur être et leurs propriétés sont même chose, considérée à différents égards': 'Essai', in Simon (1973–75), vol. 1, p. 97.

[36] 'l'être ne puisse exister que dans les modes qui lui sont propres': ibid., p. 113.

[37] 'l'ignorance où nous sommes de la véritable nature de nos esprits et de nos corps': ibid., p. 132. 'nous ne connaissons l'être que par ses attributs': ibid., p. 97.

[38] See Boulainviller's *Traité sur l'immortalité de l'âme* (1704), in Simon (1973–75), vol. 1, pp. 292–306. The criticized view is expressed at p. 300: '...l'homme sent en lui-même un maître de la maison qui dit moi, qui juge, qui veut et qui exécute, et qui est tout différent du corps.' Compare Davies (1990), pp. 79–80.

[39] 'mon corps et mon esprit ne composent qu'un même individu, ou qu'une même modalité d'existence, qui peut être considérée tantôt sous l'attribut d'étendue corporelle, et tantôt sous l'attribut de la pensée...supposant l'unité de notre être et le sentiment intime qui en doit résulter': 'Essai', in Simon (1973–75), vol. 1, p. 154. See also p. 157, where Boulainviller speaks of 'l'unité individuelle de l'esprit et du corps'. Elsewhere, at p. 164, he uses 'le sentiment de soi-même' for 'sentiment intime'. For the latter expression he also uses the term 'conscience': 'Essai', in Simon (1973–75), vol. 1, p. 135. On the latter, see Davies (1990), p. 68.

[40] This, again, is the view of Davies (1990): see pp. 82–3, 96. I have used Deschamps's *Oeuvres philosophiques*, 2 vols., ed. Bernard Delhaume (1993), and there is also an earlier edition edited by Thomas and Venturi (1963)—the edition used by Davies (1990). There does not seem to be much philosophical commentary on Deschamps. The most important item is Robinet, *Dom Deschamps: Le maître des maîtres du soupçon* (1974): see, especially, the short chapter, 'L'illusion du moi et de la personne', pp. 259–61.

topic are scattered over various writings. Importantly, his account of the self belongs to a metaphysics of the totality of being or *le tout universel*. The 'universal whole' is the foundation of which sensible beings are 'nuances' (aspects). *Le tout universel* is of a different nature from each of its parts, and so one cannot see it but only conceive of it. Deschamps distinguishes between the universal whole and 'particular wholes', such as an individual human being. By contrast to the universal whole, these are said to be of the same nature as their parts.[41] It is perhaps because of this latter claim, which suggests that there is no self or subject in the case of human beings but only a bundle of parts, that some have ascribed a bundle view to Deschamps.[42] Deschamps distinguishes, however, between three distinct aspects of the self, or *moi*: the physical self, the moral self, and the metaphysical self (*Oeuvres*, vol. 1, pp. 129–30). The self in a metaphysical sense is the self insofar as it is part of the totality of being, or *le tout universel*; the self in a physical sense is the individual human being. The latter includes the self in a moral sense, insofar as human beings are social beings.[43] These distinctions, however, are not even vaguely reminiscent of a Humean bundle view of the self. When Deschamps says that the person or self is the sum of its parts, it must be remembered that it is at the same time thought of as belonging to a larger totality.[44] In the last analysis it belongs to the *tout universel*.

---

[41] '*Le Tout* universel est un être qui existe. C'est le *fond* dont les êtres sensibles sont les nuances': Deschamps, *Oeuvres*, vol. 1, p. 121. '*Le Tout* universel, ou l'univers, est d'une autre nature que chacune de ses parties, et conséquemment, on ne peut que le concevoir, et non pas le voir ou se le figurer. Un tout particulier, comme un homme ou la généralité des hommes, est de la même nature que ses parties': ibid., p. 126. 'Le métaphysique est ce qui est général de toute généralité... il est les êtres dans ce qu'ils sont très également.... Le physique... est ce qui est particulier, ce qui est telle ou telle chose, est un homme, un arbre': ibid., p. 129.

[42] Robinet ascribes to Deschamps a psychology without a subject ('antipersonalism'), but does not relate this to Hume: Robinet (1974), pp. 260–1. Davies ascribes to Deschamps the view that any notion of the self other than that of a sum of physical parts is 'a self-imposed fiction'. Therefore, she thinks that Deschamps's view 'resembles Hume's empirical scepticism': Davies (1990), p. 83. Given Deschamps's metaphysics of *le tout*, however, his system seems to be an unlikely candidate for any version of 'empirical scepticism'.

[43] 'Ce que nous disons *notre moi* est ces deux genres, dont l'un, qui est métaphysique, est commun à tous les êtres, et dont l'autre, qui est le physique, nous est personnel, est nous comme hommes. C'est du *moi métaphysique*, si on peut l'appeler ainsi, et aussi de notre *moi physique*, des ressorts de notre machine que nous avons fait une âme, et c'est du *moi métaphysique* et de notre *moi moral* que nous avons fait un Dieu métaphysique et moral. Je distingue notre *moi moral* de notre *moi physique*, mais ils rentrent entièrement l'un dans l'autre: aussi avons-nous fait un Dieu métaphysique, physique et moral, tel que nous sommes': Deschamps, *Oeuvres*, vol. 1, pp. 129–30. 'Si nos langues sont un composé de termes métaphysiques, physiques et moraux, c'est que nous existons métaphysiquement, physiquement, et moralement: métaphysiquement, comme liés à tout, comme ne formant qu'un même être avec le reste des êtres; physiquement, comme paraissant séparés de tout, comme hommes; et moralement, comme hommes en société, sous l'état de lois, état qui en nous donnant des vertus et des vices, par le juste et l'injuste, le bien et le mal moraux qui dérivent de lui nécessairement, nous a fait une moralité ou, ce qui va au même, une façon d'être sociale, dépourvue de toute raison, et qui rend le mal moral infiniment plus onéreux que le mal physique': ibid., p. 130.

[44] 'Ce que nous appelons notre personne est un composé de parties qui en appartenant le unes aux autres, appartiennent de primauté physique au globe de la terre, soit qu'on prenne ce globe en détail, soit qu'on le prenne en général; et de primauté métaphysique au globe de la totalité universelle, à l'universel': quoted from Robinet (1974), p. 261.

In accordance with these distinctions, Deschamps speaks of the metaphysical soul and the physical soul. These must not be confounded with one another. 'Metaphysical soul' does not refer to a supernatural being but to those features that we have in common with other beings. Moreover, the metaphysical soul exists necessarily as a physical entity, in a body.[45] Deschamps states quite clearly that our self is the body—that the self is the whole of one's body. When we are dealing with the self as a human being, the word 'self' expresses nothing else but 'le tout de notre corps'.[46] Identifying the self with the body, however, is not the same as endorsing a Humean bundle theory. Deschamps speaks of the bodily self as that which 'has' sensations or perceptions. And even when he says that the self is all sensation, and that 'self and sensation are the same thing'[47], it does not follow that he envisages a subjectless self, as the passage does not indicate that there is no subject having the sensation. Most importantly, the notion of a whole made up of parts is not part of the bundle view or no-owner view of the self. Certainly, in Hume there is no metaphysics of *le tout* to back up the bundle of perceptions. Like Régis and Boulainviller, Deschamps too seems to be closer to Spinoza than he is to Hume.

It seems, then, that there is little evidence for 'anticipations' of the bundle view. No early modern philosopher prior to Hume seems to have argued for the view that the real nature of the mind consists in a subjectless collection of perceptions or experiences. Does Hume hold such a view? Some passages cited above seem to suggest that he does, and most writers on Hume seem to assume, without much argument, that he explicitly subscribes to this view of the mind. We have to look at Hume more closely, however, to see what his own view is that he thinks is so 'peculiar to himself'.

---

[45] Deschamps says: 'Il y a l'âme physique et l'âme métaphysique. L'âme physique est la vie, est le jeu des ressorts qui constituent la machine de notre corps. L'âme métaphysique, cet être qu'on a toujours confondu avec l'âme physique, et dont on a toujours parlé si absurdement, est ce que nous avons de rigoureusement commun avec tous les êtres, est l'existence métaphysique même. Cette existence est nécessairement cachée sous l'enveloppe de l'existence physique, soit qu'elle soit réputée corps, soit qu'elle soit réputée âme, et elle peut être réputée l'un et l'autre, car il n'est point de corps dans la nature qui n'ait vie à sa façon, qui n'ait une âme physique, l'âme physique n'étant en effet que le corps même': Deschamps, *Oeuvres*, vol. 1, p. 376.

[46] 'Quand nous nous distinguons de ce qui est de nous, c'est nôtre tout particulier et rien de plus que nous distinguons de telle et telle de ses affections, façons d'être, ou parties. Le *moi* est le tout de mon corps, et quand je dis, par exemple, que j'ai telle sensation, je ne dis rien sinon que mon tout, que l'ensemble de mes parties, qui est moi, a telle sensation. Nous pouvons nous distinguer de telle ou telle chose qui nous constitue, mais nous ne le pouvons pas du tout ce qui nous constitue, car ce serait distinguer notre tout de lui-même. Tout ce qui est de nous est nous, mais non pas telle ou telle chose qui est de nous, car elle n'est jamais que plus ou moins nous. Vouloir que le mot *moi* exprime autre chose que le tout de notre corps, quand il s'agit de nous comme hommes, c'est vouloir une absurdité': Deschamps, *Oeuvres*, vol. 1, p. 381.

[47] 'je suis tout sensation par ma nature, ou si l'on veut, tout mouvement nommé sensation . . . moi et sensation sont la même chose': Deschamps, *Oeuvres*, vol. 1, p. 383.

13.3. WHAT IS HUME'S BUNDLE VIEW OF THE SELF?

As we have seen, according to Reid, Hume 'maintained, that the mind is only a succession of ideas and impressions, without any subject'.[48] It is clear from these comments that like Beattie (also cited above), Reid believes that Hume makes an ontological claim reducing the self to perceptions and denying the existence of a self beyond the perceptions. For Beattie and Reid the bundle view which includes the 'no owner' or 'no subject' view is held by Hume as a straightforward ontological position about the true nature of the mind. This is also the reading of most commentators. Indeed, it constitutes the standard view about Hume's account of the self.[49]

And yet the texts show that Hume does not deny the existence of a self apart from the perceptions. Rather, Hume says that the self, *insofar as it is accessible through inner experience*, consists of nothing but the perceptions, and therefore that any knowledge claims about the nature of the mind and its identity that go beyond the 'bundle of perceptions' view cannot be justified. They are 'false' in the sense that they lack justification. Thus, when Hume introduces the bundle view in the section on personal identity he says that this is the view that reflection or inner observation reveals. When introspecting ('when I enter most intimately into what I call *myself*') he always 'stumble[s] on some particular perception or other'. He says that he 'never can *catch*' (my italics) himself 'at any time without a perception, and never can *observe* [my italics] any thing but the perception' (*Treatise*, p. 252). His statements about the mind in this and the following paragraph (ibid., pp. 252–3) must be read against this background. When he says that the mind is 'nothing but a bundle or collection of different perceptions' (ibid., p. 252) and that no one can seriously claim to have 'a different notion of *himself*' (ibid.), he is not making statements about the real nature or essence of the self. Rather, he is saying that our *idea* of the self must be based on what introspection or reflection reveals about it, and that the self that appears to us through introspection is that of a 'bundle or collection of different perceptions' (ibid.).[50] If the standard view is mistaken and Hume does not deny the existence of a

---

[48] Reid, *Inquiry*, p. 32.
[49] It is on the basis of this reading that twentieth-century positivists count Hume as one of their predecessors. Mach, for example, thinks that Hume preceded him as someone who destroyed 'the illusion of a continuous self': Mach's letter to Mauthner, 22 October 1912, in Haller and Stadler (eds.), *Ernst Mach: Werk und Wirkung* (1988), p. 242. For recent statements of the standard view, see, for example, Noonan, who claims that for Hume 'the self is in reality nothing but a bundle of its perceptions'; indeed, he says that Hume's self is 'something like a thunderstorm': *Hume on Knowledge* (1999), pp. 197, 201. The following are just a few of the many other scholars who adopt the standard view: Garrett, *Cognition and Commitment in Hume's Philosophy* (1997), pp. 164, 186; Broackes, 'Hume, Belief and Personal Identity', in Millican (ed.), *Reading Hume on Understanding* (2002), pp. 187–210, at pp. 200–1; Pitson, *Hume's Philosophy of the Self* (2002), pp. 22–7, 172; Baxter, *Hume's Difficulty: Time and Identity in the Treatise* (2008), pp. 68, 70; Wilson, *Body, Mind and Self in Hume's Critical Realism* (2008), pp. 94, 353, 375.
[50] Thus Kemp Smith notes, rightly, that Hume is very far 'from denying the existence of a continuing self': Kemp Smith, *The Philosophy of David Hume* (1941), pp. 194, 198. Although our argument here is different in many respects, the general point against the ontological interpretation of Hume's bundle view is similar to that of Craig and Strawson: Craig, *The Mind of God and the*

self beyond the perceptions, then some of the standard objections to Hume's account miss the mark. For example, it has been argued that Hume's account of the operations of the mind, and, indeed his own account of how we come to have the idea of a self and personal identity, presuppose a self that is more than a bundle of perceptions.[51] Since Hume does not deny the existence of such a self, however, the objection is beside the point.[52]

There are some passages, however, in which Hume may seem to commit himself to the bundle view as an ontological claim; that is, to the position that the bundle view represents the real essence of the self, and that consequently there can be no self over and above the bundle.

(1) For example, Hume says at one point that 'they are the successive perceptions only, that constitute the mind', and in the same paragraph that 'there is properly no *simplicity* in it [the mind] at one time, nor *identity* in different' (ibid., p. 253). These statements, however, appear (again) in a context that concerns the *idea* of our own

---

Works of Man (1987), pp. 111–20; Strawson, 'Hume on Himself', in Egonsson, Josefsson, Petersson and Rønnow-Rasmussen (eds.) *Exploring Practical Philosophy: From Action to Values* (2001a), pp. 69–94, at pp. 71–4, 78–80; Strawson, *The Secret Connexion* (1989), pp. 128–30; and Strawson, *The Evident Connexion: Hume on Personal Identity* (2011a), pp. 33–99. Craig states, correctly, that 'Hume's remarks to the effect that the mind *is nothing more* than perceptions are closely paired with the claim that we *have no idea* of the mind beyond our idea of the perceptions': Craig (1987), pp. 113–14. Hume's position is 'not that there is no mind apart from the perceptions, but that we cannot know anything of it. But also that . . . we can as it were change gear and add our tacit ride to give the question: what is the mind *in so far as it is investigable by us?*': ibid., p. 116. Regrettably, Craig's and Strawson's readings of Hume's bundle view have been largely ignored in recent discussions of Hume's account of the self. Winkler mentions the possibility of that kind of reading but does not seem to have developed it. 'Hume leaves room for what might be called a 'sceptical realist' account of personal identity, according to which there is (or may be) a mind or self distinct from perceptions, even if we have (or can have) no contentful notion of it': Winkler, ' "All is Revolution in Us": Personal Identity in Shaftesbury and Hume', *Hume Studies*, 26 (2000), 36. Pitson mentions Craig and Strawson, but rejects their reading without engaging with it in any detail. Pitson says he sees 'no reason not to take at face value' Hume's statement in the *Abstract* that 'it must be our several particular perceptions, that compose the mind': Keynes and Sraffa (eds.), *An Abstract of A Treatise of Human Nature 1740: A Pamphlet hitherto unknown by David Hume* (1938; reprinted, 1990), p. 25; Hume, *A Treatise of Human Nature*, ed. Norton and Norton (2000), p. 414; Pitson (2002), p. 172. Pitson seems to suggest that the alternative interpretation ascribes to Hume a view that has no obvious textual basis. This charge, however, rather applies to the standard view to which Pitson subscribes. In the *Abstract*, too, Hume says explicitly that 'we *know* nothing but particular qualities and perceptions' and so 'our *idea* of any mind is only that of particular perceptions' (my italics): *Abstract* (Keynes and Sraffa), p. 25; *Treatise* (Norton and Norton) p. 414. Clearly, the passage about the mind's composition must be read against this background. Kail provides a highly original account by relating the personal identity problem of the Appendix to realism about necessary connection. He seems to reject the view, however, that for Hume there may be a mind or self distinct from the perceptions: Kail, *Projection and Realism in Hume's Philosophy* (2007), pp. 131ff.

[51] Stroud, for example, discusses this objection in *Hume* (1977), p. 140.
[52] This point would also apply, *mutatis mutandis*, to Hume's defenders who argue that a bundle could do all the work that Hume assigns to the self. See, for example, Beauchamp, 'Self Inconsistency or Mere Self Perplexity', *Hume Studies*, 5 (1979), 37–44. We are in agreement, then, with Allison's assessment of this debate, albeit for different reasons. Compare Allison, *Custom and Reason in Hume: A Kantian Reading of the First Book of the Treatise* (2008), pp. 300–1.

self. They express epistemological considerations, and do not express metaphysical truths about the real essence of the human mind.

(2) In the Appendix Hume seems to make the point that the bundle view is based not only on actual, empirical introspection, but also on what we can conceive a mind to be. He says that if we suppose 'the mind to be reduc'd even below the life of an oyster' and suppose it 'to have only one perception, as of thirst or hunger', would we then 'conceive any thing but merely that perception?' We would certainly not have 'any notion of *self* or *substance*' (ibid., p. 634). In this 'supposition' or thought experiment Hume seems to be saying that we cannot even have a conception of a self that exists apart from the perceptions. These perceptions 'therefore must be the same with self' (ibid., p. 635). These remarks would seem to commit Hume to the view that we cannot even think of a self that is not a bundle of perceptions. In fact, however, Hume makes a point about our *ideas*. He says that as '*we have no idea of external substance, distinct from the ideas of particular qualities*', so '*we have no notion of it* [the mind], *distinct from the particular perceptions*' (ibid.). The argument about a mind that is reduced below the life of an oyster merely extrapolates on what we know about our own minds through inner experience. What Hume says here about our conception of the oyster-mind, or any mind, does not commit him to the position that we are unable to speak meaningfully of a self apart from the perceptions. The conceptions he is referring to here are of course based on impressions. Insofar as Hume is concerned with the notion of a substantial self that is based on impressions, he is indeed of the view that we have no idea of it 'in that sense' (ibid., p. 633)— without, however, thereby in any way denying the existence of a self beyond the perceptions.[53]

(3) There is a passage in the section 'Of scepticism with regard to the senses' which seems to state clearly what the mind really is according to Hume. He says: 'What we call a *mind*, is nothing but a heap or collection of different perceptions, united together by certain relations, and suppos'd, tho' falsely, to be endow'd with a perfect simplicity and identity'(ibid., p. 207). He also speaks here of 'that connected mass of perceptions, which constitute a thinking being' (ibid.). Again, this may seem to suggest that, to Hume, the mind is really just a bundle of perceptions, and that it is false to ascribe simplicity and identity to it because in reality (we know) they have neither. As noted above, however, Hume thinks it is false to ascribe such attributes to the mind only because we cannot justify such ascription on the basis of introspective or impressionistic evidence.[54] It does not follow from this that he is of the view that the bundle is all there is to the self in reality.

---

[53] Strawson (2001), p. 91, has pointed out that in Hume 'no idea' means 'no perfect idea', not 'no idea of any sort'. See Hume, *Treatise*, p. 234: 'We have no perfect idea of any thing but of a perception. A substance is entirely different from a perception. We have, therefore, no idea of a substance.'

[54] A belief about matters of fact can be said to be false if we cannot provide empirical evidence for it. As Hume says, this is the reason why our identity-ascriptions to plants and vegetables are 'false': *Treatise*, p. 255.

It is true that as far as a self apart from or underlying the perceptions is concerned, Hume adopts a sceptical position: we cannot know anything about it. This must not be confused, however, with a denial of the existence of such a self. In fact, his scepticism would be inconsistent with such a denial. He points out in the Introduction to the *Treatise* that the essence of the mind cannot be known: 'For to me it seems evident, that the essence of the mind' is 'equally unknown to us with that of external bodies' (ibid., p. xvii). Regarding the latter he says that his 'intention' in the *Treatise* is not to try and 'penetrate into the nature of bodies, or explain the secret causes of their operations'. According to Hume, 'such an enterprize is beyond the reach of human understanding' (ibid., p. 64). He is concerned only with knowing 'the manner in which objects affect my senses, and their connections with each other, as far as experience informs me of them'—without of course *denying* the existence of a nature of bodies that lies 'beyond the reach of human understanding' (ibid.). As the comment in the Introduction to the *Treatise* indicates, this also applies to his treatment of the mind. He does not intend 'to penetrate into the nature' of mind, as it is not accessible to us anyway. Therefore, the philosophy of the *Treatise* deals with the mind only 'as far as experience informs' him of it. Obviously, however, to say that the essence of the mind is unknowable and that his focus is on the experientially accessible self is not to deny that the mind has an essence beyond those experientially accessible features of the mind.[55] In short, Hume is concerned not with the mind's real nature but only with its introspectively accessible features.[56]

---

[55] Baxter argues that Hume assumes 'the mind or self is what it is perceived to be': Baxter, 'Hume's Labyrinth Concerning the Idea of Personal Identity', *Hume Studies*, 24 (1998), 203–33, at 207; see also Baxter (2008), p. 75. Thus, according to Baxter, when Hume states what introspection reveals about the mind he makes a statement about the mind's essence as a bundle of perceptions, because Hume thinks 'that there is no more to the self than what is evident to careful reflection': Baxter (1998), p. 209. There seems to be no evidence for ascribing this assumption to Hume, however. On the contrary, Hume is very sceptical about introspection as a means of acquiring knowledge of the nature of the mind (*Treatise*, p. xix) and holds, as stated above, that the essence of the mind cannot be known. In support of his interpretation Baxter appeals to Hume's statement that 'consciousness never deceives': Baxter (2008), p. 75. Consciousness, however, is an immediate relating to perceptions and is said not deceive us about *them*. The claim that the nature of the mind consists in a bundle of perceptions goes beyond the evidence of immediate consciousness. Baxter does not seem to distinguish between introspection or reflection on the one hand and the reflexivity that is involved in immediate consciousness on the other ('Hume assume[s] accurate reflection in consciousness'): Baxter (2008) p. 75. See the section above: 'Hume on Consciousness and Reflection'.

[56] There is a question as to whether Hume is a materialist about the mind. Wright, for example, has argued for a materialist reading of Hume: see Wright, *The Sceptical Realism of David Hume* (1983), pp. 72–4; and Wright, 'Hume, Descartes and the Materiality of the Soul', in Rogers and Tomaselli (eds.), *The Philosophical Canon in the 17th and 18th Centuries. Essays in Honour of John W. Yolton* (1996), pp. 175–90. As Wright emphasises, referring especially to *Treatise*, I.iv.5, and the essay 'On the Immortality of the Soul', Hume points out that experience suggests a connection between thinking and material base. The question of Hume's materialism is controversial, however, to say the least. Buckle has contended for a reading of Hume in terms of a 'sceptical materialism'—a view that 'affirms materiality as the best explanation for mind as well as matter—while prescinding from any dogmatic claims about the essential nature of matter itself': Buckle, 'Hume's Sceptical Materialism', *Philosophy*, 82 (2007), 553–78. Even if a materialist view of the mind can be ascribed to Hume, however, he does not make use of this view in his discussion of

The comments in the section on personal identity about the self as a bundle of perceptions do not, and cannot, concern the mind's unknowable essence, but only those features about which inner experience 'informs' us. Therefore, these comments are consistent with the notion of a mind beyond the perceptions. The standard view that the bundle comments are meant to capture the essence of the mind is inconsistent with Hume's acknowledgement that its essence is unknown. Hume is not in any way committed to a denial of the existence of a persisting self beyond the perceptions.

In summary, then, we have argued for the following four related claims:

(1) Hume's pronouncements about the mind as a bundle of perceptions are statements about the mind insofar as it is accessible to us through inner experience.
(2) These statements are not meant to be statements about the 'real essence' of the mind, as experience and observation do not reach the real essence of bodies and minds.
(3) According to Hume, the essence of the mind cannot be known to us.
(4) As the point made in (3) concerns an epistemic claim, obviously it does not commit Hume to the view that there is no persisting self beyond the perceptions.

In this light, Beattie's and Reid's objections and the corresponding arguments in present-day discussions of Hume miss the mark. This is true, of course, of all criticisms of Hume that assume that his claim about the mind as a bundle of perceptions is meant to be a statement about the mind's real essence.[57]

---

personal identity. Strawson, too, points out that in other parts of the *Treatise* 'Hume makes explicit use of the hypothesis that the mind is based in the brain, and claims that he must do so': Strawson (2001), p. 90. He concedes, however, that Hume 'can't call on this hypothesis in the more radical dialectical context of "Of personal identity", and makes no appeal to it when he returns to the problem of personal identity in the Appendix': ibid.

[57] Strawson argues that Hume makes a stronger claim than what an interpretation such as ours suggests: Strawson (2011a), pp. 40–6, 88–95. According to Strawson, Hume accepts both of the following: (1) it is a necessary truth that a perception is impossible without a perceiver or perceiving subject—'the *Experience/Experiencer thesis*'; (2) a perceiving subject is (at least non-thetically) part of the phenomenological content of introspection. As Strawson notes, (1) does not entail (2)—'a necessary truth needn't be phenomenologically apparent'. Thus Hume could hold (1) but not (2). It is plain, however, that (2) is the important issue here, because Hume is not concerned with necessary truths and relations of ideas but with what he encounters when he enters 'most intimately' into what he calls himself. Our hesitation to ascribe (2) to Hume stems from the fact that unlike some of his contemporaries, he does not explicitly endorse it. Of course, some passages in Hume may lend themselves to an interpretation in terms of (2), but this is not sufficient, in our view, to ascribe (2) to Hume. Importantly, no matter whether or not we ascribe (1) and (2) to Hume, it remains true that Hume's version of the bundle theory does not deny the existence of a self apart from the perceptions; and on this we seem to be in agreement with Strawson.

13.4. PERSONAL IDENTITY 'AS IT REGARDS OUR PASSIONS OR THE CONCERN WE TAKE IN OURSELVES': HUME AND KAMES

It could be said in support of Beattie's and Reid's objections that even if the reading proposed in the last section is correct and Hume does not deny the existence of a self beyond the perceptions, this does not address the moral aspects of their criticisms. Even if Hume assumes a self apart from the perceptions, one might argue, this self could hardly play any significant role in issues to do with morality if we cannot know anything about it. If the self is unknowable, how can we ascribe actions to it, hold it responsible for actions, and so on? We have seen that Hume himself emphasises the issue of self-concern in his discussion of personal identity. Can he account for this, given his 'bundle view' of the experientially accessible mind?

These issues relating to self-concern and morality were emphasised not only by Beattie and Reid, but also by an early proponent of the Common Sense view, Henry Home, Lord Kames, who had a considerable influence on Reid in particular. He was a friend and a kinsman of Hume, with whom he corresponded about philosophical and other matters. Kames deals with personal identity in a section of his *Essays on the Principles of Morality and Natural Religion* which first appeared in print in 1751. He refers to Hume in that section, and argues, like Beattie and others, that there is a '*feeling* (my italics) of identity, which accompanies me through all my changes' (*Essays*, pp. 233–4). It may seem that this is the kind of, view that Hume rejects in his section on personal identity in Book I of the *Treatise*. Some years later, however, in a letter to Kames of 1746, he comments on what is probably an early manuscript version of Kames's essay on personal identity: 'I likt exceedingly your Method of explaining personal Identity as more satisfactory than any thing that had ever occurr'd to me.'[58] How can we make sense of this comment? Has Hume completely changed his mind? His rather limited self-criticism in the Appendix cannot explain his endorsement of Kames's position. Of course, a simple way of dealing with this passage in Hume's letter would be to dismiss it as a polite gesture to his friend, and not take it seriously.[59] But why, if Hume wanted to be polite, would he pick personal identity of all topics? Moreover, if he really disagreed with Kames, surely he would have been able to express his disagreement politely enough.

He does so on other occasions. In fact, he criticizes other aspects of Kames's philosophy in the same letter. The quoted passage is followed by a comment, against Kames, on the 'Idea of Substance'. According to Kames, 'substance...makes a part... of every perception of sight and touch' (*Essays*, p. 249). Hume argues that the idea of substance, 'as it has no Acess to the Mind by any of our Senses or

---

[58] Klibansky and Mossner (eds.), *New Letters of David Hume* (1954), pp. 18–21, at p. 20. The letter is dated 24 July 1746.

[59] We must assume that the 'polite gesture' reading is standard among Hume scholars, as the passage is easily accessible but has been ignored in discussions of Hume on personal identity.

Feelings', has always appeared to him 'to be nothing but an imaginary Center of Union amongst the different & variable Qualitys that are to be found in every Piece of Matter' (*New Letters of Hume*, pp. 20–1). He adds that he will keep himself 'in Suspence till I hear your Opinion' (ibid., p. 21).[60] He is happy, then, to criticize Kames's accounts of other issues, and there is thus no reason to believe that he would not have stated his objections had he disagreed with Kames on personal identity.

Assuming, then, as we must, that Hume is not merely being polite in praising Kames on personal identity, his comment raises the following questions. First, what is it that he finds so attractive in Kames's discussion of identity? Second, how does his endorsement of Kames's position relate to his account of identity in the *Treatise*? We shall argue that while it had not 'occurred' to Hume explicitly to work out a position such as Kames's, most of what Kames says about personal identity is in fact compatible with Hume's account in the *Treatise*. Book II is of special importance here, and Hume's distinction, cited above, between personal identity as it regards the imagination and 'as it regards our passions or the concern we take in ourselves' will also be relevant. Before returning to the *Treatise*, however, more needs to be said about Kames's argument. Kames expands the section on personal identity considerably for later editions of his *Essays*. Here we need only look at the main features of his first edition section on the topic, as it is probable that Hume commented on an early manuscript version of the section in the 1751 edition.

Kames holds that a consciousness or feeling of one's own self 'accompanies', at least 'for the most part', all our perceptions and actions (*Essays*, p. 231).[61] Moreover, he argues that the idea or consciousness of personal identity is derived from this feeling of self: 'It is by means of this perception [of self] that I consider myself to be the same person, in all varieties of fortune, and every change of circumstance' (ibid., p. 233). This feeling of identity 'which accompanies me through all my changes ... is the only connecting principle that binds together all the various thoughts and actions of my life' (ibid., p. 234). It is, he says, a 'natural feeling'. Importantly, his discussion is very much in terms of the practical aspects of selfhood, relating to the notion of self-concern in particular. He states that 'self-preservation is every one's peculiar duty; and the vivacity of this perception [of self] is necessary to make us attentive to our own interest, and, particularly, to shun every appearance of danger'. Thus the 'consciousness or perception of self is ... of the liveliest kind' (ibid., p. 232).[62] Kames clearly appeals to Common Sense evidence for personal identity here, and he does so by emphasising that it is the very nature of self-concern which involves a feeling of our own self and its identity.

---

[60] In his *Essays* (1751) Kames deals with the notion of substance after having discussed personal identity. Hume's comments reflect that order.

[61] This is reminiscent of Hutcheson's brief remark in the letter of 1727, in which he says that 'every one has an immediate simple perception of *self*, to which all his other perceptions are some way connected': *European Magazine* (1788), 158.

[62] To underscore the moral relevance of the issue, in the third edition (1779) of his *Essays* Kames moves the section on personal identity to part 1 of the book, which deals with moral issues.

Hume agrees. In Book II of the *Treatise*, dealing with the 'passions or the concern we take in ourselves', he makes it clear that an immediate consciousness of our own self is involved in 'passions' such as pride and humility, for example. He appeals to this consciousness of self many times in Book II. He says: "'Tis evident, that the idea, or rather impression of ourselves is always intimately present with us, and that our consciousness gives us so lively a conception of our own person, that 'tis not possible to imagine, that any thing can in this particular go beyond it' (*Treatise*, p. 317). Referring explicitly to identity, Hume speaks of the 'self or that identical person, of whose thoughts, actions, and sensations we are intimately conscious' (ibid., p. 329). We have seen that in the Book I account of personal identity Hume equates the person with the mind. In Book II, however, when he is concerned with the self 'as it regards the passions', he obviously includes the body in his conception of the self.[63] For example, he says that 'pride and humility have the qualities of our mind and body, that is *self*, for their natural and more immediate causes' (ibid., p. 303).

Hume's analysis of the passions is quite complex, and there is no need to go into the details here. The main point in the present context is that according to Hume we can account for passions such as pride only if we acknowledge that the consciousness of our own (embodied) selves 'is always intimately present with us' (ibid., p. 317). Obviously, I need to be able to relate certain qualities to myself in order to develop the feeling of pride about them. Like Kames, then, Hume emphasises that the nature of self-concern involves a *consciousness* of our own self, and that this consciousness is common to all mankind. Hume recognizes that his moral psychology must assume a sense of self and self-identity. This is what is meant by personal identity, 'as it regards the passions or the concern we take in ourselves'. Hume neither requires nor presents a distinct 'theory' of personal identity for Book II.

Of course, one can extend this argument to Book III of the *Treatise* ('Of Morals'). Just as Hume's moral psychology requires a sense of self, so does his account of justice. A self as agent, rather than a subjectless bundle of perceptions, is required for the ascription of praise and blame. Accordingly, he does not refer to the self as a bundle here. Rather, he says that 'the constant and universal object of hatred or anger is a person or creature endow'd with thought and consciousness' (ibid., p. 411). Character and dispositions are features that are 'of the person, who perform'd' the actions (ibid.). The 'person acquires ... merit or demerit from his actions' (ibid.). It remains true, however, that Hume does not discuss the specific issue of the identity

---

[63] Many commentators, of course, have noted this fact. See, for example, Bricke, *Hume's Philosophy of Mind* (1980), p. 99; Waxman, *Hume's Theory of Consciousness* (1994), p. 224; and Wilson, 'Substance and Self in Locke and Hume', in Barber and Gracia (eds.), *Individuation and Identity in Early Modern Philosophy* (1994), pp. 155–99, at pp. 186–7. As Strawson puts it, in contrast to Book I references to 'self' and 'person', those in Books II and III 'do not have a purely or even primarily mental reference': Strawson (2001), p. 92, note 21. Some writers on Hume on personal identity, however, neglect the notion of the embodied self in Hume altogether. Pears, for example, restricts his discussion of personal identity to the Book I account, and claims that the problems in the latter result from his 'neglecting the body': Pears, *Hume's System* (1990), p. 129; see also pp. 133, 149–50. Pitson notes the importance of the body in Book II, but believes that even there Hume works with the bundle view as an ontological thesis about the real nature of the self: Pitson (2002), p. 124.

of persons in Books II and III. No additional treatment of identity is to be found in those parts of the *Treatise*.[64]

It has been claimed that Hume's comments about the self in Book II are inconsistent with what he says in the section on personal identity in Book I.[65] There is no such inconsistency, however. What Hume rejects in Book I is the view of Butler, Clarke, and others, according to which we have an idea of our own selves as permanent and immaterial thinking substances or souls. In Book I he does not deny that we have a 'consciousness of our own person' (ibid., p. 318). Moreover, he explicitly says there that we have a 'natural propension' to believe in our personal identity. This belief, he suggests in Book II, 'is always intimately present with us'. It should be noted also that this argument about self-consciousness in Book II no more commits Hume to a view about the nature of the self than do his 'bundle' comments in Book I. In Book I he attempts to analyse how the imagination arrives at this belief in the first place; but this is not an issue in Book II. Here he can (and must) rely on the fact of self-consciousness (and the natural propension to believe in self-identity) in order to explain its function in the workings of the passions. The consciousness of our own self does not reveal the real nature or essence of this self, however. Therefore, his appeal to self-consciousness does not commit him to a view about the nature of the self or person.[66] What is required by the passions is only the consciousness of self and the *belief* in personal identity.[67]

---

[64] On the importance of Books II and III in this context, see McIntyre, 'Character: A Humean Account', *History of Philosophy Quarterly*, 7 (1990), 193–206. McIntyre argues that with his employment of the concept of character Hume lays the groundwork for providing the 'almost-promised account of personal identity "with regard to the passions"' (205). Character—explained in terms of mental qualities which include the passions—is 'an enduring feature of a person' (194, 205) that is 'relevant to morals'. On character and personal identity in Hume, see also Wilson (1994); Wilson (2008), pp. 403–5, 424ff.; and Pitson (2002), pp. 83–92. Wilson (1994) holds that for Hume 'one's identity as a person is constituted by one's character': p. 190. For Wilson, Books II and III provide 'the full solution of the problem of personal identity'. Book I alone cannot do it: 'The man of character is one who can "mingle and unite in society" through the establishment of conventions and social artifices. Only when this is added to the man of thought do we achieve a person, someone capable of surveying his or her own being and bringing it into harmony with the deepest standards he or she has for himself or herself alone, someone responsible for his or her own identity': ibid., p. 195. This account, too, does not square with the fact that Hume does not discuss the specific issue of personal identity at all in Books II and III. Even Hume's explicit discussion of personal identity in the Appendix to Book III does not suggest anything along the lines suggested by Wilson and McIntyre. Hume never promised—not even 'almost'—a second theory of personal identity, and he certainly does not provide one. (See also the note in the previous Chapter on this issue). It should be noted also that Hume seems to distinguish between 'person' and 'character' when he says that 'the same person may vary his character and disposition, as well as his impressions and ideas, without losing his identity': *Treatise*, p. 261.

[65] The claim about inconsistency was made by Kemp Smith (1941), pp. 73–6. For critical discussions of the inconsistency claim, see, for example, Garrett (1997), pp. 167–9; Penelhum, 'Hume's Theory of the Self Revisited', *Dialogue*, 14 (1975), 389–409, esp. 389–90, 398, 407–9; Penelhum, 'The Self of Book 1 and the Selves of Book 2', *Hume Studies*, 18 (1992), 281–91. Penelhum does not think that there is an inconsistency, but holds that there is a 'shock of transition from Book 1 to Books 2 and 3': ibid., 282.

[66] On this, see also Penelhum (1992), 286.

[67] McIntyre and Pitson believe that Book II can and does work with the notion of the self as a bundle of causally related perceptions: McIntrye, 'Personal Identity and the Passions', *Journal of the*

So far, we have argued not only that Hume's view about personal identity can be illuminated by relating it to the Common Sense position as expressed by Kames but also that he himself adopts a Common Sense position.[68] Hume's brief post-Appendix comment in his letter to Kames provided the clue for this reading.[69] Yet Hume's position is not identical with that of his Scottish critic, as can be seen from a comment in Kames's discussion.[70] Kames states, towards the end of his essay on personal identity, that 'natural feelings' (such as the feeling of identity) must be 'admitted as evidence of truth'. That is to say, he assumes that the feeling of identity is proof of the reality of identity. Natural beliefs are not only consented to by all mankind; they also represent metaphysical truths—in this case, that of personal identity. On this view, the (alleged) fact that the belief in personal identity is natural to all human beings makes this belief a true one. Hume would not accept this aspect of the Common Sense view. We have seen that Hume does not deny the existence of a persisting self beyond the perceptions; but neither does he affirm it.[71] There is

---

History of Philosophy, 27 (1989), 547; Pitson (2002), pp. 84, 124. It is not clear, however, that this idea of the self plays a role in the Book II account of the passions. For a critical discussion of McIntyre's and others' equating of the self in Book II with the bundle view, see also Ainslie, 'Scepticism about Persons in Book II of the *Treatise*', *Journal of the History of Philosophy*, 37 (1999), 469–92, at 481–3. Purviance disagrees with McIntyre on this point and argues that Book II requires a 'real self': Purviance, 'The Moral Self and the Indirect Passions', *Hume Studies*, 23 (1997), 195–212, at 204–7. But the cited comments in Book II do not require any ontological commitments about the nature of the self. Hume does not require a 'real self' for his moral psychology; he requires merely the fact of our belief in personal identity. This fact is noted and explained in Book I, and is utilized in Book II. Book I, but not Book II, is concerned with an explanation of how this belief comes about. At the same time it remains true, of course, that neither Book I nor Book II denies the existence of a 'real self' apart from the perceptions.

[68] To my knowledge, the only other discussion of Hume and Kames on personal identity is by Tsugawa, 'David Hume and Lord Kames on Personal Identity', *Journal of the History of Ideas*, 22 (1961), 398–403. Tsugawa's reading, however, is very different from the one presented here. Indeed, Tsugawa thinks that Hume could not and did not accept Kames's view of personal identity at all.

[69] McIntyre seems to be the only scholar who has attempted to trace what Hume says about the self 'after writing the Appendix to the *Treatise*': McIntyre, 'Hume's Underground Self', *Studies in Early Modern Philosophy*, 3 (1993), 110–26. However, she mentions neither Kames, nor Hume's letter to Kames. The passages which McIntyre cites from the first *Enquiry*, the essay *On the Immortality of the Soul*, and the *Dialogues concerning Natural Religion*, do not in fact deal with the specific issue of personal identity as discussed in the *Treatise*. It is true, of course, that Hume's comments in the *Enquiry* and other later works on related issues such as self-concern (117) are compatible with his *Treatise* treatment of personal identity. This fact should not, however, surprise us. Hume's occasional remarks on the unity of the self in later writings certainly do not endorse the bundle view as an ontological truth about the nature of the mind. See, for example, his comment in the *Dialogues concerning Natural Religion* that the soul of man is 'a composition of various faculties, passions, sentiments, ideas' that are 'distinct from each other' but are 'united, indeed, into one self or person': *Dialogues*, ed. Kemp Smith (1947), p. 159.

[70] We do not know, of course, whether this comment was in the manuscript or letter that Hume saw.

[71] On this point we are in disagreement with Strawson's interpretation. Strawson argues that Hume is not agnostic about the existence of a persisting self over and above the perceptions: Hume thinks merely that we have no notion of its ultimate nature: Strawson (2001), pp. 72–3, 90. According to Strawson, Hume sees that there *must* be a persisting self or mind. Hume's account of the imagination commits him to such a view. Strawson suggests that the problem Hume recognizes

a 'natural propension' to believe in personal identity, and this belief plays an important role in our everyday lives. For Hume, however, it does not follow that that belief is true—and he is, of course, right about this. We do not know whether or not it is true.[72] All we can do is try to explain how this belief arises, and analyse its role in relation to the 'concern we take in ourselves'.[73]

A second important difference between Hume and Kames (and other Common Sense thinkers) is that the latter believe that the feelings of identity, and so on, are 'instinctive'. For Hume, by contrast, such feelings develop through experience; they are due to the imagination. And in principle we can explain how the imagination arrives at these beliefs. The fact that the belief in personal identity is due to a 'natural propension' in us does not mean, for Hume, that the belief is innate. The similarity between Hume and Kames consists in this: that both hold that our natural faculties (the imagination in Hume) inevitably give rise to this belief in personal identity.[74] These considerations also allow us to relate Hume's account to the Kantian notion of the self—at least in a preliminary fashion.[75]

13.5. A NOTE ON HUME AND KANT

Kant's relation to Hume's thought is, of course, much debated. It would seem obvious that Kant's notion of the *I* of pure apperception as the 'constant logical subject of thinking'[76] or the 'logical self'[77] implies a rejection of Hume's understanding of the self in terms of a 'bundle' of perceptions. Indeed, it has been claimed that Kant in the 'Transcendental Deduction of the Categories' intends to respond to 'Hume's Heap'.[78] And yet, although Kant was clearly familiar with Hume's position, he does not so much as mention Hume in that section. Moreover, the aim of the

---

in the Appendix concerns precisely 'the evident fact there is a real unity (not imagination generated) and connection among our successive perceptions': ibid., p. 84. The fact is, however, that in his analysis of personal identity Hume nowhere positively affirms the existence of a self beyond the perceptions. If he did positively affirm it, that would be as inconsistent with his scepticism as a denial of a self beyond the perceptions.

[72] Thus, *contra* Mach and others it needs to be emphasised that the fact that Hume's account involves the notion of a fiction does not mean that he thinks the belief in personal identity is merely an 'illusion' and in that sense 'false'. As Baier has pointed out, Humean fictions are not false but unverifiable: Baier, *A Progress of Sentiments: Reflections on Hume's Treatise* (1991), p. 103.

[73] This would seem to conform to Norton's reading of Hume's philosophy as a whole. Norton argues that Hume 'is a sceptical metaphysician but a common-sense moralist': Norton, *David Hume. Common-Sense Moralist, Sceptical Metaphysician* (1982), p. x.

[74] I thank M. A. Stewart and Galen Strawson for comments on this issue. Strawson argues that there is a sense in which Hume is a nativist about our ideas of objects and cause: Strawson (1989) pp. 250ff. Hume's account of the imagination can be said to have the consequence that we *inevitably* form the ideas that the Common Sense thinkers want to call innate.

[75] As noted above, Kantian accounts of identity and self-consciousness will be dealt with in more detail in *The Enlightened Subject* (in preparation).

[76] Kant, *Critique of Pure Reason*, eds. and transl. Guyer and Wood (1997), A 350.

[77] Kant, *Gesammelte Schriften* (1902ff., abbr., AA), vol. 20, p. 270.

[78] Kitcher, *Kant's Transcendental Psychology* (1990), pp. 95–116.

'Transcendental Deduction' concerns the objective validity of the categories or fundamental *a priori* concepts of the understanding, not a rebuttal of another philosopher's view about self-consciousness. Still, it is true that if we accept Kant's arguments about pure apperception, we cannot also accept Humean ideas about self-consciousness without qualification. This was pointed out explicitly—not by Kant himself, but by an early follower of his, Ludwig Heinrich Jakob.[79]

Jakob begins by stating that no concept has caused philosophers more trouble than the concept of the self or of personal identity, and that according to Hume it is a most contradictory and problematic concept.[80] On Jakob's analysis, Hume's difficulties with personal identity are rooted in the 'main principle of his system', which states that it must be possible to find a corresponding sense-impression for all our concepts. This approach is problematic, according to Jakob, precisely because the search for a sensory impression that corresponds to the concept of identity cannot be successful. It is a futile project. The concept of an identical self would have to be considered chimerical if we think, as Hume does, that the reality of the concept of the self consists in its being rooted in an impression.[81] Indeed, Hume is right in arguing that we cannot find the impression of a self among the perceptions of inner sense. Inner sense acquaints us only with constantly changing perceptions, but not with a constant, unchanging self.[82] This corresponds, of course, to Kant's own statement that empirical consciousness provides us only with different perceptions, and is in that sense 'forever variable' and 'can provide no standing or abiding self in this stream of inner appearances' (*Critique* A 107).

The point is, Jakob argues, that Hume's whole approach is wrongheaded. The concept of the self is not grounded in the senses at all, but is a 'pure product of the understanding' (Jakob, 'Kritische Versuche', p. 783). From this perspective we find that it is a 'necessary law of our understanding' that it must think all attributes as inherent in a something that functions as the condition of the possibility of its simultaneous and successive determinations (ibid.). In other words, the understanding must think or presuppose a connecting something—a self, which unifies attributes;

---

[79] Jakob, 'Kritische Versuche über David Hume's erstes Buch der Abhandlung über die menschliche Natur', in Jakob (transl.), *David Hume über die menschliche Natur aus dem Englischen nebst kritischen Versuchen zur Beurtheilung dieses Werks*, 2 vols. (1790–91), vol. 1, pp. 529–843.

[80] 'Kein Begriff hat den Philosophen von jeher mehr zu schaffen gemacht, als der unsres Selbst, oder der persönlichen Identität. Humen selbst scheint keiner widersprechender und anstößiger zu seyn, als dieser': ibid., p. 776.

[81] 'Wenn ich diese Schwierigkeiten, welche Humen so unüberwindlich schienen, überdenke, so finde ich, dass sie wiederum alle an dem Hauptprincip seines Systems hangen, dass sich nemlich zu jedem Begriffe eine Impression in den Sinnen finden müsse. Sucht man für den Begriff der Identität einen sinnlichen Eindruck, der diesem Begriffe entspricht, und will man die Realität desselben darauf bauen; so ist es richtig, dass nicht nur die Identität der äussern Dinge, sondern auch das Selbst eine bloße Schimäre ist': ibid., p. 782.

[82] 'Der innere Sinn macht uns nur mit Vorstellungen bekannt, die jederzeit wechseln; wenn man nun mit demselben das bleibende Ich, das Selbst, oder die Substanz suchen will, so wird man dieselbe niemals finden können, und, endlich, wenn man dabei beharret, dass der Sinn diesem Begriffe Inhalt verschaffen müsse, auf den Gedanken geraten, dass er überall eine Schimäre sey': ibid., pp. 782–3.

otherwise the understanding would not be able to relate to any objects at all. That is to say, the understanding could not unify or connect qualities into notions of determinate objects (but it *is* obviously able to do that), if it did not presuppose a connecting principle ('das verknüpfende Principium'); namely, a unitary and identical self (ibid., p. 784). The understanding, then, rather than inner sense, provides the idea of a unitary and identical self. Jakob notes, like Kant, that the notion of the self as a connecting principle is both necessary and empty. It is empty because reason cannot discover the real nature of this self—what it is 'in itself'.[83] It certainly does not provide us with knowledge of the soul as a mental substance, as something permanent, simple, and identical through time (ibid., pp. 786–7).[84]

Thus, in spite of the critical nature of these remarks they indicate that there is common ground among philosophers such as Kames, Hume, and Kant. All believe that in some sense the notion of a unitary self is inevitable or necessary. Kames and other Common Sense thinkers hold that this notion has an instinctive basis. Hume thinks that it develops inevitably through the activity of the imagination operating on experiential material, while Kant and his followers argue that it is a necessity of thought. Kant agrees with Hume that direct inner experience does not reveal such a notion. He can also agree that this is not to deny the existence of a real self beyond the perceptions. Nor does he say that the notion of necessary unity proves anything about the reality of the self as a substance. Kant goes beyond Kames and Hume, however, by moving away from the question about the empirical or instinctive source of the idea to an account in terms of an *a priori* or logical condition of the possibility of thought in general.[85] This can be seen not so much as a wholesale rejection of Hume's position, but as completing it from a different systematic perspective.[86]

---

[83] 'Die Idee des Verstandes von dem verknüpfenden Princip der innern Vorstellung bleibt daher zwar *nothwendig*, aber *leer*. Er muss vermöge seiner Nature ein Etwas denken, welches der Grund der Möglichkeit der Verknüpfung der Vorstellungen in Einem Bewusstseyn ist, und dieses ist *das Selbst*. Was dieses an und für sich sey, kann die Vernunft durch ihre blosse Idee nicht bestimmen': ibid., p. 785.

[84] Jakob provides (approvingly) an exposition of Kant's discussion of the paralogisms of pure reason in his *Grundriß der allgemeinen Logik und kritische Anfangsgründe der allgemeinen Metaphysik*, third edn. (1794). pp. 391–413.

[85] According to Kant, the self of pure apperception is 'the vehicle of all concepts whatever', including the categories: *Critique* A 341–342 and B 399–400.

[86] Indeed, there can be said to be a 'Kantian twist' to Hume's analysis of the self, as Allison has stated. It does not seem to consist, however, as Allison claims, in 'Hume's tendency to connect the issue of the genuine identity or unity of the self with its substantiality' which brings Hume's account 'squarely within the framework of Kant's paralogisms': Allison (2008), p. 308. Rather, it consists in the idea of the necessity of the notion of a unitary and identical self that Hume and Kant account for in different ways.

Conclusion: beyond Hume and Wolff

Plainly, eighteenth-century debates about self-consciousness and personal identity ended neither with Hume in Britain nor with Wolffianism in Germany, as—most notably perhaps—there were important further developments at the end of the century with the philosophy of Kant and the debates about the Kantian philosophy. It would, however, be a mistake to suggest that eighteenth-century thought on these issues developed towards Kant and Kantianism as a goal. On the contrary, there was no goal towards which eighteenth-century thought on those issues developed. The rich variety of views and arguments we have examined in the previous Chapters provides sufficient evidence for this. It cannot be denied, however, that Kant's philosophy constituted a major turning point in the history of thought on self-consciousness and self-identity. Nor can it be denied that Kant and the post-Kantian debates were part of eighteenth-century thought and, indeed, need to be related to the latter as part of their historical and systematic context.[1] That is, in spite of the many differences, there is an important continuity in discussions of these issues, and awareness of this is necessary for a proper understanding of the development of these central philosophical topics. The development of debates about these issues of identity and self-consciousness in the period between Hume and Kant is of value in its own right, however, and is itself characterized by an exciting richness and variety of philosophical discussion. This vast amount of material and debate cannot be discussed here, but will be dealt with in detail in a separate volume. There is space enough, however, to indicate the general themes and development that characterize discussions of these issues during this period.

First I must add a note on the necessarily limited scope of the present volume. Although I have examined some post-Wolffian and post-Humean material in the previous Chapters, this was, for the most part, only insofar as it relates critically to earlier accounts. For example, Thomas Reid was discussed mainly as a critic of Locke and Hume, and some late eighteenth-century contributions in Germany were examined, but only insofar as they related critically or approvingly to Wolffian thought. In some cases the critical engagement with earlier views is so closely connected to their own positive views, that it made sense to discuss the latter in the context above. This was the case, for example, in our discussion of Jean Bernard

---

[1] This needs to be emphasised, as there is a tendency, especially in some German scholarship of the period, to detach Kant and the post-Kantian debate about self-consciousness from its proper eighteenth-century context.

Mérian. In most cases, however, there have been only hints at what later accounts maintain in a positive sense. These will have to be discussed more fully, and there are some strands of thought in the period between Hume/Wolff and Kant that were not considered at all.

C.1. *SENTIMENT INTIME* AND *SELBSTGEFÜHL*

From roughly the 1740s to the 1770s the notion of feeling became prominent in discussions of personal identity, with a number of philosophers appealing to a 'feeling' of unity and identity (for example, in Boulainviller and Kames) in order to account for the unity and identity of the self. As far as terminology is concerned, expressions such *sentiment intime* and *sentiment de l'existence* were used by thinkers such as Condillac, Bonnet, and Rousseau, for example, and the German *Selbstgefühl* in the accounts of Feder, Lossius, and Tetens. While *Selbstgefühl* was introduced to the philosophical discussion in the mid-1760s,[2] the French variants for inner feeling have a much longer history in philosophical terminology, dating at least to the late seventeenth century and the writings of La Forge and Malebranche, discussed in Chapter 1. Malebranche introduced the notion of *sentiment intérieur* as a philosophical concept—a term that he uses synonymously with French 'conscience' or consciousness. Moreover, we saw that the problems surrounding the translation of Lockean 'consciousness' into French early in the eighteenth century led to the introduction of a variety of terms for relating to one's own self; for example, in Leibniz. But it is only from the mid-eighteenth century onwards, it seems, that notions such as *sentiment intime* were elaborated on and used widely in discussions of the self and personal identity. The various French terms for inner feeling or inner experience do not always denote the same thing, however. And the meaning of the German *Selbstgefühl*, too, varies from author to author. It is clear, however, that the increasing ubiquity of the language of feeling suggests that there is a perceived need to emphasise the immediacy by which we relate to our own self and personal identity—but again there is a variety of meanings that attach to the notion of immediacy. The inner experience expressed in terms of an immediate feeling can be thought of as denoting a direct inner awareness of perceptions, but it can also refer to memory as our capacity to bring to consciousness past experiences, or even to an awareness of the existence of our self as a subject of experience.

Appeals to inner feeling or experience of the self were made by many philosophers, however, and from a variety of perspectives when dealing with personal identity and self-consciousness. The link of the notion of feeling to that of consciousness might suggest that these accounts are essentially Lockean in character. But Lockean thoughts are, on the whole, merely the starting point here for independent accounts

---

[2] For an account of the development of the notion of *Selbstgefühl* in German philosophy, see Thiel, 'Varieties of Inner Sense. Two Pre-Kantian Theories', *Archiv für Geschichte der Philosophie*, 79 (1997), 58–79.

of self-consciousness and personal identity. Moreover, most of the philosophers who used the notion of feeling used it against the growing tendency towards materialist accounts of the mind. It was claimed by many that our inner feeling assures us of the immateriality of our own souls. On the other hand, they did not for the most part appeal to the notion of an immaterial soul as the basis for their accounts of self-consciousness and personal identity. Further, despite their endorsement of the notion of an immaterial soul, several of those thinkers at least tended towards a materialist understanding of the mind.

As noted above, the fact that empiricist accounts of personal identity flourished during this period is no coincidence. From about the middle of the century, empirical psychology, understood in various ways, became more and more influential—so much so that in 1772 the German philosopher Christoph Meiners demanded in his *Revision der Philosophie* that philosophy as a whole be based on psychology.

C.2. MATERIALISM

This leads to a second group of thinkers: philosophers who explicitly endorse a materialist account of the human mind and attempt to deal with issues of self-consciousness and personal identity form that perspective—thinkers mainly that belong to the 1770s and 1780s: Michael Hissmann and Christoph Meiners and others in Germany; Joseph Priestley and Thomas Cooper in Britain. Of course, these would often take up ideas from earlier philosophers that tend towards materialism (Anthony Collins, for example). As materialist thinkers tended to endorse empiricist ideas, they too, often appealed to notions such as feeling in their accounts of personal identity, and in that sense there is a link to the thinkers in the previous group. They further developed some of the ideas and principles endorsed by thinkers such as Bonnet and Feder.

There were several debates about materialism in the late seventeenth and early eighteenth centuries; but as is clear from our account above, the issue of personal identity hardly featured at all.[3] The materialist cause was strengthened by the middle of the eighteenth century because of developments in physiology (for example, through David Hartley in England, and Charles Bonnet and Albrecht von Haller on the Continent), and the related development of a new concept of matter, which was no longer regarded as essentially passive or inert, but seen as containing active powers and forces.[4] Of course, although their analyses of the mind tend towards a materialist view of the self, Bonnet, Hartley, and von Haller did not commit

---

[3] The issue of identity is not discussed, for example, by early eighteenth-century materialists such as Bucher and Lau: see Bucher, *Zweyer Guten Freunde Vertrauter Brief-Wechsel vom Wesen der Seelen* (1713); and Lau, *Meditationes philosophicae de deo, mundo, homine* (1717). For German materialism of the late seventeenth and early eighteenth centuries, see Stichler, *Materialisten der Leibniz-Zeit* (1966).

[4] See Yolton, *Thinking Matter: Materialism in Eighteenth-Century Britain* (1983), chapts. 5 and 7.

themselves to a materialist metaphysics. Still, their thought was used by materialists to further the materialist cause. This seems to have been the purpose of Joseph Priestley's abbreviated edition of Hartley, entitled *Hartley's Theory of the Human Mind* (1775). It was largely through Priestley's concise edition of Hartley that the latter's physiologically-based account of the mind had a broad impact—well beyond the English speaking world, as Priestley's introductory essays were soon translated into German. And Bonnet, too, although he argued explicitly for the existence of an immaterial soul, was influential not through his endorsement of the notion of an immaterial soul, but through his mechanist, physiological account of mental phenomena. This account, with its emphasis on the activity of 'fibres in the brain', certainly tends towards materialism. And his account of our mental life influenced many thinkers who were critical of the traditional philosophy of the mind.

When materialists engage with the issue of personal identity, however, they often do not even use their materialist principles; that is, they tend not to account for diachronic personal identity in terms of a material basis of thought and action. This situation raises several obvious questions concerning why materialists did not provide such an account, what kind of view they adopted instead and how they argued for it, and why many of them were reluctant to deal with the issue in the first place.[5]

We saw in Chapter 2 that materialist accounts of the mind (among other things) were attacked in the seventeenth century, with the argument that a material mind could not be identical through time, as matter constantly changes, and that therefore, a materialist theory of mind is inconsistent with the doctrine of life after death—for the latter doctrine assumes the identity of the self in this life and in the next life. The issue of the identity of a material mind is of course linked to the issue of the identity of material substances in general, and thus also to that of the human body. The issue of identity of the human body is in turn of importance to the question of the identity of the resurrected body. But only a few materialists (such as Joseph Priestley) addressed this immaterialist challenge by attempting to show that the notion of a material mind is consistent with the unity of the self and with personal identity through time. Most materialists simply avoided the standard immaterialist argument that invokes the issue of identity. More radically, some materialists even denied the existence of personal identity and explained only how the common belief about identity arises.

C.3. COMMON SENSE

This brings us to an idea encountered in our discussion of Hume and his critics: the idea of personal identity as a matter of Common Sense in thinkers such as Hume's friend Henry Home, Lord Kames, and Hume's critic James Beattie. According to

---

[5] For discussion of aspects of this issue, see Thiel, 'Locke and Eighteenth-Century Materialist Conceptions of Personal Identity', *The Locke Newsletter*, 29 (1998a), 59–83.

this view, personal identity is to be taken for granted and unanalysable. Towards the end of the century, some of the leading thinkers of the Scottish School of Common Sense, such as Thomas Reid and Dugald Stewart, developed this idea more systematically. In previous Chapters we encountered Reid as a critic of Locke and Hume. But Reid offers a positive account of personal identity as well; indeed, his is the most detailed and sophisticated Common Sense discussion of the issue in the eighteenth-century. Like many other philosophers before them, the Common Sense thinkers regard the issue of personal identity as crucially relevant to issues relating to moral responsibility. But Reid and others link this aspect to their more fundamental concern with the 'first principles' of Common Sense. Personal identity is regarded as one of those first principles and thought of as a necessary condition of thought and action. Like Leibniz before them, the Common Sense philosophers distinguish carefully between the issues of personal identity itself and the empirical evidence we may have of it—for example, through various forms of inner experience such as memory. For the later Common Sense thinkers, however, and Reid and Stewart in particular, personal identity is not primarily an empirical issue. Thus, their accounts differ significantly from Kames's conception of personal identity in terms of an unexplained 'feeling'.

Similarly, both Reid's and Stewart's discussions of self-consciousness also differ from earlier Common Sense accounts. They argue that we must assume the existence of a subject beyond the perceptions as a necessary condition of all thought and action, but that this assumption does not arise from any direct consciousness of the self as subject. Indeed, like Hume in this regard, Reid holds that there is no such direct consciousness, arguing that we are conscious of perceptions but not of a self that binds these perceptions together.[6] Reid and Stewart maintain, however, that the consciousness of perceptions necessarily and naturally 'suggests' the existence of a self as subject. For Reid, the existence of a self beyond the perceptions must be assumed, for without such a self and its identity through time we would not be able to connect thoughts with one another; we would not be able to think or act at all.[7] We saw in previous Chapters that other thinkers (Mérian and Reimarus, for example) adopt similar ideas, but the Common Sense thinkers seem to be the first who regard the notions of a subject and of personal identity as fundamental notions that do not afford analysis.

C.4. KANTIAN THOUGHT

Manfred Kuehn has shown that Scottish Common Sense philosophy played an important role in pre-Kantian German philosophy.[8] Moreover, the Common

---

[6] Reid, *An Inquiry into the Human Mind*, ed. Brookes (2000), p. 60.
[7] Reid, *Essays on the Intellectual Powers of Man*, ed. Brookes (2002), p. 262.
[8] Kuehn, *Scottish Common Sense in Germany, 1768–1800. A Contribution to the History of Critical Philosophy* (1987). For Reid's influence in France, see Manns, *Reid and his French Disciples: Aesthetics and Metaphysics* (1994).

Sense account of the self and personal identity invites comparison with Kant's own ideas on the issue. Kant, too, argues for the notion of an *I* as a necessity of thought—if in a very different systematic context. Unlike the Common Sense thinkers, Kant introduces a fundamental distinction between a transcendental and an empirical notion of the self, and the transcendental *I think* does not afford empirical evidence or 'suggestion'. The fact that Kant's main focus is not on empirical personal identity, but on the notion of the transcendental *I*, has led some to assume that his account and the debates surrounding it are not in any important way linked to earlier eighteenth-century views, and can be dealt with independently of the latter. But this assumption is clearly mistaken. Kant was familiar with many earlier conceptions of consciousness and identity discussed in the Chapters above—if not with all the individual authors we have examined. In particular he was familiar with the views of Locke, Hume, Rousseau, Tetens, the Wolffian School, the Common Sense School, and materialist theories.[9] Although his own approach is different in kind from previous examinations of those issues, he is aware of the latter, and does comment on empirical aspects of self-consciousness and identity in some contexts.

The notions of transcendental self-consciousness or apperception and self-identity, however, play a crucial and systematic role in Kant's critical philosophy.[10] They are introduced in the 'Transcendental Deduction of the Categories'—the 'heart' of the *Kritik der reinen Vernunft*—and are also central to his critique of rational psychology in the first part of the 'Transcendental Dialectic'. Together, these chapters contain elements of a philosophy of the subject. Moreover, Kant's reflections on the soul and self-consciousness are relevant to aspects of his moral philosophy as well as to his conception of empirical psychology. Some writers have emphasised the importance of Kant's arguments here to present-day debates, relating, for example, to reductionist theories of the mind.[11] Early critical contributions to the debate about Kant's philosophy—such as those of Karl Leonhard Reinhold and Ernst Platner—can help to illuminate and critically evaluate the Kantian approach to these issues.

Insofar as the debates surrounding Kant's philosophy led to the development of German Idealism at the end of the century, they constituted the beginning of a very

---

[9] In his pre-critical period Kant adopted the Wolffian notion of consciousness in terms of distinguishing. See his *Reflexion* 1679 (AA 16.80) from the 1750s. (Falk Wunderlich has drawn my attention to this passage). Compare also *Critique of Pure Reason*, B 414, note. Kant refers to Priestley's materialism in the *Critique*, A 745/B 773. For Kant and Priestley, see Mijuskovic, *The Achilles of Rationalist Arguments* (1974), pp. 90–1. Kant's familiarity with Kames is evident from a number of passages. *Reflexion* 3160 (AA 16.688) suggests that Kant knew not only Kames's *Elements of Criticism*, but also his *Essays on the Principles of Morality and Natural Religion* with the chapter on personal identity. (A German translation of *Essays* was published in 1768).

[10] For detailed developmental studies of Kant relevant to our topic, see in particular Carl, *Der Schweigende Kant. Die Entwürfe zu einer Deduktion der Kategorien vor 1781* (1989); Klemme, *Kants Philosophie des Subjekts* (1996); and Klemme, 'Kants Wende zum Ich. Zum Einfluß von Herz und Mendelssohn auf die Entwicklung der kritischen Subjekttheorie', *Zeitschrift für Philosophische Forschung*, 53 (1999), 507–29.

[11] See, for example, Sturma, 'Die Paralogismen der reinen Vernunft in der zweiten Auflage', in Mohr and Willaschek (eds.), *Immanuel Kant. Kritik der reinen Vernunft* (1998), pp. 391–411, at 408–10.

different kind of thought about human subjectivity. Here, various notions of transcendental self-consciousness play an important role, but the issue of empirical personal identity is marginalized. 'Absolute' Idealists such as Schelling and Hegel were more concerned with their project of overcoming, in quite different ways, Kantian and Fichtean 'dualisms' in philosophy. In their 'absolute idealism' the issues of relating to oneself and of personal identity through time are no longer a major concern. Both Kantian and empiricist-inclined examinations of consciousness and identity continued to appear simultaneously, however, with the speculations of the idealists, and thereby guaranteed the continuation of the debate about the central philosophical issues of self-consciousness and personal identity.

Bibliography

PRIMARY SOURCES

Anon. *Vindiciae Mentis. An Essay of the Being and Nature of Mind: Wherein the Distinction of Mind and Body, the Substantiality, Personality, and Perfection of Mind is Asserted; and the Original of our Minds, their Present, Separate, and Future State, is freely enquir'd into, in order to a more certain Foundation for the Knowledge of God, and our Selves, and the Clearing all Doubts and Objections that have been, or may be made concerning the Immortality of our Souls. In a New Method. By a Gentleman* [Thomas Emes?] (London: 1702).

—— [Mein, Charles]. *Two Dissertations concerning Sense, and the Imagination. With an Essay on Consciousness* (London: 1728); reprinted as Pseudo-Mayne, *Über das Bewußtsein 1728*, ed. and transl. R. Brandt (Hamburg: Meiner, 1983).

—— *De natura rerum dissertatio* (Amsterdam: 1757; summarized in *Monthly Review*, 30 (1764), 536–49.

—— *An Essay on Personal Identity. In Two Parts* (London: 1769).

Aquinas, Saint Thomas. *De ente et essentia*, ed. C. Boyer (Rome: Aedes Universitatis Gregorianae, 1946).

—— *In duodecim libros metaphysicorum Aristotelis expositio*, ed. M.-R. Cathala and R. M. Spiazzi (Turin and Rome: Marietti, 1950).

—— *Commentary on the Metaphysics of Aristotle*, ed. and transl. J. P. Rowan, 2 vols. (Chicago: Henry Regnery, 1961).

—— *Summa theologiae*, ed. and transl. T. Gilby et al., 61 vols. (London: Blackfriars, Eyre and Spottiswoode, 1964–80).

—— *On Being and Essence*, ed. and transl. A. Maurer (Toronto: Pontifical Institute of Medieval Studies, 1968).

Aristotle. *Metaphysics,* ed. and transl. H. Tredennick, 2 vols. (London: William Heinemann, 1936).

—— *On the Soul*, ed. and transl. W. S. Hett (Cambridge, MA: Harvard University Press; London: Heinemann, 1957).

Arnauld, Antoine. *Des vrayes et des fausses idées* (Cologne: 1683).

—— and Nicole, Pierre. *La logique; ou l'art de penser* (1662), ed. P. Clair and F. Girbal (Paris: Presses Universitaires de France, 1965).

Augustine, Saint. *The Trinity*, transl. S. McKenna (Washington: The Catholic University Press of America, 1963).

Bacon, Francis. *Novum organum* (1620), ed. Th. Fowler (Oxford: Oxford University Press, 1878).

Baumeister, Friedrich Christian. *Philosophia recens controversa complexa definitiones theoremata et quaestiones nostra aetate in controversiam vocatas* (Leipzig and Görlitz: 1741).

Bayle, Pierre. *Dictionnaire historique et critique*, 2 vols. (Rotterdam: 1697; second edn., 3 vols., Rotterdam: 1702; fifth edn., 4 vols., Amsterdam: 1740).

—— *Oeuvres diverses*, 4 vols. (The Hague: 1727–31); reprinted, ed. E. Labrousse (Hildesheim: Olms, 1964–68).

—— *Historical and Critical Dictionary: Selections*, ed. R. H. Popkin (Indianapolis: Bobbs Merrill, 1965).

—— *Historisches und Kritisches Wörterbuch. Eine Auswahl*, ed. and transl. G. Gawlick and L. Kreimendahl, 2 vols. (Hamburg: Meiner, 2003–06).

Beattie, James. *An Essay on the Nature and Immutability of Truth* (Edinburgh and London: 1770).

Becconsall, Thomas. *The Doctrine of a General Resurrection: Wherein the Identity of the Rising Body is asserted against the Socinians and Scepticks* (Oxford: 1697).

—— *The Grounds and Foundation of Natural Religion, Discover'd in the Principal Branches of it, in Opposition to the Prevailing Notions of the Modern Scepticks and Latitudinarians. With an Introduction concerning the Necessity of Revealed Religion* (London: 1698).

Bentley, Richard. *The Folly and Unreasonableness of Atheism* (1693), fourth edn., corrected (London: 1699).

Berkeley, George. *Philosophical Commentaries, Generally Called the Commonplace Book*, ed. A. A. Luce (London: T. Nelson, 1944).

—— *The Works of George Berkeley, Bishop of Cloyne*, ed. A. A. Luce and T. E. Jessop, 9 vols. (Edinburgh and London: T. Nelson, 1948–57).

Biran, Maine de. *Rapports des sciences naturelles avec la psychologie et autres écrits sur la psychologie*, in *Oeuvres de Maine de Biran*, vol. 8, ed. B. Baertschi (Paris: Vrin, 1986).

—— *Commentaires et marginalia: dix-huitième siècle*, in *Oeuvres de Maine de Biran*, vol. 11–12, ed. B. Baertschi (Paris: Vrin, 1993).

Boethius. *The Theological Tractates*, ed. and transl. H. F. Stewart, E. K. Rand, and S. J. Tester (Cambridge, MA: Harvard University Press, 1973).

Bold, Samuel. *A Discourse on the Resurrection of the Same Body* (London: 1705).

Boulainviller, Henry de. *Traité sur l'immortalité de l'âme* (1704), in *Oeuvres philosophiques*, ed. R. Simon (The Hague: Nijhoff, 1973–75), vol. 1.

—— 'Essai de métaphysique dans les principes de B . . . de Sp . . . ', in *Réfutation des erreurs de Benoît de Spinosa*, ed. N. L. Dufresnoy (Bruxelles: 1731).

—— *Oeuvres philosophiques*, ed. R. Simon, 2 vols. (The Hague: Nijhoff, 1973–75).

Boyle, Robert. *Selected Philosophical Papers of Robert Boyle*, ed. M. A. Stewart (Manchester: Manchester University Press, 1979).

Bresser, Martin. *De conscientia libri IV* (Antwerp: 1638).

Broughton, John. *Psychologia: Or, An Account of the Nature of the Rational Soul* (London: 1703).

Browne, Peter. *The Procedure, Extent, and Limits of Human Understanding* (London: 1728).

—— *Things Divine and Supernatural conceived by Analogy with Things Natural and Human* (London: 1733).

Browne, Sir Thomas. *Religio Medici* (1643), in *Sir Thomas Browne. The Major Works*, ed. C. A. Patrides (Harmondsworth: Penguin, 1977), pp. 59–161.

Bucher, Urban Gottfried. *Zweyer Guten Freunde Vertrauter Brief-Wechsel vom Wesen der Seelen* (The Hague: 1713).

Buffier, Claude. *Traité des premières véritez, et de la source de nos jugemens* (Paris: 1724).

—— *First Truths, and the Origin of our Opinions explained*, transl. P. Buffier (London: 1780).

Burgersdijk, Franco. *Institutiones metaphysicae* (Oxford: 1675).

Burthogge, Richard. *An Essay upon Reason, and the Nature of Spirits* (London: 1694; reprinted, New York: Garland, 1976).

Bury, Arthur. *The Naked Gospel* (London: 1690).

Butler, Joseph. *Analogy of Religion* (London: 1736).

—— 'Of Personal Identity', in *The Works of Joseph Butler*, ed. W. E. Gladstone (Oxford: Clarendon Press, 1897), vol. 1, pp. 317–25.

—— *The Works of Joseph Butler*, ed. W. E. Gladstone, 3 vols. (Oxford: Clarendon Press, 1897).

Cade, Anthony. *A Sermon on the Nature of Conscience* (London: 1621).

Canz, Israel Gottlieb. *Uberzeugender Beweiß aus der Vernunft von der Unsterblichkeit sowohl der Menschen Seelen insgemein, als besonders der Kinder-Seelen* (1741), second edn. (Tübingen: 1744).

Chambers, Ephraim. *Cyclopaedia: Or, an Universal Dictionary of Arts and Sciences... The Whole intended as a Course of Antient and Modern Learning*, 2 vols. (London: 1728).

Chauncy, Charles. *Five Dissertations on the Scripture-Account of the Fall, and its Consequences* (London: 1785).

Chauvin, Stephanus. *Lexicon Philosophicum* (1692), second edn. (Leeuwarden: 1713; reprinted, Düsseldorf: Stern-Verlag Jansen, 1967).

Cherbury, Herbert of. *De veritate* (1624), third edn. (London: 1645).

Cicero, Marcus Tullius. *De finibus bonorum et malorum*, transl. H. Rackham (Cambridge, MA: Harvard University Press; London: Heinemann, 1931).

Clarke, Samuel. *A Second Defense of an Argument made use of in a Letter to Mr. Dodwell* (London: 1707).

—— *A Third Defense of an Argument made use of in a Letter to Mr. Dodwel, to prove the Immateriality and Natural Immortality of the Soul. In a Letter to the Author of the Reflexions on Mr. Clark's Second Defense* (London: 1708).

—— *A Fourth Defense of an Argument made use of in a Letter to Mr. Dodwel, to prove the Immateriality and Natural Immortality of the Soul* (London: 1708).

——and Collins, Anthony. *A Letter to Mr. Dodwell; Together with A Defence of an Argument made use of in the above-mentioned Letter to Mr. Dodwell, to prove the Immateriality and Natural Immortality of the Soul. In Four Letters to the Author of Some Remarks, &c. To which is added, Some Reflections on that Part of a Book called Amyntor, which relates to the Writings of the Primtive Fathers, and the Canon of the New Testament. By Samuel Clarke. The Sixth Edition. In this Edition are inserted The Remarks on Dr. Clarke's Letter to Mr. Dodwell, and the several Replies to the Doctor's Defences thereof* (London: 1731).

—— 'Selections from the Clarke–Collins Correspondence', ed. W. Uzgalis, in John Perry (ed.), *Personal Identity*, second edn. (Berkeley/Los Angeles/London: University of California Press, 2008), pp. 283–314.

Clauberg, Johann. *Opera omnia philosophica*, ed. J. T. Schalbruch, 2 vols. (Amsterdam: 1691; reprinted, Hildesheim: Olms, 1968).

Clendon, John. *Tractatus Philosophico-Theologicus de Persona, or, A Treatise of the Word Person* (London: 1710).

Cockburn (née Trotter), Catherine. *A Letter to Dr. Holdsworth... in which the Passages that concern Mr. Lock are chiefly considered* (London: 1726).

—— *A Vindication of Mr. Locke's Christian Principles*, in *The Works of Mrs. Catherine Cockburn*, ed. Th. Birch, 2 vols. (London: 1751), vol. 1, pp. 157–378.

Coke, Sir Edward. *The First Part of the Institutes of the Laws of England. Or, a Commentary upon Littleton* (1628), ninth edn. (London: 1684).

Collins, Anthony. *Reflections on Mr. Clark's Second Defence of his Letter to Mr. Dodwell* (London: 1707).

—— *An Answer to Mr. Clark's Third Defence of his Letter to Mr. Dodwell* (London: 1708).

Cooper, Thomas. *Tracts, Ethical, Theological and Political* (1787); reprinted in U. Thiel (ed.), *Philosophical Writings of Thomas Cooper*, 3 vols. (Bristol: Thoemmes, 2001), vol. 1.

Coste, Pierre. *Essai philosophique concernant L'entendement humain... traduit de l'anglois de Mr. Locke* (Amsterdam: 1700).

Cousin, Victor. *Premiers essais de philosophie*, third edn. (Paris: Librairie nouvelle, 1855).

Coward, William. *Second Thoughts concerning Human Soul* (London: 1702).

—— *Farther Thoughts concerning Human Soul* (London: 1703).

Creuz, Friedrich Carl Casimir von. *Versuch über die Seele*, 2 vols. (Frankfurt and Leipzig: 1754).
Crichton, Alexander. *An Inquiry into the Nature and Origin of Mental Derangement*, 2 vols. (London: 1798).
Crusius, Christian August. *Entwurf der nothwendigen Vernunft-Wahrheiten* (Leipzig: 1745).
—— *Weg zur Gewißheit und Zuverlässigkeit der menschlichen Erkenntnis* (Leipzig: 1747).
Cudworth, Ralph. *True Intellectual System of the Universe* (London: 1678; *Imprimatur*, 1671).
—— *A Treatise concerning Eternal and Immutable Morality* (London: 1731).
—— *A Treatise of Freewill*, ed. J. Allen (London: John W. Parker, 1838).
Cuenz, Caspar. *Essai d'un sisteme nouveau concernant la nature des etres spirituels, fondé en partie sur les principes du célèbre Mr. Locke, philosophe anglois, dont l'auteur fait l'apologie*, 4 vols. (Neufchatel: 1742).
de Vries, Gerard. *Exercitationes rationales de deo divinisque perfectionibus, nec non philosophemata miscellanea* (1685), new edn. (Utrecht: 1695).
—— *De catholicis rerum attributis determinatones ontologica* (Utrecht: 1687).
—— *De natura dei et humanae mentis determinationes pneumatologicae* (Utrecht: 1687), sixth edn. (Edinburgh: 1718).
—— *De R. Cartesii Mediationibus a Petro Gassendo impugnatis dissertatiuncula historico-philosophica* (Utrecht: 1691).
Descartes, René. *Oeuvres de Descartes*, ed. and transl. C. Adam and P. Tannery, 13 vols., revised edn. (Paris: Vrin, 1964–76).
—— *Conversation with Burman*, ed. J. Cottingham (Oxford: Oxford University Press, 1976).
—— *René Descartes: Philosophical Writings*, ed. and transl. J. Cottingham, R. Stoothoff, D. Murdoch, and A. Kenny, 3 vols. (Cambridge: Cambridge University Press, 1984–91).
Deschamps, Léger-Marie. *Oeuvres philosophiques*, ed. B. Delhaume, 2 vols. (Paris: Vrin, 1993).
Digby, Sir Kenelm. *Observations upon Religio Medici* (1643), second edn. (London: 1644).
Dilly, Antoine. *Traité de l'âme des bêtes* (Lyon: 1676).
Diogenes Laertius. *Lives of Eminent Philosophers*, ed. and transl. R. D. Hicks, 2 vols. (Cambridge, MA: Harvard University Press; London: Heinemann, 1925).
Dodwell, Henry. *An Epistolary Discourse, proving from the Scripture and the first Fathers, that the Soul is a Principle naturally Mortal* (London: 1706).
Drew, Samuel. *An Essay on the Identity and General Resurrection of the Human Body; in which the Evidences in Favour of these important Subjects are considered in Relation both to Philosophy and Scripture* (London: 1809).
Dryden, John. *Sylvae* (1685), in *The Works of John Dryden*, ed. E. N. Hooker, H. T. Swedenberg, and V. A. Dearing, 20 vols. (Berkeley and Los Angeles: University of California Press, 1956–2000), vol. 3 (1969), pp. 1–90.
Duns Scotus. *Quaestiones quodlibetales*, ed. and transl. A. Wolter (Indianapolis: Hackett, 1968).
—— *God and Creatures. The Quodlibetal Questions*, ed. and transl. F. Alluntis and A. B. Wolter (Princeton, NJ: Princeton University Press, 1975).
Eberhard, Johann August. *Allgemeine Theorie des Denkens und Empfindens. Eine Abhandlung, welche den von der Königl. Akademie der Wissenschaften in Berlin auf das Jahr 1776 ausgesetzten Preis erhalten hat* (Berlin: 1776).
—— *Kurzer Abriß der Metaphysik* (Halle: 1794).
Edwards, Jonathan. *The Great Christian Doctrine of Original Sin defended; Evidences of its Truth produced, and Arguments to the Contrary answered* (1758), in *The Works of Jonathan Edwards*, vol. 3, ed. C. A. Holbrook (New Haven and London: Yale University Press, 1970).

Edwards, Jonathan. *'The Mind' of Jonathan Edwards: A Reconstructed Text*, ed. L. Howard (Berkeley and Los Angeles: University of California Press, 1963).

Emes, Thomas. *A Dialogue between Alkali and Acid* (London: 1698).

—— *The Atheist turn'd Deist, and the Deist turn'd Christian: Or, The Reasonableness and Union of the Natural, and the True Christian Religion* (London: 1698).

Felton, Henry. *The Resurrection of the same Numerical Body, and its Reunion to the same Soul; Asserted in a Sermon preached before the University of Oxford, at St. Mary's on Easter-Monday, 1725. In which Mr. Lock's Notions of Personality and Identity are confuted. And the Author of the Naked Gospel is answered* (Oxford: 1725).

Francke, Georg Samuel. *Versuch einer kurzen historisch-kritischen Uebersicht der Lehren und Meinungen unserer vornehmsten neuen Weltweisen von der Unsterblichkeit der menschlichen Seele* (Leipzig and Altona: 1796).

Gassendi, Pierre. *Opera omnia*, 6 vols. (Lyon: 1658; reprinted, Stuttgart: Frommann-Holzboog, 1964).

Geulincx, Arnold. *Opera philosophica*, ed. J. P. N. Land, 3 vols. (The Hague: Nijhoff, 1891–93; reprinted, Stuttgart: Frommann-Holzboog, 1965).

Goclenius, Rudolph. *Lexicon philosophicum* (Frankfurt a. M.: 1613).

Gravesande, Willem Jacob. *Introductio ad philosophiam: metaphysicam et logicam continens* (Leiden: 1736).

—— *Introduction à la philosophie, contenant la métaphysique, et la logique* (Leiden: 1737).

Grove, Henry. *The Works of the Reverend and Learned Mr. Henry Grove, of Taunton, containing all the Sermons, Discourses, and Tracts published in his Life-Time*, 4 vols. (London: 1747).

—— *A System of Moral Philosophy* (1749), ed. T. Amory, 2 vols., second edn. (London: 1749).

—— *Ethical and Theological Writings*, ed. A. P. F. Sell, 6 vols. (Bristol: Thoemmes, 2000).

Harris, John. *Lexicon Technicum: Or, an Universal English Dictionary of Arts and Sciences Explaining not only the Terms of Art, but the Arts themselves*, 2 vols. (London: 1710).

Hartley, David. *Observations on Man, His Frame, His Duty, and His Expectations*, 2 vols. (London: 1749).

—— *David Hartleys Betrachtungen über den Menschen, seine Natur, seine Pflicht und Erwartungen aus dem Englischen übersetzet und mit Anmerkungen und Zusätzen begleitet*, ed. and transl. with a commentary by H. A. Pistorius, 2 vols. (Rostock and Leipzig: 1772–73).

—— *Observations on Man... In Two Parts... Reprinted from the Author's Edition in 1749. To which are now added Notes and Additions to the Second Part... Also A Sketch of the Life and Character, and Head of the Author* (London: 1791); containing Pistorius's comments.

Hase, Christian Heinrich. *De anima humana non medii generis inter simplicem et compositam substantiam* (Jena: 1756).

Hazlitt, William. *An Essay on the Principles of Human Action and some Remarks on the Systems of Hartley and Helvetius* (London: 1805).

Herder, Johann Gottfried. *Sämmtliche Werke*, ed. B. Suphan (Berlin: 1877–1913; reprinted, Hildesheim: Olms, 1967).

—— *Werke. Vol. 2: Herder und die Anthropologie der Aufklärung*, ed. W. Proß (Munich: C. Hanser, 1987).

Herz, Markus. *Betrachtungen aus der spekulativen Weltweisheit* (1771), ed. E. Conrad, H. P. Delfosse, and B. Nehren (Hamburg: Meiner, 1990).

Hissmann, Michael. *Psychologische Versuche* (Frankfurt and Leipzig: 1777).

Hobbes, Thomas. *Leviathan* (1651), ed. C. B. MacPherson (Harmondsworth: Penguin Books, 1968).

—— *Opera philosophica quae Latine scripsit omnia*, ed. W. Molesworth, 5 vols. (London: 1839–45; reprinted, Darmstadt: Scientia, 1966).

—— *The English Works of Thomas Hobbes of Malmesbury*, ed. W. Molesworth, 11 vols. (London: 1839–45; reprinted, Darmstadt: Scientia, 1962).

Hody, Humphrey. *The Resurrection of the (Same) Body Asserted* (London: 1694).
Holdsworth, Winch. *A Sermon preached before the University of Oxford... in which the Cavils, False Reasonings, and False Interpretations of Scripture of Mr. Lock and Others, against the Resurrection of the same Body are examin'd and answered* (London: 1720).
—— *A Defence of the Doctrine of the Resurrection of the Same Body* (London: 1727).
Hollmann, Samuel Christian. *Dissertatio prior de stupendo naturae mysterio, anima humana sibi ipsi ignota* (Greifswald: 1722; another edn., Göttingen: 1750).
—— *Ueberzeugender Vortrag von Gott und der Schrifft* (Leipzig: 1733).
—— *Der Zerstreuer* (Göttingen: 1737).
—— *Gedancken von der Beschaffenheit der menschlichen Erkäntnüß, und den Quellen der Welt-Weißheit* (Göttingen: 1737).
—— *Institutiones pneumatologiae et theologiae naturalis paulo uberioris in universam philosophiam introductionis tomo III* (Göttingen: 1741).
—— *Philosophia rationalis, quae Logica vulgo dicitur, multum aucta et emendate. Paullo uberioris in universam philosophiam introductionis* (Göttingen: 1746).
—— *Zufällige Gedanken über verschiedene wichtige Materien*, 6 vols. (Frankfurt and Leipzig: 1771–76).
Home, Henry, Kames, Lord. *Essays on the Principles of Morality and Natural Religion* (1751), third edn. (1779), ed. M. C. Moran (Indianapolis: Liberty Fund, 2005).
—— *Elements of Criticism*, 3 vols. (Edinburgh and London: 1762); ed. P. Jones, 2 vols. (Indianapolis: Liberty Fund, 2005).
—— *Versuche über die ersten Gründe der Sittlichkeit und der natürlichen Religion in zween Theilen*, transl. C. G. Rautenberg (Braunschweig: 1768).
Huet, Pierre-Daniel. *Censura philosophiae cartesianae* (Paris: 1689; fourth edn., 1691).
Hume, David. *Essais philosophiques sur l'entendement humain*, 2 vols., transl. J.-B. Mérian (Amsterdam: 1758).
—— *An Abstract of a Treatise of Human Nature 1740: A Pamphlet hitherto unknown by David Hume* ed. J. M. Keynes and P. Sraffa (Cambridge: Cambridge University Press, 1938; reprinted, Bristol: Thoemmes, 1990).
—— *Oeuvres philosophiques de Mr. D. Hume*, 5 vols., transl. J.-B. Mérian and J. B. R. Robinet (Amsterdam: 1758–60).
—— *The Letters of David Hume*, ed. J. Y. T. Greig, 2 vols. (Oxford: Oxford University Press, 1932).
—— *Dialogues concerning Natural Religion* (1779), ed. N. Kemp Smith (Indianapolis: Bobbs-Merrill, 1947).
—— *New Letters of David Hume,* ed. R. Klibansky and E. C. Mossner (Oxford: Clarendon Press, 1954).
—— *Essays Moral, Political and Literary* (Oxford: Oxford University Press, 1963).
—— *Enquiries Concerning Human Understanding and Concerning the Principles of Morals*, ed. L. A. Selby-Bigge, third edn., revised P. H. Nidditch (Oxford: Clarendon Press, 1975).
—— *A Treatise of Human Nature* (1739–40), ed. L. A. Selby-Bigge, revised P. H. Nidditch (Oxford: Oxford University Press, 1978).
—— *A Treatise of Human Nature* (1739–40), ed. D. F. Norton and M. J. Norton (Oxford: Oxford University Press, 2000).
Hutcheson, Francis. *A System of Moral Philosophy*, 2 vols. (Glasgow: 1755); reprinted in *Collected Works*, ed. B. Fabian (Hildesheim: Olms, 1969–71), vols. 5 and 6.
—— 'Letter to William Mace, 6 Sept. 1727', *The European Magazine, and London Review*, 14 (September 1788), 158–60.
Ilive, Jacob. *The Oration spoke at Trinity-Hall in Aldersgate-street: In Answer to Dr. Felton's Two Discourses on the Resurrection of the same Body* (London: 1738).

Jakob, Ludwig Heinrich. 'Kritische Versuche über David Hume's erstes Buch der Abhandlung über die menschliche Natur', in *David Hume über die menschliche Natur aus dem Englischen nebst kritischen Versuchen zur Beurtheilung dieses Werks*, transl. L. H. Jakob, 2 vols. (Halle: 1790–91), vol. 1, pp. 529–843.

—— *Grundriß der allgemeinen Logik und kritische Anfangsgründe der allgemeinen Metaphysik* (1788), third edn. (Halle: 1794).

Kant, Immanuel. *Gesammelte Schriften* (Abbr. AA), ed. Königlich Preussische Akademie der Wissenschaften, and its successors (Berlin: G. Reimer, later de Gruyter, 1900).

—— *Critique of Pure Reason*, ed. and transl. P. Guyer and A. W. Wood (Cambridge: Cambridge University Press, 1997).

Keckermann, Bartholomaeus. *Scientiae metaphysicae compendiosum systema*, in *Opera omnia*, 2 vols. (Geneva: 1614).

King, Lord Peter. *The Life of John Locke* (London: 1830).

Kippis, Andrew. Review [untitled], of *An Essay on personal Identity*. *Monthly Review*, 40 (1769), 314–17.

——Review [untitled], of Edmund Law's *A Defence of Mr. Locke's Opinion*. *Monthly Review*, 40 (1769), 318–20.

Klosse, Johann Gottlieb. *Hieronymi Aletophili Erinnerungen auf die Gegen-Meinung der Meinung Herrn Hof-Rath Wolffens Von dem Wesen der Seele und eines Geistes überhaupt* (Frankfurt and Leipzig: 1729).

Knutzen, Martin. *De humanae mentis individua natura sive immaterialitate* (Königsberg: 1742).

—— *Philosophische Abhandlung von der immateriellen Natur der Seele, darinnen theils überhaupt erwiesen wird, daß die Materie nicht dencken könne und daß die Seele uncörperlich sey, theils die vornehmsten Einwürffe der Materialisten deutlich beantwortet werden. Aus dem Lateinischen übersetzet*, transl. G. H. Püschel (Königsberg: 1744).

La Forge, Louis de. *Traité de l'esprit de l'homme* (Paris: 1666).

—— *Oeuvres Philosophiques*, ed. P. Clair (Paris: Presses Universitaires de France, 1974).

Lambert, Johann Heinrich. *Neues Organon, oder Gedanken über die Erforschung und Bezeichnung des Wahren*, 2 vols. (Leipzig: 1764); reprinted, ed. G. Schenk (Berlin: Akademie Verlag, 1990).

Lau, Theodor Ludwig. *Meditationes philosophicae de deo, mundo, homine* (Frankfurt a. M.: 1717).

Law, Edmund. *An Enquiry into the Ideas of Space, Time, Immensity, and Eternity* (Cambridge: 1734).

—— *A Defence of Mr. Locke's Opinion Concerning Personal Identity; in Answer to the First Part of a Late Essay on That Subject* (Cambridge: 1769).

——(ed.). *An Essay on the Origin of Evil by Dr. William King* (1731), fifth edn. (London: 1781).

—— *Collected Works*, ed. V. Nuovo, 5 vols. (Bristol: Thoemmes Press, 1997).

Layton, Henry. *Observations upon a Short Treatise, Written by Timothy Manlove: Intituled, The Immortality of the Soul Asserted* (London: 1698).

—— *Observations upon a Treatise intituled Vindiciae Mentis* (London: 1702).

—— *A Search after Souls*, 2 vols. (London: 1706).

Lee, Henry. *Anti-Scepticism: Or, Notes upon each Chapter of Mr. Lock's Essay concerning Humane Understanding. With an Explication of all the Particulars of which he treats, and in the same Order. In four Books* (London: 1702).

Leibniz, Gottfried Wilhem. *Nouveaux essais sur l'entendement humain* (1765), in *Die Philosophischen Schriften von Gottfried Wilhelm Leibniz*, ed. C. I. Gerhardt, 7 vols. (Berlin: Weidmannsche Buchhandlung, 1875–90; reprinted, Hildesheim: Olms, 1978), vol. 5.

——*Principes de la nature et de la grâce, fondés en raison* (1714), in *Die Philosophischen Schriften von Gottfried Wilhelm Leibniz*, ed. C. I. Gerhardt, 7 vols. (Berlin: Weidmannsche Buchhandlung, 1875–90; reprinted, Hildesheim: Olms, 1978), vol. 6, pp. 598–606.
——*Discours de métaphysique* (1686), *in Die Philosophischen Schriften von Gottfried Wilhelm Leibniz*, ed. C. I. Gerhardt, 7 vols. (Berlin: Weidmannsche Buchhandlung, 1875–90; reprinted, Hildesheim: Olms, 1978), vol. 4, pp. 427–63.
——*Die Philosophischen Schriften von Gottfried Wilhelm Leibniz*, ed. C. I. Gerhardt, 7 vols. (Berlin: Weidmannsche Buchhandlung, 1875–90; reprinted, Hildesheim: Olms, 1978).
——*Opuscules et fragments inédits*, ed. L. Couturat (Paris: Alcan, 1903; reprinted, Hildesheim: Olms, 1966).
——*Sämtliche Schriften und Briefe*, ed. Deutsche Akademie der Wissenschaften zu Berlin (Darmstadt/Leipzig/Berlin: Olms and Akademie Verlag, 1923–).
——*Leibniz: Philosophical Writings*, ed. and transl. M. Morris and G. H. R. Parkinson (London: 1934; rev. reprint, London: Dent, 1973).
——*Textes inédits d'après les manuscrits de la bibliothèque provinciale de Hanovre*, ed. G. Grua, 2 vols. (Paris: Presses Universitaires de France, 1948).
——*Principes de la nature et de la grâce, fondés en raison. Principes de la philosophie ou Monadologie* (1714), ed. A. Robinet (Paris: Presses Universitaires de France, 1954).
——*The Leibniz-Clarke Correspondence*, ed. H. G. Alexander (Manchester: Manchester University Press, 1956).
——*Nouveaux essais sur l'entendement humain* (1765), in *Sämtliche Schriften u. Briefe*, ed. Deutsche Akademie der Wissenschaften zu Berlin, VI.6, ed. A. Robinet and H. Schepers (Berlin: Akademie Verlag, 1962).
——*The Leibniz–Arnauld Correspondence*, ed. and transl. H. T. Mason (Manchester: Manchester University Press, 1967).
——*Philosophical Papers and Letters*, ed. and transl. L. Loemker (Dordrecht: Reidel, 1969).
——*New Essays on Human Understanding*, transl. P. Remnant and J. Bennett (Cambridge: Cambridge University Press, 1981).
——*De Summa Rerum. Metaphysical Papers, 1675–1676*, ed. and transl. G. H. R. Parkinson (New Haven and London: Yale University Press, 1992).
Locke, John. *Identy* [sic] *of persons*, Bodleian Library MS Locke, 5 June 1683; facsimile reprinted in U. Thiel, *John Locke* (Reinbek bei Hamburg: Rowohlt, 2000).
——*An Essay concerning Human Understanding* ('Draft C'), unpublished MS (1685), Pierpont Morgan Library.
——*An Abridgement of Mr. Locke's Essay Concerning Human Understanding* (1696), abridged by John Wynne, fourth edn. (London: 1731).
——*Essai philosophique concernant L'entendement humain*, transl. P. Coste, fifth edn. (Amsterdam and Leipzig: 1755); reprinted, ed. E. Naert (Paris: Vrin, 1972).
——*The Works of John Locke*, ed. E. Law, 4 vols. (London: 1777).
——*The Works of John Locke*, 10 vols., new edn., corrected (London: 1823; reprinted, Aalen: Scientia, 1963).
——*An Early Draft of Locke's Essay, together with Excerpts from His Journals*, ed. R. I. Aaron and J. Gibb (Oxford: Oxford University Press, 1936).
——*An Essay Concerning Human Understanding*, ed. P. H. Nidditch (Oxford: Oxford University Press, 1975).
——*The Correspondence of John Locke*, ed. E. S. de Beer, 8 vols. (Oxford: Clarendon Press, 1976–89).
——*Drafts for the Essay concerning Human Understanding and other Philosophical Writings. Drafts A and B*, ed. P. H. Nidditch and G. A. J. Rogers (Oxford: Oxford University Press, 1990).
——*Identité et différence*, ed. and transl. E. Balibar (Paris: Sevil, 1998).

Lucretius Carus, Titus. *Of the Nature of Things, In Six Books, Translated into English Verse; by Tho. Creech... In two Volumes, explain'd and illustrated with Notes and Animadversions, being a compleat System of the Epicurean Philosophy* (1682), 2 vols. (London: 1714).
—— *On The Nature of Things*, ed. and transl. W. H. D. Rouse and M. F. Smith (Cambridge, MA: Harvard University Press, 1992).
Ludlam, Thomas. *Logical Tracts, comprising Observations and Essays illustrative of Mr. Locke's Treatise upon the Human Understanding* (London: 1790).
Ludovici, Carl Günther. *Ausführlicher Entwurf einer vollständigen Historie der Wolffischen Philosophie, zum Gebrauche seiner Zuhörer* (Leipzig: 1737).
Lupton, William. *The Resurrection of the Same Body. A Sermon Preach'd before the University of Oxford* (Oxford: 1711).
Malebranche, Nicolas. *De la recherche de la vérité* (1674–75), in *Oeuvres complètes de Malebranche*, ed. G. (Rodis-)Lewis (Paris: Vrin, 1962), vol. 1.
—— *Traité de morale*, in *Oeuvres Complètes de Malebranche*, ed. M. Adam (Paris: Vrin, 1966), vol. 11.
Manlove, Timothy. *The Immortality of the Soul Asserted, and Practically Improved* (London: 1697).
Maxwell, John. *A Treatise of the Laws of Nature. By... Richard Cumberland... Made English from the Latin by John Maxwell... At the End is subjoin'd, An Appendix, containing two Discourses. 1. Concerning the Immateriality of Thinking Substance. 2. Concerning the Obligation, Promulgation, and Observance of the Law of Nature, by the Translator* (London: 1727).
Meier, Georg Friedrich. *Beweis: Daß keine Materie denken könne* (1742), second edn. (Halle: 1751).
—— *Gedancken von dem Zustande der Seele nach dem Tode* (1746), third edn. (Halle: 1762).
—— *Auszug aus der Vernunftlehre* (1752), second edn. (Halle: 1760).
Meiners, Christoph. *Vermischte Philosophische Schriften*, 3 vols. (Leipzig: 1775–76).
Meißner, Heinrich Adam. *Philosophisches Lexicon, darinnen die Erklärungen und Beschreibungen aus des... hochberühmten Welt-Weisen Herrn Christian Wolffens sämmtlichen teutschen Schrifften seines Philosophischen Systematis sorgfältig zusammen getragen* (Bayreuth and Hof: 1737); reprinted, ed. L. Geldsetzer (Düsseldorf: Stern-Verlag Janssen, 1970).
Menasseh ben Israel. *De resurrectione mortuorum* (Amsterdam: 1636).
Mendelssohn, Moses. *Ueber die Empfindungen* (Berlin: 1755).
—— *Phädon oder über die Unsterblichkeit der Seele* (1767), ed. D. Bourel (Hamburg: Meiner, 1979).
—— *Gesammelte Schriften* (Berlin: 1929); reprinted, ed. F. Bamberger (Stuttgart and Bad Cannstatt: Fromman-Holzboog, 1971).
—— *Philosophical Writings*, ed. and transl. D. O. Dahlström (Cambridge: Cambridge University Press, 1997).
Mérian, Jean-Bernard. 'Mémoire sur l'apperception de sa propre existence', in *Histoire de l'académie royale des sciences et belles-lettres. année 1749* (Berlin: 1751), pp. 416–41. Referenced as (1749a).
—— 'Mémoire sur l'apperception considerée relativement aux idées, ou, sur l'existence des idées dans l'âme', in *Histoire de l'académie royale des sciences et belles-lettres. Année 1749* (Berlin: 1751), pp. 442–77. Referenced as (1749b).
—— 'Sur le principe des indiscernables', in *Histoire de l'académie royale des sciences et belles-lettres. Année 1754* (Berlin: 1756), pp. 383–98.
—— 'Sur l'identité numérique', in *Histoire de l'académie royale des sciences et belles-lettres. Année 1755* (Berlin: 1757), pp. 461–75.
—— 'Parallèle de deux principes de psychologie', in *Histoire de l'académie royale des sciences et belles-lettres. Année 1757* (Berlin: 1759), pp. 375–91.

———'Ueber die Apperzeption seiner eignen Existenz', in *Magazin für die Philosophie und ihre Geschichte. Aus den Jahrbüchern der Akademien angelegt*, vol. 1, ed. M. Hissmann (Göttingen and Lemgo: 1778), pp. 89–132.

———'Parallel der beiden Prinzipien der Psychologie, der Empfindungs- und Vorstellungskraft', in *Magazin für die Philosophie und ihre Geschichte. Aus den Jahrbüchern der Akademien angelegt*, vol. 6, ed. M. Hissmann (Göttingen and Lemgo: 1783), pp. 175–204.

———'Sur le phénoménisme de David Hume', in *Mémoires de l'académie royale des sciences et belles-lettres depuis l'avènement de Frédéric Guillaume II au Thrône* (Berlin: 1793), pp. 417–37.

———'Parallèle historique de nos deux philosophies nationales', in *Mémoires de l'Académie Royale des Sciences et Belles-Lettres depuis l'Avènement de Frédéric Guillaume II au Thrône, Classe de philosophie spéculative* (Berlin: 1797), pp. 53–96.

———*Sur le problème de Molyneux*, ed. F. Markovits (Paris: Flammarion, 1984).

Micraelius, Johann. *Lexicon philosophicum* (1653), second edn. (Stettin: 1662).

More, Henry. *The Immortality of the Soule, So Farre Forth As It Is Demonstrable from the Knowledge of Nature and the Light of Reason* (London: 1659).

———*An Antidote against Atheism*, in H. More, *A Collection of Several Philosophical Writings*, 2 vols. (London: 1662; reprinted, New York: Garland, 1978).

Morell, Thomas. *Notes and Annotations on Locke on the Human Understanding, written by Order of the Queen* (London: 1794).

Müller, August Friedrich. *Einleitung in die Philosophischen Wissenschaften*, 3 vols. (Leipzig: 1728; second edn., 1733).

Norris, John. *An Essay towards the Theory of the Ideal or Intelligible World*, 2 vols. (London: 1701–04; reprinted, New York: Garland, 1978).

Overton, Richard. *Mans Mortalitie* (1643–44), ed. H. Fisch (Liverpool: Liverpool University Press, 1968).

d'Oyly, Robert. *Four Dissertations* (London: 1728).

Pardies, Ignace-Gaston. *Discours de la connaissance des bestes* (Paris: 1672).

Parker, Samuel (1640–88). *An Account of the Nature and Extent of the Divine Dominion, Especially as They Refer to the Origenian Hypothesis concerning the Preexistence of Souls, Together with a Special Account of the Vanity and Groundlessness of the Hypothesis It Self* (London: 1666).

Parker, Samuel (1681–1730). *Essays on Divers Weighty and Curious Subjects. Particularly on Mr. Lock's and Sir William Temple's Notions* (London: 1702).

———*A Letter to Mr. Bold, occasion'd by his late Discourse concerning the Resurrection of the Same Body* (London: 1707).

Pascal, Blaise. *Pensées* (1669), transl. A. J. Krailsheimer (Harmondsworth: Penguin, 1966).

Pearson, John. *An Exposition of the Creed* (London: 1659).

Perronet, Vincent. *A Vindication of Mr. Locke, from the Charge of giving Encouragement to Scepticism and Infidelity, and from several other Mistakes and Objections of the learned Author of the Procedure, Extent, and Limits of Human Understanding. In Six Dialogues* (London: 1736).

———*A Second Vindication of Mr. Locke, wherein his Sentiments relating to Personal Identity are clear'd up from some Mistakes of the Rev. Dr. Butler, in his Dissertation on that Subject* (London: 1738); reprinted, with a new Introduction by J. Yolton (Bristol: Thoemmes, 1991).

———*Some Enquiries, Chiefly Relating to Spiritual Beings: in Which the Opinions of Mr. Hobbes, with Regard to Sensation, Immaterial Substance and the Attributes of the Deity Are Taken Notice of; and Wherein Likewise is Examined How Far the Supposition of an Invisible Tempter is Defensible on the Principles of Natural Reason* (London: 1740).

Platner, Ernst. *Philosophische Aphorismen nebst einigen Anleitungen zur Philosophischen Geschichte* (1776), third edn. (Leipzig: 1793).
Plotinus. *Enneads*, transl. A. H. Armstrong, 7 vols. (Cambridge, MA: Harvard University Press, 1966–88).
Ploucquet, Gottfried. *Principia de substantiis et phaenomenis* (Frankfurt and Leipzig: 1764).
—— *Examen meletematum celeberrimi anglorum philosophi, Lockii, de personalitate* (Tübingen: 1760).
Plutarch. 'Life of Theseus', in *Plutarch's Lives*, transl. B. Perrin, 11 vols. (London: W. Heinemann; Cambridge, MA: Harvard University Press, 1959–62), vol. 1, pp. 1–87.
Poley, Heinrich Engelhard. *Herrn Johann Lockens Versuch vom Menschlichen Verstande. Aus dem Englischen übersetzt und mit Anmerkungen versehen* (Altenburg: 1757).
Price, Richard and Priestley, Joseph. *A Free Discussion of the Doctrines of Materialism and Philosophical Necessity in a Correspondence between Dr. Price and Dr. Priestley* (London: 1778).
Priestley, Joseph. *Hartley's Theory of the Human Mind* (London: 1775).
—— *Disquisitions relating to Matter and Spirit* (London: 1777).
—— *The Doctrine of the Divine Influence on the Human Mind* (Bath and London: 1779).
Pufendorf, Samuel. *Elementorum iurisprudentiae universalis libri duo* (1660), new edn. (Lund: 1672; reprinted, Oxford: Clarendon Press, 1931).
—— *De jure naturae et gentium* (1672), in Pufendorf, *Gesammelte Werke*, ed. W. Schmidt-Biggemann, pt. 4, vols. 1 and 2, ed. F. Böhling (Berlin: Akademie Verlag, 1998).
—— *The Law of Nature and Nations*, transl. B. Kennett (London: 1717).
Régis, Pierre-Sylvain. *Système de philosophie contenant la logique, la métaphysique, la physique, et la morale*, 3 vols. (Paris: 1690).
—— *Réponse au livre qui a pour titre, P. Danielis Huetii... Censura philosophiae cartesianæ* (Paris: 1691).
Reid, Thomas. *Curâ primâ Of Common Sense*, ed. D. F. Norton, in L. Marcil-LaCoste, *Claude Buffier and Thomas Reid* (Montreal: McGill–Queen's University Press, 1982), pp. 187–208.
—— *An Inquiry into the Human Mind on the Principles of Common Sense* (1764), ed. D. R. Brookes (Edinburgh: Edinburgh University Press, 2000).
—— Review [untitled and anonymously published] of Joseph Priestley's *Hartley's Theory of the Human Mind. Monthly Review*, 53 (1775–76), 380–90 and *Monthly Review*, 54 (1776), 41–7.
—— *Essays on the Intellectual Powers of Man* (1785), ed. D. R. Brookes, editorial annotations and introduction K. Haakonssen (University Park, PA: Pennsylvania State University Press, 2002).
Reimarus, Hermann Samuel. *Die Vornehmsten Wahrheiten der natürlichen Religion* (1754), third edn. (Hamburg: 1766), facsimile ed. G. Gawlick (Göttingen: Vandenhoeck & Ruprecht, 1985).
Robertson, William. *An Attempt to explain the Words Reason, Substance, Person, Creeds, Orthodoxy, Catholic-Church, Subscription, and Index Expurgatorius* (London: 1766).
Roche, Antoine-Martin. *Traité de la nature de l'âme, et de l'origine des connaissances. Contre le systême de M. Locke et de ses partisans*, 2 vols. (Amsterdam: 1759).
Ross, Alexander. *Medicus Medicatus: Or the Physicians Religion Cured, by a Lenitive or Gentle Potion: With some Animadversions upon Sir Kenelme Digbie's Observations on Religio Medici* (London: 1645).
Rüdiger, Andreas. *Herrn Christian Wolffens Meinung von dem Wesen der Seele und eines Geistes überhaupt; und D. Andreas Rüdigers Gegen-Meinung* (Leipzig: 1727); reprinted, with a preface by M. Albrecht (Hildesheim: Olms, 2008).
Scharf, Johannes. *Metaphysica exemplaris, seu Prima philosophia* (1625), fourth edn. (Wittenberg: 1643).
Scheibler, Christoph. *Metaphysica* (Geneva: 1636).
Schulze, Gottlob Ernst. *Psychische Anthropologie* (Göttingen: 1816; third edn., 1826).

Seneca, Lucius Annaeus. *Ad Lucilium Epistulae Morales*, ed. and transl. R. M. Gummere (London and Cambridge, MA: Harvard University Press, 1953).
Sergeant, John. *The Method to Science* (London: 1696).
——*Solid Philosophy Asserted, against the Fancies of the Ideists: Or, The Method to Science Farther illustrated. With Reflections on Mr. Locke's Essay* (London: 1697; reprinted, New York: Garland, 1984).
——*Transnatural Philosophy, or, Metaphysicks demonstrating the Essences and Operations of all Beings whatever... and shewing the Perfect Conformity of Christian Faith to Right Reason, and the Unreasonableness of Atheists... and other Sectaries: with an Appendix giving a Rational Explication of the most B. Trinity* (London: 1700).
Servetus, Michael. *De trinitatis erroribus libri septem* (Hagenau: 1531).
——*Two Treatises of Servetus on the Trinity*, transl. E. M. Wilbur (Cambridge, MA: Harvard University Press, 1932).
Shaftesbury, Anthony Ashley Cooper, Earl of. *Philosophical Regimen*, in *The Life, Unpublished Letters, and Philosophical Regimen of Anthony, Earl of Shaftesbury*, ed. B. Rand (London: Swan Sonnenschein, 1900).
——*Characteristics*, ed. J. M. Robertson, 2 vols. (London: Grant Richards, 1900).
——*Characteristics of Men, Manners, Opinions, Times*, ed. L. E. Klein (Cambridge: Cambridge University Press, 1999).
Sherlock, William. *A Vindication of the Doctrine of the Holy and Ever Blessed Trinity* (London: 1690).
——*A Defence of Dr. Sherlock's Notion of a Trinity in Unity* (London: 1694).
——*Auserlesene Zeugnisse von den wichtigsten Grundwahrheiten der Christlichen Religion* (Berlin: 1744). A translation of thirty of Sherlock's sermons, with a preface by F. E. Rambach.
Smith, John. *Select Discourses* (1660), third edn., corrected (London: Rivingtons and Cochran, 1821).
South, Robert. *Animadversions upon Dr. Sherlock's Book, Entituled A Vindication of the Holy and Ever Blessed Trinity* (London: 1693).
——*Tritheism Charged upon Dr. Sherlock's New Notion of the Trinity* (London: 1695).
Spinoza, Baruch de. *Short Treatise on God, Man, and His Well Being* (c. 1660), ed. and transl. A. Wolf (London: Adam and Charles Black, 1910).
——*Ethica* (1677), in *Spinoza Opera*, ed. C. Gebhardt, 4 vols. (Heidelberg: C. Winter, 1925), vol. 2.
——*Spinoza Opera*, ed. C. Gebhardt, 4 vols. (Heidelberg: C. Winter, 1925).
——*The Collected Works of Spinoza*, ed. E. Curley (Princeton, NJ: Princeton University Press, 1985).
Stanley, Thomas. *The History of Philosophy, the Eighth Part, Containing the Stoick Philosophers* (London: 1656).
Stewart, Dugald. *Collected Works*, ed. W. Hamilton, 11 vols. (Edinburgh: T. Constable, 1854–60), facsimile ed. K. Haakonssen (Bristol: Thoemmes, 1994).
Stillingfleet, Edward. *The Doctrine of the Trinity and Transubstantiation Compared... The Second Part* (London: 1687).
——*A Discourse in Vindication of the Doctrine of the Trinity: With an Answer to the Late Socinian Objections against it from Scripture, Antiquity and Reason* (London: 1697).
——*An Answer to Mr. Locke's Second Letter; Wherein his Notion of Ideas is Prov'd to be Inconsistent with It Self, and with the Articles of the Christian Faith* (London: 1698).
Strähler, Daniel. *Prüfung der Vernünftigen Gedancken des Herrn Hoff-Rath Wolffes von Gott, der Welt und der Seele des Menschen, auch allen Dingen überhaupt*, 2 vols. (Jena and Leipzig: 1723; reprinted, Hildesheim: Olms, 1999).
Suárez, Francisco. *Disputationes metaphysicae* (1597), 2 vols. (Hildesheim: Olms, 1965).

Suárez, Francisco. *De legibus* (1612), in *Opera omnia*, ed. C. Berton, 28 vols. (Paris: Vivès, 1856–78), vols. 5 and 6.
—— *De unitate individuali eiusque principio / Über die Individualität und das Individuationsprinzip*, ed. and transl. (German) R. Specht, 2 vols. (Hamburg: Meiner, 1976).
—— *Suarez on Individuation. Metaphysical Disputation V: Individual Unity and Its Principle*, ed. and transl. J. J. E. Gracia (Milwaukee, WI: Marquette University Press, 1982).
Sulzer, Johann Georg. 'Sur l'apperception, et son influence sur nos jugemens', *Histoire de l'academie royale des sciences et belles-lettres. Année 1764* (Berlin: 1766), 415–34.
—— *Allgemeine Theorie der Schönen Künste* (1771–74), fourth edn., enlarged, with supplements by C. F. von Blanckenburg, 4 vols. (Leipzig: 1796–98).
—— 'Von dem Bewußtseyn und seinem Einflusse in unsre Urtheile', in *Vermischte Philosophische Schriften*, vol. 1 (Leipzig: 1773), pp. 199–224.
—— *Vermischte Philosophische Schriften*, 2 vols. (Leipzig: 1773–81; reprinted, Hildesheim: Olms, 1974).
Tetens, Johann Nicolas. *Philosophische Versuche über die menschliche Natur und ihre Entwicklung*, 2 vols. (Leipzig: Weidmanns Erben und Reich, 1777; reprinted, Hildesheim: Olms, 1979).
Thomasius, Christian. *Einleitung zu der Vernunftlehre* (Halle: 1691; reprinted, Hildesheim: Olms, 1968).
Thümmig, Ludwig Phillip. *Institutiones philosophiae Wolfianae* (Frankfurt and Leipzig: 1725–26); reprinted in Ch. Wolff, *Gesammelte Werke*, pt. 3, vol. 19 (Hildesheim: Olms, 1982).
Tiedemann, Dietrich. *Untersuchungen über den Menschen*, 3 vols. (Leipzig: 1777–78).
Tillotson, John. *The Possibility of the Resurrection asserted and proved* (1682), in *The Works of... Dr. John Tillotson... Published from the Originals by Ralph Barker*, 3 vols. (London: 1728), vol. 3, pp. 248–55.
Timpler, Clemens. *Metaphysicae systema methodicum* (Steinfurt: 1604).
Tucker, Abraham. *Man in Quest of Himself: Or A Defence of the Individuality of the Human Mind, or Self* (published 1763 under the pseudonym 'Cuthbert Comment'), in S. Parr (ed.), *Metaphysical Tracts by English Philosophers of the Eighteenth Century* (London: 1837; reprinted, Hildesheim: Olms, 1974), pp. 171–210.
—— *The Light of Nature Pursued* (1768–78), second edn., 7 vols. (London: 1805; reprinted, New York and London: Garland, 1977).
Turner, John. *The Middle Way Betwixt Necessity and Freedom* (London: 1683).
—— *A Discourse concerning the Messias... To Which is Prefixed a Large Preface, Asserting and Explaining the Doctrine of the Blessed Trinity, against the Late Writer of the Intellectual System* (London: 1685).
Valla, Lorenzo. *De linguae latinae elegantiae* (Cambridge: 1688).
Voltaire, François-Marie Arouet de. *Letters concerning the English Nation* (London: 1733).
—— *Lettres écrites de Londres sur les Anglois, et autres sujets* (Basle: 1734).
—— *Traité de métaphysique* (1734), ed. H. T. Patterson, second edn. (Manchester: Manchester University Press, 1957).
—— *Oeuvres complètes de Voltaire*, 72 vols. (Paris: 1784–89).
—— *Lettres philosophiques*, ed. G. Lanson, third edn., 2 vols. (Paris: Hachette, 1924).
Wallace, George. *A System of the Principles of the Laws of Scotland* (Edinburgh: 1760).
Ward, Seth. *A Philosophical Essay towards an Eviction of the Being and Attributes of God. The Immortality of the Soule. The Truth and Authority of Scripture* (Oxford: 1652).

Warren, Edward. *No Praeexistence: Or a Brief Dissertation against the Hypothesis of Humane Souls, Living in a State Antecedaneous to This* (London: 1667).
Watts, Isaac. *Philosophical Essays on Various Subjects... With Remarks on Mr. Locke's Essay on the Human Understanding. To which is subjoined A Brief Scheme of Ontology* (1733), third edn. (London: 1742; reprinted, Bristol: Thoemmes Press, 1990).
Whichcote, Benjamin. *Select Sermons* (London: 1698).
Whitehead, John. *Materialism Philosophically Examined* (London: 1778).
Wilkins, John. *Of the Principles and Duties of Natural Religion* (London: 1677).
Willis, Thomas. *De anima brutorum quae hominis vitalis ac sensitiva est, exercitationes duae* (1672), transl. as *Two Discourses Concerning the Souls of Brutes, which is also that of the Vital and Sensitive Part of Man* by S. Pordage (London: 1683).
Winckler, Johann Heinrich. *Institutiones philosophiae Wolfianae* (Leipzig: 1735).
—— *Die Frage, ob die Seelen der Thiere Verstand haben* (Leipzig: 1742).
Wolff, Christian. *Vernünftige Gedancken von den Kräften des menschlichen Verstandes und ihrem richtigen Gebrauche in Erkenntnis der Wahrheit* (1713), in Ch. Wolff, *Gesammelte Werke*, pt. 1, vol. 1, ed. H. W. Arndt (Hildesheim: Olms, 1965; reprinted, 1978; following the 1754 edn.; abbr. *Deutsche Logik*).
—— *Vernünfftige Gedancken von Gott, der Welt und der Seele des Menschen, auch allen Dingen überhaupt* (1719), in Ch. Wolff, *Gesammelte Werke*, pt. 1, vol. 2, ed. Ch. A. Corr (Hildesheim: Olms, 1983; reprint of the 1751 edn.; abbr., *Deutsche Metaphysik*).
—— *Der Vernünfftigen Gedancken von Gott, der Welt und der Seele des Menschen, auch allen Dingen überhaupt, Anderer Theil, bestehend in ausführlichen Anmerckungen* (1724), in Ch. Wolff, *Gesammelte Werke*, pt. 1, vol. 3, ed. Ch. A. Corr (Hildesheim: Olms, 1983; reprint of the 1740 edn.).
—— *Discursus praeliminaris de philosophia in genere*, in Ch. Wolff, *Philosophia rationalis sive logica* (1728), in Ch. Wolff, *Gesammelte Werke*, pt. 2, vol. 1.1–1.3 (Hildesheim: Olms, 1983; reprint of the 1740 edn.), vol. 1.1.
—— *Philosophia prima, sive ontologia* (1730), in Ch. Wolff, *Gesammelte Werke*, pt. 2, vol. 3, ed. J. École (Hildesheim: Olms, 1962; reprint of the 1736 edn.).
—— *Psychologia empirica* (1732), in Ch. Wolff, *Gesammelte Werke*, pt. 2, vol. 5, ed. J. École (Hildesheim: Olms, 1968; reprint of the 1738 edn.).
—— *Psychologia rationalis* (1734), in Ch. Wolff, *Gesammelte Werke*, pt. 2, vol. 6, ed. J. École (Hildesheim: Olms, 1972; reprint of the 1740 edn.).
—— *Psychologie ou Traité sur l'ame, contenant les connoissances, que nous en donne l'experience* (Amsterdam: 1745); reprinted in, Ch. Wolff, *Gesammelte Werke*, pt. 3, vol. 46, ed. J. École (Hildesheim: Olms, 1998).
—— *Redenkundige bedenkingen over God, de wereld, en de menschelyke ziele... doar Christian Wolff*, transl. J. Ch. Sprögel, 2 vols. (Amsterdam: 1767–68).
—— *Gesammelte Werke*, ed. J.École et al. (Hildesheim/Zürich/New York: 1962–).

SECONDARY SOURCES

Ainslie, Donald. 'Scepticism about Persons in Book II of the *Treatise*', *Journal of the History of Philosophy*, 37 (1999), 469–92.
—— 'Hume's Reflections on the Identity and Simplicity of Mind', *Philosophy and Phenomenological Research*, 62 (2001), 557–78.
—— 'Hume on Personal Identity', in E. S. Radcliffe (ed.), *A Companion to Hume* (Oxford: Blackwell, 2008), pp. 140–56.
Alanen, Lilli. *Descartes's Concept of Mind* (Cambridge, MA: Harvard University Press, 2003).

Alger, William Rouneville. *A Critical History of the Doctrine of a Future Life* (Philadelphia: George W. Childs, 1864).

Allison, Henry. *Custom and Reason in Hume: A Kantian Reading of the First Book of the Treatise* (Oxford: Oxford University Press, 2008).

Alston, William and Bennett, Jonathan. 'Locke on People and Substances', *Philosophical Review*, 97 (1988), 25–46.

Altmann, Alexander. *Moses Mendelssohns Frühschriften zur Metaphysik* (Tübingen: J. C. B. Mohr, 1969).

Ancillon, Jean Pierre Frédéric. 'Éloge historique de J.-B. Mérian', in *Abhandlungen der Königlichen Akademie der Wissenschaften zu Berlin, Historische Einleitung* (Berlin: G. Reimer, 1810), pp. 52–90.

Anderson, David J. 'Susceptibility to Punishment: A Response to Yaffe', *Locke Studies*, 8 (2008), 101–6.

Aner, Karl. *Gottfried Ploucquets Leben und Lehren* (Halle: Niemeyer, 1909).

Annas, Julia. *Hellenistic Philosophy of Mind* (Berkeley/Los Angeles/London: University of California Press, 1992).

Anstey, Peter. '*De Anima* and Descartes: Making up Aristotle's Mind', *History of Philosophy Quarterly*, 17 (2000), 237–60.

—— *The Philosophy of Robert Boyle* (London and New York: Routledge, 2000).

Antognazza, Maria Rosa. *Leibniz: An Intellectual Biography* (Cambridge: Cambridge University Press, 2009).

Aquila, Richard E. 'The Cartesian and a Certain "Poetic" Notion of Consciousness', *Journal of the History of Ideas*, 49 (1988), 543–62.

Ariew, Roger. *Descartes and the Last Scholastics* (Ithaca and London: Cornell University Press, 1999).

Armogathe, Jean-Robert. *Theologia Cartesiana. L'explication physique de l'Eucharistie chez Descartes et Dom Desgabets* (The Hague: Nijhoff, 1977).

Arnaud, Thierry. 'Où commence la "Métaphysique allemande" de Christian Wolff?', in O.-P. Rudolph and J.-F. Goubet (eds.), *Die Psychologie Christian Wolffs* (Tübingen: Niemeyer, 2004), pp. 61–73.

Aspelin, Gunnar. *Ralph Cudworth's Interpretation of Greek Philosophy. A Study in the History of English Philosophical Ideas* (Gothenburg: Wettergren & Kerber, 1943).

Assenmacher, Johannes. *Die Geschichte des Individuationsprinzips in der Scholastik* (Leipzig: Meiner, 1926).

Atherton, Margaret. 'Locke's Theory of Personal Identity', *Midwest Studies in Philosophy*, 8 (1983), 273–93.

Ayers, Michael R. *Locke*, 2 vols. (London and New York: Routledge, 1991).

Baertschi, Bernard L. 'La conception de la conscience developpée par Mérian', in M. Fontius and H. Holzhey (eds.), *Schweizer im Berlin des 18. Jahrhunderts* (Berlin: Akademie Verlag, 1996), pp. 231–48.

Baier, Annette. *A Progress of Sentiments: Reflections on Hume's Treatise* (Cambridge, MA: Harvard University Press, 1991).

Baillie, James. 'Recent Work on Personal Identity', *Philosophical Books*, 34 (1993), 193–206.

Baker, Gordon. 'Seventeenth Century Philosophy', *British Journal of the History of Philosophy*, 8 (2000), 353–73.

—— and Morris, Katherine J. *Descartes' Dualism* (London and New York: Routledge, 1996).

Balibar, Étienne. *John Locke: Identité et différence* (Paris: Editions de Seuil, 1998).

Ball, Bryan W. *The Soul Sleepers: Christian Mortalism from Wycliffe to Priestley* (Cambridge: James Clarke, 2008).

Balz, Albert G. A. *Cartesian Studies* (New York: Columbia University Press, 1951).

Barber, Kenneth F. and Gracia, Jorge J. E. (eds.). *Individuation and Identity in Early Modern Philosophy: Descartes to Kant* (Albany, NY: State University of New York Press, 1994).

Barber, William Henry. *Leibniz in France. From Arnauld to Voltaire. A Study in French Reactions to Leibnizianism, 1670–1760* (New York: Oxford University Press, 1955).
Barth, Christian. 'Bewusstsein bei Descartes', *Archiv für Geschichte der Philosophie*, 93 (2011), 162–94.
Bartha, Paul. 'Substantial Form and the Nature of Individual Substance', *Studia Leibnitiana*, 25 (1993), 43–54.
Baxter, Donald L. M. 'Hume's Labyrinth Concerning the Idea of Personal Identity', *Hume Studies*, 24 (1998), 203–33.
—— *Hume's Difficulty: Time and Identity in the Treatise* (London and New York: Routledge, 2008).
Beauchamp, Tom L. 'Self Inconsistency or Mere Self Perplexity', *Hume Studies*, 5 (1979), 37–44.
Beck, Lewis White. *Early German Philosophy. Kant and his Predecessors* (Cambridge, MA: Belknap Press, 1969).
Behan, David P. 'Locke on Persons and Personal Identity', *Canadian Journal of Philosophy*, 9 (1979), 53–75.
Bella, Stefano di. *The Science of the Individual: Leibniz's Ontology of Individual Substance* (Dordrecht: Springer, 2005).
Belfrage, Bertil. 'A New Approach to Berkeley's *Philosophical Notebooks*', in E. Sosa (ed.), *Essays on the Philosophy of George Berkeley* (Dordrecht: D. Reidel, 1987), pp. 217–30.
Berlioz, Dominique. 'L'esprit comme principe individuel chez G. Berkeley', in G. M. Cazzaniga and Y. Ch. Zarka (eds.), *L'Individu dans la pensée moderne* (Pisa: Edizioni ETS, 1995), pp. 391–403.
Berman, David. 'Anthony Collins: Aspects of his Thought and Writings', *Hermathena*, 119 (1975), 49–70.
Bettcher, Talia. 'Berkeley on Self-Consciousness', in S. H. Daniel (ed.), *New Interpretations of Berkeley's Thought* (Amherst, NY: Humanity Books, 2008), pp. 197–220.
—— 'Berkeley and Hume on the Self and Self-Consciousness', in J. Miller (ed.), *Topics in Early Modern Philosophy of Mind* (Dordrecht: Springer, 2009), pp. 195–224.
Black, Deborah. 'Consciousness and Self-Knowledge in Aquinas's Critique of Averroes's Psychology', *Journal of the History of Philosophy*, 31 (1993), 349–85.
—— 'Avicenna on Self-Awareness and Knowing that One Knows', in S. Rahman, T. Hassan, and T. Street (eds.), *The Unity of Science in the Arabic Tradition* (Dordrecht: Springer, 2008), pp. 63–87.
Blackwell, Richard J. 'Christian Wolff's Doctrine of the Soul', *Journal of the History of Ideas*, 22 (1961), 339–54.
Blakey, Robert. *History of the Philosophy of Mind: embracing the Opinions of all Writers on Mental Science from the Earliest Period to the Present Time*, 4 vols. (London: Longman, Brown, Green and Longmans, 1850).
Bobro, Marc Elliott. 'Is Leibniz's Theory of Personal Identity Coherent?', *The Leibniz Review*, 9 (1999), 117–29.
—— *Self and Substance in Leibniz* (Dordrecht: Kluwer Academic Publishers, 2004).
Bolton, Martha Brandt. 'Locke on Identity: The Scheme of Simple and Compounded Things', in K. F. Barber and J. E. Gracia (eds.), *Individuation and Identity in Early Modern Philosophy: Descartes to Kant* (Albany, NY: State University of New York Press, 1994) pp. 103–31.
Bowin, John. 'Chrysippus' Puzzle about Identity', *Oxford Studies in Ancient Philosophy*, 24 (2003), 239–51.
Bradish, Norman C. 'John Sergeant, A Forgotten Critic of Descartes and Locke', *The Monist*, 39 (1929), 571–92.
Brands, Hartmut. *'Cogito ergo sum'. Interpretationen von Kant bis Nietzsche* (Freiburg i. Br.: Alber, 1982).
Brandt, Reinhard. 'Rousseau und Kants "Ich denke"', *Kant-Forschungen*, 5 (1994), 1–18.

Brandt, Reinhard. 'Selbstbewusstsein und Selbstsorge. Zur Tradition der οἰκείωσις in der Neuzeit', *Archiv für Geschichte der Philosophie*, 85 (2003), 179–97.
—— 'John Lockes Konzept der persönlichen Identität. Ein Resümee', *Aufklärung*, 18 (2006), 37–54.
Brentano, Franz. *Psychology from an Empirical Standpoint*, transl. A. C. Rancurello, D. B. Terrell, and L. L. McAlister (London: Routledge and Kegan Paul, 1973).
Bricke, John. *Hume's Philosophy of Mind* (Edinburgh: Edinburgh University Press, 1980).
Brinkmann, Klaus. 'Consciousness, Self-consciousness, and the Modern Self', *History of the Human Sciences*, 18 (2005), 27–48.
Briscoe, Peter. 'On the Phenomenalism of David Hume', *Hume Studies*, 23 (1997), 178–91.
Brissenden, Robert Francis. '"Sentiment": Some Uses of the Word in the Writings of David Hume', in R. F. Brissenden (ed.), *Studies in the Eighteenth Century* (Canberra: Australian National University Press, 1968), pp. 89–107.
Broackes, Justin. 'Hume, Belief and Personal Identity', in P. Millican (ed.), *Reading Hume on Understanding* (Oxford: Oxford University Press, 2002), pp. 187–210.
Brown, Clifford. *Leibniz and Strawson: A New Essay in Descriptive Metaphysics* (Munich and Vienna: Philosophia, 1990).
Brown, S. C. 'Berkeley on the Unity of the Self', *Royal Institute of Philosophy Lectures*, 5 (1971), 64–87.
Buckle, Stephen. 'Hume's Sceptical Materialism', *Philosophy*, 82 (2007), 553–78.
Buickerood, James G. '*Two Dissertations concerning Sense, and the Imagination. With an Essay on Consciousness* (1728): A Study in Attribution', *1650–1850: Ideas, Aesthetics, and Inquiries in the Early Modern Era*, 7 (2002), 51–86.
—— '"The whole exercise of reason": Charles Mein's Account of Rationality', *Journal of the History of Ideas*, 63 (2002), 639–58.
Burford, Thomas O. 'A Theater of Memory: Vico's View of Personal Identity', *South Atlantic Philosophy of Education Society Yearbook*, 32 (1987), 69–76.
Burge, Tyler. 'Memory and Persons', *The Philosophical Review*, 112 (2003), 289–337.
Bürger, Peter. *Das Verschwinden des Subjekts* (Frankfurt a. M.: Suhrkamp, 1998).
Burns, Norman T. *Christian Mortalism from Tyndale to Milton* (Cambridge, MA: Harvard University Press, 1972).
Busche, Hubertus. 'Apperzeption und Intellekt', *Allgemeine Zeitschrift für Philosophie*, 19 (1994), 53–63.
Bynum, Caroline Walker. 'Material Continuity, Personal Survival, and the Resurrection of the Body: A Scholastic Discussion in its Medieval and Modern Contexts', in C. W. Bynum (ed.), *Fragmentation and Redemption. Essays on Gender and the Human Body in Medieval Religion* (New York: Urzone Publishers, 1991), pp. 239–97.
—— *The Resurrection of the Body in Western Christianity, 200—1336* (New York: Columbia University Press, 1995).
Carl, Wolfgang. *Der schweigende Kant. Die Entwürfe zu einer Deduktion der Kategorien vor 1781* (Göttingen: Vandenhoeck & Ruprecht, 1989).
Carruthers, Peter. 'HOP over FOR, HOT Theory', in R. J. Gennaro (ed.), *Higher Order Theories of Consciousness: An Anthology* (Philadelphia: John Benjamins, 2004), pp. 115–58.
Carter, Benjamin. 'Ralph Cudworth and the Theological Origins of Consciousness', *History of the Human Sciences*, 23 (2010), 29–47.
Carus, Friedrich August. *Geschichte der Psychologie* (Leipzig: 1808); reprinted, with an introduction by R. Jeschonnek (Berlin: Deutscher Verlag der Wissenschaften, 1990).
Cassirer, Ernst. *The Platonic Renaissance in England*, transl. J. P. Pettegrove (Austin: University of Texas Press, 1953).

Caston, Victor. 'Aristotle on Consciousness', *Mind*, 111 (2002), 751–815.
Cazzaniga, Gian Mario and Zarka, Yves Charles (eds.). *L'individu dans la pensée moderne xvie–xviiie siècle*, 2 vols. (Pisa: Edizioni ETS, 1995).
Chadwick, Henry. *Boethius: The Consolations of Music, Logic, Theology, and Philosophy* (Oxford: Oxford University Press, 1981).
Chappell, Vere. 'Locke and Relative Identity', *History of Philosophy Quarterly*, 6 (1989), 69–83.
Chisholm, Roderick M. *Person and Object: A Metaphysical Study* (London: Allen & Unwin, 1976).
Conn, Christopher Hughes. 'Locke's Organismic Theory of Personal Identity', *Locke Studies*, 2 (2002), 105–35.
—— *Locke on Essence and Identity* (Dordrecht and Boston: Kluwer Academic Publishers, 2003).
Cooney, Brian. 'John Sergeant's Criticism of Locke's Theory of Ideas', *The Modern Schoolman*, 50 (1973), 143–58.
Corcoran, Clive M. 'Do we have a Shaftesburean Self in the *Treatise?*', *Philosophical Quarterly*, 23 (1973), 67–72.
Corr, Charles A. 'Cartesian Themes in Wolff's German Metaphysics', in W. Schneiders (ed.), *Christian Wolff 1679–1754. Interpretationen zu seiner Philosophie und deren Wirkung* (Hamburg: Meiner, 1983), pp. 113–20.
Cottingham, John. 'Descartes on "Thought"', *Philosophical Quarterly*, 28 (1978), 208–14.
Coventry, Angela and Kriegel, Uriah. 'Locke on Consciousness', *History of Philosophy Quarterly*, 25 (2008), 221–42.
Cover, Jan A. and O'Leary-Hawthorne, John. *Substance and Individuation in Leibniz* (Cambridge: Cambridge University Press, 1999).
Craig, Edward. *The Mind of God and the Works of Man* (Oxford: Oxford University Press, 1987).
Cramer, Konrad. 'Die Stunde der Philosophie. Über Göttingens ersten Philosophen und die philosophische Theorielage der Gründungszeit', in J. v. Stackelberg (ed.), *Zur Geistigen Situation der Zeit der Göttinger Universitätsgründung 1737* (Göttingen: Vandenhoeck & Ruprecht, 1988), pp. 101–43.
—— 'Einfachheit, Perzeption und Apperzeption. Überlegungen zu Leibniz' Theorie der Substanz als Subjekt', in R. Cristin (ed.), *Leibniz und die Frage nach der Subjektivität* (Stuttgart: Franz Steiner, 1994), pp. 19–45.
Curley, Edwin M. 'Leibniz on Locke on Personal Identity', in M. Hooker (ed.), *Leibniz: Critical and Interpretive Essays* (Minneapolis: University of Minnesota Press, 1982), pp. 302–26.
—— *Behind the Geometrical Method: A Reading of Spinoza's Ethics* (Princeton, NJ: Princeton University Press, 1988).
Daniel, Stephen H. *The Philosophy of Jonathan Edwards* (Bloomington and Indianapolis: Indiana University Press, 1994).
Davies, Catherine Glyn. *'Conscience' as Consciousness: The Idea of Self-Awareness in French Philosophical Writing from Descartes to Diderot* (Oxford: Voltaire Foundation, 1990).
Delahaye, Karl. *Die 'memoria interior'-Lehre des heiligen Augustinus und der Begriff der 'transzendentalen Apperzeption' Kants. Versuch eines historisch-systematischen Vergleichs* (Würzburg: C. J. Becker, 1936).
Den Uyl, Douglas and Rice, Lee. 'Spinoza and Hume on Individuals', *Reason Papers*, 15 (1990), 91–117.
Dessoir, Max. *Geschichte der Neueren Deutschen Psychologie* (Berlin: Carl Duncker, 1902).

Dierse, Ulrich. 'Nachträge zu G. F. Meiers Religionsphilosophie', in L. Kreimendahl (ed.), *Aufklärung und Skepsis. Festschrift für Günter Gawlick* (Stuttgart-Bad Cannstatt: Frommann-Holzboog, 1995), pp. 33–46.
Ducharme, Howard M. 'Personal Identity in Samuel Clarke', *Journal of the History of Philosophy*, 24 (1986), 359–83.
Eleutheropulos, Abr. *Friedrich Carl Casimir von Creuz's Erkenntnistheorie* (Leipzig: Oswald Schmidt, 1895).
Ellis, Jonathan. 'The Contents of Hume's Appendix and the Source of his Despair', *Hume Studies*, 32 (2006), 195–231.
Engfer, Hans-Jürgen. *Philosophie als Analysis. Studien zur Entwicklung philosophischer Analysiskonzeptionen unter dem Einfluß mathematischer Methodenmodelle im 17. und frühen 18. Jahrhundert* (Stuttgart-Bad Cannstatt: Frommann-Holzboog, 1982).
Erickson, Robert A. 'Situations of Identity in the *Memoirs of Martinus Scriblerus*', *Modern Language Quarterly*, 26 (1965), 388–400.
Euler, Werner. 'Bewußtsein–Seele–Geist. Untersuchungen zur Transformation des Cartesischen "Cogito" in der Psychologie Christian Wolffs', in O.-P. Rudolph and J.-F. Goubet (eds.), *Die Psychologie Christian Wolffs* (Tübingen: Niemeyer, 2004), pp. 11–50.
Fabbianelli, Faustino. 'Tatsachen des Bewußtseins und "nexus rerum" in Christian Wolffs Psychologie', in J. Stolzenberg and O.-P. Rudolph (eds.), *Christian Wolff und die Europäische Aufklärung*, 5 vols. (Hildesheim and New York: Olms, 2007–10), vol. 2, pp. 355–66.
Falkenstein, Lorne. 'Hume and Reid on the Simplicity of the Soul', *Hume Studies*, 21 (1995), 25–45.
Ferguson, James P. *The Philosophy of Dr. Samuel Clarke and its Critics* (New York: Vantage Press, 1974).
Flage, Daniel. 'Berkeley, Individuation, and Physical Objects', in K. F. Barber and J. J. E. Gracia (eds.), *Individuation and Identity in Early Modern Philosophy: Descartes to Kant* (Albany, NY: State University of New York Press, 1994), pp. 133–54.
Flew, Antony. 'Locke and the Problem of Personal Identity', *Philosophy*, 26 (1951), 53–68; reprinted in C. B. Martin and D. M. Armstrong (eds.), *Locke and Berkeley: A Collection of Critical Essays* (Garden City, NY: Doubleday, 1968), pp. 155–78.
Forschner, Maximilian. *Die Stoische Ethik* (Stuttgart: Klett-Cotta, 1981).
——'Der Begriff der Person in der Stoa', in D. Sturma (ed.), *Person. Philosophiegeschichte–Theoretische Philosophie–Praktische Philosophie* (Paderborn: Mentis, 2001), pp. 37–57.
Forstrom, K. Joanna S. *John Locke and Personal Identity: Immortality and Bodily Resurrection in Seventeenth-Century Philosophy* (London and New York: Continuum, 2010).
Fox, Christopher. *Locke and the Scriblerians: Identity and Consciousness in Early Eighteenth-Century Britain* (Berkeley, CA: University of California Press, 1988).
Frank, Manfred. *What is Neo-Structuralism?* (Minneapolis: University of Minnesota Press, 1989).
——(ed.). *Selbstbewußtseinstheorien von Fichte bis Sartre* (Frankfurt a. M.: Suhrkamp, 1991).
——*Selbstgefühl* (Frankfurt a. M.: Suhrkamp, 2002).
——'Non-objectal Subjectivity', *Journal of Consciousness Studies*, 14 (2007), 152–73.
Freedman, Joseph S. *European Academic Philosophy in the Late Sixteenth and Early Seventeenth Centuries: the Life, Significance, and Philosophy of Clemens Timpler (1563/4–1624)*, 2 vols. (Hildesheim: Olms, 1988).
Fritz, Anita D. 'Berkeley's Self: its Origin in Malebranche', *Journal of the History of Ideas*, 15 (1954), 554–72.

Fuhrmann, Manfred. 'Persona, ein Römischer Rollenbegriff', in O. Marquard and K. Stierle (eds.), *Identität* (Munich: Wilhelm Fink, 1979) pp. 83–106.
Furth, Montgomery. 'Monadology', in H. Frankfurt (ed.), *Leibniz: A Collection of Critical Essays* (Garden City, NY: Double Day, 1972), pp. 99–136.
Gallie, Roger. 'The Same Self', *The Locke Newsletter*, 18 (1987), 45–62.
Garber, Daniel. 'Leibniz and the Foundations of Physics: The Middle Years', in K. Okruhlik and J. R. Brown (eds.), *The Natural Philosophy of Leibniz* (Dordrecht: Reidel, 1985), pp. 27–130.
—— 'Soul and Mind: Life and Thought in the Seventeenth Century', in D. Garber and M. Ayers (eds.), *The Cambridge History of Seventeenth-Cenutry Philosophy* (Cambridge: Cambridge University Press, 1998), pp. 759–95.
—— and Ayers, Michael (eds.). *The Cambridge History of Seventeenth-Century Philosophy* (Cambridge: Cambridge University Press, 1998).
—— and Wilson, Margaret. 'Mind–Body Problems', in D. Garber and M. Ayers (eds.), *The Cambridge History of Seventeenth-Cenutry Philosophy* (Cambridge: Cambridge University Press, 1998), pp. 833–67.
Garrett, Don. 'Spinoza's Theory of Metaphysical Individuation', in K. F. Barber and J. J. E. Gracia (eds.), *Individuation and Identity in Early Modern Philosophy: Descartes to Kant* (Albany, NY: State University of New York Press, 1994), pp. 73–101.
—— *Cognition and Commitment in Hume's Philosophy* (Oxford: Oxford University Press, 1997).
—— 'Locke on Personal Identity, Consciousness and "Fatal Errors"', *Philosophical Topics*, 31 (2003), 95–125.
—— 'Representation and Consciousness in Spinoza's Naturalistic Theory of the Imagination', in Ch. Huenemann (ed.), *Interpreting Spinoza: Critical Essays* (Cambridge: Cambridge University Press, 2008), pp. 4–25.
—— 'Difficult Times for Humean Identity?', *Philosophical Studies*, 146 (2009), 435–43.
Gaukroger, Stephen (ed.). *The Uses of Antiquity* (Dordrecht: Kluwer, 1991).
Gawlick, Günther. 'G. F. Meiers Stellung in der Religionsphilosophie der deutschen Aufklärung', in N. Hinske (ed.), *Zentren der Aufklärung I: Halle: Aufklärung und Pietismus* (Heidelberg: Schneider, 1989), pp. 157–76.
Gennaro, Rocco J. 'Leibniz on Consciousness and Self-Consciousness', in R. J. Gennaro and Ch. Huenemann (eds.), *New Essays on the Rationalists* (Oxford: Oxford University Press, 1999), pp. 353–71.
—— (ed.). *Higher Order Theories of Consciousness: An Anthology* (Philadelphia: John Benjamins, 2004).
Gilead, Amihud. 'Spinoza's *Principium Individuationis* and Personal Identity', *International Studies in Philosophy*, 15 (1983), 41–57.
Gill, Christopher. 'Personhood and Personality: The Four Personae Theory in Cicero, *De Officiis* I', *Oxford Studies in Ancient Philosophy*, 6 (1988), 169–99.
—— *The Structured Self in Hellenistic and Roman Thought* (Oxford: Oxford University Press, 2006).
Glauser, Richard. 'John Sergeant's Argument against Descartes and the Way of Ideas', *The Monist*, 71 (1988), 585–95.
Gloy, Karen. 'Platons Theorie der "episteme heautes" im *Charmides* als Vorläufer der modernen Selbstbewußtseinstheorien', *Kant-Studien*, 77 (1986), 137–64.
Goubet, Jean-François. 'In welchem Sinne ist die Wolffsche Psychologie als Fundament zu verstehen? Zum vermeintlichen Zirkel zwischen Psychologie und Logik', in O.-P. Rudolph and J.-F. Goubet (eds.), *Die Psychologie Christian Wolffs* (Tübingen: Niemeyer, 2004), pp. 51–60.

Grabmann, Martin. *Mittelalterliches Geistesleben*, 3 vols. (Munich: M. Hueber, 1926–56).
Gracia, Jorge J. E. *Introduction to the Problem of Individuation in the Early Middle Ages* (Munich and Vienna: Philosophia, 1984).
—— 'The Centrality of the Individual in the Philosophy of the Fourteenth Century', *History of Philosophy Quarterly*, 8 (1991), 235–51.
—— 'Christian Wolff on Individuation', *History of Philosophy Quarterly*, 10 (1993), 147–64.
—— (ed.). *Individuation in Scholasticism: The Later Middle Ages and the Counter-Reformation* (Albany, NY: State University of New York Press, 1994).
—— and Kenneth F. Barber (eds). *Individuation and Identity in Early Modern Philosophy: Descartes to Kant* (Albany, NY: State University of New York Press, 1994).
Grau, Kurt Joachim. *Die Entwicklung des Bewusstseinsbegriffes im XVII. und XVIII. Jahrhundert* (Halle: Niemeyer, 1916).
Grave, Selwyn Alfred. *The Scottish Philosophy of Common Sense* (Oxford: Clarendon Press, 1960).
Grean, Stanley. *Shaftesbury's Philosophy of Religion and Ethics: A Study in Enthusiasm* (Athens, OH: Ohio University Press, 1967).
Green, Michael. 'The Idea of a Momentary Self and Hume's Theory of Personal Identity', *British Journal for the History of Philosophy*, 7 (1999), 103–22.
Greshake, Gisbert. 'Die theologische Herkunft des Personbegriffs', in G. Pöltner (ed.), *Personale Freiheit und Pluralistische Gesellschaft* (Vienna: Herder, 1981), pp. 75–86.
Grossklaus, Dirk. *Natürliche Religion und Aufgeklärte Gesellschaft. Shaftesbury's Verhältnis zu den Cambridge Platonists* (Heidelberg: Universitätsverlag C. Winter, 2000).
Güzeldere, Güven. 'Is Consciousness the Perception of What Passes in a Man's Own Mind?', in T. Metzinger (ed.), *Conscious Experience* (Paderborn: Schöningh; Thorverton: Imprint Academic, 1995), pp. 335–58.
Haakonssen, Knud. *Natural Law and Personhood: Pufendorf and Social Explanation*, Max Weber Lecture No. 2010/06; published online at http://cadmus.eui.eu/handle/1814/14934.
Hacking, Ian. 'Individual Substance', in H. G. Frankfurt (ed.), *Leibniz: A Collection of Critical Essays* (Garden City, NY: Doubleday, 1972), pp. 137–53.
Hall, Roland. 'Hume's Use of Locke on Identity', *The Locke Newsletter*, 5 (1974), 56–75.
Hampshire, Stuart. *Spinoza* (Harmondsworth: Penguin, 1951).
Harnack, Adolf. *Geschichte der Königlich Preussischen Akademie der Wissenschaften zu Berlin*, 3 vols. (Berlin: Reichsdruckerei, 1900).
Harré, Rom. 'Knowledge', in G. S. Rousseau and R. Porter (eds.), *The Ferment of Knowledge: Studies in the Historiography of Eighteenth-Century Science* (Cambridge: Cambridge University Press, 1980), pp. 11–54.
Harrison, John and Laslett, Peter. *The Library of John Locke*, second edn. (Oxford: Oxford University Press, 1971).
Hartz, Glenn A. *Leibniz's Final System: Monads, Matter and Animals* (London and New York: Routledge, 2007).
Häseler, Jens. 'Johann Bernhard Merian: ein Schweizer Philosoph an der Berliner Akademie', in M. Fontius and H. Holzhey (eds.), *Schweizer im Berlin des 18. Jahrhunderts* (Berlin: Akademie Verlag, 1996), pp. 217–30.
Hauser, Christian. *Selbstbewußtsein und personale Identität* (Stuttgart-Bad Cannstatt: Frommann-Holzboog, 1994).
Hedley, Douglas and Hutton, Sarah (eds.). *Platonism at the Origins of Modernity* (Dordrecht: Springer, 2008).
Heinz, Marion. *Sensualistischer Idealismus. Untersuchungen zur Erkenntnistheorie des jungen Herder* (Hamburg: Meiner, 1994).
Helm, Paul. 'John Locke and Jonathan Edwards. A Reconsideration', *Journal of the History of Philosophy*, 7 (1969), 51–61.

——'Jonathan Edwards and the Doctrine of Temporal Parts', *Archiv für Geschichte der Philosophie*, 61 (1979), 37–51.
——'A Forensic Dilemma: John Locke and Jonathan Edwards on Personal Identity', in P. Helm and O. D. Crisp (eds.), *Jonathan Edwards: Philosophical Theologian* (Aldershot: Ashgate, 2003), pp. 45–59.
Hennig, Boris. *'Conscientia' bei Descartes* (Freiburg: Alber, 2006).
——'Cartesian *Conscientia*', *British Journal for the History of Philosophy*, 15 (2007), 455–84.
Henrich, Dieter. 'Fichte's Original Insight', *Contemporary German Philosophy*, 1 (1982), 15–52; first published as 'Fichte's ursprüngliche Einsicht', in D. Henrich and H. Wagner (eds.), *Subjektivität und Metaphysik, Festschrift für Wolfgang Cramer* (Frankfurt a. M.: Klostermann, 1966), pp. 188–232.
——'Die Identität des Subjekts in der transzendentalen Deduktion', in H. Oberer and G. Seel (eds.), *Kant: Probleme, Analysen, Kritik* (Würzburg: Königshausen und Neumann, 1988), pp. 39–70.
——'The Identity of the Subject in the Transcendental Deduction', in E. Schaper and W. Vossenkuhl (eds.), *Reading Kant: New Perspectives on Transcendental Arguments and Critical Philosophy* (Oxford: Blackwell, 1989), pp. 250–80.
——'Die Anfänge der Theorie des Subjekts', in A. Honneth, T. McCarthy, C. Offe, and A. Wellmer (eds.), *Zwischenbetrachtungen Im Prozeß der Aufklärung. Jürgen Habermas zum 60. Geburtstag* (Frankfurt a. M.: Suhrkamp, 1989), pp. 106–70.
Herrick, James A. *The Radical Rhetoric of the English Deists. The Discourse of Skepticism, 1680–1750* (Columbia, SC: University of South Carolina Press, 1997).
Hight, Marc A. 'Berkeley and Bodily Resurrection', *Journal of the History of Philosophy*, 45 (2007), 443–58.
Holbrook, Clyde A. 'Jonathan Edwards on Self-Identity and Original Sin', *The Eighteenth Century: Theory and Interpretation*, 25 (1984), 45–63.
Hölscher, Ludger. *The Reality of the Mind. Augustine's Philosophical Arguments for the Human Soul as a Spiritual Substance* (London: Routledge & Kegan Paul, 1986).
Hoopes, James. *Consciousness in New England: From Puritanism and Ideas to Psychoanalysis and Semiotic* (Baltimore and London: Johns Hopkins University Press, 1989).
Horn, Christoph. 'Selbstbezüglichkeit des Geistes bei Plotin und Augustinus', in J. Brachtendorf (ed.), *Gott und sein Bild. Augustins 'De Trinitate' im Spiegel gegenwärtiger Forschung* (Paderborn: Schöningh, 2000), pp. 81–103.
——'Seele, Geist und Bewusstsein bei Augustinus', in K. Crone, R. Schnepf, and J. Stolzenberg (eds.), *Über die Seele* (Berlin: Suhrkamp, 2010), pp. 77–93.
Hufnagel, Alfons. 'Die Wesensbestimmung der Person bei Alexander von Hales', *Freiburger Zeitschrift für Philosophie und Theologie*, 4 (1957), 148–74.
Hunter, Ian. *Rival Enlightenments. Civil and Metaphysical Philosophy in Early Modern Germany* (Cambridge: Cambridge University Press, 2001).
Hunter, William B., Jr. 'The Seventeenth Century Doctrine of Plastic Nature', *Harvard Theological Review*, 43 (1950), 197–213.
Hutchison, Ross. *Locke in France, 1688–1734* (Oxford: Voltaire Foundation, 1991).
Irwin, Terence H. 'Stoic Individuals', *Philosophical Perspectives*, 10 (1996), 459–80.
Israel, Jonathan I. *Radical Enlightenment: Philosophy and the Making of Modernity 1650–1750* (Oxford: Oxford University Press, 2001).
Jacob, Alexander. 'The Neoplatonic Conception of Nature in More, Cudworth, and Berkeley', in S. Gaukroger (ed.), *The Uses of Antiquity* (Dordrecht: Kluwer, 1991), pp. 101–21.

Jolley, Nicholas. *Leibniz and Locke: A Study of the New Essays On Human Understanding* (Oxford: Clarendon Press, 1984).
—— *Locke: His Philosophical Thought* (Oxford: Oxford University Press, 1999).
Jones, Peter. *Hume's Sentiments* (Edinburgh: Edinburgh University Press, 1982).
Jorgensen, Larry M. 'The Principle of Continuity and Leibniz's Theory of Consciousness', *Journal of the History of Philosophy*, 47 (2009), 223–48.
Jung, Gertrud 'Syneidesis, Conscientia, Bewußtsein', *Archiv für die Gesamte Psychologie*, 89 (1933), 525–40.
Kahn, Charles H. 'Sensation and Consciousness in Aristotle's Psychology', *Archiv für Geschichte der Philosophie*, 48 (1966), 43–81.
Kail, Peter J. E. *Projection and Realism in Hume's Philosophy* (Oxford: Oxford University Press, 2007).
Kaufman, Dan. 'The Resurrection of the Same Body and the Ontological Status of Organisms: What Locke Should Have (and Could Have) Told Stillingfleet', in P. Hoffman, D. Owen, and G. Yaffe (eds.), *Contemporary Perspectives on Early Modern Philosophy: Essays in Honor of Vere Chappell* (Peterborough, ON: Broadview Press, 2008), pp. 191–214.
Kemmerling, Andreas. *Ideen des Ichs: Studien zu Descartes* (Frankfurt a. M.: Suhrkamp, 1996).
—— 'Was macht den Begriff der Person so besonders schwierig?', in G. Thomas and A. Schüle (eds.), *Gegenwart des Lebendigen Christus* (Leipzig: Evangelische Verlagsanstalt, 2007), pp. 541–65.
Kemp Smith, Norman. *The Philosophy of David Hume* (London: Macmillan, 1941).
Kerby-Miller, Charles (ed.). *Memoirs of the Extraordinary Life, Works, and Discoveries of Martinus Scriblerus* (New Haven: Yale University Press, 1950; reprinted, New York: Oxford University Press, 1988).
Kerferd, George B. 'The Search for Personal Identity in Stoic Thought', *Bulletin of the John Rylands University Library of Manchester*, 55 (1972), 177–96.
Kitcher, Patricia. *Kant's Transcendental Psychology* (Oxford: Oxford University Press, 1990).
Kittsteiner, Heinz D. *Die Entstehung des modernen Gewissens* (Frankfurt a. M.: Suhrkamp, 1995).
Klemme, Heiner F. *Kants Philosophie des Subjekts* (Hamburg: Meiner, 1996).
—— 'Kants Wende zum Ich. Zum Einfluß von Herz und Mendelssohn auf die Entwicklung der kritischen Subjekttheorie', *Zeitschrift für Philosophische Forschung*, 53 (1999), 507–29.
Kobusch, Theo. *Die Entdeckung der Person. Metaphysik der Freiheit und Modernes Menschenbild* (Darmstadt: Wissenschaftliche Buchgesellschaft, 1997).
—— *Christliche Philosophie. Die Entdeckung der Subjektivität* (Darmstadt: Wissenschaftliche Buchgesellschaft, 2006).
Kort, Eva D. 'Stillingfleet and Locke on Substance, Essence, and Articles of Faith', *Locke Studies*, 5 (2005), 149–78.
Krailsheimer, Alban John. *Studies in Self-Interest. From Descartes to La Bruyère* (Oxford: Oxford University Press, 1962).
Kreuzer, Johann. 'Der Begriff der Person in der Philosophie des Mittelalters', in D. Sturma (ed.), *Person Philosophiegeschichte–Theoretische Philosophie–Praktische Philosophie* (Paderborn: Mentis, 2001), pp. 59–77.
Kriegel, Uriah. 'Consciousness as Intransitive Self-Consciousness: Two Views and an Argument', *Canadian Journal of Philosophy*, 33 (2003), 103–32.
Krieger, Martin. *Geist, Welt und Gott bei Christian August Crusius* (Würzburg: Königshausen und Neumann, 1993).
Krook, Dorothea. *John Sergeant and his Circle* (Leiden: Brill, 1993).

Kuehn, Manfred. *Scottish Common Sense in Germany, 1768–1800. A Contribution to the History of Critical Philosophy* (Kingston and Montreal: McGill–Queen's University Press, 1987).
Kulstad, Mark. *Leibniz on Apperception, Consciousness and Reflection* (Munich: Philosophia, 1991).
Kurze, Therese. *Die Metaphysik des Samuel Clarke* (Paderborn: Schöningh, 1929).
Lähteenmäki, Vili. 'Orders of Consciousness and Forms of Reflexivity in Descartes', in S. Heinämaa, V. Lähteenmäki, and P. Remes (eds.), *Consciousness: From Perception to Reflection in the History of Philosophy* (Dordrecht: Springer, 2007), pp. 177–201.
——'The Sphere of Experience in Locke. The Relations between Reflection, Consciousness and Ideas', *Locke Studies*, 8 (2008), 59–100.
——'Cudworth on Types of Consciousness', *British Journal for the History of Philosophy*, 18 (2010), 9–34.
Laird, John. *Hume's Philosophy of Human Nature* (North Haven, CT: Shoe String Press, 1967).
Lännström, Anna. 'Locke's Account of Personal Identity: Memory as Fallible Evidence', *History of Philosophy Quarterly*, 24 (2007), 39–56.
Laursen, John Christian. 'Swiss Anti-skeptics in Berlin', in M. Fontius and H. Holzhey (eds.), *Schweizer im Berlin des 18. Jahrhunderts* (Berlin: Akademie Verlag, 1996), pp. 261–81.
——and Popkin, Richard H. 'Hume in the Prussian Academy: Jean-Bernard Mérian's "On the Phenomenalism of David Hume"', *Hume Studies*, 23 (1997), 153–91.
Leinkauf, Thomas. 'Substanz, Individuum und Person. Anthropologie und ihre metaphysischen und geisttheoretischen Voraussetzungen im Werk von Leibniz', *Internationale Zeitschrift für Philosophie*, 1 (1999), 24–45.
Leinsle, Ulrich Gottfried. *Reformversuche Protestantischer Metaphysik im Zeitalter des Rationalismus* (Augsburg: Maro Verlag, 1988).
Lennon, Thomas M. 'The Problem of Individuation among Cartesians', in K. F. Barber and J. J. E. Gracia (eds.), *Individuation and Identity in Early Modern Philosophy: Descartes to Kant* (Albany, NY: State University of New York Press, 1994), pp. 13–39.
Lewalter, Ernst. *Spanisch-jesuitische und deutsch-lutherische Metaphysik des 17. Jahrhunderts*, second edn. (Darmstadt: Wissenschaftliche Buchgesellschaft, 1967).
Lewis, Clive Staples. *Studies in Words* (Cambridge: Cambridge University Press, 1960).
Lewis, Eric. 'The Stoics on Identity and Individuation', *Phronesis*, 40 (1995), 89–108.
Libera, Alain de. 'When did the Modern Subject Emerge?', *American Catholic Philosophical Quarterly*, 82 (2008), 181–220.
Lindemann, Ruth. *Der Begriff der Conscience im französischen Denken* (Jena: W. Gronau, 1938).
Lloyd, Anthony C. 'On Augustine's Concept of a Person', in R. A. Markus (ed.), *Augustine: A Collection of Critical Essays* (Garden City, NY: Doubleday, 1972), pp. 191–205.
——'The Self in Berkeley's Philosophy', in J. Foster and H. Robinson (eds.), *Essays on Berkeley: A Tercentennial Celebration* (Oxford: Clarendon Press, 1985), pp. 187–209.
Long, Anthony Arthur. 'Hierocles on *oikeiōsis* and self-perception', in A. A. Long, *Stoic Studies* (Cambridge: Cambridge University Press, 1996), pp. 250–63.
——*Stoic Studies* (Cambridge: Cambridge University Press, 1996).
Loptson, Peter. 'Locke, Reid, and Personal Identity', *The Philosophical Forum*, 35 (2004), 51–63.
——'Man, Person, Spirits in Locke's *Essay*', *Eighteenth-Century Thought*, 3 (2007), 359–72.

Lowe, Edward Jonathan. 'Review of Christopher Hughes Conn, *Locke on Essence and Identity*', *Locke Studies*, 4 (2004), 243-53.
Luce, Arthur Aston. *Berkeley and Malebranche* (London: Oxford University Press, 1934).
—— *The Dialectic of Immaterialism* (London: Hodder and Stroughton, 1963).
Lund, Roger D. 'Martinus Scriblerus and the Search for the Soul', *Papers in Language and Literature*, 25 (1989), 135-50.
Lycan, William G. 'Consciousness as Internal Monitoring', in N. J. Block, O. Flanagan, and G. Güzeldere (eds.), *The Nature of Consciousness: Philosophical Debates* (Cambridge, MA: MIT Press, 1997), pp. 755-71.
Lyttle, David. 'Jonathan Edwards on Personal Identity', *Early American Literature*, 7 (1972), 163-71.
McCann, Edwin. 'Locke on Identity: Matter, Life, and Consciousness', *Archiv für Geschichte der Philosophie*, 69 (1987), 54-77.
McCullough, Laurence B. 'Leibniz and Traditional Philosophy', *Studia Leibnitiana*, 10 (1978), 254-70.
—— 'Leibniz on Individuals and Individuation: How the Mature Philosophy Resolves Problems of the Earliest Philosophy', in A. Heinekamp (ed.), *Leibniz. Tradition und Aktualität. V. Internationaler Leibniz-Kongress. Vorträge* (Hannover: Gottfried-Wilhelm-Leibniz-Gesellschaft, 1988), pp. 542-6.
—— *Leibniz on Individuals and Individuation* (Dordrecht: Kluwer, 1996).
MacDonald, Paul S. *History of the Concept of Mind. Speculations about Soul, Mind and Spirit from Homer to Hume* (Aldershot: Ashgate, 2003).
—— *History of the Concept of Mind, Volume 2. The Heterodox and Occult Tradition* (Aldershot: Ashgate, 2006).
McDowell, John. 'Reductionism and the First Person', in J. Dancy (ed.), *Reading Parfit* (Oxford: Blackwell, 1997), pp. 230-50.
Mach, Ernst. 'Brief an Mauthner, 22 Okt 1912', in R. Haller and F. Stadler (eds.), *Ernst Mach: Werk und Wirkung* (Wien: Hölder-Pichler-Tempsky, 1988) p. 242.
McIntyre, Jane L. 'Personal Identity and the Passions', *Journal of the History of Philosophy*, 27 (1989), 545-57.
—— 'Character: A Humean Account', *History of Philosophy Quarterly*, 7 (1990), 193-206.
—— 'Hume's Underground Self', *Studies in Early Modern Philosophy*, 3 (1993), 110-26.
—— 'Hume: Second Newton of the Moral Sciences', *Hume Studies*, 20 (1994), 3-18.
Mackie, John Leslie. *Problems from Locke* (Oxford: Oxford University Press, 1976).
MacLean, Kenneth. *John Locke and English Literature of the Eighteenth Century* (New York: Russell and Russell, 1962).
McMurrich, James Playfair. 'The Legend of the "Resurrection Bone"', *Transactions of the Royal Canadian Institute*, 9 (1913), 45-51.
McRae, Robert. *Leibniz: Perception, Apperception and Thought* (Toronto: University of Toronto Press, 1976).
Madonna, Luigi Cataldi. 'Die Erkenntnis der Existenz in der Philosophie von Christian Wolff', in L. C. Madonna (ed.), *Macht und Bescheidenheit der Vernunft. Beiträge zur Philosophie Christian Wolffs. Gedenkband für Hans Werner Arndt* (Hildesheim: Olms, 2005), pp. 133-50.
Manns, James W. *Reid and his French Disciples: Aesthetics and Metaphysics* (Leiden: E. J. Brill, 1994).
Markovits, Francine. 'Diderot, Mérian et l'Aveugle', in J.-B. Mérian, *Sur le problème de Molyneux* (Paris: Flammarion, 1984), pp. 193-281.

Marshall, John. 'Locke, Socininanism, "Socinianism", and Unitarianism', in M. A. Stewart (ed.), *English Philosophy in the Age of Locke* (Oxford: Clarendon Press, 2000), pp. 111–82.
Martens, Ekkehard. *Das selbstbezügliche Wissen in Platons 'Charmides'* (Munich: C. Hanser, 1973).
Martin, Raymond and Barresi, John. *Naturalization of the Soul: Self and Personal Identity in the Eighteenth Century* (London and New York: Routledge, 2000).
—— *The Rise and Fall of Soul and Self. An Intellectual History of Personal Identity* (New York: Columbia University Press, 2006).
Mates, Benson. *The Philosophy of Leibniz: Metaphysics and Language* (Oxford: Oxford University Press, 1986).
Mattern, Ruth. 'Moral Science and the Concept of Persons in Locke', *Philosophical Review*, 89 (1980), 24–45.
Matthews, Gareth B. 'Si fallor, sum', in R. A. Markus (ed.), *Augustine. A Collection of Critical Essays* (Garden City, NY: Anchor Books, 1972), pp. 151–67.
Mauss, Marcel. 'A Category of the Human Mind: The Notion of Person; the Notion of Self', transl. W. D. Halls, in M. Carrithers, S. Collins, and S. Lukes (eds.), *The Category of Person: Anthropology, Philosophy, History* (Cambridge: Cambridge University Press, 1985), pp. 1–25.
Michael, Emily and Michael, Fred S. 'Corporeal Ideas in Seventeenth Century Psychology', *Journal of the History of Ideas*, 50 (1989), 31–48.
Mijuskovic, Ben L. 'Hume and Shaftesbury on the Self', *Philosophical Quarterly*, 21 (1971), 324–6.
—— *The Achilles of Rationalist Arguments* (The Hague: Nijhoff, 1974).
Miller, Jon. 'The Status of Consciousness in Spinoza's Concept of Mind', in S. Heinämaa, V. Lähteenmäki, and P. Remes (eds.), *Consciousness: From Perception to Reflection in the History of Philosophy* (Dordrecht: Springer, 2007), pp. 203–20.
Milton, John R. 'John Locke and the Nominalist Tradition', in R. Brandt (ed.), *John Locke: Symposium 1979* (Berlin and New York: de Gruyter, 1981), pp. 128–45.
Mishori, Daniel. 'Locke on the Inner Sense and Inner Observation', *Locke Studies*, 4 (2004), 145–81.
Mugnai, Massimo. 'Leibniz on Individuation: From the Early Years to the "Discourse" and Beyond', *Studia Leibnitiana*, 33 (2001), 36–54.
Nadler, Steven M. 'Arnauld, Descartes, and Transubstantiation: Reconciling Cartesian Metaphysics and Real Presence', *Journal of the History of Ideas*, 49 (1988), 229–46.
—— *Arnauld and the Cartesian Philosophy of Ideas* (Manchester: Manchester University Press, 1989).
—— 'Spinoza and Consciousness', *Mind*, 117 (2008), 575–601.
Naert, Émilienne. *Mémoire et conscience de soi selon Leibniz* (Paris: Vrin, 1961).
Noonan, Harold W. *Personal Identity* (London: Routledge, 1989).
—— *Hume on Knowledge* (London and New York: Routledge, 1999).
Norton, David Fate. *David Hume. Common-Sense Moralist, Sceptical Metaphysician* (Princeton, NJ: Princeton University Press, 1982).
Noxon, James. 'Senses of Identity in Hume's Treatise', *Dialogue*, 8 (1969), 367–84.
Nuovo, Victor. 'Aspects of Stoicism in Locke's Philosophy', in S. Hutton and P. Schuurman (eds.), *Studies on Locke: Sources, Contemporaries, and Legacy* (Dordrecht: Springer, 2008), pp. 1–25.
O'Daly, Gerard James Patrick. *Plotinus' Philosophy of the Self* (Shannon, Ireland: Irish University Press, 1973).
—— *Augustine's Philosophy of Mind* (London: Duckworth, 1987).

Oehler, Klaus. *Subjektivität und Selbstbewußtsein in der Antike* (Würzburg: Königshausen und Neumann, 1997).
O'Higgins, James. *Anthony Collins: The Man and His Work* (The Hague: Nijhoff, 1970).
Olson, Eric T. *The Human Animal: Personal Identity without Psychology* (Oxford: Oxford University Press, 1997).
Owens, Joseph. 'The Self in Aristotle', *Review of Metaphysics*, 41 (1988), 707–22.
Palme, Anton. *J. G. Sulzers Psychologie und die Anfänge der Dreivermögenslehre* (Berlin: W. Fussinger, 1905).
Palmer, Robert Roswell. *Catholics and Unbelievers in Eighteenth-Century France*, second edn. (New York: Cooper Square, 1961; first edn., Princeton, NJ: Princeton University Press, 1939).
Parfit, Derek. *Reasons and Persons* (Oxford: Clarendon Press, 1984).
Passmore, John. *Ralph Cudworth: An Interpretation* (Cambridge: Cambridge University Press, 1951).
Pears, David. *Hume's System* (Oxford: Oxford University Press, 1990).
Penelhum, Terence. 'Hume on Personal Identity', *Philosophical Review*, 64 (1955), 571–89.
—— 'Hume's Theory of the Self Revisited', *Dialogue*, 14 (1975), 389–409.
—— *Butler* (London: Routledge & Kegan Paul, 1985).
—— 'The Self of Book 1 and the Selves of Book 2', *Hume Studies*, 18 (1992), 281–91.
Perkins, Jean A. *The Concept of the Self in the French Enlightenment* (Geneva: Librairie Droz, 1969).
Perler, Dominik. 'Graduelle oder Kategorische Unterschiede? Leibniz über das Verhältnis von Tieren und Menschen', in E. Barke, R. Wernstedt, and H. Breger (eds.), *Leibniz neu denken* (Stuttgart: F. Steiner, 2009), pp. 76–95.
Perrett, Roy W. *Death and Immortality* (Dordrecht: Nijhoff, 1987).
Phemister, Pauline. *Leibniz and the Natural World: Activity, Passivity and Coporeal Substances in Leibniz's Philosophy* (Dordrecht: Springer, 2005).
Pitassi, Maria-Cristina. 'Une résurrection pour quel corps et pour quel humanité? La réponse lockienne entre philosophie, exégèse et théologie', *Rivista di storia della filosofia*, 53 (1998), 45–61.
Pitson, A. E. *Hume's Philosophy of the Self* (London and New York: Routledge, 2002).
Pohlenz, Max. *Die Stoa. Geschichte einer geistigen Bewegung* (Göttingen: Vadenhoeck und Ruprecht, 1949).
Poser, Hans. 'Innere Prinzipien und Hierarchie der Monaden', in H. Busche (ed.), *Gottfried Wilhelm Leibniz: Monadologie* (Berlin: Akademie Verlag, 2008), pp. 81–94.
Potts, Timothy C. *Conscience in Medieval Philosophy* (Cambridge: Cambridge University Press, 1980).
Prantl, Carl von. 'Johann Bernard Mérian', in *Allgemeine Deutsche Biographie*, vol. 21, (Leipzig: Duncker und Humblot, 1885), pp. 428–30.
Principe, Walter H. *Alexander of Hales' Theology of the Hypostatic Union* (Toronto: Pontifical Institute of Medieval Studies, 1967).
Purviance, Susan. 'The Moral Self and the Indirect Passions', *Hume Studies*, 23 (1997), 195–212.
Radner, Daisie. 'Thought and Consciousness in Descartes', *Journal of the History of Philosophy*, 26 (1988), 439–52.
Raynor, David. 'Hume and Berkeley's *Three Dialogues*', in M. A. Stewart (ed.), *Studies in the Philosophy of the Scottish Enlightenment* (Oxford: Oxford University Press, 1990), pp. 231–50.

Renz, Ursula. *Die Erklärbarkeit von Erfahrung. Realismus und Subjektivität in Spinozas Theorie des menschlichen Geistes* (Frankfurt a. M.: Klostermann, 2010).
Rescher, Nicolas. *Leibniz: An Introduction to his Philosophy* (Totowa, NJ: Rowman & Littlefield, 1979).
Rey, Anne-Lise. 'Ontologie et psychologie dans la pensée de Christian Wolff: la raison de l'actualisation', in O.-P. Rudolph and J.-F. Goubet (eds.), *Die Psychologie Christian Wolffs* (Tübingen: Niemeyer, 2004), pp. 99–118.
Rheinfelder, Hans. *Das Wort 'Persona'. Geschichte seiner Bedeutungen mit besonderer Berücksichtigung des Französischen und Italienischen Mittelalters* (Halle: Max Niemeier, 1928).
Rice, Lee C. 'Spinoza on Individuation', in M. Mandelbaum and E. Freeman (eds.), *Spinoza: Essays in Interpretation* (La Salle, IL: Open Court, 1975), pp. 195–214.
—— 'Reflexive Ideas in Spinoza', *Journal of the History of Philosophy*, 28 (1990), 201–11.
Robinet, André. *Dom Deschamps: Le maître des maîtres du soupçon* (Paris: Seghers, 1974).
—— 'Suárez im Werk von Leibniz', *Studia Leibnitiana*, 13 (1981), 76–96.
Röd, Wolfgang. 'Erhard Weigels Lehre von den entia moralia', *Archiv für Geschichte der Philosophie*, 51 (1969), 58–84.
(Rodis-)Lewis, Geneviève. *Le problème de l'inconscient et le Cartésianisme* (Paris: Presses Universitaires de France, 1950).
Rosenfield, Leonora Cohen. *From Beast-Machine to Man-Machine. Animal Soul in French Letters from Descartes to La Mettrie* (New York: Octagon Books, 1968).
Ruello, Francis. 'Remarques sur la notion thomiste de personne', *Revue des Faculté Catholique de l'Ouest*, 2 (1963), 3–32.
Russell, Paul. 'Hume's Treatise and the Clarke–Collins Controversy', *Hume Studies*, 21 (1995), 95–115.
—— *The Riddle of Hume's Treatise. Skepticism, Naturalism, and Irreligion* (Oxford: Oxford University Press, 2008).
Rutherford, Donald. 'Idealism Declined. Leibniz and Christian Wolff', in P. Lodge (ed.), *Leibniz and His Correspondents* (Cambridge: Cambridge University Press, 2004), pp. 214–37.
Salomon, Lewin. *Zu den Begriffen der Perzeption und Apperzeption von Leibniz bis Kant* (Bonn: Carl Georgi, 1902).
Saw, Ruth. 'Personal Identity in Spinoza', *Inquiry*, 12 (1969), 1–14.
Schaffrath, Josef. *Die Philosophie des Georg Friedrich Meier. Ein Beitrag zur Geschichte der Aufklärungsphilosophie* (Eschweiler: Herzog, 1940).
Scharp, Kevin. 'Locke's Theory of Reflection', *British Journal for the History of Philosophy*, 16 (2008), 25–63.
Schechtman, Marya. *The Constitution of Selves* (Ithaca and London: Cornell University Press, 1996).
Scheffler, Samuel. 'Leibniz on Personal Identity and Moral Personality', *Studia Leibnitiana*, 8 (1976), 219–40.
Schenk, Günter. *Leben und Werk des Halleschen Aufklärers Georg Friedrich Meier* (Halle: Hallescher-Verlag, 1994).
Schepers, Heinrich. *Andreas Rüdigers Methodologie und ihre Voraussetzungen. Ein Beitrag zur Geschichte der deutschen Schulphilosophie im 18. Jahrhundert* (Cologne: Kölner Universitäts-Verlag, 1959).
Schmaltz, Tad M. *Malebranche's Theory of the Soul: A Cartesian Interpretation* (Oxford: Oxford University Press, 1996).

Schmaltz, Tad M. 'The Cartesian Refutation of Idealism', *British Journal for the History of Philosophy*, 10 (2002), 513–40.
Schmaus, Michael. *Die Psychologische Trinitätslehre des Hl. Augustinus* (Münster: Aschendorff, 1927).
Schmitt, Arbogast. 'Synästhesie im Urteil aristotelischer Philosophie', in H. Adler and U. Zeuch (eds.), *Synästhesie. Interferenz-Transfer-Synthese der Sinne* (Würzburg: Königshausen und Neumann, 2002), pp. 109–47.
Schüßler, Werner. *Leibniz' Auffassung des menschlichen Verstandes (intellectus). Eine Untersuchung zum Standpunktwechsel zwischen 'système commun' und 'système nouveau' und dem Versuch ihrer Vermittlung* (Berlin and New York: de Gruyter, 1992).
Schwyzer, Hans Rudolf. '"Bewusst" und "unbewusst" bei Plotin', in E. R. Dodds (ed.), *Les Sources de Plotin* (Geneva: Foundation Hardt, 1960), pp. 343–90.
Sedley, David. 'The Stoic Criterion of Identity', *Phronesis*, 27 (1982), 255–75.
Seel, Otto. 'Zur Vorgeschichte des Gewissens-Begriffes im altgriechischen Denken', in H. Kusch (ed.), *Festschrift Franz Dornseiff zum 65. Geburtstag* (Leipzig: Bibliographisches Institut, 1953), pp. 291–319.
Shin, Kyungwon. 'Search for Personal Identity in Locke and Wordsworth', *Journal of English Language and Literature*, 35 (1989), 627–50.
Shoemaker, Sydney. 'Persons and their Pasts', *American Philosophical Quarterly*, 7 (1970), 269–85.
Sihvola, Juha. 'The Problem of Consciousness in Aristotle's Psychology', in S. Heinämaa, V. Lähteenmäki, and P. Remes (eds.), *Consciousness: From Perception to Reflection in the History of Philosophy* (Dordrecht: Springer, 2007), pp. 49–65.
Simmons, Alison. 'Changing the Cartesian Mind: Leibniz on Sensation, Representation and Consciousness', *Philosophical Review*, 110 (2001), 31–75.
Sleigh, Robert C. *Leibniz and Arnauld: A Commentary on Their Correspondence* (New Haven, CT: Yale University Press, 1990).
Snobelen, Stephen D. 'Socinianism, Heresy and John Locke's *Reasonableness of Christianity*', *Enlightenment and Dissent*, 20 (2001), 88–125.
Snowdon, Paul F. 'Persons, Animals, and Ourselves', in C. Gill (ed.), *The Person and the Human Mind* (Oxford: Oxford University Press, 1990), pp. 83–107.
Sommer, Robert. *Grundzüge einer Geschichte der Deutschen Psychologie und Ästhetik von Wolff-Baumgarten bis Kant-Schiller* (Würzburg: Stahel, 1892).
Sorabji, Richard. *Self: Ancient and Modern Insights about Individuality, Life and Death* (Oxford: Clarendon Press, 2006).
Southgate, Beverly. '"Beating Down Scepticism": The Solid Philosophy of John Sergeant, 1623–1707', in M. A. Stewart (ed.), *English Philosophy in the Age of Locke* (Oxford and New York: Oxford University Press, 2000), pp. 281–315.
Stelzenberger, Johannes. *Conscientia bei Augustinus: Studien zur Gechichte der Moraltheologie* (Paderborn: Schöningh, 1959).
Stephens, John. 'Edmund Law and his Circle at Cambridge: Some Philosophical Activity of the 1730s', in G. A. J. Rogers and S. Tomaselli (eds.), *The Philosophical Canon in the 17th and 18th Centuries* (Rochester, NY: University of Rochester Press, 1996), pp. 163–73.
Stewart, M. A. 'Berkeley and the Rankenian Club', in D. Berman (ed.), *George Berkeley: Essays and Replies* (Dublin: Irish Academic Press, 1986), pp. 25–45.
——'Reid on Locke and Personal Identity: Some lost Sources', *The Locke Newsletter*, 28 (1997), 105–16.
Stewart, Roy A. *Rabbinic Theology* (Edinburgh and London: Oliver and Boyd, 1961).

Stiehler, Gottfried (ed.). *Materialisten der Leibniz-Zeit* (Berlin: VEB Deutscher Verlag der Wissenschaften, 1966).

Stolzenberg, Jürgen. '"Wie wir erkennen, daß wir sind". Überlegungen zu Wolffs Beweis des Satzes "Ich bin" im ersten Kapitel der *Deutschen Metaphysik*', in L. C. Madonna (ed.), *Macht und Bescheidenheit der Vernunft. Beiträge zur Philosophie Christian Wolffs. Gedenkband für Hans Werner Arndt* (Hildesheim: Olms, 2005), pp. 123–31.

Strawson, Galen. *The Secret Connexion* (Oxford: Clarendon Press, 1989).

——'Hume on Himself', in D. Egonsson, J. Josefsson, B. Petersson, and T. Rønnow-Rasmussen (eds.), *Exploring Practical Philosophy: From Action to Values* (Aldershot: Ashgate Press, 2001), pp. 69–94.

——*The Evident Connexion: Hume on Personal Identity* (Oxford: Oxford University Press, 2011a).

——*Locke on Personal Identity* (Princeton, NJ: Princeton University Press, 2011b).

Stroud, Barry. *Hume* (London: Routledge and Kegan Paul, 1977).

Sturma, Dieter. 'Die Paralogismen der reinen Vernunft in der zweiten Auflage', in G. Mohr and M. Willaschek (eds.), *Immanuel Kant. Kritik der reinen Vernunft* (Berlin: Akademie Verlag, 1998), pp. 391–411.

Swain, Corliss Gayda. 'Personal Identity and the Skeptical System of Philosophy', in S. Traiger (ed.), *The Blackwell Guide to Hume's Treatise* (Oxford: Blackwell, 2006), pp. 133–50.

Teichert, Dieter. *Personen und Identitäten* (Berlin and New York: de Gruyter, 2000).

Teichmann, Jenny. 'The Definition of Person', *Philosophy*, 60 (1985), 175–85.

Tennant, R. C. 'The Anglican Response to Locke's Theory of Personal Identity', *Journal of the History of Ideas*, 43 (1982), 73–90.

Thiel, Udo. 'Locke's Concept of a Person', in R. Brandt (ed.), *John Locke. Symposium Wolfenbüttel 1979* (Berlin: de Gruyter, 1981), pp. 181–92.

——*Lockes Theorie der personalen Identität* (Bonn: Bouvier, 1983).

——*John Locke* (Reinbek bei Hamburg: Rowohlt, 1990; second edn., 2000).

——'Cudworth and Seventeenth-Century Theories of Consciousness', in S. Gaukroger (ed.), *The Uses of Antiquity* (Dordrecht: Kluwer, 1991), pp. 79–99.

——'Hume's Notions of Consciousness and Reflection in Context', *British Journal for the History of Philosophy*, 2 (1994a), 75–115.

——'Leibniz and the Concept of Apperception', *Archiv für Geschichte der Philosophie*, 76 (1994b), 195–209.

——'Hauser, Christian: *Selbstbewusstsein und Personale Identität*', *Das Achtzehnte Jahrhundert*, 19 (1995), 243–5.

——'Between Wolff and Kant: Merian's Theory of Apperception', *Journal of the History of Philosophy*, 34 (1996), 213–32.

——'Varieties of Inner Sense. Two Pre-Kantian Theories', *Archiv für Geschichte der Philosophie*, 79 (1997a), 58–79.

——'"Epistemologism" and Early Modern Debates about Individuation and Identity', *British Journal for the History of Philosophy*, 5 (1997b), 353–72.

——'Locke and Eighteenth-Century Materialist Conceptions of Personal Identity', *The Locke Newsletter*, 29 (1998a), 59–83.

——'Individuation', in D. Garber and M. Ayers (eds.), *The Cambridge History of Seventeenth-Century Philosophy*, 2 vols. (Cambridge: Cambridge University Press, 1998b), vol. 1, pp. 212–62.

——'Personal Identity', in D. Garber and M. Ayers (eds.), *The Cambridge History of Seventeenth-Century Philosophy*, 2 vols. (Cambridge: Cambridge University Press, 1998c), vol. 1, pp. 868–912.

Thiel, Udo. 'The Trinity and Human Personal Identity', in M. A. Stewart (ed.), *English Philosophy in the Age of Locke* (Oxford: Oxford University Press, 2000), pp. 217–43.

—— 'Kant's Notion of Self-Consciousness in Context', in V. Gerhardt, R.-P. Horstmann, and R. Schumacher (eds.), *Kant und die Berliner Aufklärung*, 5 vols. (Berlin and New York: de Gruyter, 2001), vol. 2, pp. 468–76.

—— 'Abraham Tucker', in H. Holzhey and V. Mudroch (eds.), *Grundriss der Geschichte der Philosophie. Die Philosophie des 18. Jahrhunderts. Band 1: Grossbritannien und Nordamerika, Niederlande* (Basel: Schwabe, 2004), pp. 411–14.

—— 'Der Begriff der Intuition bei Locke', *Aufklärung*, 18 (2006), 95–112.

—— 'Das "Gefühl Ich". Ernst Platner zwischen Empirischer Psychologie und Transzendentalphilosophie', *Aufklärung*, 19 (2007a), 139–61.

—— 'Zum Verhältnis von Gegenstandsbewußtsein und Selbstbewußtsein bei Wolff und seinen Kritikern', in J. Stolzenberg and O.-P. Rudolph (eds.), *Christian Wolff und die Europäische Aufklärung*, 5 vols. (Hildesheim and New York: Olms, 2007–10), vol. 2 (2007b), pp. 377–90.

—— 'Sulzer über Bewußtsein im Kontext', in F. Grunert and G. Stiening (eds.), *Johann Georg Sulzer. Aufklärung zwischen Christian Wolff und David Hume* (Berlin: Akademie Verlag, 2011), pp. 21–36.

—— 'Religion and Materialist Metaphysics: Some Aspects of the Debate about the Resurrecton of the Body in Eighteenth-Century Britain', in R. Savage (ed.), *Philosophy and Religion in Enlightenment Britain: New Case Studies* (Oxford: Oxford University Press, 2012), pp. 90–111.

Thornton, Mark. 'Same Human Being, Same Person?', *Philosophy*, 66 (1991), 115–18.

Thweatt, Vivien. *La Rochefoucauld and the Seventeenth-Century Concept of the Self* (Geneva: Librairie Droz, 1980).

Todd, Denis. *Imagining Monsters: Miscreations of the Self in Eighteenth-Century England* (Chicago and London: University of Chicago Press, 1995).

Tonelli, Giorgio. 'Analysis and Synthesis in XVIIIth Century Philosophy Prior to Kant', *Archiv für Begriffsgeschichte*, 20 (1976), 178–213.

Trendelenburg, Adolf. 'Zur Geschichte des Wortes Person', *Kant-Studien*, 13 (1908), 1–17.

Tsugawa, Albert. 'David Hume and Lord Kames on Personal Identity', *Journal of the History of Ideas*, 22 (1961), 398–403.

Tuveson, Ernest. 'Locke and the Dissolution of the Ego', *Modern Philology*, 52 (1955), 155–74.

—— *The Imagination as a Means of Grace: Locke and the Aesthetics of Romanticism* (Berkeley: University of California Press, 1960).

Uehlein, Friedrich A. *Kosmos und Subjektivität. Lord Shaftesbury's Philosophical Regimen* (Freiburg and Munich: Alber, 1976).

Uzgalis, William. 'Locke and Collins, Clarke and Butler, on Successive Persons', in J. Perry (ed.), *Personal Identity*, second edn. (Berkeley/Los Angeles/London: University of California Press, 2008), pp. 315–26.

Vailati, Ezio. 'Leibniz's Theory of Personal Identity in the New Essays', *Studia Leibnitiana*, 17 (1985), 36–43.

—— 'Clarke's Extended Soul', *Journal of the History of Philosophy*, 31 (1993), 387–403.

—— *Leibniz and Clarke: A Study of their Correspondence* (Oxford: Oxford University Press, 1997).

Vidal, Fernando. 'Un "desir de corps mort". Résurrection et identité des evangiles au cyberspace', *Equinoxe*, 15 (1996), 139–52.

—— *Les sciences de l'ame xvie–xviiie siecle* (Paris: Honore Champion, 2006).

Vleeschauwer, Herman Jean de. 'Les antécédants du transcendantalisme: Geulincx et Kant', *Kant Studien*, 45 (1954), 245–73.
Vogel, Cornelia J. de. 'The Concept of Personality in Greek and Christian Thought', *Studies in Philosophy and the History of Philosophy*, 2 (1963), 20–60.
Wahrman, Dror. *The Making of the Modern Self. Identity and Culture in Eighteenth-Century England* (New Haven and London: Yale University Press, 2004).
Walker, Nigel. *Crime and Insanity in England*, 2 vols. (Edinburgh: Edinburgh University Press, 1968).
Wallace, Thomas. *A Review of the Doctrine of Personal Identity: In which are Considered and Compared the Opinions of Locke, Butler, Reid, Brown, and Stewart, upon that Subject* (London and Dublin: Longman, Rees, Orme, Brown, and Green; and R. Milliken, 1827).
Warren, Edward W. 'Consciousness in Plotinus', *Phronesis*, 9 (1964), 83–97.
Warren, James. 'Lucretian *Palingenesis* Recycled', *Classical Quarterly*, 51 (2001), 499–508.
Watson, Richard A. 'Transubstantiation among the Cartesians', in T. M. Lennon, J. M. Nicholas, and J. W. Davis (eds.), *Problems of Cartesianism* (Kingston and Montreal: McGill–Queen's University Press, 1982), pp. 127–48.
—— *The Breakdown of Cartesian Metaphysics* (Atlantic Highlands, NJ: Humanities Press International, 1987).
Watt, Ian. *The Rise of the Novel* (Berkeley: University of California Press, 1957).
Waxman, Wayne. *Hume's Theory of Consciousness* (Cambridge: Cambridge University Press, 1994).
Wedeking, Gary. 'Locke on Personal Identity and the Trinity Contorversy of the 1690s', *Dialogue*, 29 (1990), 163–88.
Weinberg, Shelley. 'The Coherence of Consciousness in Locke's *Essay*', *History of Philosophy Quarterly*, 25 (2008), 21–39.
Weiser, Christian Friedrich. *Shaftesbury und das Deutsche Geistesleben* (Berlin: B. G. Teubner, 1916).
Wellman, Robert R. 'The Question posed at *Charmides* 165a–166c', *Phronesis*, 9 (1964), 107–13.
Wertz, Spencer and Wertz, Linda. 'Some Correlations between Swift's Gulliver and Locke on Personal Identity', *Journal of Thought*, 10 (1975), 262–70.
Wiggins, David. *Sameness and Substance* (Oxford: Blackwell, 1980).
—— *Sameness and Substance Renewed* (Cambridge: Cambridge University Press, 2001).
Wilkins, Kathleen Sonia. *A Study of the Works of Claude Buffier* (Geneva: Institut et Musée Voltaire, 1969).
Williams, Bernard. *Problems of the Self* (Cambridge: Cambridge University Press, 1973).
Wilson, Catherine. *Leibniz's Metaphysics: A Historical and Comparative Study* (Princeton, NJ: Princeton University Press, 1989).
Wilson, Fred. 'Substance and Self in Locke and Hume', in K. F. Barber and J. J. E. Gracia (eds.), *Individuation and Identity in Early Modern Philosophy: Descartes to Kant* (Albany, NY: State University of New York Press, 1994), pp. 155–99.
—— *Body, Mind and Self in Hume's Critical Realism* (Frankfurt/Paris/Ebikon/Lancaster/New Brunswick, NJ: Ontos, 2008).
Wilson, Margaret Dauler. 'Leibniz: Self-Consciousness and Immortality in the Paris Notes and After', *Archiv für Geschichte der Philosophie*, 58 (1976), 335–52.
—— 'Objects, Ideas and "Minds": Comments on Spinoza's Theory of Mind', in M. D. Wilson, *Ideas and Mechanism: Essays on Early Modern Philosophy* (Princeton, NJ: Princeton University Press, 1999), pp. 126–40.
Winkler, Kenneth P. *Berkeley: An Interpretation* (Oxford: Clarendon Press, 1989).
—— 'Locke on Personal Identity', *Journal of the History of Philosophy*, 29 (1991), 201–26.

Winkler, Kenneth P. '"All is Revolution in Us": Personal Identity in Shaftesbury and Hume', *Hume Studies*, 26 (2000), 3–40.
Woolhouse, Roger S. 'The Nature of an Individual Substance', in M. Hooker (ed.), *Leibniz: Critical and Interpretive Essays* (Minneapolis: University of Minnesota Press, 1982), pp. 45–64.
—— *Descartes, Spinoza, Leibniz. The Concept of Substance in Seventeenth-Century Metaphysics* (London and New York: Routledge, 1993).
Wright, John P. *The Sceptical Realism of David Hume* (Manchester: Manchester University Press, 1983).
——'Locke, Willis, and the Seventeenth-Century Epicurean Soul', in M. J. Osler (ed.), *Atoms, Pneuma, and Tranquillity: Epicurean and Stoic Themes in European Thought* (Cambridge: Cambridge University Press, 1991), pp. 239–58.
——'Hume, Descartes and the Materiality of the Soul', in G. A. J. Rogers and S. Tomaselli (eds.), *The Philosophical Canon in the 17th and 18th Centuries. Essays in Honour of John W. Yolton* (Rochester, NY: University of Rochester Press, 1996), pp. 175–90.
Wunderlich, Falk. 'Kant's Second Paralogism in Context', in W. Lefèvre (ed.), *Between Leibniz, Newton, and Kant* (Dordrecht: Kluwer, 2001), pp. 175–88.
—— *Kant und die Bewußtseinstheorien des 18. Jahrhunderts* (Berlin and New York: de Gruyter, 2005).
——'Christian Wolff über Bewußtsein, Apperzeption und Selbstbewußtsein', in J. Stolzenberg and O.-P. Rudolph (eds.), *Christian Wolff und die Europäische Aufklärung*, 5 vols. (Hildesheim and New York: Olms, 2007–10), vol. 2 (2007), pp. 367–75.
Wundt, Max. *Die Deutsche Schulmetaphysik des 17. Jahrhunderts* (Tübingen: J. C. B. Mohr, 1939).
—— *Die Deutsche Schulphilosophie im Zeitalter der Aufklärung* (Tübingen: J. C. B. Mohr, 1945).
Yaffe, Gideon. 'Locke on Ideas of Identity and Diversity', in L. Newman (ed.), *The Cambridge Companion to Locke's Essay Concerning Human Understanding* (Cambridge: Cambridge University Press, 2007), pp. 192–230.
Yarbrough, Stephen R. 'The Beginning of Time: Jonathan Edwards's Original Sin', in K. Z. Derounian-Stodola (ed.), *Early American Literature and Culture* (Newark: University of Delaware Press, 1992), pp. 149–64.
Yolton, John W. 'Locke's Unpublished Marginal Replies to John Sergeant', *Journal of the History of Ideas*, 12 (1951), 528–59.
—— *John Locke and the Way of Ideas* (Oxford: Oxford University Press, 1956).
—— *Thinking Matter: Materialism in Eighteenth-Century Britain* (Minneapolis: University of Minnesota Press, 1983).
—— *Locke and French Materialism* (Oxford: Oxford University Press, 1991).
Zahavi, Dan. 'The Heidelberg School and the Limits of Reflection', in S. Heinämaa, V. Lähteenmäki, and P. Remes (eds.), *Consciousness: From Perception to Reflection in the History of Philosophy* (Dordrecht: Springer, 2007), pp. 267–85.
Zart, Gustav. *Einfluss der englischen Philosophen seit Bacon auf die deutsche Philosophie des 18. Jahrhunderts* (Berlin: F. Dümmler, 1881).
Zucker, Friedrich. *Syneidesis-Conscientia* (Jena: Gustav Fischer, 1928).

Index

Aaron, R.I. 97n, 133n
Adam 132, 262, 263, 265, 284n
Adam, Charles 9n, 36n, 82n
Adam, Michel 51n
Adler, Hans 15n, 307n
afterlife 19, 24, 25, 30, 35, 59, 61, *81–6*, 90, 91, 93, 99, 132, 133, 134, 137n, 138, 147, 156, 161, 167, 168, 172, 180, 225, 227n, 228, 236, 237, 249, 261, 267, 273, 275, 291, 314, 316, 318, 319, 323, 325, 332, 336, 409n, 434
agency 1, 2n, 27, 122, 126n, 173, 247, 270, 275, 425
aggregate/s 76, 105, 287n, 288n, 289, 411
Ainslie, Donald 383n, 386n, 393n, 394n, 399n, 427n
Alanen, Lilli 46n
Albrecht, Michael 344n
Alexander, H.G. 282n
Alexander of Hales 28
Alger, William Rouneville 85n, 90
Allison, Henry 383n, 390n, 395n, 399n, 400n, 419n, 430n
Alluntis, F. 20n
Alston, William 107n
Ancillon, F. 366n
Anderson, David J. 128n, 215n
Aner, Karl 316n
Annas, Julia 2n, 15n
Anstey, Peter 41n, 44n
Antognazza, Maria Rosa 279n
apperception 18, 279, 295–301, 302, 303n, 304–5, 306, 310, 311, 316, 326, 330, 343, 350, 351n, 352, 354, 355, 356, 360, 361, 365–7, 368, 371, 372–6, 377–9, 428, 429, 430n, 436
  in Kant 330n, 376, 377, 378, 379, 428, 429, 430n, 436
  in Leibniz *295–301*, 303n
  in Mérian 316, 356, *365–7*, 368, 371, *372–6*
  in Wolff 302, *304–5*, 306, 311
  see also consciousness; *conscientia*; intuition; self-consciousness
appetite 12, 13n, 65, 287
Aquila, R.E. 46n, 47
Aquinas, Thomas 2n, 15, 19, 20, 23, 29, 37, 44n, 86, 283, 284
Ariew, Roger 39n

Aristotelianism 2, 19, 22, 23, 25, 28, 81n, 102, 191
Aristotle 11, 12, 15, 19, 20, 117n, 307n, 410
Armogathe, Jean-Robert 39n
Armstrong, D.M. 107n, 122n, 201n
Arnauld, Antoine 12, 23, 39, 45, 52, 53, 54, 66n, 99, 117, 118, 282n, 285n, 288, 289, 404
Arnaud, Thierry 310n
Aspelin, G. 68n
Assenmacher, Johannes 19n, 22n
Atherthon, Margaret 107n
atoms, atomism 83, 87, 91n, 102, 103, 104, 105, 161, 162, 244, 273, 280, 285, 287, 323;
  see also corpuscles, corpuscularianism
Augustine of Hippo 16, 27, 44n, 49n, 53n, 56n
Averroes 22, 25
Averroism 20, 64
Avicenna 16, 22
Ayers, Michael R. 2, 37n, 39n, 41n, 62n, 108n, 125n, 127n, 191n

Bacon, Francis 23
Baertschi, Bernhard L. 366n, 367n, 376n
Baier, Annette 428n
Baillie, James 108n
Baker, Gordon 44n, 59n
Balibar, Étienne 46n
Ball, B.W. 83n, 91n, 133n, 229n
Balz, A.G.A. 5n, 23n, 50n
Barber, Kenneth 5n, 23n, 26n, 62n, 72n, 108n, 177n, 261n, 397n, 413n, 425n
Barber, W.H. 302n
Barbeyrac, Jean 78n, 80n
Barke, E. 299n
Barresi, John 3n, 4, 5, 179n, 221n, 225n, 230n, 233n, 234n, 274n, 397n
Barth, Christian 48n, 49n
Bartha, Paul 281n, 287n
Baumeister, Friedrich Christian 314
Baxter, Andrew 410
Baxter, Donald 383n, 394n, 398n, 399n, 406n, 418n, 421n
Bayle, Pierre 24n, 25n, 50, 54, 180n, 385, 393, 410, *411–12*
Beattie, James 197, 383n, 384, *407–9*, 411, 418, 422, 423, 434

Beauchamp, Tom L. 419n
Becconsall, Thomas 156, 157, *172–4*
Beck, Lewis White 365n
Behan, David P. 99n, 191n
Bella, Stefano Di 284n, 287n, 289n
Bennett, Jonathan 107n, 112n, 280n
Bentley, Richard 84n, 225n
Berkeley, George 4n, 10n, 31n, *176–7*, 187, 210, *211–13*, 214, 217, 224n, 226, 248, *251–2*, *258–62*, 264, 275, 408n, 410, *412*;
  see also consciousness; personal identity
Berman, David 144n, 408n
Bettcher, Talia 252n, 412n
Bible 92n, 136, 137, 138, 166n, 167
Biran, Maine de 367, 376
Birch, Thomas 166
Black, Deborah 16
Blakey, Robert 3n
Blackwell, Richard J. 306n
Block, N.J. 112n
Bobro, Marc 294n
body 23, 39, 40, 42, 62, 63, 74, 75, 76, 84, 90, 103, 104, 105, 163, 225, 262, 294, 326, 327, 356, 392, 410, 415;
  see also identity; individuation
  human 19, 20, 22, 25, 28, 29, 30, 37, 38, 39, 40, 41, 42, 43, 55, 59, 60, 61, 62, 63, 64, 66, 67, 74, 76, 77, 78, 80, 85, 90, 99, 101n, 105, 109, 125, 126n, 136, 142, 163, 164, 167, 171, 175, 193, 194, 204, 205, 225, 227, 228, 230, 236, 238, 244, 245, 246, 250, 256, 267, 270, 271, 273, 274, 275, 287, 288, 290, 294, 313, 317, 321, 322, 336, 337, 339, 341, 345, 346n, 351, 354, 358–61, 362, 365, 393, 405n, 411, 413, 415, 417, 425, 434;
  see also identity, 'of the human body'; organism; resurrection
Boethius 19, 28, 29, 30, 35, 36, 55, 99, 184
Bold, Samuel 154n, 166, 221
Bolton, Martha Brandt 108n
Bonnet, Charles 162, 311, 339, 432, 433, 434
Boulainviller, Henri de 410, *413–15*, 417, 432
Bourdin, Pierre 46, 47
Bourel, D. 330n
Bowin, John 24n
Boyle, Robert 41, 72, 74, 75, 87, 89, 91, 98n, 102, 103, 106;
  see also identity
Brachtendorf, Johannes 16n
Bradish, N.C. 191n
Brands, Hartmut 373n
Brandt, Reinhard 7n, 13n, 14n, 19n, 23n, 100, 102, 122n, 127n, 191n, 253n, 378n
Breger, H. 299n

Brentano, Franz 117
Bresser, Martin 44n
Bricke, John 405n, 425n
Brinkmann, Klaus 1n, 15
Briscoe, Peter 367n, 370n
Brissenden, R.F. 405n
Broackes, Justin 418n
Brookes, Derek R. 112n, 122n, 189n, 197n, 407n, 408n, 435n
Broughton, John 225
Brown, Clifford 287n
Brown, J.R. 288n
Brown, S.C. 252n, 261n
Brown, Thomas 5n
Browne, Peter 203, 248, *249–51*, 252, 275, 405n;
  see also self-consciousness
Browne, Thomas 86, 87n
Bucher, Urban Gottfried 433n
Buckle, Stephen 409n, 421n
Buffier, Claude 385, 390, *392–3*;
  see also identity
Buickerood, James 7n, 253n, 255n
Burford, Thomas 1n
Bürger, Peter 60n
Burgersdijk, Franco 23
Burman, Frans 45, 46, 47, 48, 49n
Burns, N.T. 83n
Burthogge, Richard 36, 54, 56n, *73*, *165–6*;
  see also identity
Bury, Arthur 90, 135
Busche, Hubertus 301n, 304n
Butler, Joseph 5n, 125n, 169, 184, 190, *198–205*, 206, 208, 220, 221, 226, 230n, 231, 232, *266–9*, 270, 272, 274, 275, 286, 302, 317, 328, 384, 385, 386, 389, 396, 410, 426;
  see also identity; personal identity; self-consciousness
Bynum, Caroline Walker 85n, 86n, 87n

Cade, Anthony 9
Cambridge Platonism 8, 56, 61, *67–8*, 84n, 99, 225, 230n, 242, 247;
  see also Cudworth, Ralph; More, Henry; Smith, John; Whichcote, Benjamin
Campbell, George 212n
Canz, Israel Gottlieb 315, *316–22*, 325, 326, 328, 376;
  see also identity; personal identity; self-consciousness
Capella, Werner 23n
Carl, Wolfgang 330n, 377n, 379, 436n
Carrithers, M. 26n
Carruthers, P. 112n
Carter, Benjamin 68n

Cartesianism, Cartesians 3, 16, 35, 36, 41, 53, 55, 59n, 60, 64, 67, 68, 72, 76, 82, 83, 99, 102, 104n, 109, 117, 121, 122, 128, 163, 165, 167, 193, 195, 196, 226, 227, 229, 230, 237, 241, 258, 259, 267, 268, 270, 275, 280, 288n, 294, 304n, 307n, 316, 324, 346, 349, 350, 351, 371, 373, 413, 415;
  see also consciousness; Descartes, René; self-consciousness
Carus, Friedrich August 3n
Caston, Victor 11, 12n, 117n
Cathala, M.-R. 20n
Cazzaniga, G. M. 5n, 252n
Chadwick, Henry 28n
Chambers, Ephraim 154
Chappell, Vere 108n
character 21, 26, 179, 192, 209, 395, 397n, 425
Chauncy, Charles 265
Chauvin, Stephanus 36
Cherbury, Herbert of 9n
Chisholm, Roderick 263n, 265n
Christian, Christianity 19, 25, 27, 30, 81, 85, 90, 132, 133, 135, 136, 261, 262, 280, 407
christology 27, 28
Chrysippus 12, 14, 15n, 24, 101n
Church, early 27
Church Fathers 2n
Cicero, Marcus Tullius 13, 14n, 15n, 26, 77, 80, 81, 101, 129n, 208
Clair, Pierre 10n, 23n
Clarke, Samuel 6n, 144, 145, 147, 169, 191, 203, 205, 225n, 226, *229–34*, 235, 237, 267, 272, 273, 275, 282, 283, 285, 302, 303, 339, 384, 385, 396, 410, 426;
  see also consciousness, personal identity
Clauberg, Johannes 24, 72, 75, 102;
  see also identity
Clendon, John 28n, 36
Cockburn (née Trotter), Catherine 166
cogito 16, 38n, 178, 227n, 228, 327, 349, 350, 351, 373
Coke, Edward Sir 130, 131n
Collins, Anthony 6n, *144–7*, 150, 154n, 169, 198, 199, 221, 226, 229, 230n, 231, 232, 233n, 234, 267, 292, 284, 385n, 396, 410, 433;
  see also consciousness; personal identity
Collins, S. 26n
Combach, Johannes 21n
Common Sense, Scottish School of 32, 196–7, 384, 393, 396, 407, 408, 423, 424, 427, 428, 430, *434–6*
composite, compounded beings 20, 22, 25, 29, 62, 63, 103, 104, 281, 272, 303
conceptualism, *see* nominalism

Condillac, Étienne Bonnot de 1n, 5n, 412, 432
Congreve, William 253
Conn, Christopher Hughes 122n, 125n, 126n
conscience 7, 8, 9, 10, 11, 14, 43, 44n, 68n, 70, 71, 99, 141, 172–5, 234, 235, 236, 256, 350
conscientia 7, 8, 9, 10, 13, 43, 44, 45n, 46, 47, 49n, 52, 54, 59n, 65, 256, 304, 305, 346, 350, 351, 356
consciousness:
  in Aristotle 11–12
  in Berkeley 176–7, 252
  in Clarke 229–34
  in Collins 144–6
  'creature consciousness' 12
  in Creuz, von 321–2, 352–3
  in Crusius 347–9
  in Cudworth 67–71
  in Descartes and Cartesians 43–54, 59
  in the *Essay on Consciousness* 253–8
  of external objects 6, 11, 15, 16, 297, 304, 306–11, 328, 339, 348, 353, 354, 365, 373
  first/ higher order accounts of 11, 12, 15–16, 45, 47, 48, 50, 53, 56, 70, 113, 117, 297–301, 406n
  in Grove 234–6
  in Hume 403–6
  and infinite regress 11, 12, 48, 53, 113, 114, 296n, 301n, 375, 406
  in Lee 195
  in Leibniz 295–301
  in Locke 109–19, 121–6, 168–86, 202
  in Mérian 372, 378
  in Reimarus 336–8
  in Sergeant 193–4
  in the seventeenth and eighteenth centuries 5–15, 30, 31, 35, 54
  in Sherlock and South 55–9
  in Spinoza 65–7
  in Sulzer 355, 356–8, 361–5
  in Wolff 304–11, 330, 336, 343–8, 349, 352
  see also apperception; *conscientia*; intuition; memory; reflection; self-consciousness; *Selbstgefühl*; *sentiment intérieur*, *sentiment intime*
Cooney, B. 191n
Cooper, Thomas 86n, 91, 167, 268, 433
Corcoran, Clive M. 391n
corpuscles, corpuscularianism 73, 74, 102, 285;
  see also atoms, atomism
Corr, Charles A. 9n, 302n, 306n
Coste, Pierre 9, 10, 103n, 184
Cottingham, John 9n, 36n, 45n

Cousin, Victor 367
Couturat, L. 283n
Coventry, Angela 114n, 117n
Cover, J.A. 282n, 284n, 287n, 291n, 293n
Coward, William 90–2
Craig, Edward 418n, 419n
Cramer, Konrad 297n, 298n, 301n, 349n, 351, 352n
Creech, Thomas 24n, 82, 83, 84, 99
Creuz, Friedrich Carl Casimir von 316, *321–2*, 323, 332, 349, *352–4*;
see also consciousness, personal identity, self-consciousness
Crichton, Alexander 57n
Cristin, Renato 297n
Crone, Katja 16n
Crusius, Christian August 302, 343, 344, *346–9*, 352;
see also consciousness
Cudworth, Ralph 8, 9, 12, 13, 14, 56, 59n, *67–71*, 81, 83, 84, 89, 99, 117, 133, 168, 225, 242, 243, 244, 291, 328, 409, 410;
see also Cambridge Platonism; consciousness; self-consciousness
Cuenz, Caspar 144, *148–50*, 181, 183, 203, 221;
see also self-consciousness
Cumberland, Richard 6n
Curley, Edwin 61n, 64n, 293n, 294n

Dahlström, D.O. 142n, 331
Dancy, J. 190n
Davies, Catherine Glyn 4n, 10n, 53n, 68n, 412n, 414n, 415n, 416n
De Beer, E.S. 119, 130n, 165n
De natura rerum dissertatio 271, 272n
De Vries, Gerard 10, 36, 252n
Delahaye, Karl 16n
Delhaume, Bernard 415n
Den Uyl, D. 63n
Derounian-Stodola, K.Z. 262n
Des Bosses, Bartholomaeus 304n
Descartes, René 1, 4, 8n, 9, 14, 15, 16, 17, 18, 21, *36–48*, 49n, 51, 52, 53n, 55, 56, 58, 59, 61, 62, 67, 68, 71, 82, 89, 90, 98n, 103, 120, 128, 160, 178, 193, 227, 230, 305, 327, 349, 350, 402;
see also Cartesianism; consciousness; identity; personal identity; self-consciousness
Deschamps, Léger-Marie 410, 413, *415–17*
Dessoir, Max 303n, 344n, 365n, 366n
Diderot, Denis 5n
Dierse, Ulrich 324n
Digby, Kenelm Sir 41, 89
dignity 28, 411n
Dilly, Antoine 49, 50
Diogenes Laertius 12, 14, 101n

Dodwell, Henry 6n
D'Oyly, Robert 156, 157
Drew, Samuel 86n, 167
drunkenness 130–1, *172–4*
Dryden, John 83n
Dufresnoy, Nicolas Lenglet 414n
Duns Scotus, John 19, 20, 23, 281n
Durandus 281n

Eberhard, Johann August *332–5*, 337, 339, 340, 343, 379;
see also personal identity; self-consciousness
Edwards, Jonathan 6n, 132n, 211n, 226, *262–5*, 275;
see also personal identity
Egonsson, D. 384n, 419n
Ellis, Jonathan 399n, 400n
Emes, Thomas 228, 229, 230, 258, 259, 275
empiricism, empiricist 15, 32, 224, 274, 323, 342, 361, 367, 376, 378, 379, 433, 437
Engfer, Jürgen 367n
Epicureanism 24, 82, 109n
Erickson, Robert A. 154n
Eriugena, John Scotus 19
essence 14, 19, 20, 21, 23, 28, 37, 42, 58, 59, 60, 75, 105, 109, 120, 121, 133, 136, 137n, 181, 192, 200, 203, 227, 228, 270, 272, 273, 281, 284, 285, 289, 290, 336, 402, 415, 418, 419, 420, 421, 422, 426
real and nominal essence in Locke 103, 104
Eucharist 19, 39, 40; see also transubstantiation
Euler, Werner 306n, 307n
experience 6n, 14n, 15, 43, 82, 83, 115, 116, 117, 118n, 120, 122, 123, 128, 149, 50, 193, 209, 229, 275, 283, 287, 292, 306, 307n, 334, 340, 341, 351, 361, 367, 368n, 387, 392, 408, 409, 421, 422, 428

Fabbianelli, Faustino 305n
Falkenstein, Lorne 387n
Feder, Johann Georg 432, 433
Felton, Henry 156, *157–60*, 161, 167, 168, 169, 220
Ferguson, James P. 144n, 230n
Fichte, Johann Gottlieb 3n, 17, 354, 437
Ficino, Marsilio 68n
Fisch, H. 83n
fission 211n, 225, 230n, 233, 235, 262n
Flage, Daniel 177n, 261n
Flanagan, O. 112n
Flew, Anthony 107n, 122n, 127n, 201, 209
Fontius, Martin 366n
form (and matter) 19, 20, 21, 22, 23, 25, 29, 35, 281, 288n, 289
Formey, Jean-Henri-Samuel 367n
Forschner, Maximilian 12n, 14, 26n
Forstrom, K. Joanna S. 98n, 214n

Index

four-dimensionalism 125n, 126n, 264n
Fowler, Th. 23n
Fox, Christopher 4n, 8n, 154n
Francke, Georg Samuel *327–8*, 329n, 330n
Frank, Manfred 4n, 6n, 17n, 257, 366n, 373n, 376n
Frankfurt, Harry G. 46n, 287n, 300n
Freedman, Joseph S. 21n
freedom 28, 77, 78, 81, 128, 129, 236, 254
Freeman, E. 63n
Fritz, Anita D. 252n
Fuhrmann, Manfred 26n

Gallie, Roger 107n
Garber, Daniel 37n, 39n, 41n, 62n, 82n, 108n, 127n, 191n, 282n, 288n
Garrett, Don 62n, 66n, 218–20, 383n, 398n, 399n, 406n, 418n, 426n
Gassendi, Pierre 23, 109
Gastrell, Francis 54
Gaukroger, Stephen 2n, 6n, 67n, 68n
Gawlick, Günter 25n, 324n, 335n
Gebhardt, Carl 13n, 61n
Gennaro, R.J. 112n, 296n, 297n, 300n
Gerhardt, C.I. 64n, 113n, 280n, 373n
Gerhardt, Volker 330n
German Idealism 3, 354, 436–7
Geulincx, Arnold 42, 72, 73
Gibb, J. 97n, 133n
Gibieuf, Guillaume 37n
Gilby, Thomas 15n
Gilead, Amihud 63n
Gill, Christopher 13n, 14, 24, 25, 26n, 82n, 99n, 100n, 101n, 108n
Girbal, François 23n
Gladstone, W.E. 198n, 386n, 396n
Glauser, R. 191n
Gloy, Karen 11n
Goclenius, Rudolph 9n, 23n, 45n
God 17, 18, 19, 21, 22, 30, 36, 42, 44n, 51, 63, 66, 67, 81, 83, 87, 90, 91, 103, 132, 133n, 134, 138, 141, 142, 147, 149, 161, 172, 181, 205, 228, 240, 242, 249, 252, 263, 264, 265, 273, 284n, 292, 293, 321, 323
Goubet, Jean-François 306n, 310n
Grabmann, Martin 21n
Gracia, J.J.E. 5n, 19n, 21n, 23n, 26n, 27n, 62n, 72n, 108n, 177n, 261n, 303n, 397n, 413n, 425n
Grau, Kurt J. 4n, 303n, 307n, 348n, 403n
Grave, S.A. 408n
Gravesande, Willem Jacob 148, 149
Grean, Stanley 179n, 180n, 245n
Green, Michael 401n
Greig, J.Y.T. 398n
Greshake, Gisbert 26n

Grove, Henry 11n, 24n, 211n, *234–7*, 275; see also consciousness
Grua, G. 291n
Guzeldere, G. 112n

Haakonssen, Knud 78n
Hacking, Ian 287n
haecceitas 21, 281, 289
Hall, Roland 384n
Haller, Albrecht von 433
Haller, R. 418n
Halls, W.D. 26n
Hampshire, Stuart 65n
Harnack, Adolf 365n, 366n, 380n
Harré, Rom 3n
Harris, John 153
Harrison, John 100n
Hartley, David 141, 205, 339, 409n, 433, 434
Hartz, Glenn A. 287n, 289n
Häseler, Jens 366n
Hassan, T. 16n
Hauser, Christian 5n
Hazlitt, William 5n
Hedley, D. 2n
Hegel, Georg Wilhelm Friedrich 437
Heidelberg School 17, 18n; see also Henrich, Dieter
Heinämaa, S. 11n, 18n, 48n, 65n
Heinz, Marion 363, 364, 365n
Hellenistic philosophy 2, 24
Helm, Paul 263, 264, 265
Helvetius, Claude Adrien 334
Hennig, Boris 8n, 9n, 44n, 46n, 47n
Henrich, Dieter 3n, 17, 18n, 308n, 366n
Henry of Ghent 22
Herder, Johann Gottfried *363–4*
Herrick, James A. 160n
Herz, Markus 331n, 377
Hicks, R.D. 14n
Hight, Marc A. 261n, 262n
Hinske, N. 324n
Hirtius 80n
Hissmann, Michael 354n, 357n, 361n, 362n, 364n, 366, 371n, 276, 378, 379, 433
Hobbes, Thomas 4n, 12, 23, 24, 27n, 29, 44n, 48, 72, 74, 75, *76–81*, 83, 98n, 102, 103, 104, 133n, 203, 257, 385n, 392; see also identity
Hody, Humphrey 87, 88
Hoffman, P. 138n
Hoffmann, A.F. 344
Holbrook, Clyde A. 262n, 265n
Holdsworth, Winch 156, 157, 166
Hollmann, Samuel Christian 10, *349–52*
Hölscher, Ludger 16n
Holzhey, Helmut 272n, 366n

Home, Henry, Lord Kames 197, 384, 423–8, 430, 432, 434, 435, 436n
Honneth, A. 3n, 308n
Hooker, Michael 287n, 293n
Hoopes, James 264n
Horn, Christoph 16n
Horstmann, R.-P. 330n
Howard, Leon 6n, 211n, 262n
Huenemann, Charles 66n, 296n
Huet, Pierre–Daniel 53, 54n
Hufnagel, Alfons 28n
Hume, David 1, 3, 4, 5n, 10n, 32, 199, 241, 244n, 254n, 258, 339, 355, 367n, 370, 380, *383–406, 407–30*;
 see also consciousness; identity; personal identity; self-consciousness
Hunter, Ian 68n, 80n, 81n
Hutcheson, Francis 399n, *410–11*, 424n
Hutton, Sarah 2n, 100n

idea/s 51, 52, 63, 64, 65, 66, 67, 105, 106, 107, 108, 110, 111, 113, 115
 association of 339, 390, 392, 394
 ideas of ideas 66, 67
identity:
 in Boyle 74–5
 in Buffier 392–3
 in Burthogge 73
 in Butler 267–8
 in Canz 317
 in Clauberg 72–3
 in Descartes 38–41
 in Hobbes 75–6
 of the human body 25, 26, 30, 39, 40, 41, 43, 62, 63, 88, 90, 91, 92, 137, 317 336;
  see also body, 'human'; resurrection
 in Hume 388–93
 of indiscernibles 282–5, 302–3, 347, 365n, 368n
 in Lee 195
 in Leibniz 282–9, 302–3
 in Locke 102–6
 of persons, *see* personal identity
 of physical objects/bodies 18, 21, 23, 24, 25, 26, 62, 73, 74, 75, 102, 103, 104, 105, 106, 107, 388–93
 in Sergeant 192–3
 in the seventeenth and eighteenth centuries 18, 23–6, 72–6
 in Spinoza 62–3
 transitivity of 210–11, 214
 in Wolff 303
identity condition (of immortality) 30n, 81, 84, 86, 126n, 128, 133, 134, 168
imagination 63, 246, 249, 320, 321, 339, 373, 390–2, 394

individuation *18–25*, 29, 30, 39–42, 43n, 54, 56, 57, 58, 59, 62, 63, 72–6, 82, 98, 102–4, 135–7, 159, 163, 191–4, 196, 228, 230n, 243, 268, *279–94*, 302–3
indivisibility 149, 160, 230, 232, 233, 255, 259, 267, 287, 288, 321, 336, 361, 362, 384, 386, 387, 411, 412n
inner sense 6, 7, 11, 17, 50, 109, 110, 111, 114, 115, 120, 131, 147, 148, 149, 163, 233, 249, 250, 292, 298, 309, 323, 336, 345, 346, 348–52, 353, 361, 385–8, 393, 401, 403, 406, 418, 420, 422, 429, 430, 432, 433, 435
introspection 250, 336, 353, 376, 385, 387, 388, 405, 406, 418, 420, 421, 422n
intuition 18, *118–20*, 252, 298
Irwin, T. 24n
Israel, Jonathan 413n, 414n

Jacob, Alexander 68n
Jakob, Ludwig Heinrich 429–30
Jessop, T.E. 10n, 211n, 251n, 412n
Jolley, Nicholas 213n, 214, 216, 293n, 294n
Jones, Peter 393n
Jorgensen, Larry M. 300n, 301n
Josefsson, J. 384n, 419n
Jung, G. 8n

Kahn, Charles 11n
Kail, P.J.E. 419n
Kames, *see* Home, Henry, Lord Kames
Kant, Immanuel 2n, 4n, 13n, 16, 17n, 32, 230n, 233n, 255, 302, 326n, 328, 330, 331n, 332, 333, 344, 352, 354, 355, 363, 365, 373n, 376, 377, 378, 379, 380, 428–30, 431, 432, *435–7*;
 see also apperception
Kaufman, Dan 138n
Keckermann, Bartholomaeus 23, 282n
Kemmerling, Andreas 40n, 46n, 110n
Kemp Smith, Norman 418n, 426n, 427
Kennett, Basil 78n
Kenny, Anthony 9n, 36n
Kerby-Miller, Charles 154, 410n
Kerferd, G.B. 14, 100n
Keynes, J.M. 402n, 419n
King, Peter Lord 118n
Kitcher, Patricia 428n
Kittsteiner, Heinz D. 8n, 140n, 141
Klein, Lawrence E. 178n, 241n
Klemme, Heiner F. 310n, 331n, 436n
Klibansky, R. 423n
Klosse, Johann Gottlieb 343–7
Knutzen, Martin *329–31*, 332, 334
Kobusch, Theo 2n, 28, 29n, 79n, 80n, 81n
Kort, E.D. 137n

Krailsheimer, A.J. 60n
Kreimendahl, Lothar 25n, 324n
Kreuzer, Johann 26n, 27n
Kriegel, Uriah 114n, 117n
Krieger, Martin 348n
Krook, Dorothea 191n
Kuehn, Manfred 435
Kulstad, Mark 110n, 113, 298n, 300n
Kurze, Therese 230n

La Forge, Louis de 10, 52, 54, 99, 117, 432
La Rochefoucauld, François de 60
Lähteenmäki, Vili 11n, 18n, 48n, 49n, 65n, 69n, 70n, 71n, 111n, 113n, 115n
Laird, John 393n
Lambert, Johann Heinrich 302, 377
Lamy, François 53
Land, J.P.N. 42n
Lännström, Anna 122n, 125n, 229n
Laslett, Peter 100n
Lau, Theodor Ludwig 433n
Laursen, John Christian 366n, 367n
Law, Edmund 129n, 154, 186, 202, *205–10*, 214, 220, 221, 272;
see also personal identity
Layton, Henry 83, 166, 229
Lee, Henry *163–5*, 166, 167, 168, *170–3*, 179, *195–8*, 220;
see also identity;
personal identity
Leibniz, Gottfried Wilhelm 1, 4n, 5n, 9, 12, 8, 21, 23, 24, 25, 32, 64, 71, 75, 87n, 112, 113, 114, 125n, 135, 169, 226, 230n, 276, *279–314*, 316, 319, 322, 332, 343, 347, 359, 365n, 373n, 411, 412n, 432, 435
on 'complete notion' 284, 286, 287, 290, 293
on indiscernibles 282–5
on monad/s 259, 287, 288, 290, 294, 295
on minute perceptions 290, 292, 296, 301n, 319, 332, 363
on principle of continuity 300
on principle of sufficient reason 283, 285, 303, 320–2
see also apperception; identity; consciousness;
personal identity;
self-consciousness
Leibniz's Law 214
Leinkauf, Thomas 294n
Leinsle, Ulrich Gottfried 344n
Lennon, Thomas M. 39n, 43n, 413
Lenz, Martin 115n
Lewalter, E. 21n, 35n
Lewis, C.S. 8n, 10n
Lewis, E. 24n
Libera, Alain de 2n

Lindemann, Ruth 4n
Lloyd, A.C. 27n, 251n, 252n
Locke, John 1, 4, 5, 9, 10, 11, 13n, 14, 18, 23, 24, 25, 31, 32, 54, 59, 76, 81, 93, *97–120*, *121–52*, 153–89, 190–221, 262, 295, 297, 298, 385, 397; see also consciousness; essence; identity; personal identity; self-consciousness
Loemker, L. 64n, 280n
Long, A.A. 14n
Loptson, Peter 107n, 129n
Lossius, Johann Christian 432
Lowe, E.J. 126n
Luce, A.A. 10n, 176n, 221n, 251n, 252n, 260, 261, 412
Lucretius 24, 82, 83, 84, 99, 100n, 237n, 273
Ludlam, Thomas 197, 198, 202n
Ludovici, Carl Günther 315n
Lukes, S. 26n
Lund, Roger D. 154n
Lupton, William 156, 157n
Lycan, William 112
Lyttle, David 264

McAlister, L.L. 117n
McCann, Edwin 125n
McCarthy, T. 3n, 308n
McCullough, Laurence B. 280n, 282n, 286n, 287n, 289n, 293n
McDonald, Paul S. 3n
McDowell, John 191
Mace, William 410, 411n
Mach, Ernst 418n, 428n
McIntyre Jane L. 383n, 385n, 397n, 426n, 427n
McKenna, Stephen 16n
Mackie, John 123, 124n, 215n, 216, 217
MacLean, Kenneth 154
McMurrich, J.P. 87n
Macpherson, C.B. 23n, 76n
McRae, Robert 296n, 298n
Madonna, Luigi Cataldi 306n
Malebranche, Nicolas 10, 42, 50, 51, 52, 181, 248, 249, 280, 432
man, idea of 77, 82, 105, 106, 107–9, 126, 137, 156, 193
Mandelbaum, M. 63n
Manlove, Timothy 84, 85n
Markovits, Francine 365n
Markus, R.A. 16n, 27n
Marquard, Odo 26n
Marshall, John 133n
Martens, Ekkehard 11n
Martin, Raymond 3n, 4, 5, 179n, 107n, 122n, 201n, 221n, 225n, 230n, 233n, 234n, 274n, 397n

materialism 31, 32, 77, 82, 83, 84, 85, 90–3, 133n, 144, 145, 148, 150, 154, 163, 166, 167, 181n, 203, 224, 225, 226, 228, 229, 232, 233, 235, 239, 241, 242, 244, 245n, 273, 279, 311, 325, 328, 330, 336, 339, 340, 342, 344, 351, 352, 358, 361, 362, 371, 384, 408, 409, 410, 411, 412, 421n, 433–4, 436
Mates, Benson 287n, 294n
Mattern, Ruth 107n, 129n
Matthews, Gareth B. 16n
Mauss, Marcel 26n
Maxwell, John 6
Medieval philosophy 18, 19;
    see also Scholastic philosophy
Meier, Georg Friedrich 316, 322–7, 349;
    see also self-consciousness
Mein, Charles 7, 18, 226, *253–8*, 275
Meiners, Christoph 339, 362, 433
Meißner, Heinrich Adam 314
Melanchthon, Philipp 36
memory 16, 27, 59n, 60, 63, 64, 82, 83, 85, 99, 100, 109, *121–9*, 147, 148, 155, *168–80*, 183, 184, 185, 186, 187, 188, 189, 191, 197, 200, 201, 204, 207, 209–13, 216, 217, 219, 220, 226, 231, 233, 238–40, 247, 256, 261, 263, 273, 291, 292, 295–7, 301, 309, 312–14, 318–23, 324, 325, 327, 328, 331, 332, 337n, 338, 339, 341, 345, 362, 363, 368, 369, 373–5, 394–6, 405, 408, 432, 435
Menasseh ben Israel 87n
Mendelssohn, Moses 142, *329–31*, 332
Mérian, Jean-Bernard 18, 306n, 315, 316, 343, 344, 354, 355, 361, *365–76*, 435;
    see also apperception; consciousness; personal identity; self-consciousness
Mesland, Denis 39
Metzinger, T. 112n
Micraelius, Johann 9n, 23n, 35
Mijuskovic, Ben L. 4, 30n, 179n, 233n, 241n, 252n, 259n, 386n, 391n, 412n, 436n
Miller, Jon 65n, 412n
Millican, Peter 418n
Milton, John 23n
mind 27, 31, 37, 38, 41, 64, 66
    bundle theory of 258, 259, 388, 395n, 398n–9n, 401, 403, 406, *407–20*, 421n, 422, 423, 425, 426, 427n, 428
    immaterialist theories of 31, 92, 144, 150, 154, 168, *224–42*, 247, 261, 262, 266, 267, 269, 274–6, 317, 321, 336–7, 340, 352, 408, 409, 412, 434;
        see also materialism; soul
miracle/s 139, 141–3
Mishori, Daniel 111n, 114n
Mohr, Georg 436n

Molyneux, William 97, 130, 131, 154, 172, 173, 365n, 366
Montaigne, Michel 60
More, A. 84n
More, Henry 68n, 85, 98n
Morell, Thomas 197, 198
Morris, Mary 44n, 295n, 296n
Mossner, E.C. 423n
Mugnai, Massimo 282n, 284n, 286n
Müller, August Friedrich 316, 323–5, 347;
    see also self-consciousness
Murdoch, D. 9n, 36n

Nadler, Steven M. 39n, 53n, 65n, 66, 67
Naert, Émilienne 297n
natural law 27
Newman, L. 127n, 214n
Nicole, Pierre 23n
Nidditch, P.H. 23n, 97n, 120n, 121n, 351n, 384n
Nizolius, Marius 281
nominalism, nominalists 21, 23, 74, 277, 278, 284
Noonan, Harold W. 123n, 125n, 201n, 210n, 216n, 217n, 389n, 398n, 402n, 418n
Norris, John 45n, *248–9*, 251, 252
Norton, David F. 384n, 402, 410, 419n, 428n
Norton, Mary J. 384n, 402, 410, 419n, 428n
Noxon, J. 405n
Nuovo, Victor 100n

Oberer, Hariolf 366n
occasionalism 181
Ockham, William of 21
O'Daly, G.J.P. 8n, 27n, 68n
Oehler, Klaus 11n, 15n
Offe, C. 3n, 4n, 308n
O'Higgins, James 144n
oikeiosis 13, 14, 100, 101
Okruhlik, K. 288n
O'Leary-Hawthorne, John 282n, 284n, 287n, 293n
organism, organic body 42, 43, 88, 137, 138, 245, 288, 413
Osler, M.J. 109n
Overton, Richard 83, 90, 133n
Owen, D. 138n
Owens, Joseph 15n

Palmer, R.R. 181n
Pardies, Ignace-Gaston 49, 50
Parfit, Derek 190n
Parker, Samuel (1640–1688) 85
Parker, Samuel (1681–1730) 156, 157, 166
Parkinson, G.H.R. 282n, 284n, 295n, 296n
Pascal, Blaise 60
Passmore, John 81n, 242n

Patrides, C.A. 87n
Patterson, H. Temple 146n, 147n
Paul, apostle 85, 138
Pears, David 424n
Pearson, John 86
Penelhum, Terence 201n, 209n, 266n, 267n, 383n, 397n, 426n
Perkins, Jean A. 4n
Perkins, William 68
Perler, Dominik 299n
Perrett, Roy W. 30n
Perrin, B. 24n, 75n
Perronet, Vincent 202, *203–5*, 206, 220, 221
Perry, John 144n, 230n
person, personality 26, 27, 28, 29, 31, 35, 36, 54, 55, 56, 57, 58, 60, 64, 71, 97, 98, 108, 120, 122, 129, 130, 140, 141, 143, 147, 149, 158, 160, 164, 167, 182, 183, 184, 190, 194, 196, 199, 201, 205, 208, 209, 210, 213, 215, 230, 238, 256, 260, 291, 312, 313, 314, 319, 322, 325–6, 327, 322, 341n, 345, 362n, 369
personal identity 1, 18, 24, 26, 27, 72, 80, 83, 97, 98, 106, 137, 138, 144, 149, 150, 157, 158, 189, 203, 204, 205
  in Berkeley 176–7, 197, 211, 258–62
  in Butler 198–201, 266–9
  in Canz 318–19
  in Clarke 169, 229–34
  in Collins 145–6
  in Creuz, von 321–2
  in Descartes 38–40
  in Eberhard 332–5
  in Edwards 262–6
  in *Essay on Personal Identity* (anon.) 186–8, 212, 269–72
  in Hume 383–8, 393–403, 423–30
  in Law (Edmund) 205–9
  in Lee 170–2, 194, 195
  in Leibniz 289–95, 301
  in Locke 121–44, 201–9, 213–20
  in Mérian 368–72
  in Reid 197, 212–13
  in Reimarus 335–9
  in Sergeant 193–4
  in the seventeenth and eighteenth centuries 30, 31–2, 432–6
  in Shaftesbury 177–80, 240–7
  in Sherlock and South 54, 59
  in Spinoza 63–4
  in Sulzer 361–3
  in Tiedemann 340–2
  in Tucker 272–5
  in Voltaire 146–8
  in Watts 160–3, 237–40
  in Wolff 312–14
  see also afterlife; identity; resurrection; soul, 'immortality'
Petersson B. 383n, 419n
Petrus Aureolus 281
Phemister, Pauline 287n
phenomenology 16, 117
Pistorius, Hermann Andreas 141, 142
Pitson, A.E. 383n, 394n, 418n, 419n, 425n, 426n, 427n
Platner, Ernst 127n, 335, 362n, 367, 376, 436
Plato, Platonism 2, 8n, 11, 12, 19, 25, 56, 67, 68, 71, 99;
  see also Cambridge Platonism
Plotinus 8n, 12, 13, 67, 68, 71, 99
Ploucquet, Gottfried *184–6*, 187, 199, 316n, 376, 377
Plutarch 24, 75n
Pohlenz, Max 13n
Poley, Heinrich Engelhard 316, 319–21, 344n
Pöltner, G. 26n
Pope, Alexander 154
Popkin, Richard H. 25n, 50n, 366n, 367n, 411n
Pordage, S. 109n
Porphyry 16n
Poser, Hans 301n
Potts, Timothy C. 8n
Prantl, Carl von 366n
Price, Richard 225n
Priestley, Joseph 1n, 7, 90, 142n, 145, 162, 239, 409n, 433, 434, 436n
Principe, Walter 28n
Proß, W. 363n
psychology 27, 57n, 60, 310, 316, 357n, 365n, 377, 416n
  empirical 7, 32, 57n, 304, 307, 311, 339, 355, 433, 436
  moral 425, 427n
  rational 233n, 307, 310, 311, 327, 328, 344, 436
Pufendorf, Samuel 29, *76–81*, 108, 128, 129, 149
Purviance, Susan 397n, 427n
Püschel, Georg Heinrich 329n

Radner, Daisie 46n
Rahman, S. 16n
Rambach, E. 57n
Rancurello, A.C. 117n
Rand, Benjamin 242n, 245, 246
Rand, E. K. (ed. of Boethius) 28n
Raynor, David 398n, 408n, 409n, 410n, 411n, 412n
realism 19, 20, 23, 25

reflection, reflecting 16, 17, 18, 45, 46, 47, 49, 50, 51, 52, 53, 54, 56, 71, 109, 111, 112, 113, 114, 115, 116, 118, 292, 295, 296, 297, 298, 299, 300, 301, 302, 309, 337n, 346, 352, 359, 365, 372, 373, 374, 375, 376, 379n, 399, 403–6, 418, 421n
Régis, Pierre Sylvain 42, 43, 53, 410, 413
Reid, Thomas 1n, 5n, 107n, 109, 112n, 122n, 189n, 197–8, 211–14, 216, 217–18, 220, 302, 384, 387n, 393, 407–9, 411, 418, 422–3, 431, 435;
see also personal identity
Reimarus, Hermann Samuel 226, 315, 328, *332–9*, 340, 343, 379, 435;
see also consciousness; personal identity; self-consciousness
Reinhold, Karl Leonhard 1n, 18n, 311n, 354n, 436
Remes, P. 11n, 18n, 48n, 65n
Remnant, P. 112n, 280n
Renz, Ursula 65n
repentance 139–43
representation 296, 305n, 320, 326, 329–31, 332, 335, 339, 340, 348, 350–2, 357–9, 361, 363, 364, 365, 377
res cogitans 37, 42, 330
Rescher, Nicolas 296n, 297n
responsibility, moral/ legal 1, 19, 27, 29, 35, 76, 78, 127–8, 149
resurrection 19, 20, 25, 26, 30, 81–93, 98, 135, 136, 139, 140, 146n, 155, *156–69*, 220, 221, 229, 232, 234, 236, 237, 239, 261, 262, 273;
see also body, 'human'; identity; organism
rewards and punishments 30, 81, 83, 84, 86, 92, 99, 127n, 128, 140, 143, 168, 180, 213, 214, 215, 225, 229, 232, 316, 325;
see also afterlife
Rey, Anne-Lise 310n
Rheinfelder, Hans 26n, 28n, 36n
Rice, Lee C. 63n, 64n, 65n
rights 27, 28, 293
Robertson, William 28n
Robinet, André 280n, 296n, 297n, 299n, 367n, 415n, 416n
Roche, Antoine-Martin *181–4*
Röd, Wolfgang 80
Rodis-Lewis, Geneviève 4n, 10n, 37n, 39n, 42n, 46n, 50n, 53n, 54n, 65n, 82n
Rogers G.A.J. 120n, 205n, 421n
Roman law 26, 27
Rønnow–Rasmussen T. 383n, 419n
Rorarius 50n, 411n
Rosenfield, Leonora Cohen 49n, 50n
Ross, Alexander 86, 87, 90
Rouse, W.H.D. 24n
Rousseau, G.S. 3n

Rousseau, Jean Jacques 334, 380n, 412n, 432, 436
Rowan, J.P. 20n
Rüdiger, Andreas 322, 329n, *343–8*, 350, 352, 372, 375, 376;
see also self-consciousness
Rudolph, Oliver-Pierre 305n, 306n, 307n, 310n
Ruello, Francis 29n
Russell, Bertrand 385n
Rutherford, Donald 279

Salomon, Lewis 303n, 377n
Saw, Ruth 63n
sceptics, scepticism 24, 58, 60, 180n, 226, 241, 243, 245, 269, 324, 325, 355, 367n, 415, 416n, 419n, 420, 421, 428n
Schaffrath, Josef 324n
Schaper, Eva 366n
Scharf, Johannes 23, 35n
Scharp, Kevin 112n, 115n
Schechtman, Marya 124n, 127n, 143n, 215, 216n
Scheibler, Christoph 21n, 23, 35, 36
Scheffler, Samuel 291n, 294n
Schelling, Friedrich Wilhelm Joseph 437
Schenk, Günter 324n, 377n
Schepers, Heinrich 280n, 296n, 299n, 344n, 346n, 367n
Schmaltz, Tad M. 38, 43n, 52n
Schmaus, Michael 27n
Schmidt-Biggemann, Wilhelm 78n
Schmitt, Arbogast 15n, 307n
Schneiders, W. 306n
Schnepf, R. 16n
Scholastic, Scholasticism 3, 8, 18, 19, 20, 21, 27, 28, 29, 35, 36, 40, 41, 50, 54, 60, 64, 67, 72, 73, 75, 81, 98, 102, 122, 136, 137, 280, 282, 286, 289, 300, 311, 344
Schotan, Johann 54n
Schüle, A. 40n
Schulze, Gottlob Ernst 354–6, 367
Schumacher, R. 330n
Schüßler, Werner 299n
Scheweling, Eberhard 54n
Schwyzer, H.R. 8n, 68n
Scotism, Scotists 21, 285, 293
Scott, George L. 408n
Scriblerians 153, 410
Sedley, David 24n
Seel, Gerhard 366
Seel, O. 8n
Selbstgefühl 57n, 361, 432–3
Selby-Bigge, L.A. (ed. of Hume) 254n, 384n, 398, 403n

self-concern 14, 100, 121–2, 127–8, 144, 398, 412, 422–5
self-consciousness
  69, 70, 71, 139
  in Bentley 84n
  in Browne, Peter 250
  in Butler 266
  in Canz 317, 318
  in Creuz, von 322, 352–4
  in Cudworth 69–71
  in Cuenz 149, 150
  in Descartes and Cartesians 16, 17, 61
  in Eberhard 332
  in the *Essay on Consciousness* 257
  in Hume 383, 426, 429
  in Leibniz 294, 296, 297, 301
  in Locke 118–20
  in Meier 327
  in Mérian 355, 372–6, 378–80
  in Müller 323
  reflection theory of 17, 18
  in Reimarus 335, 337
  in Rüdiger 346
  in the seventeenth and eighteenth centuries 6, 7, 11, 14–18, 15, 30, 31, 32, 35, 224–5, 279, 302, 343, 376–8, 431–7
  in Sherlock and South 54–9
  in Spinoza 65n
  in Sulzer 355, 356–61, 363–4
  in Tiedemann 340
  in Wolff 303, 304–12
  see also apperception; consciousness; *conscientia*; intuition; *Selbstgefühl*; *sentiment intime*
self-determination 1, 70, 71
self-knowledge 43, 56, 57, 59n, 65, 71, 181, 249, 251, 297n, 306, 307n, 373; *see also* self-consciousness
self-preservation 13, 14, 424
Sell, Alan P. 11n, 24n, 234n, 236n
Seneca, Lucius Annaeus 13n, 14n, 15n, 101
sensus communis 9n
sentiment intérieur 10, 42, 50, 52
sentiment intime 415, 432–3
Sergeant, John 41, 102, 103n, *191–5*, 196, 197, 198, 201, 202, 220, 230n, 286; *see also* consciousness; identity; personal identity
Servetus, Michael 35, 36
Shaftesbury, Anthony Ashley Cooper, 3rd Earl *177–80*, 226, *240–7*, 261, 269, 275, 385, *390–1*, 400n; *see also* personal identity
Sherlock, William *54–60*, 98, 117, 136, 156, 163, 167, 168, 195, 209, 345n;
  see also consciousness; personal identity; self-consciousness
Shin, Kyonwong 154n
Siger of Brabant 25
Sihvola, Juha 11n
Simmons, Alison 46n, 300n, 301n
Simon, Renée 414n, 415n
sin 140, 142, 143
  original *131–2, 262–3*, 265
Sleigh, R.C. 282n, 284n
Smith, John 84n, 225n,
Smith, M.F. 24n
Snobelen, Stephen D. 133n
Sommer, Robert 303n
Sorabji, Richard 16n, 82n, 99n, 100n
Sosa, E. 260n
soul:
  animal souls 49, 50, 101, 183, 299, 312, 313, 330n, 344
  extended soul 148, 181, 182, 203, 230, 237, 339, 344, 348, 371
  immaterialist theories of 31, 92, 144, 150, 154, 168, *224–42*, 247, 261, 262, 266, 267, 269, 274–6, 317, 321, 336–7, 340, 352, 408, 409, 412, 434
  immateriality of 32, 35, 37, 38, 42, 58, 69, 67, 68, 71, 73, 76, 82–5, 91, 92, 104, 105, 109, 120, 122, 128, 133, 136, 137n, 139, 144, 145, 150, 160, 163, 165, 168, 169, 175, 176, 181, 183, 186, 187, 203, 204, 206, 246, 247, 249, 254, 258, 259, 260, 261, 267, 268, 269, 270, 273, 274, 276, 279, 287, 289, 290, 291, 294, 295, 311, 316, 324, 328, 330, 331, 332, 336, 341, 351, 362, 369, 371, 384, 385, 387, 388, 396, 411, 426, 433, 434
  immortality of 19, 20, 25, 30, 42, 51, 64, *81–5*, 90, 97–9, 132, 33, 134, 137, 147, *166–9*, 225, 229, 234, 254, 280, 291, 304, 312–14, 315–17, 321–5, 327–8, 330, 332, 339n, 344, 352, 376, 399n, 407, 409
  indestructibility of 37, 133, 312, 313, 314, 316, 317, 319, 321–4, 327, 328
  universal soul 25, 64, 240, 242–3, 246–7, 275, 280n; *see also* mind
South, Robert *54–60*, 98, 117, 136, 167, 179, 190, 195, 209, 345n;
  see also consciousness; personal identity; self-consciousness
Southgate, Beverly 191n
space and time 23, 74, 102, 103, 104, 125n, 135, 192, 205, 372, 394
Spazier, Karl 335
Spiazzi, R.S. 20n

Spinoza, Baruch de 13, 25, *61–7*, 71, 72, 280, 286, 367, 393, 413n, 414, 417;
  see also consciousness; identity; personal identity; self-consciousness
spirit, spiritual 20–2, 25, 31n, 42, 43, 49, 51, 55, 58, 64, 73, 92, 103–4, 106–7, 109, 129n, 148–9, 164–77, 181, 203, 252, 259–61, 263n, 274–5, 280, 294n, 297, 317, 327–8, 412, 413, 415
Sraffa, P. 402n, 419n
Stackelberg, Jürgen V. 349n
Stadler, F. 418n
Stahl, Daniel 23, 281
staminal particles *162*, 167, 239
Stanley, Thomas 12–13
Stelzenberger, Johannes 8n
Sterne, Laurence 153
Stewart, Dugald 5n, 197, 198n, 407, 435
Stewart, H.F. 28n
Stewart, M.A. 10n, 41n, 55n, 74n, 97n, 133n, 191n, 212n, 213, 398n, 402n, 408n, 428n
Stewart, Roy 87n
Stiehler, G. 433n
Stierle, Karl-Heinz 26n
Stillingfleet, Edward, Bishop of Worcester 36n, 54, 56n, *134–9*, 154–6, 157, 161, 163, 165, 167, 168, 191, 286
Stoicism 2n, 12–15, 24, 100, 101, 102, 127n
Stolzenberg, Jürgen 16n, 305n, 306n, 307n
Stoothoff, R. 9n, 36n
Strähler, Daniel 10, 343
Strawson, Galen 139n, 140, 143n, 383n, 399n–400n, 409n, 418n, 419n, 420n, 421n–2n, 425n, 427n, 428n
Street, Tony 16n
Stroud, Barry 383n, 400n–1n, 419n
Sturma, Dieter 26n, 436n
Suárez, Francisco 21–3, 25, 26, 29, 30, 35, 40, 41, 75, 79n, 89n, 102, 280–2, 284–5, 289
subjectivity 1, 2n, 3, 8n, 15, 27, 68, 437
substance 22, 25, 27, 28, 29, 37, 38, 41, 42, 43, 60, 61, 62, 64, 73, 78–9, 81, 84, 87, 93, 103–5, 108, 120, 122, 129, 133, 134, 136, 137, 139, 143, 146, 159, 171, 177, 185, 187, 189, 193, 194–7, 199, 208, 209, 214, 224, 226, 233, 247, 253, 276, 280, *282–91*, 302, 314, 331, 333, 384
Sulzer, Johann Georg *354–65*, 372, 380;
  see also consciousness; personal identity; self-consciousness
Suphan, B. 363n
synaisthesis 8, 12n, 13, 70, 71, 99
syneidesis 8, 12, 236
Swain, Corliss Gayda 395n
Swift, Jonathan 153–4

Tannery, Paul 9n, 36n, 82n
Teichert, Dieter 3n
Teichmann, Jenny 26n
temporal parts, see four-dimensionalism
Tennant, R.C. 153n
Terrell, D.B. 117n
Tertullian 27
Tester S.J. 28n
Tetens, Johann Nicolas 5n, 344, 367, 377, 380n, 432, 436
Thiel, Udo 5n, 6n, 8n, 23n, 26n, 39n, 42n, 43n, 55n, 56n, 57n, 62n, 67n, 72n, 86n, 97n, 98, 99n, 108n, 113n, 114n, 119n, 120n, 122n, 127n, 153n, 167n, 191n, 202n, 230n, 272n, 298n, 303n, 307n, 311n, 330n, 361n, 366n, 377n, 386n, 409n, 413n, 432n, 434n
thinking matter 144–50;
  see also materialism
Thomas, G. 40n
Thomasius, Christian 9n, 344–6, 348
Thomasius, Jakob 23
Thomist/s 22, 23, 25, 289
Thornton, Mark 108n
Thweatt, Vivien 60n
Tiedemann, Dietrich 335, 339–42;
  see also personal identity; self-consciousness
Tillotson, John 89
Timpler, Clemens 21n
Todd, Denis 154n
Tomaselli, S. 205n, 421n
Tonelli, Giorgio 367n
Traiger, S. 395n
transubstantiation 19, 39, 89n;
  see also Eucharist
Tredennick, H. 20n
Trendelenburg, Adolf 26n, 36n
Trinity 16, 18, 19, 21, 27, 28, 29, 31, 35, 54, 55, 98, 135, 190
tritheism 21
Tsugawa, Albert 427n
Tucker, Abraham 24n, 197, 210n, 226, 269, *272–6*;
  see also personal identity
Turner, John 56n, 140–2
Tuveson, Ernest 153n–4n

Uehlein, Friedrich A. 245n
universals 19, 21, 23, 73, 286n, 289n
Uzgalis, W. 144n, 146n, 230n

Vailati, Ezio 230n, 233n, 293n, 294n
Valla, Lorenzo 35, 36, 291n
Venturi, F. 415n
Vidal, Fernando 3n, 85n, 86n
Vogel, C.J. de 26n

Voltaire, F.-M. Arouet de 144, *146–8*, 150, 220, 221;
see also personal identity
Vossenkuhl, Wilhelm 366n

Wagner, Hans 17n
Wahrmann, Dror 4n
Walker, Nigel 130n
Wallace, George 408n
Wallace, Thomas 5n
Ward, Seth 82n
Warren, Edward 85
Warren, E.W. 8n, 68
Warren, James 99n, 100n
Watson, Richard A. 39n
Watt, Ian 154
Watts, Isaac 10n, 150n, *160–2*, 168, *175–7*, 179, 188, 203, 205, 220, 226, *237–40*, 245, 270, 271, 274, 275, 370;
see also personal identity
Waxman, Wayne 397n, 403n, 425n
Wedeking, Gary 55n, 57n, 58n
Weigel, Erhard 80
Weinberg, Shelley 113n, 114n, 117n
Weiser, Christian Friedrich 241n, 244n
Wellman, R.R. 11n
Wellmer, A. 3n, 308n
Wernstedt, R. 299n
Wertz, Linda 154n
Wertz, Spencer 154n
Wesley, Charles 203
Wesley, John 203
Whichcote, Benjamin 242n
Whitehead, John 225, 226
Wiggins, David 108n, 190n, 210n
Wilbur, E.M. 35n
Wilkins, John 110
Wilkins, K.S. 393n
Willaschek, Marcus 436n
Willis, Thomas 109n

Wilson, Catherine 287n, 293n
Wilson, Fred 384n, 397n, 418n, 425n, 426n
Wilson, Margaret 41n, 65n, 291n, 294
Winckler, Johann Heinrich 334, 335n, 336, 337
Winkler, Kenneth 107n, 122n, 129n, 179n, 180n, 217n, 218, 241n, 246n, 247, 252n, 261n, 383n, 391n, 395n, 399n, 400n, 419n
Wolff, Christian 1, 3, 4n, 7, 9, 15, 32, 279, *301–14*, *316–19*, 321, 322, 323, 325, 326, 327, 328, 329, 330, 332, 335, 336, 337, 339, 340, 343, 344, 345, 346, 347, 348, 349, 351, 352, 354, 355, 356, 357, 358, 359, 360, 362, 363, 364, 365, 372, 373, 375, 376, 378, 431–2;
see also apperception; consciousness; identity; personal identity; self-consciousness
Wolter, Allan 20n
Woolhouse, Roger 62n, 287n
Wright, John P. 109n, 409n, 421n
Wunderlich, Falk 4n, 304n, 305n, 306n, 309n, 330n, 331n, 363n, 366n, 373n, 377n, 379n, 436n
Wundt, Max 21n, 23n, 35n, 307n, 344n, 345, 349n
Wynne, John 103n, 119

Yaffe, Gideon 127n–8n, 138n, 214–15
Yarbrough, Stephen R. 262n
Yolton, John 144n, 146n, 148n, 181, 191n, 203n, 204n, 230n, 421n, 431n, 433n

Zahavi, Dan 18n
Zarka, Y. Ch. 5n, 252n
Zart, G. 355n
Zeuch, Ulrike 15n, 307n
Zucker, Friedrich 8n

Lightning Source UK Ltd.
Milton Keynes UK
UKOW04f0503090514

231375UK00001B/1/P